THE VICTORIA HISTORY OF THE COUNTIES OF ENGLAND

A HISTORY OF YORKSHIRE: EAST RIDING

VOLUME IX

THIS HISTORY IS DEDICATED BY GRACIOUS PRIVILEGE TO

QUEEN ELIZABETH II

IN CELEBRATION OF HER MAJESTY'S DIAMOND JUBILEE

AND INSCRIBED TO THE MEMORY OF HER LATE MAJESTY

QUEEN VICTORIA

WHO GRACIOUSLY GAVE THE HISTORY ITS TITLE

THE VICTORIA HISTORY OF THE COUNTIES OF ENGLAND

ALAN THACKER CONSULTANT EDITOR

ELIZABETH WILLIAMSON EXECUTIVE EDITOR

THE UNIVERSITY OF LONDON

INSTITUTE OF HISTORICAL RESEARCH

Frontispiece *All Saints' church, Great Driffield, from the south-east, 2006.*

A HISTORY OF THE COUNTY OF YORK: EAST RIDING

VOLUME IX

HARTHILL WAPENTAKE, BAINTON BEACON DIVISION

GREAT DRIFFIELD AND ITS TOWNSHIPS

GRAHAM KENT
WITH DAVID NEAVE AND SUSAN NEAVE

PUBLISHED FOR THE

INSTITUTE OF HISTORICAL RESEARCH

BY BOYDELL & BREWER · 2012

First published 2012

A Victoria County History publication
in association with The Boydell Press
an imprint of Boydell & Brewer Ltd
PO Box 9, Woodbridge, Suffolk IP12 3DF, UK
and of Boydell & Brewer Inc.
668 Mt Hope Avenue, Rochester, NY 14620, USA
website: www.boydellandbrewer.com
and with the
University of London Institute of Historical Research

ISBN 978 1 904356 11 0

A catalogue record for this book is available
from the British Library

Papers used by Boydell & Brewer Ltd are natural, recyclable products
made from wood grown in sustainable forests

Typeset by Tina Ranft, Woodbridge, Suffolk
Printed and bound by CPI Group (UK) Ltd, Croydon, CR0 4YY

CONTENTS OF VOLUME IX

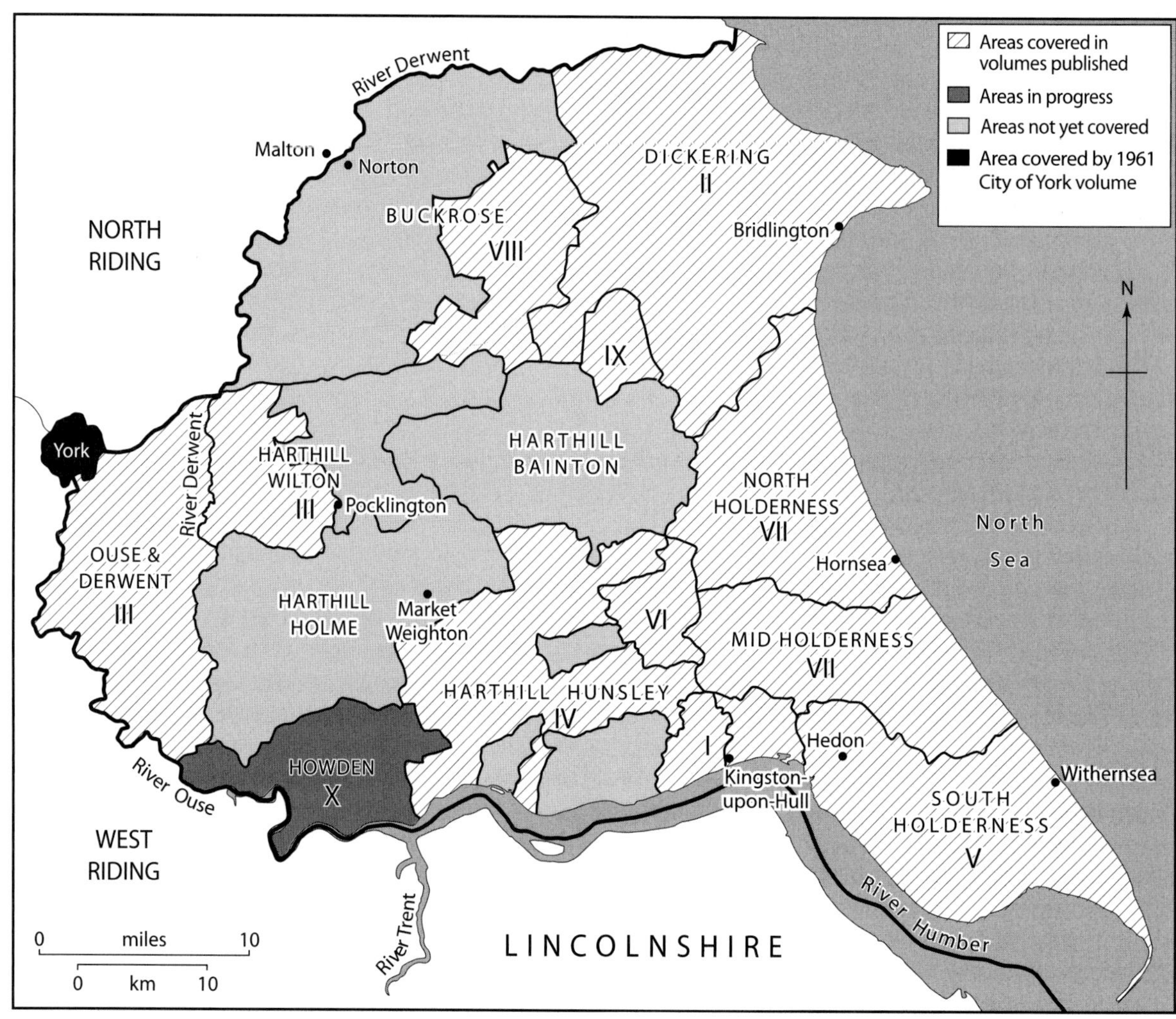

Key to volumes published and forthcoming.

LIST OF ILLUSTRATIONS

LIST OF MAPS AND PLANS

LIST OF TABLES

The cost of research for this volume was met largely by

East Riding of Yorkshire Council,

University of Hull

and the

County History Trust

whose support is gratefully acknowledged

UNIVERSITY OF Hull

FOREWORD AND ACKNOWLEDGEMENTS

The research for this volume was carried out in two phases, the first by Dr Graham Kent between 2000 and 2006, and the second by Dr David Neave and Dr Susan Neave between 2008 and 2010. Some two-thirds of the volume had been written by Graham Kent before his retirement in 2006, and the work was revised and completed by David and Susan Neave.

We are most grateful for the financial support established by the former East Riding County Council in 1974 and continued by the present East Riding of Yorkshire Council and North Yorkshire County Council. Accommodation and other assistance was provided by the University of Hull. The Marc Fitch Fund generously supported the publication of this volume.

Numerous institutions and individuals gave access to documents or buildings, or shared information. Many of these are mentioned in the notes, and all are thanked for their invaluable help. Special thanks must go to the staff of the East Riding Archives and Local Studies Service, Hull History Centre, the Borthwick Institute for Archives, North Yorkshire County Record Office and the National Archives. Particularly useful were the research papers of the late Norman Creaser, in private hands, and information generously provided by the late Chris Ketchell. We are most grateful to Leslie Webster for much helpful comment on the Early Settlement section and especially for guidance on the dating and interpretation of the early-medieval finger-rings.

The help and encouragement of Professor John Beckett, Dr Alan Thacker, Elizabeth Williamson, Jessica Davies and Matthew Bristow of the Victoria County History Central Office in the preparation of this volume are much appreciated. Maps were drawn by Cath D'Alton.

Further information about the VCH is available on the website www.victoriacountyhistory.ac.uk.

David and Susan Neave

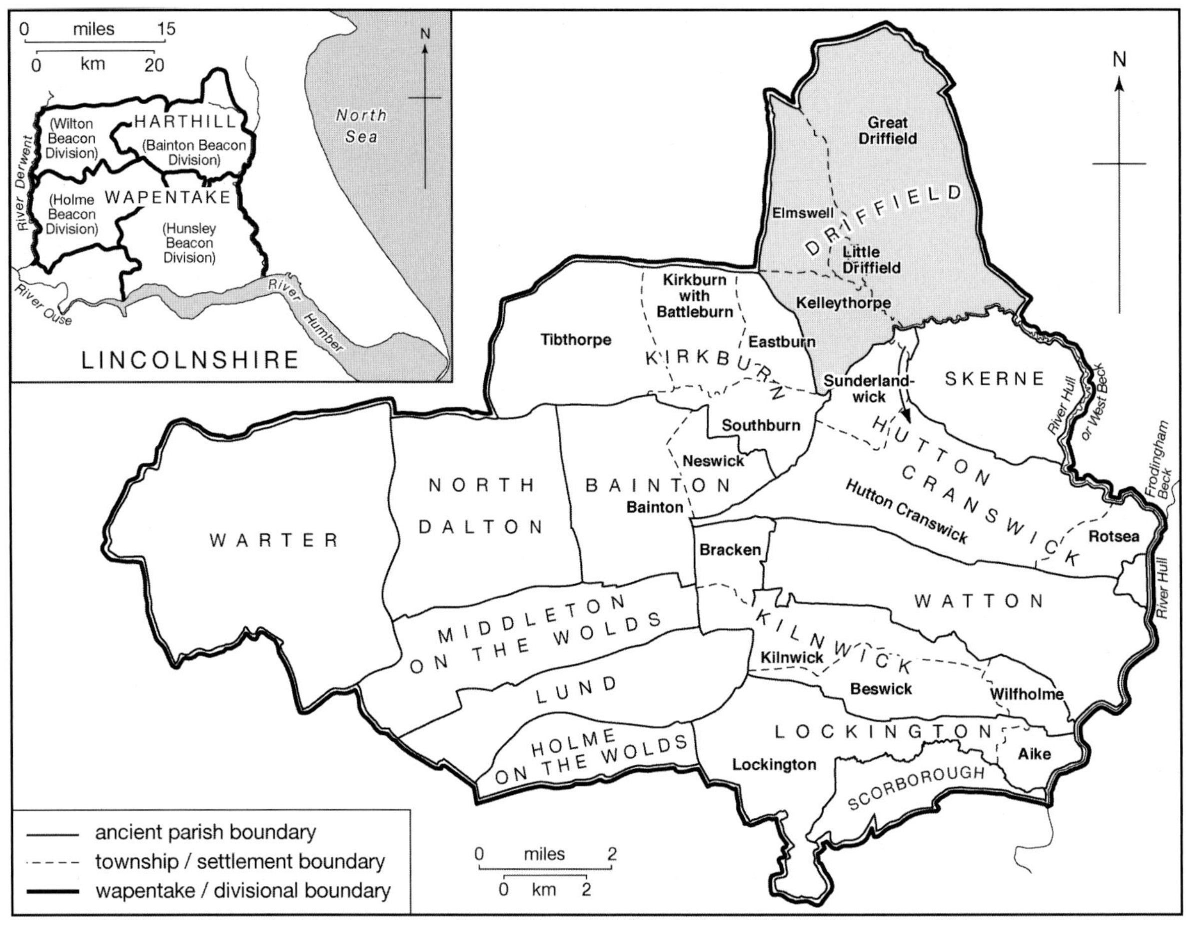

1. *Harthill Wapentake: Bainton Beacon Division.*

GREAT DRIFFIELD AND ITS TOWNSHIPS

THIS VOLUME CONCERNS the ancient parish of Great Driffield in the former East Riding of Yorkshire, comprising the market town of Great Driffield, and its rural townships of Little Driffield, Elmswell and Kelleythorpe, an area of 7,600 a. (3,076 ha.).

In 1086 Driffield, Kelleythorpe and part of Elmswell lay in Driffield hundred, the rest of Elmswell was in Turbar hundred. The whole parish became part of Harthill wapentake during the 12th century, and in the Bainton Beacon division of the wapentake in Elizabeth I's reign.[1]

On the abolition of the East Riding County Council in 1974 Driffield and its former townships became part of the Borough of North Wolds, later renamed East Yorkshire, in the newly-created county of Humberside, and in 1996 they became part of the East Riding of Yorkshire unitary authority.

Because of the intricacies of their past history Great Driffield and Little Driffield are dealt with together in this volume. They were parts of a single manor and parish, had one field system and are within one civil parish. Separate accounts are given of the townships of Elmswell and Kelleythorpe.

LANDSCAPE

Great Driffield and the smaller settlements of Little Driffield and Elmswell are sited at the foot of the Yorkshire Wolds, close to the 75 ft (23 m.) contour, at the headwaters of the River Hull.[2] To the south a band of flatter land shelves down to about 35 ft (11 m.) above sea level, while north of the settlements the wold slopes rise to 361 ft (110 m.) at Maiden's Grave on the northern parish boundary. The higher ground, which occupies two-thirds of the parish, is divided by steep-sided valleys; Elmswell slack, or valley, and Monks Dale separates Elmswell and Driffield wolds, and Slaysdale and Danesdale the wolds of Driffield and Nafferton.

Below the high chalk wold land in the north, the middle of the parish is largely covered by boulder clay. Some glacial gravel occurs in the valley bottoms there, and a larger deposit of gravel and sand provided Great Driffield with its site. The lowest land in the south is also covered with gravel and, alongside the main drains, with alluvium.[3] The soil is mostly strong loam. On the higher wold land the loam thins, and there and on the level ground in the south of the parish it is mixed with much chalk gravel.[4]

The availability of water evidently determined the location, and in Great Driffield's case also the layout, of the settlements. The town was established beside a stream which rises in the lower reaches of Monks Dale and flows south-eastwards down the middle of the parish. The lesser settlements, including Kelleythorpe in the south of the parish, were all sited at springs, the resultant streams draining from Elmswell and Little Driffield forming several of the parish's internal boundaries. Other boundary streams were the small watercourse of Nafferton slack, or valley, in the south-east of Great Driffield, and the stream forming the entire southern boundary of the parish. The latter flowed north-eastwards along the southern boundary of Kelleythorpe; received water from Elmswell and Little Driffield through Driffield Beck; then meandered eastwards along the southern limit of Great Driffield, and a mile or so downstream from Driffield parish formed the main tributary of the River Hull. Its course has evidently changed, or been changed, with the result that by the 19th century boundary and stream no longer coincided.[5] The several mills on the stream probably account for some of the alterations. Bell Mill existed in the 1570s, when it was claimed to have suffered because of the building of a new cloth mill at Bull Crook; an old mill race and a ditch dug through common land nearby were then recorded, and perhaps in consequence of such changes stones then marked part of the boundary between Skerne and Driffield.[6] A greater alteration to the natural drainage was effected in the 18th century, when the town's stream and lesser drains, which until

1 For an account of Harthill wapentake see *VCH Yorks. ER*. iii. 129–32.

2 Para. based on OS Map 1:25,000, SE 95–6, TA 05–6 (1953–4 edn).

3 Geol. Survey Map 1:63,360, solid and drift, sheet 64 (1858 edn, reprinted 1954).

4 ERAO, DX/100.

5 OS Map 1:10,560, Yorks. CLXI–II, CLXXVIII (1855 edn).

6 TNA, E 178/2594.

then had fed into the southern boundary stream, were diverted into the new canal.[1]

The clearance of the natural vegetation, of oak and scrub woodland, is believed to have begun early on the chalk uplands, probably in the Neolithic period, and by the Bronze Age much of the Wolds at least probably comprised open pastoral land interrupted by residual woodlands.[2] Much of that land, as well as some lower down, where clearance may have been slower, was later used for the growing of cereals. Most of the land lay in the open fields of the two Driffields and of Elmswell until they were inclosed in 1742 and 1771 respectively. As well as land regularly sown, the fields included poorer, wold land, which seems often to have been used as rough grazing for sheep and ploughed only occasionally. Grassland was otherwise to be found mainly in the south, adjoining the streams and especially in Kelleythorpe. That settlement had an open field or fields in the 16th century but they seem to have been inclosed before the mid 17th century; a common pasture remained, and was then valued locally for the grazing of cattle and sheep. The final date of inclosure at Kelleythorpe is not known.[3] Inclosure in the Driffields, where there were many proprietors, resulted in the usual pattern of rectangular fields crossed by new, straight roads, but in Elmswell earlier arrangements were hardly disturbed by the allotments made to the two owners, one of whom, the lord of the manor, received almost the whole settlement. The fields in Elmswell were reorganized into larger units in the later 19th century, when the Denisons, Lords Londesborough, the owners, also added new farmhouses away from the hamlet; in modified form, the old layout of the farmlands has, however, largely survived there.[4] Outlying farms were also built on newly-inclosed land in the Driffields, and there and in Elmswell small plantations of trees were added to the open landscape to shelter farmhouses and game, and mark boundaries.[5] Apart from the growth of the town, there were then no great changes to the landscape until the earlier 20th century, when an airfield was made in the south-west of the parish.

AREA AND BOUNDARIES

In 1850–1 Driffield parish contained 7,600 a., of which 4,814 a. lay in Great Driffield township, later civil parish. The settlements of Elmswell, of 1,293 a., and Kelleythorpe, with 1,105 a., together formed the 2,398-a. township of Elmswell with Kelleythorpe.[6] The remaining 388 a. of the parish comprised Little Driffield township, the grounds of which were intermingled with those of Great Driffield.[7]

A mixture of natural features and man-made constructions were used for the boundaries of the ancient parish. In the north-west, the boundary ran along the bottom of a dry valley called Ewe Dale, and stones were placed as markers there and on the higher northern boundary. Boundary stones were also employed within the parish, two marking a detached part of Little Driffield near Clitheroe Farm.[8] The northern parish boundary had evidently been formed by an ancient way, the route of which is confirmed by earthworks in neighbouring parishes; that road probably also accounts for the location beside the Driffield boundary of a large Iron-Age cemetery called Danes' Graves and land nearby called Maiden's Grave.[9] The western parish boundary was formed by a wide field division, Garton balk, and the possibly ancient road running along it which was confirmed at the inclosure of Elmswell in 1771.[10] Other balks separated Elmswell from Kelleythorpe,[11] and Great and Little Driffield. In the southern half of the parish, below the spring line, settlement and parish boundaries were formed largely by streams, although by the mid 19th century that origin had been confused by changes in the meandering courses.

The western boundary of Kelleythorpe was described in some detail in the early 18th century, when it was disputed.[12] From the south-western corner of Elmswell, it led along part of a track called York Gate; turned southwards to another road, Brick Kiln Gate, and then continued across the pastures as far as Laug Hill and the boundary with Southburn, in Kirkburn parish. York Gate was presumably part of an ancient trackway leading to Huggate, Pocklington, and beyond,[13] while the later Brick Kiln corner identifies Brick Kiln Gate as

1 ERAO, IA. 41; OS Map 1:10,560, Yorks. CLXI–CLXII (1855 edn); below, this section, communications.

2 T. G. Manby, 'Bronze Age Settlement in Eastern Yorkshire', in J. Barrett and R. Bradley (eds), *Settlement and Society in the British Later Bronze Age* (Brit. Archaeol. Rep., Brit. Ser. 83, 1980), ii. 313.

3 Below, Kelleythorpe.

4 Below, Elmswell.

5 OS Map 1:10,560, Yorks. CXLIV, CLXI (1854–5 edn).

6 The modern spelling of Elmswell, rather than Emswell, is used throughout the Driffield account.

7 OS Map 1:10,560, Yorks. CXLIV, CLXI (1854–5 edn).

8 OS Map 1:2,500, Yorks. CXLIV. 16 (1910 edn).

9 N. Loughlin and K. R. Miller, *Survey of Archaeol. Sites in Humbs.* (1979), 120.

10 RDB, AN/196/12.

11 Best, *Farming Bks*, ed. Woodward, p. xxiii.

12 Following based on HUL, DDHO/39/1–2; below, Kelleythorpe.

13 T. Jefferys, *Map of Yorks.* (1775); below, this section, communications.

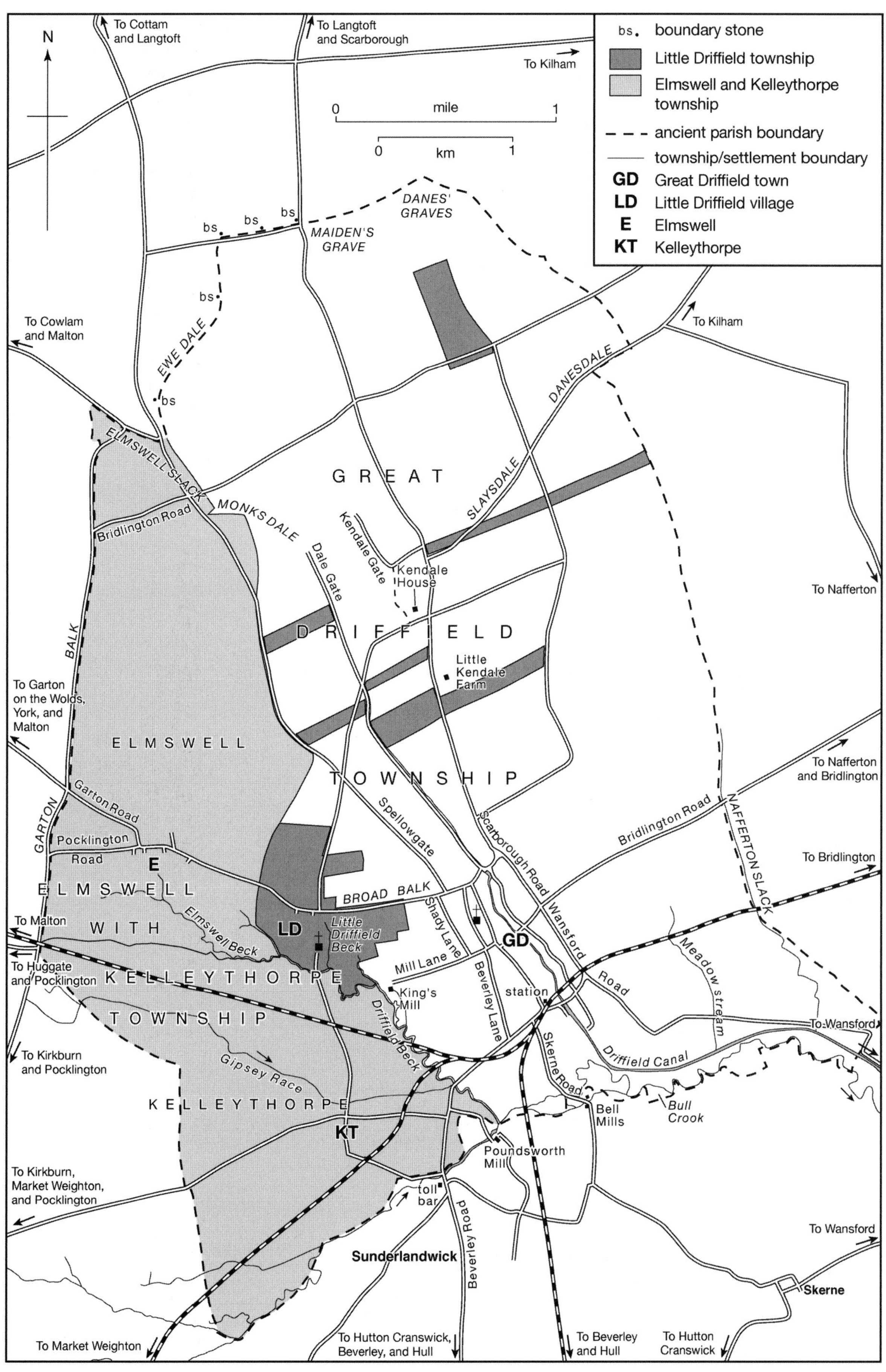

2. *Driffield parish in 1850.*

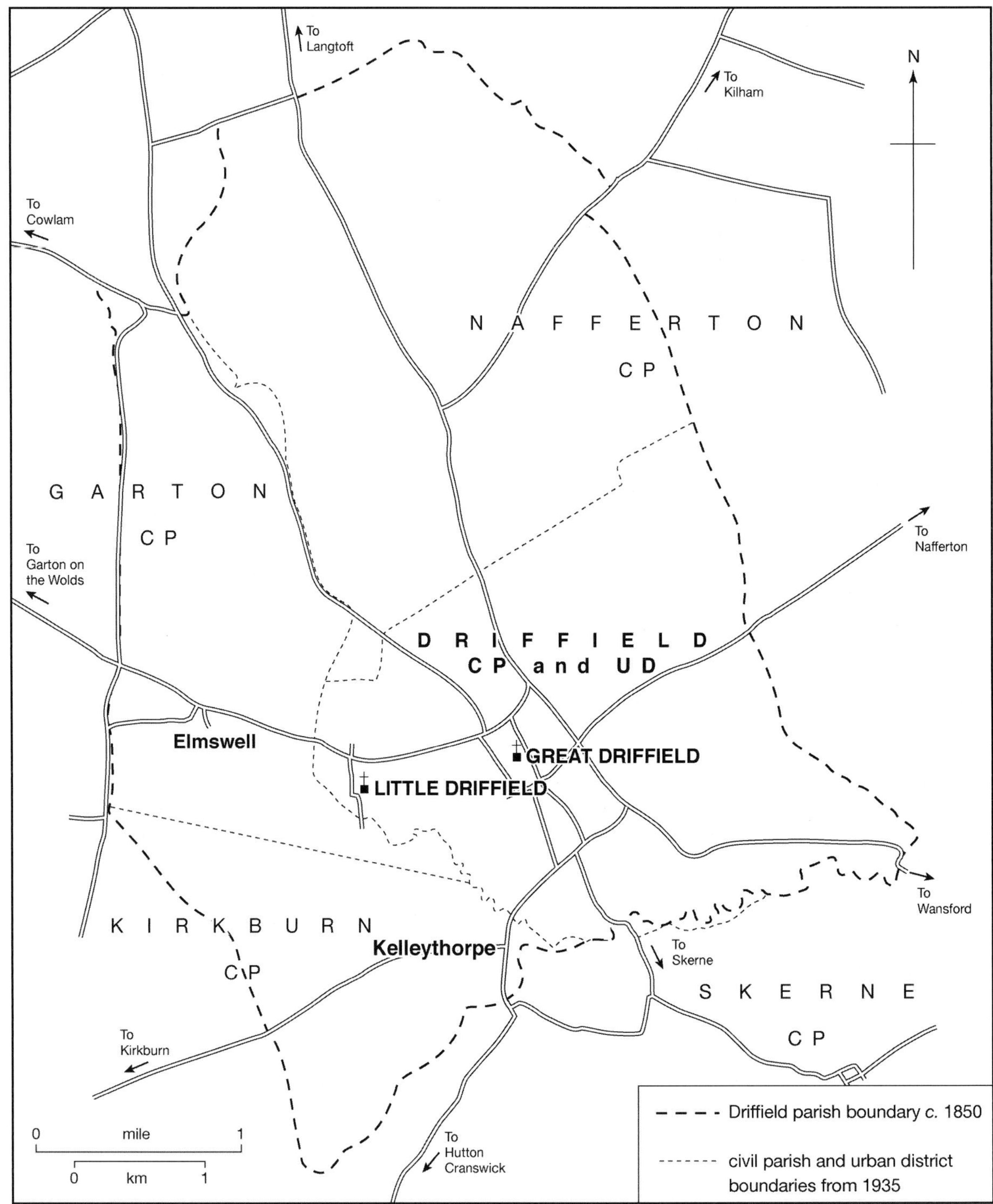

3. *Driffield parish: Civil parish and urban district boundaries from 1935.*

the present Driffield-Market Weighton road.[1] In the 17th century the land on either side of the boundary, in the greets in Kelleythorpe and the outfield of Eastburn, comprised a single, uninclosed pasture, and part of the boundary between the two settlements was a headland created for that purpose. The pastures were later divided by embankments topped by fences or hedges which were made in the later 17th and early 18th centuries, probably in connection with the rabbit warrens then being established in Kelleythorpe.[2]

In 1866 three separate civil parishes of Great Driffield, Little Driffield, and Elmswell with Kelleythorpe were

1 OS Map 1:10,560, Yorks. CLXI (1855 edn).

2 Below, Kelleythorpe.

created.[1] Little Driffield was divided between the other two civil parishes in 1885. The greater part, with the village of Little Driffield, was added to Elmswell with Kelleythorpe, which was then renamed Elmswell with Little Driffield civil parish and subsequently comprised 2,590 a.; the rest of Little Driffield was amalgamated with Great Driffield civil parish, later also an urban district, which, as a result, had an area of 5,004 a.[2]

A new urban district and civil parish of Driffield was created in 1935 from 2,230 a. of Great Driffield urban district and civil parish, 194 a. of Elmswell with Little Driffield civil parish, including the village of Little Driffield, and 44 a. of Skerne civil parish. There remained 2,774 a. of the dissolved Great Driffield civil parish and urban district, and 2,396 a. of Elmswell with Little Driffield civil parish; the 2,774 a. were then added to Nafferton civil parish, and the Elmswell with Little Driffield area was shared between the new civil parishes of Garton and Kirkburn, 1,466 a. going to Garton and 930 a. to Kirkburn.[3] The area of Driffield civil parish was virtually unchanged in 2001, at 1,000 ha. (2,471 a.).[4]

EARLY SETTLEMENT

The early history of settlement in what was to become Driffield parish goes back long before its written record begins in the 11th century.[5] It is part of a wider pattern in a region whose wealth and density of settlement rendered it of far more than local importance from Neolithic times right down to the Norman Conquest. The material evidence of this activity includes scattered finds and at least one important settlement site, but is above all funerary in nature, being dominated by burial mounds (barrows) of the Bronze and Iron Age. Excavation of these features began as early 1721 and reached a peak with the activities of J. R. Mortimer, a Driffield corn merchant, in the 19th century.[6] Much has been lost. It has been estimated that about a quarter of the funerary mounds in the Driffield area were destroyed by ploughing and other agricultural operations in the later 19th century;[7] others fell victim to the railway and, in the 20th century, often after hurried investigation, to the wartime airfield and other building works.[8] To an extent those losses have been balanced by more recent finds and by the development of aerial photography.[9]

The quantity of flint and stone implements, including axes, arrow-heads, scrapers and knives collected from the Wolds by Mortimer and other archaeologists since the 1840s indicates that the region had a population which was large, and perhaps also enduring, in the Neolithic period (from about 4000 to 2500 BC). Although pits containing occupation debris have been discovered, the post-holes and hearths likely to have been associated with them have not been found, presumably because such shallow features are likely to have been destroyed by erosion.[10] In the Driffield area Neolithic finds are rare, but they include a few significant sites. Worked flint tools together with fragments of late Neolithic pottery were discovered on the western side of the modern town, in St John's Road,[11] and a rare Neolithic house with a hollow floor and post-hole settings has been identified slightly further north, in Mill Street.[12] Although no Neolithic barrows have been found in the area covered by the modern town, a number have been excavated to the west in the area of dense activity stretching from Kelleythorpe to Wetwang. They include a long barrow to the east of Elmswell and round barrows on the site of the former airfield and at Eastburn Warren Farm.[13] In general, the evidence suggests that the rich and well-drained soil, so suitable for arable cultivation, already attracted farmers in Neolithic times. The long-cleared landscape was indeed responsible for the area's Anglo-

1 F. A. Youngs, *Guide to the Local Administrative Units of England*, v. 2 Northern England (1991), 536, 541.

2 *Census*, 1891, 1921. An order of 1883 seems not to have been effective: ERAO, QAT/21.

3 *Census*, 1931 (pt ii).

4 Ibid. 1981; inf. from Office for National Statistics, 2004.

5 This section is by Alan Thacker. It provides an overview of the archaeology and early settlement of the whole area covered by this volume. Details of the archaeology and early settlement of each township will be found in the relevant topographical sections for the Driffields, Elmswell and Kelleythorpe.

6 For general surveys of the archaeology of the area, see J. R. Mortimer, *Forty Years' Researches in British and Saxon Burial Mounds of E Yorks.* (1905); A. J. Challis and D. W. Harding, *Later Prehistory from the Trent to the Tyne* (Brit. Archaeol. Rep., Brit. Ser., 20, 1975); N. Loughlin and K. R. Miller, *Survey of Archaeol. Sites in Humbs.* (1979), 89–90, 97–8, 112–13, 120 (where Mortimer's reference numbers are cited incorrectly); C. Fenton-Thomas, *Forgotten Landscapes of the Yorks. Wolds* (2005); J. S. Dent, *Iron Age in E. Yorks.* (Brit. Archaeol. Rep. 508 Brit. Ser., 2010); S. Harrison, *History of Driffield* (2002), chaps 1 and 2.

7 E.g. *VCH Yorks.* i. 399; Mortimer, *Forty Years' Researches*, 272.

8 T. Sheppard, 'Excavations at Eastburn, E Yorks.', *YAJ* 34 (1939), 37–8, 41–5; T. G. Manby, 'A Neolithic Site at Driffield, ER of Yorks.', *YAJ* 39 (1956–8), 169–78; below, Kelleythorpe.

9 Manby, 'Bronze Age Settlement', in Barrett and Bradley, ii. 307–370, at 314; C. Stoertz, *Ancient Landscapes of the Yorkshire Wolds* (1997).

10 T. G. Manby, 'Neolithic Occupation Sites on the Yorkshire Wolds', *YAJ* 47 (1975), 23–6.

11 Manby, 'Neolithic Site', 169–78; Loughlin and Miller, *Survey*, 90, treat the finds as Bronze Age; fig. 4, no. 2.

12 T. G. Manby, S. Moorhouse and P. Ottaway (eds), *Archaeology of Yorks.* (Yorks. Arch. Soc., 2003), 52–3; *DT* 22 Oct. 1992; fig. 4, no. 1.

13 Harrison, *Driffield*, 17; fig. 4.

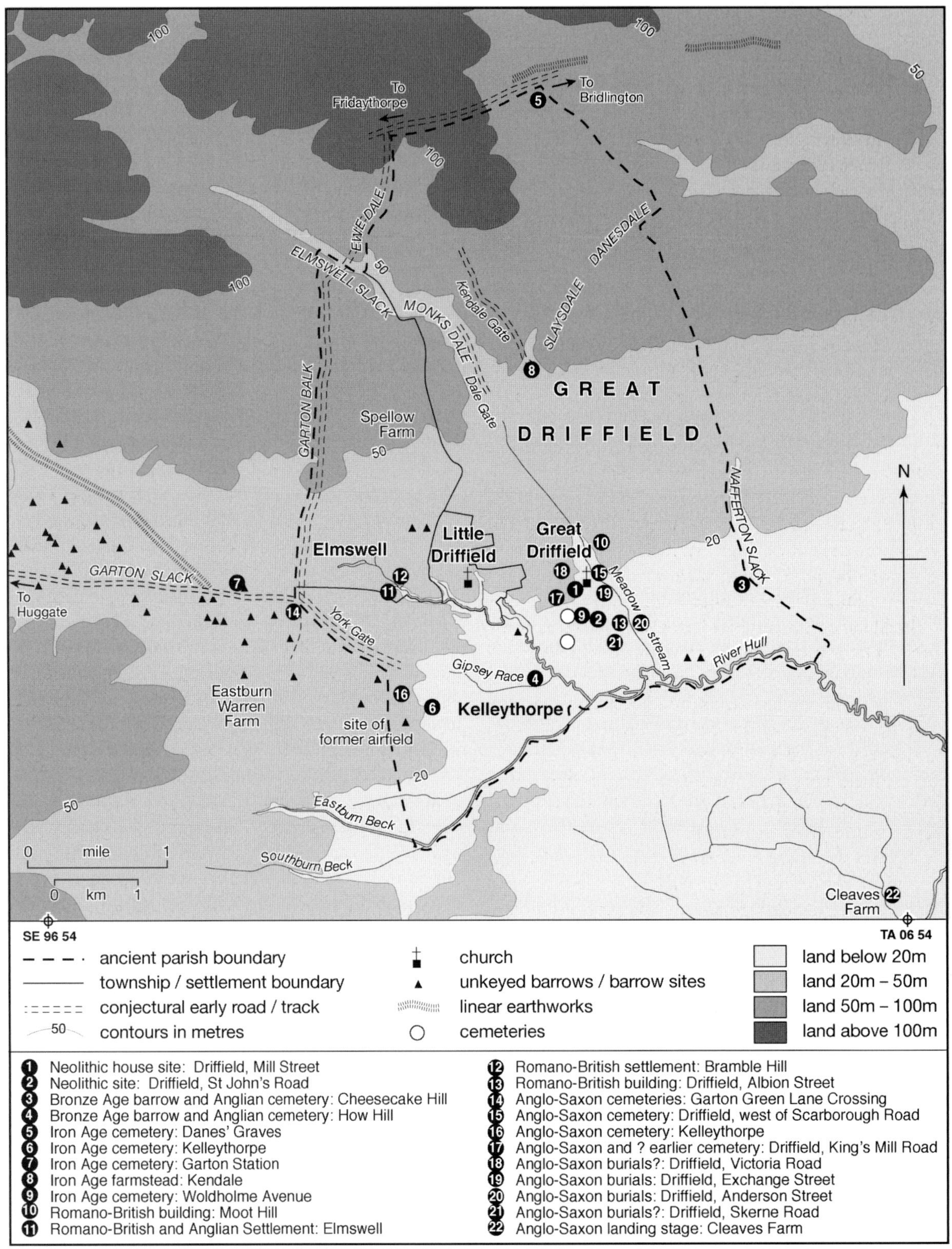

4. *Prehistoric, Romano-British and Anglo-Saxon sites in and around Driffield ancient parish.*

Saxon name: Driffield means 'open land, characterized by dirt' (presumably in the sense of manure) or characterized 'by fields of stubble'.[1]

Knowledge of Bronze Age settlement (roughly 2500–700 BC) comes very largely from burial sites, similar in distribution to the long barrows but by then characteristically round. The evidence from Driffield is unusually rich and relates mostly to the earlier part of the period, before 1400 BC. The main focus of the barrows extends westwards from the recreation ground, to the south of King's Mill Road, in the west of the modern town, along the valley running through Elmswell into Garton slack.[2] Among the nine barrows which Mortimer assigned to a Driffield group, were two large round Bronze Age barrows which became the focus of later cemeteries: the now destroyed How Hill, on the north side of the Gipsey Race in Kelleythorpe, and Cheesecake Hill, on the parish boundary to the east of the modern town.[3] At least another five Bronze Age barrows were located in Elmswell.[4] At the centre of How Hill, lay a late Neolithic or early Bronze Age cist burial, evidently of high status; the grave goods included a bronze chisel or adze, a stone bracer, amber buttons and a beaker.[5] Other Bronze Age finds from Driffield include an imported bronze palgrave, a bronze sword and pottery.[6] The barrows which yielded such material became much less dominant in the late Bronze Age, perhaps because barrow-building had ceased.[7] By then the principal landscape features were the linear earthworks, known locally as dykes, and represented in the Driffield area by a feature running roughly east-west, just north of the Danes' Graves plantation on the north boundary of the parish.[8] Another such feature, the Garton slack dyke, ran eastwards from the Wetwang towards Elmswell along the valley of Garton slack. Probably an embanked roadway, it became the focus of numerous burials.[9]

THE ARRAS CULTURE

During the Iron Age (*c.* 700 BC to 1st century AD), from around the mid 5th century BC, significant cultural changes occurred in east Yorkshire, reflected in new forms of burial, the characteristic features of which were the small round barrow, surrounded by a square ditch, and the square barrow. Many of the interments were characterized by distinctive burial practices: uncoffined graves with the bodies often buried in a contracted or crouched position. Most distinctive of all was the cart, or chariot, burial, a type reserved for those of high status, in which the remains were accompanied by a two-wheeled vehicle. Some graves were furnished with food, pottery, weapons and items of jewellery which have allowed the sites to be dated and have provided evidence of contemporary economy and society. Named after a rich cemetery near Market Weighton, the Arras culture is especially evident in the Driffield area in three important cemeteries, that known as Danes' Graves, on the northern boundary of the parish, that at Kelleythorpe (originally published as Eastburn), in the south of the parish, and that at Garton Station, just to the west.[10]

The Danes' Graves cemetery, which lay just to the south of the linear earthwork already mentioned, is one of the largest of its period in east Yorkshire. Although much has been lost since excavation began in 1721, some 300 barrows can still be located and it may originally have comprised as many as 400–500 burials.[11] Most were relatively modest, of a single individual with few if any grave goods, but they do include a cart burial which contained two contracted inhumations, a dismantled two-wheel cart and some horse harness, but, as far as is known, no weapons.[12] Kelleythorpe, by contrast, where some fifty small grave mounds were excavated, rather summarily, just before the Second World War, and more since, has yielded *inter alia* shield fragments, a spear head and a sword.[13] Both Danes' Graves and Kelleythorpe have produced pottery, in the form of simple jars of coarse material.[14] At Garton Station, a group of square barrows focused upon a large square enclosure included an elaborate cart burial.[15]

Although no Iron Age domestic site has been conclusively identified in the Driffield area, material indicative of settlement has been discovered. At

1 V. Watts (ed.), *Camb. Dict. of Eng. P-N* (2004), 195; *PN Yorks. ER* (EPNS), 154; C. Loveluck, 'The Development of the Anglo-Saxon Landscape: Economy and Society 'On Driffield', E Yorks., 400–700 AD', *Anglo-Saxon Studies in Archaeology and History* 9 (1996), 25.

2 Harrison, *Driffield*, 18–19.

3 Barrows C 38 and C 44: Mortimer, *Forty Years' Researches*, 271–83, 286–93; barrow C38 is called 'How Hill' in a report of its excavation in 1870, *HP* 7 Oct. 1870; below, this section; fig. 4, nos 3 and 4.

4 Below, Elmswell, early settlement.

5 Mortimer, *Forty Years' Researches*, 272–5 (barrow C 38); Manby, Moorhouse and Ottaway (eds), *Archaeology of Yorks.* 59, 61, 74; Loughlin and Miller, *Survey*, 113, where Mortimer's barrow no. is given wrongly as 138; below, Kelleythorpe, early settlement.

6 Below, Great and Little Driffield, early settlement.

7 H. G. Ramm, *The Parisi* (1978), 9; Manby, 'Bronze Age Settlement', 319–20.

8 Harrison, *Driffield*, 28.

9 Loughlin and Miller, *Survey*, 95-7; below, Elmswell, early settlement.

10 Ramm, *Parisi*, 13–21; I. M. Stead, *Arras Culture* (1979); I. M. Stead, *The La Tène Cultures of E Yorks.*, Yorks. Philosophical Soc. (1965); I. M. Stead, *Iron Age Cemeteries in E. Yorks.* (1991), esp. 17–24; P. Halkon (ed.), *New Light on the Parisi* (1989); P. Halkon (ed.), *Further Light on the Parisi* (1998); Dent, *Iron Age*, 72, 77; fig. 4, nos 5–7.

11 Loughlin and Miller, *Survey*, 120; below, Great and Little Driffield, early settlement; fig. 4, no.5.

12 Stead, *Arras Culture*, 16–18, 20–21; Stead, *La Tène Cultures*, 7, 92, 105–10; Loughlin and Miller, *Survey*, 120.

13 Stead, *Arras Culture*, 18; Stead, *La Tène Cultures*, 74, 110; Sheppard, 'Excavations at Eastburn', 35–42; Loughlin and Miller, *Survey*, 112; below, Kelleythorpe, settlement; fig. 4, no. 6.

14 Stead, *La Tène Cultures*, 66; Challis and Harding, *Later Prehistory*, ii. 16, fig. 31.

15 Stead, *Iron Age Cemeteries*, 29–30, 40–1, 58–61; fig. 4, no. 7.

Kelleythorpe, in 1952, Iron Age ditches and native pottery from the immediately pre-Roman period were found on a site adjoining the cemetery.[1] At Kendale, to the north of the modern town of Driffield, evidence of what may have been an early Iron Age farmstead has been discovered in the form of a flint floor and pits for storing corn.[2] Taken with the extensive funerary evidence, all this suggests that the Driffield area was intensively occupied and exploited well before the arrival of the Romans.[3]

Arras culture burials belong to the La Tène group of Iron Age cultures. Named after an archaeological site in Switzerland and based in eastern France and central Europe, they flourished between *c.* 450 BC and the 1st century AD. Although there is at least one object from an Arras culture burial which may date from early in the La Tène period (before 400 BC), most of the artefacts yielded by these graves seem to date from the 2nd and 1st centuries BC. In particular, the large cemeteries with numerous small barrows, such as Danes' Graves and Kelleythorpe, appear mostly to date from this late period. Kelleythorpe, which contains non-native material, is the latest of all the Yorkshire La Tène cemeteries; Danes' Graves, however, includes some larger barrows with shallow interments which may well be as early as the 4th century BC.[4]

It has been suggested that the distinctive continental practices, in particular square barrows and cart burial, were introduced into east Yorkshire with the arrival of the immigrants in the 5th century BC, since thereafter, for perhaps four centuries, there is no evidence of contact with other continental La Tène cultures.[5] But, while the burials suggest an intrusive culture, perhaps that of an immigrant group, it is clear that, even in the earliest phases, they included a native as well as a continental element.[6] The immigrants are more likely to have been agriculturalists and herdsmen rather than warrior aristocrats and may well have integrated peacefully with the native population. The cart or chariot burials are important here. Once thought to have contained no armour or weaponry,[7] that view has had to be revised since the 1980s with the discovery at sites such as those at Wetwang and Garton, not far from Driffield, of rich assemblages including swords, spear heads, shields, and a chain mail shirt.[8] Such elaborate burials probably commemorate early Iron Age chieftains, but not necessarily warriors.[9] The spears in particular seem to have been used as part of the burial rite rather than as indicators of warrior status.[10]

The immigrants themselves may not have been particularly numerous; perhaps initially they influenced the burial practices of a native elite or tribe, and then eventually, through this, the native population as a whole. Elite cart burials probably ceased in the late Iron Age, when we find large cemeteries, with many small mounds containing few grave goods indicative of people of relatively modest status.[11] The change in funerary practice represented by the abandonment of square barrows, and indeed the virtual disappearance of funerary evidence altogether, may reflect changes in belief associated with economic developments.[12]

The distinctive Arras burial culture has been identified with the arrival in Yorkshire of a people known the Parisi, probably the tribe which gave its name to Paris. They are first mentioned as established in Yorkshire by the Egyptian geographer Ptolemy, writing in the 2nd century AD. Ptolemy's account indicates that the Yorkshire Parisi lived near the Brigantes in an area which can be identified as lying between the Humber in the south and the limestone hills on the north side of the Vale of Pickering, and extending from the coast in the east to the River Derwent in the west.[13] This is very much the area in which the Arras culture occurs, but, as has been observed, the argument for linking it with the Parisi, although attractive, can only be speculative: the first record of the latter is so long after the arrival of the former.[14]

ROMAN SETTLEMENT

Arras culture burial had come to an end before the arrival of the Romans.[15] In the Driffield area, however, the cemeteries at Danes' Graves and Kelleythorpe appear to have continued in use almost up to the Roman conquest.[16] Evidence of the survival of native burial customs into the Anglian period has been found at a cemetery at Garton Green Lane Crossing, about a mile to the west of Elmswell.[17] It seems likely, then, that whatever changes in religious, cultural and economic practice it may have undergone, the native population in and around Driffield had survived.[18] That is also suggested by the evidence for continuity of settlement.[19] In the Roman period the only identifiable urban

1 Stead, *La Tène Cultures*, 75; J. T. Philips, 'An Iron Age Site at Driffield, E Yorks.', *YAJ*, 40 (1959–62), 183–91.

2 Below, Great and Little Driffield, early settlement; fig 4, no. 8

3 Stead, *La Tène Cultures*, 75; Stead, *Arras Culture*, 89.

4 Stead, *La Tène Cultures*, 75, 82–3; Dent, *Iron Age*, 81–2; Harrison, *Driffield*, 35.

5 Stead, *Arras Culture*, 89–93.

6 Ibid., 39, 92; Challis and Harding, *Later Prehistory*, i. 173.

7 Stead, *La Tène Cultures*, 5, 85.

8 Stead, *Iron Age Cemeteries*, 29–34; J. Dent, 'Three Cart Burials from Wetwang, Yorks.', *Antiquity* 59 (1985), 85–92.

9 Dent, *Iron Age*, 81.

10 Stead, *Iron Age Cemeteries*, 33.

11 Stead, *La Tène Cultures*, 85, 88; Stead, *Iron Age Cemeteries*, 184.

12 Dent, *Iron Age*, 80–2. Cf. Stead, *Iron Age Cemeteries*, 184.

13 Ramm, *Parisi*, 21–5; Ptolemy, *Geographia*, ed. C. F. A. Nobbe (1898) II, 3, 10.

14 Stead, *Arras Culture*, 92–3. Cf. Stead, *La Tène Cultures*, 88.

15 Stead, *Iron Age Cemeteries*, 184.

16 Ramm, *Parisi*, 14.

17 Ibid. 135.

18 Dent, *Iron Age*, 77.

19 Challis and Harding, *Later Prehistory*, i. 187.

5. *The Elmswell plaque repoussé bronze sheet (restored) attached to an enamelled cast bronze strip. Made* c. *70AD, it perhaps decorated a wooden casket. (9.5 in x 3.1 in).*

settlements in the territory of the Parisi were, in the south, Petuaria (Brough on Humber), which may have been the main administrative centre, and, in the north, the fort of Malton. Another, Delgovicia, as yet unidentified, lay between these two.[1] Although the Driffield area, then, probably lay some way from a town, it did include a significant nucleated settlement, at Elmswell just to the west of the modern Driffield. This settlement seems to have been occupied throughout the Roman period. Roman Elmswell was evidently a place of some significance. Although engaged mainly in mixed pastoral and arable farming, with fields, drove roads and a corn-drying kiln, its inhabitants were also involved in metal working, and perhaps in making pottery. The site has yielded evidence of smithing and the remains of furnaces with considerable quantities of slag.[2] It has also produced the celebrated Elmswell plaque, a repoussé bronze panel with fine late La Tène ornament, British in style but also showing Roman influence and probably manufactured around 70 AD.[3] Evidence of imported products, including late Roman glass and pottery, suggests that the community had generated a surplus sufficient to buy such commodities or at least to be able to obtain them in exchange for its own products.[4] Elmswell thus looks very much like a native site, probably already established in the late Iron Age and continuing under Roman occupation; it may indeed have outlasted the Romans' departure. Pottery, in the form of Huntcliff ware, suggests occupation in the late 4th century and possibly into the 5th.[5]

Other Romano-British settlement sites include Bramble Hill, a little to the north of Elmswell, perhaps a cult site connected with the springs which gave Elmswell its name,[6] and Eastburn, to the south, where field-walking 1997-8 identified at least eight sites, all interpreted as small farmsteads dating from the 2nd to the 4th century, but with roots perhaps in the pre-Roman past.[7]

There is now growing evidence of Romano-British settlement within the area of the modern town. A building which perhaps survived until the late 4th century has been found at the base of Moot Hill, the motte of the Norman castle.[8] A large quantity of roofing tiles, apparently from a substantial Roman building, were discovered near Albion Street, together with pits containing a variety of debris, including pottery which may be dated to the 4th century. Evidence of Romano-British occupation, perhaps of another substantial building, has been found on Eastgate Street South.[9]

ANGLO-SAXON SETTLEMENT

Pre-Viking

An Anglian settlement, dateable to the 5th or 6th century, lay immediately to the east of Romano-British

1 Ramm, *Parisi*, 21–5.

2 Ibid., 80, 120; C. Loveluck, 'Anglo-Saxon Landscape', 28–9; A. L. Congreve, *A Roman and Saxon Site at Elmswell, 1935–6* (Hull Museum Publication, no. 193, 1937); idem, *1937* (Hull Museum Publication, no 198, 1938); P. Corder, *Excavations at Elmswell, E Yorks., 1938* (Hull Museum Publication no. 207, 1940); below; Elmswell, early settlement; fig. 2, no. 11.

3 Ramm, *Parisi*, 80; P. Corder and C. F. C. Hawkes, 'A Panel of Celtic Ornament from Elmswell, E Yorks', *Antiquaries Jnl.* 20 (1940), 338–57; C. Fox, *Pattern and Purpose. A Survey of Celtic Art in Britain* (1958), 105–6.

4 Loveluck, 'Anglo-Saxon Landscape', 28–9.

5 Ramm, *Parisi*, 134; Loveluck, 'Anglo-Saxon Landscape', 28.

6 Below, Elmswell, early settlement; fig. 4, no. 12.

7 Stead, *La Tène Cultures*, 75; Harrison, *Driffield*, 47–8.

8 Below, Great and Little Driffield, early settlement; fig. 4, no. 10.

9 Harrison, *Driffield*, 44–5, based on excavations by Humberside Archaeological Unit, 1992, 1993; fig. 4, no. 13.

Elmswell.[1] Finds from it and from nearby include a 6th-century brooch, a comb, three bone knives and some Anglian pottery.[2] About a mile to the south-east, in Kelleythorpe by the Gipsey Race, lay a cemetery established at much the same time and focused upon How Hill (Mortimer's barrow C38), with its early Bronze Age cist burial.[3] All the Anglian burials that were found were inhumations. The finds include a post-Roman penannular brooch, of a type thought to be native although buried 'in a recognizably Anglo-Saxon manner'. That has been interpreted as evidence of that in the Driffield area the 'native population adopted German fashions of cultural expression'.[4]

Besides the early cemetery at How Hill may be put a similar cemetery at Cheesecake Hill, which lay to the east of modern Driffield, again focused upon a Bronze Age barrow.[5] This is probably of the same date, from the late 5th to the early 7th century. Unlike Kelleythorpe, however, it was found to contain a small number of cremations. These were the only two burial sites of this period to yield significant numbers of graves (41 have been excavated at Kelleythorpe, 35 at Cheesecake Hill). Other Bronze Age and later barrows in the area contained early Anglo-Saxon secondary interments but cannot be shown to have been associated with large-scale cemeteries.[6]

The two main early cemeteries contained significant numbers of furnished burials – *c.* 59 per cent at Kelleythorpe, 46 per cent at Cheesecake Hill. The grave goods suggest a population of some material wealth. At Kelleythorpe they included many silver, copper alloy and iron artefacts, while at Cheesecake Hill there was a preponderance of amber and rock crystal beads and one grave with imported European cowrie shells. In general, those buried at Kelleythorpe appear to have been wealthier than those at Cheesecake Hill but to have been less interested in imported materials such as beads and amulets. The preponderance of metalwork perhaps suggests a population still endowed with native iron-making skills whereas the imported materials at Cheesecake Hill suggest a Germanic population in contact with northern Germany and Scandinavia.

Close to Elmswell, which bears an early (7th-century) English name, a number of rather later cemeteries, of mid 7th- to early 8th-century date, were established, not focused upon Bronze Age barrows but aligned along or next to prehistoric linear earthworks.[7] Just over a mile to the west, in Garton parish, numerous inhumations have been found dating from the mid to late 7th century. At Garton Green Lane Crossing there were two cemeteries, one furnished (and containing the native style burials already mentioned), the other unfurnished (and perhaps Christian), lying aligned along an earthwork running north-east to south-west and at the northern edge of an almost obliterated long barrow.[8] A little to the west, the Iron Age square barrow cemetery at Garton Station included 35 Anglian burials, many well furnished, of which 11 lay within the central square enclosure and were of exceptional richness.[9] The grave goods included fine 7th-century jewellery, a hanging bowl and quite exceptional ironwork assemblages.[10] A further cemetery lay at Kelleythorpe near the boundary with Eastburn in Kirkburn parish.[11] These sites have yielded much metalwork, including some high-status gold and garnet jewellery, penannular brooches, weapons, imported glass and amethyst beads. The ironwork includes iron tools perhaps used in smithing. Here, then, is further evidence that a continuing tradition of iron working lay behind the wealth of the area immediately to the west of modern Driffield, around Elmswell and Garton.[12]

Other putative Anglo-Saxon burials are very difficult to date. Several skeletons found near the gas works and eastwards to the Scarborough road appear to belong to an extensive cemetery lying on the eastern side of Driffield town centre, which may have been Anglian.[13] On the west side of the town at King's Mill Road, a further site, perhaps connected with a barrow, yielded burials apparently of Anglo-Saxon date, some of them contracted.[14] Other burials of uncertain date but possibly Anglo-Saxon occur scattered along or just off Eastgate South and at Skerne Road, just south of the town centre.[15]

All this provides a context for the famous annal in the Anglo-Saxon Chronicle recording the burial of the Northumbrian king Aldfrith at Driffield in 705.[16] Aldfrith's death occurred on 14 December and it has

1 Loveluck, 'Anglo-Saxon Landscape', 28; fig. 4, no. 11.

2 Ramm, *Parisi*, 134, 136; Loughlin and Miller, *Survey*, 98.

3 Fig. 4, no. 4.

4 Loveluck, 'Anglo-Saxon Landscape', 30–1.

5 For this and the following paragraph see Loveluck, 'Anglo-Saxon Landscape', 32–9; fig. 4, no. 3.

6 Loveluck, 'Anglo-Saxon Landscape', 34; Loughlin and Miller, *Survey*, 90.

7 Loveluck, 'Anglo-Saxon Landscape', 33; Fenton-Thomas, *Forgotten Landscapes*, 88–9.

8 Loveluck, 'Anglo-Saxon Landscape', 40. The division of the two cemeteries was marked by the long barrow C 34, incorporated into the earthwork, see Mortimer, *Forty Years' Researches*, 246–57; Ramm, *Parisi*, 135; fig. 4, no. 14.

9 I. M. Stead, 'Garton Station', *Current Archaeology* 103 (1987), 234–7; Stead, *Iron Age Cemeteries*, 21–2, 24. Stead raises the possibility that several of the square barrows, which appear to have contained no Iron Age burials, were in fact added to the existing Iron Age cemetery by the Anglians.

10 Personal communication from Leslie Webster.

11 Sheppard, 'Excavations at Eastburn, E Yorks.', 44–7; fig. 4, no. 16.

12 Loveluck, 'Anglo-Saxon Landscape', 39–42.

13 Loughlin and Miller, *Survey*, 90; below, Great and Little Driffield, early settlement; fig. 4, no. 15.

14 Mortimer, *Forty Years' Researches*, 294; below, Great and Little Driffield, early settlement; fig. 4, no. 17.

15 Harrison, *Driffield*, 53–64; fig. 4, nos 19–21.

16 It occurs only in D and E texts, which are based on northern annals: *Two Anglo-Saxon Chronicles Parallel*, ed. J. Earle and C. Plummer (1892, 1899), i. 41; ii. 35; *A-S. Chron.*, ed. D. Whitelock (1961), 25.

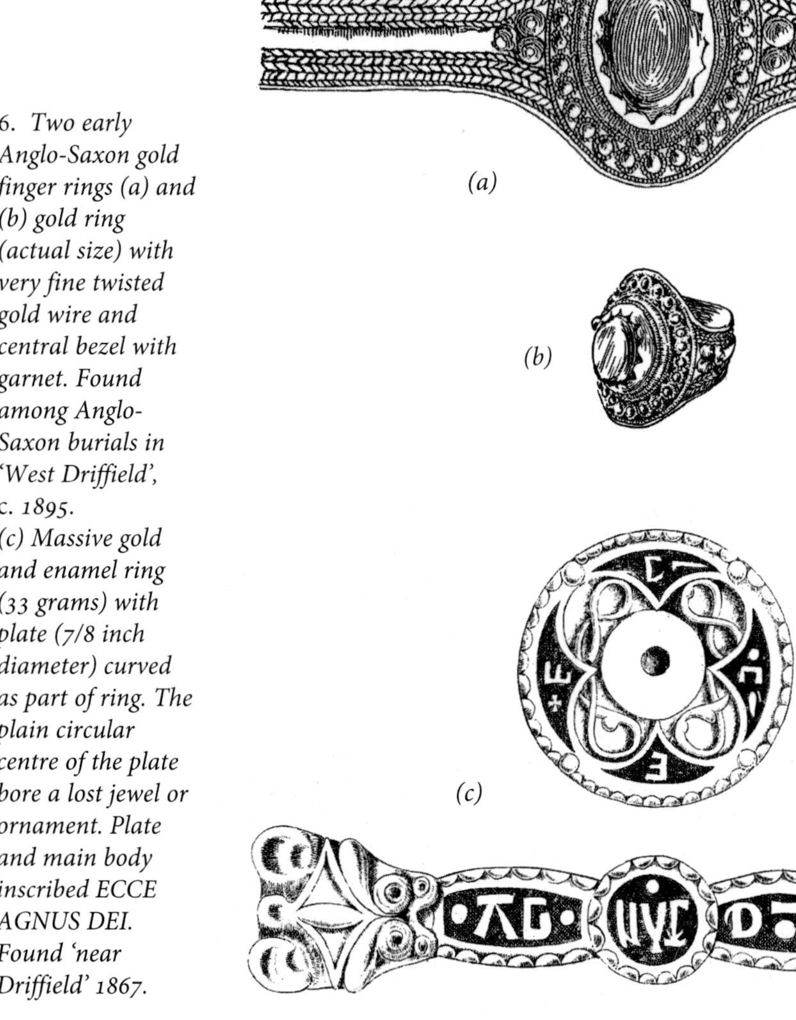

6. *Two early Anglo-Saxon gold finger rings (a) and (b) gold ring (actual size) with very fine twisted gold wire and central bezel with garnet. Found among Anglo-Saxon burials in 'West Driffield', c. 1895. (c) Massive gold and enamel ring (33 grams) with plate (7/8 inch diameter) curved as part of ring. The plain circular centre of the plate bore a lost jewel or ornament. Plate and main body inscribed ECCE AGNUS DEI. Found 'near Driffield' 1867.*

been suggested that he intended to spend Christmas in Driffield, if true an indication that it was a centre to which he attached especial significance.[1] Aldfrith, the learned Irish-educated successor of King Ecgfrith (d. 685), issued a coinage, silver *sceattas*, which, most unusually, bear a Latinized form of his name and which occur in some concentration on the Yorkshire coast, at Whitby, and around the Humber estuary. *Sceattas* of a similar date, although not inscribed with Aldfrith's name, have been found to the west of modern Driffield at Garton slack and others to the north-west and north-east. Such silver *sceattas* do not occur elsewhere in Northumbria until the 730s and their restricted distribution in the south-east of the kingdom suggests that Aldfrith's Driffield estate may have been an important centre for their promotion and circulation.[2] Other evidence relevant to Driffield's connections with Northumbria's kings comes in the form of two gold rings discovered there. One, probably found in an area of burials west of Driffield Beck and adorned with a fine garnet and with twisted gold wire, dates probably from the later 7th century; the jewel's distinctive dogtooth setting belongs to a type which emerges in that period. It is sufficiently grand to have belonged to a member of the royal kindred or to a royal official or counsellor.[3] The other ring is later, probably mid 9th century. A massive object, weighing some 33 grams, it was inscribed with a text from St John's Gospel, ECCE AGNUS DEI ('Behold the lamb of God'),[4] and also bore schematized animal heads and Trewhiddle style nielloed ornament. The

1 B. Yorke, *'Rex Doctissimus': Bede and King Aldfrith of Northumbria*, Jarrow lecture, 2009, 16.

2 Yorke, *'Rex Doctissimus'*, 6, 14–15; Loveluck, 'Anglo-Saxon Landscape', 43–4.

3 T. Sheppard, 'A Saxon Gold Ring Found at Driffield', *TERAS* 24 (1921–2), 43–50.

4 John 1, 29.

central element of the bezel was missing, but may well have comprised an image of the Agnus Dei. The nearest analogue is a ring which had belonged to a Queen Æthelswith, almost certainly the wife of King Burgred of Mercia. Inscribed with her name and title and also adorned with an Agnus Dei, it was a ring of office, dating from her regnal years in Mercia (853/4–874) and presumably left behind when she accompanied her husband into exile.[1] The Driffield ring was thus clearly of the highest status. While it may have been brought to Driffield and lost or deposited there in or after the Viking invasions, it is perhaps more likely that it reflected the area's continuing royal associations.

The Landing Place at Cleaves Farm

An important site probably closely linked with the royal estate at Driffield was excavated recently at Cleaves Farm, in Skerne, on the east side of the River Hull, some 2½ miles south-east of the modern town. The excavated finds and remains, dating from between the 7th and 11th centuries, relate to an artificial causeway and two structures, a wooden jetty or landing place and a wooden platform, possibly part of a river crossing. The earliest of the timber structures could date from the time when the Driffield estate was held by the kings of Northumbria. Standing at the limit of the tidal range of the River Hull, it may have been a landing-place for imported commodities serving the needs of the royal vill. Skerne was a soke under the jurisdiction of the lord of Driffield in 1066 and could have been a constituent member of the 7th-century royal estate, which is likely to have been larger than that recorded in the Domesday survey. The place-name Brigham, 'village by a bridge', which lay a little to the west of Skerne is Anglian and may relate to the structures found at Cleaves Farm. Skerne's own place-name, however, is Scandinavian, and many of the finds and remains from the excavation are probably from the Anglo-Scandinavian period, i.e. from the later 9th to the early 11th century. They suggest the continuing importance of the Driffield estate during the period between its disappearance from the record in the 8th and century and its re-emergence in 1086.[2]

The Late Anglo-Saxon Estate

Almost certainly Anglo-Saxon Driffield was a large estate with many settlements. That is suggested by the fact that in 1066 it was a large manor assessed with its berewicks at some 23 carucates[3] and the jurisdictional focus of a large group of sokelands, assessed at over 50 carucates.[4] It was then in the possession of Earl Morcar of Northumbria. Comparison with other comital estates suggests that its size and its possession by Morcar are further indications that the estate had been part of Northumbrian royal patrimony.[5] Also significant is the fact that it gave its name to a hundred, one of those which constituted the later wapentake of Harthill. In many cases, these hundreds, which from the later 10th century may already have been grouped into larger administrative units similar to the medieval wapentakes, coincided with earlier soke manors. That certainly seems to have been the case at Driffield.[6] The hundredal meeting-place was probably at Spellow, whose place-name derives from Old English words *spell*, meaning 'speech', and *haugr*, meaning 'mound'. The exact location of the meeting place is unknown, but it was approached from Driffield and Elmswell by ancient trackways, both known as Spellowgate, and the name survives today in Elmswell, as Spellow Farm and Spellow Clump. That it lay in Elmswell is perhaps a further indication of the early local importance of the settlement there.[7]

Location of the Estate Centre

The fact that in early Anglo-Saxon times the name Driffield designated an area which probably included many settlements makes it difficult to be certain that the main estate centre lay in or near the site of the modern town. Nevertheless, it seems likely that the two churches known to stand on the estate in Earl Morcar's day were in fact the Driffields' two ancient churches and that they provide evidence relating to the whereabouts of settlement. In early Anglo-Saxon times settlement in Driffield was perhaps focused upon the western margins of the modern town at or just west of the Driffield beck. The garnet ring found there may have come from a cemetery in that area or, perhaps, from a royal complex. Burials also occur on the other side of the beck, off King's Mill Road, and in Shady Lane (later Victoria Road).[8] Such evidence sits well with the probability that the church at Little Driffield, which lay a little to the north-west on a tributary of the Driffield beck, goes back at least to the 10th century and is, almost certainly, the earliest church in the area. It has

1 J. T. Fowler, 'An Account of the Anglo-Saxon Gold Ring Discovered near Driffield, Yorks., now in the possession of the Revd Geo. Welby, Barrowby, Grantham', *Proceedings of the Geological and Polytechnic Society of the West-Riding of Yorks.* 5 (1870), 157-62; L. Webster and J. Backhouse (eds), *The Making of England* (1991), no. 244. The author is grateful to Leslie Webster for much help with the discussion of the gold rings.

2 R. Van de Noort and S. Ellis, *Wetland Heritage of the Hull Valley* (2000), 217–42; *VCH Yorks.* ii. 197; Watts (ed.), *Camb. Dict. P-N.* 86, 553; fig. 4, no. 22.

3 Of these 17½ were said to be in Driffield parish. The summary, however, assigns an assessment of 32½ carucates just to Great and Little Driffield: *VCH Yorks* ii. 197, 320.

4 *VCH Yorks.* ii. 197, 224, 225, 292.

5 R. Sharpe, *The Earls of York and Bamburgh*, Chadwick Lecture, 2009, forthcoming.

6 It comprised the Domesday manors of Great and Little Driffield, belonging to the king and the count of Mortain: *Yorks. Domesday* (Alecto Domesday, 1992), 52, 61, 62.

7 *Yorks. Domesday*, 67; fig. 4. The place-name 'Moot Hill', which might be thought to offer a rival site, probably derives from the castle motte.

8 Below, Great and Little Driffield, early settlement; fig. 4, nos 17–18.

yielded late 9th- or 10th-century sculpture and according to a long-standing local tradition is the church in which King Aldfrith was buried.[1]

Evidence from the Norman castle motte and from High Street suggests that settlement later moved eastwards.[2] After a period in which soil had accumulated, pits were dug, and then a ditch, which cut through the floor of the Roman building beneath; eventually a bank was created in association with the ditch. These features came into existence between *c.* 550 and the creation of the Norman motte (perhaps in 1069);[3] they may be connected with a move which eventually occasioned the establishment of a second church, at Great Driffield, probably by the mid 11th century, even if the settlement around it was later remodelled under the Normans.[4]

CONCLUSIONS

The Driffield area seems, then, to have been rich in both agricultural and mineral resources and industrially productive from Roman times if not before. In the early Anglo-Saxon period, it was evidently inhabited by a mixture of Germanic settlers and a continuing native population, of some wealth, involved not only in farming but in the iron working which they had inherited from their Romano-British predecessors. They included people, particularly in the east of the parish, with a taste for imported beads and other objects likely to have from Germanic Europe.

By the late 7th century, perhaps because of its wealth and productivity, the Driffield area had become a favoured and probably extensive royal estate, perhaps then focused around Elmswell and Little Driffield and with a landing-place at Cleaves Farm. Aldfrith evidently stayed there at important festivals and promoted there an experimental coinage, including an issue which bore his name. The Agnus Dei ring suggests that the area continued to have important royal associations until the mid 9th century. With the Danish invasion and the demise of the Northumbrian kingship, elements of the royal estate may have become separate, no longer looking to the former royal *caput* as their focus; the main centre of settlement perhaps moved eastwards. The estate was clearly still a major territorial unit when it was in Earl Morcar's hands in 1066, but in 1086, after the harrying of the north it was classified as 'waste', and clearly had at least temporarily been reduced in value. Although it subsequently recovered,[5] it probably never again achieved the regional dominance that it had enjoyed in the days of Aldfrith.

POPULATION

There is no good evidence as to numbers in the parish or its constituent settlements before the late 14th century when Driffield was one of the most populous settlements in the East Riding, lying tenth in number of taxpayers in 1377.[6] Those liable to pay the poll tax in the parish that year numbered 456, of whom 348 lived in Great and Little Driffield combined, 92 at Elmswell, and 16 in Kelleythorpe.[7] The number of taxpayers in the two Driffields was greater than in the other small market towns in Harthill wapentake, Pocklington with 341 taxpayers and Market Weighton with 235, and the nearby market villages of Hutton Cranswick with 318 and Nafferton with 240, but it had less than the number in Kilham, 363 and Bridlington, 379.[8]

Driffield had probably reduced in population and wealth by the early 16th century, but the two Driffields with Kelleythorpe still ranked eighth out of 105 places in Harthill wapentake in the amount of tax paid in 1524, 89*s.* 2*d.*, and fifth in the number of listed taxpayers, 46. This was considerably less than the 193*s.* 10*d* tax paid, and fewer than the 90 taxpayers, recorded for Pocklington or the 54 tax payers at Hutton Cranswick.[9] There are no figures for Kilham or Nafferton in 1524, but in 1525 Kilham was taxed at 66*s.* 6*d.* and Nafferton at 50*s.* 2*d*, compared to 72*s.* 10*d.* for the Driffields and Kelleythorpe.[10] This suggests that Driffield was on equal ranking with Kilham, but in 1539 only 23 able-bodied men are returned in the muster roll for Great and Little Driffield, compared to Kilham, 49, Hutton Cranswick, 50, Market Weighton, 58 and Pocklington, 109.[11] Had Driffield suffered a severe drop in population since the mid 1520s or is there another explanation? If there had been such a decline the parish had recovered by 1584 when 54 men were returned on the muster roll for Great Driffield, 8 for Little Driffield and 6 for Elmswell. The number returned for Great Driffield was similar to that for Kilham, 51 and Hutton Cranswick, 57.[12]

An analysis of Great Driffield parish registers

1 J. Lang, *Corpus of Anglo-Saxon Sculpture III: York and Eastern Yorks.* (1991), 179; below, Great and Little Driffield, religious history: Middle Ages.

2 Loveluck, 'Anglo-Saxon Landscape', 45; fig. 4, no. 10.

3 M. R. Eddy, 'Excavations at Moot Hill, Driffield', *ER Archaeologist* 7 (1983), 40–51.

4 Below, Great and Little Driffield, development.

5 Below, Great and Little Driffield, economic history: agriculture.

6 C. C. Fenwick, *The Poll Taxes of 1377, 1379 and 1381*, pt 3 (2005), 160–9.

7 TNA, E 179/202/59, mm. 24, 32–3.

8 Fenwick, *Poll Taxes*, 161–4.

9 J. Sheail, *The Regional Distribution of Wealth in England as Indicated in the 1524/5 Lay Subsidy Returns*, II (1998), 399–401.

10 Sheail, *Regional Distribution*, 399–400.

11 TNA, E36/39.

12 *Miscellanea* v (YAS Rec. Ser. 116), 72, 82–3, 90.

Year	*Estimated population*
1672	715
1700	661
1720	706
1740	682
1760	742
1780	924
1800	1,190

Sources: Purdy, *Yorks. Hearth Tax*, 56; Noble, 'Growth and development', 285.

Table 1. *Great Driffield: Estimated Population 1672–1800*

suggests that the population was in decline for over a hundred years from the later 16th century, interrupted by a slight rise in the 1640s.[1] There were crisis periods such as 1591 when the 45 burials were more than twice the annual average for the decade, and in the early 1620s when the annual average of 12 burials rose to 33 in 1623 and about 65 in 1624. Ten of the burials in the latter year took place in October and the description 'poor' was applied to several of the deceased.[2]

The first trustworthy estimate of the population can be calculated from the hearth tax list of 1672 when there were 159 households in the two Driffields, which using the standard multiplier of 4.5 gives a population of around 715, of which about 650 lived in Great Driffield. The settlement then ranked eighth in number of households in the East Riding; the largest town was Beverley with 620 households, then Bridlington, 352, Cottingham, 289, Howden, 207, Holme on Spalding Moor, 176, Pocklington, 168 and Hunmanby, 167. Driffield had more households than Market Weighton with 141, Hutton Cranswick, 128, Kilham, 110, Nafferton, 102, and the market village of North Frodingham with 85.[3]

Comparing the number of households in 1672 with the number of families calculated by incumbents in response to a visitation questionnaire in 1743 there was a decrease of over 20 per cent in the population of the wapentake division of Bainton Beacon between the two returns.[4] Comparable figures are not available for Driffield, as no return was made by the incumbent in 1743, but an estimated population figure of 682 in 1740 suggests a decrease of less than 5 per cent.[5] The natural decrease was greatest in the period 1670–99 when there were 147 more burials than baptisms recorded in the parish registers of Great and Little Driffield. A number of crisis years occurred at this time, most significantly 1679–81 when burials were up to twice the average. In the period 1700–39 there was a modest natural increase, with baptisms exceeding burials in each decade except 1720–29 when there were futher crisis years and 94 more burials than baptisms.[6]

Driffield's limited drop in population compared to its natural decrease in the late 17th century and 1720s indicates that the settlement experienced in-migration rather than the out-migration that accounted for the loss of over a third of the population elsewhere in Bainton Beacon.[7] The freeholder community of Driffield would attract villagers from the more restrictive closed settlements, where the actions of landowners led directly to population decline.[8] In-migration probably increased after the inclosure of the open fields in 1742, which led to an increase in the number of freeholders. This and the general acceleration of population growth experienced nationwide from the mid 18th century meant that Driffield was already expanding with an estimated population of around 800 by the time the navigation opened in 1770.[9]

Thereafter the population rose rapidly, reaching about 1,331 at the first census in 1801, an increase of around 66 per cent over 30 years. The rate of increase escalated in the first half of the 19th century, with the population doubling by 1831 to 2, 660, and increasing by a further 50 per cent to 3,963 in 1851 (Table 2). With the exception of Hull, no town in the area grew faster.[10] Between 1801 and 1851 Great Driffield's population increased by 198 per cent, whilst that of most of the other East Yorkshire towns rose between 60 and 70 per cent.[11] Over a third of the increase in the period 1801–51 can be attributed to in-migration, and probably much more considering the increased mobility of the population and the periods of overseas migration.[12] In 1830 the Revd Richard Allen, vicar of Driffield, recorded that 'the strength of this nation [is] removing very fast into

1 D. Foster, 'Population,' in B. Dyson (ed.), *A Guide to Local Studies in E Yorks.* (1985), 132, 134.

2 ERAO, PE10/1.

3 J. D. Purdy, *Yorks. Hearth Tax Returns* (1991), 51, 54–9.

4 S. Neave, 'Rural settlement contraction in the ER of Yorks. *c.* 1660–1760' (Hull Univ. PhD thesis, 1990), 37. There was a decrease of around 19% for the East Riding as a whole.

5 M. K. Noble, 'Growth and development of country towns: the case of eastern Yorks., *c.* 1700–1850' (Hull Univ. PhD. thesis, 1983), 285; Table 1.

6 ERAO, PE 10/2–3; PE11/1–2.

7 Neave, 'Rural settlement', 38; Noble, 'Growth and development', 286.

8 Neave, 'Rural settlement', 84–133, 276–8.

9 Estimate noted by John Browne *c.* 1848: ERAO, DDX/17/15. In 1764 the non-resident curate unhelpfully said that there were over a hundred families in the parish, probably a very misleading underestimate: *Drummond's Visit.* i, p. 139.

10 M. Noble, 'Urban Development', in Dyson (ed.) *Guide to Local Studies*, 112.

11 *VCH Yorks.* iii. 488–99.

12 Noble, 'Growth and development', 288.

	DRIFFIELD PARISH	Great Driffield township	% change	Elmswell with Kelleythorpe township	Little Driffield township
1801	1,483	*c.* 1,331*		72	*c.* 80
1811	2,025	1,857	39.5%	86	82
1821	2,471	2,303	24%	93	75
1831	2,854	2,660	15.5%	102	92
1841	3,477	3,223	21%	100	154
1851	4,259	3,963	23%	110	186
1861	4,734	4,405	11%	132	197
1871	5,423	5,067	15%	154	202
1881	6,323	5,937	17%	168	218

* 1, 411 in Gt and Little Driffield. There were *c.* 80 inhabitants in Little Driffield: Ross, *Driffield*, 80.
Source: *VCH Yorks*. iii. 490.

Table 2. *Driffield: Parish Population 1801–81*

	DRIFFIELD PARISH	Great Driffield civil parish/urban district (5,004 a.)	% change	Elmswell with Little Driffield civil parish (2,590 a.)
1891	6,037	5,703	-4%	334
1901	6,036	5,766	+1%	270
1911	5,951	5,676	-1.5%	275
1921	5,975	5,674	0%	301
1931	6,208	5,915	4%	293

Source: *Census*, 1891–1931.

Table 3. *Driffield: Parish and Civil Parishes Population 1891–1931*

America'.[1] The parish officers of Great Driffield were directed to assist the emigration to Australia of John Robson, his wife, and three children, paupers, in 1849.[2]

Only a quarter of working males in Great Driffield in 1851 were born in the town, 45 per cent were born elsewhere in the East Riding, 15 per cent in the rest of Yorkshire, and 9.5 per cent in the rest of England and Wales.[3] The area of influence of the town and its role as a focal point for migratory movement is indicated by the origin of marriage partners for residents who came from 84 places in the period 1790–1850. In 24 per cent of marriages one partner came from outside the parish, all but 16 per cent from within the East Riding.[4]

Whilst most villages in the Driffield area reached their peak population in 1851 or 1861 the population of the town, despite a slowing down in the 1850s, continued to rise significantly until the 1880s.[5] It was still a focus for in-migration at a time when overall the Driffield superintendent registrar's district experienced considerable out-migration. During the period 1881–1900 the impact of the agricultural depression led to increased out-migration to the extent that for the first time in the 19th century the population of the district declined, with many going abroad.[6] In March 1883 the local paper reported that a 'large party' had left Driffield station for Liverpool and Canada, and the newspaper owner then advertised a scheme of cheap emigration to New York.[7]

Great Driffield's population was static rather than in decline between 1881 and the 1920s; most of the 4 per cent fall in the 1880s was due to the re-organization of the civil parishes in 1885 when Little Driffield was detached from Great Driffield and joined with

1 ERAO, PE/10/T. 84, s.a. Mar. 1830.
2 Ibid. PE/10/T. 99, s.a. 1849.
3 Howorth, *Driffield*, 84.
4 Noble, 'Growth and development', 291.
5 Foster, 'Population', 133; *HP* 3 May 1861.
6 Foster, 'Population', 135–6.
7 *DT* 31 Mar. 1883.

	Driffield civil parish/urban district (2,468 a./999 ha.)	*% Change*
1951	7,006	18.5%
1961	6,892	-1.5%
1971	7,895	14.5%
1981	9,100	15%
1991	9,912	9%
2001	11,477	16%

Sources: *Census*, 1951–91; inf. from Office for National Statistics, 2004.

Table 4. *Population: Driffield Civil Parish 1951–2001*

Elmswell. The introduction of new industries in the 1920s–30s and the impact of the airfield on the periphery probably account for the population rise to 1951. The creation of a smaller urban district in 1935 made little difference to the town's population, involving as it did the loss of a rural area inhabited in 1931 by only 94 people.[1]

After a modest fall in population in the late 1950s, there has been a steady rise, at first encouraged by expanding industries then sustained by the town's popularity as a residential centre. In 2001 about 60 per cent of the population (6,957) were over 16 and under 65 years old, with 2,138 children and 2,382 older people. The population was 98.5 per cent white British and only 0.5 per cent of ethnic origin. The average household size was 2.28 in 2001, compared with 4.29 in 1901.[2]

COMMUNICATIONS

ROADS

The better drained and more easily cleared Wolds are believed to have been crossed by regularly used tracks, possibly as early as the Neolithic period, between *c.* 4,000 and 2,000 BC. Linear embankments and burial mounds mark stretches of the early ways, but less certain is their progress into the lower areas, where the wetter ground and the later concentration of human activity have together combined to remove what evidence there may have been. For those reasons, little can be said about early routes in Driffield parish, much of which lies down the Wold slope or in the Hull Valley. However, one of the lower Wold roads identified, that from York and Fridaythorpe to Bridlington, ran along the slope, some 3 miles north of the present town of Driffield, there later forming the northern boundary of both Driffield parish and the Bainton division of Harthill wapentake. Its course is aligned with linear earthworks in the neighbouring parishes, and a large Iron-Age cemetery, made sometime between the 8th and the 1st century BC, and ground nearby called Maiden's Grave, also testify to the antiquity and significance of the boundary there.[3] Another early route across the Wolds was evidently that which led from the south of Driffield parish over the Wolds to Huggate, and then presumably descended into the Vale of York. Once again the route is marked by an embankment, just to the west of Driffield parish, in neighbouring Garton on the Wolds, and was flanked formerly by many prehistoric burial sites. It was later an important local boundary, marking the northern limit of Tibthorpe and Kirkburn townships and the Bainton division of Harthill wapentake, besides defining a stretch of the boundary between Kelleythorpe township and Kirkburn parish.[4] Much later the way was called York Gate, or Road, and it is now represented by very minor roads. The way to Huggate was probably crossed from an early date by another route, proceeding northwards from Kirkburn along Garton balk and later forming much of Driffield parish's western boundary.

The process by which the lower land in the parish was settled, and the nature of the early communications between those and other populated areas in the district, is obscure. It is not possible to describe comprehensively the roads linking places within and beyond the parish boundaries until the 18th century, but one or two of the roads recorded then may be suggested as very early routes. There is believed to have been a settlement at Kendale on the lower slope of the Wolds, to the north of the present town, from the late Iron Age into the Middle Ages, and there was later a way leading up the slope there, presumably to give access to fields but perhaps also to join the British trackway or the Roman road on the higher ground. Variously called Kendale Gate, or Kendale Road, and High Peter Lane, it was partly discontinued as a highway at inclosure in 1742, but remained later as a field road.[5] Another old way nearby called Dale Gate, leading to wold land in the north-west of the parish, was confirmed in part at

1 *Census*, 1931 (pt ii).

2 ER of Yorks. 2001 Census Area Profile: Driffield.

3 Notes by Revd E. Maule Cole in *Proc. Yorks. Geol. and Polytechnic Soc.* N.S. 13 (1897–9), 299; OS Map 1:25,000, SE 96, TA 06 (1953–4 edn).

4 OS Map 1:25,000, SE 85, 95 (1953 edn).

5 RDB, B/153/42, *see* Ric. Langley's allotment of 145 a. 3 r. 21 p.; ERAO, IA. 41; OS Map 1:10,560, Yorks. CLXI (1855 edn); OS Map 1:10,000, TA 06 SW (1983 edn).

inclosure in 1742, and was later known also as Low Peter Lane.[1] That lane was evidently continued southwards to Great Driffield, its lower part being represented later by a footpath which followed both a stream and the close boundaries made at inclosure.[2]

By the mid 18th century most of the present roads serving the parish existed. Four roads led from the town onto the higher ground: one went north-eastwards by way of Nafferton to Bridlington; a second northwards to a main road between Bridlington and York, and then on to Langtoft and eventually Scarborough; the third north-westwards through the small settlements of Little Driffield and Elmswell to Garton on the Wolds, where the road divided to continue to Malton and York; and the last south-westwards by way of Kirkburn to Market Weighton and Pocklington in the Vale of York. Another road across the Wolds, York Gate, the ancient route to the Pocklington and the Vale through Huggate, was apparently then also still used. The town's other roads led into the Hull Valley and Holderness, one southwards to Hutton Cranswick, and then on to Beverley and Hull, and the other south-eastwards to Wansford, North Frodingham, Skipsea, and the North Sea coast.[3] That the former way was early is suggested by the name of its ford through Driffield Beck, Alamanwath, or Hallimanwath, which is believed to have been Anglo-Scandinavian.[4]

At the inclosure of the Driffields in 1742[5] and Elmswell in 1771[6] some of the existing highways in the parish were improved. That to Langtoft and Scarborough, comprising roads called Duggleby Trod and Scarborough Gate, was confirmed by the former award but its width was increased to 40 ft. The same width was also ordained for the road to Malton and York in Elmswell, as well as for lesser roads, like Spellowgate, which connected Driffield with part of Elmswell and small settlements on the Wolds. Other roads confirmed at the inclosure of Elmswell included Pocklington and Bridlington Roads, earlier known as Pocklington and Kilham Gates.[7] The former led westwards from the hamlet along Maskill balk[8] before turning south into Garton balk, which formed the western boundary,[9] to reach the south-western corner of Elmswell; there it joined the ancient way called York Gate, which continued westwards across the Wolds to Pocklington and York. That the Kilham or Bridlington road was another early route is suggested by its use across Driffield of a field division which was connected to the balk forming the western parish boundary, and like it was called Garton balk.[10]

More significantly, several new roads were made at inclosure. Apart from their characteristic straight courses, they are identifiable from the boundary descriptions of adjacent allotments. One object of the new roads was to relieve congestion in the growing town by constructing lateral by-passes to its east and west. The eastern road, later Scarborough Road and Wansford Road, served the routes to the north and east of Driffield, while two western roads were made to link the route to York and Malton with that to Beverley and Hull. The more northerly of the western roads was later called Shady Lane and Victoria Road in turn,[11] and the southern stretch[12] Beverley Lane, or Street, and now St John's Road.[13] Beyond the lateral roads, new courses were also made for the roads to Nafferton, later Bridlington Road,[14] Beverley,[15] and Wansford.[16] The Wansford road also replaced the nearby 'ancient highway to the south end of Great Driffield', primarily an outgang giving access to the town's pastures.[17]

Lesser roads awarded at inclosure include Skerne Road, which leads south from the town. It was awarded as a private way, in large part to give inhabitants of Driffield and Little Driffield access to Bell Mill, just across the boundary stream in Skerne parish; the new road, called Factory Lane in the mid 19th century, probably replaced a route to the east of the beck by way of the outgang, which was then extinguished.[18] Similarly, another minor road awarded in 1742 was the new lane leading westwards from Driffield town to King's Mill, later in turn called Mill Lane and King's Mill Road. Part of its purpose was to give the inhabitants of the town and of Little Driffield access to the mill; another way then awarded led directly to the mill from the York road at Little Driffield, and that was perhaps the earlier route which Mill Lane was intended to supplement.[19]

1 RDB, B/153/42 [roads]; OS Map 1:10,560, Yorks. CLXI (1855 edn).

2 ERAO, IA. 41; OS Map 1:10,560, Yorks. CLXI (1855 edn).

3 T. Jefferys, *Map of Yorks.* (1775).

4 Ross, *Driffield*, 192–3; OS Map 1:10,560, Yorks. CLXI (1855 edn).

5 RDB, B/153/42; ERAO, IA. 41.

6 RDB, AN/196/12.

7 Best, *Farming Bks*, ed. Woodward, 40, 99.

8 BIA, CC. Pr. 11/3.

9 OS Map 1:2,500, Yorks. CLXI. 10 (1910 edn).

10 OS Map 1:2,500, Yorks. CXLIV. 16 (1910 edn).

11 RDB, B/153/42, see Thomas Etherington's allotment of 25 a. 3 r. 23 p.; ERAO, IA. 41. OS Map 1:10,560, Yorks. CLXI (1855 edn); OS Map 1:2,500, Yorks. CLXI. 12 (1910 edn).

12 RDB, B/153/42, see Ric. Langley's allotment of 50 a. 2r. 1p.

13 RDB, CH/301/480; ERAO, NV/1/107; OS Map 1:10,560, Yorks. CLXI (1855 edn); OS Map 1:2,500, Yorks. CLXI. 12 (1893 edn).

14 See Ric. Langley's allotment of 32 a. 0 r. 26 p.

15 See Ric. Langley's allotment of 17 a. 2 r. 6 p.

16 See George Colbatch's allotment as vicar of 3 a. 3 r. 18 p. OS Map 1:2,500, Yorks. CLXI. 12 (1893 edn).

17 See allotments to Chappilow (2 a. 2 r. 25 p.); Hudson, Ann (3 a. 3 r. 31 p.), and Langley (10 a. 3 r. 38 p. in 33 a. 1 r. 14 p.).

18 RDB, B/153/42 [roads]; LH/153/213; ERAO, IA.41. The course of the outgang was later followed by Beechwood Lane.

19 RDB, B/153/42 [roads] *and see* Ric. Langley's allotment of 50 a. 2 r. 1 p.; ERAO, IA. 41; OS Map 1:10,560, Yorks. CLXI (1855 edn); OS Map 1:2,500, Yorks. CLXI. 12 (1893 edn).

The busiest of the parish's roads in the 18th century were probably those to Beverley, Bridlington, and Scarborough, though the significance of that to York and Malton is suggested by the milestones which stood until the mid 20th century in Little Driffield and Elmswell.[1] The road from Beverley and the first mile or so of the Scarborough road, from Driffield to Kendale House, were turnpiked in 1766, the promoters including Beverley Corporation.[2] A bar was sited just south of Driffield parish, close to the junction with the Beverley road of lanes leading to Sunderlandwick, in Hutton Cranswick, and Skerne; milestones formerly stood north of the town near Little Kendale Farm[3] and close to Great Driffield's southern boundary.[4] The road was subsequently improved by the building of Hallimanwath bridge to replace the ford through Driffield Beck,[5] and in 1768 Arthur Young reckoned it comprised the best turnpike road in Yorkshire.[6]

In 1866 the trustees of the Beverley to Kendale House turnpike took over the financially-unviable road from Beverley to Kexby Bridge, aware that its closure as a turnpike would damage the Driffield route: both trusts were discontinued in 1881.[7]

The main roads were later the responsibility of the county council, which, to cope with the increasing volume of traffic, improved several of them in the mid 20th century. In 1982 the particular problem of the congestion of the town with holiday traffic was addressed by the opening of a by-pass.[8]

In 1792 a diligence ran from Hull to Scarborough, through Driffield, three times a week, returning the same day, and two common stage wagons or carts went from Driffield to Hull every Monday and Friday night and returned the next day.[9] In 1823 the turnpike road was used by the Wellington, a coach service running between Hull, Bridlington, and Scarborough; a coach left Driffield for the resorts each morning in summer and three days a week in winter, and another went daily to Hull.[10]

Omnibus services were run from Driffield to villages in the region in the later 19th century.[11] The horse-drawn buses mostly left from public houses and yards in the town on the evening of market day, Thursday.[12] Motor vehicles were introduced in the early 1920s, one of the first operators was W. Allen who ran a service from Middleton to Driffield on Thursdays and Saturdays with three motor buses. The route and vehicles were purchased by Alan Lawson of Walkington in 1925, who later the following year sold the service to the newly formed East Yorkshire Motor Services Ltd (EYMS).[13] By the mid 1920s services to Hull, Beverley, Bridlington, Langtoft, Hornsea, Fridaythorpe, and villages *en route* were provided by three companies, EYMS, Driffield & District Motor Services, and Green Bus Service. EYMS acquired the last two in 1928–9, and Everingham Bros of Pocklington, who had been operating to the town for over 20 years, in 1953.[14] In 2010 EYMS was running regular services to Hull, Beverley, Bridlington, Scarborough, and York, besides one or two local services.[15] The company acquired a garage in Westgate, Driffield as a depot *c.* 1926; the present bus station and garage at the bottom of Middle Street South, close to the railway station, was built in 1957.[16]

NATURAL WATERWAYS

Streams flowing from the Wolds united in Driffield to form the main tributary of the River Hull. In the early 14th century at least some of the corn grown on the estate of St Mary's abbey at Elmswell seems to have been carried to York by water, presumably along the Hull,[17] and in the 17th century the river was said to be used by 'great' sailing boats for carrying barley from Wansford, about a mile downstream from the Driffield boundary.[18] In 1621, when Henry Best of Elmswell sold some barley, it was agreed that he should deliver it to the boatman and pay for the hire of the boat, the buyer accepting the hazards of carriage by water; the latter included the stakes and mud banks which obstructed the river's course between Wansford and Hull. At least one Wansford man, Robert Bonwick, seems to have been providing a regular weekly service to Hull in the earlier 17th century.[19] Later the system was reckoned to be navigable only from North Frodingham, some four or five miles south-east of Driffield, where there were landings at Emmotland and on Frodingham Beck, another of the river's tributaries. Nevertheless, part of

1 OS Map 1:10,560, SE 95 NE, TA 05 NW (1956 edn).

2 Following based on K. A. MacMahon, *Roads and Turnpike Trusts in Eastern Yorks.* (E Yorks. Local Hist. Ser. 18, 1964), 29–30, 59, 66–7; *Beverley Corp. Min. Bks (1707–1835)* ed. K. A. MacMahon (YAS Rec. Ser. 122), 46; OS Map 1:10,560, Yorks. CLXI (1855 edn).

3 OS Map 1:10,560, TA 05 NW (1956 edn).

4 T. Jefferys, *Map of Yorks.* (1775). In the 1780s the road to Bell Mills and beyond was used to avoid paying toll on the turnpike road, apparently with the connivance of the miller: MacMahon, *Roads and Turnpike Trusts*, 51.

5 RDB, B/153/42; OS Map 1:10,560, Yorks. CLXI (1855 edn); Ross, *Driffield*, 81, 192–3.

6 A. Young, *Six Months Tour through the North of* England (1770), i. 1.

7 MacMahon, *Roads and Turnpike Trusts*, 66–7.

8 Below, loc. govt, pub. services (roads).

9 *Universal Brit. Dir.* (*c.* 1792), ii. 827; *HP* 21 Jan. 1800.

10 Baines, *Hist. Yorks.* (1823), ii. 198; *HP* 4 Oct 1823, 18 July 1826.

11 Following based on directories.

12 Illus. in *BG* 9 Mar. 1978.

13 K. A. Jenkinson, '*Twixt Wold, Carr & Coast: E Yorks Motor Services Ltd and its Associates* (1992), 11–12.

14 Ibid. 15–16, 18–20, 36.

15 EYMS website, 2010.

16 Jenkinson, *'Twixt Wold, Carr & Coast*, 14, 23; ERAO, UDDR/1/8/54, Building...Cttee, 7 Aug. 1957; ibid. CRWP/9.

17 TNA, LR 11/51/732.

18 *Yorks. Ch. Notes* (YAS Rec. Ser. 34), 164.

19 Best, *Farming Bks*, ed. Woodward, 116–17, 167.

the trade of the growing town of Driffield with Hull was conducted by way of the river, corn being sent downstream from North Frodingham, and coal and other goods returned.[1] In the 1760s William Porter of Driffield exported corn from Emmotland, Frodingham Bridge and Corps Landing in Hutton Cranswick parish.[2]

DRIFFIELD NAVIGATION (CANAL)

In 1767 an Act of Parliament was obtained to extend navigability to Driffield and to improve the River Hull by dredging and making cuts.[3] Opposition was met from the lord of Skerne manor, who seems already to have begun another canal to Driffield, the route for which was surveyed by John Smeaton *c.* 1764.[4] The tolls allowed under the Act reflected the essentially agricultural purpose of the waterway. The goods mentioned specifically were corn, peas, beans, hay, rapeseed, malt, flour, building materials, coal, and manures. Work was begun in 1767; by the end of the next year tolls began to be levied on the southern part of the navigation, and by 1770 the construction of the five miles of canal and dredging of the river and of the Frodingham Beck branch were largely complete. The navigation opened then, and the work was finally completed in 1772. The engineer of the canal was John Grundy, and others involved included James Pinkerton who was evidently helped by his brother John, later a renowned canal contractor.[5] Financially, the canal was a disappointment to the subscribers of the £15,175 for its construction, in part due to the policy of charging low tolls on goods such as coal, which was used for lime burning, and the materials needed for improving the roads of the region. Concessions were also granted to foster carpet making at Wansford and other local industry, and land around the canal head was let on long building leases to encourage the construction of warehouses and granaries. Despite the lack of profit, the canal was much used for the exportation of grain and the importation of manures and general goods; by 1791 a public carrying service from Hull employed 2–3 vessels, and about 1800 a ship of 44 tons ran along the waterway to Hull and Leeds. The previous year Richard Langley, lord of the manor of Driffield and the chief creditor of the 18th-century undertaking, with the other creditors, petitioned for another Act to allow the tolls to be increased. That Act was passed in 1817, and from then until 1850 there were often net balances of £1–2,000 a year, enabling much of the debt to be redeemed.

Another Act had been obtained by the commissioners in 1801 to improve the navigation below Driffield. The work, designed by William Chapman, included the construction of a new lock at Hempholme, in Leven; the cutting of a new channel for the river below Emmotland, and the rebuilding and heightening in 1803 of the troublesome low bridge at Hull Bridge, near Beverley.[6] The 'New Navigation' was apparently completed in 1805, and by 1823 its relatively modest cost, £6,000, had been paid off; tolls, which produced £1,547 in 1822–3, were subsequently lowered considerably to a level sufficient to maintain the system. About the date that the New Navigation was made, the system was also extended by a small, private branch leading off Frodingham Beck to mills in Foston, and later public wharves were made at Frodingham Bridge and on the River Hull at Corps Landing, in Hutton Cranswick parish. The main cargoes were coal, grain, and flour; other commodities carried included rapeseed, lime, and bricks.[7]

In 1817 a new steam packet, the *Countess of Scarborough*, ran thrice weekly in each direction between Hull and Driffield.[8] That venture may have failed soon afterwards, but three boats were providing a public goods service between the two places in 1823.[9] In 1825 J. Steel announced the re-commencement of his service for goods and passengers aboard the improved *Express* steam packet; it too operated thrice weekly in each direction.[10]

The opening of railway lines in 1846 and 1853 undermined the prosperity of the Driffield navigation, but, by lowering its tolls, it survived, and thereby kept the cost of railway freight down. The toll on coal on the Old Navigation was only 6*d.* a ton from 1846 and from 1851 all corn was charged at 1*d.* a quarter. The railways eventually killed the general carrying services along the waterway, the last vessels, the *Queen* and the *Princess* being taken out of service about 1860. The opening of the linseed cake mill in 1862 gave a boost to navigation and three years later it was reported that there were 30 keels or sloops at River Head, more than ever before, with many more on their way, most laden with linseed.[11] Twenty or more broad boats, or keels, each with a capacity of 60 to 80 tons were sometimes to be seen loading and unloading at

1 B. F. Duckham, *Inland Waterways of E Yorks. 1700–1900* (E Yorks. Local Hist. Ser. 29, 1973), 17.

2 *Journals of the House of Commons*, xxxi, 186.

3 Following based on Duckham, *Inland Waterways*, 16–34. The bill is printed in Ross, *Driffield*, 101–5; minute books of the commisioners and other records of the navigation are at ERAO, DDIN, DDX/237 and DDBD/89-90.

4 *Reports of the late Mr John Smeaton* (1797), i. 207–8. 'Mr Brown's new cutt' in Skerne was shown on John Grundy's plan and scheme of 1766: HUL, DDX/16/250. It was later called 'New river': OS Map 1:10,560, Yorks. CLXXIX (1854 edn).

5 S. R. Broadbridge, 'John Pinkerton and the Birmingham Canals', *Transport History*, IV, i (1971), 33–4.

6 *Beverley Corp. Min. Bks (1707–1835)*, 57, 82–3, 87.

7 Below, econ. hist., trade and ind. (1770–1851 & corn trade).

8 *HP* 14 Jan. 1817; *HA* 22 Mar. 1817.

9 Baines, *Hist. Yorks.* (1823), ii. 198.

10 *HA* 11 Mar. 1825.

11 ERAO, DDX/17/15; *DT* 2 Dec. 1865.

7. *Great Driffield: Railway station yard,* c. *1910. On the left is the station master's house.*

the canal head.[1] In 1880–1 the Old Navigation was used to transport some 23,000 tons, besides 155,000 bricks. Linseed and linseed oil; cotton-seed; locust beans, and cake accounted for half of the tonnage, and coal for much of the rest, but corn, then including maize, was relatively unimportant. By the 1930s the main commodity carried was corn for Bradshaws at Bell Mills. There were four keels left using the canal in the early 1940s, and the last commercial boat to reach Driffield was the keel 'Caroline', carrying 50 tons of wheat, on 16 March 1945.[2] The commissioners recognized the end of the navigation's working life and sold off the warehouses at River Head in 1949.[3] The canal was dredged as part of an improvement of the local sewerage system undertaken by the UDC and Hull Corporation in the 1950s,[4] but thereafter the navigation was for years the decaying preserve of pleasure craft[5] and fishermen.

The drainage commission eventually failed for lack of appointments, but two bodies came into existence in its stead in the mid 20th century.[6] Driffield Navigation Amenities Association was founded in 1968, granted charitable status in 1974, and had some eighty members *c.* 2000. Driffield Navigation Ltd, later Driffield Navigation Trust, was set up afterwards.[7] Much of the derelict canal was restored by the two bodies between 1996 and 2009, including the five locks.[8]

RAILWAYS

A railway from York to Bridlington through Driffield was proposed in 1834 when the engineer John Rennie surveyed the route.[9] Nothing came of this but in 1845 the proposal was revived with Driffield residents supporting a memorial that was sent to the directors of the York & North Midland Railway who had proposed a line from York to Pocklington.[10] Again it was not pursued but by this date work was underway by the Hull & Selby Railway Co. on a branch line from Hull to Bridlington, through Driffield.[11]

The line which skirted the south of the town was opened on 6 October 1846. The station was built at the bottom of Middle Street, just to the west of the canal head. Less than a year later in July 1847 work began at

1 Ross, *Driffield*, 106; E. Paget-Tomlinson, *Britain's Canal & River Craft* (1979), 54–61.

2 J. Grainger, 'On a Canal Barge', in *E Yorks. Within Living Memory* (1998), 13–14; A. D. Biggin and R. Squires, *Driffield Navigation Guide* (1975), 10.

3 RDB, 814/588/483; 818/304/252.

4 ERAO, UDDR/1/8/54, Public Health Cttee, 4 Nov. 1957.

5 *VCH Yorks. ER.* ii. 177. A rate for pleasure boats using the navigation had been set in 1767: Ross, *Driffield*, 105.

6 The last commissioner died in 1972, then resident in Southern Rhodesia: Biggin and Squires, *Driffield Navigation*, 11.

7 *BG* 15 June 1978; *DT* 28 Nov. 1991; 21 Jan. 1998; DNAA website, 2004.

8 Inf. from Driffield Navigation Trust, 2010; *ERM* 29 July 2003; *HDM* 16 Dec. 2000; 5 Sept. 2003; *YP* 20 Nov. 2008.

9 K. A. MacMahon, *Beginnings of E Yorks. Railways* (E Yorks. Local Hist. Ser. 3, 1953), 8–9; *HP* 23 May 1845.

10 *HP* 23 May 1845.

11 Ibid. 27 Sept. 1844.

Driffield on a railway line to Malton, but owing to financial difficulties construction was intermittent and the line was not opened until 19 May 1853.[1] It crossed the parish south of Elmswell and Little Driffield to join the Bridlington line close to Driffield station. Although much agricultural produce, particularly corn, was carried to Driffield the line was not a financial success and it was said to be the 'poorest' in England in 1864.[2] Another line was opened on 1 May 1890 from Driffield to Market Weighton.[3] The track led from the Malton line near Kelleythorpe and afforded via Selby a more direct connection with Leeds and the West Riding.[4]

The Malton–Driffield line was closed to passengers in 1950 and entirely in 1958; the track has been lifted and the land sold.[5] The line to Market Weighton was closed in 1965, and its track has also been removed.[6] The Hull-Bridlington line, with an extension to Scarborough, was still operated in 2010.

1 W. Burton, *Malton and Driffield Junction Railway* (1997), 5–21.

2 *HP* 21 Oct. 1864.

3 MacMahon, *Beginnings of E Yorks. Railways*, 38.

4 OS Map 1:2,500, Yorks. CLXI. 12 (1893 edn); MacMahon, *Beginnings of E Yorks. Railways*, 11–13, 19, 25. A proposed direct line from Driffield to Scarborough was never built: Ross, *Driffield*, 87, 195.

5 RDB, 1206/505/445; 1259/358/322; Burton, *Malton and Driffield Junction Railway*, 70–3.

6 ERAO, UDDR/1/1/39, Gen. Purposes Cttee, 4 May 1965; C. Clinker and J. M. Firth, *Closed Passenger Stations and Goods Depots* (1971), 95 [s.v. Market Weighton].

GREAT AND LITTLE DRIFFIELD

GREAT DRIFFIELD stands at the foot of the Yorkshire Wolds, 11 miles (18 km.) north of Beverley and the same distance south-west of Bridlington. The nearest cities are Hull, 16 miles (26 km.) to the south and York, 24 miles (39 km.) to the west.

As noted above the townships of Great and Little Driffield are dealt with jointly in this volume. Because the settlement did not have a separate field system the physical extent of Little Driffield is uncertain before the mid 19th century. At that date it covered 388 a. of which 185 a. was in six detached parts, lying dispersed in the fields of Great Driffield.[1] This land was awarded at inclosure, as was much of the rest of the land in Little Driffield township.[2]

In 1066 Driffield was a large and regionally important manor in the hands of Earl Morcar, probably with its origins in a much earlier Anglo-Saxon estate associated with Aldfrith, king of the Northumbrians.[3] It is possible that Little Driffield was the original settlement, and may have been the vill recorded in Domesday Book, when the manor was held by the king. If so then Great Driffield is a later, possibly planned, settlement of the 12th century associated with the royal castle.

The economy of the medieval manor was based on agriculture, at least four water-mills and the profits of the market and four fairs, the latter held at Little Driffield. Although favourably situated at the junction of two agricultural districts, the Wolds and Holderness, with a good water supply and tenants who for a time leased the manor and had the freedoms associated with an ancient demesne, Driffield had seemingly failed as a trading centre before the 17th century.

Despite not having a market of any significance, if one at all, Great Driffield remained one of the largest settlements in the area in the late 17th century, more populous than the nearby market villages of Kilham and North Frodingham. This and its location on one of the main routes from the south to the increasingly fashionable resort of Scarborough, and the popularity amongst the gentry of field sports, particularly for hunting on the Wolds and angling in the local trout streams, in the early-mid 18th century, can be seen as the foundation for the town's later development. The two or three inns evidently built or rebuilt there to accommodate travellers and sportsmen provided a base for the corn trade which rapidly expanded in the later 18th century following agricultural improvements, partly consequent upon the inclosure of the open fields, sheep walks and rabbit warrens on the Wolds.

The opening in 1770 of the navigation linking Driffield to Hull and the expanding market of the West Riding was the trigger that transformed the large village into a boom town. The long decayed weekly market was revived and corn, coal and timber merchants, professionals, tradesmen and craftsmen poured in. An attempt to set-up a textile industry failed, but milling, malting, brewing, tanning, bone crushing and other trades processing the products of, or providing for, the farming community flourished. A cattle market was established, hastening the decline of the annual fairs except for the hiring fair at Martinmas, the high point for trade and pleasure in the town's calendar along with the summer agricultural show.

Driffield grew much faster than any other market town in the East Riding in the first half of the 19th century and it was soon the most populous town after Beverley and Bridlington, servicing an extensive hinterland.[4] Its economy was boosted by the opening of the railway in 1846 and the third quarter of the 19th century was a particularly prosperous time when town's main industries were the manufacture of artificial manure and cattle cake, the vital ingredients of the high farming of the 'Golden Age' of agriculture. Two other industries, printing and cabinet making, expanded rapidly thanks to the entrepreneurs involved and the availability of skilled labour, male and female, rather than any local demand.

The confident market town had all the usual mid-Victorian trappings: a Union workhouse, a corn exchange, a Mechanics' Institute, a temperance hall, National and Board schools, a gas works, a cemetery, brass bands, friendly societies, freemasons, local newspapers and, the focus for many, Nonconformist chapels. Driffield was a dissenting town and, as it became increasing politicised from the 1870s onwards, more Liberal than Tory. Support for the latter came from a revived Anglican church and the residents of the grander houses.

In the late 19th and early 20th century the town stagnated, its prosperity undermined by the depressed state of agriculture and outside competition. Many of

1 OS Map 1:10,560, Yorks. CLXI (1855 edn).

2 RDB, B/153/42; ERAO, IA. 41. Much of the detached land, 144 a., was awarded to the Prebendary of Driffield.

3 *A.-S. Chron.* ed. D. Whitelock (1961), 25.

4 M. Noble, 'Urban Development' in Dyson (ed.), *Guide to Local Studies*, 112.

the main firms closed including old-established corn merchants and flour mills, all the breweries, and the large printing and cabinet making works. The building of a military airfield on the edge of the town and agricultural prosperity during the First World War gave a boost to the local economy but it was short lived. New industries were introduced between the wars and these and Driffield's importance as a retail and service centre, along with the re-establishment of the RAF airfield, helped retain population despite the continuing decline of the town's rural hinterland.

The town attracted a number of new firms in the third quarter of the 20th century, some with agricultural connections, such as those processing turkeys, but most were unconnected, including manufacturers of light clothing, cake decorations and spectacles, who drew on the availability of female labour. The closure of the airfield and most of these industries in the decade from the mid-1990s was partly compensated for by the development of an industrial estate at Kelleythorpe.

In 2010 Great Driffield retained its old significance as the region's retail and service centre with a minor administrative role within East Yorkshire. Perhaps more importantly, it had become a dormitory town, with many of its citizens working in Beverley, Hull and Bridlington.

SETTLEMENT

The earliest part Great Driffield known to have been settled was land lying to the west of the beck in the later town. Skeletons have been unearthed on the west side of St John's Road, and the animal remains, pottery, and worked stones found by subsequent excavation have been interpreted as belonging to a Neolithic, agricultural settlement.[1] Slightly further north, in Mill Street, traces of a house from the same period have been found.[2] Some worked flints, thought to date from about the beginning of the Neolithic period, have been recovered on the east side of the beck at Moot Hill.[3]

Settlement in the west of the town may have been continued into the Bronze Age, or resumed then, for a burial ground discovered in King's Mill Road included one possibly Neolithic grave and evidence of cremation in the Bronze Age.[4]

Other early settlement sites in the later territory of Great Driffield may have lain away from the modern town. One of the early barrows was situated on a rise called Cheesecake Hill, about a mile to the east of the present town and close to the boundary with Nafferton.[5] Some 90 ft in diameter and probably raised during the Bronze Age, it was used over a long period.[6] Among miscellaneous local finds of Bronze-Age artefacts have

8. *Great Driffield: View across Moot Hill from near Pinfold to All Saints' church in 1950s.*

1 Above, vol. intro., early settlement.

2 Ibid.

3 M. R. Eddy, 'A Roman settlement and early medieval motte at Moot-Hill, Gt Driffield, N Humbs.', *ER Archaeologist* 7 (1983), 44.

4 Mortimer, *Forty Years' Researches*, 294; *VCH Yorks*. ii. 86–7.

5 OS Map 1:10,560, Yorks. CLXII (1855 edn).

6 Mortimer's barrow C 44. Mortimer, *Forty Years' Researches*, 286–93; *VCH Yorks*. ii. 84–5.

been an imported bronze celt or adze, possibly from Moot Hill, and a bronze sword discovered in Bridlington Road.[1]

Perhaps the most renowned of Great Driffield's archaeological sites is the large Iron-Age cemetery which was popularly assumed to contain the bodies of Scandinavians killed in a battle, and was consequently called Danes' Graves.[2] Some three miles north of the present town on the higher ground, the burial ground was sited beside the ancient road from Fridaythorpe and perhaps the Vale of York to Bridlington[3] which probably then, as later, formed the boundary of Driffield's territory. About half a mile further west, the track passed another probable burial ground, land later called Maiden's Grave. The number of square barrows at Danes' Graves was much reduced by ploughing,[4] but almost two hundred remained protected by their woodland location in the later 19th century, and some were then excavated.[5] The barrows were arranged roughly in lines, each being 1–3½ ft high and 9–33 ft in diameter. Those excavated in the 1890s revealed oval or oblong depressions in the ground, mostly with the remains of one person, buried in a contracted position. The graves also contained animal remains; bronze and iron artefacts, and a little pottery. An enamelled bronze pin found then was dated to 300 or 400 BC, but later assessment of the finds indicated that the ground may have been in use rather later, from the 3rd or 2nd centuries BC and perhaps until the coming of the Romans in the 1st century AD.[6] Two of the graves had more than one occupant: five skeletons were found in one of them, while the other had the remains of two adults together with the iron and bronze gear of a chariot and its horses, indicating a high status burial. A quern stone, or hand mill, discovered on the Driffield site in 1860 suggests, moreover, the growing of cereal crops locally.

In much the same period as the Danes' Graves cemetery was in use there is believed to have been a settlement down the slope near the later Great Kendale, or Kendale House, Farm,[7] and evidence for the continued settlement of land in the west of the present town during the Iron Age has been provided by a number of skeletons unearthed in Woldholme Avenue.[8]

Until recently there was little evidence in Great Driffield of the succeeding Roman period. Mortimer had excavated two barrows near the southern boundary, discovering possible Romano-British burials, besides recording a find elsewhere of pottery which may have been Romano-British.[9] In 1975, however, a floor made of chalk blocks was found, together with Romano-British pottery, at the base of the medieval motte at Moot Hill; that evidence indicates the presence of a Romano-British building which was abandoned in the late 4th century AD. Other discoveries of the period have included evidence of a possible farmstead off Albion Street[10] and pottery shards from the Cranwell Road area.[11]

Among the first signs of Anglo-Saxon settlement were burials inserted into the earlier barrows, graves which are believed to have been made in the late 5th or early 6th centuries.[12] In Great Driffield the Cheesecake Hill barrow was found to contain, besides the Bronze-Age burials, Anglo-Saxon interments richly accompanied by goods including a pair of brooches dated to *c.* 550 AD.[13] Another existing burial site reused by the Anglo-Saxon population was that on the west side of the town, off King's Mill Road. The evidences of its earlier use are slight, and all or most of the 12 skeletons discovered there, some contracted and including children, were believed on the basis of the accompanying pottery to be those of Anglo-Saxons.[14]

Other Anglo-Saxon interments, some of them of cremated remains, were made in new burial grounds. One such burial ground in Great Driffield has been found in the south of the present town, north of Anderson Street. Other burials, possibly contemporary but devoid of dateable evidence, have been found further north, off Exchange Street and in Bridge Street, and on the west side of the town in Shady Lane, later Victoria Road.[15]

Some of the archaeological evidence suggests that the early focus of the later town was to the west of the beck, around King's Mill Road: the scattered nature of the Anglo-Saxon finds and paucity of later archaeology make that conclusion very speculative, however.[16] What is clear is that by the 8th century the neighbourhood of Driffield was heavily settled. The name Driffield is Anglian and believed to mean 'stubble field', perhaps an early allusion to the importance of corn production. Early Northumbrian silver coins have been found locally, some of them

1 Above, vol. intro., early settlement.

2 Following based on *Archaeol. Jnl.* 22 (1865), 108–12, 264; J. R. Mortimer, 'The Danes' Graves', *Ann. Rep. Yorks. Philosophical Soc.* (1897), 1–8; J. R. Mortimer, 'Danes' Graves', *Proc. Yorks. Geol. and Polytechnic Soc.* N.S. 8 (1897–9), following p. 286; *Reliquary* 3 (Oct. 1897), 224–30.

3 Above, communications (roads).

4 The former extent of the burial ground is evident from crop marks: Loughlin and Miller, *Survey*, 120.

5 At least twenty other barrows there had been opened earlier in the century: Mortimer, 'Danes' Graves', 288–92. A. Bryant, *Map of ER Yorks.* (1829); OS Map 1:10,560, Yorks. CXLIV (1854 edn).

6 Challis and Harding, *Later Prehistory*, i. 68–70, 74–5, 170; ii, fig. 31.

7 Below, Kendale.

8 *HDM* 21 Sept. 1988.

9 Mortimer's barrows 212A and B: Mortimer, *Forty Years' Researches*, 285, 297; OS Map 1:2,500, Yorks. CLXI. 16 (1910 edn).

10 *DT* 22 Oct. 1992.

11 Eddy, 'Moot-Hill', 40–51.

12 Loveluck, 'Anglo-Saxon Landscape', 30.

13 Mortimer, *Forty Years' Researches*, 286–93; *VCH Yorks.* ii. 84–5, 87; Loveluck, 'Anglo-Saxon Landscape', 34.

14 Mortimer, *Forty Years' Researches*, 294; *VCH Yorks.* ii. 86–7.

15 *VCH Yorks.* ii. 86–7; Mortimer, *Forty Years' Researches*, 293–4; Loughlin and Miller, *Survey*, 90.

16 Loveluck, 'Anglo-Saxon Landscape', 45.

attributed to King Aldfrith, who died in Driffield in 705 AD. Though attempts to find a royal residence in Driffield have been fruitless, Driffield's significance at the Conquest, as a large manor held by Earl Morcar, may well have had its origins in or before the 8th century.[1]

Kendale There seems to have been an early farm or settlement at Kendale in Great Driffield. Near Great Kendale Farm, a burial was discovered in the mid 19th century, and later a floor of flint stones and many pits dug into the chalk there, 6–20 ft in diameter and 3 ft deep, were commented on.[2] The pits are thought to have been for the storage of corn, and have yielded pottery and other finds, possibly ranging from as early as the 5th century BC to the 1st century AD.[3] The attraction of the site is evident in the Scandinavian or Anglo-Scandinavian name, which describes a valley with a spring.[4] A spring or well west of the farmhouse was enlarged into a pond before it was drained in the 20th century.[5]

Kendale had a distinct identity within Great Driffield in the Middle Ages: in 1086 the land belonging to Driffield manor included 6 carucates at 'Cheldal', and Little Keldale was recorded as a field name in 1202.[6] No later indications of settlement there have been found, and there were certainly no buildings there at inclosure in 1742, although an old way, Kendale Gate, was then mentioned.[7] Great Kendale Farm was built there soon after inclosure.

DEVELOPMENT

GREAT DRIFFIELD

If the settlements of Great and Little Driffield both existed in the 11th century they were not separately identified in the Domesday Book where they were seemingly counted as one vill. They were part of a single manor, and then or later part of a single ecclesiastical parish and they shared a single open field system in the Middle Ages and later. Could there have been only one settlement in 1086? Only the single place name, variously Drifelt, Drifeld, Driffields or Driffeud, was used then and into the 13th century; the earliest use of the epithets Great (Magna, Much, Mich, Mykel, or Mykil) and Little (Parva), so far discovered, was in the late 13th century.[8]

It can be assumed that there were two settlements in 1086 if the two churches then recorded in the manor were those at Great and Little Driffield.[9] The tradition of it being the burial place of King Aldfrith in 705 and the presence of fragments of a late 9th- or 10th-century cross support the existence of a pre-Conquest church at Little Driffield, but there is no such evidence relating to the church at Great Driffield.[10] It is likely that the church at 'Driffield' granted by Henry I to the archbishop and York minster in the first decade of the 12th century, and soon afterwards used to endow the prebend of Driffield, was that at Little Driffield.[11] The prebendary had his manor house at Little Driffield in the late 13th century probably, as later, adjacent to the church.[12]

From c. *1100–1700*

Was Great Driffield a 12th-century new settlement planned or developed alongside the castle, typical of Norman new towns?[13] The town's fairly regular layout is characteristic of a planned settlement.[14] It has a simple core plan, which comprises three streets running in a south-easterly direction parallel to the beck or stream with connecting cross lanes. As shown on the first known plan of 1742 the streets on either side of the beck extended, as now, for ¾ mile.[15] It is likely that the early settlement was smaller, with its focus at the northern end. Here was the Norman castle whose motte survives on the east side of the beck, and probably the later manor house on the adjacent site known as Hall Garth, west of the beck.[16] The main street, now Middle Street North, also west of the beck, was then probably of equal length with its western back lane, later Westgate, and the church stood between the two, about half way along. The southern end of the medieval settlement was probably an open area used, as later, for a market place

1 Ibid. 43–4.
2 Sheahan and Whellan, *Hist. York & ER.* ii. 503; Ross, *Driffield*, 2–3; OS Map 1:2,500, Yorks. CLXI. 7 (1910 edn).
3 Loughlin and Miller, *Survey*, 120; Challis and Harding, *Later Prehistory*, i. 25, 57, 75, 77, 164; ii, fig, 27.
4 *PN Yorks. ER* (EPNS), 154.
5 ERAO, DDX/17/15; OS Map 1:2,500, Yorks. CLXI. 12 (1910 edn).
6 *VCH Yorks.* ii. 197; *Yorks. Fines, John* (Surtees Soc. 94), p. 41.
7 RDB, B/153/42.
8 TNA, C 1/568, no. 54; C 1/838, no. 52; YAS, MD 161/c/j; *PN Yorks. ER* (EPNS), 153–4; *A.-S. Chron.* ed. G. P. Cubbin (1996), pp. xi, 9. Magna is used in 1277 and Parva in 1290: TNA, CP/25/1/266/56/16; *Yorks. Inq.* ii, 95.
9 Another possibility for the second church on the manor is that at Kirkburn (Burn or Westburn), in the soke of Driffield, where there was a church *c.* 1119 and probably in the late 11th century: K. A. MacMahon, *Church of St Mary Kirkburn* (1953), 21, 24–5.
10 Below, buildings, relig. buildings.
11 *EYC.* i, pp.123, 333–6; *VCH Yorks.* iii. 13.
12 *Miscellanea*, iv (YAS Rec. Ser. 94), 27. The land awarded to the prebend at inclosure in 1742 was deemed to be in Little Driffield township: RDB, B/153/42; ERAO, IA/ 41; OS Map 1:10,560, Yorks. CLXI (1855 edn).
13 M. Beresford, *New Towns of the Middle Ages* (1967), 334–5.
14 Ibid. 142–78.
15 ERAO, IA /41
16 Below, manors and estates, Driffield manor.

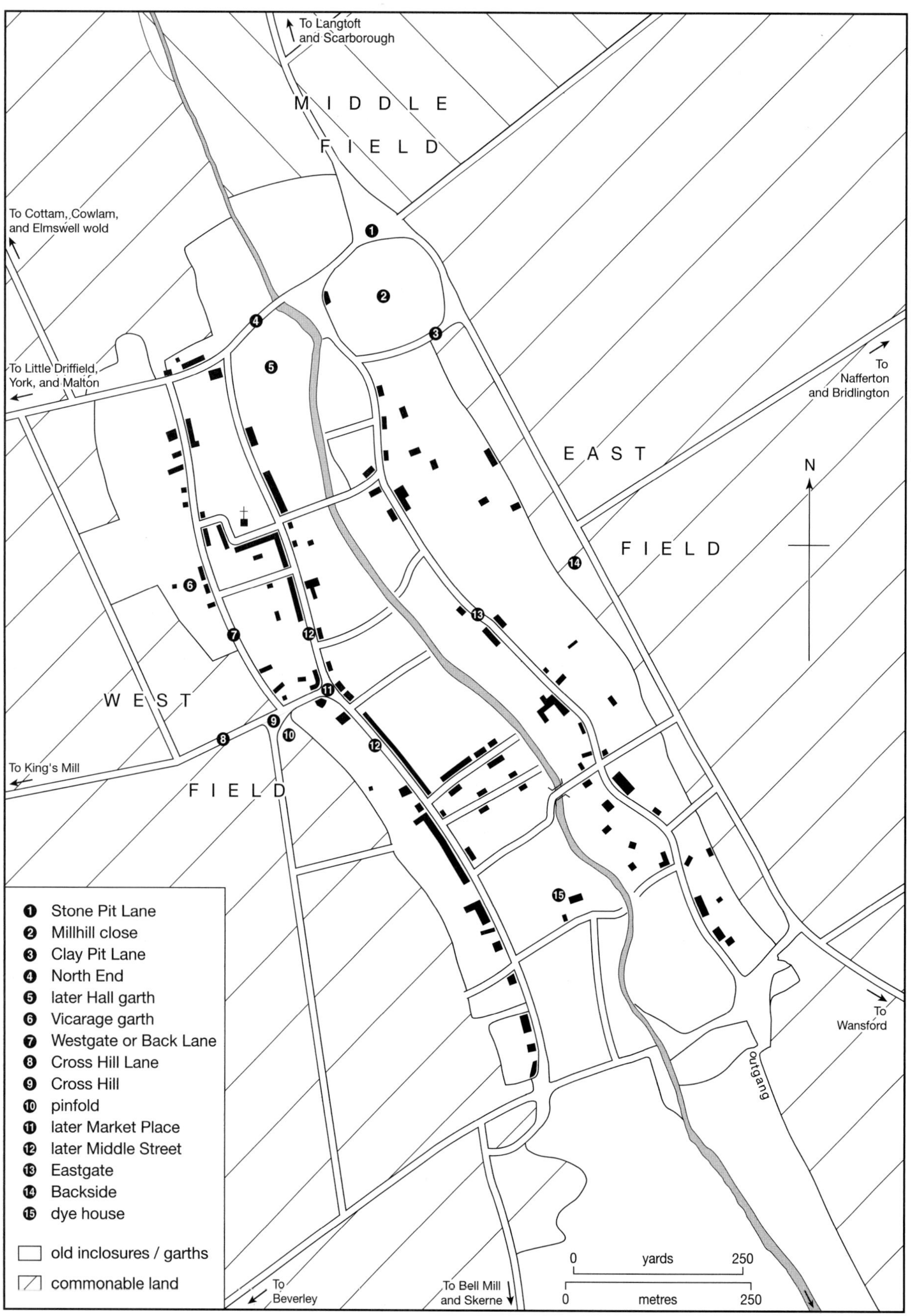

9. *Great Driffield: The town in 1742.*

and the pinfold, or pound, and now represented by Cross Hill and Market Place.

If not an entirely new settlement in the 12th century, it was then that Great Driffield expanded and became a potential town. There was probably a castle by the early or mid 12th century, the church was built or rebuilt *c.* 1180–1200, and a market existed by 1199. As a royal manor in 1086 Driffield had the status of ancient demesne giving the tenants freedom from tolls in all markets and custom houses and other privileges, and in 1201 they obtained from King John the right of farming the vill.[1] The tenants had the lease of the manor with the right of collecting the rents and other proceeds of the manor and paying to the king a fixed sum yearly, leaving them with either a profit or a loss.[2] There were many similarities between these various rights and the franchises granted to boroughs but evidently Driffield had no legal claim to the status of a borough although it is referred to as such in 1226–8.[3]

The extent of the medieval settlement is uncertain, but there appear to have been buildings around River Head, in an area known as Southorpe, suggesting a subsidiary settlement. Burials and other finds were made in the 19th century in the grounds of the former Southorpe Lodge and an adjacent field was called Chapel Nook.[4] More recently a medieval building platform was uncovered at River Head.[5]

By the late 15th century some houses had been built away from the main street in the parallel back lanes, then named as Eastgate and Westgate.[6] The buildings there later included two of the largest houses in the town, both the chief houses of estates regarded as manors, and possibly also several related lesser houses. The house of the Cromptons, apparently the largest house in Great Driffield in the later 17th century, stood between the beck and Eastgate, on land afterwards also named as Hall Garth.[7] On the other side of the town was the house of the Etheringtons, later represented by Westgate Hall.[8] An impression of Great Driffield and its buildings on the eve of the town's growth is given by the hearth tax evidence of 1672. Virtually all of the 159 households then recorded there and in the neighbouring and very small settlement of Little Driffield lived in cottages with one or two hearths each; about half of the buildings were too modest to be taxed at all, and a mere six dwellings were more substantial, with more than two hearths.[9]

From c. *1700*

The inclosure plan of 1742 provides the earliest information on the layout of the town, although the state of the map when copied has clearly led to omissions and discrepancies.[10] By then the main streets were of their present length, ending close to where the canal head would be constructed later in the century. All three streets had buildings along both sides, but the line of garths was broken at the end of Middle Street, and building was generally thinner and more scattered in the south and east of the town.

The main street was called variously Highgate, Middlegate, Fore Street, and Town Street in the 18th and 19th centuries, but the modern name of Middle Street was also in use by 1774.[11] The subsidiary nature of Eastgate and Westgate resulted in both continuing to be known also as Back Lane, and the southern end of Eastgate was still called Back Street in the mid 19th century.[12] West Street, recorded in 1793, was evidently yet another name for Westgate.[13] North End was used by 1742 for one of the cross lanes linking the streets.[14]

Driffield's medieval market lapsed at unknown date, and its site was very probably much reduced subsequently by building. Parts of the old market place may have been represented in 1742 by the triangular widening in the chief street, and further west by ground at the bottom of Westgate.[15] That stretch of the main street was known, nevertheless, as Market Place or Middle Street into the early 19th century,[16] but the former gradually became the accepted name there. The other probable remnant of the old market area was next to one of the town's open fields, and also contained the settlement's pinfold into the 18th century.[17] Formerly called Pinfold Hill, it has been known since the 19th century as Cross Hill,[18] possibly because of the intersection there of four of the town streets. After the revival of the market, Cross Hill was also used by the traders, and was sometimes called 'back market place'.[19]

1 *Pipe R.* 1201 (PRS, N.S. 14), 144–5; *Rot. Chart.* (Rec. Com.), 85; *Yorks. Hund. and Quo Warr. R* (YAS Rec. Ser. 151), 10, 117; P. Vinogradoff, *Villainage in England* (1892), 92. The tenants of the prebendary of Driffield were also exempt from paying tolls. *Cal. Chart. R.*1381–5, 165; 1399–1402, 1–2.

2 A. Ballard, 'The English Boroughs in the Reign of John', *English Historical Review* 14 (no. 53), 97.

3 Ibid. 97, 104; *Bk of Fees* i. 356.

4 ERAO, DDX/17/15.

5 *DP* 18 Sept. 1996.

6 TNA, C 141/4, no. 45; C 142/36, no. 67; E 150/224 [last].

7 Below, manors, Driffield (Crompton).

8 Ibid. (Etherington).

9 Above, vol. intro., population; below, soc. hist., soc. structure.

10 ERAO, IA. 41. Another copy is at BIA, CC. Pr. 11/1. The building differences between the two are slight.

11 RDB, O/236/583; AU/8/15; FZ/303/358; ERAO, EB/1/108; HUL, DDLG/30/622.

12 RDB, B/153/42, s.v. Thomas Etherington's allotment of 3 a. 1 r. 35 p.; ibid. DD/259/354; HA/352/389; OS Map 1:10,560, Yorks. CLXI (1855 edn).

13 RDB, BS/184/278.

14 Ibid. B/153/42.

15 ERAO, IA. 41. The 'market place' was mentioned in 1751: HUL, DDLG/30/622.

16 Baines, *Hist. Yorks.* (1823), ii. 197, s.v. Dandy, Hannah.

17 It was later re-located: below, this section.

18 Cf. RDB, B/153/42 (Ann Gray's allotment 2 a. 0 r. 38 p.); ERAO, IA. 41; *1st Rep. Royal Com. Mkt Rights and Tolls* (Parl. Papers, 1888 [C. 5550-I], liii), Vol. II, p. 261.

19 HUL, DDSH(2)/3/1.

10. *Great Driffield: No. 23 Exchange Street, 2006. Built c. 1805 and occupied as a solicitor's office and residence soon afterwards.*

The thinly developed nature of much of the town determined the character of the growth which occurred following the opening of the canal in 1770. Some additional accommodation was created by dividing houses, like those in Middle Street and Back Street in the 1770s.[1] About 1800 new streets were laid out, connecting the centre of the town with the new roads made alongside the town at inclosure. On the eastern side, an old lane from Market Place to the beck was extended to Eastgate, and then on across former open-field land to the eastern inclosure road, later Scarborough Road, and that to Bridlington. The work is said to have been begun in 1799, and was evidently complete by 1801, when the new road to Nafferton was mentioned.[2] The new way, including the former lane, was called New Road, or Burlington (Bridlington) Street, by 1803.[3] The Independent chapel had been built in New Road by 1803; building plots north and south of the street were bought the same year, and one of the purchasers, Thomas Atkinson, bricklayer, sold a newly-built house there in 1804.[4] After the building of the Corn Exchange in 1842, the stretch to Eastgate became Exchange Street, and New Road was used only for the continuation to Scarborough Road. To the north of New Road, Washington Street was developed in the 1840s, at least in part, by the surgeon Washington Harrison, who lived in the nearby Hill Cottage, later Chestnut Villa.[5]

On the west side of the town, the prominent mercantile family, the Etheringtons, developed new streets, extending the town westwards across former commonable land to the new inclosure road to Beverley, variously called Beverley Lane, or Street, Back Lane,[6] and later St John's Road. In 1805 George Etherington and other members of the family were selling building plots on the west side of Middle Street, one of them with two new houses on it, and the abuttals then included 'a new street now staked out and intended to be called Adelphi Street'.[7] In 1848 the family's development was described as lying between Middle Street and Beverley Street, and comprising new streets called George Street, Union Street, and The Adelphi.[8]

A number of grander houses were built around the town in the late 18th-early 19th century, some by tradesmen and professionals, others by gentry attracted by field sports. At the south end there were Old White Hall, New White Hall, Grove Cottage, Southorpe Lodge and Rose Villa, on New Road, Easterfield House, and nearby Garden Cottage, later Sunnycroft.[9]

1 RDB, AW/192/319; AY/320/518.

2 Ibid. CD/244/361; Pevsner and Neave, *Yorks. ER*, 442–3.

3 RDB, CE/501/751; CO/192/305; DD/259/353.

4 Ibid. CE/501/751; CF/386/607; CF/386/608; CG/478/796.

5 Ibid. FZ/26/35; FZ/27/36; TNA, HO 107/2366; ERAO, PE/10/T. 120; ibid. TA/13; OS Map 1:10,560, Yorks. CLXI (1855 edn); OS Map 1:2,500, Yorks. CLXI. 12 (1893 edn).

6 RDB, CD/238/353.

7 Ibid. CH/397/646; CH/398/647; CH/399/648.

8 Ibid. KP/107/153. The last was also known, less glamorously, as Back or Little George Street. George Street and Little George Street were adopted as public streets *c.* 1840, when they had been in use for more than twenty years: ERAO, PE/10/T. 99, s.a. 1839, 1841; OS Map 1:10,560, Yorks. CLXI (1855 edn); OS Map 1:2,500, Yorks. CLXI. 12 (1893 and 1910 edns).

9 Below, buildings, domestic buildings.

11. *Great Driffield: Easterfield House, New Road, 2011. Built* c. *1820 for Dr Francis Forge.*

By the 1850s the older streets and garths were becoming more closely built with modest housing, among which were several terraces of cottages in or near Eastgate, at North End, and in Boggle Lane, close to the new railway station.[1] Promise Square, off Westgate, then comprised 20 houses.[2] Developers probably included George Wrangham, a Bridlington draper, and his sons; about 1850 the Wranghams had four houses in Middle Street, and behind them, in Wrangham Row, nearly 30 houses, the premises of an agricultural chemist, F. C. Matthews, and a malt kiln.[3] More modestly, Richard Clark Dosser owned a terrace of eight cottages in Westgate, called Dosser's Place, in the 1840s,[4] and in 1854 the millwright John Harker bought seven cottages, and was then building another eight, at the junction of Cranwell Street and Eastgate North.[5]

Large houses were also put up for the middle classes, mostly on the edge of the town. In 1859 it was noted that a considerable number of middle-class houses had been erected and that the town was a 'desirable place of residence for invalids, persons of limited income, and those fond of a retired and rural life, and quiet social society where no rancorous feelings prevail through political and religious animosity'.[6]

Probably because of building development in the centre of the town,[7] the pinfold was removed from Cross Hill to the northern edge of Driffield, apparently before 1805,[8] and in 1851 twelve houses called Pinfold Place stood on or close to its former site.[9] Parts of the town, nevertheless, remained unbuilt *c.* 1850, land in the south, for instance, being then used as a nursery garden.[10]

The Expanding Town, c. *1850 – c.1950*

The building up and extension of the town continued in the second half of the 19th century, when the population grew more slowly but had reached nearly 6,000 in the slightly enlarged civil parish by 1891. Much of the development occurred on the west side of the town, between Westgate and Shady Lane; along King's Mill Road, and further south between Middle Street South and Beverley Street. Church Street was laid out and developed with modest houses, many of them terraced, in 1861–2,[11] and cottages were built on Shady Lane in 1863.[12] There were said to be an unprecedented number of houses under construction in 1865, adding to the 'wealth, beauty and importance' of the town.[13]

G. R. Wrangham and T. G. Marshall bought property formerly belonging to the Etheringtons in 1873, and

1 OS Map 1:10,560, Yorks. CLXI (1855 edn).
2 TNA, HO 107/2366.
3 RDB, GY/378/456; ERAO, PE/10/T.120; below, econ. hist., trades and ind. (bone crushing and manure manufacture).
4 ERAO, TA/13; ibid. PE/10/T. 120.
5 Then described as Cranwell Lane and East Back Street: RDB, HD/55/77.
6 *HP* 16 Dec. 1859.
7 e.g. RDB, CD/311/468; CD/312/469; CF/426/674; CG/476/792.
8 RDB, CH/301/480; OS Map 1:10,560, Yorks. CLXI (1855 edn). The pinfold, a brick and pantile barn, was restored by the UDC in 1973: ibid. UDDR/1/1/47, Housing...Cttee, 2 Apr. 1973. Photographs of 1957 by Bob Allen at ERAO, PH/4/11.
9 TNA, HO 107/2366.
10 ERAO, TA/13; ibid. PE/10/T. 120.
11 *DT* 21 Dec. 1861; Ross, *Driffield*, 82.
12 *DT* 18 Apr. 1863.
13 Ibid. 23 Dec. 1865.

divided and developed it soon afterwards, making a new road, afterwards Etherington Road, or Lane, between Westgate and Shady Lane.[1] Further south, large detached and semi-detached houses were put up by the prosperous middle classes in Lockwood Street. That street was laid out by James Harrison, corn merchant of Driffield and Hull, and the Beverley ironfounder Alfred Crosskill in 1873, when the building plots there and adjacent ones in Beverley Lane were sold at auction to prominent professionals and tradesmen. Similar housing was also strung along Beverley Road, close to the railway station, together with the more modest South Parade (1867) and other terraces.[2] On the east side of the town, there was development alongside and to the west of Scarborough Road. Downe Street, named from the title borne by the Dawnays, lords of Driffield manor, was laid out by 1865;[3] the former Claypit Lane was improved and renamed Gibson Street, and the margins of the adjoining Moat or Moot Hill were covered with terraced houses. Moat Hill, also known as Snowden Hill, belonged in the mid 19th century to Edward Gibson, the iron and brass founder, who evidently put up Moot Hill Terrace between 1873 and 1884.[4] Five of the new houses on the west side of Scarborough Road were erected in or soon before 1883 by the Driffield builder and timber merchant Joseph Berry.[5] Further east, detached houses for the middle classes were being put up *c.* 1890 in The Avenue, off Bridlington Road.[6] At the north end of the town its most imposing house was developed during the period, Millfield House being built for a wealthy shopkeeper, Henry Angas, in the 1860s, and later enlarged and remodelled for Harrison Holt, a Hull industrialist, as Highfield.[7] The town's public and commercial buildings were also added to, as well as rebuilt. Thus by 1892 a new school had been built at the junction of Scarborough Road and Bridlington Road, and further east, along Bridlington Road, a hospital, a new workhouse, and a cemetery. Similar new building on the other side of the town included a Roman Catholic church.[8] The town's second Anglican church, put up at the junction of Lockwood Street and Beverley Street in the late 1870s as a temporary church but later retained as a mission church dedicated to St John, was replaced by a new building in 1900, and it was probably then that Beverley Street became St John's Road.[9] Shady Lane, planted with 'fine trees' and 'being rapidly built up' *c.* 1890 became Victoria Road about the date of the queen's death in 1901.[10] The town's chief industrial building, the linseed cake mill, was put up in the 1860s, and in the late 19th century the south end of the town was said, with some over-simplification, to be its 'chief commercial quarter' in consequence of the canal and the railway station there.[11]

Driffield continued to grow, but relatively slowly, in the earlier 20th century.[12] The building evidence reflects a population which increased little between the late 19th century and the Second World War.[13] Much of what new building there was comprised ribbon development along existing roads. In the 1920s and 1930s semi-detached houses and bungalows were thus strung loosely along the east side of Wansford Road and Scarborough Road, and the south side of Beverley Road. The few terraced and other houses put up along the south side of York Road in the later 19th century,[14] were similarly added to, while along the north side ribbon development with semi-detached houses extended the built area of the town westwards. Incursions were, however, also made into the open ground on either side of the town, beyond the boundary roads. In 1925 the builder Arthur Leason put up houses on the south side of Manorfield Road, laid out to the east of Wansford Road on land belonging to G. T. Beal.[15]

The building of Manorfield Road was continued after the Second World War by David Naylor, and Manorfield Avenue laid out in the 1930s was then developed, apparently by Frank Whiteley 'architect'.[16] Further south part of Meadow Lane was built up as Meadow Road. On the west side of Driffield, a field road leading to Pomona Fruit Farm, later Woldholme Avenue, began to be built along with large detached and

1 RDB, LD/335/389; NU/286/423; OS Map 1:2,500, Yorks. CLXI. 12 (1910 edn). Marshall still had much property in the town in 1910: ERAO, NV/1/107.

2 *DT* 18 Jan. 1873, 17 Oct., 5 Dec. 1874, 2 Mar. 1878; RDB, KQ/273/350; LD/334/388; LD/360/416; LD/388/458, etc. The street was probably named from W. F. Lockwood, who preceded the Harrisons at (Old) White Hall, River Head: TNA, HO 107/2366; RDB, LB/196/267. It was said to have been opened in 1876, and was almost built up c. 1890: Ross, *Driffield*, 82.

3 *DT* 25 Mar. 1865.

4 RDB, LD/335/389; *Kelly's Dir. N & ER Yorks.* (1872), 354; Mortimer, *Forty Years' Researches*, 294; J. Nicholson, 'Moot Hill at Driffield', *Notes & Queries* 6th ser. ix. 205; Ross, *Driffield*, 194.

5 RDB, NR/91/122; 67/493/459 (1894).

6 Ibid. 19/451/431 (1887); 26/370/329 (1888). The development was completed about 1960 by Eileen Moss and the builder David L. Naylor: ibid. 1180/391/345, etc.

7 Below, buildings, domestic buildings.

8 OS Map 1:2,500, Yorks. CLXI. 12 (1893 edn); below, buildings.

9 Below, relig. hist., 1840 to 1940 (Anglicanism).

10 Ross, *Driffield*, 81; see under Raylor in *Kelly's Dir. N & ER Yorks.* (1901), 467; (1905), 485.

11 There was, however, also some industry in the north of the town, and middle-class housing was then being built close to the station: Ross, *Driffield*, 81.

12 Following based on OS Map 1:2,500, Yorks. CLXI. 12 (1910 edn); OS Map 1:25,000, TA 05 (1953 edn); fieldwork, 2003–4.

13 Above, vol. intro., population.

14 OS Map 1:10,560, Yorks. CLXI (1855); OS Map 1:2,500, Yorks. CLXI. 12 (1893 and 1910 edns).

15 *DT* 2 Jan. 1926

16 RDB, 358/441/355; 648/207/166; 926/240/200; 1074/272/244; 1828/374/287.

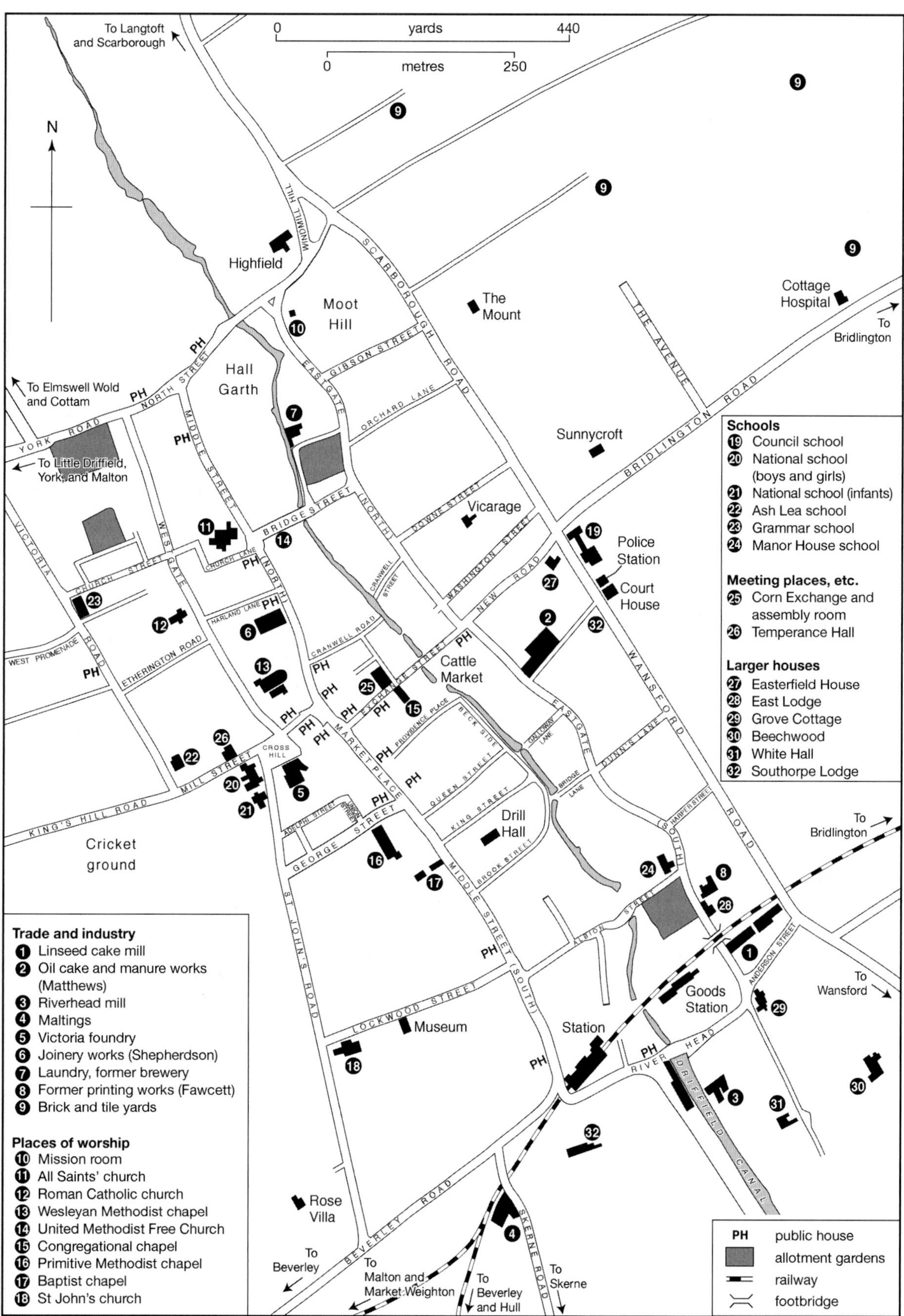

12. *Great Driffield; The town in 1909.*

semi-detached houses in the 1930s, and new side roads were also made there then, later Wold View Road, North and South. One of the developers was Herbert Holmes (d. 1937), a wholesale grocer.[1]

Increased Expansion c. *1950–2010*

The great expansion of Driffield occurred in the later 20th century, and was continuing in 2010. From a pre-war total of nearly 6,000, the town's population rose steadily until the 1970s, and then accelerated to reach some 9,900 in 1991 and almost 11,500 in 2001. In 2002 the town council declared itself against any further development until local services were enlarged to cope with the greater numbers in Driffield and its district.[2] Building had resumed after the war in the 1950s. One of the largest projects was that begun by the urban district council before the war and continued later by that council and its successors, an undertaking which eventually provided almost five hundred dwellings, mostly to the east of Scarborough Road, where the new streets made included Eastfield and Northfield Roads.[3] The building firms used by the council also put up much private housing in and around the town. To the south of the council estate, a house called The Mount was demolished and its name given to a new street laid out and built along in the later 1950s and 1960s by the local firms of W. E. Naylor & Son, joiners, and D. Naylor & Son, builders.[4] Other estates of the 1960s and 1970s included Park Avenue, put up by the Leasons, Greenways and Greenlands, and Highfield Avenue.[5] Eventually much of the land bounded by Bridlington Road and Scarborough Road, and extending north to the new by-pass and east as far as the hospital, was covered with housing, and the 138-home Fieldfare estate has carried the built area across to the southern side of Bridlington Road. In all, some 1,100 homes were erected in the north-east of Driffield between the Second World War and 2003.[6]

On the other side of Driffield, most of the ground bounded by St John's Road and Victoria Road; Beverley Road; Driffield Beck; and the new by-pass was similarly used for housing. Some of the earliest building there, elaborating the pre-war beginnings of Woldholme Avenue, took place in Spencer's Way and Spencer's Mead, added about 1955.[7] Later some 700 dwellings were put up along an extended Woldholme Avenue; in Bracken Road, completed in 2004, and their side turnings. Further north, between King's Mill Road and York Road, about 300 homes were added in Mill Falls, Newland Avenue, and their side closes. Newland Avenue was begun by Messrs. Naylors in the early 1950s;[8] Mill Falls estate, another Naylor development, named in 1968,[9] and Reina Drive was in progress there in 2004. The town was similarly extended northwards by the building of another 200 or so homes in the Whitelands and Lowndes Park estates off Spellowgate, and to the south by the *c.* 90-home Elm Road estate, off Skerne Road. Lowndes Park, by Naylors, was begun about 1965;[10] Elm Road by Barratts a decade later, and the Whitelands development after 1982.[11]

By the end of the century it was chiefly the south-east of the town, to the east of Wansford Road, which was being developed. An estate of almost 130 homes served by a new road called New Walk was built then,[12] and in 2004 building was continuing on The Beechwood, the Verity Way estate, and a small development off Meadow Road. The largest of those enterprises, the Verity Way estate, was being put up by Persimmon Homes.[13] Altogether about 80 units in and off The Beechwood and Verity Way had been occupied by the end of 2003.[14]

To a much lesser extent, the town grew in the later 20th century by the infilling and re-development of its older core. In the south, around the canal, about 60 houses were put up in Watersedge, Riverside Close, Riverside Mews,[15] and Riverhead Drive. Other buildings were cleared away and their sites re-developed. The 19th-century terraced houses of Washington Street were demolished and replaced with 40 homes by the council about 1980;[16] Sawyers Court was built, evidently about 1990, on the site of a burned-out sawmill at North End;[17] and in the late 1990s nearly 30 dwellings comprising Fawcett Gardens were put up on the site of Benjamin Fawcett's home, East Lodge, his printing works, and a later food-processing factory beside Wansford Road.[18]

1 Wold View Road was apparently completed or taken over by the UDC in 1957: ERAO, UDDR/1/8/31, Highways...Cttee, 4 Mar. 1935; UDDR/1/8/32, Highways...Cttee, 7 Oct. 1935; RDB, 1086/319/289.

2 *HDM* 18 Apr. 2002.

3 Below, loc. govt, public services (housing).

4 RDB, 1432/339/310; 1477/103/95; 1494/295/265; ERAO, UDDR/1/8/53, Housing...Cttee, 4 Mar.1957; UDDR/1/8/57, Public Health Cttee, 23 May 1960; UDDR/1/1/36, Housing...Cttee, 2 Apr. 1962; OS Map 1:25,000, TA 05 (1953 edn).

5 ERAO, UDDR/1/8/57, Public Health Cttee, 23 May 1960; UDDR/1/1/37, Housing...Cttee, 9 Sept. 1963; UDDR/1/1/40, Housing...Cttee, 6 Feb. 1967; UDDR/1/1/46, Housing...Cttee, 4 Sept. 1972.

6 The figures are based on the street totals in *Register of Electors* (2004).

7 ERAO, UDDR/1/8/53, Public Health Cttee, 9 Apr. 1956; UDDR/1/8/56, Housing...Cttee, 27 Apr. 1959.

8 Ibid. UDDR/1/8/49, Housing...Cttee, 7 Apr. 1952; 2 Feb. 1953; UDDR/1/1/38, Public Health Cttee, 7 Dec. 1964.

9 Ibid. UDDR/1/1/42, Housing...Cttee, 2 Dec. 1968; RDB, 1613/347/300.

10 ERAO, UDDR/1/1/39, Housing...Cttee, 27 Apr. 1965; UDDR/1/1/40, Housing...Cttee, 2 Jan. 1967; RDB, 1828/375/288.

11 RDB, 1881/213/194; *DT* 5 Aug. 1982.

12 *DT* 5 Aug. 1982.

13 Advertisement for firm at rugby club.

14 *Register of Electors* (2004).

15 *DT* 22 Sept. 1994.

16 Ibid. 6 July 1978.

17 RDB, 997/488/434; plaques on building.

18 *DP* 29 Jan. 1997; *HDM* 14 Oct. 1998; below, econ. hist., indiv. trades and ind. (printing).

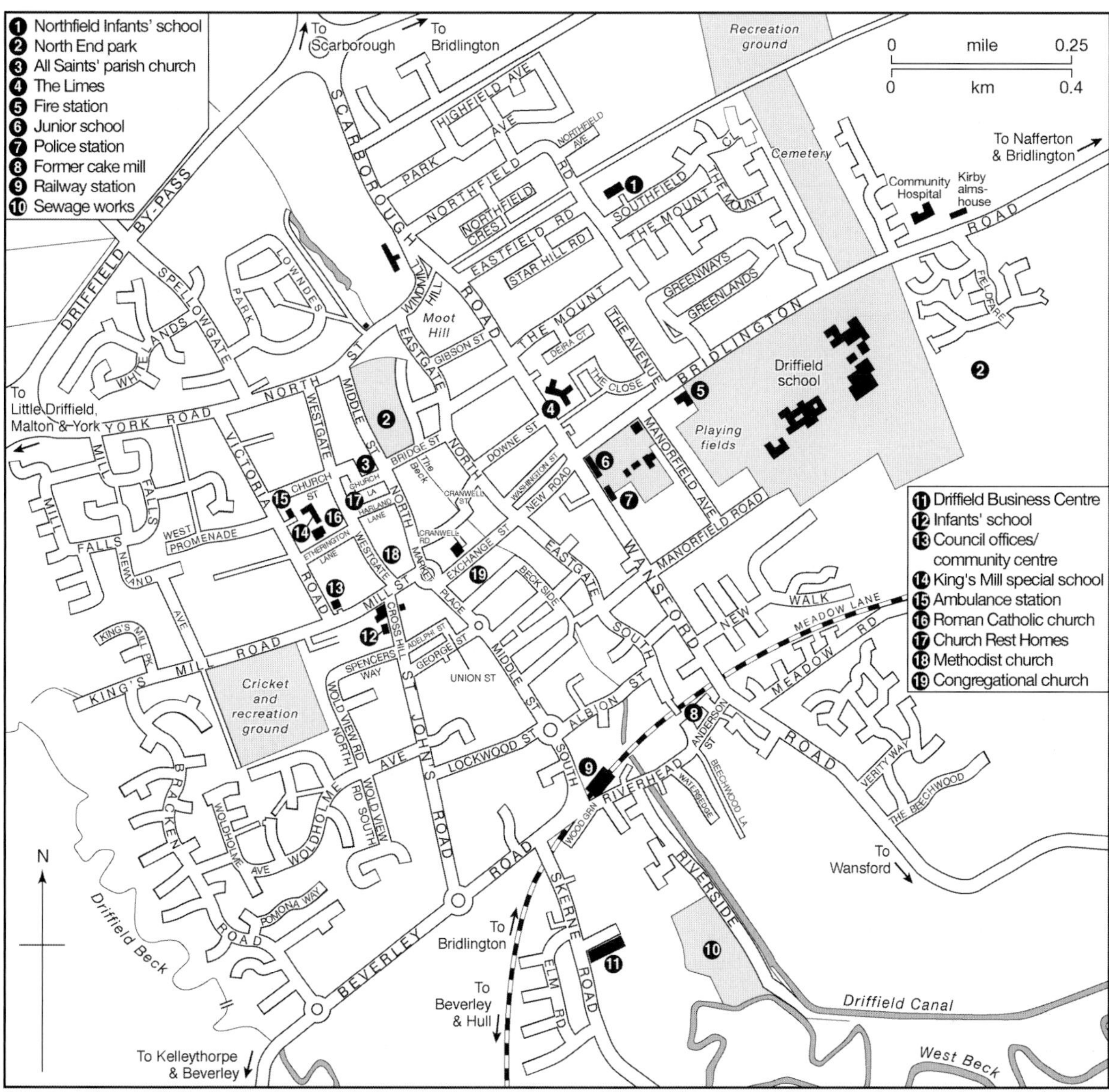

13. *Great Driffield: The town in 2000.*

Early in 2004 the former goods station near by had been cleared and work begun on Riverhead Gardens,[1] similar work was then under way in New Road, and in 2006 the tall Dewhirsts factory in Westgate was being turned into flats. Concern over the nature of some of the changes led to the designation of two conservation areas in the town by East Yorkshire Borough Council in 1980.[2] One included the area around the canal head, where a former mill has been remodelled as some 20 flats,[3] and warehouses[4] and another industrial building similarly converted for housing.

At the beginning of the 21st century the town presented two very different faces, the older, commercial and domestic core, constructed between the later 18th century and the earlier 20th, and the later, wholly domestic, periphery.

LITTLE DRIFFIELD

Little Driffield's early history is poorly documented. Its church is by tradition the burial place of Aldfrith, king of the Northumbrians. More surely, the architecture of the church suggests that it was one of the two churches on Driffield manor in 1086.[5] The prefix Parva or Little was used from the late 13th century to distinguish the

1 *DP* 24 Apr. 1998.
2 *DT* 12 Mar., 7 May 1981; inf. from Planning Dept, ER of Yorks. Council, 2006.
3 *HDM* 3 Nov. 1993.
4 RDB, 1763/3/3; HUL, DX/99/24; ERAO, UDDR/1/1/46, Housing...Cttee, 8 May 1972; *Register of Electors* (2004).
5 Below, relig. hist., Middle Ages (Little Driffield).

14. *Little Driffield in the 1950s. Looking north across the village pond to the Downe Arms public house.*

small village from its larger neighbour of Great Driffield, which stands less than a mile away to the east.[1] Sixteen cottagers in Little Driffield were recorded in 1290,[2] and in 1672 the settlement had 12 householders liable for hearth tax.[3] In 1742 there were some 25 houses, half of them standing to one or other side of a wide green, which was bounded to the east by the beck and closed at its southern end by the church and its yard. The beck, flowing from a spring-fed pond in the north of the green, had presumably attracted the first settlers to the site. In the 18th century the other houses of Little Driffield were strung along the road running east-west across the north of the green from Driffield to Garton, York, and Malton, later York Road. The street leading north from the church through the green, presumably then the main street and now called Church Lane, was continued beyond the Driffield road by a road called Little Driffield Trod, or Gate, which led into the fields, and eventually to Kilham. Since the 14th century fairs had been held in Little Driffield on the green,[4] but at inclosure in 1742 the trod was enlarged for the horse fair, and former open-field land north-west of the village was designated for the sale of sheep.[5] Little Driffield Trod has since been called Horsefair Lane.[6]

In the early 21st century the village was small, domestic, well cared for, and quiet. The tranquillity of the village was due largely to the modern by-pass, which ran around the eastern and northern edges of the village, removing through traffic and isolating Little Driffield from the nearby town by severing York Road.

Most of the domestic buildings date from the 20th century, and comprise a mixture of houses and bungalows. Older houses include one or two 19th-century terraces and a former vicarage house in York Road, and in Church Lane the large Springfield House, remodelled and extended in the 19th century, and the former Downe Arms. Beyond the church, two slate-roofed, gabled cottages stand close to Elmswell Beck, evidently built in the 1840s by the Denisons, later Lords Londesborough, owners of the Elmswell estate. The larger was called Trout Stream Cottage, and the smaller was presumably the cottage held in 1884 by Driffield Fishing Club as lessee of Lord Londesborough.[7] Little non-residential building remains. A building put up by the 1950s on the site allotted for the horse fair was used for packing eggs[8] and then as a clothing factory, but that, and some offices in York Road, stood recently abandoned in 2004, and, apart from a plumbing and heating concern, commercial and industrial activity was then absent from the village.

1 *PN Yorks. ER* (EPNS), 154–5.
2 *Yorks. Inq.* ii, p. 96.
3 TNA, E 179/205/504.
4 Below, econ. hist., mkts and fairs.
5 RDB, B/153/42; ERAO, IA. 41.
6 RDB, HK/317/333.
7 RDB, NW/171/238; OS Map 1:10,560, Yorks. CLXI (1855 edn).
8 OS Map 1:10,560, TA 05 NW (1956 edn); OS Map 1:10,000, TA 05 NW (1970 edn); ERAO, UDDR/1/8/54, Housing...Cttee, 3 Feb. 1958.

THE MARKET TOWN AND ITS HINTERLAND

The status, economy and society of a market town depend on a constant interaction with its hinterland, the extent and prosperity of which is of paramount importance.

Nothing is known of the catchment area of Driffield's medieval market, but it would have been constrained in the early 14th century by the plethora of settlements in the locality granted market charters; there were nine such places within 6 miles of Great Driffield.[1] In some cases a market may never have become established, but in others the market perhaps failed because of the competition for traders. This may have been the reason why Great Driffield's market had apparently closed by the later 17th century, when only the markets at Kilham and North Frodingham were active locally, and even these were of little consequence. The Frodingham market was not recorded in Blome's *Britannia* in 1673 and Kilham was said to have only a 'mean market'.[2]

At that date Great Driffield, with around 145 households, was larger than Kilham or North Frodingham.[3] It was the eighth most populous settlement in the East Riding and with the presence of grocers and mercers and other tradesmen it had some urban characteristics, but it was not a town because it did not have an active market.[4] The chief local market towns in the late 17th century were Beverley, Bridlington and Malton (NR), all at least twice the size of Driffield, and further afield there were the large trading centres of Hull and York.[5]

The situation was much the same in the mid 18th century when Driffield was emerging as a trading and service centre, a position that was formalised when its market was revived following the turnpiking of the road from Beverley and the opening of the navigation in 1770.[6] The already decayed markets at Kilham and North Frodingham offered no competition to the 'new' market town which was well placed to exploit a wide catchment area. The rivalry came from Malton and Bridlington whose merchants controlled the corn trade

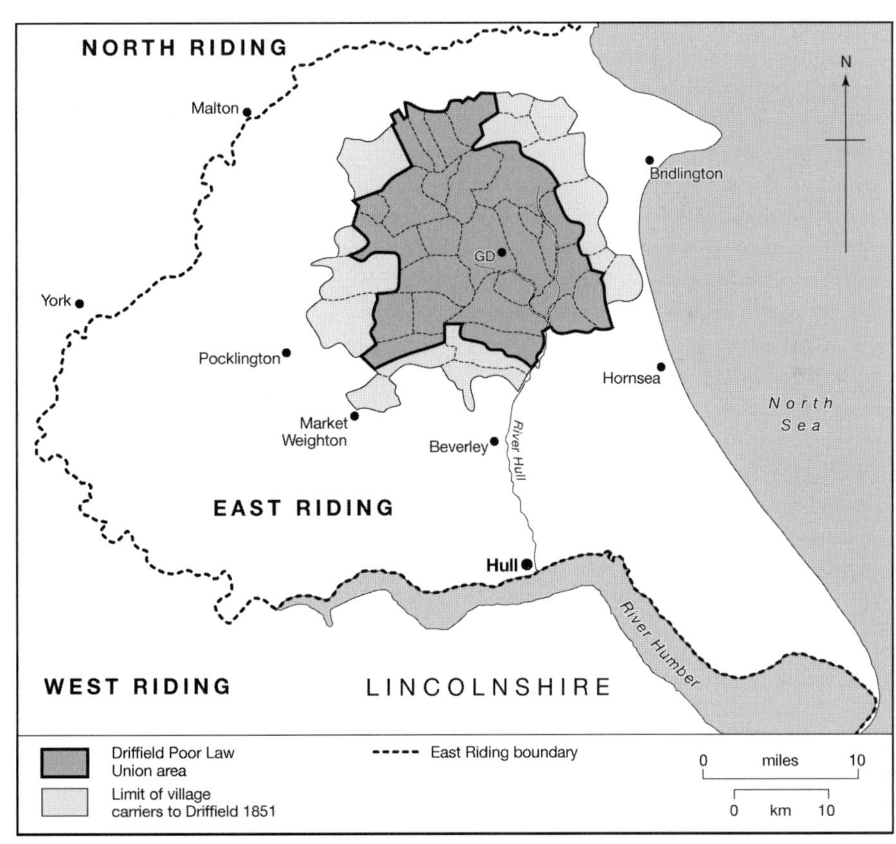

15. *Great Driffield: Catchment area in 1851.*

1 Beresford, *New Towns*, 288–9, figs. 51–2; Gazetteer of Markets and Fairs in England and Wales to 1516 website: www.history.ac.uk/cmh/gaz. North Frodingham is included in the nine although no market charter is recorded: *VCH Yorks. ER.* vii. 266.

2 R. Blome, *Britannia* (1673), 255.

3 Purdy, *Hearth Tax*, 55–6, 61.

4 Below, econ. hist., trade and ind. (1600–1770). As Penelope Corfield has noted, at this period 'all towns had markets, but not all markets created towns'. P. J. Corfield, *The Impact of English Towns 1700–1800* (1982), 21.

5 Purdy, *Hearth Tax*, 51, 54, 94; Blome, *Britannia*, 254–5.

6 R. R. *A new description of all the counties in England and Wales* (1752), 214; *Nomina Villarum Eboracensum* (1768), 93–9.

with established trading links and access to water transport, but Driffield's more central position in relation to the ever-increasing arable acres, the flexibility of the town's early corn factors and the direct link to Hull, and from there to the West Riding, gave it the advantage. By the late 1780s Driffield had overtaken its rivals in both the corn and coal trade of much of the northern half of the East Riding.[1] The rapid rise of the town, its popularity as a social centre, and its central location meant that when around 1800 the site for a new sessions house for the East Riding was being considered, Driffield was suggested and only lost by one vote to Beverley.[2]

The success of the market, not just in corn but also in other agricultural produce and a wide range of goods, attracted merchants, professionals, tradesmen and craftsmen to settle in the town. They came to service the area's rapidly expanding agricultural community, particularly the tenants of the large new farms on the Wolds and Holderness. When the tenant farmers attended the weekly market, they also patronised the shops and inns, consulted the attorneys and apothecaries, bought seeds and artificial manure, commissioned machinery from the implement makers and suits and boots from the tailors and shoemakers. Here their sons and daughters attended private schools, younger sons entered the trades and professions, and it was to here that many farmers or their widows retired.[3] Driffield was also the social and retail centre for the farm workers, especially the young unmarried farm servants who would congregate in their thousands at Martinmas, seeking work through the hirings, entertainment from the many sideshows and public houses, and new clothes, footwear, and other provisions from the well-supplied stores.

The interaction with the hinterland was not one sided; tradesmen and craftsmen went out into the surrounding area, selling their goods and working on the farms and great estates.[4] New ideas spread from the town to the countryside, particularly religious dissent with Nonconformist preachers from Driffield evangelising local villages.[5] In the late 1830s officers of affiliated order friendly societies in Driffield promoted the movement by opening Oddfellows' lodges at Nafferton and Weaverthorpe, and Foresters' courts at Middleton on the Wolds and Hutton Cranswick.[6] Less welcome was the criminal activity. Two men taken poaching in Cowlam Warren in 1804 were said to be part of a 'gang of scamperers, that have long committed depredations from Driffield' and in 1842 a spate of thefts in local villages were blamed on an organized gang of thieves from the town who had 'free warren to rob the town and countryside'.[7]

AREA OF INFLUENCE

In 1848 it was estimated that about fifty villages 'depended on Driffield for their supply of coals, seeds, bone and other manures and shop goods'.[8] A more accurate guide to town's catchment area comes from the coverage of the carriers' carts that came from local villages on market day.[9] In 1851 some 86 carriers from 46 places went to Driffield, this reached a peak of 55 places and 111 carriers by 1901.[10] In the mid 19th century no other town in eastern Yorkshire had more carrier services than Driffield nor more places covered.[11] The villages served by them lay up to 10 miles away to the north, east and west, but only about 6 miles to the south because of the proximity of Beverley.

Much the same area was included in Driffield Poor Law Union, set up in 1836, comprising 44 townships and covering 165 square miles.[12] The area had an 89 per cent increase in population between 1801 and 1851 from 7,563 to 14, 293, despite experiencing constant out-migration.[13]

ADMINISTRATIVE CENTRE

Driffield's position as the focal point for an extensive rural area made it the obvious place to head a poor law union. This was the first of a number of official administrative roles attached to market towns in the 19th century that increased their interaction with their hinterland. From 1837 the town was the location for the office of the superintendent for the new civil registration district, coterminous with the poor law union area, and in 1842 it was selected for the site of a police station and lock-up with a paid superintendent constable for the Bainton Beacon petty sessions division.[14] A county court, dealing with small debts, and covering the registration district area was based in the town from 1847. The fortnightly magistrates' court for

1 Below, econ. hist., indiv. trades and ind. (corn trade).

2 ERAO, DDX/128/27.

3 The chemist James Elgey, the brewer David Holtby, the draper Henry Angas, and the newspaper proprietor George Jackson in the mid-Victorian town, and later the solicitor, Thomas Holtby, came from farms on the Wolds and Hull Valley: Census Returns.

4 HUL, DDSY/98/2, 111, 115, 125–40.

5 Below, relig. hist., nonconformity (1740–1840; 1840–1940).

6 *HA* 15 June 1838; 22 Feb., 8 Mar. 1839.

7 *HP* 31 Jan. 1804; 11 Mar. 1842.

8 ERAO, DDX/17/15.

9 Fig. 15.

10 White, *Dir. Hull & York* (1851), 606–7; *Kelly's Dir. N & ER Yorks.* (1901), 463–4. The number of places covered fell back to 44 in 1921, 27 in 1933 and 22 in 1937: Directories.

11 From a study of 23 towns, excluding Hull and York, in an area bounded on the south by the Humber, the east by the North Sea, the north by the southern edge of the North Yorks Moors, and to the west by the Vale of York: M. Noble 'Growth and development in a regional urban system: the country towns of eastern Yorkshire, 1700–1850', *Urban History Yearbook* 1987, 14.

12 Fig. 15; below, loc. govt, Driffield poor law union.

13 Great Driffield is not included in the figures. *VCH Yorks.* iii. 487–90, 495.

14 White, *Dir. Hull & York* (1851), 598–9; below, loc. govt, police.

the division which by 1840 was meeting alternately at the New Inn, Bainton and Driffield, was held solely at the latter from 1858.[1] To these was added a coroner's court for much of the East Riding and part of the North Riding in 1862.[2]

From 1872 the poor law union guardians acted as the rural sanitary authority, the basis for the Driffield Rural District Council formed in 1894 with offices in the town. A polling centre for parliamentary elections since the 1830s, Driffield became the centre for the new Buckrose constituency from 1885, and the election results were declared there.[3]

Other non-government bodies had headquarters in the town. The Methodists, for example, organized their work in the area through a circuit (later Wesleyan) from 1809, and a Primitive Methodist circuit from 1837, with superintendents and other ministers resident in Driffield. The former circuit covered some 26 centres and the latter about 30 in the 1870s.[4]

CHANGING STATUS

Driffield retained its key administrative role with regard to its hinterland until the mid 20th century after which it was steadily eroded. There was much dissatisfaction in the town when in 1945 it was decided to move the declaration of the poll at parliamentary elections to Bridlington.[5] The town's police station was demoted and placed under the Pocklington division in 1947, and then under Bridlington in 1968. In the latter year the town's Post Office was reduced from a head office to that of a salaried sub-office under Scarborough.[6] Local government re-organization in 1974 brought an end to the urban and rural district councils and the area was then administered by the Borough of North Wolds (later East Yorkshire) based at Bridlington and from 1996 by the East Riding of Yorkshire Council based in Beverley. In 2001 the magistrates' court was closed after which local cases were dealt with at Bridlington or Beverley.[7] It was only in education that Driffield's links to the surrounding area were strengthened with the development of the county secondary school from 1947, attended by pupils from local villages.

Other changes affected the town's relationship with its hinterland. Its status as a railway junction was hit by the closing of the railway lines to Malton in 1958 and Market Weighton in 1965, cutting the numbers travelling to the town by rail from local villages. The decline of the corn market and its closure in 1964, and end of the cattle market in 2001, meant the town had less of a focus for the farming community. Its role as an important employer of local labour, particularly female, was hit by the closure of a number of the town's major industries in 1994–2005.[8] Despite these set-backs Driffield remained in the early 21st century an important and popular centre for retail and services, with a wide range of shops and facilities.

MANORS AND OTHER ESTATES

PATTERN OF LANDHOLDING

Driffield was probably the centre of a large estate long before the 11th century, when the first known record of landholding there was made as part of the Domesday survey. King Aldfrith of Northumbria's death and burial there in 705 suggests that it was a royal vill,[9] and archaeological remains have indicated some high-status burials very much earlier.[10] In 1066 most of the parish and much land in the district comprised the manor of Driffield held by Earl Morcar.[11] Morcar, who played a leading part in English affairs in the mid 11th century, was a younger brother of Eadwine, earl of Mercia; brother-in-law to Harold Godwineson, King Harold II, and, after his election in 1065, earl of Northumbria.[12] Morcar also held many other estates in the north and the midlands; in Yorkshire he had in all twelve large manors in the East Riding, and Easingwold and Pickering in the North Riding. He lost his lands in the turbulent years of the 1060s. In 1066 Morcar and his brother were defeated by the ousted earl of Northumbia, Tostig Godwineson, and his ally Harald Hardrada, king of Norway, at Fulford near York, and, though soon afterwards that defeat was reversed by

1 *HP* 9 Apr. 1847; 8 Oct 1858.
2 Below, loc. govt, courts.
3 Ibid. politics.
4 Below, relig. hist., nonconformity (1740–1840; 1840–1940); *Wesleyan Methodist Church Souvenir of the Centenary of the Driffield Circuit* (1909), 11.
5 *DT* 8 Aug. 1945.
6 ERAO, DDX/980/2/4 (P. A. Shaw, 'Driffield: A geographical analysis', 1969), pp. 65–6.
7 Below, loc. govt., courts.
8 Below, econ. hist., trade and ind.
9 Above, vol. intro., early settlement; below, relig. hist., Middle Ages (Little Driffield).
10 Above, vol. intro., early settlement .
11 Unless otherwise said, this introduction is based on the information and sources given below under the named estates.
12 *DNB*, *s.v.* Morcar.

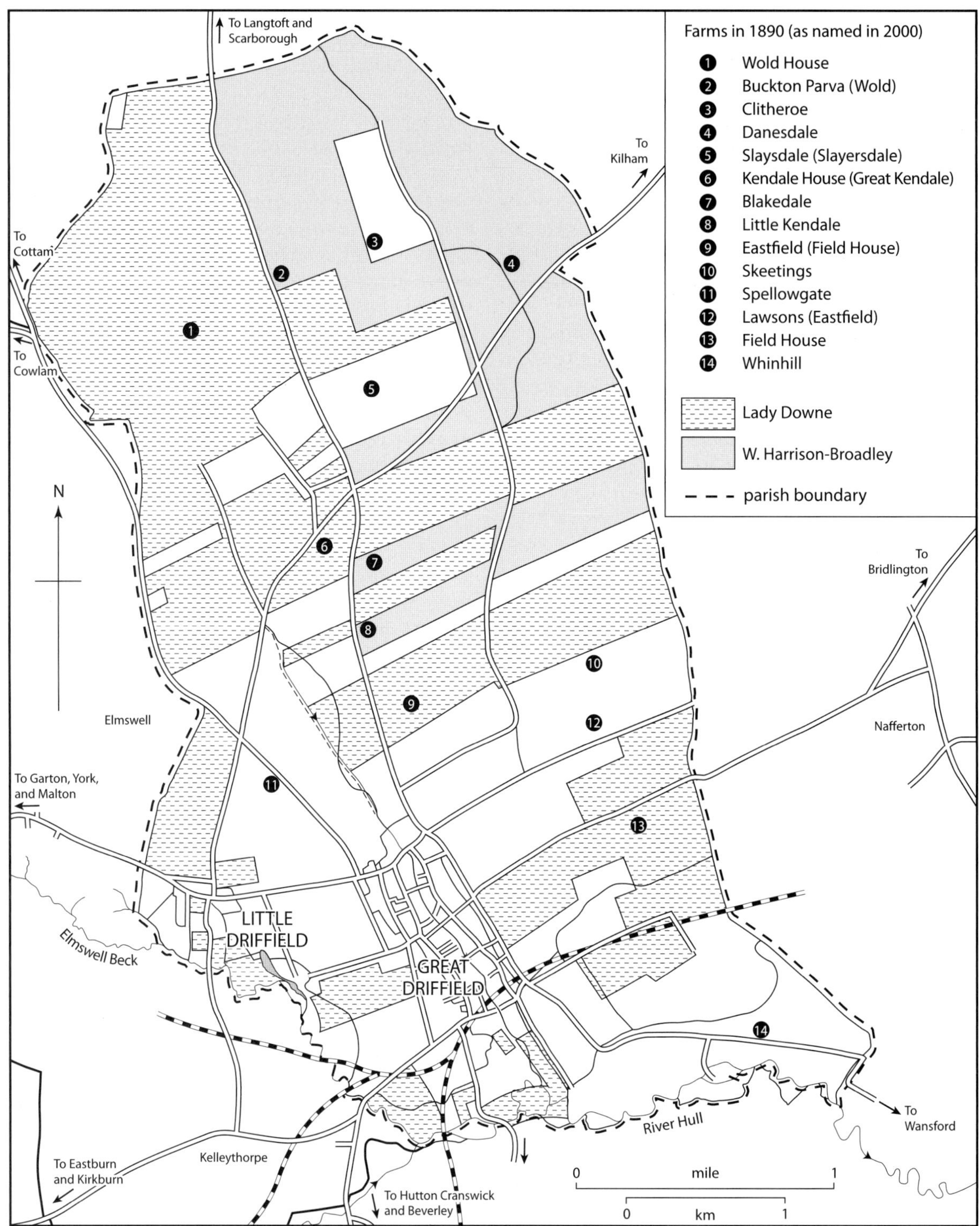

16. *Great and Little Driffield: Major estates in the late 19th century.*

Harold II at Stamford Bridge, Morcar and his brother were later equivocal in their support for Harold and, after Harold's defeat at Hastings, for William I. Following Morcar's rebellion in 1068 and again in 1071, he was imprisoned and evidently stripped of his estates.[1]

Apart from Morcar's manor, the only other holdings recorded in 1086 were a tiny holding of the archbishop of York and a manor at Elmswell held at the Conquest by Norman.[2] The name Norman was English, and referred either to a North Country man or more particularly to someone of Scandinavian nationality or descent.[3]

By 1086 both Driffield and Elmswell manors had passed to the king. Driffield manor's berewicks at Elmswell and Kelleythorpe were relatively unimportant parts of the manor later, the former apparently being absorbed into the estate of St Mary's abbey, York, and the latter becoming a sub-manor of Driffield. Driffield manor was later usually called Great (Magna) Driffield manor, but its inclusion of land in Little Driffield led to a reputed manor of Little (Parva) Driffield being recorded as well on occasion, or to the whole estate being regarded as the manor of Driffields Ambo. From the mid 12th century the manor was usually occupied by Crown grantees, of whom the Scropes held between the 14th and the 16th centuries, and their heirs, the Danbys, until the early 18th century. The manor belonged from the 1730s to the Langleys, and then to their heirs, the Dawnays, Viscounts Downe, until it was divided and sold in the early 20th century.

Little is known about the manor house after the 13th century, when it would seem to have been a fortified house, or castle, in Great Driffield. Later in the Middle Ages the house fell into disrepair and was apparently demolished. Probably no large house was built in its place by the lords of the manor, who without exception lived elsewhere, from the 14th century mostly in the North Riding. The Lords Scrope were seated at Masham and Upsall;[4] the Danbys a few miles from Masham at Thorpe Perrow;[5] the Langleys at Wykeham Abbey near Scarborough,[6] and the Dawnays at Baldersby Park near Ripon.[7]

The only other estate that was rightly reckoned a manor was the rectory. Comprising tithes and a carucate of land in the Driffields, the rectory was given with the church in the 12th century to York minster, and later assigned to officers of the cathedral church. It was sold by the Church in the mid 19th century, when it comprised almost 200 a. in two farms. There were several other estates which were sometimes described as manors. One farm, Routh Hall, seems to have been subtracted from Driffield manor to form part of the settlement of a wife of one of the Lords Scrope. Others would seem to have been either large freeholdings, successors perhaps to earlier holdings of sokeland, or larger farms on the lord's holding let to tenants.

The number of tenants on the manor or manors is usually unknown, but from the 18th and 19th century sources do provide an increasingly comprehensive view of landownership in the two Driffields. Some idea of the nature and extent of the chief manor, and of its tenurial structure, is afforded by a deed of 1723. The demesne, the lord's own holding, then comprised 4 carucates and 5½ oxgangs, or about 870 a., in Great and Little Driffield, all shared among 19 tenants. The rest of the 5,200 a. in Great and Little Driffield townships was probably held largely by the 46 freeholders of the manor, who then owed rents amounting to £24 a year.[8] The size of the lord's share was doubled by a purchase of the early 18th century, and later enlarged further. At inclosure in 1742, eighty-eight owners were allotted 4,778 a. in the Driffields. About 4,025 a. went to 11 owners in allotments totalling more than 100 a. each; they included the lord of the manor who received 1,760 a., Thomas Etherington with 430 a., and the rector with 178 a. A further 430 a. was allotted to 11 proprietors in awards of 20–99 a. each, and the remaining 320 a. was shared by the 66 smallest proprietors, 42 of whom received less than 5 a. each.[9]

Land tax returns indicate that there was an increase of 27 per cent in the number of landowners between inclosure and the end of the century, with a more marked rise in the last decade. There were some ninety-seven proprietors in 1787, a 10 per cent increase since inclosure, and 112 proprietors in 1802, a further rise of 15.5 per cent.[10]

The rapid growth of the town in the first half of the 19th century led to a greatly increased number of property owners, 252 appearing on the tithe award schedule for Great and Little Driffield in 1845. The greatest rise was amongst the lesser property owners, those with houses rather than land. More than two-thirds of the property owners had less than 1 a.[11] The eight holdings of more than 100 a. then comprised in all almost 3,900 a., of which the lord of the manor had just over 2,000 a., Etherington's successor *c.* 630 a., and Henry Broadley 516 a. The number of middling holdings, of 20–99 a. and containing in all some 780 a., was 19, and there were 32 holdings of 5–19 a. each,

1 Ibid.; *VCH Yorks.* ii. 150.

2 Below, Elmswell, Elmswell manor.

3 O. von Feilitzen, *Pre-Conquest Personal Names of Domesday Book* (Uppsala, 1937), 332.

4 *Complete Peerage*, s.v. Scrope.

5 *Visitation of Yorks. 1584–5 and 1612*, ed. J. Foster, 262–3.

6 *VCH Yorks. NR.* ii. 500.

7 J. Foster, *Pedigrees of Yorks.* iii.

8 Some of the freeholders also held demesne land: RDB, H/392/807.

9 RDB, B/153/42.

10 ERAO, QDE/1 Driffields Ambo; M. Noble, 'The Land Tax Returns in the Study of the Physical Development of Country Towns', in M. Turner and D. Mills (eds), *Land and Property the English Land Tax 1692–1832* (1986), 99. Noble's figures show a surprising if modest decline to 108 proprietors in 1832.

11 Noble, 'Growth and development', 277–8.

containing 315 a., and 21 of 1–5 a., comprising together almost 60 a. The remaining 170 proprietors held houses and other buildings but little land; while some of the holdings were small, comprising a single house, they were often more substantial, with several houses and a variety of commercial and industrial premises. Robert Wrangham, for instance, owned the premises of an agricultural chemist, F. C. Matthews, a malt kiln, and nearly 30 houses.[1] Apart from the lord of the manor's own holding, one other sizeable estate was slowly created in the Driffields following inclosure, that eventually exceeding 1,000 a. and belonging in the later 19th century to the Harrison-Broadleys. However, like the chief estate, it too was broken up in the early 20th century, and no one landowner was predominant thereafter.

DRIFFIELD MANOR

The large manor of Driffield passed soon after 1066 from Earl Morcar to the king. It then included land in Driffield and four dependent estates, or berewicks, together assessed at 23 carucates, and some 50–60 carucates of sokeland held by free tenants of the manor.[2] The berewicks were at Elmswell and Kelleythorpe, in Driffield parish, Brigham, in Foston parish, and in Kilham parish. Information from the summary in Domesday Book, adjusted by the deduction of sokeland, suggests that the 23 carucates were made up of 14 in Driffield, 5 in Kilham, 2 in Elmswell, 1½ in Kelleythorpe, and ½ carucate in Brigham. The sokeland in Driffield parish comprised 6 carucates at Cheldal (later Kendale) and 3 carucates in Kelleythorpe. Further afield there was sokeland at Cranswick, in Hutton Cranswick, at Eastburn, Westburn (later Kirkburn), Southburn, and Tibthorpe, all in Kirkburn parish, and in Kilham, Kilnwick, and Skerne parishes.[3] In Beswick, in Kilnwick, 6 carucates in two manors, one of them held by Morcar, seem also to have been regarded as parts of Driffield's soke by 1086,[4] and almost 4 carucates more, at Middleton on the Wolds, were then also claimed as sokeland of Driffield, although that was disputed.[5]

The Crown may have occupied Driffield manor until the mid 12th century, but thereafter the estate was usually held by its grantees in return for their fealty, that is, the duty of fidelity to the king as feudal lord, and the occasional nominal rent.[6]

It was evidently Henry II who granted Driffield manor to William le Gros, count of Aumale, the tenant by 1156 and at his death in 1179.[7] Driffield then reverted to the Crown.[8] In the mid 1190s it was assigned to Richard I's brother John, later King John.[9] William de Forz, count of Aumale, apparently claimed Driffield 'as his right', presumably because of his grandfather's tenure, and he obtained possession from King John in 1215. Forz's tenure was confirmed by Henry III in 1217, and again, following the count's rebellion, in 1221, but the Crown seems to have repossessed Driffield from Easter 1222.[10] The manor was held between 1236 and her death in 1238 by Henry III's sister Joan, queen of Scotland, in return for a hawk each year,[11] and in 1241 was given by the same king to William de Forz, the son and shortly afterwards successor of the earlier tenant, and his wife Christine, in exchange for Christine's share of the earldom of Chester. She had died by 1246 without issue,[12] and her sister Devorgild and her husband John de Balliol (d. by 1268) inherited Driffield. The Balliols gave the manor to their son, Hugh de Balliol,[13] but by 1271 he was dead without issue, and Driffield evidently reverted to his mother Devorgild.[14] She was succeeded, perhaps before her death in 1290, by another son, Sir John de Balliol, king of Scotland from 1292.[15] In the later 13th century the manor comprised 22½–24 carucates in Driffield.[16] It was later forfeited, with the rest of Balliol's lands, to Edward I,[17] and in 1306, by grant or confirmation of an earlier assignment in the Exchequer,

1 ERAO, PE/10/T. 120; below, econ. hist., bone crushing and manure manufacture.

2 The assessment of Driffield at 32½ carucates in the summary cannot be explained: *VCH Yorks.* ii. 320.

3 *VCH Yorks.* ii. 197, 320, 323.

4 Ibid. 197, 225, 320.

5 Ibid. 224–5, 292.

6 *Cal. Chart. R.* 1226–57, 222–3; *Cal. Inq. Misc.* vii, p. 288; *Yorks. Inq.* ii, p. 95.

7 *Pipe R.* 1156–8 (Rec. Com.), 26; 1179 (PRS 28), 16, 23. The grant may have been part of the agreement which Henry II reached with the count at York in 1155: R. W. Eyton, *Itin. of Hen. II* (1878), 5; B. English, *Lords of Holderness, 1086–1260* (1979), 23.

8 *Pipe R.* 1187 (PRS 37), 91.

9 *Chancellor's R.* 1196 (PRS, N.S. vii), 164; *Pipe R.* 1197 (PRS, N.S. 8), 42; 1199 (PRS, N.S. 10), 38.

10 *Rot. Litt. Claus.* (Rec. Com.), i. 347, 458; *Rot. Litt. Pat.* (Rec. Com.), i (1), 154; *Pipe R.* 1221 (PRS, N.S. 48), 118; 1222 (PRS, N.S. 51), 133; English, *Lords of Holderness*, 43–6.

11 *Cal. Chart. R.* 1226–57, 222–3; *Cal. Pat.* 1232–47, 158, 210, 214; *DNB, s.v.* Joan, queen of Scotland.

12 *Cal. Chart. R.* 1226–57, 262–3; *Yorks. Fines*, 1232–46, p. 175; *Complete Peerage*, s.v. Aumale.

13 *Close R.* 1247–51, 161; *Yorks. Inq.* i, pp. 107–8; *Complete Peerage*, s.v. Balliol.

14 *Feudal Aids*, vi. 51; *Yorks. Hund. and Quo Warr. R.* (YAS Rec. Ser. 151), 58.

15 *Yorks. Inq.* ii, pp. 95–6; *Complete Peerage*, s.v. Balliol; *Yorks. Hund. and Quo Warr. R.* 211–12.

16 *Yorks. Inq.* i, pp. 107–8; ii, p. 96; *Feudal Aids*, vi. 51.

17 *Cal. Pat.* 1334–8, 195.

it was assured to the king's nephew, John of Brittany, earl of Richmond.[1] The grant was ratified by Edward II and enlarged to include John's heirs in 1308,[2] and in 1318 the earl was granted free warren in, or the right to hunt over, the demesne of his manor of Driffield.[3] He was returned as the lord of Driffield and its members in 1316,[4] but lost the estate temporarily to the Crown in 1326.[5] Early in the 1330s, the earl granted his regained manor for her life to his niece, Mary de Valence (d. 1377), countess of Pembroke, in exchange for her lands in France.[6] The countess seems also to have held as part of her dower rents from Driffield and other places; after her death they were divided between her husband's heirs, Elizabeth, wife of Sir Thomas Percy, and Phillipa, wife of Sir Ralph Percy.[7]

By his death without issue in 1334, the earl of Richmond's estates were held to have reverted to the Crown,[8] which in 1336 granted the manor of Driffield to Geoffrey le Scrope and his heirs, subject to the countess's life grant.[9] Geoffrey's son, Henry le Scrope, Lord Scrope, held Driffield by lease of the countess of Pembroke from 1374,[10] and obtained full possession at her death in 1377.[11] He (d. 1392) was succeeded in the manor, then sometimes called Great Driffield manor, by his son Stephen, Lord Scrope (d. 1406), and Stephen by his widow Margery.[12] The forfeiture and execution of Henry le Scrope, Lord Scrope, in 1415, and the death of his mother Margery in 1422, caused the manor to revert once again to the Crown. In 1425, however, Henry's brother, John le Scrope, Lord Scrope (d. 1455), claimed that the estate had been settled on him, and the Crown earlier and later seems to have committed Driffield manor to appointees of Lord Scrope,[13] and later allowed the Scropes full possession.[14] In the 15th century the manor was largely occupied by freeholders and other tenants, the lord's own holding, the demesne, being of only 3½ carucates.[15]

The heirs of the last Lord Scrope, Geoffrey le Scrope (d. 1517), were his sisters. Alice le Scrope married Sir James Strangways (d. 1521), and another sister Margery married Sir Christopher Danby (d. 1518),[16] and in the 1520s the lords of Great Driffield manor were named as Sir Thomas Strangways and Lady (Margery) Danby.[17] In 1534 William Strangways, clerk, was dealing with property in Driffield,[18] but most of the Scropes' holding, including the manor, evidently passed to the Danby family. It may have been the Danbys' son Christopher[19] who, as Sir Christopher Danby, held the manor by 1533 and died in 1571, leaving as heir his son Sir Thomas. The manor was then called Driffield upon the Wold, and part lay in the unlocated Costerdale.[20] Sir Thomas Danby settled the manor on his son Thomas and Thomas's bride Elizabeth Wentworth in 1577,[21] and, following her husband's death in 1582, Elizabeth Danby held the manor of Great (Magna) Driffield until at least 1624. Her heir was her grandson Thomas Danby.[22] It was presumably he who, as Sir Thomas Danby, with Thomas Danby, esq., and Francis Danby mortgaged the demesne estate in Driffield in 1642. Sir Thomas and Francis Danby, variously said to be the son of Sir Thomas or of Thomas Danby, esq., were Royalists, and their estate in Driffield was further burdened with payment of a fine to Parliament in the 1640s. It was then worth £80 a year[23] and included a reputed manor of Little (Parva) Driffield.[24] Sir Thomas died in 1660 and under his will the manors of Great and Little Driffield were left to trustees to be sold to benefit his younger children, but that was not done, and there was later prolonged litigation in Chancery which was only resolved in the early 18th century. Margaret Danby, widow of Sir Thomas's son Thomas (d. 1667) had obtained dower in Driffield, allegedly by deceit, and her interest passed at her death in 1688 to her sister Mary Palmes. In 1704, before the final decree, Sir Thomas's grandson, Sir Abstrupus Danby, and his son Abstrupus, sold the manor or manors to James Rickinson,[25] who also bought premises in Driffield from William Palmes, probably about the same date.[26]

1 Ibid. 1301–7, 470; *Complete Peerage*, s.vv. Balliol, Richmond. The grant may have originated in 1299: Ross, *Driffield*, 18.

2 *Cal. Chart. R.* 1300–26, 121.

3 Ibid. 1300–26, 406.

4 *Feudal Aids*, vi. 165.

5 *Cal. Fine R.* 1319–27, 383; *Complete Peerage*, s.v. Richmond.

6 *Complete Peerage*, s.vv. Pembroke, Richmond; *Cal. Pat.* 1330–4, 124, 404; 1334–8, 195; 1370–4, 417.

7 *Cal. Inq. p.m.* xiv, pp. 330, 337; *Cal. Fine R.* 1377–83, 5.

8 *Cal. Inq. Misc.* ii, p. 342; *Cal. Pat.* 1334–8, 199–200.

9 *Cal. Pat.* 1334–8, 195; *Complete Peerage*, s.v. Richmond.

10 *Cal. Pat.* 1370–4, 417.

11 *Complete Peerage*, s.v. Pembroke.

12 *Cal. Inq. p.m.* xvii, pp. 110, 113, 115; xix, pp. 40, 43–4; *Cal. Close*, 1405–9, 30.

13 TNA, C 145/307, no. 2; *Cal. Fine R.* 1422–30, 28; 1437–45, 49; *Complete Peerage*, s.v. Scrope of Masham.

14 TNA, C 139/161, no. 14; C 142/30, no. 30; *Cal. Inq. p.m. Hen. VII*, iii, pp. 87–8; *Test. Ebor.* iv, pp. 72–4; *Complete Peerage*, s.v. Scrope. John issued a charter regarding his 'town and franchise of Driffield' in 1428: Ross, *Driffield*, 19–20.

15 TNA, C 139/4, no. 34.

16 *Complete Peerage*, s.v. Scrope, which mistakenly makes Margery Margaret; cf. *Visit. Yorks. 1563 and 1564*, ed. C. B. Norcliffe (Harl. Soc. 16), 88–9.

17 TNA, C 142/36, no. 67; C 142/48, no. 161; E 150/224 [last].

18 *Complete Peerage*, s.v. Scrope; *L&P Hen. VIII*, vii, p. 56.

19 *Complete Peerage*, s.v. Scrope; for the Danbys, T. D. Whitaker, *Hist. of Richmondshire* (1823), ii [between 98 and 99].

20 TNA, C 142/157, no. 68; *Cal. Pat.* 1569–72, p. 488.

21 *Cal. Pat.* 1578–80, p. 239.

22 TNA, C 142/199, no. 74; C 142/239, no. 121; C 142/404, no. 118.

23 HUL, DDBA/4/114; DDBA(2)/6/1, 45; *Cal. Cttee for Compounding*, ii, pp. 1014–16; *Yorks. Royalist Composition Papers*, ii (YAS Rec. Ser. 18), pp. 160–1; iii (YAS Rec. Ser. 20), p. 86.

24 TNA, CP 25(2)/612/1650–1 Hil. no. 37; CP 25(2)/752/12 Chas II Trin. no. 4.

25 ERAO, DDCC/134/13; TNA, C 78/1441, no. 1; ibid. CP 25(2)/754/19 Chas II Trin. [10 from end]; CP 25(2)/756/24 Chas II Trin. [no. 53]; CP 25(2)/983/2 Anne Hil. no. 34.

26 RDB, D/7/9.

Rickinson, a master mariner of Scarborough, died in 1711, and was succeeded by his widow Elizabeth[1] and their son, William Rickinson of Scarborough, later also of Malton. Rickinson's holding as lord of the manor, comprising 4 carucates and 5½ oxgangs, or some 870 a., all let to tenants,[2] was enlarged in 1722. His mother then conveyed to him an estate which she had bought in 1716 from Charles Hudson and others; it included 4 carucates in five farms and nine cottages in Great Driffield, besides other houses and ½ oxgang in Little Driffield.[3] In 1733 William and Elizabeth Rickinson sold the manor, then called Driffields Ambo, and the estate formerly belonging to the Hudsons to Richard Langley (formerly Hutchinson) and the trustees of the will of his uncle, Thomas Langley of North Grimston.[4] Langley, of Wykeham Abbey (NR), may also have inherited land in Driffield from Thomas Langley, who had been recorded as a freeholder of the manor in 1723.[5] At inclosure in 1742 Richard Langley (formerly Hutchinson) was awarded 1,760 a. for his commonable lands in Great and Little Driffield.[6] He died in 1755[7] and his son and successor, Boynton Langley, in 1772.[8] Driffield descended to Boynton's son, Richard Langley, who died in 1817 without issue,[9] being succeeded, at the death of his widow Dorothy in 1824 by his cousin, Marmaduke Dawnay. Dawnay then took the surname Langley and died unmarried in 1851.[10] Marmaduke Langley's successor was his nephew, William. H. Dawnay, Viscount Downe, who then had, besides the manor, 2,045 a. in Great and Little Driffield.[11] He (d. 1857) left the estate for her life to his widow Mary Dawnay, Viscountess Downe, later the wife of Sidney Leveson Lane. Lady Downe (d. 1900) was succeeded by her son, Hugh Richard Dawnay, Viscount Downe,[12] who sold the estate in many lots, mostly in 1907 and 1918. In the earlier year Herbert Tennant bought Wold House Farm, of 609 a. and occupied by Samuel Tennant; Samuel Tennant bought Great Kendale Farm with 529 a., and James Reed, a Driffield grocer, the 378-a. Eastfield Farm.[13] The rest of the estate was disposed of mostly in 1918, though small sales continued until 1925.[14] Field House Farm, with *c.* 265 a. in Driffield, was sold to Walter Walmsley in 1918.[15] The following year the manors of Great and Little Driffield, comprising the freehold of all manorial lands in the two places; rents amounting to nearly £5 10*s.* a year; grazing rights on waste lands in Driffield parish; and mercantile and fishing rights, were bought by an association of farmers from the area, including James Reed and C. A. Goodlass of Great Driffield. The association was later named the Driffield Farmers' Union, and in 1933 was described as the Driffield branch of the East Yorkshire Farmers' Union.[16] In 1964 Robert Megginson, the remaining trustee, sold the premises bought in 1919 to the urban district council.[17]

The purchaser of the largest lot, Wold House Farm, Herbert Tennant (d. 1944) was succeeded by Percy, Stanley, and Kenneth Tennant, whose son R. W. Tennant had the farm in 2006.[18] Great Kendale was sold by Samuel Tennant in 1918 to George Beal, and most of the land, *c.* 239 ha. (590 a.), was bought from his grandson, Peter Beal, by R. W. Tennant in 2000. With 267 ha. (660 a.) of the Pockthorpe Hall estate, in neighbouring Nafferton and Kilham, bought in the 1980s, the Tennants had some 809 ha. (2,000 a.) in 2006.[19]

Castle and Manor House

The earliest chief house of the manor for which there is real evidence is the Norman castle, the motte of which survives as Moot Hill on the east side of the beck.[20] The motte was constructed at an unknown date after the Conquest on a natural elevation, a base of turves being built up with layers of boulder clay, gravel, and chalk rubble; the material came from nearby, much of it probably from the ditch dug around the motte.[21] The earthwork was much reduced in the 19th century,[22] but in the 1970s it remained about 40 m. in diameter and 3–4 m. high.[23] In 2010 the mound and the land around it was covered with rough grass and scrubby bushes.

The Norman castle, which was not referred to in 1086, is believed to have been abandoned and then revived, perhaps *c.* 1140, during the troubles of King Stephen's reign.[24] The area of the bailey of the castle, the eastern ditch or moat of which was mentioned in 1208,[25]

1 Ibid.; ERAO, DDX/17/15.
2 RDB, H/391/806; H/392/807; K/701/1493.
3 Ibid. F/32/71; H/290/609.
4 Ibid. M/377/602; N/79/160; *VCH Yorks. ER* viii. 28–9.
5 RDB, H/392/807. For the Langleys, J. Foster, *Pedigrees of Yorks.* iii, s.v. Boynton; *VCH Yorks. NR.* ii. 500.
6 RDB, B/153/42.
7 HUL, DDCV/42/2.
8 RDB, AB/283/505.
9 Ibid. BF/405/668; BI/83/128; CG/579/938; DB/490/689.
10 Ibid. DS/351/376; for the Dawnays, J. Foster, *Pedigrees of Yorks.* iii.
11 RDB, GX/105/109; HM/74/71.
12 Ibid. NR/360/517; 190/395/336.
13 Ibid. 91/189/176; 91/206/191 (1906); 97/511/461(1907).
14 Ibid. 292/257/222; 296/592/495.
15 Ibid. 189/510/452.
16 Ibid. 192/489/431; *Kelly's Dir. N & ER Yorks.* (1921), 497; (1933), 451.
17 RDB, 1388/16/16.
18 RDB, 681/68/53; 685/119/104; inf. from Mr R. W. Tennant, 2006.
19 RDB, 185/229/184; inf. from Mr Tennant and Mr Beal, Driffield, 2006.
20 TNA, C 60/504, no. 18. Mude or Mud Hill were said later to be variants of Moot Hill: Mortimer, *Forty Years' Researches*, 295.
21 Eddy, 'Moot-Hill', 40–51.
22 *VCH Yorks.* ii. 45; Mortimer, *Forty Years' Researches*, 294–5.
23 Eddy, 'Moot-Hill', 43; Loughlin and Miller, *Survey*, 90.
24 Eddy, 'Moot-Hill', 50.
25 *Yorks. Fines, John* (Surtees Soc. 94), p. 120. The source does not indicate that the bailey was then abandoned nor support the more easterly location mentioned in Eddy, 'Moot-Hill', 42, 50.

is uncertain but it is possible that it extended to include Hall Garth, the large, moated site on the western side of the beck. King John presumably stayed in the castle or possibly a replacement manor house on Hall Garth during his visits to Driffield in January 1201, and again in January and February 1213,[1] and much building work was done then. In or shortly before 1211, nearly £206 was spent on the king's 'houses' at Driffield, and in the following year just over £385 was claimed for work on the buildings and a fish pond, done under the supervision of William of Driffield and William of Scalby.[2] Henry III was at Driffield in December 1227 and the following year he ordered new barns and cowsheds to be built there.[3] Nevertheless, by 1268 the chief house of Driffield was valued at only £1 a year, and in 1290 it was evidently out of repair, the 'chief manor' then being said to be 'enclosed' but 'not sufficient for keeping it up'.[4] Edward III visited Driffield in December 1332 and May 1334, but he may not have slept there.[5] The manor house had probably been demolished by 1423, when a value of 5*s.* a year was put on 'the site of the manor' with the grazing and fruit of an orchard.[6] In 1742 Hall Garth belonged to the lord of the manor and was of almost 5 a.[7] Earthworks remained in the early 20th century, but they were largely destroyed in the mid century, when the Hall Garth site was landscaped to form North End Park.[8] Nevertheless, there was a very evident mound in the north-western corner of the park in 2010.

In 1856 Great Kendale farmhouse, described as 'an ancient brick building', was regarded as the manor house, possibly because it was where Lord Downe's rents were collected. The township of Beswick, in Kilnwick, part of Driffield's soke and perhaps for that reason enjoying freedom from tolls at the lord's fairs at Little Driffield, was then said to pay an annual rent there.[9]

RECTORY

The rectorial estate in the parish belonged to York minster by Henry I's grant of Driffield parish church and its chapel or chapels to the archbishop of York and the cathedral church early in the 12th century.[10] Then or soon afterwards one of the canonries in the minster was endowed with the estate in Driffield, which was subsequently known as the prebend of Driffield.[11] The prebendal estate was valued at £100 in 1291.[12] In 1484 the prebendary's estate, reckoned a manor of Driffield,[13] was annexed to the precentorship of York.[14] In 1853 the then precentor agreed, in return for an annuity, to release his estate to the Ecclesiastical Commissioners for England, who were due to succeed him under the Cathedrals Act of 1840,[15] and in 1854 they sold much of the rectory.[16]

The rectory, which comprised glebe land and tithes, was usually let by the precentor, his lessee paying a money rent and becoming responsible for certain out-payments and, more importantly, for the maintenance of the chancels of Great and Little Driffield churches.[17] From 1636 the Huttons, presumably relatives of Matthew Hutton, archbishop of York (d. 1606), held the estate. Elizabeth Hutton, recorded as the lessee about 1650,[18] was succeeded by Thomas Hutton, who obtained a new lease, for the usual term of three lives, from the precentor in 1704. In 1722 Hutton assigned his lease to William Rickinson of Malton, then also lord of the chief manor of Driffield, who took out new leases between 1725 and 1736. Dr Francis Topham, a legal officer in the diocesan bureaucracy, had acquired Rickinson's interest by 1757, when a new lease was made to him,[19] and the Tophams retained the estate until at least 1796.[20]

Before the 19th century the lessee of the rectory evidently divided the estate and sub-let the parts.[21] In 1825, however, a new leasing policy was introduced, the single head lease being divided by the precentor into four particular leases; one allowed the collection of rents owed in lieu of tithes in the two Driffields, two others concerned the uncommuted tithes of Elmswell and Kelleythorpe, and the last was a lease of the rectory land.[22]

1 Itin. of King John in *Rot. Litt. Pat.* (Rec. Com.), i (1).
2 *Pipe R.* 1211 (PRS, N.S. 28), 32; 1212 (PRS, N.S. 30), 26.
3 *Cal. Lib.* 1226–40, 62; H.M. Colvin (ed.), *The History of the King's Works*, ii (1963), 924.
4 *Yorks. Inq.* i, p. 108; ii, p. 95.
5 *Cal. Pat.* 1330–4, 380, 545.
6 TNA, C 139/4, no. 34.
7 Motte Hill (then Millhill Close) belonged to another proprietor: ERAO, IA. 41.
8 OS Map 1:2,500, Yorks. CLXI. 12 (1910 edn); Loughlin and Miller, *Survey*, 90.
9 RDB, GX/105/109; Sheahan and Whellan, *Hist. York & ER.* ii. 503.
10 *EYC.* i, pp. 333–6.
11 Ibid. ii. 123; *VCH Yorks.* iii. 13.
12 *Tax. Eccl.* 297,321.
13 W. Page (ed.), *Yorks. Chant. Surv.* i (Surtees Soc. 111), p. 98.
14 Le Neve, *Fasti, 1541–1857, York*, 33.
15 *Lond. Gaz.* 14 June 1853, pp. 1650–1; 3 & 4 Vic. c. 113.
16 Below, this section, glebe land.
17 BIA, CC. P./Dri. 10, Dri. 1.
18 Lamb. Pal. Libr., COMM. XIIa/17/484–6; *TERAS* 2 (1894), 26–7.
19 BIA, CC. P./Dri. 10, Dri. 1, 5; RDB, H/348/720.
20 HUL, DDSY/23/171.
21 Below, this section.
22 BIA, CC. P./Dri. 10, Dri. 9–12.

TITHES

Most of the value of the rectory came from the tithes of corn, hay, wool, and lambs.[1] From the earlier 17th century the estate was let for a base rent of £62 a year, the tithes accounting for £56 of that sum and the land for £6. About 1650 the real value of the tithes from Great and Little Driffield was reckoned to be about £200 a year, and that of those in Elmswell and Kelleythorpe £80.[2] The collection of the rectorial tithes seems to have been sub-let. William Browne who was involved in a tithe dispute in 1564 was described as farmer, or lessee, of Driffield rectory, but was perhaps in fact a sub-lessee.[3] More certainly sub-lessees were William Spink and Stephen Dawson, farmers of the rectory of Great and Little Driffield from 1600, and in 1618 Robert Salvin of Skerne and his later wife Margaret Spink, widow of Driffield.[4] The interest of Salvin and Spink passed, probably in 1619, to the Peirsons of Mowthorpe, in Kirby Grindalythe.[5] About 1640 it was alleged that John Peirson was the sub-lessee of John Dent, farmer of the rectory.[6] Sometimes called the proctor of Driffield, Peirson or his son, also John, was the lessee under Elizabeth Hutton about 1650; Mrs Peirson of Mowthorpe had the tithes in 1664,[7] and the farmers in 1677 were Matthew and Thomas Peirson.[8] Ann Drinkrow, widow, later Ann Boyes, was sub-lessee under Thomas Hutton *c.* 1720.[9]

Great and Little Driffield The wool tithes in Driffield and neighbouring Skerne were said to be governed by the custom that the whole tithe fell to the rector of the parish in which the sheep were pastured at Candlemas (2 February). Since that was not necessarily where they were kept at other times or clipped in the summer, the wool tithes were disputed in the 17th century.[10] The rectorial tithes in Great and Little Driffield were commuted for annual rents at inclosure there in 1742; except for the allotments made for the glebe, all of the land then inclosed was charged with rents amounting to £276 a year for the corn and hay tithes, and £28 10*s.* for those of wool and lambs. The same tithes due from the garths and old inclosures were similarly extinguished for a rent sum of £5 5*s.* a year.[11]

Elmswell The corn tithes of Little Driffield and Elmswell were held by Edward Fisher, probably as a sub-lessee, about 1600.[12] By then many of the tithes in Elmswell were not taken in kind but were settled by cash payments. All the rectorial tithes from the demesne, or lord's holding, then valued at £20, were compounded for by an annual rent of 18*s.*, obviously set long before[13] and challenged by the lessee of the tithes in the mid 16th century.[14] In the mid 19th century the composition rent exempted 512 a. in Elmswell from the payment of tithes.[15] So far as the 'town land' was concerned, the corn and hay tithes were then commuted for cash on the basis of the number of oxgangs held, the rates being 10*s.* to 12*s.* an oxgang for corn tithe and 4½*d.* an oxgang for that of hay.[16] Lambs were still counted and wool weighed each year for tithe in the 17th century, but, once again, settlement was often in cash rather than kind. The lord, Henry Best, was liable for some lamb and wool tithes, presumably for 'town land' held by him, but by 1625 he seems often to have paid a customary composition of £2 5*s.* a year instead of tithing.[17]

On the renewal of William Rickinson's lease of the rectory in 1736, the tithes of Elmswell and the 18*s.* composition rent were sub-let to Francis Best, the lord there, and that arrangement was evidently continued by later lessees and the Bests.[18] In 1825, when the leasing of the rectory was reformed, the rector himself let most of the Elmswell tithes to the Revd Francis Best for a money rent and assumption of the rector's duty of maintaining the chancel of Little Driffield church. The rest of the Elmswell tithes, due from some 90 a. belonging to Robert Moyser, were let by the rector that year to Moyser.[19] At the commutation of the tithes by award of 1844, all of the rectorial tithes there, including the ones covered by the composition rent, were extinguished for rent charges totalling £184.[20]

In the 14th century St Mary's abbey, York, was rendered tithes in kind at Elmswell, some 7 quarters of wheat, 8½ quarters of barley, nearly 8 quarters of oats, and 4 quarters of peas being received in 1320–1. The reason for the render is not known, but those tithes may have come from a nearby parish, such as Burton Agnes, in which the abbey had the rectory.[21]

1 *Miscellanea*, iv (YAS Rec. Ser. 94), 27.
2 Lamb. Pal. Libr., COMM. XIIa/17/324–6, 483, 486; BIA, CC. P./Dri. 10, Dri. 1.
3 BIA, D/C. CP. 1564/1.
4 Ibid. D/C. CP. 1601/5; Best, *Farming Bks*, ed. Woodward, 172; *YAJ* 17 (1903), 177.
5 *VCH Yorks ER* viii. 130, 134.
6 BIA, CP. H. 2315.
7 Best, *Farming Bks,* ed. Woodward, 172, 187–8, 193, 241; *TERAS* 2 (1894), 26–7.
8 BIA, D/C. CP. 1677/6.
9 TNA, E 126/23.
10 BIA, CP. H. 2315; D/C. CP. 1601/5.
11 RDB, B/153/42.
12 BIA, D/C. CP. 1608/4.
13 Best, *Farming Bks*, ed. Woodward, 172, 187, 202. The tithes of the demesne were valued at £28 about 1650: Lamb. Pal. Libr., COMM. XIIa/17/324–6.
14 BIA, D/C. CP. 1564/1.
15 Ibid. TA. 36M.
16 Best, *Farming Bks*, ed. Woodward, 113, 187–8, 192.
17 Ibid. 28, 176, 187, 193, 198.
18 RDB, O/359/881–2.
19 BIA, CC. P./Dri. 10, Dri. 10, 12.
20 Ibid. TA. 36M.
21 TNA, LR 11/51/732; *VCH Yorks. ER.* ii. 114.

Kelleythorpe As in Elmswell, so in Kelleythorpe the chief proprietor usually leased the tithes in the 18th and 19th centuries. In the 1730s James Moyser obtained a lease of the Kelleythorpe tithes from William Rickinson, the lessee of the rectory,[1] and the tithes there were let in 1825 by the rector to Robert Moyser, who under the lease assumed the rector's responsibility for the upkeep of the chancel of Great Driffield church.[2] Moyser sold his interest, with the estate, to W. J. Denison in 1836.[3] By award of 1844, the tithes due from the *c.* 1,100 a. in Kelleythorpe, or Driffield Greets, were extinguished for a rent charge of £250 15*s.*[4]

GLEBE LAND

The glebe land of the rectory comprised 9 oxgangs or 1 carucate in Great or Little Driffield.[5] There were about 25 tenants on the rectorial manor of Driffield in the late 13th century. They held plots of land, perhaps mostly their tofts, in return for cash rents totalling some £3 a year, 55 chickens, attendance at the manor court, and a succession due called relief.[6] The poultry rents were still being paid in the 16th century.[7] The land was a relatively unimportant part of the rectory: *c.* 1650 it was reckoned to be worth just £20 a year, as opposed to an annual value of almost £300 put on the tithes.[8] The manor was said *c.* 1700 to have 19 tenants.[9]

At inclosure in 1742, the land and its appurtenant common rights were exchanged for allotments amounting to 178 a.[10] Nothing is known of the farmers who cultivated the rectory farm or farms before 1825, when the rector let his landed estate in Driffield to David Holtby.[11] Following the transfer of the rectory to the Ecclesiastical Commissioners in 1853, the estate was sold in 1854; it then comprised two farms situated in Little Driffield township. Robert Holtby bought one with 110 a., perhaps that near the church, and Robert Hornby the 75-a. Clitheroe Farm, standing on an outlier of Little Driffield township in the north-east of Driffield parish.[12]

The rectorial estate at Little Driffield included a 'manor house' in the late 13th century,[13] but that had evidently gone by 1636, when a lease of the estate referred to the manor-house site. The chief house in 1649, the 'parsonage house', was a modest farmhouse in good repair.[14] It was probably represented later by Tythe Farm, which stood on the east side of Little Driffield village street, in the 1820s,[15] and by the rectory farm situated immediately south of Little Driffield church on the east side of the lane to Kelleythorpe in 1854.[16] That farmhouse was removed in the mid 20th century.[17]

OTHER MANORS AND ESTATES

TOLEY FEE

Toli of Driffield was recorded in the earlier 12th century,[18] and it may have been one of his descendants, Toly (Tholi, Tholy) son of Thorsten, who had been succeeded in an estate in Driffield by his son William by 1224.[19] From 1277 Peter Tholy held ½ carucate and rents of nearly £1 16*s.* a year in Great Driffield as the tenant of John Marshall and his wife Agnes.[20] Land lately held by a Peter Toly had passed to Walter Ake, who then sold it to Hugh Arden (Ardern) in 1386.[21] Other land at Driffield granted by Walter Ake to Hugh Arden in 1383 lay next to land held by Beatrice Arden, daughter and heir of Peter Toly, who was probably the wife of Hugh.[22] There was later a Toley (Toly, Tuley) fee manor there with appurtenances in Little Driffield and other places. It seemingly passed to Sir Peter Arden (d. 1467) of Latton, Essex, Chief Baron of Exchequer, probably the son or grandson of Hugh Arden, then to his daughter Ann who married Sir John Bohun (d. 1494) of Midhurst, Sussex.[23] The manor was inherited by their daughter Mary who married Sir David Owen illegitimate son of Sir Owen Tudor, the grandfather of Henry VII.[24] Their son Sir Henry Owen sold the estate in

1 RDB, O/57/120; O/359/881; O/360/883.
2 BIA, CC. P./Dri. 10, Dri. 12.
3 RDB, FB/198/212; FB/199/213.
4 BIA, TA. 36M.
5 Ibid. Bp. Dio. 3, ER. p. 102; TNA, C 142/238, no. 41; *Cal. Inq. p.m. Hen VII*, i, p. 151; *Feudal Aids*, vi. 51; *Miscellanea*, iv (YAS Rec. Ser. 94), 27.
6 *Miscellanea*, iv (YAS Rec. Ser. 94), 27.
7 TNA, C 142/238, no. 41.
8 Lamb. Pal. Libr., COMM. XIIa/17/324–6.
9 BIA, Bp. Dio. 3, ER. p. 102.
10 RDB, B/153/42.
11 BIA, CC. P./Dri. 10, Dri. 11.
12 RDB, HE/11/13; HE/13/14; *Lond. Gaz.* 2 Dec. 1853, pp. 3549–50; OS Map 1:10,560, Yorks. CXLIV, CLXI (1854–5 edn).
13 *Miscellanea*, iv (YAS Rec. Ser. 94), 27.
14 Lamb. Pal. Libr., COMM. XIIa/17/482, 484.
15 A. Bryant, *Map of ER Yorks.* (1829). The scale of the map makes it impossible to identify Tythe Farm absolutely with the later farm.
16 RDB, HE/13/14; OS Map 1:10,560,Yorks. CLXI (1855 edn); OS Map 1:2,500, Yorks. CLXI. 11 (1893 edn).
17 OS Map 1:10,560, TA 05 NW (1956 edn); OS Map 1:10,000, TA 05 NW (1970 edn).
18 *EYC.* ii, p. 496.
19 *Rot. Litt. Claus.* (Rec. Com.), i. 625; *Cur. Reg. R.* xi, p. 439.
20 *Yorks. Fines, 1272–1300*, p. 12.
21 *Cal. Close*, 1385–9, 153.
22 Ibid. 1381–5, 589. Hugh Arden of Driffield was probably one and the same as Hugh Arden (Ardern) escheator in Yorkshire in the 1390s: *Cal. Close*, 1392–5, 554.
23 TNA, PROB/11/5; *Test. Ebor.* iv, 102–3; *Complete Peerage*, ii. 201–2.
24 *DNB*, *s.v.* Owen Tudor ; *Complete Peerage*, ii. 201–2.

1522 to Ralph Swillington (d. 1525).[1] Swillington, recorder of Leicester and Coventry and for a short-time Attorney-General to Henry VIII, was born at Great Driffield, the son of William Swillington.[2] Ralph Swillington left his lands at Great Driffield to his nephew George Swillington of Sutton Bonington (Notts.), and Liddington (Rutland), a servant of Thomas Cromwell, who had succeeded his grandfather William Swillington in two houses and a carucate in Great and Little Driffield.[3] George Swillington (d. *c.* 1558–60) left his Driffield land to his daughter Margaret, the wife of Francis, or Faustinius Feilding, who held the manor about 1570.[4] Following the death of Feilding Margaret remarried, and as the wife of Thomas Bird she sold the manor to Stephen Dawson in 1597.[5] No more is known of the manor.

ROUTH HALL

A sub-manor of Great Driffield manor was held by fealty of the Scropes and their heirs by Elizabeth, the relict of Thomas le Scrope, Lord Scrope (d. 1493).[6] By Elizabeth's settlement of 1513, her manor of Routh (Rauffes, Raffes) Hall in Driffield, together with 16 houses and 3 carucates and 2 oxgangs, passed at her death in 1517 to her niece Lucy Browne and Lucy's husband, John Cutt (d. 1528). Lucy survived both her husband and her son, Sir John Cutt (d. 1555), and at her death in 1558 she was succeeded by her grandson John Cutt.[7] In 1570 Lucy's grandson or another John Cutt sold the manor, which then included 25 houses, to Thomas (d. 1582) and Richard Michelbourne (d. 1583), who held it in undivided half shares. Variously named the manor of Raffulles Hall, Routh Hall, Great Driffield, or Great and Little Driffield, in the later 16th and early 17th century, the holding evidently descended like the manors of Routh and Tansterne, in Aldbrough, before being sold by Sir Richard and Thomas Michelbourne in 1614 to (Sir) George Etherington.[8] The manor was then worth just over £37 a year 'in divers farms'.[9] Etherington (d. 1622) was succeeded in Great Driffield manor by his son Richard.[10] The manor was not mentioned again, perhaps being combined with other land belonging to the Etheringtons.[11]

Routh Hall manor was presumably named after the Rouths, and held by them as sub-tenants. The Rouths (Raufs) were evidently established in Driffield by the mid 14th century, when William Routh and a chaplain, Thomas Routh, were active in the violent politics of the district. Thomas Routh, probably another, was serving as constable of either Great or Little Driffield in 1377.[12] John Routh (Reuthe) of Driffield, esquire, was mentioned in 1445, and his brother Brian, of Great Driffield, gentleman, in 1449 and 1465.[13] At Brian Routh's death in 1483 he held the manor, then called Great Driffield manor, and all the other parts of Elizabeth Scrope's estate.[14] He was succeeded by his daughter Elizabeth and her husband Sir John Cutt (d. 1521), and the estate was settled on their son John (d. 1528) and his wife Lucy Browne. John Cutt and Lucy Browne succeeded also to the interest of Lady Scrope, whereby the two tenancies were presumably merged.[15] The tenant in the early 16th century may have been the Henry Routh of Great Driffield then recorded.[16]

Manor House Routh Hall was later said to have stood on Eastgate, and to have been the residence in the early 17th century of the Spinks, lessees of the rectory.[17] An inscription uncovered during the restoration of All Saints' church in 1878–80 read 'William Spinke Routhe Hall His seat A.D. 1616'.[18]

DRIFFIELD (ETHERINGTON)

The Etheringtons, who served the Danbys in their administration of the manor and town of Driffield in the 16th century,[19] also had an estate there which may have been regarded as a sub-manor of Driffield. The founder of the estate was William Etherington (d. 1562), who came from Holme on Spalding Moor, probably on his marriage to Alice, daughter and heir of Brian Skerne.[20] Around 1540, Etherington claimed that a house and 60 a. of land in Great Driffield that he had by right of his wife was held from Sir Christopher

1 *Yorks. Fines*, i. 39; J. W. Clay (ed.), *N Country Wills* (Surtees Soc. 96), 119–20.

2 S. T. Bindoff (ed.), *History of Parliament: The House of Commons 1509–58* (1982), iii. 412–13.

3 TNA, C 1/568, no. 54; C 1/1070, no. 60. Cf. ibid. C 66/1446, mm. 42–4; Bindoff, *Ho. of Commons 1509–58*, 411–12.

4 TNA, C 3/68/9; R. M. Glencross (ed.) *Administrations in the Prerogative Court of Canterbury 1559–1571* (1912), 86; *Yorks. Fines*, i. 372.

5 *Yorks. Fines*, iii. 145; iv. 76. Margaret Fyldinge married Thomas Byrde at All Sts, Derby on 2 Apr. 1589: IGI.

6 *Complete Peerage*, s.v. Scrope.

7 TNA, C 142/36, no. 67; C 142/48, no. 161; C 142/134, no. 225; E 150/224 [last].

8 TNA, C 142/214, nos. 205, 221; *Yorks. Fines*, i. 382; *1603–14*, 143; *1614–25*, 12; *VCH Yorks. ER*. vii. 14, 352.

9 ERAO, DDRI/35/29.

10 TNA, C 142/391, no. 59; *Yorks. Fines, 1614–25*, 205.

11 Below, this section, Driffield (Etherington).

12 Below, soc. hist., soc. structure.

13 *Cal. Pat.* 1441–6, 380; 1446–52, 239; *Cal. Close*, 1461–8, 321–2.

14 Cf. TNA, C 141/4, no. 45; C 142/48, no. 161. *Test. Ebor*. iii, p. 347.

15 TNA, C 142/36, no. 67; C 142/48, no. 161; E 150/224 [last]; *VCH Yorks. ER*. vii. 14.

16 TNA, C 1/354, no. 37.

17 Ross, *Driffield*, 50; below, this section, rectory.

18 *DT* 6 Nov. 1880.

19 Below, loc. govt.

20 BIA, precentorship wills, William Eddrinton, 1562 (inventory); Thomas Etherington, 1589 (will); *VCH Yorks. ER*. ii. 274. Alice Skerne was said to be the widow of Sir Thomas Danby for which there is no evidence: J. W. Walker (ed.), *Yorks. Pedigrees A–F* (1942), 176.

Danby, not George Swillington.[1] He acquired a house, cottage and land at Great Driffield from Ralph Arden in 1542 and on his death twenty years later he had at least nine oxgangs there, besides an estate at Cattleholmes, in the neighbouring parish of Lowthorpe.[2] William Etherington's son Thomas, along with his brothers George and William, was dealing with an estate in Great Driffield in 1566, the other parties being Sir Christopher Danby, his wife and son.[3] When Thomas Etherington died in 1589, he held freely under Driffield manor a large estate comprising a 'manor or chief house', 15 other houses, some two carucates of farmland, mills, and free rents. Etherington's estate included unspecified lands bought from William Gaskin (Gascoigne), the reputed manor of the Gascoignes.[4] Under Thomas Etherington's will, the estate was divided between his sons Richard and George, both later knighted.[5] Sir George Etherington who inherited the Driffield estate died in 1622 and his son Richard (d. 1628) succeeded to the property there and at Newton Garth in Paull parish, where he lived. It was possibly his widow Jane, daughter of Sir George Throckmorton who occupied the six-hearthed house in Great Driffield in 1672.[6] Richard Etherington (d. 1696), who with his wife Mary (d. 1690) is commemorated by a grave slab in Driffield parish church, was probably the son of Richard and Jane Etherington and father of John Etherington (d. 1720), mercer.[7] Thomas Etherington, evidently John's son, was awarded 430 a. for his commonable lands in Great and Little Driffield at inclosure in 1742. He married Anne Stork, eventually the heir to her father John and brother Thomas, who was awarded some 340 a. at inclosure, probably in lieu in part of another Etherington holding that had passed down to the Storks from Marmaduke Etherington (d. 1638) son of George, brother of Thomas Etherington (d. 1589).[8] Thomas Etherington (d. 1767) was succeeded by his son, the Revd George Etherington (d. 1802), and he by his son Richard, a Hull merchant. The estate in Driffield then comprised *c.* 585 a. Richard Etherington (d. 1804) divided his estate in the Driffields and Skerne between his brothers George (d. 1830), John (d. 1820), and Henry of Dantzig, merchant, and a sister, Jane, who married another Hull merchant, J. B. La Marche (d. 1839).[9] All or most of the estate in the parish had fallen to the share of Mrs La Marche by the 1840s, when she had *c.* 630 a. in the two Driffields.[10] She died in 1850, and much of the land was settled in 1853 on her daughter Jane Stork La Marche and her prospective husband, Thomas Holden, a Hull solicitor (d. 1863).[11] Mrs Holden died in 1871,[12] and her stepson Thomas Holden sold almost 600 a. in Driffield in several lots in 1872 and 1873. The largest purchase, amounting, besides land in adjoining Kilham, to some 370 a. in Driffield and including Blakedale Farm and that on Driffield Wold called Buckton Parva, was made by W. H. Harrison-Broadley.[13] The farms later descended with the larger holding of the Harrison-Broadleys.[14]

Manor House At his death in 1589, Thomas Etherington had a large and luxuriously-appointed house in Driffield.[15] That may have been the house held by Mrs Etherington in 1672, and represented later by Westgate Hall. Thomas Etherington's old inclosures in 1742 included several houses, the chief of them occupying a site of an acre, on the west side of Westgate.[16] In the mid 19th century the estate included some 25 houses and cottages in Westgate, most of them on the east side of the street; to the west a 5-a. site was occupied by Westgate Hall and three cottages, and abutting that to the north was another house, no longer part of the estate, but formerly owned by a John Etherington. The Etheringtons' house was later described as a mansion in Westgate, 'for...long...one of...only three brick and tiled houses in the then village'.[17] Westgate Hall, sold in 1873 to G. R. Wrangham and T. G. Marshall, and subsequently occupied by Wrangham,[18] was later bought for the presbytery of the Roman Catholic church, and in 1892 it was described as the 'old manor house'.[19] It was later demolished and a new presbytery built on part of its site in 1926.[20]

DRIFFIELD (GASCOIGNE)

A manor of Driffield upon the Wold, lying in Great and Little Driffield, and including 5 houses and 1 carucate

1 TNA, C1/1070/60–62.

2 *Yorks. Fines*, i. 99; BIA, precentorship wills, William Eddrinton, 1562 (inventory).

3 *Yorks. Fines*, i. 327.

4 BIA, precentorship wills, Thomas Etherington, 1589 (will and inventory); below, this section, Driffield (Gascoigne).

5 TNA, C 142/220, no. 73; BIA, precentorship wills, Thomas Etherington, 1589 (will and inventory); W. C. Metcalfe, *A Book of Knights Banneret, Knights of the Bath, and Knights Bachelor* (1885), 146, 175. Sir Richard Etherington inherited the manor of Ebberston (NR) from his father: HUL, DDHO/52/4/ 64, 87; *VCH Yorks NR.* ii. 435–6.

6 TNA, E 179/205/504.

7 Ross, *Driffield*, 132; BIA, precentorship wills, John Etherington 1720 (inventory); HUL, DDMC/99/1.

8 RDB, B/153/42; AE/535/1025; FF 1654

9 Ibid. AI/503/987; F/250/404; F/353/551; CF/354/552; G/402/662; H/397/646; K/50/87; KP/107/152; *YH* 8 Apr. 1820.

10 ERAO, PE/10/T. 120.

11 Ross, *Driffield*, 133.

12 ERAO, DDHB/7/44; RDB, HC/187/253.

13 RDB, KW/213/261; KY/96/121; KY/205/267; KY/359/481; KY/363/483; KZ/261/364; KZ/262/365; KZ/263/366; KZ/263/367; LD/335/389; ERAO, DDHB/7/38, 42.

14 Below, this section, Danesdale Farm.

15 Below, buildings.

16 ERAO, IA. 41. The house is numbered in the key but that number does not appear on the map itself; the succeeding numbers are however shown on the west side of Westgate.

17 Ross, *Driffield*, 132.

18 RDB, HC/187/253; LD/335/389; NU/286/423.

19 Bulmer, *Dir. E Yorks.* 166.

20 J. A. Barry, *A Hundred Years at Our Lady and St Edward's* (*c.* 1986) [2]

and 2 oxgangs, was held of the Danbys by fealty and payment of £1 6*s.* 8*d.* a year by the Gascoigne family. It was evidently acquired through the marriage of John Gascoigne and Elizabeth Swillington, perhaps niece of Ralph Swillington (d. 1525).[1] Elizabeth widow of John Gascoigne evidently remarried and as Elizabeth Redman (d. 1530) was succeeded in the manor by her son William Gascoigne (d. 1538). William's heir was his son, also William Gascoigne, followed in turn by his son William Gascoigne who with his wife Jane sold his Driffield estate to Thomas Etherington in 1577.[2] The manor then seemingly became part of the Etherington estate.

DRIFFIELD (CROMPTON)

An estate in the district was evidently assembled by Thomas Crompton, auditor to Elizabeth I.[3] He bought and leased respectively the Crown's manors of Elmswell and Kelleythorpe in the 1590s, and his grandson, Walter Crompton (d. 1714), had a holding in those townships and in Sunderlandwick, in Hutton Cranswick parish, in 1664.[4]

More important may have been the family's interest in Driffield itself. Walter's father Robert Crompton, esq., another Royal official as a clerk in the Alienation Office, described as of Great Driffield, was licensed to marry as his second wife Ceziah Strickland of Boynton in 1628, and in the 1630s he was prominent enough to be fined for not taking a knighthood.[5] After his death in 1646, Ceziah Crompton (d. 1667) held lands in Driffield worth £100 a year, the reversion after her death belonging to her stepson, Thomas Crompton, a Royalist officer.[6] The same Thomas Crompton with his wife Mary was dealing with the holding as a manor of Great Driffield in 1668.[7] It was probably their son Thomas who was the Major Crompton who died *c.* 1695, leaving a daughter, the wife of Mathew Hodgson. After Mrs Hodgson's death about 1705, the chief house and land were let to Henry Emers (Amers, Amars). Ownership of the chief house, other houses, closes, and 7½ oxgangs passed to Thomas Holmes, a Beverley mercer, who was married to Elizabeth, only surviving daughter of Thomas Crompton.[8] In 1714 Holmes, together with his son Thomas, sold the estate to a Gainsborough mercer, Henry Revell. In 1719 Revell and his wife Susannah resold it to James Manuel of Malton, tallow chandler, and his wife Mary. Manuel (d. 1731)[9] was succeeded by his three daughters, and at inclosure in 1742 some 225 a. were duly allotted to Frances Lister, wife of a Malton grocer, and Mary and Jane Manuel. They also had about 10 a. of garths in the town, including the site of the medieval castle, and 'Amar's house', formerly that of the Cromptons.[10] The estate was held in undivided third shares by the heirs who, by the marriage of Jane Manuel, later included the Kirkby family.[11] It has not been traced further, but in 1845, the 3-a. site of the chief house on Eastgate, then called Hall Garth, was owned by Emanuel Kirby.[12]

Manor House In 1672 Thomas Crompton's house, which stood on the west side of Eastgate, on the cattle market site, was the largest in the town, with 11 hearths.[13] The house had been demolished by the 1840s.[14]

A farmhouse which was built on former open-field land allotted to the Manuel heirs at inclosure in 1742,[15] standing to the north-west of the town, beside Spellowgate, was known as Manor Farm, or Manor House, in the 20th century.[16]

DANESDALE FARM

A large estate, comprising just over 500 a. in Driffield and based on Danesdale Farm, was assembled by purchase and exchange after the inclosure of the Driffields in 1742 by William Paul of Nafferton, later of Danesdale (d. *c.* 1780). His son, also William,[17] sold the holding in 1786 to R. C. Broadley (d. 1812),[18] and it duly passed to his nephew Henry Broadley, who had 516 a. in the Driffields in the 1840s.[19] Broadley (d. 1851) was eventually succeeded by his nephew, W. H. Harrison-Broadley. He bought *c.* 370 a. of the former Etherington estate in 1872, including Buckton Parva and Blakedale farms,[20] and Little Kendale with 40 a. in 1879.[21] W. H. Harrison-Broadley (d. 1896) was succeeded by his

1 F. W. Dendy (ed.), *Visitation of the North* (Surtees Soc. 133), 36.

2 TNA, C 142/61, no. 31; C 142/51, no. 63; *Yorks. Fines* ii. 100.

3 W. Dugdale, *Visitation of Co. of York, 1665–6* (Surtees Soc. 36), 322.

4 TNA, CP 25(2)/753/16 Chas II Trin. [no. 25]; BIA, York Wills, Walter Crompton Mar. 1714; below, Elmswell and Kelleythorpe. Walter was the son by Ceziah Strickland of Robert Crompton, son to Thomas: J. W. Clay (ed), *Dugdale's Visitation of Yorkshire*, iii (1917), 482; Ross, *Driffield*, 129–30.

5 *YAJ* 17 (1903),191; *Miscellanea*, i (YAS Rec. Ser. 61), 105.

6 *Cal. Cttee for Compounding*, ii, p. 1002; *Yorks. Royalist Composition Papers*, ii (YAS Rec. Ser. 18), p. 191 ; Clay, *Dugdale*, iii, 482.

7 TNA, CP 25(2)/754/20 Chas II Mich. [20 from end]; CP 43/343, rott. 197–8.

8 HUL, DDSY/34/96.

9 RDB, D/227/373; F/389/838; L/414/762; BIA, CP. I. 694.

10 RDB, B/153/42; ERAO, IA. 41.

11 RDB, AO/329/511; AR/193/380; AR/295/576. The registrations erroneously make Jane Mary: cf. ERAO, DDHB/7/28.

12 ERAO, PE 10/T. 120; ibid. TA/13. Manuel Kirkby of Great Driffield, gentleman, was perhaps the same: RDB, FQ/372/363.

13 TNA, E 179/205/504; ERAO, IA. 41.

14 ERAO, PE 10/T. 120; ibid. TA/13.

15 RDB, B/153/42; ERAO, IA. 41.

16 RDB, 122/470/433; 619/444/312; 1652/298/267.

17 ERAO, DDHB/30/51.

18 Ibid. DDHB/30/54, 57. For the Broadleys and Harrison-Broadleys, see *Burke's Landed Gentry* (1937), 242–3; *VCH Yorks. ER*. v. 59–60.

19 ERAO, PE/10/T. 120.

20 Ibid. DDHB/7/38, 42; above, this section, Driffield (Etherington).

21 ERAO, DDHB/7/48.

nephew, H. B. Harrison, who assumed the additional name of Broadley, and he (d. 1914) by his son, J. B. Harrison-Broadley.[1] Most of the estate was sold to the tenants in 1920, Arthur, Albert, and Arthur Edward Dixon buying Danesdale with 565 a., and Newark and William Walker the 228-a. Buckton Parva Farm.[2] Other sales included Blakedale Farm with 46 a., then bought by G. T. Beal.[3] J. B. Harrison-Broadley died in 1944, and in 1954 his widow Doris and the other administratrix sold Little Kendale, then of 128 a., to Kenneth and Mary Walgate.[4]

Danesdale Farm was sold by Arthur Dixon, then retired, to John Henry Boynton of Danesdale, evidently his tenant, and John Herbert Boynton of Field House Farm, in neighbouring Kilham, in 1955. In 1965 the Boyntons added Clitheroe Farm, of some 60 a., which John Herbert Boynton and his wife, by then of Danesdale, conveyed to their son John Michael Boynton in 1973.[5] In 2006 the last-named had a holding of 244.9 ha. (605 a.) based on Danesdale Farm.[6]

The farmhouse was rebuilt in the mid 20th century but an early 19th-century foldyard remains.

MINOR HOLDINGS

Ecclesiastical

Beverley minster was granted £5 a year out of Driffield manor by King Stephen *c.* 1150,[7] and seems to have had another property in the parish; after the suppression, one or more freeholders of Great Driffield owed £1 a year to the minster's successor, the Crown's manor of Beverley Chapter.[8]

Watton priory had land in Driffield until its dissolution in 1539. The holding was included in the life grant of the former priory made by the Crown in 1540 to the last prior, Robert Holgate, afterwards archbishop of York. The reversion after Holgate's death was granted to John Dudley, duke of Northumberland, in 1552,[9] but no more is known of the holding in Driffield.

Until it was dissolved in 1539, Monk Bretton priory (WR) had an estate in Driffield. It was worth £1 13*s.* 4*d.* a year in 1563, when the Crown granted it to William Horne.[10]

An estate in Great Driffield belonged to the Knights Hospitaller, and formed part of their preceptory of the Holy Trinity at Beverley. It presumably included the land and rents from four houses in Great Driffield which, following the suppression of the order, the Crown granted to William Ramsden in 1546 as former property of the Hospitallers.[11] Another part of the Hospitallers' estate may have been St John's Garth, which was mentioned earlier, together with a former tenant, a chaplain, Thomas Austin,[12] and there was a St John's Close in Kelleythorpe in 1576.[13]

Other

According to the summary in Domesday Book, William I's half-brother, Robert, count of Mortain, held 6 oxgangs in Driffield in 1086.[14] Possibly the same were the 6 oxgangs held 'by charter' and rent of 12*s.* a year of the lord of Driffield manor by Stephen Hammond in 1268.[15]

Land of Driffield manor valued at £3 a year was given by King John at or soon after his accession in 1199 to a royal official, Brian the usher (*hostarius, ostiarius*).[16] The holding was later said to be in Driffield itself, and to comprise ½ carucate and almost 2 carucates more occupied by tenants. By 1231 it had passed to Roger de Argentoem, the husband of Brian's daughter, who then owed a Norwegian goshawk for it each year.[17]

Roger Arundel, clerk, an officer of Whitby abbey and royal justice, held 3 carucates in Driffield in 1203–4. An estate belonging to him and comprising land and mills was later said to be worth nearly £32 a year in rents; it may have been or have included the holding in Driffield. He died in 1210 leaving Thomas of Holme as his heir.[18]

1 RDB, 83/43/42 (1896); 86/501/471 (1906); 169/96/71.
2 Ibid. 223/214/180; 225/520/429.
3 Ibid. 223/190/161; 223/192/162.
4 Ibid. 732/54/42; 978/494/433.
5 Ibid. 1019/548/486; 1423/87/80; 1844/397/283.
6 Inf. from Mr J. M. Boynton, 2006.
7 *EYC.* i, pp. 96–7.
8 HUL, DDCV/16/5, 8; ERAO, DDX/683/16, ff. 1–2, 10.
9 *VCH Yorks.* iii. 255; *Cal. Pat.* 1550–3, 117–18.
10 *VCH Yorks.* iii. 94; *Cal. Pat.* 1560–3, 588–90.
11 *L&P Hen. VIII*, xxi (I), p. 356.
12 TNA, C 141/4, no. 45; C 142/36, no. 67; E 150/224 [last].
13 ERAO, DDCC/111/214.
14 *VCH Yorks.* ii. 321.
15 *Yorks. Inq.* i, p. 108.
16 *Pipe R.* 1201 (PRS, N.S. 14), 144; *Rot. Chart.* (Rec. Com.), 85, where ewerer (*aquarius*) is given in error.
17 *Bk of Fees*, ii. 1354–5.
18 *Pipe R.* 1204 (PRS, N.S. 18), 206; 1211 (PRS, N.S. 28), 32; *EYC.* ii, pp. 376–7; L. L. Norsworthy, 'The Yorks. Arundels II. The East Riding', *Notes & Queries* 29 May 1948, 221–3.

ECONOMIC HISTORY

For much of its history the chief occupation in Driffield parish was agriculture, but from an early date the processing of agricultural produce and the sale of foodstuffs, livestock, and other goods also played their part in the local economy.

Some idea of the relative importance of agriculture, commerce, and industry in the parish as a whole is to be had from valuations of the manor of Driffield made in the later 13th century. In 1268 most of the value of the manor, reckoned at just over £104 a year, came from the lands occupied by the tenants, and presumably farmed by them; the only other activities were suggested by the valuation of £33 put on four water mills and the markets and fair.[1] In 1290 Driffield's value was about £80, of which land accounted for £55 and the mills and the markets for £20.[2]

Agriculture continued to dominate the economy of Driffield until the opening of the canal in 1770. An analysis of all occupational entries in the Anglican baptism and burial registers from that date indicates a sharp drop in the number engaged directly in agriculture by the early 19th century. Just under 7 per cent of the occupations recorded in the period 1821 to 1840 were related to agriculture, almost 16 per cent were retail or service occupations and over 42 per cent were manufacturing.[3]

More accurate figures obtained from census enumerators' returns (Table 5) confirm the decline in agricultural occupations and rise in manufacturing by the mid 19th century. Some forty years later it was noted that Driffield presented 'with its array of lofty chimneys, at least the semblance of a manufacturing town'.[4] By this date however its role as the retail and service centre for a wide area was probably of greater significance. The numbers working in retail showed a marked rise in the later 19th century as did those involved in transport, particularly the railway.

	1851	*1901*
Agriculture	10.7	8.9
Building	6.1	8.3
Retail/service	9.6	22.5
Manufacturing	27.2	25.7
Professions	9.3	5.2
Maritime/transport	3.8	6.4
Domestic	18.7	15.0
Miscellaneous	9.0	8.0

Sources: 1851: Noble, 'Growth and development', 295; 1901: TNA, RG13/4518–9.

Table 5. *Great Driffield: Occupational Structure 1851 and 1901*

The decline in agricultural employment continued throughout the second half of the 20th century, but agriculture, because of its regional significance, has remained important to the economy of the town.[5] In 2001 there were 218 residents between the ages of 16 and 74 employed in the broad category of agriculture, hunting or forestry, compared to 896 in manufacturing, 676 in health and social work and 371 in education.[6]

AGRICULTURE

BEFORE INCLOSURE

The manor of Driffield, which extended into several other parishes, was badly affected by the Norman depredations in Yorkshire following the Conquest. The 'home farm' or farms with four 'berewicks', or dependent estates, were reckoned to include land for 12 ploughteams, and to have been worth in all £40 a year in 1066; by 1086 no value was asigned to that part of the manor. The extensive and scattered holdings of the manorial tenants called sokemen were likewise returned in 1086 as waste.[7] There had evidently been a recovery by the 1150s, when the manor was valued at £68 a year.[8]

1 *Yorks. Inq.* i, p. 108.

2 Ibid. ii, pp. 95–6. The fairs were presumably included but were not specifically mentioned in 1290: below, this section, mkts and fairs.

3 Noble, 'Growth and development', 295.

4 Ross, *Driffield*, 30.

5 The number of full-time hired farm workers employed in Driffield declined from 64 in 1951 to only 24 in 1981: TNA, MAF68/4368, MAF68/5781.

6 Great Driffield urban area, 2001 Census Area Profiles, ERYC website.

7 *VCH Yorks.* ii. 197.

8 *Pipe R.* 1156–8 (Rec. Com.), 26.

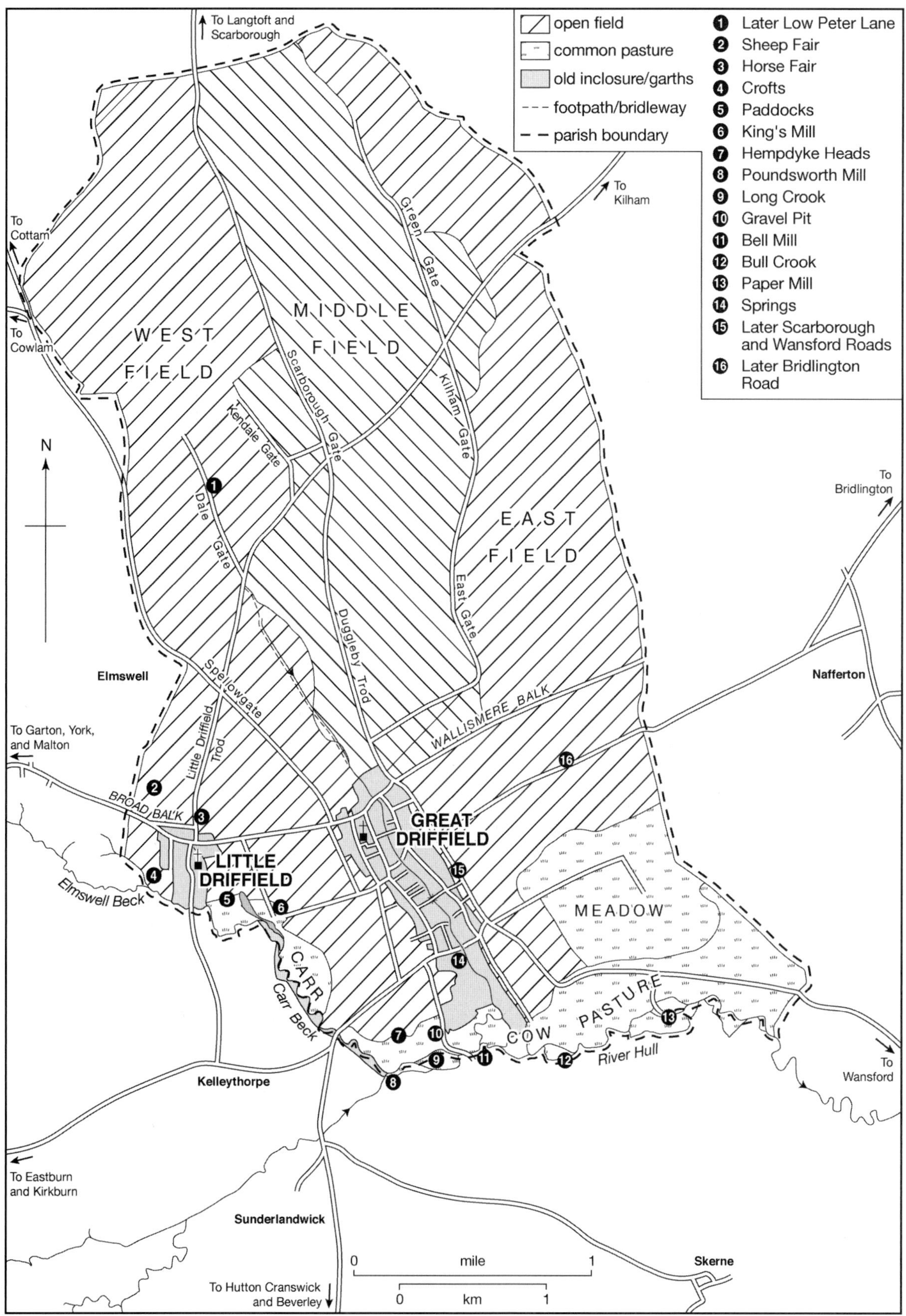

17. *Great and Little Driffield before inclosure in 1742.*

Tenants and Land Tenures

In 1201 the tenants of Driffield obtained a lease of most of the manor, making them directly responsible for paying over the manorial income to the sheriff of Yorkshire for transmission to the king's treasury. The annual sum expected, composed of the rents, market profits, and other proceeds of the manor, and known as the 'farm', was then increased to £72 a year net.[1] In 1268 the manor was valued at just over £104 a year in Driffield, and at about £120 including Kelleythorpe and the dependencies outside the parish; the total value in 1290 was put at just over £98.[2] The manor was let for £100 a year in the 1320s.[3] In the earlier 15th century its value, including its members outside Driffield parish, was less than £30 a year after the deduction of administrative and other costs,[4] and net values ranging from £10 to £40 a year were given in the 16th and 17th centuries.[5]

The demesne land of the manor, the lord's own holding, comprised 3½ carucates;[6] a carucate comprised 8 bovates, or, to use the local term, oxgangs, each of which seems to have varied between about 12 a. and 26 a.[7] The demesne may have been neglected during the count of Aumale's tenure of the manor; following his death in 1179, the Crown made good the stocking by providing eleven oxen. Similarly, five ploughs and four oxen had to be supplied about 1200, when a change in the administration of the estate was caused by the accession of King John.[8] From the early 13th century the demesne was not farmed directly by the lord but was let with the other appurtenances of the manor to the tenants. The lease evidently included the stock and equipment on the demesne.[9] The manor was taken back into the king's hands in 1228, when the sheriff of Yorkshire was ordered to allow the tenants their crops growing on the demesne. The estate was evidently then given over largely to the growing of corn.[10] By 1268, however, the demesne was once again let to tenants at the will of the lord; the annual value put on each oxgang was then £1 5*s*., producing in all a value of £35.[11] By 1723 the demesne estate had been enlarged to comprise 4 carucates and 5½ oxgangs, or some 870 a., all in Great or Little Driffield. It was then held by 19 tenants for rents amounting to *c*. £100 a year; there were eleven farms in all, six of them of 4–6 oxgangs each, and five 2-oxgang holdings.[12]

Most of the tenant farmers on the manor were freeholders of various sorts. Much of the land was sokeland, Driffield including 16 carucates of sokeland in 1268, each valued or rented at 16*s*. 10*d*. a year, and almost 14 carucates being held in socage in 1290.[13] Though free tenants, the sokemen were bound to provide labour for the cultivation of the lord's land. In 1290 a value of £3 1*s*. was put on the 61 ploughing, harrowing, weeding, and corn-reaping and corn-carrying works owed by the sokemen. The leasing of the demesne probably meant that those services were not demanded but instead were settled by each sokeman paying an extra money rent. The sokeman's tenure also involved the payment to the lord of merchet and relief, taxes due respectively when the tenant's daughters were married and on succession to the holding. Relief was then charged at 16*s*.

Other farmers in the late 13th century held land on the manor by a tenure known as drengage. In 1290 just over 4 carucates in Driffield were held in drengage, each valued at the same annual rate of 16*s*. 10*d*. as the sokeland. The tenure, which involved the payment of relief at the rate of £1 6*s*. 8*d*., was almost certainly superior to that of the sokemen who owed labour services.[14] A local surname was derived from drengage tenure, John and Thomas Dring (Drenge) of Driffield occurring, for example, in the 14th century.[15] It was presumably another group of proprietors who in 1268 held 3 carucates 'by charter', their land being then valued at the higher rate of either 12*s*. or £1 an oxgang.[16] By 1423 the earlier distinctions between the freeholding tenants on the chief manor may have ceased to have much meaning, and in a valuation of that date a sum of £11 was given simply for all the free rents of the tenantry.[17] Much of Driffield manor was occupied three centuries later by 46 freeholders for rents totalling some £24 a year.[18]

The 13th-century sources are mostly silent as to the number of tenants in Driffield, and to the size of their holdings, but in 1290 the number of tenants there with little or no land, the cottagers, was recorded. Twenty-nine cottagers owing rents totalling £1 10*s*. 6*d*. and each bound also to do three harvesting works for the lord presumably lived in Great Driffield. Their works, valued at 1*d*. each, were, like those of the sokemen, probably then discharged by a cash payment. At Little Driffield there were 16 cottagers in 1290, owing rents amounting to £2 3*s*. 8*d*. but not apparently agricultural works.[19]

As on other estates belonging to the king, the tenants

1 Ibid. 1201 (PRS, N.S. xiv), 144–5; *Rot. Chart.* (Rec. Com.), 85.
2 *Yorks. Inq.* i, pp. 107–9; ii pp. 95–6.
3 *Cal. Pat.* 1324–7, 336.
4 TNA, C 139/4, no. 34; *Cal. Inq. Misc.* vii, p. 288.
5 TNA, C 142/30, no. 30; C 142/157, no. 68; C 142/404, no. 118.
6 *Feudal Aids*, vi. 51; *Yorks. Inq.* ii, p. 95.
7 ERAO, DDCC/111/214.
8 *Mem. R.* 1200 (PRS, N.S. 21), 61; *Pipe R.* 1180 (PRS 29), 62; 1199 (PRS, N.S. 10), 55; 1200 (PRS, N.S. 12), 102.
9 *Pipe R.* 1201 (PRS, N.S. 14), 161.
10 *Close R.* 1227–31, 60, 75; *Cal. Lib.* 1226–40, 62–3, 82, 241.
11 *Yorks. Inq.* i, p. 108.
12 RDB, H/392/807.
13 Para. based on *Yorks. Inq.* i. p. 108; ii, p. 96.
14 *Yorks. Inq.* ii, p. 96; R. Faith, *The English Peasantry and the Growth of Lordship* (1997), 94–5.
15 *Cal. Pat.* 1334–8, 222; *Cal. Close*, 1385–9, 499.
16 *Yorks. Inq.* i, p. 108.
17 TNA, C 139/4, no. 34.
18 RDB, H/392/807. One or two rents may have been mistranscribed: cf. ibid. M/377/602.
19 *Yorks. Inq.* ii, p. 96.

of Driffield manor were liable to occasional taxation, in addition to the regular rents and services attached to their holdings. Though called tallage – a levy more commonly exacted from unfree tenants – on the royal demesne it was evidently taken from all the tenants, and, perhaps for that reason, was also referred to euphemistically as a 'gift'.[1] The sum to be paid was assessed by royal justices. Such taxation was frequent in the late 12th and earlier 13th century, when money was needed urgently for military campaigns in Scotland and France. The earliest recorded tallage in Driffield amounted to almost £26, the first half being paid in 1186–7.[2] More than one levy was made in the mid 1190s, when the money to ransom Richard I was being raised.[3] In the first decade of the 13th century there were two tallages amounting to almost £60, and another levy, for nearly £27, was made in or by 1219.[4] Besides the compounded charge on the whole community, sums seem to have been raised also from an individual holding or named inhabitants, as in 1229–30, when Driffield with its 'fair' was rated at £13 6*s*. 8*d*., and two of the inhabitants, Richard Heyrun and Robert of Kilham, at £2 and £1 6*s*. 8*d*. respectively.[5] The payment of tallage may have ended in the 13th century, when Driffield ceased to be part of the royal demesne,[6] and the public records lack further details of the tax because of the change of lordship.

Common Lands

The early history of land-use in Great and Little Driffield is not well-documented, and the best idea of the commonable lands of the settlements comes from their description at inclosure in 1742.[7] The two townships shared the open fields and one agricultural system.

East Field and a Middle Field were recorded in the 16th century, and West Field in 1601.[8] East Field lay east and north-east of Great Driffield, extending from the northern parish boundary almost as far as the southern boundary stream. Also running practically from one end of the parish to the other was West Field, which in the south encompassed Little Driffield and separated that settlement and Great Driffield. Middle Field occupied rising ground between the other fields, to the north of Great Driffield. The size of the open fields meant that they included some poor soils on the chalk Wolds, and in consequence an infield-outfield system was evidently employed, the worst land being left mostly as grassland and only tilled occasionally. Certainly infield and outfield balks in Driffield were referred to in 1638.[9] The extensive fields were divided into flatts or falls, the Lord's flatt in Middle Field being recorded in the 17th century.[10] As elsewhere, the basic unit of land in the common fields, the strip, land, or selion, varied in its width; 'broad' and 'narrow' lands, with common rights, made up an oxgang, which in the Driffields evidently contained 24 a.[11] A typical holding was that of some 23 a., purchased by Richard England in 1720, which consisted of at least 33 lands, denoted by their position in individual flatts, dispersed through East, Middle and West Fields.[12]

Grassland was mostly in the south of the settlements, adjoining or close to the western and southern boundary streams of Great Driffield. It was used as meadow, or 'ing', and perhaps more importantly as grazing.[13] Common meadow land was not specifically referred to at the inclosure of the Driffields in 1742, but the common pastures were then named; the chief were the Meadow, the Cow Pasture, and the Carr. Of the lesser pastures, the Parks and Long Crook lay in or adjoined the Cow Pasture, and the Paddocks in or close to the Carr.[14] At least some of the grazing was shared with the neighbouring parish of Skerne, possibly as a solution to the confusion of boundaries and grounds made by earlier changes in the watercourses. About 1575 Driffield farmers were said to enjoy grazing in some of the southern grasslands between Lady Day (25 March) and Lammas Day (1 August). From Lammas they apparently had the right to put as many as 200 cattle into the 'crooks', or meanders, of the streams, and other grasslands, all of which were intercommoned with Skerne farmers.[15] In 1735 a Skerne man was punished in Driffield manor court for putting cattle into 'our common crooks before Lammas', and possibly similar were other intrusions on Driffield's 'common' by men of Skerne and Wansford.[16] At inclosure in 1742 the award mentioned 'Lammas ground' on the west side of Carr Beck and a part of the Cow Pasture intercommoned by Skerne farmers.[17] At inclosure an old route from the town to the southern pastures, the Outgang, was extinguished and awarded;[18]

1 H. S. Bennett, *Life on the English Manor* (1937), 138 ff.; A.L. Poole, *From Domesday Book to Magna Carta 1087–1216* (1955), 418–19.

2 *Pipe R.* 1187 (PRS 37), pp. xxiv, xxix–xxx, xxxv, 91.

3 *Pipe R.* 1195 (PRS, N.S. 6), pp. xv, 98, 261; *Chancellor's R.* 1196 (PRS, N.S. v7), pp. xvii, xxi, 173; 1197 (PRS, N.S. 8), pp. xiii, 59–60.

4 *Pipe R.* 1204 (PRS, N.S. 18), pp. xliii, 206; 1206 (PRS, N.S. 20), pp. xxiii, 207; 1207 (PRS, N.S. 22), p. 89; 1219 (PRS, N.S. 42), p. 198.

5 *Pipe R.* 1230 (PRS, N.S. 4), p. 32.

6 Above, manors, Driffield manor.

7 Award at RDB, B/153/42; plan at ERAO, IA. 41.

8 TNA, C 2/ELIZ/E2/54, m. 1; Ibid. C 3/399/161; BIA, D/C. CP. 1601/5, 1636/9.

9 TNA, C 3/399/161.

10 BIA, D/C. CP. 1601/5; RDB, G/437/942, H/152/316.

11 RDB, D/209/344, H/392/807, H/606/1223.

12 Ibid. G/437/942.

13 TNA, E 178/2594.

14 RDB, B/153/42.

15 TNA, E 178/2594.

16 HUL, DDCV/42/4, s.a. 1733, 1735.

17 RDB, B/153/42 (*see* James Moyser's allotment of 9 a. 3 r. 9 p. *and* Ric. Langley's of 20 a. 2 r. 28 p.).

18 Ibid. (*see* Ric. Langley's allotment of 33 a. 1 r. 14 p.); ERAO, IA. 41; OS Map 1:10,560, Yorks. CLXI (1855 edn).

it was presumably the same as the way for cattle, the 'Neteoutegang', leading to a mill dam which had been mentioned in 1383.[1]

Away from the southern streams, other grassland was provided in the open fields. In 1638 the lord of the manor was in dispute with the freeholders over the pasturage of the field balks, which was also claimed variously to be let by the constables by general consent or to be commonable by all inhabitants from 1 August.[2] The grass on the balks was mentioned again in 1736, when the constables were fined for mowing it,[3] and several surreptitious hay crops were taken from the commons and balks during that decade.[4] The probable lack of meadow ground in particular may have led to tillage being laid down to grass; part of West Field called the Tofts, or Crofts, at Little Driffield lay in strips in the 18th century, but at least some of it was then being used for hay.[5] Grazing was also available in the fallow field, which, following the harvest, was evidently opened to animals on Michaelmas Day (29 September).[56]

Parts of the high wold land were perhaps not cultivated often[7] or at all, and that grassland supplemented the settlements' rough grazing. In 1600 the conversion of grassland to tillage was specified as a possible waste of an estate in Driffield and Lowthorpe, perhaps reflecting both a scarcity of meadow and grazing and the need to protect thinner upland soils from over use for corn.[8] In the 18th century sheep and cattle grazed the wold pastures, which, like other commons in the Driffields, were opened for grazing on 1 August.[9] The common grasslands were valued also as sources of fuel. In 1733, besides hay, turves were taken from the common land, and later dried dung, or cassons, were collected from the Wolds contrary to a by-law.[10]

To the south of the town, much of the land on either side of the beck had already been inclosed by 1742, probably from the common pasture. A small area there called Springs remained commonable but was virtually surrounded by closes, including a Spring Close.[11]

Stock and Crops

The most detailed information on the stock and crops of Driffield farmers is provided by probate inventories. All but one of 15 farming inventories for the period 1558–1638 record sheep, with an average flock size of 130. The largest flocks of 480 and 440 sheep were respectively those of William (d. 1562) and Thomas Etherington (d. 1589), then the leading resident landowners. They also had the largest number of cattle, 36 and 41, pigs, 26 and 30, and horses 34 and 23. Thomas Etherington's farm of at least 15½ oxgangs was unusually large.[12] In the early 18th century, when the lord's holding, the demesne, was reckoned to comprise some 870 a., it was held in eleven farms of 2–6 oxgangs, each.[13] A more typical farm was that of Richard Nicholson (d. 1638), who had 8 oxgangs of arable land, a flock of 100 sheep, 13 cattle, 9 pigs, 7 horses and 4 oxen.[14] As was common in the Bainton Beacon division Driffield farmers used both draught horses and oxen for ploughing.[15] Crops were often more valuable than stock, but only occasionally are wheat, rye, oats and barley itemised in inventories, with the first two referred to most frequently.[16] The 'wheat and ryefield' and the 'oatfield' were mentioned in 1632.[17] The produce from orchards and gardens in Great Driffield, including walnuts, filberts, pears, plums, damsons, and red roses (probably for rose water), was tithed in 1595 suggesting commercial sales not just household use.[18]

A dozen inventories of the late 17th century to early 18th show little change in farming. Farms were smaller, flocks ranged from 30 to 300 sheep, averaging 93, and farmers had around 9 cattle, 6 horses, and a few pigs and poultry; most had oxen.[19] Again there is little information on the differing quantities of crops grown although John Knaggs (d. 1695) had, as well as corn (growing and thrashed and unthrashed), 8 bushels of pease, 4 bushels of wheat and rye, 4 bushels of barley and 7 quarters of malt.[20] Barley, chiefly grown for malting, appears more prominent. In 1696 John Thompson harvested 30 stooks of rye or maselin, 40 stooks of peas and 60 stooks of barley at Driffield.[21]

INCLOSURE

From the 16th century onwards there were periodic attempts to inclose parts of the common land, most likely where it adjoined closes around the town. In 1594 Stephen Dawson and Edward Fisher were ordered by the manor court to lay open closes from Michaelmas to Lady Day and in 1617 John Edwards was ordered to open a 'new intack' every year in 'averidge time ... as it hath been before times'.[22] Similar action was taken against George and Marmaduke Etherington for four pieces of

1 *Cal. Close*, 1381–5, 589; Best, *Farming Bks*, ed. Woodward, 306.
2 TNA, C 3/399/161.
3 HUL, DDCV/42/4, s.a. 1736.
4 Ibid. s.a. 1733, 1734, 1737.
5 RDB, A/235/334.
6 HUL, DDCV/42/4, s.a. 1733, 1735.
7 Above, this section.
8 TNA, C 142/259, no. 33.
9 HUL, DDCV/42/4, s.a. 1734, 1735, 1743.
10 Ibid. s.a. 1733, 1741; J. Wright, *Engl. Dialect Dict.* (1923), i. 530.
11 ERAO, IA. 41; RDB, B/153/42 (*see* allotments to Thomas Stork and John Gray the younger).
12 Best, *Farming Bks*, ed. Woodward, 251–4.
13 ERAO, DDCC/111/214.
14 Best, *Farming Bks*, ed. Woodward, 251–4.
15 Royal Society, C.P. x (3)26).
16 Best, *Farming Bks*, ed. Woodward, 252.
17 Harrison, *Driffield*, 156.
18 J. Thirsk, *Alternative Agriculture* (1997), 36.
19 BIA, precentorship wills 1692–1729.
20 Ibid. Aug 1695, John Knaggs.
21 BIA, CPH/4475.
22 HUL, DP/4.

ground in 1629, and Edward Dawson and William Whitehead for closes in 1627. John Leason and William Thorley were fined 10*s* for every month that their respective walls encroached on the common in 1655.[1]

The desire for more enclosed land around the growing settlement as well as a wish to benefit from improvements in farming are likely to have been behind what was the particularly early inclosure by Act of Parliament of the open fields of Great and Little Driffield in 1742. It was only the fourth inclosure act concerning an East Riding settlement, and the first dealing with a substantial freeholder community.[2]

A tripartite agreement between Richard Langley, lord of the manor, the owner and lessee of the great tithes, and the other proprietors of Great and Little Driffield, for the dividing and inclosing of open fields, pastures and commons, was drawn up on 29 October 1740. An Act confirming the agreement and appointing three commissioners to oversee the process was passed in 1741 and the award signed 26 June 1742.[3] In all 4,778 a. were allotted, of which 1,301 a. came from West Field, 1,086 a. from East Field, and 1,003 a. from Middle Field. Allotments in the common pastures included 158 a. from the Cow Pasture, 139 a. from the Meadow, and 10 a. in the Carr. The remaining 1,081 a. was almost entirely composed of allotments from more than one part of the commonable lands which makes it impossible to determine the extent of individual fields or pastures. Besides those already named, allotments came from grasslands called Long Crook, Hempdyke Heads, the Paddocks, the Springs, and Messenger's Leys, and a few old inclosures were also involved in exchanges. All three fields extended onto the high ground, and much of the land was allotted as 'wold land'; so designated were 542 a. in West Field, 210 a. in Middle Field, and 191 a. in East Field, and much of a further 168 a. lay jointly in East and Middle Fields.

Allotments were made to 88 proprietors, most with relatively small holdings. Forty-two received less than 5 a. each, and 24 between 5 a. and 19 a. Eleven others were each awarded 20–99 a., and 7 between 115 a. and 225 a. each. George Colebatch, vicar, was allotted 285 a. on his own account, Thomas Stork 343 a., Thomas Etherington 430 a., and Richard Langley, lord of the chief manor, 1,760 a.

Several of the smaller owners evidently sold their holdings at inclosure: some transfers were mentioned in the award, and others can be deduced from differences between the award and the later plan. Mary and Ann Oliver had transferred a small holding to William Long before the award, and by the time the map was made he had added 28 a. more, representing four proprietors' shares in the Cow Pasture.[4] Richard Langley similarly enlarged his estate with a house before the award, and soon afterwards with three proprietors' allotments totalling about 10 a. Thomas Etherington bought estates from four proprietors before the award, and subsequently added 11 a. allotted to two owners in the Cow Pasture. Two interests bought by William Byass, innkeeper, were later enlarged by the 3-a. allotment of Elizabeth Owram, widow. Some differences, like the 75 a. allotted to Ann Boyes but shown on the plan as part of her son John Drinkrow's estate, probably resulted from succession rather than sale.[5] The consolidation of holdings after inclosure is perhaps best illustrated by the Danesdale estate, of *c.* 500 a. in Driffield and 80 a. in Nafferton, which William Paul of Nafferton created by purchase and exchange between 1748 and 1776. The largest component, of 124 a., was bought from the Colebatch family, and 60 a. more was acquired by exchanging other land formerly belonging to the Colebatches.[6]

It was a particularly unusual inclosure. Under the terms of the Act, all the open fields and commons of the two townships were to be 'flatted and divided', and held in severalty, but only those lands in the West Field to the south of the balk called Broad Balk, leading from Great Driffield to Little Driffield and those in the East Field to the south of the balk called Wallis Mear, were to be inclosed immediately as directed by the inclosure commissioners. The greater part of the open fields to the north of the settlements were to be inclosed whenever those allotted the land 'shall respectively please'. In the case of the allotments to the south of Broad Balk and Wallis Mear common rights were extinguished by the inclosure act, but to the north the lands whilst uninclosed remained subject to 'such stint or common right' as settled by the commissioners. Once an owner had inclosed any part of his land, then it would be held 'free and discharged ... from all manner of common right', and the owner would lose in proportion any right of common in the yet uninclosed lands. Until the whole of the lands were inclosed they were to be 'kept and continued in a regular course of tillage'. There were several owners who had only houses or cottages for which they received small allotments in lieu of common rights, and it was determined that they be allotted lands to the south of Broad Balk and Wallis Mear as such small

1 Ibid.

2 V. Neave, *Handlist of ER Enclosure Awards* (1972).

3 14 Geo. II, c. 11 (Priv. Act); award at RDB, B/153/42. The original plan of 1742 may not have survived, but at least two copies were made in the 19th century. One of them was re-copied carefully in 1956, and that version (ERAO, IA. 41) has been used throughout this volume. The other 19th-century copy is at BIA, CC. Pr. 11/1. The two copies seen were clearly derived from the same, original plan, the differences between them reflecting the difficulty of transcribing the earlier versions. Variations between the award and the plan are discussed below.

4 RDB, R/116/279; Q/470/1166.

5 For the relationship, ERAO, DDHB/30/51.

6 ERAO, DDHB/30/51, 57.

holdings to the north would have been 'inconvenient and prejudicial to the course of husbandry'.[1]

The continuation of the communal nature of some aspects of farming after the inclosure award is evidenced by agricultural offences dealt with by the manor court. In 1752 stinted pasture was reported to have been overstocked with 50 sheep; in 1756 a farmer had broken the pasturage rules by 'bailing' his oxgang in the corn field, possibly meaning that he tethered beasts on his own land too soon after harvest,[2] and in 1772 the grazing after harvest, or average, had been begun before the field was clear of corn. As late as 1783 a by-law was issued against cattle and pigs being put onto the arable land before all the crops were in.[3]

AFTER INCLOSURE

Post-Inclosure Farming

With no great rush to inclose all the allotted lands part of the farming of Great and Little Driffield continued to be undertaken from farmsteads within the settlements until the end of the 18th century.[4] Some new farms were built and of the 14 farms in the parish in 1768, four had been recently erected on the Wolds to the north of the village.[5] Kendale (Great Kendale), Wold House (Buckton Parva), Danesdale, and one unnamed (Middlefield Farm, now Field House, Scarborough Road), are shown on Jeffreys' plan of 1772.[6] Middlefield Farm and Kendale were built by Richard Langley. Post and rails were provided for the farm at Kendale Well in 1759.[4] Wold House, later called Buckton Parva or Wold Farm, was built in the bottom left-hand corner of the 129 a.-allotment made to Thomas Etherington in 1742.[7] Danesdale was the centre of the 500 a. estate built up since 1742 by William Paul who was living there by 1768.[9] Langley had probably built another farm, Field House, to the east of the town and south of the Nafferton/Bridlington Road by 1774.[10] None of Langley's farms was particularly large in 1774, ranging from Little Driffield Farm of 144 a. to Kendale of 288 a.[11] Most had their land spread through two or three of the former open arable fields plus meadow and pasture, and they had sheep 'gates' on Langley's uninclosed wold, similar to the pre-inclosure system.[12] There was some farm re-organization by 1796, probably to provide more compact holdings, but the sheep walk on the wold was still open.[13]

A lease for what appears to be Middlefield Farm in 1752 between Richard Langley and Thomas Harrison details the cropping of the 250 a.-holding. A third of the land 'commonly used in tillage' was to lie fallow each year. The fallow was to be sown with turnips the next year, then barley and clover, followed by wheat or rye 'or any other sort of grain'.[14] The emphasis on turnips and clover, the new crops associated with agricultural improvement, was particularly significant. When Arthur Young reported on the farming of Driffield in 1768 he noted that a more traditional four-course system was practised; fallow, followed by wheat or barley, then peas or beans, and finally oats. Only a very few turnips were grown for sheep and clover was sown with oats and mown for hay twice. Young makes no mention of inclosure, but records that there were 300 a. of sheep walk, and 1,200 sheep in the parish which were kept 'all winter in the field, their turnips being too trifling to mention'. He praised the dairies and provided a summary of the stock and crops of three of the 14 farms. One of 280 a. in extent was divided equally between grass and arable, of the arable 25 a. were planted with wheat and 30 with barley. The farmer had a flock of 100 sheep, 21 cattle, comprising 5 cows, 8 beasts and 8 young cattle, 8 working horses and 8 oxen. On a second farm of 200 a., 80 a. were of grass and 120 arable. The stock here consisted of 400 sheep, 3 cows and 8 young cattle, and there were 6 horses and 6 oxen. A smaller farm of 70 a., of which 40 a. were arable and 30 grass, had 100 sheep and 2 cows, with 2 working horses and 4 oxen. Driffield farmers still regarded both oxen and horses as 'absolutely necessary', and they used 6 oxen and 8 horses for 120 a. of arable land.[15]

Sainfoin was being grown on Danesdale Farm in 1783. The terms of a lease that year for this wold farm of almost 600 a. reveal the care which was then being taken not to exhaust the tillage with too frequent or too extensive use; no more than three crops were to be taken before land was fallowed, and the area growing corn was not to exceed 200 a.[16] The same concern led to the insertion in leases of the rectorial farm of a clause forbidding the tenant from inclosing any remaining open land without the permission of the rector, on pain of automatic voidance of the lease.[17]

Turnips and grass seeds were more generally grown

1 14 Geo. II, c. 11 (Priv. Act)

2 Wright, *Engl. Dialect Dict.* i. 132.

3 HUL, DDCV/42/2, s.a. 1756, 1772, 1783; ibid. DDCV/42/4, s.a. 1752.

4 Below, map 9.

5 Young, *Six Months Tour*, ii. 6.

6 T. Jefferys, *Map of Yorks.* (1772).

7 NYRO, ZDS/XVII/5.

8 ERAO, IA. 41

9 ERAO, DDHB/7/16.

10 Harrison, *Driffield*, 200. The presence since the early 20th century of two Field House Farms, one off Scarborough Road, the other off Bridlington Road causes confusion. The 1850s Ordnance Survey plan names the former as Middlefield Farm and the latter as Field House, and this designation is followed here. OS Map 1:10,560, Yorks. CLXI (1855 edn). For a time in the later 19th century Middlefield Farm was called Eastfield Farm, a name also used on occasions for the smaller Skeetings and Lawson Farms. OS Map 1:2,500, Yorks. CLXI. 12 (1893 edn); ibid. (1910 edn); HRO, DDHT/9/689.

11 Harrison, *Driffield*, 200.

12 NYRO, ZDS/IV/1/6/1–2.

13 Ibid. ZDS/IV/1/6/1; Howorth, *Driffield*, 32–5.

14 Harrison, *Driffield*, 195.

15 Young, *Six Months Tour*, ii. 1–7.

16 ERAO, DDHB/30/54, 58.

17 BIA, CC. P./Dri. 10, Dri. 5.

by 1796 when Sir Frederick Eden commented on the farming at Driffield. He also noted that 'several experiments have been tried, by planting potatoes, and then sowing a crop of wheat immediately after; but this has not answered the expectation of the farmers'.[1] In 1801 there were said to be 1,954 a. under crops in Great and Little Driffield: wheat accounted for just over 700 a., barley for almost 400 a., oats and turnips or rape for nearly 300 a. each, and peas for just over 200 a., and the crops were described as the most abundant ever seen.[2]

Inclosure and better husbandry greatly increased the value of the land and the landlord's income. The annual rent from the Langley estate at Driffield rose from £273 or about 3*s*. an acre in 1741–2, to £659 or 7*s*. 6*d*. an acre in 1774, and £1,558 or 17*s*. 6*d*. an acre in 1796.[3] The value of the low lying Allimond Wharf Close alongside Driffield Beck rose from 6*s*. in 1774 to 40*s*. in 1796 which may suggest great improvements in drainage of the area.[4] In 1774 pasture was generally valued per acre at twice that of arable, but in 1796 the rents per acre were more equal.[5] The increase in the value of the arable land reflected the high price of corn during the Napoleonic wars. There was much pressure throughout the area to increase the extent of arable land, this encouraged inclosure and the ploughing out of grassland including sheep walks and rabbit warrens.[6] Richard Langley appears to have inclosed his remaining open wold land in Driffield parish between 1796 and 1802, much to the annoyance of a fellow gentleman, evidently keen on hunting, who broke down a fence immediately after it had been erected.[7] In 1794 200,000 quick-wood plants were purchased for hedging on the wolds and by 1802 part of the former open sheep-walk, covering 326a. had been attached to a much enlarged Great Kendale Farm.[8] The proportion of the farmland that was arable in Great and Little Driffield rose from two-thirds to three-quarters between the 1790s and the mid-1840s, when additional farmsteads were built outside the town and existing farms re-organized.[9]

The present Wold House Farm, which possibly began as a high barn for Great Kendale Farm *c.* 1800, had become a separate 600-a. farm by 1840.[10] By 1845 the following small farms were sited in the northern two-thirds of the parish: Clitheroe, Slaysdale, Blakedale, Little Kendale, Eastfield (later Skeetings) and Lawson Farm (later Eastfield) and along Wansford Road were Chimney or Chesney Farm and Whin Hill Farm. There were some 12 farms of over 50 a. in 1845, the five largest were Field House, 284 a., Middlefield, 391 a., Great Kendale, 449 a., Danesdale, 486 a., and Wold House, 624 a.[11]

Just prior to and during the boom years of Napoleonic Wars the landowners and farmers of Driffield and area showed an active interest in the improvement of stock and crops. An annual show of bulls established at Great Driffield by 1787 was possibly linked to the Driffield Agriculture Society that by 1792 was offering annual premiums for the best sheep, cattle and pigs.[12] The society, evidently refounded in 1795, met four times a year under the chairmanship of a local member of the landed gentry such as Edward Topham from Wold Cottage, Thwing and Thomas Grimston of Kilnwick.[13] More often referred to as the East Riding Agricultural Society it offered 'rewards' at its regular meetings for such diverse achievements as to 'the cottager who shall have planted the greatest number of apple trees', 'the mechanic who shall produce the best swathe rake upon improved principles', and the person who shall produce 'the best method of curing the curl top in the potatoe'.[14] In 1800 discussions were held and resolutions were passed seeking the establishment of an experimental farm in the East Riding under the patronage of the Board of Agriculture, encouraging 'the mowing of young clovers and other seeds, and giving them to cattle in the fold yard', and declaring that 'oxen, are in many respects as useful as horses for the plough and other agricultural purposes'.[15] The society's main event was an annual show of cattle and sheep that is said to have been held on land in Eastgate North later occupied by Lora Cottages.[16] The society met in the Hunt Room; the secretary throughout was William Drinkrow and the organizing committee consisted of local landed gentry.[17] The last mention of this society was in 1812 and its demise may have coincided with the end of the Driffield Hunt club *c.* 1811 and the sale of the Hunt Room.[18]

George Coates, the tenant at Middlefield Farm (now Field House) *c.* 1799–1811, was amongst the local

1 F. M. Eden, *The State of the Poor*, iii (1797), 818.

2 TNA, HO 67/26/125.

3 Harrison, *Driffield*, 199; Howorth, *Driffield*, 32–5.

4 Howorth, *Driffield*, 33.

5 Harrison, *Driffield*, 203.

6 A. Harris, '"A rage of plowing": The reclamation of the Yorks. Wolds', *YAJ* 68 (1996), 217; *VCH Yorks. ER*. viii. 31.

7 HUL, DDSY/101/73 (undated letter from Digby Legard to Tatton Sykes).

8 Harrison, *Driffield*, 197; NYRO, ZDS/IV/1/6/3.

9 Eden, *State of the Poor*, iii. 818; ERAO, PE/10/T. 120; Baines, *Hist. Yorks*. (1823), ii, 196.

10 C. Hayfield, 'Manure factories? The post-enclosure high barns of the Yorks. Wolds', *Landscape History* 13 (1991), 33–45; H. Teesdale, *Map of Yorks*. (1828); White, *Dir. E.R Yorks* (1840), 206; ERAO, TA/13; ibid. PE/10/T. 120.

11 ERAO, PE/10/T.120.

12 *YC* 19 June 1787; *Annals of Agriculture*, 19 (1793), 58.

13 *HA* 2 May 1795; *VCH Yorks. ER*. ii. 325; Ross, *Driffield*, 174.

14 *HP* 15 Apr. 1800.

15 Ibid. 12 Aug. 1800.

16 *St James' Chronicle* 3 Oct 1797; *Annals of Agriculture*, 32 (1799), 538; *HP* 12 Aug. 1800; 25 June 1805; 23 June 1807; 21 June, 9 Aug. 1808; 8 Aug. 1809; 17 Sep. 1810; *Agricultural Magazine* 8 (1803), 383; 10 (1804), 380–1; 12 (1805), 50; Ross, *Driffield*, 88; OS Map 1:10,560, Yorks. CLXI (1855 edn).

17 *HP* 17 Sep. 1810.

18 H. E. Strickland, *Gen. View of Agric. of ER of Yorks*. (1812), 301; ERAO, DDX/128/27; below, soc. hist., hunting.

farmers involved with the Agricultural Society.[1] At the cattle show at Driffield in 1803 Coates gained prizes for the best yearling heifer, the second-best two-year old bull, and the second- best shearing ram. All three bulls that won prizes at the show were bred by him.[2] Coates, who became renowned as a breeder of Shorthorn cattle and Leicester sheep, had introduced the former into the East Riding from the 'vicinity of the Tees'.[3] He bred the famous bull Patriot, sold for 500 guineas in 1804, and a cow for which he is said to have refused an offer of 1,000 guineas.[4] This was no doubt 'the Driffield Cow', a print of which Coates dedicated to his landlord Richard Langley.[5] In 1822, by which time he had moved to Carlton near Pontefract (WR), Coates compiled a herd book of registered pedigrees of shorthorns, the first for any animal.[6] Coates Herdbook, still published, was said to have 'joined the Bible and Book of Martyrs upon many a farmhouse table'.[7]

Turnip was the most important of the new crops, providing winter fodder for sheep who fed in the fields and thereby manured the land. In 1805, David Anderson, nursery and seedsman at River Head, Driffield, was selling five types of turnip seed, including some brought from Norfolk and Scotland, and also cole, rape and parsley seed.[8] It was the introduction of bone manure, crushed bone, or bone dust, that enabled turnips to be grown so successfully on the light soils of the Wolds. Samples of bone dust were sent to Driffield by James Clark of Hull in 1810, and that same year the use of bone manure was said to have been pioneered by Tatton Sykes (later 4th Bt) on his farm at Pockthorpe, adjoining Great Driffield.[9] In 1826 a bone mill was established at Driffield.[10]

By 1800 the local agricultural society was offering premiums for 'mechanical inventions that might be useful in husbandry'.[11] The first thrashing machine had been introduced into the East Riding from Northumberland by Miles Smith, owner of the Sunderlandwick estate adjoining Driffield, in 1787, but it was not until some twenty-five years later that thrashing machines were in general use throughout the region.[12] Mark Foley was making portable thrashing machines and turnip and corn drills at Driffield by 1823, and there were three machine makers there by 1840.[13]

Cereal prices fell sharply at the end of the Napoleonic Wars and much distress was felt periodically in the local farming community, amongst tenants and farm workers, until the early 1850s.[14] Prices fluctuated; sheep and wool prices were at a low point in 1826 with lambs being sold for only 8*s.* 6*d.* each at Driffield August Fair, but two years later they sold for 24*s.* and soon afterwards the Revd Richard Allen, vicar of Driffield noted that wheat had 'advanced beyond the reach of the poor'.[15] He considered that the distress had been heightened by the increased use of portable threshing machines.[16] Just over a year later in January 1830 Allen wrote that a 'gloom pervades almost every countenance in consequence of the general depression of trade and agriculture', and then in May recorded that 'poverty is the complaint of all ranks and degrees'.[17] Money was scarce, sales were common, and many from the area emigrated to America.[18] A soup kitchen was established at Driffield in December 1830. The following month two straw stacks were burnt in the parish and fearing unrest a great number of special constables were sworn in for the East Riding.[19] The hardship for the tenant farmers was alleviated to some extent by the landlords returning a proportion of the rents. In 1831 Marmaduke Langley reduced his tenants' rents by 20 per cent and made a further return of 10 per cent.[20]

The difficulties faced by farmers were clearly behind the initiative of Thomas Scotchburn in 1826, when he called a meeting at the Red Lion inn to establish an association for the protection 'of the cultivators of the soil' and to defend 'their just claims before the legislature'.[21] Two hundred farmers attended the first meeting. The 'Driffield Agricultural Association' was flourishing in 1834, with E. H. Reynard as president, George Hopper, vice-president, James Harrison, corn merchant, as treasurer, and Scotchburn as secretary.[22] The association provided two barrels of ale for the populace when the foundation stone of the Corn

1 *HA* 26 Jan. 1811.

2 *YH* 20 Aug. 1803, 15 Aug. 1807.

3 Strickland, *Gen. View*, 223.

4 Sheahan and Whellan, *Hist. York & ER.* ii. 497, 503; *YH* 26 Oct. 1811; G. Coates, *The General Short-Horned Herdbook* (1822), 12, 48, 105.

5 *The Driffield Cow*, painted by Benjamin Gale of Hull, engraved by John Whessel (Driffield, 1804).

6 P. J. Perry, 'The Shorthorn Comes of Age (1822–1843): Agricultural History from the Herdbook', *Agricultural History* 56 (1982), 561; J. R. Walton. 'The Diffusion of the Improved Shorthorn Breed of Cattle in Britain during the Eighteenth and Nineteenth Centuries', *Transactions of the Institute of British Geographers*, N.S. 9 (1984), 23.

7 Walton, 'Diffusion of the Improved Shorthorn Breed', 23.

8 *HP* 5 Mar. 1805. Anderson was resident at Driffield by 1799: RDB, BZ/314/505.

9 A. Harris, 'Bones for the land: the early days of an East Yorkshire industry', *E Yorks. Loc. Hist. Soc. Bulletin* 31 (Spring 1985), 10–11.

10 ERAO, DDX/17/15; below, this section, bone crushing

11 *HP* 15 Apr. 1800.

12 Strickland, *Gen. View*, 88.

13 Baines, *Hist. Yorks.* (1823), ii.197; White, *Dir. E. & N.R Yorks* (1840), 206; below, this section, metal working.

14 *Yorks. ER.* viii. 34.

15 *YH* 30 Aug. 1828; ERAO, DDX904/1/1, entries for 25 Aug., 9 Oct. 1828.

16 ERAO, DDX904/1/1, 6 Sept. 1828.

17 Ibid. DDX904/1/2, 28 Jan., 7 May 1830.

18 Ibid. 23 Mar., 15 May 1830; *YG* 24 Apr., 4 May 1830; *HA* 8 Apr. 1830; 10 May 1833.

19 *YG* 24 Dec. 1830; YAS, DD147/88.

20 *HA* 30 Sept. 1831.

21 *YH* 2 Dec. 1826.

22 Howorth, *Driffield*, 54–5; *HP* 24 Jan., 14 Feb. 1834.

Exchange was laid in 1841.[1] Its members would have been solidly in support of the Corn Laws, the repeal of which in 1846 led to a sharp fall in grain prices from 1848 to 1850.[2] A correspondent from Driffield in November 1849 commented on the 'depressed state of the agricultural interest', and the many agricultural servants that were then unhired.[3] Emigration fever hit the area, and the newspapers have a number of reports of Driffield residents migrating to Australia in 1849 and America in 1852.[4] In July 1850 many small farmers and tradesmen and their families from around Driffield, Market Weighton and Bridlington sailed for South Africa under the 'Natal scheme' promoted by Henry Boast, farmer and Wesleyan lay preacher, from North Dalton, 6 miles south-west of Driffield.[5] The extent of the local farmers' hardship led Marmaduke Langley to return 10 per cent of the rent to his tenants in 1851.[6]

High Farming 1850–1877

James Caird made no reference to agricultural distress when he visited Driffield and the Yorkshire Wolds as a special commissioner from *The Times* in December 1850. Instead he saw 'large and numerous corn ricks' which gave 'an air of warmth and plenty', and 'turnip fields, crowded with sheep'.[7] Here he found 'high farming' in practice on the large farms by tenants who were 'probably the wealthiest men of their class in the county'. From 'their social position' they 'were men of education and liberal mind, alive to the improvements which recent times' had produced, and they commanded the capital which 'enabled them to take advantage of those improvements'.[8] These were the men who founded the Driffield Farmers Club in 1851 and the Driffield Agricultural Society in 1854. Thomas Hopper of Kelleythorpe, president, and Robert Hornby of Driffield Wold, treasurer, of the Farmers Club, were also vice-presidents of the Agricultural Society along with Thomas Dawson of Poundsworth Mill, Francis Jordan of Eastburn, Henry Hill of Sledmere Field and William Angas of Neswick.[9] The last was the son of Caleb Angas, a leading authority and writer on agriculture, who lived in Driffield from *c.* 1849 until his death in 1860.[10]

High farming and the so-called golden age of agriculture, which lasted from the early 1850s until the late 1870s, brought great prosperity to the town. Farmers, who recorded profits almost every year, and landowners, with their higher rental income, could obtain at Driffield all the 'raw' materials for high farming, the aim of which was increased output of meat and grain. It depended on feeding cattle and sheep with large amounts of oil-cake, the extensive use of artificial fertilizers and reduction in labour costs by mechanisation.[11] A local chemist F. C. Matthews established an artificial or chemical fertilizer works at Driffield in 1847 and oil-cake, initially brought from Hull by canal, then rail, was manufactured in the town by 1860.[12]

Mechanisation, an important element of high farming, was adopted by farmers on the Wolds beginning with portable threshing machines and corn drills, in use and available from Driffield machine makers by the early 1820s. Legard noted in 1848 that drilling, as distinct from broadcasting seed by hand, had become universal on the Wolds, as well as the use of the clod crusher patented by William Crosskill of Beverley.[13] Crosskill manufactured on licence Hussey's mechanical horse-drawn reaper which performed so well at a demonstration arranged by Driffield Farmers Club 1851 that several members took the machine on loan.[14] The following year the club organized a competition at Kelleythorpe between Hussey's and McCormick's reapers, judged by Thomas Hopper, Francis Jordan, Caleb Angas, J. Staveley of North Dalton and Thomas Craven of Field House Farm, Driffield.[15] The reaper was gradually adopted and by 1870 was said to have 'almost entirely superseded the scythe' in the Driffield area.[16] Steam thrashing machines were introduced at the same period, one made by Clayton, Shuttleworth & Co., Lincoln, and owned by Messrs. Foley, machine manufacturers at Driffield, was demonstrated in a field near the Market Place in October 1851.[17] Early the following year the local farmer, miller and corn merchant Thomas Dawson told fellow members at the first annual meeting of the Farmers Club that it was no use 'crying' over the repeal of the Corn Laws, and 'if they wished to mend their position they must betake themselves to the advantages to be obtained by means of various ingenious instruments'.[18] At the first two shows arranged by the Agricultural Society in 1854–5, manufacturers from Driffield won prizes for clod crushers, a seed sowing machine, a seed drill, a chaff

1 *HA* 11 June 1841.

2 R. Perren, *Agriculture in Depression 1870–1940* (1995), 2–3.

3 *HA* 16, 30 Nov. 1849.

4 Ibid. 9 Jan., 13 July, 3 Aug. 1849, 16 Apr. 1852; D. Neave, 'Friendly Societies in the Rural ER 1830–1912' (Hull Univ. PhD thesis 1986), 168–9.

5 A. F. Hattersley, *The British Settlement of Natal* (1950), 149–61.

6 *HA* 18 Apr. 1851.

7 J. Caird, *English Agriculture in 1850–51* (2nd edn, 1852), 297, 310.

8 Ibid. 310–11.

9 *HP* 18 Apr., 1851; 26 Jan. 1855.

10 *DNB*, *s.v.* Caleb Angas; *HP* 17 Feb. 1860.

11 Perren, *Agriculture in Depression*, 2.

12 Below, this section, artificial manure; seed crushing and animal feed.

13 G. Legard, 'Farming of the ER of Yorks.', *Jnl of the Royal Agricultural Soc. of England* 9, ii. (1848), 109, 116.

14 *HA* 12 Sept. 1851; Howorth, *Driffield*, 89. The American inventor Hussey was present at the demonstration having attended the Great Exhibition.

15 *HP* 20, 27 Aug. 1852.

16 Ibid. 2 Sept. 1870.

17 Ibid. 31 Oct. 1851.

18 Howorth, *Driffield*, 89.

Year	% of total area of crops and grass returned								Number per 1000 acres				
	Wheat	Barley	Oats	Trnps	Other crops	Clover	Perm grass	Total area	Horses	Cattle	Sheep	Pigs	Poultry
1866	26	6.5	13	20	N/D	14.5	20	3881 a.	N/D	75	627	97	N/D
1881	16.5	10	18	17.5	3.5	12.5	22.5	4446 a.	48	92	633	102	N/D
1891*	14.5	11	16.5	16	6.5	14	21	4390 a.	52	99	1063	151	N/D
1901	15	13	15	15	5	14.5	23	4573 a.	53	101	799	90	N/D
1911	14	13	15.5	15.5	4.5	14	23.5	4617 a.	57	116	976	119	N/D
1921	15	17.5	14.5	15	2	14	22	4541 a.	55	92	679	78	919
1931	14.5	13.5	15	15	3.5	15	23.5	4472 a.	48	108	986	95	1084
1941	15	20	11	13.5	3.5	12	24.5	5279 a.	42	170	891	79	839

Source: 1866–1931 TNA, MAF 68/77–8, 780, 1350, 1920, 2490, 3051, 3591; 1941 figures are a combination of the returns for the post-1935 parish (below Table 8) and the 1941 returns for 8 farms in Nafferton parish formerly in Gt Driffield: TNA, MAF68/3998; MAF32/1065/20.
* Gt Driffield and Sunderlandwick N/D no data

Table 6. *Great Driffield: Crops and Stock 1866–1941*

cutter, and an improved turnip drill for nitro-phosphate.[1] The last was exhibited by F. C. Matthews who later ran a depot at his fertilizer works for the North of England Implement Co. selling, drills, horse hoes, winnowing machines, prize ploughs, cultivators and self-raking reapers.[2]

Matthews, first secretary of both the Farmers Club and the Agricultural Society, had a farm on Wansford Road where he was able to demonstrate the benefits of artificial manures and machinery to his prospective customers.[3] His success was often referred to in the local press. The benefits of top dressing fertilizer were noted in a report on the hay harvest in 1859 which praised 'the abundant crops yearly reaped by Mr F. C. Matthews who pays attention to the cultivation of his grass which is always the first ready for the scythe'. Matthews was the first to introduce improved hay-making implements, including Samuelson's double-acting hay making machine and the same inventor's leveraged horse rake that did the work of seven or eight hand rakers.[4] In 1861 a crop of wheat grown by Matthews on former 'cold barren land' was described as the best in the East Riding, and his turnips were more forward than any in the neighbourhood.[5] A few years later Matthews' crop of mangold was said to be perhaps the finest 'in the country'.[6]

The changes between 1866 and 1881 for crops and stock at Great Driffield (Table 6) reflect general trends during the period of high farming, where the basis of prosperity was a move within mixed farming from corn to livestock.[7] Overall with crops there was a sharp drop in the acreage of wheat, and falls in the extent of turnips and clover, but significant rises in the acreage of barley, oats and permanent grass. By 1881 however the agricultural depression was making an impact. The same pattern occurs in figures for the whole of Bainton Beacon division, which included Driffield at its north-eastern corner. The farmland of this division, from the low-lying often waterlogged meadows along the upper stretches of the River Hull to the well-drained thin-soiled chalk Wolds, was representative of that worked by the farmers from a much wider area who frequented Driffield's markets and fairs. In Bainton Beacon between 1867 and 1880 the acreage of wheat declined, but by only 5 per cent and this was after 1875, the extent of barley rose over the whole period by 82 per cent, most sharply in the early 1870s, whilst the acreage of oats fluctuated, rising overall by 10 per cent. Permanent grassland rose by 18 per cent with the greatest increase before 1875.[8]

The grassland along with oats was needed for the increase in stock, particularly cattle, shown in the figures for Great Driffield (Table 6), and Bainton Beacon.[9] Numbers fluctuated not least because of the severe outbreak of rinderpest in 1865–6, when 10 per cent of the East Riding's cattle died, and foot and

1 *Farmers Magazine* 6 (1854), 152; *HP* 27 July 1855; below, this section, metal working.
2 *HP* 17 Dec. 1858.
3 Ibid. 18 Apr. 1851; 4 Nov. 1853; 12 July 1861.
4 Ibid. 8 July 1859.
5 Ibid. 14 June 1861.
6 Ibid. 1 July 1870.
7 E. J. T. Collins, 'Did mid-Victorian agriculture fail?' *Refresh* 21 (1995), 1.
8 M. G. Adams, 'Agricultural change in the ER of Yorks. 1850–80' (Hull Univ. PhD thesis, 1977), 192, 195.
9 Ibid. 199, 207.

mouth disease that occurred locally in 1869 and 1875.[1] Nevertheless the stock of beef and other cattle rose by 84 per cent in Bainton Beacon between 1869 and 1880.[2] The rise in sheep numbers at Driffield was less marked, but there had almost certainly been a drop in the later 1870s. In Bainton Beacon sheep numbers rose by 66 per cent between 1866 and 1875 but then dropped by 4 per cent by 1880.[3] Leicester sheep were the favoured breed in the Driffield area, and it was claimed that there was 'no part of the world in which they arrive at greater perfection, or where the breeding of them is better understood'.[4] The area was also renowned by the 1850s for the 'very superior quality' of the cattle and the 'excellent breed of carriage horses'.[5]

The Driffield show, especially famed for its horses, was the great showcase for local stock, and it thrived in the 1860s–70s, with attendances of over 6,000.[6] It was not held in 1875, because that year Driffield hosted the Yorkshire show, a recognition of the area's prominence in the agriculture of the county.[7] Two years later the golden age had ended.

Agricultural Depression 1877–1914

Local farmers meeting at Driffield in 1892 agreed that the agricultural depression had begun in 1877 and was still going on.[8] Although 1876 had been a 'lean year' on the Wolds it was the very wet harvest of 1877 that began the real decline.[9] Almost continuous rain fell for a fortnight soon after harvest had begun on a Driffield farm, the standing wheat began to sprout and that which had been cut lay 'in a deplorable condition'.[10] Local farmers had 'rather a trying time' and Robert Hornby of Driffield Wold, 'who everyone thought well to do', failed in February 1878.[11] That spring began a period of two and a half years of exceptional wet and cold. The lean years of 1876–8 were followed by the 'disaster' of 1879.[12] Farmers laid off workers and it was reported at Driffield that 'never within the memory of the 'oldest inhabitant' of the district has such an amount of distress been so markedly prevalent as just now ... Worn-out men and women, with as many as half a dozen haggard-looking children, are common sights.'[13] Five years of exhaustion and partial recovery followed in 1880–4, then conditions deteriorated again and autumn 1885 was 'about the worst season ever known' on the Wolds.[14] In

	Wheat *s. per qtr*	*Oats* *s. per qtr*	*Barley* *s. per qtr*
1881	50	19	36
1886	32	16	30
1891	34	17	32
1896	25	15	26
1901	26	17	28
1906	27	16	27
1911	33	19	31

Source: S. B. A. Parrott, 'Agricultural conditions in the ER of Yorks. in the late 19th and 20th centuries' (Leeds Univ. MPhil thesis, 2002), 179.

Table 7. *Driffield Corn Market: Autumn Corn Prices 1881–1911*

the 1880s as a consequence of the distress large numbers, chiefly labourers and craftsmen and their families, left the Driffield area for Canada and Australia.[15] There was another very bad harvest in 1892, a year that was described in a report from Driffield Primitive Methodist circuit as being one of 'general and unprecedented agricultural depression'.[16] More disastrous for the farmers than the weather was the prolonged fall in the prices of cereals and wool due to the great increase in imports.[17] At the weekly corn market at Driffield the price of wheat fell sharply in the early 1880s and remained low for some thirty years, whilst the fall in the price of oats and barley was less drastic.

Wool prices fell locally from 35*s*. a stone in 1864 to 14*s*. in 1879 and 12*s*. in 1894, giving the leading local farmer, Francis Jordan of Eastburn, a drop in income from wool sales from £1,925 for 1,500 fleeces in 1864, to only £508 for 1, 260 fleeces in 1894.[18]

Not only were farmers hit by low prices but also by periodic outbreaks of disease amongst their animals. There was an extensive outbreak of foot and mouth throughout the area in 1881 that was traced to Canadian cattle sold at Driffield cattle market by a dealer from the west of England. At the same time swine fever occurred in farms at Great and Little Driffield and at

1 *DT* 27 Oct. 1988, 9 July 2003.
2 Adams, 'Agricultural change', 199.
3 Ibid. 207.
4 Sheahan and Whellan, *Hist. York & ER.* ii. 497.
5 Ibid.
6 *HP* 3 Aug. 1860; 25 July 1879.
7 Ibid. 9 July 1875.
8 *DT* 12 Nov. 1892.
9 *Royal Commission on Agricultural Depression*: Assistant Commissioner R. Hunter Pringle's Report (Parl. Papers 1895 [C 7735], xvi), pp. 8–10; *Hull News* 19 July 1879.
10 *HP* 31 Aug. 1877.
11 HUL, DDSY/101/94, Letters to Sir Tatton Sykes 15 Feb., 6 Mar. 1878.
12 *Royal Commission on Agricultural Depression*, Pringle's Report, p. 9.
13 *HP* 19 Sept. 1879.
14 *Royal Commission on Agricultural Depression*, Pringle's Report, p. 9; HUL, DDSY/101/96. For the impact of the depression on the Wolds to the west of Driffield see *VCH Yorks. ER.* viii. 35–7.
15 *DT* 31 Mar. 1883; ERAO, MRD 2/4/3.
16 *DT* 12 Nov. 1892; ERAO, MRD/2/4/4.
17 *Royal Commission on Agricultural Depression*: Pringle's Report, pp. 8–10.
18 Ibid. p. 10.

18. *Great Driffield: Farmworkers at Great Kendale Farm, 1916. There were nine or ten hired men living-in on the farm, and five labourers paid by the week.*

Sunderlandwick.[1] Four years later 50 cattle were suspected of being affected by foot and mouth on James Hopper's large farm at Kelleythorpe and the movement of cattle in the area was halted.[2] Anthrax was a problem in the 1890s with cases at Nicholson's fellmongers at Little Driffield and two farms at Elmswell.[3]

Faced by such ongoing problems James Hopper and others founded a new Driffield Farmers Club in 1885 to provide lectures and a forum for discussion on agricultural issues.[4] The club functioned until about 1900.[5]

In the particular case of Driffield and its district, the depression of the late 19th century may have had less impact on the balance between arable and livestock farming than it did elsewhere in the riding. In 1905 the area of arable land in the ecclesiastical parish was still much greater than that of grassland, 5,441 a. as against 1,714 a. respectively,[6] and that imbalance was even greater on the higher, Wolds farms: in 1907 Wold House had 516 a. of arable land and only 54 a. of grassland; Great Kendale 475 a. and 46 a. respectively, and the 378-a. Eastfield Farm was practically wholly under crops.[7]

Agricultural returns for Driffield from 1881 to 1911 (Table 6) show no great fluctuations, but indicate a limited continuation in the move from cereals to livestock that was already evident in 1881. The acreage of wheat, after a further drop, stabilised as did that of barley after a modest rise. Somewhat surprisingly the acreage of oats and turnips (both fed to animals) and permanent grassland declined, although some recovery was made by 1911, particularly in the extent of grassland. The move to livestock was most evident in 1911, with high numbers of cattle, sheep and pigs. A fall in cereal prices helped the livestock farmer by reducing the cost of purchased feedstuffs.[8]

Those with smaller farms on the lower Wolds or the now better drained areas of the Hull Valley fared best during the depression because their land was more suitable for livestock farming.[9] The tenants of the large Wolds farms survived only because they could draw on the capital that had been accumulated during more prosperous times, and on the support of their landlords, who gave rent rebates and allowances for cattle cake and fertilizer in order to retain good

1 *YH* 30 Sept. 1881.

2 *HP* 1 May 1885.

3 *DT* 23 Sept., 2 Dec. 1893; 15 May 1896. Cattle disease and the steps being taken to protect native stock from imported beasts were prominent issues in the local parliamentary election of 1890: HUL, DDSY/104/157.

4 Ross, *Driffield*, 32, 89. Harrison, *Driffield*, 358 has 1884, apparently in error.

5 *Kelly's Dir. N & ER Yorks.* (1901), 466.

6 Acreage Returns, 1905.

7 RDB, 91/189/176; 91/206/191 (1906); 97/511/461 (1907).

8 Perren, *Agricultural in Depression*, 12.

9 S. B. A. Parrott, 'Agricultural conditions in the ER of Yorks. in the late 19th and 20th centuries' (Leeds Univ. MPhil thesis, 2002), 57, 64.

tenants.[1] A gathering of leading local farmers, including James Hopper of Kelleythorpe, informed H. Rider Haggard that the only farmers who had done well 'were those who had some speciality, such as breeding of hackneys'.[2] Hackneys, or roadsters as they were originally called, were prominent at the Driffield show from the early 1870s.[3] S. R. Tennant of Great Kendale was a leading hackney breeder, winning prizes all over the country including the Hackney Horse Society's gold medal for the best mare or gelding in 1907.[4] Specialist breeders of cattle and sheep also fared well, particularly when selling their stock abroad. This included the many local farmers breeding Leicester sheep, described by a visitor to the Wolds in 1910 as 'the aristocrats among British sheep ... still showing a quality in their looks and action which has been rivalled by no other breed'.[5] The Improved Leicester Sheep Breeders' Association has had its office at Driffield since its foundation *c.* 1892. Its first flock book, printed in the town by Benjamin Fawcett, was issued in 1893 listing around 100 members from all over the country but with a concentration on the Yorkshire Wolds.[6]

Revival 1914–21

The First World War brought about a temporary revival in agriculture. The prices achieved by farmers on the Wolds for their cereals increased sharply between 1914 and the peak year of 1917. Wheat rose from 28*s*. to 80*s*. per quarter, barley from 31*s*. to 74*s*. and oats 20*s*. to 50*s*.[7] The impact on farming at Driffield is borne out by comparison of the figures for stock and crops for 1911 and 1921 (Table 6). There was a noticeable fall in livestock numbers, particularly of sheep which decreased from 976 per 1000 a. to 679, and a fall in the area of permanent grassland. The crops used for animal feed, oats and turnips declined whilst wheat and, particularly, barley increased in area.

It was the government's guarantee of minimum cereal prices in 1917 that encouraged the expansion of cereal growing at the expense of livestock and permanent pasture.[8] This was evident on the 592-a. Danesdale Farm on the Wolds, where the area of grassland fell from 87 a. in 1915–17, to 45 a. in 1918–19, and the extent of cereals rose from 224 a. in 1915 to 363 a. in 1918. Barley, which unusually had not been grown at all on the farm in 1913–14, covered 94 a. in 1918 and 105 a. in 1919. Wheat increased from 77 a. in 1915 to 149 a. in 1919, but oats decreased from a highpoint of 146 a. in 1914 to 86 a. in 1919. There was also a significant fall in turnips from 143 a. in 1915 to 64 a. in 1919, and clover or seeds from 123 a. in 1914 to 83 a. in 1919.[9]

Depression, 1920s and 1930s

The post-war boom came to an end in 1921 when prices for agricultural produce fell markedly for two years.[10] By December 1921 the price of barley at Driffield was at its lowest since pre-war.[11] Farmers moved to cut costs by laying off labourers and requiring others to work over 55½ hours a week instead of 50 hours for 2*s*. less. Early in 1922 farm workers in the Driffield district went on strike holding large gatherings in the town and the vicar reported that there was much unemployment.[12]

The drop in cereal prices by the early 1930s to figures lower than in 1914 was most disastrous, and periodic outbreaks of foot and mouth in 1922, 1923 and 1926 hit local farmers.[13] Many cattle, sheep and pigs were slaughtered and Driffield cattle market was regularly closed. In 1926 arrangements were made for dealing with between 100,000 and 200,000 sheep at an improvised abattoir at the disused Albion corn mill at Driffield.[14] One of the Driffield farms affected was Blakedale, where the 88 cattle in buildings were healthy, but three-quarters of the 629 sheep and lambs in the fields were infected, including 134 pedigree Oxford Down sheep.[15] Cattle and pigs at Great Kendale were clear but not the 500 sheep.[16] Edward and Albert Dixon who farmed at Danesdale were fined for not reporting the existence of the disease in their flock of 400 sheep.[17]

In 1932, after more than half a dozen years of things 'getting worse', the adverse impact of the 'prevailing agricultural depression' on congregrations was commented on by the superintendent of Driffield Primitive Methodist circuit.[18] The same year, and for the next four years it was decided not to hold the Driffield Agricultural Show because of the state of farming.[19] In 1934 a local newspaper reported that 'Owners of large estates have been called on to make great sacrifices ... Tenants have lost fortunes ... and hundreds of those who survive are down to the limit of their resources.'[20]

1 *VCH Yorks. ER*. viii. 37; H. Rider Haggard, *Rural England*, ii. (1906 edn), 365; Parrott, 'Agricultural conditions', 99–103; HUL, DDSY/101/95, 98.
2 Rider Haggard, *Rural England*, ii. 365.
3 E. H. Milner, *Centenary Brochure of the History of the Driffield Agricultural Soc.* (1973), 12.
4 *The Times* 29 June 1907; HRO, DBHT/9/899.
5 *The Times* 17 Oct. 1910.
6 ERAO, DDX 909/1, 18, 36, 56.
7 S. Harrison, A *Time to Reap* (2000), 56.
8 Perren, *Agriculture in Depression*, 33–4.
9 ERAO, DDTH/9.
10 Perren, *Agriculture in Depression*, 41.
11 *The Times* 21 Dec. 1921.
12 ERAO, DDX 831/1/1; BIA, V. 1912–22/Ret.
13 Harrison, *Time to Reap*, 57–8; *The Times* 3 Feb. 1922; 15 Dec. 1923; 30 Mar., 20, 26 Apr. 1926.
14 *The Times* 30 Mar.; 22 Apr. 1926; *HT* 3 Apr. 1926.
15 *The Times* 1 Apr. 1926.
16 Ibid. 31 Mar. 1926; *Lond. Gaz.* 9 Apr. 1926, 2491.
17 *The Times* 30 Apr. 1926.
18 J. A. S. Watson, *Rural Britain To-day and To-Morrow* (1934), 73; ERAO, MRD/2/4/14.
19 Milner, *Driffield Agric. Soc.* 24–5.
20 *Malton Messenger* 10 Feb. 1934, quoted in Harris, 'Hard times', 14.

Wolds farmers were said to be in a 'parlous condition' in 1937 having 'experienced some degree of depression since 1924, after which date barley prices dropped to a lower level and wage rates rose to a higher'.[1] They also suffered from the decline in demand for heavy sheep, such as Leicester Longwools, the labour intensiveness of turnips and their lack of capital.[2] Farmers were more vulnerable than they had been in the later 19th century as most were owner occupiers by the 1920s, some with mortgages, and they could no longer rely on relief from their landlord through rent rebates or allowances. The great estates had been broken up. Lord Downe had sold three farms – Wold House, Great Kendale and Middlefield – in 1907 and Field House Farm in 1918. The first and last were sold to the tenants, as were Kelleythorpe by Lord Londesborough in 1911 and Danesdale and Buckton Parva farms by W. H. Harrison-Broadley in 1920. The whole Elmswell estate, comprising three farms, was sold by Lord Londesborough in 1911 to one of the tenants, Robert Holtby.[3]

In the 1920s the significant changes in crops and stock at Driffield were a drop in the acreage of barley, a slight rise in permanent grassland and an increase in the numbers of sheep, cattle, pigs and poultry (Table 6). The expansion of sheep farming was surprising at a time when the demand for the heavy sheep bred on the Wolds was in decline, but increases in the other livestock were to be expected.[4] By the 1930s the most important sources of farm income nationally were milk, cattle, pigs, poultry and eggs, in that order.[5] Most local farms were keeping some dairy cattle by the early 1940s but of the larger farms it was only Middlefield (Field House) Farm that specialised in dairying with a herd of 30 dairy cows.[6] There were ventures such as Springfield Dairy, River Head, and at various times the small dairy farms along Wansford Road, at Chestnut Cottage, California and Oakhurst Cottage.[7] The increase in milk production locally, encouraged by the Milk Marketing Board set up in 1933, was no doubt the reason why Glaxo opened a milk processing plant in Driffield in 1937.[8]

There was little opportunity for the Wolds farmer to change from the traditional sheep and barley farming but on the lower lands around and to the south and east of the town there was some diversification.[9] It was here by the early 1940s that small acreages of sugar beet, rape, mustard, beans and potatoes were being grown.[10] Sugar beet, evidently introduced into the parish in the 1920s, covered some 63 a. in 1941.[11] A proposal to establish a sugar beet factory at Driffield in 1927 was not implemented.[12] There was seemingly little attempt at vegetable growing, one of the few lucrative aspects of inter-war farming. The acreage of potatoes grown in the parish declined from 17.5 in 1901, to 7.5 in 1921 to only 4.75 in 1941. Only two market gardeners or fruit growers were recorded in the 1920s–30s, one had a fruit farm to the west of St John's Road where a jam factory was opened in 1928.[13]

Second World War

Farming prospered during the war years but in the early stages many local farmers were in the position of the tenant of Little Kendale Farm whose finances had 'deteriorated considerably' during the previous twenty years. When the farm was inspected for the National Farm Survey in 1941 it was given a B grade, and noted that it could be made much more productive by greater expenditure on manure and labour. The farmer was said to lack 'ambition and foresight'.[14] Most of the Driffield farms were graded A, but B grades were given to Great Kendale, Buckton Parva, Whin Hill and Poundsworth because of the rough state of their cultivation.[15]

In 1941 the three largest farms in the parish, Great Kendale, 610 a., Danesdale, 519 a., and Wold House, 591 a., with land on the Wolds were almost 90 per cent arable. Over 25 per cent of their acreage, 41 per cent in the case of Wold House, was devoted to barley, with from 12 to 18 per cent wheat, 5 to 12 per cent oats, 17 to 19 per cent turnips and 12 to 19 per cent clover. Wold House on the highest ground was emphatically a traditional sheep and barley farm. There was a large flock of 586 sheep, but only 6 cattle and some 90 poultry. The other two farms averaged around 350 sheep, 50 cattle, 30 pigs and 140 poultry and were more typical of Wolds mixed farms.

The range of stock and crops on the smaller low-lying 142-a.Whin Hill Farm, on Wansford Road, was not that dissimilar but here wheat occupied 24 per cent of the acreage, and barley and oats around 18 per cent. Cattle, of which there were 31, were proportionately more important, and there were 51 sheep.[16]

Table 8, with information from the agricultural returns for 1941 and 1951, illustrates little of the changes to be expected by the emphasis on arable farming

1 TNA, MAF 38/47.
2 Ibid.
3 Above, manors and estates; below, Elmswell and Kelleythorpe.
4 TNA, MAF38/47.
5 Perren, *Agriculture in Depression*, 48.
6 TNA, MAF32/1057/5.
7 Ibid. MAF32/1057/5/19; directories.
8 Perren, *Agriculture in Depression*, 58–9; H.D. Watts, 'The industrial geography of rural E Yorks.' (Hull Univ. MA thesis, 1964), 85, 96.
9 G. I. Ramsdale, '25 years of agricultural change in the ER, 1931–56' (Hull Univ. MA thesis, 1957), 127.
10 TNA, MAF68/3998.
11 Ibid. MAF68/3591, 3998.
12 *HT* 3 Dec. 1927.
13 Directories; Watts, 'Industrial geography', 96.
14 TNA, MAF32/1065/20.
15 Ibid.
16 Ibid.

Year	Crop: % of total area of crops and grass returned								Stock: Number per 1000 acres				
	Wheat	Barley	Oats	Trnps	Other crops	Clover	Perm grass	Total area	Horses	Cattle	Sheep	Pigs	Poultry
1941	13.5	13	12.5	9.5	5	10	36.5	2707 a.	51	258	1053	112	1276
1951	11	12	9	8	13	16	30	2717 a.	22	284	767	134	4,667
1961	12.5	21	7.5	6	4	21	28	2464 a.	-	243	1171	93	15,933
1981	27	39.5	0.5	0	10.5	0	22.5	2099 a.	-	189	875	4,543	132
1988	39	20.5	0	0	20.5	0	20	2081 a.	-	252	405	10,695	1708

Source: TNA, MAF 68/3998, 4368, 4571, 5781, 6139
*figures relate to the post-1935 parish

Table 8. *Great Driffield: Crops and Stock 1941–1988**

during the war. The figures cannot be compared with those in Table 6 because they are for the smaller urban district of Great Driffield created in 1935 when 2,774, almost all wolds land, of the former civil parish and urban district was transferred to Nafferton parish. The greater part of the new urban district comprised land on the lower edge of the Wolds and upper Hull Valley and had a different farming profile than that of larger pre-1935 Great Driffield.

The fall in the acreage of permanent grassland, with ploughing out encouraged by the War Agricultural Committee, was not balanced by an increase in the acreage of cereals. There may have been an increase in wheat growing, as was experienced on the Wolds, but if so it had been reversed by 1951. More land was put down to clover and other crops, the latter included 45 a. of mangolds and 16 a. of kale, both for animal feed, 21 a. of beans, 10 a. of peas, and 30 a. of potatoes. The smaller farms on the lower land were clearly diversifying, and the acreage of orchards and small fruit growing was at an all time high of 21a. The decrease in the number of sheep per 1000 a. by 27 per cent between 1941 and 1951, no doubt reflected the emphasis on arable during the war.

Mechanisation, which had made great advances in local farms during the war, developed rapidly in the years after.[1] As a result the number of horses per 1000 a. on Driffield farms fell from 51 in 1941 to 22 in 1951 and only 8 four years later. Tractors which did the work of 8–10 horses had taken over, and by the early 1950s the larger arable farms had combined harvesters, potato planters and sugar beet lifters.[2]

Later 20th century

In the 1950s the farming at Driffield reverted for a time to the traditional emphasis on sheep and barley (Table 8). The number of sheep rose from 2,083 in 1951 to 2,885 in 1961, and the acreage of barley from 322 to 515. The area of wheat and clover also increased but that of oats, turnips, and permanent grass declined. There was a drop in the number of cattle and pigs but a great increase in poultry.[3] An egg packing station was opened at Little Driffield *c.* 1956 and Twydale's turkey processing factory at Great Driffield in 1958.[4]

The 1970s saw the greatest changes in local farming with the beginning of the dominance of arable farming. There was a great expansion in malting barley, particularly after the introduction of a higher-yielding winter barley in the later 1970s. By 1981 almost 40 per cent of the arable area at Driffield was devoted to barley. Wheat growing, after an initial drop after the war, also increased rapidly and in the 1980s expanded at the expense of barley which was no longer as profitable. Oats, a century earlier the second cereal crop in the parish, were hardly grown by 1981, and not at all in 1988, the last date for which returns are available for individual parishes. Clover and seeds, a major crop in 1961, had gone 20 years later, as had turnips, which had been in decline from before the Second World War.[5] The new crops of the later 20th century were oilseed rape, potatoes and vining peas. Between 1981 and 1988 the acreage of rape grown in Driffield rose from 104 a. to 114 a., potatoes from 82 a. to 158 a., and peas from 27 a. to 129 a.

With nearly all the arable land on the 288-a. Field House Farm, Bridlington Road devoted to wheat and barley in 1979, it was typical of the area. The rotation was broadly two years of wheat, followed by two or three years of barley, then roots, followed by barley undersown to one year ley grazed by sheep. Although specialising in cereals the farmer had a flock of 400 Suffolk Cross ewes and around 200 beef cattle.[6] The

1 Every farm of 100 a. or more at Driffield had at least one tractor, and the larger farms two, in 1941: TNA, MAF32/1065/20.

2 Ramsdale, '25 years of agricultural change', 136.

3 TNA, MAF68/4368, 4571.

4 Watts, 'Industrial geography', 87; Shaw 'Driffield', 83.

5 Ramsdale, '25 years of agricultural change', 84.

6 ERAO, DDFU/4/33 (*ER Farmers Jnl* 31, 1979), pp. 22–32.

extent of the livestock on the farm was unusual as there was a marked fall in the number of cattle and sheep in the parish between 1961 and 1981. By the latter date the emphasis locally was on pig farming, which had all but replaced commercial poultry keeping. Large-scale intensive pig farming was centred on Field House Farm, Scarborough Road, the headquarters of Yorkwold Pigro Ltd founded by James A. R. Dewhirst (d. 2008) who started with 140 sows in 1972. By the early 21st century it had become one of the largest pig businesses in Britain, with units from Lincolnshire to Northumberland, as well as in America and Canada.[1]

The number of sheep continued to decline in the 1980s and by the end of the century had virtually disappeared from local farms. The fattening of cattle remained significant, with an increase in numbers in the 1980s, but stock rearing suffered a major set-back with the severe foot and mouth epidemic in 2001, which led to the closure, for good, of the town's cattle market.[2]

Holdings

In the 19th and earlier 20th century there were, besides smaller holdings, usually about 18–20 farms in the parish,[3] several of them large. In 1851 the areas of 25 agricultural holdings were recorded. The largest were the 550-a. Driffield Wold Farm and Danesdale and Wold House Farms, each with 530 a. The other holdings comprised one of 460 a. two of 300–399 a., three of 100–149 a., four of 50–99 a., seven of 20–49 a., and five of 6–19 a. each.[4] The number of smallholdings was increased in 1911, when the county council bought 114 a., comprising most of East Field Farm, and let it as one holding of 50 a., including the farm buildings, and six others of 4–19 a. each.[5] In 1937 of the 15 farms in the Driffield, eight were of 150 a. or more. In 1955 for Driffield civil parish, *c.* 2,730 a., lay in four larger farms, one of over 500 a., eight farms of 50–149 a., and no less than 41 holdings of less than 50 a. The reorganization of agriculture with help from the European Commission in the later 20th century resulted in a great reduction in the number of agricultural holdings, the largest units growing at the expense of the medium and smaller units. By 1988 the three largest farms in Driffield civil parish included one of more than 300 ha. (*c.* 740 a.), and there were then five others with 20–49 ha. (49–121 a.) each and only seven holdings of less than 19 ha. (47 a.).[6] The East Field Farm holding, slightly reduced by the building of the new by-pass to 40 ha. (*c.* 100 a.), was still held by the successor authority, the East Riding of Yorkshire Council, in the early 21st century, but it had been consolidated and was then let as one holding to the tenant of the farm.[7]

Woodland

After the initial clearance of the land, woodland seems to have been of little importance in the parish. In 1845 woodland with shelter belts on the wold covered some 90 a.[8] The Etheringtons and their successors may have planted much of the woodland in the north-east of the Driffields, and in 1872 their farm called Buckton Parva was described as well wooded.[9] In 1881 Driffield civil parish had about 71 a. of woodland and in 1988 the area returned under the smaller civil parish included 18 ha. (45 a.).[10]

The sewage works, to the south of the town produced revenue from the grass and willows there, the latter apparently being sold by the ton in 1895, and in 1897 being bought by tender by Hull Blind Institution.[11]

TRADE AND INDUSTRY

Medieval to 1600

Driffield's location between the differing agricultural economies of the Wolds and the lower grounds of the Hull Valley and Holderness made it an obvious place to trade. By the late 12th century a market was being held on Driffield manor, and a market and a fair were granted early in the 14th century.[12]

Corn seems always to have been an important commodity, if not the chief one. In the 1320s Alexander de Berewys, who had a ship at Scarborough, may have been a merchant of Driffield,[13] and in 1337 Adam Butler of Driffield with other merchants was engaged in the purchase and shipping from Hull to Middelburg, Zeeland (Netherlands) of corn for the king.[14] Corn trading, perhaps outside the market, was also one of the sources of the Etherington family's wealth in the 16th century, along with their farming, milling, and administrative interests.[15] In 1562 William Etherington left personal property valued at nearly £400, of which

1 *DT* 12 Jan. 2009.
2 TNA, MAF68/5781, 6139; *ERG* 5 Aug. 2004.
3 Directories.
4 TNA, HO 107/2366.
5 RDB, 135/430/380; ER CC *Mins* 1911–12, 218–19, 309–10, 317–18. 'East Field' may be Skeetings.
6 TNA, MAF 68/4516; MAF 68/6139.
7 Humbs. CC *Mins* 1980–1, D 1204; 1984–5, J 327; inf. from ERYC, 2006.
8 ERAO, PE10/T.120.
9 ERAO, DDHB/7/38.
10 TNA, MAF 68/780; MAF 68/6139.
11 ERAO, UDDR/1/1/1, pp. 66, 103, 147.
12 Below, this section, mkts and fairs.
13 *Cal. Pat.* 1327–30, 276.
14 Ibid. 1334–8, 414.
15 Below, soc. hist., soc. leadership.

19. *Great Driffield: King's Mill* c. *1900. The watermill, enlarged and converted to steam in the late 19th century, was closed after a fire in 1906.*

some £70 represented money owing to him, much of it for corn sales.[1]

Milling, utilising the various streams in the parish, is the only known medieval industry. There were eight mills on the extensive manor of Driffield in 1086.[2] The four mills recorded in the later 13th century and in the early 17th century are likely to have been in or on the borders of the parish, perhaps represented later by King's Mill, Bell Mill, Poundsworth Mill and Walk Mill.[3] As well as grinding corn, one or more of the medieval mills may have been used for fulling locally produced cloth as occurred in the parish in the later 16th century.[4]

1600–1770

Driffield's market seems to have been given up or to have become insignificant by the 17th century, although its fairs continued to play their part in the local economy.[5] Kilham and North Frodingham were the local active markets in the late 17th century although Driffield was the more populous settlement.[6] Its occupational profile in the 17th and early 18th century, drawn from stray references in parish registers, deeds, wills and probate inventories, was more akin to that of a small market town than a purely agricultural village. As well as the usual rural trades - millers, blacksmiths, carpenters, shoemakers, tailors, weavers, butchers, innkeepers and a ploughwright – there were grocers, mercers, oatmealmakers, paper makers, tanners, glovers, flaxdressers, clothmakers, bleachers, and a dyer.[7] Most significant are the grocers and mercers recorded periodically from the 1660s onwards, including members of the influential Etherington and Drinkrow families.[8] The move by the grocer Thomas Drinkrow from Kilham to Great Driffield in the 1670s may indicate the beginning of the latter's rise at the expense of the former place.[9] The market at Kilham was described as 'mean' in 1673 and the tolls of the market and two fairs there were let for £10 a year around 1720 whilst the tolls and profits of two fairs at Little Driffield, together with a house, were let for £14.[10]

Although referred to as a 'market town' in the 1730s–40s there is no record of an active market at Driffield at this period, and this status may relate to its range of trades and services, which included an apothecary and twelve licenced alehouses in the 1740s, and its emergence as a sporting centre and a stopping-

1 BIA, precentorship wills, William Eddrinton, 1562 (inventory).

2 *VCH Yorks.* ii. 197.

3 *Yorks. Inq.* i, p. 108; ii, p. 95; *Yorks. Fines* 1614–25, 205; below, this section, milling.

4 Below, this section, textiles.

5 Ibid. mkts and fairs.

6 Above, Gt and L Driffield [intro.], mkt town and its hinterland.

7 ERAO, PE 10/1; DDBD/16/1; RDB, B/153/42; HUL, DDHO/14/1a; Neave, 'Rural settlement contraction', 204; BIA, CPH, 4475; precentorship wills, Robert, Archer 1675; John Leason, 1681, Richard Preston, 1693.

8 RDB, E/28/48; BIA, precentorship wills, John Etherington, 1720.

9 HUL, DDDU/11/64–5; ERAO, RDB E/23/39; E/28/48; BIA, CPH. 4475.

10 D. Woodward, *Descriptions of East Yorkshire: Leland to Defoe* (E Yorks. Local Hist. Ser. 39, 1985), 29; RDB, H/392/807; *VCH Yorks. ER.* ii. 258.

off point for those rushing to take the waters at Scarborough.[1] The open fields were inclosed in 1742 increasing agricultural income and freeing land immediately around the town for development. A further boost came with improved transport links through the building of a bridge over the beck at Sunderlandwick in 1765 and the turnpiking of the road from Beverley to Driffield and Kendale House the following year.[2] Driffield's location on a busy routeway accounts for the presence of three prominent inns there by the 1760; the Red Lion, the Nag's Head and the Blue Bell.[3] They provided accommodation and entertainment for local gentry families and passing visitors and became the focal point for merchants and other traders. Trade in the increasing output of grain from the Wolds had begun there by 1767 when the landlord of the Blue Bell, William Porter, who was also a corn factor, gave evidence in London in support of the bill to make the River Hull navigable up to Driffield.[4] The main financial support for the canal came from the principal landowner and lord of the manor, Boynton Langley, who subscribed £5,300 of the initial £11,870. Eight residents of Driffield subscribed a further £1,100, including £450 from William Paul of Danesdale, £200 from Henry Drinkrow, and £50 from William Porter.[5]

1770–1851

Following the opening of the canal in 1770 Driffield was rapidly transformed into a thriving trading town and inland port. The weekly market was re-established and merchants and professionals flocked to the bourgeoning town. Two of the early solicitors, Thomas Cator and William Conyers, and one of the corn merchants, James Harrison, relocated from Malton (NR), up until then the main centre for the corn trade in eastern Yorkshire.[6]

By 1784 there were numerous specialist merchants at Driffield dealing in goods carried on the canal, including five coal merchants, three of whom also dealt in corn, a brandy, corn and seed merchant, a flour merchant, a butter and bacon factor, two dealers in hams, a timber merchant and a woolstapler. Local farmers also found a market for their produce with a maltster, three brewers, two tanners, a currier and two furriers.[7] Amongst the retailers were six grocers (three of whom were also haberdashers and two were mercers), two hardwaremen, a tallow chandler, two sadlers and cap makers, a leather breeches maker and a watchmaker. Professionals were represented by two attorneys and three apothecaries and surgeons, one also a man-midwife.[8]

Urbanisation continued apace and by 1792 the town could also boast six tailors and drapers, five shoemakers, four wine and spirit merchants, two peruke makers, a gunsmith, a milliner, a staymaker and a bookseller; the last was also a druggist and Driffield's first postmaster and printer. There were now three attorneys, four surgeons, two watchmakers and eight grocers.[9] In 1792 Richard Porter, a coal, corn and spirit merchant, in partnership with his brother William, a grocer and mercer, and two Leeds clothiers, built a large worsted yarn factory at Bell Mills, on the southern border of the township. This first attempt a industrialisation failed and in just over ten years the Porters were bankrupt.[10]

Bankruptcy was one of hazards facing traders at Driffield during this period of rapid expansion, when the population of the town rose by 75 per cent between 1801 and 1821.[11] During the first decade four corn factors, two grocers, a vintner, a flaxdresser, a carrier and a tin-plate worker went bankrupt.[12] During the next decade 1810–19, seven bankruptcies involved two druggists, one also a bookseller and stationer, a tanner, a currier, a grocer and draper, a miller, and a cabinet maker, and there were six more in 1820–23, including another cabinet maker, a silversmith, a plumber, a coal merchant, a grocer and a money scrivener.[13]

Despite these setbacks the town was evidently flourishing in the early 1820s (Table 9). During the previous thirty years there had been an increase in the number and range of professionals with the addition of auctioneers, bankers and numerous school teachers, and an expansion in retailing, most significantly in the clothing trades. There was a rise in the number of corn millers, maltsters and brewers, processing some of corn growing in abundance in the newly inclosed fields of the Wolds. The rest was sent to the West Riding, from where the returning sloops and keels brought coal, and also carried imported timber from Hull. The economy was still dominated by the activities of the twenty or so wholesale merchants, dealing in coal, corn, flour, and timber. The distribution of coal from

1 *Journey from London to Scarborough* (1734), 27; ERAO, QSF/147/D/4; below, soc. hist., soc. life.

2 Howorth, *Driffield*, 42; MacMahon, *Roads and Turnpike Trusts*, 30.

3 Below, soc. hist, inns and public houses.

4 *Journals of the House of Commons*, xxxi, 185–6.

5 HRO, DFP/748–9.

6 *DT* 23 Apr. 1892; *Browne's General Law List* (1782); below, this section, corn trade.

7 *Bailey's Brit. Dir.* (1784), iii. 526–7. The furriers, Bethel Boyes and Francis Brown, had their own rabbit warrens at Eastburn and Kelleythorpe: A. Harris, 'The rabbit warrens of E Yorks. in the 18th and 19th centuries', *YAJ* 42 (1967–70), 432–3, 436, 442; below, Kelleythorpe.

8 *Bailey's Brit. Dir.* (1784) iii, 526–7.

9 *Universal Brit. Dir.* (*c.* 1792), ii. 827–8.

10 Below, this section, textiles.

11 Above, vol. intro., population.

12 *HP* 28 Jan. 1800; 18, 25 Oct., 13 Dec. 1803; 13 Mar., 14 Aug., 11 Sept. 1804; 10, 17 Mar. 1807; 24 Oct. 1809.

13 *HP* 24 Oct. 1809; 12 May 1812; 28 Feb. 1815; 12 May, 29 Sept. 1818; 9 Nov. 1819; *The Examiner*, June 1817; Mar. 1820; Mar., Apr., June 1821; *Newcastle Magazine* May 1823; Howorth, *Driffield*, 54.

Trade/Profession	*1792*	*1823*	*1851*	*Trade/Profession*	*1792*	*1823*	*1851*
Timber merchant	0	3	2	Linen manufacturer	0	2	2
Coal & corn mercht	5	4	9	Flax spinner	0	1	0
Bone crusher	0	0	3	Paper maker	1	1	0
Chem. manure manuf	0	0	1	Lime burner	0	0	3
Corn miller	3	5	7	Brickmaker	0	2	3
Flour dealer	0	12	0	Bricklayer/builder	2	4	5
Wine & spirit mercht	4	5	9	Joiner/carpenter/builder	3	7	14
Grocer & draper	8	10	22	Painter, plumber & glazier	2	6	7
Shopkeeper	0	2	33	Stone & marble mason	0	3	2
Butcher	3	10	11	Cabinet maker	0	6	7
Baker/confectioner	2	5	10	Wood turner	0	0	3
Maltster	1	5	7	Wheelwright	0	0	6
Brewer	1	3	6	Iron and brass founder	0	0	3
Cooper	1	2	3	Machinemkr/millwright	0	5	6
Innkeeper/victualler	9	18	25	Ironmonger/hardwareman	3	3	6
Fellmonger/tanner	2	2	2	Glass & pot dealer	2	2	4
Currier	0	1	2	Smith	3	8	7
Hosier & glover	0	1	0	Farrier	1	0	0
Saddler	2	4	6	Tinner & brazier	1	2	3
Shoemaker	5	16	20	Gunsmith	1	0	2
Breeches maker	1	0	0	Clock & watchmaker	2	3	6
Tallow chandler	2	2	2	Bookseller	1	3	3
Tailor/draper	6	12	22	Printer	0	2	4
Staymaker	1	2	4	Druggist	1	2	6
Milliner	1	7	24	Surgeon & apothecary	4	5	6
Hatter	0	3	4	Veterinary surgeon	0	0	2
Straw hat maker	0	5	8	Attorney	3	5	6
Basket maker	0	1	2	Auctioneer	0	3	2
Peruke maker	2	0	0	Banker	0	2	4
Hairdresser	0	1	6	Clergy	4	7	7
Ropemaker	1	2	1	Schoolmaster/school	1	7	10

Sources: *Universal Brit. Dir.* (*c.* 1792), ii, 827–8; Baines, *Hist. Yorks.* (1823), ii, 195–8; White, *Dir. Hull & York* (1851); 600–607.

Table 9. *Great and Little Driffield: Trades and Professions 1792, 1823 and 1851*

Driffield by cart over a wide area led, by the late 1820s, to the virtual end in seaborne coal imported into Bridlington from the Tyne.[1]

Industrial developments were closely linked to the needs of the farming community from the 1820s, commencing at Bell Mills where bone crushing took the place of paper making and flax spinning. By 1846 there were three bone crushing mills in Driffield and the following year F. C. Matthews began the manufacture of artificial manure there.[2] The increase in mills in the town and neighbourhood provided work in 1823 for the five millwrights and machine makers; the latter included Mark Foley, who supplied the more progressive farmers with portable threshing machines and turnip and corn drills.[3] Another development was the establishment of two brickworks on the east side of the town, and the growth of building firms such as that of William Clark who had 20 employees in 1851.[4]

There was plenty of work for builders for, as John Browne noted in 1848, during the previous 15 years there had been erected in the town 180 cottages, 47 houses, 27 houses with shops, three public houses, a

1 D. Neave, *Port, Resort and Market Town: A history of Bridlington* (2000), 104, 158; *Report of the Select Committee from the House of Lords on the State of the Coal Trade* (Parl. Papers 1830 (9), viii) p. 96.

2 Below this section, bone crushing and manure manufacture.

3 Baines, *Hist. Yorks.* (1823), ii, 197.

4 TNA, HO 107/2366.

20. *Great Driffield: Market Place, print of 1860. Pickering, ironmonger, Blakeston, printer and bookseller, and Cross Keys inn on left, Creaser, druggist and Bell Hotel on right, and Elgey, grocer in centre.*

brewery, an iron foundry, a bone mill, two steam flour mills, a gas works, the Corn Exchange, the Union workhouse and the police station and lock-up.[1] There was also the railway station on the Hull to Bridlington line opened in 1846. The building of the railway brought plenty of work to Driffield with 'cartmen, bricklayers, joiners, masons, excavators and bricklayers' labourers ... in full employ' and 'the brickyards, lime-kilns and sand-pits ... all in active operation'.[2] Soon after the opening of this line consent was given for the Malton to Driffield railway on which work began in July 1847.[3]

The coming of the railway further enhanced Driffield's role as the focal point for the people of the Wolds and north Holderness. This position had been acknowledged when Driffield was chosen as the location for the workhouse for the poor law union encompassing some 44 townships, covering most of the town's catchment area.[4] In 1823 the 24 carriers coming to Driffield on market day served 21 places; by 1851 this had risen to over 80 carriers serving 46 places.[5] From 1847, in addition to attending the general and corn markets on a Thursday, farmers gathered on alternate Wednesdays for the cattle market. Shops and service providers benefited by these developments, particularly the clothing trades, the dozen tailors' concerns and the same number of hat makers' shops recorded in 1823 rising to 20 and over 30 respectively by 1851. [6] In that year almost 200 tailors and drapers, hatters, and dressmakers lived in the town, and about 70 shoemakers. Provisioning and building each employed about 120 people. Growth was accompanied, moreover, by a widening in the range of goods offered beyond the necessities of life, and at least some of the outlets became specialist shops. 'General' shops remained, however, like the seven combining drapery and grocery in 1851. The increasing sophistication of the shops is evident in the case of watchmakers, with 3 in 1823 and 6 in 1851, some also described as jewellers and employing in all 13 workers. There had been a move to large working units and a greater proportion of tradesmen and craftsmen employed labour at Driffield in 1851 than in other local market towns. Altogether 64 persons employed labour with 25 employing three or more men.[7]

1851–1918

Driffield probably had its period of greatest prosperity during the so-called golden age of agriculture in the third quarter of the 19th century, when industries providing the raw materials for high farming were introduced or expanded. Bone crushing was further developed with four concerns in the town by the early 1860s and at least three artificial manure manufacturers, the largest of the latter, Matthews, was also crushing oil seed and producing cattle cake. James Harrison, corn merchant and miller, had begun the manufacture of oil-cake at Driffield by 1860, but the following year concerns over purity led local farmers and others to establish the Driffield & East Riding Pure Linseed Cake Co. Ltd, soon to become the town's major employer.[8]

1 ERAO, DDX/17/15.

2 Howorth, *Driffield*, 71; *HP* 9 Jan. 1846.

3 Burton, *Malton & Driffield Junction Railway*, 10; *HP* 3 Sept. 1847.

4 White, *Dir. Hull & York* (1851), 598.

5 Baines, *Hist. Yorks.* (1823), ii. 198; White, *Dir. Hull & York* (1851), 606–7; Fig. 15.

6 This summary is based on directories and the 1851 census enumerators' returns: TNA, HO 107/2366.

7 Noble, 'Growth and development', 299.

8 *HP* 24 Jan. 1862; below, this section, seed crushing and animal feed.

Trade/industry/crafts	*1851*	*1871*	*1901*
Cabinet maker/wood turner/carver	11	12	117
Carpenter/joiner	55	72	77
Sawyer	10	15	13
Coach/carriage builder/painter	3	20	9
Oil & cake miller/labourer	0	35	57
Manure manufacturer	1	11	0
Grocer/tea dealer	54	64	73
Bricklaying/building/plasterer	29	40	72
Painter/plumber/glazier	16	19	35
Stonemason	10	13	12
Brewer/maltster	21	14	7
Cooper	7	5	2
Tailor	35	54	49
Dressmaker/milliner/straw bonnet maker	126	126	130
Shoemaker	65	59	40
Saddler	12	11	16
Corn/flour miller	21	34	16
Brickmaker	16	16	14
Blacksmith	26	39	28
Iron founder/iron moulder/engineer/millwright/ machine maker/smith	27	58	39
Brazier/tinner/whitesmith	13	8	12
Ironmonger	6	7	16
Printer/engraver/colourer/binder	30	46	22
Ropemaker	2	1	7
Draper	31	48	40
Shopkeeper/shop assistant/apprentice	0	12	32
Waterman/mariner	14	9	27* (*10 on board)
Railway worker	13	35	74
Fellmonger	5	5	8
Tanner	0	12	8
Currier	3	4	1
Victualler/publican/beerhousekeeper	23	22	19
Baker/confectioner	12	9	25
Butcher	23	26	36
Druggist/chemist/medicine dealer	17	18	14
Watchmaker/jeweller	13	9	11

Sources: Census Returns TNA, HO 107/2366; ibid. RG10/4806–7; ibid. RG13/4518–9.

Table 10. *Great and Little Driffield: Trades and Industries, 1851, 1871 and 1901*

An increase in the use of agricultural machinery partly explains the rise in numbers of foundry workers engineers and machine makers (Table 10). The number of foundries increased from two in 1849 to five in 1857.[1] The largest concern in 1871 was that of Thomas Pickering with 40 employees; he was also an ironmonger and supplied a wide range of cast-iron goods.[2] Allied to the machinery manufacturers were the coach builders of which there were three firms in 1871 making phaetons, light four-wheeled open carriages, and

1 *Slater's Royal Nat. Com. Dir. of Yorks. & Lincs.* (1849), 83; *Post Office Dir. N & ER Yorks.* (1857), 1239–40.

2 These included pumps and gateposts of which a number survived in the area in the early 21st century. e.g. at Marramatte Farm and Top Row, Bridlington Road, Sledmere.

gigs for the wealthier tradesmen, professionals and gentlemen farmers, and also 'whitechapels' used by shopkeepers for local deliveries.[1]

Retail trades, which were generally on the increase, saw a particular rise in the number working as tailors or in drapers' shops from 66 in 1851 to 102 in 1871. The larger shops were combined grocers and drapers such as Henry Angas with ten employees in 1861 and John Robinson who ran the East Riding House of Commerce in Market Place with eight men, eight women and six boys in 1861.[2] The Driffield Working Men's Co-operative Industrial and Provident Society founded in 1868 had a store, first in Doctor (Doctor's) Lane then in Middle Street South which did not rival these larger concerns until later in the century.[3] Of tailors and outfitters the largest business in 1881 was that of William Dewson who employed 16 men and 4 women.[4] The main change in retail in the last three decades of the century was the increase in numbers working in food shops, especially butchers, bakers and confectioners, and grocers (Table 10). This probably reflects the decline in food prices, the modest increase in wages for the working class and the greater use of town shops by local villagers.[5]

Driffield was particularly noted for its wholesale provision trade and it was claimed in 1875 that the business of the wholesale grocers had increased thirty-fold.[6] They supplied village shopkeepers with large quantities of bacon, butter, cheese, lard, tea, coffee and other groceries for '50 or 60 miles round'.[7] The leading wholesale grocers and provision dealers were Lance & Co., established in 1856 by Robert Excell Lance (d. 1870).[8] In 1865–6 the firm built extensive premises in Middle Street North. The distribution of wholesale goods was facilitated by improved railway services. After long delays the line to Malton was opened in 1853 and that to Market Weighton in 1890. There was a marked rise in railway workers at Driffield from 13 in 1851 to 35 in 1871 and 74 in 1901, and the transportation of linseed by canal for the oil mill increased the number of watermen.

Somewhat surprisingly two of the major industries in the later 19th century, printing and cabinet making, were not linked to agriculture or to the particular needs of the locality. Benjamin Fawcett's printing firm, begun in the 1830s, saw great developments from the 1850s because of the quality of his coloured wood engravings. In 1881 he was employing 18 men, 15 girls and 9 boys; the girls coloured-in the engravings. The firm of George Shepherdson & Son, cabinet makers, ecclesiastical woodworkers and house furnishers, also began earlier in the century but it was only after J. F. Shepherdson took on the business in 1872 that it expanded to employ 12 men in 1881, 60 in 1892 and at least 100 in 1901. The firm were also building contractors and benefited by the continuing prosperity locally of the building industry in the late 19th century. The number of builders, bricklayers, plasterers, plumbers, glaziers, painters, carpenters and joiners rose from 100 in 1851, to 131 in 1871 and 184 in 1901. One of the larger building firms employing 14 in 1881 was that of William Leason, the second generation of a family of builders that still existed in Driffield in 2010.[9] As well as numerous commercial and public buildings, many houses were erected in the later 19th century, particularly for the

21. *Great Driffield: Former Lance & Co., wholesale grocers, Market Place, 2006. Designed by William Hawe and built 1865–6.*

1 P. Howorth, A *Year Gone By: A Yorks. Town 1871* (1991), 37.

2 TNA, RG9/3607. Robinson's claimed to be over 160 years old in 1949: *Driffield Official Guide* (1949), 1.

3 J. E. Smith, *The Shop for the People: Two centuries of Co-operative Enterprise in Hull and E Yorks.* (1998), 143. The Driffield Co-operative Society was wound up in 1972.

4 TNA, RG11/4793.

5 B. S. Rowntree and M. Kendall, *How the Labourer Lives* (1913). 185, 193–4.

6 *HP* 16 July 1875.

7 ERAO, DDX/128/27; *HP* 16 July 1875.

8 *The Century's Progress* (1893), 221; D. Petch, *Driffield Cemetery MIs* (2002), 35.

9 TNA, RG11/4794; *DT* 4 Nov. 2008.

22. Great Driffield: River Head, 2011. Late 19th-century hand-operated crane and Riverhead Mill, built 1842.

upper working and middle classes.[1] The number of houses in the town rose from 873 in 1851 to 1,505 in 1901, a 72 per cent increase at a time when the population rose by 45 per cent.[2]

Under 5 per cent of the houses in Driffield were standing empty in 1881 but this had risen to over 13 per cent by 1891, remaining high at just over 11 per cent in 1901.[3] This was evidence that the agricultural depression that began in the late 1870s was having an impact on the market town. The older industries processing agricultural produce and servicing the farming community were particularly affected. In the 1890s the two largest and oldest corn merchant firms, Harrisons and Dawsons, closed and corn milling declined, hit by the increasing reliance on imported wheat from 1870 onwards. This concentrated activity in the ports; locally that meant Hull. The milling capacity in the Driffield area decreased from 50 sacks an hour in 1870 to only 10 sacks an hour in 1902.[4] Poundsworth Mill closed in the 1890s, the steam mill at River Head in 1901, and King's Mill following a major fire in 1906. The last two had been updated with roller mills, to produce the increasingly popular white flour, but this was not enough to make them viable with transport costs.[5] This left only Bell Mills which was enlarged by a new owner who in 1880s–90s fitted it with roller mills, electric lighting, steam power and water turbine. Bone crushing came to an end in the 1890s and artificial manure manufacture *c.* 1912, but oil-seed crushing and the manufacture of cattle cake continued. Landowners helped their tenant farmers with allowances of cattle cake instead of reducing rents. Brewing, which had been in decline since the 1860s, was said to have 'entirely disappeared' by 1900.[6] Malting however continued on Skerne Road and at a new malt kiln built on Eastgate North. All three tanneries, one at Great Driffield and two at Little Driffield, were evidently no longer working as such by 1901, the owners being listed as fellmongers.

The two major industries unconnected with agriculture also came to an end. Fawcett's printing works was insolvent on the founder's death in 1893 and closed soon afterwards.[7] A fire in 1905 that destroyed Shepherdson's works on Middle Street North was the beginning of the end of this important woodworking firm. Around 1912 Herbert Shepherdson relocated the reduced business to Stockport, Cheshire. That left the Driffield Pure Linseed, Cotton & Union Cake Co. with a staff of 92 as the town's major employer on the eve of the First World War.[8]

The number of men working at the linseed oil mill was reduced to 32 by 1916, but generally the war boosted Driffield's flagging economy.[9] Tradesmen and shop-

1 Below, buildings.
2 Census.
3 Ibid.
4 H. D. Watts, 'Agricultural Industries: The Decline of the Small Business', *Business History* 9 (1967), 121.
5 Watts, 'Industrial geography',78.
6 HRO, DBHT/5/304, newspaper cutting Jan. 1900; below, this section, brewing.
7 R. and A. McLean, *Benjamin Fawcett, Engraver and Colour Printer* (1988), 23; below, this section, printing.
8 P. Howorth, *The Impact of War: Driffield and the Wolds 1914–1919* (2002), 63.
9 Howorth, *Impact of War*, 63.

keepers, still dependent largely on the local farming community, benefited by the sharp rise in the price of corn and other agricultural produce, and from the construction of an airfield in Eastburn township to the west of the town from early in 1916. RAF Driffield as it was called from February 1919, when building work was complete, had a manning establishment of 839 although this is unlikely to have been reached.[1]

Inter-War, 1919–45

Local agriculture boomed during the war and immediately post-war, but the prosperity was short-lived. The war evidently had an adverse impact on Little Driffield's September fair which, after a move to Great Driffield, was held for the last time in 1920.[2] That year also saw the closure of RAF Driffield, and the subsequent demolition of its buildings.[3] Prices for agricultural produce fell sharply from 1921, and the following year action to reduce farm workers' wages led to strikes, and the vicar reported that there was much unemployment.[4] The main employers in the 1920s were the two seed-crushing mills, Bradshaw's flour mills and the timber yards.[5] A proposal to open a sugar beet factory in 1927 was not implemented, and the two industries set up at this time, a rug factory and a jam factory, mainly employed women.[6] The latter was established by the large grocery firm of Fields of Hull off St John's Road in 1928, using produce from the adjacent Pomona fruit farm.[7]

The intensification of the agricultural depression in the early 1930s led to increased unemployment at Driffield which reached a serious level in 1933.[8] The closure of Matthews' seed crushing mill at this time must have contributed to the problem, to alleviate which allotments were provided for those out of work at the beginning of 1934.[9] That year Howard Leason, builder and chairman of the urban district council housing committee, declared that Driffield could no longer be considered an 'industrial community' and that its future lay as a residential centre.[10] Plans for developing a 15-a. 'Garden Village' off Scarborough Road came to nothing but there was plenty of work for construction workers and others when the Air Ministry decided to establish a permanent military airfield on the former site of RAF Driffield in 1935, officially opened the following year.[11] Other employment was provided by a milk processing plant opened by Glaxo at Great Driffield in 1937.[12] Basically a bulk collection point with facilities to convert the surplus milk to powdered form it employed 20 local men and dealt with 3,000–4,000 gallons a day.[13] Older established industries slumped, local foundries and agricultural implement makers were hit by the introduction of tractors and more sophisticated machinery and brickmaking had ended by the late 1930s, as had the jam factory.[14]

The population of the rural district fell by 9 per cent between 1911 and 1931, and although this was offset by a modest 4 per cent rise in the town, there was an overall fall in the catchment area which would have reduced the customers for the town's retailers, who must have suffered also by the decline and eventual end of the Martinmas hirings.[15] The total number of grocers, small shopkeepers, boot and shoemakers, tailors, drapers and outfitters, fell from 65 in 1921 to 50 in 1937, although the number of boot and shoe repairers, as distinct from makers, increased from one to nine.[16] The fall in number of tailors and shoemakers would have been greater had not these craftsmen virtually disappeared from local villages.[17]

The Second World War, as with the first, brought a period of prosperity for farmers, and RAF Driffield, which was operational throughout the war, except between autumn 1942 and July 1944, brought employment and trade for local shops, pubs, cinemas and dance halls.[18] One casualty of the war was the Driffield Pure Linseed, Cotton & Union Cake Co.'s mill closed in 1942 as a result of government policy to concentrate certain industries.[19]

Post-War

The town's economy was hit when RAF Driffield was placed on a care and maintenance basis at the end of the war, but in September 1946 it became active again with a succession of flying schools, before transference to Fighter Command in 1955. Two years later it became a Fighter Weapons School before being closed in March 1958. Mothballed for a short time it re-opened by the end of that year as headquarters of a Thor international ballistic missile complex, a role it played until 1963 when the strategic missile force was abandoned.

1 G. Simmons, 'Then and Now, pt. iv: Royal Flying Corps Eastburn/Royal Air Force Driffield', *E Yorks. Historian* 4 (2003), 81–6; G. Simmons and B. Abraham, *Strong Foundations: Driffield's Aerodrome from 1917 to 2000* (2001), 13–22; *HT* 22 Feb. 1919.

2 Below, this section, later fairs.

3 Harrison, *Driffield*, 414.

4 ERAO, DDX 831/1/1; BIA, V. 1912–22/Ret.

5 *DT* 28 Dec. 1929.

6 For rug factory below, this section, textiles.

7 Watts, 'Industrial geography', 96.

8 *HT* 13 Sept. 1930, 21 Feb. 1931, 6 May 1933.

9 Ibid. 13 Jan. 1934.

10 Ibid. 3 Nov 1934.

11 Below, Kelleythorpe.

12 *HT* 10 Apr. 1937; *DT* 10 Oct. 1958.

13 Watts, 'Industrial Geography', 85, 96.

14 E. T. Carr (ed.), *Driffield Capital of the Wolds* (1948), 19. The fruit farm surrounding the Pomona jam factory was for sale in 1937: HRO, DBHT/9/1096.

15 Above, vol. intro., population; below, this section, hirings.

16 *Kelly's Dir. N & ER Yorks.* (1921), 501–4; *Kelly's Dir. N & ER Yorks.* (1937), 446–50.

17 *VCH Yorks. ER.* viii. 49.

18 Harrison, *Driffield*, 415–6, 419–20.

19 Watts, 'Industrial geography', 94, 96–7.

Although closed the married quarters continued to be occupied by staff from RAF Leconfield, near Beverley, and with up to 900 people living there it remained important to the economy of Driffield.[1]

After the Second World War the corn market closed but the cattle market thrived, and there was a transformation of the industrial profile of the town. Of the older industries only the saw mills with associated timber trades, particularly active after the war, and milling remained by the mid 1960s.[2] Although Bradshaw's Bell Mills was destroyed by fire in 1949, it was soon rebuilt on a grander scale and fitted with the most modern equipment and Driffield retained its position as the most important centre for milling in rural East Yorkshire.[3] The maltings on Skerne Road continued to operate until 1962 when they were closed as a consequence of the opening of the large modern works at Knapton near Malton.[4] Other old established concerns that closed were the two remaining foundries, Wood's went *c.* 1957 and Taylor's in 1964, and the steam laundry, in Laundry Lane, established 1910, that once employed 70 people, mostly women, closed *c.* 1969.[5] Of more recent firms the rug factory of John Beever & Son, in Westgate closed in the mid 1950s and Glaxo Laboratories closed in 1962 because there was less milk produced locally and nationally there was a bigger demand for fresh rather than powdered milk.[6]

New industries took their place. White's Sugar Mills Ltd, manufacturers of speciality caster and icing sugars and cake decorations, bombed out of Hull in 1941, took over the former Driffield Pure Linseed Cake & Union Co. works in 1947.[7] By 1956 they had a staff of 150–200 depending on the season.[8] The firm, then owned by Charles Southwell Ltd, closed *c.* 1969 and that year the former manager Michael Shepherdson set up Shepcote Ltd with a factory in Church Street making edible cake decorations and *petit fours*.[9]

There was an increase in poultry farming locally and an egg packing station was opened at Little Driffield by 1956, and then two years later Twydale turkey packing factory founded by Raymond Twiddle was established with five employees.[10] The firm took over the former Glaxo factory on Wansford Road in 1968 and the following year there was a staff of 120. A former employee established the rival Broadacres turkey factory on Skerne Road in 1964 with 20 staff.[11] Twydale Turkeys, part of the Bibby feed company from 1969, took over Broadacres in 1977 and merged with Hillsdown Holdings in 1986 of which the successive firms based in Driffield, Moorlands then Buxted Foods, were part. Processing of turkeys ended at the Wansford Road works in 1991, which were then used for offices before being abandoned in 1995 and demolished for housing in 1997.[12] In 2004 the Skerne Road factory was operated by Uniq Prepared Foods and Frontline Foods.

Other new firms had no link with agriculture; they were 'footloose' industries that could be located anywhere with a good labour supply and suitable accommodation.[13] In 1950 I. J. Dewhirst Ltd, a light clothing manufacturer from Leeds (WR) opened a small workshop in Driffield employing eight young women. Initially functioning under the brand name Duwear and based in a former furniture showroom in Exchange Street and then in the former rug factory in Westgate, the firm had 60 employees in 1956 and 290 in 1969, almost all female.[14] The main customers were Marks & Spencer and mail-order firms; in 1966 the workshop was producing 18,000 shirts a week.[15] It was a Driffield man's experience in the optical trade that led to the establishment of Vertex (Optical) Ltd in the town in 1956. The firm producing spectacle frames and lenses benefited from the demand for glasses as a result of the introduction of the National Health Service and the increasing desire for more fashionable products. Skilled workers were imported to train local people and by 1963 the firm had 83 workers, some employed by a recently established subsidiary Cindico which made 'baby bouncers'.[16] Six years later there were 160 employees.[17] Another smaller firm making spectacle frames, Kenra Frames, was set up in the town by 1972.[18]

The new firms largely relied on female labour, with a significant number working part-time. Between 1951 and 1964 male employment declined in the Driffield employment area by 1,200 but there was a dramatic increase of 850 in female employment. The increase in female workers rose more rapidly than in Britain as a whole, and the number who worked part-time was much higher than the national average.[19] Agricultural employment in the area was in decline and the trades linked to it in the town.[20]

Despite the closure of the railway line to Malton, to passengers in 1950 and all traffic in 1958, the closure of the line to Market Weighton in 1965 and the final disappearance of the village carrier Driffield retained

1 Census; Harrison, *Driffield*, 421–2.
2 Carr, *Driffield*, 19.
3 Watts, 'Industrial geography', 89.
4 Ibid. 121.
5 M. Wynn, *Driffield* (2004), 143
6 Shaw 'Driffield', 82.
7 *Dalesman*, vol. 28 (1966), 468.
8 *Driffield Town Guide* (1956), 23.
9 *DT* 10 Nov. 2006; *Driffield Souvenir Guide* (1972), 61; www.shepcote.co.uk
10 Watts, 'Industrial geography', 87.
11 Shaw, 'Driffield', 83.
12 *DP* 29 Jan. 1997; *YP* 10 May 2007; 14 July 2009; *Poultry World* 1 Dec. 2008.
13 F. N. Burton, *The Changing Economic Structure and Development Potential of Driffield and its Region* (*c.* 1966), 7.
14 Shaw, 'Driffield', 83; *Driffield Town Guide* (1956), 30.
15 Shaw, 'Driffield', 83; *Dalesman*, vol.28 (1966), 467.
16 Watts, 'Industrial geography', 102–3.
17 Shaw, 'Driffield', 82.
18 *Driffield Souvenir Guide* (1972), 75.
19 Burton, *Changing Economic Structure*, 7, 22.
20 Ibid. 25.

its position as the centre for retail goods and services for a wide area thanks to the growth in motor transport.[1] Villagers from up to 6 miles away went there for their groceries, the first supermarket, Jackson's, opening in 1963.[2]

Retailers and service providers benefited from the town's increasing popularity as a dormitory town for residents working in Bridlington, Beverley, Hull, and further afield. The town's population rose by two thirds from 6,892 in 1961 to 11,477 in 2001, but that of the catchment area fell steadily throughout. This was partly due to the withdrawal of armed forces and their families from RAF Driffield and its successor, the Alamein Barracks.[3]

Kelleythorpe industrial estate was developed by Derek Megginson on 85 a. that he purchased adjoining the airfield in 1975. Work began on the site in 1986 and the first building was occupied in 1988. The first phase covering 30 a. was fully occupied by 2000, a second phase of 20 a. was filled by 2004 when there some 50 companies on the estate employing over 600 people.[4]

The industrial estate was the economic driving force for Driffield in the late 20th – early 21st century and provided the base for much needed employment at a time when industries were closing in the town. Vertex Ltd went into receivership in 1994 with the loss of 60 jobs, then there was the closure in 1997 of Cindico, with over 100 employees, and Swan Optical spectacles, with 45 employees.[5] Dewhirst Ltd, which was employing 530 people in its two factories in Driffield in 1992, stopped production there in 2002.[6] Grampian Foods, which was processing turkeys in the former Twydale Turkey plant on Skerne Road, closed in 2005 with the loss of 220 jobs.[7] Shepcote with a workforce of 40, one of the town's largest employers, relocated to the Kelleythorpe industrial estate in 2007.[8]

The development of the periphery made the older core of Driffield even more of a marketing and service centre, what industry there was in the town being small in scale and unobtrusive.[9] Retailing in Driffield changed greatly in the later 20th century. Existing shops were challenged by competition from new businesses, in particular from the four small supermarkets and nine charity shops which then established themselves in the town. As a result, the food shops had been reduced to about thirty and outfitters to a dozen by 2004; of about one hundred and forty shops in Driffield then, some twenty stood empty, several of them in a closed arcade called the Viking Centre. On the other hand, increasingly mobile shoppers were retained and attracted by the new grocers, and by the large car parks laid out on some of the vacant land to the east of the main street, and the town's rising population also helped to keep the centre generally prosperous. Several of the remaining food shops distinguished themselves from the larger retailers by specializing in whole or farm foods, and in 2004 the town still boasted two general ironmongers and R. Morris & Son, a butcher's run by the same family for more than 170 years.[10] Many of the other concerns offered non-essential goods and services, responding to the greater leisure and income of their patrons. Besides fourteen hairdressers, there were a dozen shops selling newspapers and fancy goods, seven businesses providing leisure equipment and amusements of various kinds, three florists, three jewellers, three computer accessory shops, five pet shops, and three travel agents. An internet café was opened at the railway station in 2004. Social change was reflected also in the provision of meals and drink, the efforts of nearly twenty public houses being supplemented by the same number of 'fast food' shops and restaurants, offering English, Mediterranean, and Asian dishes.

A traditional base of the local economy, mercantile activity linked to agriculture, was also much altered in the mid 20th century. Most of the 14 concerns still trading in corn, flour, seeds, and coal in 1937 were given up as a result of the substitution of natural gas and oil for coal, and the difficulties of competing with larger regional and national firms. By 2004 there was only one coal merchant and one seed corn merchant left.[11] Two agricultural merchants then operated from premises in the town and on the industrial estate, and there was another concern trading in straw. Trade in another of the traditional bulk commodities, timber, conversely continued and developed as other building products were introduced. In 1937 there were three timber merchants, a cement merchant, and a general builders' merchant in Driffield. By 2004 there were twelve merchants, four of them located on the industrial estate; they included, besides local concerns, branches of larger national firms and specialist suppliers of windows and components for bathrooms and kitchens. The increase in the significance of builders' merchants reflected the housing boom of the late 20th century, which also probably accounts for the presence on the industrial estate of engineering concerns making portable accommodation for building sites and several small-scale joinery works. Though much of the new building was done by large regional or national

1 Burton, *Malton and Driffield Junction Railway*, 72.

2 J. R. Tarrant, *Retail Distribution in Eastern Yorkshire in Relation to Central Place Theory*, Univ. of Hull Occasional Papers in Geography No. 8 (1967), 34; Shaw, 'Driffield', 58.

3 Below, Kelleythorpe.

4 Inf. from Derek Megginson, Eastburn, 2011; *Driffield Town Guide* (*c.* 2004), 7; *DT* 10 Jan. 2008.

5 Wynn, *Driffield*, 168; *YP* 1 Dec. 1994.

6 Wynn, *Driffield*, 168.

7 *YP* 10 May 2007. The processing of turkeys at the Wansford Road factory had ceased in 1991: *DP* 29 Jan. 1997.

8 *YP* 7 Feb. 2002; www.shepcote.co.uk

9 This section by Graham Kent, 2004.

10 *DT* Jan. 2000 (millennium edn).

11 The remaining corn miller, at Bell Mills, dealt in seed corn too, but from other premises: inf. from Mr M. Robson, Driffield, 2004.

Commerical/industrial concern	*'Town'*	*Peripheral*	*Total*
Merchants:			
builders	8	4	12
agricultural	2	1	3
fuel	1	1	2
scrap metal	1	-	1
Food processors: (miller, confectioner, makers of prepared foods, petfoods)	2	7	9
Industrial chemists/optical engineers	-	5	5
Engineers:			
Motor	11	4	15
Computer	-	2	2
Others (electrical, agricultural,.mechanical.)	4	8	12
Builders, plumbers, electricians etc.	10	3	13
Woodworkers	1	6	7
Other manufacturers: (clothing, glass items)	2	-	2
Inns, cafés	36	1	37
Food shops	30	-	30
Clothing and shoe shops	16	-	16
Other 'shops':			
Hairdressers	14	-	14
Stationers, printers, newsagents, fancy goods	12	2	14
Furniture, furnishings	12	-	12
Charity	9	-	9
Amusements, sports shops, gym, etc.	7	1	8
Ironmongery, tools, DIY, equip. hire	7	1	8
Pet shops	5	-	5
General shops (Woolworth, Boyes etc.)	4	-	4
Cycles, mobility equipt., etc.	3	1	4
Computer accessories/business equipt.	3	1	4
Electrical shops	4	-	4
Jewellers	3	-	3
Chemists	3	-	3
Florists	3	-	3
Travel agents	3	-	3
Advice centres	3	-	3
Motor accessories	1	-	1
Saddlery	1	-	1
Sign shop	1	-	1
Funeral director	1	-	1
Dental supplies	-	1	1

Sources: fieldwork winter 2003–4; advertisements; www.kellysearch.com. (Nov. 2003). Detailed lists deposited at ERAO, DDX/1095.

Table 11. *Driffield Parish: Commercial and Industrial Concerns in 2004*

firms, some was the work of the dozen concerns of local builders and allied tradesmen.

In 2004 new businesses recently established on the periphery of the town included seven preparing foodstuffs, ranging in size from an extensive factory on Skerne Road to small operations in the units on the industrial estate. A dozen engineers also worked on the Kelleythorpe estate, several of them making buildings for agriculture and for the building industry, and one or two as motor engineers. There was a handful of high technology enterprises included a food-hygiene laboratory and two optical factories on the industrial estate, and at Driffield Business Centre on Skerne Road two software engineers and a water-treatment chemist.

MARKETS AND FAIRS

Medieval Markets and Fairs

A market (*forum*) was being held on Driffield manor by 1199, when its dues may have been worth £12 a year,[1] and *c.* 1280 John de Balliol claimed the right to a market and fairs at Driffield; the market was then held on Monday, and the fairs on the day before and feast days of the Assumption of St Mary (14–15 August) and either her Purification (1–2 February) or, more probably, Nativity (7–8 September). The claim was disputed by Balliol's overlord, the Crown, as not included in the earlier grant to his predecessors, and it was then alleged that the family had also infringed Crown rights by increasing the ancient toll there and levying a new one.[2] The market and fairs were effectively confirmed in 1318, when the Crown granted the then lord of Driffield, John of Brittany, earl of Richmond, a market and a four-day annual fair, though the market was to be held on Friday, and the fair from the second Monday after Easter.[3] The market and fair ground may have been from the outset in Little Driffield, where in 1392 two fairs and the market were held, producing tolls worth £2 a year.[4] That income was valued at only £1 a year in 1423.[5] The tolls charged on traders attending Driffield's markets and fairs were disputed soon afterwards by those from Beverley, whose claim of exemption by royal grant was allowed by John le Scrope, Lord Scrope, the lord of Driffield, in 1428.[6]

The four fair days were altered after the 13th century, those on the feast days of St Mary being kept but the days preceding them being re-allocated, presumably to achieve a better spread of fairs across the spring and summer. By the 1490s fairs were being held at Little Driffield on Whit Monday and the Nativity of St Mary (8 September),[7] and another on Easter Monday was recorded about the same time.[8] In the 17th century the date of the fourth fair was given as the Assumption of St Mary (15 August). The August and September fairs were called the Lady Day fairs;[9] evidently as a result of the mid 18th-century reform of the calendar, they later fell on 26 August and 19 September.[10]

Two of the fairs, those on Whit Monday and in September, were policed by men from neighbouring villages, who came armed with clubs. Those fairs were accordingly sometimes called the Club fairs.[11] Late in the 15th century the tenants of the earl of Northumberland's manor of Nafferton claimed to have assisted the officers of the lord of Driffield in keeping order 'according to custom' at the fair held at Little Driffield on the Nativity of St Mary (8 September). An alternative view was that the arrival of the bailiff of Nafferton manor with some sixty 'unarmed' people to police the fair and to trade had caused a riot. The trouble seems to have had at its core the claim of the inhabitants of Nafferton to freedom from tolls and stallage in Driffield.[12] In the 17th century both the September and the Whit Monday fairs were recorded as policed by men from Nafferton and Lowthorpe, then said to come armed with clubs and preceded by a piper.[13]

Goods traded at the fairs *c.* 1500 included sheep, leather, cheese, fish, and 'smithy ware', and toll was also then charged on carts bringing turves and hay into Driffield from Nafferton.[14]

Later Fairs

The 17th-century fairs were, as they may have been earlier, largely for livestock. Cattle, lambs and other sheep, and horses sold well at Easter, especially to Holderness graziers buying stock to fatten. The summer and autumn fairs were more general in character, with household goods and hardware on sale, as well as livestock.[15] Early in the 18th century the tolls and profits of two of the fairs were let for £14 a year, together with the 'stallger house'. The house, perhaps the place where hurdles and other gear were stored, evidently stood west of the street at Little Driffield.[16] Although cattle continued to be brought to the fairs,[17] they seem by the mid 18th century to have been chiefly for sheep and horses. The fairs were held on the village green[18] until the 18th century, when much of the activity was removed to the northern edge of Little Driffield. At inclosure in 1742 Richard Langley, lord of the manor, was thus charged with setting aside parts of some 70 a. allotted to him for the holding of the usual sheep fairs, and in 1856 a close of some 10 a. was being

1 *Pipe R.* 1199 (PRS, N.S. 10), 55; 1230 (PRS, N.S. 4), 32; *Yorks. Inq.* i, p. 108; ii, p. 95.

2 *Yorks. Hund. and Quo Warr. R.* (YAS Rec. Ser. 151), 61, 211–12.

3 *Cal. Chart. R.* 1300–26, 406.

4 *Cal. Inq. p.m.* xvii, p. 115.

5 TNA, C 139/4, no. 34.

6 For a later defence by Beverley Corporation, see ERAO, BC/II/7/5, f. 158v.; Ross, *Driffield*, 19–20.

7 *Yorks. Star Chamber Proc.* iii (YAS Rec. Ser. 51), pp. 18, 37–8; *Complete Peerage*, s.v. Scrope.

8 TNA, STAC 2/20/27.

9 Best, *Farming Bks*, ed. Woodward, 117–19.

10 K. L. McCutcheon, *Yorks. Fairs and Markets* (Thoresby Soc. 39), 175. In the 19th century the dates were given, probably in error, as 16 Aug. and 29 Sept.: Baines, *Hist. Yorks.* (1823), ii. 194; *1st Rep. Royal Com. Mkt Rights and Tolls*, Vol. I (Parl. Papers, 1888 [C. 5550], liii), p. 220.

11 Ross, *Driffield*, 94.

12 TNA, STAC 2/20/27; *Yorks. Star Chamber Proc.* iii, pp. 18, 37–8.

13 Best, *Farming Bks*, ed. Woodward, 118. Perhaps related were the fines laid in Driffield manor court on people from Nafferton and Foston for 'not answering the clubs': HUL, DDCV/42/4, s.a. 1733.

14 TNA, STAC 2/20/27; *Yorks. Star Chamber Proc.* iii, pp. 37–8

15 Best, *Farming Bks*, ed. Woodward, 118–19.

16 RDB, H/392/807; HL/158/170.

17 Baines, *Hist. Yorks.* (1823), ii. 194.

18 Sheahan and Whellan, *Hist. York & ER.* ii. 503.

so used.[1] Horses and leather were also sold at the September fair in the mid 18th century,[2] the horse fair being kept in a part of the road leading north-eastwards from Little Driffield which was ordered in 1742 to be 132 ft wide for that purpose.[3]

The four annual fairs on Easter Monday, Whit Monday, 26 August and 19 September were still active in the mid 19th century for the sale of sheep and cattle, but all were 'seriously injured' by the opening of a fortnightly livestock market at Driffield in 1847.[4] The two so-called Harvest fairs in August and September continued to be important for the sale of sheep. Some 5,000 lambs and 500 grazing ewes were for sale at the first fair, and 6,000 sheep and a few rams and cattle at the second in 1871.[5] As well as the thousands of Lincoln and Leicester lambs and sheep and a few cattle and horses sold at the September fair, the main feature in the 1870s–90s was the sale and letting of rams.[6] By this date the Easter and Whitsun fairs, the latter once a great pleasure fair, were of 'very minor importance'.[7] Two toll-collectors were employed by Viscountess Downe, the lady of the manor, about 1890, and a court of pie-powder was held at the Red Lion in Driffield at noon on fair days to hear and adjudicate upon trading disputes.[8]

Although all four fairs were still listed in 1913 only the September fair, when hundreds of Lincoln and Leicester rams and thousands of store lambs were said to sold by dealers and auctioneers, probably still functioned to any extent. [9] The fair was held for the last time at Little Driffield in 1918, and then for the next two years, following the sale of the right to hold the fairs and the market, it was held in a field on the east side of Great Driffield.[10] The last fair was evidently held in 1920 but the proclamation of the fairs continued at Little Driffield up to and including 1924.[11]

Later Markets

A reference *c.* 1535 to Market Driffield, presumably Great Driffield, may indicate that the Friday market was still active, but it was probably discontinued before the early 17th century when it was not among the local markets used by Henry Best of Elmswell.[12] Best did however buy seed peas at Great Driffield in 1647.[13] In the 1730s ale-tasters and market searchers were appointed in the manor court, but they may have controlled other retailing and the fairs.[14] A visitor called Driffield a 'market town' in 1733 and some ten years later the leading townspeople referred to it as such, but neither market nor market place are mentioned in the inclosure award in 1742.[15] The central, triangular enlargement of the main street, later called Market Place, did then exist, and was presumably the 'market place' mentioned in 1751.[16] A local resident born in 1759 later stated that there had been a market ever since he could remember; 'old women used to sell butter & there was beef & other things exhibited for sale'.[17] A Thursday market was in existence by 1773, probably having been transferred from North Frodingham by that date.[18] In 1792 it was said to be a 'good market on Thursdays for corn, meat, calves, and pigs in the season, and divers other things, and is well supplied with sea-fish'.[19] The market place was laid out in 1799 when the buildings on the west side were set back; the last vacant plot there was for sale in 1804.[20]

In 1808 the weekly market was said to be 'disorderly', causing Driffield inhabitants to petition the lord of the manor, Richard Langley, to regulate it and appoint a market supervisor.[21] The petitioners suggested that the tradesmen and 'country people' coming to market be assigned distinct parts of the market place. The west side was to be occupied from north to south by butchers, livestock dealers, and carriers' carts. Other areas were proposed for coopers and ropers, horse dealers, and sellers of pottery and hardware, cloth, books, toys, butter, fruit and vegetables, and confectionery. Pinfold or Cross Hill was to be a station for empty carts, and the market place was to be swept weekly from 1 October to 1 May. The lady of the manor in 1822 ordered the butchers to stand on the east side of Market Place, extending northwards from Exchange Street; butter, eggs, and poultry to be displayed on the west side of Market Place, and ploughs and such like to be sold on Cross Hill.[22] The sale of butter and eggs was evidently later moved across Market Place, to the yard of the

1 RDB, B/153/42; HK/313/328.
2 McCutcheon, *Yorks. Fairs and Mkts.* 175.
3 RDB, B/153/42; OS Map 1:10,560, Yorks. CLXI (1855 edn).
4 *HP* 16 May 1845; 9 Apr., 3 Sep. 1847; 5 Apr. 1850; 16 Aug. 1856; *1st Rep. Royal Com. Mkt Rights and Tolls*, Vol. II (Parl. Papers, 1888 [C.5550-1], liii) p. 268.
5 Howorth, *Year Gone By*, 85.
6 *HP* 23 Sep. 1870; 25 Sep. 1874; 22 Sep. 1876; 22 Sep. 1882; 21 Sep. 1883; *YH* 21 Sept. 1891; 23 Sept. 1893; 20 Sept. 1900.
7 *Final Rep. Royal Com. Mkt Rights and Tolls*, Vol. XIII, Pt 2 (Parl. Papers, 1890–1 [C. 6268-VI. A], xl), pp. 560–7; *Kelly's Dir. N & ER Yorks.* (1872), 351.
8 Ross, *Driffield*, 94.
9 *Kelly's Dir. N & ER Yorks.* (1913), 511; *Borough Guide to Driffield* (1913), 18.
10 RDB, 190/395/336; 192/489/431; M. W. Barley (ed.) *History of Great and Little Driffield* (1938), 26–7. Manorfield Road is on the site of the later fairground.
11 Barley, *Great and Little Driffield*, 27.
12 TNA, C1/838/52–3; Best, *Farming Bks*, ed. Woodward, 105–6, 110.
13 Best, *Farming Bks*, ed. Woodward, 106.
14 HUL, DDCV/42/2.
15 *Journey from London to Scarborough* (1734), 27; ERAO, QSF/147/D/4.
16 HUL, DDLG/30/622.
17 ERAO, DDX/17/15.
18 *DT* 23 Apr. 1892; *1st Rep. Royal Com. Mkt Rights and Tolls*, Vol. II, p. 265; Sheahan and Whellan, *Hist. York & ER.* ii. 410.
19 *Universal Brit. Dir.* (*c.* 1792), ii. 827.
20 ERAO, DDX/17/15; *YH* 4 Feb. 1804.
21 Howorth, *Driffield*, 38–9; HUL, DDCV/42/12.
22 *DT* 18 Feb. 1998.

23. *Great Driffield: Market Place from the south-east c. 1900. Thursday market in progress with covered stalls and carriers' carts.*

Black Swan.[1] In 1836 the lord was petitioned again about the room being taken by the pottery sellers, evidently on the west side of Market Place. It was then requested that they be removed further down the street, below the Buck inn, and that carts should go instead into George Street or to the 'back market place', evidently meaning Cross Hill.[2] The market was held on a Thursday afternoon until 1840 when it was resolved that the market for butter, fruit, and poultry should commence at 10 a.m. and that the corn market be held from 11 a.m. to 2 p.m.[3]

The Market Place had become too small by 1840 with nearly the whole space occupied by the dealers in butter, fruit, and vegetables, and other small tradesmen, so that the cornfactors and farmers were driven into the centre of the public street.[4] This led to the building of the Corn Exchange on New Road, later Exchange Street, in 1841–2.[5] However it was soon deserted because one of principal corn factors, probably James Harrison, refused to use the building, and farmers preferred to transact business in the street or inn doorways.[6] There were further complaints about the overcrowded Market Place in 1861 with stallholders obstructing the footpaths.[7]

By the end of the century there was also a market on Saturdays. From 1876 or 1877 the local board ran the markets and took the tolls as lessee of the lady of the manor, Viscountess Downe, to whom it paid £25 a year. The board subsequently supplied the stalls and employed a market inspector. Besides corn, the goods traded included poultry, eggs, butter, meat, fruit and vegetables, timber, hardware and pottery, clothing, and manures.[8] The board's successor, the urban district council (UDC), also held the markets, paying Lord Downe £30 a year for them in the early 20th century.[9]

Ownership of the markets continued to descend with the manor, eventually being sold to Driffield UDC in 1964.[10] The following year the council moved the markets out of Market Place to their later location on Cross Hill.[11] In 1973 the UDC bought a former foundry adjoining Cross Hill, and then proposed adapting one of its buildings to move the markets indoors.[12] The conversion of the market hall and the re-organization of local government probably delayed matters, and not until 1975 did the succeeding North Wolds District Council finally move the markets indoors.[13] Within twenty years the market hall was in a poor state of repair, and in 1995 the markets were once again moved outdoors, onto Cross Hill; the hall was demolished soon afterwards for more car parking. Markets were still being held twice a week, on Thursday and Saturday, although in 1995 that on Saturday was described as dead, and the off-street site was regarded as largely responsible for the decline.[14] By 1998 there were usually less than five stalls in the market.[15] In 2001 the East Riding of Yorkshire Council allowed the Thursday market to be returned to Market Place and released its

1 Ibid. 15 Nov. 1963, copy at HUL, DDX/16/126.
2 HUL, DDSH(2)/3/1; Mortimer, *Forty Years' Researches*, 271. Carts later stood on Cross Hill or in pub yards: *DT* 18 Feb. 1998.
3 *YH* 30 May 1840.
4 *Farmers Magazine* Nov. 1840, 343.
5 *HP* 11 June 1841, 27 Jan. 1843; below, buildings.
6 *HP* 12 June 1874.
7 Ibid. 15 Feb. 1861.
8 *Final Rep. Royal Com. Mkt Rights and Tolls*, Vol. XIII, Pt 2, pp. 560–7; *Kelly's Dir. N & ER Yorks.* (1872), 351; Ross, *Driffield*, 32, 94.
9 ERAO, NV/1/107; ibid. UDDR/1/1/1, p. 6, etc. Illus. of market c. 1910 at HUL, DX/144/3 (A 5068/12; A 5071/1).
10 RDB, 1388/16/16; above, manors and estates, Driffield manor.
11 *DT* 18 Feb. 1998.
12 RDB, 1826/585/484; ERAO, UDDR/1/1/46, Housing...Cttee, 1 Jan. 1973; UDDR/1/1/47, Housing...Cttee, 7 May 1973; Public Health Cttee, 20 Aug. 1973.
13 *DT* 3 Dec. 1981 (illus.); 27 Oct. 1988; 18 Sept. 2002.
14 ERAO, EYEY/1/4/8/3, Environmental...Cttee, 21 Nov. 1994; 5 Feb. 1996; *DT* 20 July 1994; *DP* 7 June 1995; *HDM* 22 Dec. 1994; 28 May 1997.
15 *HDM* 27 Aug. 1998.

management to Driffield Town Council. The move successfully revived the market, which subsequently had about thirty stalls offering fish, fruit and vegetables, clothes, and miscellaneous household goods.[1] The town council's plan to close the main street on Saturdays to hold the second market there as well was vigorously and successfully opposed by local shopkeepers,[2] and it has remained on Cross Hill, where in 2005 a few traders were selling garden plants, clothing, and household items.

The reduction in the town's food markets was to an extent made good in 2000, when a monthly farmers' market was begun outside the town on the show-ground.[3]

Livestock Markets

Until the mid 19th century livestock from Driffield and its district was marketed in Leeds or Wakefield (WR), or in local fairs, including those at Little Driffield.[4] A fortnightly cattle market on a Thursday 'for the sale of fat and lean stock of every description' was established at Driffield in 1808, but it was evidently short-lived.[5]

By 1833 there was a weekly pig market on a Thursday with usually 200–300 pigs for sale.[6] That year a public meeting under the chairmanship of the solicitor Thomas Scotchburn resolved to establish a fortnightly cattle market on Thursdays.[7] The first market was held in April 1833, and the following two years it was well attended but with a better supply of sheep than beasts.[8] It was found that Thursday was too late in the week and by April 1838 it had been moved to a Monday but it failed soon after.[9]

The pig market was being held at the Dog and Duck public house by 1844. William Jarratt then bought the house, later the Falcon, and its extensive yard between the beck and Market Place,[10] and in 1847 he opened a livestock market there which was operated on alternate Wednesdays.[11] During its first six months 6,596 sheep and 975 beasts were offered for sale there.[12]

After objecting in 1853 to the venture as an infringement of his market, the lord of the manor agreed informally to the continuation of the cattle market for the good of the manor and the wider area. In 1856–8 the market, then ranked amongst the best in Yorkshire, was extended with pens capable of holding 200 beasts and 1,500 sheep.[13] Some 30,000 head of cattle were sold there in 1858.[14]

Jarratt (d. 1875) was succeeded by his son, William Otley Jarratt, who in 1883 successfully opposed the setting up of a rival cattle market near the railway line, and the acquisition by the proposed company of an exclusive right to hold markets and fairs in the parish; the challenge came from another Driffield solicitor and member of the local board, G. B. Tonge, apparently supported by another legal firm, Jennings & Co.[15] In 1888 Jarratt believed that his market was again threatened, on that occasion by the 'speculators' who had recently built the waterworks. Jarratt's market, which he boasted was 'likely to become equal, if not superior, to any other market in the riding', then accommodated upwards of 4,000 sheep and about 450 cattle in sheds and pens, and included a covered market for pigs and sheep.[16] Usually there were some 1,500 sheep in the market, and between 1875 and 1877 on average 43,000 sheep a year and almost 5,000 cattle passed through it, besides large numbers of pigs, many of which were bought for Hull and the West Riding.[17] In 1913 it was claimed that as many as 4,000 sheep were sold in one day.[18]

Initially, selling had been by private contract, but about 1870 auctions were introduced, and by the 1880s fat stock was always sold in that way; lean stock, however, continued to be sold by contract. In the late 19th and early 20th century cattle and sheep were traded in the Wednesday markets, and pigs on Thursdays, apparently in Jarratt's market and on the premises of Jane Ransom at the Black Swan. Charges borne by farmers using the market comprised auctioneering fees and a payment for the accommodation of animals, 1*s.* 4*d.* being charged for a pen for four head of cattle, for example. Jarratt's interest passed at his death in 1895 to his son, also William Otley Jarratt, who in 1914 appointed his brother Alfred and sister Rose Williams as fellow trustees. In 1918 the market was finally confirmed to the Jarratts by the lord of the manor. It was to be for livestock and other goods, and tolls and dues might be charged, but the market site was not to be further enlarged. By then though, the market site had been extended from the yard behind Market Place

1 *DP* 9 Feb., 31 Aug. 2001; *DT* 20 June 2001; *HDM* 12 Mar. 2002; inf. from Claire Binnington, Driffield Town Council, 2005.

2 *DP* 6 Sept. 2002; *DT* 25 Sept. 2002.

3 Harrison, *Driffield*, 405.

4 For the following, RDB, 186/566/482; *1st Rep. Mkt Rights and Tolls*, Vol. II, pp. 260–8; *Final Rep. Mkt Rights and Tolls*, Vol. XIII, Pt 2, pp. 560–3.

5 *HP* 30 Apr., 3 May 1808.

6 *YH* 2 Mar. 1833, 21 Jan., 11 Feb., 13 May 1837.

7 *HP* 22 Feb. 1833; *YH* 2 Mar. 1833.

8 *HP* 29 Mar. 1833; *YH* 20 Sep., 4, 18 Oct. 1834; 21 Feb., 16 May, 13 June, 3 Oct. 1835; Pigot, *Nat. Com. Dir.* (1834), 710.

9 ERAO, DDX/17/15; *YH* 7 Apr.; 28 July 1838; White, *Dir. E.R Yorks* (1840), 202.

10 RDB, FZ/303/358.

11 Sheahan and Whellan, *Hist. York & ER.* ii. 498; *Kelly's Dir. N & ER Yorks.* (1872), 351.

12 *HP* 17 Sept. 1847.

13 Ibid. 7 Dec. 1856; 4 Feb. 1859.

14 Ibid. 4 Feb. 1859.

15 ERAO, QDP/229; *Kelly's Dir. N & ER Yorks.* (1889), 377.

16 For the 'market house' with its salerooms and bars, see RDB, 95/163/144 (1897).

17 *1st Rep. Mkt Rights and Tolls*, Vol. II, pp. 266–7; *Kelly's Dir. N & ER Yorks.* (1893), 407.

18 *Borough Guide to Driffield* (1913), 18

24. *Great Driffield: Cattle Market with sheep for sale, 1957.*

across the beck to cover in all about an acre.[1] In 1920 the Jarratts sold the market to local auctioneers, among them William Wilberfoss of Driffield and Walter Dee, then of Sledmere but soon afterwards of Garton on the Wolds. The consortium's venture was incorporated as Driffield Cattle Market Co. Ltd in 1921, and it was presumably then or in the preceding year that cattle and sheep sales were made weekly and moved to Tuesday.[2]

In the 1920s and 30s cattle and sheep were brought in on foot from an area of up to 12 miles; the buyers were the many small butchers from local villages with their own slaughter houses, as well as larger traders from Hull, Malton and Scarborough. By the 1950s there was covered accommodation for 650 beef cattle and over 1000 pigs. Trade increased when the market day was moved to a Thursday with animals brought from up to 25 miles away. There were five firms of auctioneers at the market and on one occasion in the 1960s as many as 1,000 fat cattle sold in a single day.[3]

The market was moved to a Monday towards the end of the century and was in decline when it was closed as a disease precaution during the foot and mouth crisis in 2001. In 2003, when it was of almost 2 a., the cattle market site was offered for sale. It was then said that it was the cattle market that made Driffield a market town, and that its loss ended an era both in the economy of the town and in East Riding agriculture, which had experienced a big decline in livestock farming.[4] There were plans to redevelop the cattle market site as part of a general regeneration of the beckside area in 2004.[5]

The firm of Cook & Dee, agricultural auctioneers and valuers, of Garton on the Wolds, moved its office to Driffield in 1945, and subsequently diversified into selling houses and, from 1964, antiques, fine art, and other household goods.[6] In 1951 the partnership, then of no. 22 Exchange Street, bought the Mechanics' Institute there.[7] At the beginning of the 21st century the auctions of Dee, Atkinson, & Harrison were an important element in the town's character, and attracted dealers from a wide area of northern England.

Wool Market

Wool dealers were advised of the facilities for the trade at Great Driffield in 1775 but no market was established until 1850.[8] Then it was estimated that 150,000 sheep were annually clipped in the vicinity of the town.[9] There was a good attendance of dealers at the first wool market but no record of it in later years has been found.[10]

Hiring Fairs

Martinmas The hiring of servants took place at labour markets which were held each November at Martinmas under the supervision of the Chief

1 OS Map 1:2,500, Yorks. CLXI. 12 (1893 edn); RDB, 238/208/176.

2 RDB, 238/208/176; 315/595/481; *Kelly's Dir. N & ER Yorks.* (1913), 511; (1921), 497. Illus. of mkt. in Harrison, *Driffield*, 245 *and* pl. 13.

3 P. S. Atkinson, *The Winds of Change* (privately printed, 2001), 171–2.

4 *DT* 12 Feb. 2003; *DP* 14 Feb. 2003; *ERM* 14 Feb. 2003.

5 *ERG* 5 Aug. 2004.

6 Dee, Atkinson, & Harrison website, 2003.

7 RDB, 900/311/263.

8 *YC* 23 May 1775.

9 *HP* 7 June 1850.

10 Ibid. 14, 28 June 1850.

Constable of each wapentake or division who was responsible by statute for regulating local wages.[1] In the mid 17th century the statute days, sessions, or fairs for the Bainton Beacon division of Harthill wapentake were held at Kirkburn, and there were other sittings nearby, at Kilham and Sledmere, in Dickering and Buckrose wapentakes respectively.[2]

Statute hirings or 'statties' were held at Driffield in 1777, and were probably held there annually from the late 18th century.[3] In 1828 the vicar noted on 17 November 'not many hired', but there was a particularly successful hirings in 1834.[4] The opening of the railway made an important difference to the attendance. In 1848 around 1,000 farm servants arrived by train, and the following year 'many thousands' were present at the hirings with an 'ungovernable and boisterous' crowd at the station.[5] By the mid 19th century the hirings at Driffield were probably the most important in the East Riding. The figures for Hull and Beverley hirings are unknown but 1,800 men and 790 women attended the first hirings at Driffield in 1860, more than twice the number that two days later were at Bridlington, the second largest hirings in the riding.[6] Farm servants, male and female, as well as farmers and their families, attended the hirings from a radius of 10–12 miles around the town, with many others coming for the pleasure fair and other entertainments.[7]

By the mid 19th century there were three hiring days at Driffield, the first on the Monday nearest Martinmas day, 11 November, the second, two weeks later, on the Monday nearest Old Martinmas day, 23 November, with the third on the following Thursday.[8] The last was largely a pleasure fair. The hirings, and in particular Martinmas week when the farm servants had their annual week's holiday, were vital to the economy of the town. It was the most important time in the year for the tradesmen and publicans with some shopkeepers selling more goods at Martinmas than in the rest of the year.[9] Thousands of young men and women, with the greater part of their year's wages, gathered in the town. From the tailors the men would buy a suit, shirts and trousers, from the shoemaker two pairs of boots, one working pair the other for Sunday, and from the stalls and jewellers, they bought trinkets, musical instruments and gifts for friends and families.[10] Much time and money was spent in the many pubs and there was often unrest.[11]

The decline in the hirings began after the First World War. In 1923 it was noted that the hirings appeared 'to be losing a good deal of interest', but the streets were still crowded with men and boys in the later 1930s.[12] The hirings were last held in 1939, and although that year 'a good number of farm hands' attended the cattle market in Martinmas week and shops were busy, there were no roundabouts or other amusements.[13] It was the Agricultural Wages (Regulation) Act and changing agricultural practice, in particular the end of working farm horses, as much as the Second World War, that brought an end to the hirings.[14]

Harvest hirings In August many men, mostly from the North Riding, attended Driffield market to be hired for harvest work in the fields.[15] In 1841 vast numbers from Ireland sought work.[16] The increased use of reaping machines reduced the use of the scythe and the need for skilled harvesters, but employment was found for the many who poured into the town from the grazing districts of north-west Yorkshire and Westmorland in 1863.[17] There were still many labourers, including Irish, seeking harvest work in 1891.[18]

CORN TRADE

In the mid 18th century the principal corn markets for the Yorkshire Wolds, and adjacent areas, were at Malton, from where the grain was taken to the West Riding via the River Derwent, and at Bridlington, from where it was transported by ship to London.[19] By the 1760s at least one corn factor, William Porter, landlord of the Blue Bell, was trading in Driffield, but he had the inconvenience and expense of having to carry goods overland for some five or six miles to reach a navigable stretch of the River Hull.[20] Following the opening of the

1 J. J. Clarke, *Hist. of Local Govt of UK* (1955), 18.

2 Best, *Farming Bks*, ed. Woodward, 140–1, 165.

3 C. T. Holderness, *Some Driffield Incidents 117 Years Ago* (1908), 32.

4 ERAO, DDX/904/1/1; *HA* 16 Nov. 1849.

5 *YH* 21 Nov. 1846; *HA* 17 Nov. 1848; 16 Nov. 1849; G. Moses, *Rural Moral Reform in 19th-Century England* (2007), 114.

6 J. Skinner, *Facts and Opinions Concerning Statute Hirings* (1861), 21.

7 *Yorks. Gazette* 18 Nov. 1854, quoted in G. Moses, 'Rustic and Rude': Hiring Fairs and their Critics in E Yorks.', *Rural History* 7 (2), 158.

8 S. Caunce, *Amongst Farm Horses: The Horselads of E Yorks.* (1991), 55–6, 62.

9 S. Caunce, 'Twentieth-Century Farm Servants: The Horselads of the ER of Yorks.', *Agricultural History Review* 39 (1991), 158.

10 H. Reffold, *Pie for Breakfast: Reminiscences of a Farmhand* (1984), 58; Moses, *Rural Moral Reform*, 109–10; J. Fairfax-Blakeborough, *Yorks.: East Riding* (1951), 50–1.

11 Below, soc. hist., fairs, feasts and galas.

12 *DT* 21 Nov. 1923 quoted in S. Parrott, 'The Decline of Hiring Fairs in the ER of Yorks.: Driffield *c.* 1874–1939', *Jnl of Regional and Local Studies* 16 (1996), 20; *DT* 25 Oct. 1930; ERAO, UDDR/1/8/32, Highways...Cttee, 7 Oct. 1935; E. Pontefract and M. Hartley, *Yorks. Tour* (1939), 66.

13 *DT* 2 Dec. 1939 quoted in Parrott, 'Decline in Hiring Fairs', 28.

14 Caunce, *Amongst Farm Horses*, 209–18.

15 ERAO, DDX/904/1/3; *HP* 27 Aug. 1841; 2 Sept. 1853.

16 *HP* 27 Aug. 1841.

17 Ibid. 21 Aug. 1863; 2 Sept. 1870.

18 *YH* 21 Aug. 1891.

19 W. Marshall, *The Rural Economy of Yorkshire*, vol. 2 (1788), 257; T. Hinderwell, *History and Antiquities of Scarborough* (1798), 254.

20 *Journal of the House of Commons*, xxxi. 185–6.

Year	*Wheat quarters*	*Barley quarters*	*Oats quarters*	*Total*
1820	9,533	4,558	14,795	28,886
1830	13,191	17,933	5,884	37,008
1840	14,354	19,430	6,300	40,084
1850	17,829	21,327	10,426	49,582
1860	16,358	20,953	9,830	47,141
1870	16,722	26,647	9,915	53,284

Source: Harrison, *Driffield*, 242–3. For other figs. see B. F. Duckham, *The Inland Waterways of E Yorks. 1700–1900*, (1973), 30.

Table 12. *Corn exported by canal from Driffield 1820–70*

Driffield navigation, and with the advantage of a more central location in an increasingly arable area, the town soon outstripped its rivals and by the late 1780s was the region's principal corn market.[1]

By 1792 over 20,000 quarters of corn were carried annually on the navigation via Hull to the West Riding, rising to over 30,000 quarters in the 1830s, and 40,000 in the 1840s.[2] In addition large quantities of wheat ground into flour by the numerous local millers were exported, totalling 8,000 sacks in 1819, 32,000 in 1838, 19,700 in 1844 and 23,000 in 1846.[3]

The claim by a resident that in 1848 over 70,000 quarters and in 1862 some 100,000 quarters of grain, were sent from Driffield to Wakefield and other West Riding markets may be an exaggeration but would include grain sent via the railway.[4] For many years before the late 1840s the corn market at Bridlington was entirely in the hands of Driffield factors and millers, who purchased at least 90 per cent of the corn sold there.[5]

The corn market continued to thrive throughout the rest of the 19th and early 20th century.[6] With the sale of 39,775 quarters of wheat, 48,699 quarters of barley, and 28,627 quarters of oats in 1915, Driffield was second only to Hull in quantity of corn sold in any Yorkshire market. Nationally Driffield lay 10th as regards sale of oats, 13th for sale of barley and 22nd for wheat, out of 160 corn markets.[7] In 1919 more barley and oats were sold at Driffield than anywhere else in Yorkshire.[8] The corn market remained in a reasonably flourishing state until the 1940s.[9]

Corn factors and merchants William Marshall noted in 1788 that the corn trade at Malton was in the hands of a few merchants 'who can generally make their own price', whilst at Driffield the numerous buyers were chiefly factors, who bought on commission, some of whom made £300 or £400 a year on 'the low commission of sixpence a quarter'.[10] The terms factor and merchant were used interchangeably for Driffield's early corn traders who included Jeremiah Jarratt, William Ushaw and Richard Porter, jun., in 1784.[11] They were soon afterwards joined by William and Richard Dunn, who initially had dealt in butter and bacon.[12] By 1784 Jarratt and Ushaw had warehouses at River Head and the Dunns built a warehouse there in 1787–9, on land leased from the navigation commissioners.

25. *Great Driffield: Mortimer's warehouse at River Head, 2011. Built 1877 for James Gidlow, soot merchant.*

1 Marshall, *Rural Economy*, 257; Hinderwell, *Scarborough*, 254; S. Neave and S. Ellis (eds), *An Historical Atlas of E Yorks.* (1996), 66–7; Harris, 'A rage of plowing', 209–10.
2 *Universal Brit. Dir.* (*c.* 1792), ii. 827; Table 12.
3 Legard, 'Farming ER Yorks.' 108.
4 ERAO, DDX/17/15, DDX/128/27.
5 Ibid. DDX/17/15.
6 Directories.
7 *Board of Agriculture and Fisheries: Agricultural Statistics 1915* (Parl. Papers 1916 [Cd. 8391] xxxii), pp. 119–23.
8 *Ministry of Agriculture and Fisheries: Agricultural Statistics 1919* (Parl. Papers 1920 [Cmd. 902] i) p. 94.
9 Atkinson, *Winds of Change*, 173. The market is said to have finally closed in 1964: Wynn, *Driffield*, 181.
10 Marshall, *Rural Economy*, 257.
11 *Bailey's Brit. Dir.* (1784), iii. 526–7.
12 Ibid. 526; *Universal Brit. Dir.* (*c.* 1792), ii. 828; ERAO, PE10/4 (Richard Dunn, cornfactor, 1785).

Additional warehouses built by the commissioners in 1792 were let to the Dunns and Jarratt.[1]

To avoid the canal tolls William Ushaw built a wharf and warehouse 12 miles from Driffield, on the River Hull at Baswick Steer in Brandesburton parish and sold his house, River Head House, and warehouses at Driffield to James Harrison, a corn merchant from New Malton, in 1802.[2] Following the bankruptcy in 1803 of Richard Porter, who had overstretched himself with the textile mill at Bell Mills, Harrison and the Dunns dominated the corn trade at Driffield.[3]

Richard Dunn died in 1811 and William Dunn four years later.[4] The former, described in his obituary as 'truly honest and upright in all his dealings', had a son Richard who became a partner in the Malton bank of Pease, Dunn & Pease, which had opened a branch in Driffield by 1815.[5] When the bank was taken over in 1820 Dunn returned to the corn trade regularly attending Wakefield market from Malton.[6] By the late 1820s he had moved to Wakefield, where he became one of the town's leading corn merchants living rather grandly at Heath House, Heath, by 1840.[7] Richard Dunn retained his Driffield connections, acquiring shares in Driffield Corn Exchange and he and his son, Richard Dacre Dunn, probably acted as the Wakefield agent for his brother-in-law Thomas Dawson, miller, of Poundsworth Mill, who had taken over the Dunns' Driffield cornfactoring business.[8] R. D. Dunn did act as agent for Dawson's sons, Richard Dunn Dawson (d. 1875) and Thomas Dawson (d. 1877), who with their brother George Robert Dawson (d. 1849) succeeded to the business on the death of their father in 1847.[9]

This family connection was important, for much of the corn traded at Driffield was destined for the Wakefield market. James Harrison (d. 1846), Driffield's leading corn dealer, was an attender at the corn market at Wakefield in 1822, and he had established a branch office there by 1834, run by his second son George W. Harrison.[10] His eldest son James, described as a corn, coal, seed and bone merchant and miller at Driffield in 1851, opened another office at Sculcoates, Hull where he was succeeded by his three sons James, George, and Edward Harrison.[11] The firm evidently closed, at both Driffield and Hull, not long before Edward's death in 1902. Thomas Dawson & Sons also closed at the end of the century, having survived being charged with fraud in 1870.[12]

Harrisons and Dawsons were the only corn merchants at Driffield in the 1850s, but the following decade they were joined by the antiquary John Robert Mortimer, who had built a grain warehouse and corn drying kiln at Fimber station on the Driffield to Malton line around 1856. From 1863 he appears to have concentrated his business at Driffield, extending a warehouse at the station there.[13] Mortimer (d. 1911) was declared bankrupt in 1887, but the business continued being eventually taken over by his son James who was killed during the First World War.[14] James Mortimer & Co., corn and seed merchants still existed in 2010 with an office and warehouse at River Head.

Other corn merchants in the 20th century were Thomas Wilson & Son, *c.* 1901–29, who attended on Thursdays from Bridlington, Daniel Byass & Sons, *c.* 1921–72, and the corn millers Bradshaws of Bell Mills.[15]

CORN MILLING

The streams of Driffield parish were used to drive several mills, but references to them before the 16th century are slight and difficult to interpret, and their sites are unknown. Eight mills were recorded on the extensive manor of Driffield in 1086, but some of those would have been on appurtenant lands outside Driffield parish.[16] The mills of Driffield were mentioned again in the late 12th century;[17] four water mills working in the later 13th century may have been in or adjoining Driffield parish,[18] and in 1423 there were two on the manor, worth £4 net a year.[19] One of the mills may have been Crawe Mill, whose dam had been recorded in 1383.[20] A water mill on the Routh Hall manor in 1570[21] was perhaps among the four mills which Richard Etherington, the lord of that manor, had in 1622.[22] There were water mills at Kelleythorpe and Elmswell.[23]

Most of the early mills were probably for the grinding of corn but cloth was fulled in some of them.

1 ERAO, DDX/1040/5; DDX/17/15.

2 Ibid. DDX/1318/5.Ushaw went bankrupt in 1808: *HP* 23 Aug. 1808.

3 *HP* 5 Oct. 1803.

4 E Yorks. Family Hist. Soc., *Driffield Monumental Inscriptions* (2003), 21.

5 *YH* 7 Sept. 1811; 12 Oct. 1816; 1 Aug. 1818.

6 Baines, *Hist. Yorks.* (1822), i. 437; below, this section, banking.

7 Pigot, *Nat. Com. Dir.* (1828–9), ii. 1120; *HP* 30 Oct. 1840; TNA, HO107/1272/11.

8 Dunn had a farm at Kilham. *LM* 4 Feb., 10 Mar., 22 Apr., 27 May 1843. Thomas Dawson had married Mary the eldest daughter of Richard Dunn, sen., in 1805: *YH* 12 Oct. 1805; Pigot, *Nat. Com. Dir.* (1822), 606.

9 *YH* 3 Nov. 1849; 31 Mar. 1877; *HP* 15 July 1870; 15 Jan. 1875.

10 Directories; *YH* 6 June 1846; *LM* 9 Aug. 1823.

11 TNA, HO107/2366; directories.

12 Directories; *HP* 15 July 1870.

13 Burton, *Malton & Driffield Junction Railway*, 45; directories.

14 S. Harrison, 'John Robert Mortimer' *E Yorks. Local Hist. Soc. Bulletin* 55 (Winter 1996–7), 20; *Lond. Gaz.* 14 Feb. 1888, 1029; directories. James Mortimer served in the Boer War and had risen to the rank of Lt-Colonel when he was killed in 1916: P. Howorth, *The Impact of War: Driffield and the Wolds 1914–1919* (2002), 16, 18, 74, 116–8.

15 Directories; *Driffield Souvenir Guide* (1972), 69; ibid. (1974), 42–3, 70; below, this section, milling.

16 *VCH Yorks.* ii. 197.

17 *Pipe R.* 1182 (PRS 31), 35–6; 1199 (PRS, N.S. 10), 55.

18 *Yorks. Inq.* i, p. 108; ii, p. 95.

19 TNA, C 139/4, no. 34.

20 *Cal. Close*, 1381–5, 589.

21 *Yorks. Fines*, i. 382.

22 Ibid. 1614–25, 205.

23 Below, Elmswell and Kelleythorpe.

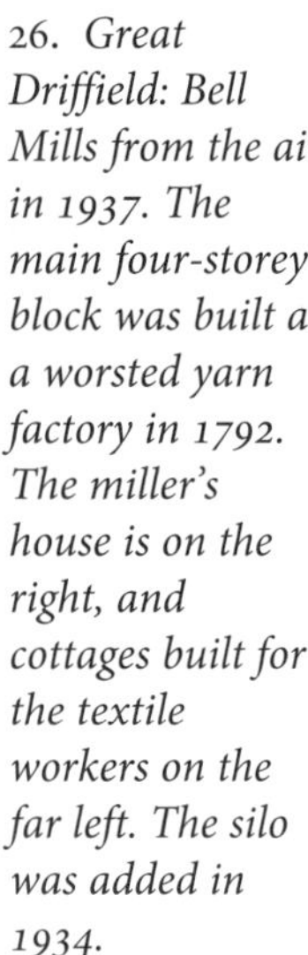
26. *Great Driffield: Bell Mills from the air in 1937. The main four-storey block was built as a worsted yarn factory in 1792. The miller's house is on the right, and cottages built for the textile workers on the far left. The silo was added in 1934.*

Other processes were carried on in the mills later, and in the 1790s a short-lived attempt was made to produce cloth industrially. Those changes, and the need later to compete with large modern concerns elsewhere, led to some of the mills being much improved technically, particularly as regards the source of power. In 1847 there were four water mills, two windmills, and three steam flour mills in Driffield.[1]

Despite their situation in a rural part of the Riding, Driffield's modernised mills survived longer than most because of their proximity to the good communications secured for the town in the 18th and 19th centuries. Eventually though, most of the mills were closed in the face of competition from national milling concerns; only one of them, Bell Mills, was still operating as a flour mill in 2010.[2]

Water Mills

Bell Mill(s) Bell Mill stood close to the town of Driffield but on the far side of the southern boundary stream, in Skerne parish, until a change of boundary brought it into Driffield.[3] One of the eight mills recorded on Driffield manor in 1086 may have stood on the site.[4] The water mill was owned by Watton priory by the early 14th century, and at the Dissolution it passed to the Crown.[5] The queen's mill called 'the Bell mill' was mentioned in 1574 relating to a dispute over another mill erected nearby.[6] The tenant was John Dawson, possibly a member of the family whose long connection with milling in the neighbourhood continued into the 19th century. In the later 16th century Dawson claimed that Bell Mill was damaged by the building then of a fulling mill or mills downstream at Bull Crook, particularly by changes made to the watercourse common to both enterprises.[7] At the inclosure of the two Driffields in 1742, Bell Mill was evidently a flour mill used by the inhabitants of Driffield parish, who were then made partly responsible for the maintenance of the road to Bell Mill.[8]

Bell Mill was held by Francis Dawson before 1753, when the occupier was William Long, a paper maker. Long and his son, also William, evidently developed the premises. By 1774 they had rebuilt Bell Mill, still described as a water corn mill, and there was then also a new house there.[9] All or part of the old corn mill may have been retained for paper making, for the corn mill was later said to adjoin a paper mill, as well as being close to the house; the location of the present mill house suggests that the early mills stood on the west side of Skerne Road.[10] Bell Mills was sold to James Boddy, *c.* 1773, and then to Thomas Baxter, both paper makers, before it was purchased by Richard and William Porter and Joseph and Whittell Sheepshanks in 1792.[11] They built a large textile factory close by, but to the east of the

1 *HP* 15 Oct. 1847. A fourth steam mill then under construction became a brewery and then a steam laundry: below, this section, brewing.

2 K. J. Allison, *ER Water-Mills* (E Yorks. Local Hist. Ser. 26, 1970), 17.

3 OS Map 1:10,560, Yorks. CLXI (1855 edn); OS Map 1:25,000, TA 05 (1953 edn).

4 *VCH Yorks.* ii. 197. A tradition with no support in the records has a Templar chapel standing there later, and the chapel's bell giving the mill its name: *BG* 4 Aug. 1977; *DT* 15 June 1994.

5 Allison, *ER Water-Mills*, 7–8; HUL, DDCV/199/2; DDCV2/53/1.

6 TNA, E178/2494; E134/23 Eliz/East13.

7 Ibid. E 123/5, f. 374b; E 178/2594; below, this section, textiles.

8 RDB, B/153/42; ERAO, IA. 41.

9 RDB, W/309/644; AS/401/667.

10 *LM* 10 Oct. 1818; 27 Mar. 1824.

11 RDB, AU/123/199; AU/124/200; BC/172/255; BQ/329/516; *Bailey's Brit. Dir.* (1784), iii. 526; *YC* 15 Apr. 1783; 27 Apr. 1790.

27. Great Driffield: Bell Mills, 2011. The mill was rebuilt after a fire in 1949.

road.[1] There were now three mills, described in 1804 as 'one used as a worsted thread manufactory, another formerly used as a bolting mill, but now or lately used as a paper mill and the other as a corn or flour mill'.[2] Following the bankruptcy and deaths of Richard and William Porter the mills were sold to Richard William Moxon of Hull, banker, and John Carrick of Welton in 1807.[3] They were leased in 1808, then sold in 1813, to Samuel Milbourn.[4] The mills were occupied in 1823 by Robert Fidler, corn miller, William Carrick, flax spinner, and Lawrence Duxbury, paper maker.[5] In 1825 all three mills were bought by Richard Arkwright, the lord of Skerne manor and son of the inventor Sir Richard Arkwright,[6] and the whole Skerne estate passed by a purchase of 1852 to Albert Denison, Lord Londesborough.[7]

Thomas Scotchburn, a Driffield solicitor, took on Bell Mills in 1826, and it was evidently for him that the former four-storey textile mill was converted for bone crushing and corn milling.[8] The bone mill and corn mill were under the one roof but driven by separate water wheels. The corn mill was fitted with new machinery by Hewes & Wren of Manchester, and included three pairs of French millstones and one pair of grey stones and a bolting mill.[9] The older corn mill and paper mill were then either demolished or converted to other uses. Scotchburn initially appears to have run both the corn and bone mills, but then only the bone mill.[10]

Following Scotchburn's death in 1837, the corn mill was let to Thomas and William Dunning and the bone mill to John Brigham from Beverley by 1840.[11] William Dunning, miller 1846–50, emigrated to America and was followed at Bell Mills by William Wrigglesworth (d. 1861) who moved from Albion Mill, Driffield.[12] Wrigglesworth was succeeded by his widow Charlotte, then his son John who was declared bankrupt in 1880.[13] The mill used only for corn milling was leased from *c.* 1882 by Richard Topham Kirby, who was living at Hull,

1 RDB, BQ/329/516; below, this section, textiles.

2 RDB, CH/2/3.

3 ERAO, DDX/17/15.

4 Ibid.

5 Baines, *Hist. Yorks.* (1823), ii. 196–7; *LM* 27 Mar. 1824. Fidler was a discharged debtor in 1830: *YH* 10 June 1830.

6 RDB, BQ/329/516; DY/19/23; *DNB*, *s.v.* Richard Arkwright; below, this section, textiles.

7 RDB, GX/322/387.

8 ERAO, DDX/17/15; below, this section, bone crushing.

9 Described as 'recently erected' in 1838: *YH* 12 May 1838. A breast-shot waterwheel that still existed in 1921 was said to have been erected by Hewes and Wren in 1828: *A Model Country Mill* (reprinted from *Milling*, 24 Dec. 1921), [3].

10 Pigot, *Nat. Com. Dir.* (1828–9), ii. 930; Pigot, *Nat. Com. Dir.* (1834), 711; White, *Hull & District Dir.* (1831), 248.

11 White, *Dir. N & ER Yorks* (1840), 213; below, this section, bone crushing.

12 Directories; *YH* 3 Aug. 1850; E Yorks. Family Hist. Soc., *Skerne Monumental Inscriptions* (1981), 6; *Lond. Gaz.* 7 Mar. 1851, 676; TNA, HO107/2366.

13 TNA, RG9/3608; *Lond. Gaz.* 19 Mar. 1880, 2161.

1871–81, and Selby in 1891.[1] At the time of his death in 1894 he was said to be of Bell Mills, Driffield and Victoria Mills, Wilmington, Hull.[2] Bell Mills was taken over by the manager Eleazer B. Bradshaw who had worked for Kirby since 1875.[3] Bradshaw bought Bell Mills from W. F. H. Denison, earl of Londesborough, in 1909.[4] He died in 1921 and was succeeded by his three sons.[5]

It was probably the proximity of the canal and the railways which made it worth repeatedly improving Bell Mills to enable them to compete with larger, regional millers.[6] Rollers were installed in 1882, making it possible to process North American corn imported by way of the canal. The mill was assisted by steam by 1889; in 1893 one of the mill's two water wheels was replaced with a water turbine, and in 1921 the whole of the milling machinery was replaced.[7] By 1938 electricity, which had been used for lighting since 1886, was also running machinery. Steam ceased to be used following a fire in 1949, and in 1994 the turbine ceased to operate.[8] The mill was enlarged in 1890 re-equipped then and about 1920, and in 1934 new warehouses and a silo were added.[9] A fire damaged part of the complex in 1949, though the mill building, warehouses, and office block were all saved. The mill was nevertheless rebuilt as a six-storeyed block in 1951–2 and 1955.[10] A new plant for making animal feed was built in 1968, replacing the company's mill at River Head in Driffield.[11] The rebuilt and enlarged plant was again refitted in 1990, when over 69,000 tonnes of flour, were produced annually at Bell Mills.[12] E. B. Bradshaw & Sons Ltd, still a family firm in 2010, deals in flour, seeds, and fertilisers and has a garden centre.

King's Mill In 1589 Thomas Etherington held a half share in a water mill called King's Mill, which he then left to his son George.[13] Probably the same was the corn mill called Barber Mill, which was held in half shares by other members of the Etherington family in the late 16th and earlier 17th century. A half share in the mill had been bought by Marmaduke Etherington and his son George before 1654, when George sold his interest to a Driffield baker, John Stork.[14] King's Mill was recorded again at inclosure in 1742, when it stood between Great and Little Driffield, and evidently served both communities; the proprietors were then Joseph Todd and others.[15] Major building works were carried out on the mill in 1778 when John Dickon (d. 1805) took over the mill; he was followed by his son William (d. 1841).[16] William Witty was miller *c.* 1849–60, then Henry Dickon Marshall (d. 1910), grandson of William Dickon, who was employing seven men in 1881.[17] The mill was driven by water diverted into a mill dam from the nearby Driffield Beck until a new four-storey mill, equipped with rollers and powered by steam, was built in the later 19th century. A serious fire at the mill in 1906 caused milling to be abandoned in favour of farming.[18] The mill house and other buildings were later occupied as a private house.

Walk/Dye Garth Mill A former fulling, or walk, mill in Dye(house) Garth Lane was left by John Drinkrow in 1776 to Thomas Drinkrow who in turn sold it to William Jarratt in 1797.[19] Jarratt bequeathed the mill in 1806 to Mark Laybourne, turner, who is said to have used it for wood turning, but it was in use as a flax works by 1810.[20] The mill was sold to Robert Fisher, miller, in 1813, who that year sold it to John Sever of Garton, farmer, who had it as a corn mill in 1823 under the name of Dye Garth Mill.[21] The mill was bought by Henry Abbey of Garton, farmer, in 1836, and Philip Abbey was the miller 1845–52, his son Thomas in 1861.[22] It was known as Abbey's Mill or Walk Mill.[23] The mill was later run as part of Albion Mill, and had become a storehouse by 1903.[24]

1 *Model Country Mill*, [1]; *Kelly's Dir. N & ER Yorks.* (1889), 454; TNA, RG10/4780; RG11/4758; RG12/3877.

2 *YH* 19 Feb. 1894; Bulmer, *Dir. E Yorks.* (1892), 271, 1211.

3 TNA, RG11/4758; *Model Country Mill*, [1]; *BG* 4 Aug. 1977; *DT* 15 June 1994; *Kelly's Dir. N & ER Yorks.*(1897), 533.

4 RDB, 113/335/312.

5 *Model Country Mill*, [1–2].

6 Illus. at HUL, DX/144/3 (A 5069/17). Following based on Allison, *ER Water-Mills*, 16–18, 42–3.

7 *Kelly's Dir. N & ER Yorks.* (1889), 454; *Model Country Mill*, [2–3].

8 Inf. from H. Graham Mackrill, Elmswell, 2004.

9 Illus. at HUL, DX/144/3 (A 5068/17; A 5070/5–6); datestone for 1934 on rebuilt premises.

10 Datestones, including that of the 1792 building ; *BG* 4 Aug. 1977; R. Wood, *Policing from Wansford Road* (Driffield Crime Prevention Panel, 1997), 81 (illus.); inf. from S. Bradshaw, Driffield, 2006.

11 *BG* 4 Aug. 1977; below, this section, seed crushing and animal feed.

12 *BG* 4 Aug. 1977; *DT* 15 June 1994.

13 TNA, C 142/220, no. 73; BIA, precentorship wills, Thomas Etherington, 1589 (will).

14 TNA, C 142/238, no. 41; C 142/259, no. 33; C 142/391, no. 59; ibid. CP 25(2)/614/1654 Trin. no. 77; ERAO, DDX/585; *Yorks. Royalist Composition Papers*, iii (YAS Rec. Ser. 20), p. 206; Ross, *Driffield*, 27–8. Thomas Etherington had a daughter named Barbara (Berberye): BIA, precentorship wills, Thomas Etherington, 1589 (will).

15 RDB, B/153/42; ERAO, IA. 41; OS Map 1:10,560, Yorks. CLXI (1855 edn).

16 Holderness, *Some Driffield Incidents*, 21; *YH* 17 Apr. 1841.

17 *HP* 20 Aug. 1841, 27 Oct. 1854; 25 Aug. 1876; *YH* 10 Nov. 1849; TNA, RG11/ 4794/ 44; directories.

18 Allison, *ER Water-Mills*, 43; directories; illus. at HUL, DX/144/3 (A 5071/11); *DT* 22 May 1986 (illus.); C. Clubley, *Driffield in Old Picture Postcards* (1985), pl. 60.

19 ERAO, DDX/17/15.

20 Ibid.; RDB, CP/342/525.

21 Baines, *Hist. Yorks.* (1823), ii. 196; *HP* 21 Feb. 1834; below, this section, textiles.

22 ERAO, TA/13; ibid. PE/10/T. 120; TNA, RG9/3608; *YH* 3 Apr. 1852, 9 Apr. 1853.

23 TNA, HO 107/2366; ERAO, PE/10/T. 120; ibid. TA/13; OS Map 1:10,560, Yorks. CLXI (1855 edn); White, *Dir. Hull & York* (1851), 603; (1858), 661.

24 Below, this section; J. Nicholson, *The Capital of the Yorkshire Wolds* (1903), 27; Clubley, *Driffield*, pl. 62.

Dawson's Riverhead Mill By 1823 Thomas Dawson of Poundsworth Mill tenanted a corn mill in Driffield, then described as at River Head but evidently standing further south, on the west side of the canal.[1] Originally a water mill it had probably been converted to steam by 1847 when it was being used as a bone mill.[2]

Poundsworth (Pounceford) Mill Poundsworth Mill, fed by the stream running along the south-western boundary of Driffield parish, stood just across that boundary in Hutton Cranswick parish. It may have existed in 1589 when the lease of 'Pownsworthe' was left by Thomas Etherington to his son Richard.[3] The mill had evidently been owned by the Crompton family in the 17th century, and was sold in 1702 to James Rickinson of Scarborough.[4] In 1733 Poundsworth Mill and associated land was sold by William Rickinson, along with the manor of Driffield, to Richard Langley. It then passed down with the Langley estate until sold in 1918.[5] In 1742 it was called Red Mill, and it or an earlier structure was then commemorated by the nearby Burnt Mill bridge.[6] Corn was ground in Poundsworth or Red Mill by several generations of the Dawson family from at least 1760 when Thomas Dawson was the tenant. He was followed by his son George and grandson Thomas Dawson (d. 1847).[7] The last was also a leading cornfactor, a business carried on by his three sons George Robert, Richard Dunn and Thomas Dawson along with Poundsworth mill and farm.[8] Two years after the death of Thomas Dawson in 1877, the farm and water and steam powered corn mill was leased to Stephen and William Duggleby.[9] In 1889 John Dunn, miller and lime burner, held the premises.[10] They were evidently given up soon afterwards.[11] The large mill, of four storeys and an attic, very likely had more than one set of stones, and was sometimes called Poundsworth Mills.[12] The building had been demolished by the 1960s.[13]

Windmills

North End Mill A windmill presumably once stood in Millhill Close, on the motte of medieval castle at the north end of Driffield, but it had gone before 1742.[14] A smock windmill had been built nearby on North End Close by the end of 1804.[15] It was sold by Thomas G. Lawson, surgeon to John Wilkinson of Huggate, yeoman and Joseph Clement of Driffield, surgeon, in 1808.[16] William Parkin was evidently the owner by 1819, having improved the mill at a cost of £1,200, and he was the miller there in 1823.[17] The mill was let that year when it is described as a tower wind corn mill 'containing seven floors, three pair of French and one pair of Grey stones, five regulating sails (Hooper's patent) with 'flies' and gallery'.[18] It later had a Lincolnshire-style ogee cap.[19] John Simpson was the miller *c.* 1828–31, when it was called Mount Pleasant Mill.[20] In 1845 it was owned by the surgeon Washington Harrison and occupied by Chambers Sproxton, miller.[21] Steam power was added by 1856.[22] The work was probably carried out by John Harker, millwright, who claimed £7 7*s.* from Harrison, the balance of account for work at the mill then held by William Witty.[23] North End Mill,[24] sometimes known instead by the names of its millers, lost its top and sails in a gale in 1860, but apparently continued to be operated for a few years more, presumably as a steam mill.[25] In 1864 the premises were sold to Henry Angas, a retired draper, who then cleared the site and built a house, successively called Millfield and Highfield, there. The earlier use is recalled by the street name Windmill Hill.[26]

Wansford Road Mill A post mill was built south-east of the town, apparently *c.* 1825.[27] It ground corn until at least 1858,[28] but evidently ceased to be used soon afterwards. The building has been removed.[29]

1 Baines, *Hist. Yorks.* (1823), ii. 196; ERAO, TA/13; ibid. PE/10/T. 120.
2 Below, this section, steam mills.
3 BIA, precentorship wills, Thomas Etherington, 1589 (will).
4 HUL, DDSY/34/96, DDCV/87/3(a).
5 HRO, DBHT/9/890.
6 RDB, B/153/42 [roads]; T. Jefferys, *Map of Yorks.* (1775).
7 NYRO ZDS/IV/1/6/1; *YH* 4 Dec. 1847; 2 Sept 1848; ERAO, DDX983/1/7.
8 *YH* 3 Nov. 1849; *HP* 15 July 1870; 15 Jan. 1875. For more on the Dawsons see above, this section, corn trade.
9 *YH* 31 Mar 1877; 22 Aug. 1878; NYRO, ZDS IV/IV/4/6.
10 Directories.
11 Watts, 'Industrial geography', 95.
12 OS Map 1:10,560, Yorks. CLXI (1855 edn).
13 Allison, *ER Water-Mills*, 43; illus. at HUL, DX/144/3 (A 5068/2; A 5069/8); Clubley, *Driffield*, pl. 61.
14 ERAO, IA. 41.
15 *HP* 15 Jan. 1805; HUL, DDMC/26/26.
16 RDB, CH/302/481.
17 HUL, DDLG/15/59; Baines, *Hist. Yorks.* (1823), ii. 196; *DT* 15 Jan. 1997, which erroneously has the windmill built in 1819.
18 *YH* 11 Oct 1823; *HA* 30 Jan. 1824
19 Illus. at NMR (Swindon), BB84/2699; Clubley, *Driffield*, pl. 40.
20 Pigot, *Nat. Com. Dir.* (1828-9), ii. 931; White, *Dir. Hull & District* (1831), 248.
21 ERAO, PE10/T120.
22 Sheahan and Whellan, *Hist. York & ER.* ii. 498.
23 *HP* 30 July 1858.
24 H. Teesdale, *Map of Yorks.* (1828); OS Map 1:10,560, Yorks. CLXI (1855 edn).
25 (John Simpson) RDB, HX/246/280; A. Bryant, *Map of ER. Yorks.* (1829). (Robert Oxtoby & Son) White, *Dir. E.R Yorks* (1840), 205; (William Wilson) White, *Dir. Hull & York* (1851), 603. (Tate & Son) White, *Dir. Hull & York* (1858), 661. (John Hill) *Slater's Royal Nat. Com. Dir. of Yorks.* (1864), 117; *HP* 2 Mar. 1860.
26 Ross, *Driffield*, 97, 180; *DT*, 15 Jan. 1997; OS Map 1:2,500, Yorks. CLXI. 12 (1893 edn); below, buildings [Highfield].
27 Baines, *Hist. Yorks.* (1823), ii. 196; H. Teesdale, *Map of Yorks.* (1828).
28 White, *Dir. Hull & York* (1851), 603; (1858), 661.
29 Ross, *Driffield*, 97 is apparently incorrect in dating the demolition to *c.* 1855.

28. *Great Driffield: Albion Mill, Albion Street, 1975. Built as a steam flour mill in 1847, the building was demolished in 1989.*

Steam Mills

Riverhead Mill In 1842 John Harker millwright built a steam powered mill, of four storeys and an attic, for James Harrison & Sons, corn merchants, on the east side of the canal at River Head.[1] Initially a bone mill, it was also used for corn milling in 1849–64.[2] Riverhead Mill was given up about 1900,[3] and in 1902 the Harrison heirs sold the premises, comprising a house, mills, warehouses, and some 4 a., to the Driffield Pure Linseed, Cotton & Union Cake Co. Ltd, which had a large mill nearby. The company evidently used the former mill as a warehouse, before selling it in 1949 to E. B. Bradshaw & Sons Ltd, who re-equipped it and used it for flour milling for a few years following the destruction of Bell Mills.[4] It was then used by Bradshaws for making animal feed until 1968.

Albion Mill A large steam flour mill was built in 1847 on Dye(house) Garth Lane (Albion Street) for Chambers Sproxton and William Wrigglesworth, who were then leasing Poundsworth Mill.[5] The partnership was dissolved in 1851 and Sproxton remained as miller for a few years. He was followed *c.* 1860 by William Witty who took over the neighbouring Walk Mill and ran it as part of Albion Mill, which also gave its name to the street.[6] In 1872 and 1889 Albion Mill was being used as a saw mill, but by the 1890s corn was being ground there again by Thomas Holtby, also a brewer and maltster in Driffield. Milling evidently ceased about 1905, though corn and flour dealing continued from the premises.[7] The building taken over by East Yorkshire Farmers Ltd *c.* 1947 had been bought by 1972 for a Farmway Country Store, dealing in animal feeds,

1 Above, this section, corn trade.
2 Directories.
3 Directories; OS Map 1:10,560, Yorks. CLXI (1855 edn); ERAO, TA/13; ibid. PE/10/T. 120; TNA, HO 107/2366.
4 RDB, 49/27/26 (1902); 824/576/492; below, this section, seed crushing and animal feed; Watts, 'Industrial geography', 97.
5 Allison, *ER Water-Mills*, 42; *HP* 15 Oct. 1847.
6 Directories; Nicholson, *Capital of the Yorks. Wolds*, 27; OS Map 1:2,500, Yorks. CLXI. 12 (1893 edn).
7 Ross, *Driffield*, 81; directories. R. T. Holtby was described as a miller in 1903: RDB, 55/474/451 (1903).

29. *Great Driffield: The Driffield & East Riding Pure Linseed Cake Co. mill, print of 1878. A major extension including a clock tower was added in 1870 to the south of the original four-storey range built alongside the railway line in 1862.*

equestrian supplies, and other country goods.[1] The concern demolished the former mill in 1989, and have erected new buildings on the extensive site.[2]

Other The third steam-driven corn mill that existed in 1847 has not been definitely identified although it was possibly the Riverhead Mill owned by Marmaduke Langley and tenanted by Thomas Dawson of Poundsworth Mill.[3] Built as a water mill before 1823 it may have been converted to steam in the 1840s.[4] It was used for bone crushing by 1828.[5] Taken over by Brighams in 1877 the bone mill was demolished *c.* 1900.[6]

SEED CRUSHING AND ANIMAL FEED

By the end of the 19th century the crushing of corn, linseed, and cotton seed to obtain oils and produce cake for cattle had become Driffield's chief industry.[7] James Harrison & Sons had established an oil-seed crushing mill at canal head by 1860. Early the following year William Jackson, a farmer at Garton on the Wolds, purchased three lots of Harrison's oil-cake which he fed to his cattle and sheep. When animals died Jackson claimed that the cake was adulterated and took Harrison to the Exchequer court seeking compensation. The case was lost but it highlighted the problem of adulterated feedstuffs.[8]

Driffield & East Riding Pure Linseed Cake Co. Concern about the quality of the feedstuffs available led substantial farmers and others from the locality to found at the end of 1861 the Driffield & East Riding Pure Linseed Cake Co. Ltd 'for the manufacturing of unadulterated linseed cake ... for rearing and fattening cattle'.[9] The first chairman was Thomas Hopper, farmer, of Kelleythorpe, and the other directors were the farmers Francis Jordan of Eastburn and Richard Holtby of Haywold, Huggate, and James Elgey, chemist, and William Jarratt, bank manager, both of Driffield. The company acquired an acre of land to the south of the railway line, extending from Eastgate to the Wansford road. It was close to the railway station and canal head. Here a mill designed by Joseph Wright of Hull was erected in 1862 at a cost of £6,000, comprising a four-storeyed range, 220 ft long by 150 ft wide. At the end of the decade the business was booming and 30–40 men were employed there. In 1870, when William Jarratt was chairman of the company, the mill was enlarged with a southern range along Anderson Street, and buildings connecting that to the earlier northern block, crowned by a tower containing a clock and five bells.[10] Richard Davison, company secretary, perfected and patented a cotton seed cleaning machine in 1876

1 *DT* 23 Aug. 1947; ERAO, UDDR/1/1/46, Housing...Cttee, 5 June 1972.
2 Inf. from Farmway Country Store, 2003; *DT* 12 Oct. 1989.
3 ERAO, DDX/17/15; ibid. TA/13; ibid. PE/10/T. 120.
4 Above, this section, water mills.
5 H. Teesdale, *Map of Yorks.* (1828).
6 Below, this section, bone crushing.
7 Bulmer, *Dir. E Yorks.* (1892), 165.
8 *Court of Exchequer Feb. 13th 1862: Jackson v Harrison* (1862), copy at Hull History Centre.
9 *HP* 24 Jan. 1862.
10 Ibid. 18 Feb. 1870; W. Jarratt, *The Character and Condition of the Linseed Cake Trade* (1870); H. W. Brace, *History of Seed Crushing in Great Britain* (1960), 57–8.

and the company began manufacturing cotton cake two years later when it was claimed that the mill was 'one of the largest and most complete' in England, 'if not Europe'.[1] It was fitted up with electric light in 1885 and soon after it was said to be employing about 100 workers.[2] A three-storeyed oil refinery was added in 1887 shortly before the greater part of the works was destroyed by fire.[3] The company, then under the chairmanship of William Jarratt's son, William Otley Jarratt, was forced into liquidation, but in 1888 the premises were taken over and rebuilt on a slightly reduced scale by a new company, the Driffield Pure Linseed, Cotton & Union Cake Co. Ltd, still with the same chairman and secretary.[4]

New products dealt in included artificial manures, said to have been made there from 1889, and clover and other seeds.[5] Described as 'the most important commercial undertaking in the town' in 1892, the mill continued to produce animal feeds until 1940 when seed crushing ceased.[6] In 1952 the company sold its 'recently occupied' mills, and other premises at River Head, to White's Sugar Mills Ltd, a Hull concern which had already established itself in the mill as a lessee by 1947.[7] White's was succeeded by Charles Southwell & Co. Ltd which made sweets in the works until its closure about 1970.[8] The extensive building was used for a time as a billiard hall and nightclub but later stood empty.[9] Demolition was under way in 2006 when the clock tower came down, but some buildings still stood in 2010.[10]

Messrs F. C. Matthews, Son & Co. Ltd (Eastgate Mills)
Francis Matthews was making animal feed cakes from various sorts of corn finely ground and mixed with locust and spices by 1864 at his Eastgate works. He was an early maker of compound cakes, corn and oil-cake being mixed and pressed in box presses.[11] In 1866 Matthews was advertising his new corn feeding cake for beasts and sheep as a substitute for linseed cake and five years later was claiming the patronage of the Prince of Wales and leading agriculturists.[12] The company was producing linseed and cotton cakes as well as corn cake by 1878.[13] In the late 1890s the chairman of F. C. Matthews, Son & Co. was Harrison Holt, a partner in the large seed crushing firm of Willows, Holt & Willows in Hull, which in 1899 merged with like concerns in Hull to form British Oil & Cake Mills (BOCM).[14] It was probably due to Holt that new Anglo presses for producing feed cakes were installed around 1909.[15] The firm ceased seed crushing in the early 1930s.[16]

BONE CRUSHING AND MANURE MANUFACTURE

Bone Crushing

The 19th century saw notable additions to the traditional soil improvers used in the Driffield area. The chief fertiliser *c.* 1800 was farmyard manure, although lime, soot, pigeon dung, and rape dust were also applied, and the navigation allowed the importation of night soil, stable manure, and sweepings from Hull. The great innovation was crushed bone, or bone dust which was found particularly successful for cultivating turnips, after which a good crop of wheat was obtained on even the worst land. Bone manure was in use in 'great abundance' on the Yorkshire Wolds by 1822 when the solicitor Thomas Scotchburn (d. 1837) noted that it had 'long been a matter of surprise' in the neighbourhood 'that no mill or machine for grinding bones' had ever been erected at Driffield.[17] He remedied this by leasing Bell Mills, evidently for this purpose, in 1826.[18] Two years later Scotchburn sold Sir Tatton Sykes 214 quarters of bones at £147 for the Sledmere estate.[19] Another 'bone dust manufacturer' Benjamin Dodsworth was based at River Head in 1828–9, to be followed there by Robert Middleton by 1834.[20] They were almost certainly based at the bone mill, later tenanted by Thomas Dawson, which was situated on the west side of the navigation about ⅓ mile from River Head.[21] Bones would be procured by John Simpson, bone merchant, who had moved from Wilmington, Hull to Driffield where he died in 1835.[22] Some would have been

1 *Lond. Gaz.* 28 Apr. 1876; *Driffield and East Riding Pure Linseed Cake Company's Quarterly Jnl*, Oct. 1878, copy at HRO, DBR/2212.

2 Harrison, *Driffield*, 278; *HP* 13 Feb. 1885.

3 Ross, *Driffield*, 33–4.

4 RDB, 18/372/352 (1887); 25/668/496; 27/211/200 (both 1888); *Lond. Gaz.* 3 July 1888, 3650; ibid. 16 Sept. 1892; Brace, *Seed Crushing*, 105–6; illus. Harrison, *Driffield*, pl. 11.

5 Directories; Harrison, *Driffield*, 281. There is no mention of artificial manures in the detailed account of the firm in *The Century's Progress*, 222.

6 Ross, *Driffield*, 97; *Kelly's Dir. N & ER Yorks.* (1893), 406; Brace, *Seed Crushing*, 106.

7 *Kelly's Dir. N & ER Yorks.* (1937), 443; RDB, 910/126/99; Harrison, *Driffield*, 281. The Driffield Pure Linseed, Cotton & Union Cake Co. Ltd was wound up voluntarily in 1965: *Lond. Gaz.* 7 May 1965, 4498.

8 NMR (Swindon), Wailes 225/69 21/22.

9 *DP* 11 Oct. 1995; *HDM* 24 Aug. 1999.

10 *DT* 25 Oct. 2006; 22 Apr. 2009.

11 Brace, *Seed Crushing*, 89, 105.

12 *HP* 14 Sept. 1866; 7 July 1871; A. Harris, 'Francis Cook Matthews of Driffield', *E Yorks. Local Hist. Soc. Bulletin* 43 (Winter 1990–1), 10; below, this section, artificial manure.

13 *HP* 10 May 1878.

14 Hull History Centre, unbound pages from *Men of the Period: England* [1897], 223–4; Brace, *Seed Crushing*, 134. Holt moved to Driffield from Hull by 1879 when he was living at no. 30 New Road, and moved to Highfield in the 1880s: Directories; G. K. Brandwood, *Temple Moore* (1997) 21.

15 Brace, *Seed Crushing*, 53–4, 105.

16 Below, this section, artificial manure.

17 ERAO, DDX/17/15.

18 Ibid.; Holderness, *Some Driffield Incidents*, 66–7; Pigot, *Dir.* (1828–9), 390; (1834), 711; *YH* 3 Mar. 1827.

19 HUL, DDSY/98/110.

20 Pigot, *Nat. Com. Dir.* (1828–9), 390; (1834), 711.

21 H. Teesdale, *Map of Yorks.* (1828); ERAO, PE10/T120

22 *HP* 23 Jan. 1835; *YH* 3 Aug. 1844.

30. *Great Driffield: Riverhead Mill, 2011. A steam-powered mill built in 1842 for crushing bones and grinding corn. The large metal tie plates were made at Harker's foundry.*

collected locally but most would have come via the navigation from Hull that 'great emporium of bones'.[1]

In 1840 there were two bone dust manufacturers at River Head, William and John Brigham, from Beverley, who had also taken over the bone mill at Bell Mills, and Thomas Dawson, the miller at Poundsworth Mills, who was tenanting the bone mill on the west side of the navigation.[2] Another bone mill was erected by the corn merchant James Harrison at River Head, on the east side, in 1842.[3] Later F. C. Matthews began bone crushing at his Eastgate works and by 1864 there were four concerns in the town.[4]

Dawson's canal-side bone mill was taken over by Brighams in 1877, having moved from Bell Mills.[5] The partnership of Brigham & Co., bone crushers, was dissolved in December 1879, but a firm of that name was listed as manure merchants at River Head in 1889.[6] Harrisons were last listed as bone crushers in 1892, but Matthews, after a gap, were recorded as such 1905–25.[7]

Artificial Manure

From the mid-19th century until the First World War the manufacture of artificial fertilizers was one of Driffield's main industries.

F. C. Matthews, Son & Co. Francis Cook Matthews (1812–84), established as a chemist and druggist in 1835, began the commercial production of artificial fertilizer in 1847.[8] Although declared bankrupt in 1848, he continued to make chemical fertilizers and sold them through Kagenbusch, Dent, Matthews & Co. based in his premises in Middle Street.[9] The fertilizer had been 'devised' by P. Kagenbusch, a pupil of the German chemist Justus von Liebig, who in 1848 had lectured on the subject at the Corn Exchange to 'a tolerably numerous audience, amongst whom were some of the leading farmers of the neighbourhood'.[10] In 1850 Matthews disposed of what remained at Driffield of Kagenbusch's fertilizer and announced his intention of manufacturing 'a new artificial manure', this time in conjunction with Hodgson & Simpson of Wakefield.[11]

Using bones Matthews made ammonia-phosphate for corn and grass and nitro-phosphate for root crops and rape, in new works in Eastgate South, where he was

1 Harris, 'Bones', 8; *HA* 13 July 1849.
2 White, *Dir. N & ER Yorks.* (1840), 202, 205, 213; *YH* 29 July 1854; ERAO, PE10/T120; above, this section, milling.
3 HUL, DDSY/98/113; above, this section, milling.
4 *Slater's Royal Nat. Com. Dir. of Yorks.* (1864), 114.
5 NYRO, ZDS IV/10/4/8.
6 HUL, DDSY/101/85; directories. The bone mill still stood in 1890 but was demolished within the following 20 years: OS Map 1:2,500, Yorks. CLXI. 16 (1893, 1910 edn).
7 Directories.
8 Token at Southburn Archaeological Museum 2010; White, *Dir. N & ER Yorks* (1840), 205; Harris, 'Matthews', 10.
9 *Lond. Gaz.* 3 Nov 1848; Harris, 'Matthews', 10.
10 *HP* 28 Apr. 1848.
11 Harris, 'Matthews', 10.

employing three men in 1851.[1] The new fertilizers were offered at prices lower than guano, crushed bones and superphosphate of lime, the other favoured manures. The company flourished and by 1856 it was reckoned that its artificial manures were being used on at least 15,000 a. in the district.[2] In the early 1860s Matthews' son, an analytical chemist, joined the firm which by then had 10 employees.[3] By 1866 the company was also making livestock feeds from imported corn, linseed and cottonseed and crushing bones, and by 1871 enjoyed the patronage of the Prince of Wales and 'other leading agriculturists'.[4] On Matthews' death in 1884 the works in Eastgate comprised a four-storey mill equipped for crushing oilseeds and making animal feeds, sheds where bones were ground and manures prepared, warehouses, workshops, a laboratory, extensive stables and houses for a clerk and foreman.[5] In 1885 the firm was incorporated as F. C. Matthews, Son & Co. Ltd. and still produced artificial manure in 1912.[6] and remained in business, latterly only as seed crushers, until the early 1930s.[7] The company was in voluntary liquidation in 1934 when its Eastgate premises were sold. The buildings have been largely demolished and a builders' merchant occupied the remaining buildings in 2010.

Other Manufacturers By the 1860s there were two, or possibly three, other local manufacturers of artificial manures.[8] John Sterriker, with premises in the Market Place, had before 1852 purchased from Matthews his business as a druggist and manufacturer of lemonade and soda water, and the right to sell sulphuric acid and nitrate of soda for agricultural purposes.[9] Soon he was advertising himself as an agricultural chemist and by 1864 was making chemical manures. In the late 1870s he was selling bone manure.[10] Nothing further is known of the artificial manure works in Middle Street, put up for sale by Elijah Temple in 1869.[11] By 1864 and until the late 1890s a tanner, William Foster, made chemical fertilizers at Little Driffield.[12] After rebuilding, the Driffield & East Riding Pure Linseed Cake Co. was said to have prepared artificial manures.[13]

BREWING AND MALTING

Brewing

Driffield was well-situated for brewing, with plentiful supplies of local barley and good quality water of the right sort, 'unimpregnated with mineral particles'.[14] As elsewhere, brewing was at first small-scale, and carried on for consumption at home or for sale in the house where it was made. Gradually some licensed victuallers began to supply other public houses, and eventually larger-scale breweries were developed. Those who ran the breweries and sold beer on wholesale terms to publicans and private customers in quantities larger than a cask or gallon were termed common brewers.[15]

Among the earliest common brewers in the town were Thomas Barmby, *c.* 1784–92, Jeremiah Laybourne, *c.* 1795–1807, and John Dobson *c.* 1801–7.[16] There were three breweries in 1823, five in 1845 and six in 1851 when around 30 people were employed as brewers or maltsters in the town.[17] Three Driffield brewers went bankrupt in the 1850s, but there were still six breweries in the town in 1864.[18] Brewing remained 'considerable' in 1892, but declined soon afterwards as larger, regional brewers like John Smith's of Tadcaster (WR) bought up the licensed houses and breweries.[19] In 1900 it was noted that the brewing industry at Driffield, 'formerly of some importance' had entirely disappeared; 'the breweries most recently closed are turned into warehouses and bottling stores, and all the beer consumed is brought by rail or road from Hull, Scarborough and other towns'.[20]

Holtby's (Eastgate Brewery) Probably the largest brewery in Driffield was that built up by the Holtbys.[21] It may have originated in the malting business run by Milburn Allison in Doctor Lane, now Queen Street, in 1823. In 1832 David Holtby leased a malting for 14 years from William Dickon of King's Mill, in Doctor Lane, and he set up a brewery that year.[22] Holtby (d. 1838) was succeeded by his widow Mary. Between 1848 and 1851 the brewing and malting operation was removed from

1 Ibid.; Harrison, *Driffield*, 356; TNA, HO 107/2366. Matthews later had a second 'mill', possibly in Eastgate North, known as the 'Little Mill': Howorth, *Year Gone By*, 35.
2 Sheahan and Whellan, *Hist. York & ER*. ii. 498.
3 Harris, 'Matthews', 10.
4 Ibid.; Slater, *Dir.* 1864 – see advert; *HP* 12 Feb. 1864; 7 July 1871; 5 May 1875; 10 May 1878.
5 Harris, 'Matthews', 10–11; HUL, DDSY/101/88.
6 *DT* 20 Apr. 1912.
7 Directories; *Lond. Gaz.* 11 Apr. 1933, 2509.
8 *Slater's Royal Nat. Com. Dir. of Yorks.* (1864), 117.
9 *HP* 30 July 1852.
10 *Post Office Dir. N & ER Yorks.* (1857), 1240; (1872), 355; *Slater's Royal Nat. Com. Dir. of Yorks.* (1864), 117; Atkinson, *Winds of Change*, 64.
11 *DT* 31 July 1869.
12 Directories; Howorth, *Year Gone By*, 35; Atkinson, *Winds of Change*, 64, 73.
13 Above, this section, seed crushing.
14 *Post Office Dir. N & ER Yorks.* (1857), 1238.
15 E. M. Sigsworth, *The Brewing Trade During the Industrial Revolution* (1967), 3.
16 ERAO, PE10/4; RDB, CH/368/598; *Bailey's Brit. Dir.* (1784), iii, 526–7; *Universal Brit. Dir.* (*c.* 1792), ii. 828; *Yorks. Poll Book* (1807), 167; *HP* 15 Sept. 1801; *YH* 19 Oct. 1816.
17 Baines, *Hist. Yorks.* (1823), ii, 195; White, *Dir. Hull & York* (1851), 602; ERAO, PE/10/T120; TNA, HO 107/2366.
18 *YH* 3 Apr. 1852, 5 Nov. 1859; *HP* 13 Mar. 1857; *Slater's Royal Nat. Com. Dir. of Yorks.* (1864), 115.
19 By 1910 Smith's owned, besides many of the public houses, an 'old brewery', a malt kiln, and the market house in the cattle market: ERAO, NV/1/107.
20 HRO, DBHT/5/304, newspaper cutting Jan. 1900.
21 P. Aldabella and R. Barnard, *Hull and E Yorks. Breweries* (1997), 9, 24.
22 ERAO, PE/10/T120; ibid. DDX904/1/3, 6–7, 28 June 1832.

31. *Great Driffield: Holtby's brewery, Laundry Lane, 1957. The building with the tall chimney was a brewery for some 50 years from c. 1850, before its conversion to a steam laundry and baths. The nearer range was part of a maltings.*

Doctor Lane to larger premises on a lane, now Laundry Lane, off Eastgate North, where three men were employed in 1851 and seven by 1871.[1] Mrs Holtby was succeeded *c.* 1880 by her son Thomas, who was elected one of the first two county councillors for Driffield in 1889.[2] He was apparently still brewing and malting at Eastgate brewery in 1897, but in that year he sold his public houses in Driffield to John Smith's Tadcaster Brewery Co. Ltd.[3] The Eastgate brewery closed and part became a steam laundry and baths soon afterwards and the malting was rebuilt for Daniel Byass in 1898–9.[4]

Westgate Brewery Situated on the north side at the western end of Harland Lane, at its junction with Westgate, the brewery and malting was evidently occupied by George Stephenson in 1823 and Richard Seller by 1828.[5] The brew house was said to be 'new erected' in 1836 when it was put up for sale by Seller who was retiring through ill health.[6] George Taylor, brewer and maltster, was the owner by 1843, and he was in partnership with William Hewitt by 1846.[7] The brewery, with horse-driven pumps, and malt kiln were sold in 1847, possibly to Robert Liddell, brewer, who was owner by 1850.[8] He died early the next year and the business was taken over by his widow Caroline Liddell, but the increase in costs of malt, barley and hops, particularly the latter, led to her bankruptcy in 1857.[9] She was followed by William Turner, described as a brewer of Harland Lane in 1858, and he by John William Turner (d. 1888).[10] The family's enterprises, which also included a wine and spirits business in Market Place and brickmaking, were being run in 1892 by Emily Turner, widow.[11] The Turners evidently rebuilt the Westgate brewery further down Harland Lane.[12] As the

1 The Eastgate site had been occupied in 1845 by Robert Skelton's tannery and malt kiln: ERAO, TA/13; ibid. PE/10/T. 120; OS Map 1:10,560, Yorks. CLXI (1855 edn); OS Map 1:2,500, Yorks. CLXI. 12 (1893 edn); TNA, HO 107/2366; TNA, RG10/4806.

2 *Post Office Dir. N & ER Yorks.* (1879), 384; TNA, RG11/4793.

3 *YH* 10 Apr. 1889; RDB, 94/16/16 (1897), etc.

4 ERAO, NV/1/107, s.v. R. T. Holtby; *YH* 24 July 1899; illustration in *Borough Guide to Driffield* (1913), 6; below, this section, malting.

5 Baines, *Hist. Yorks.* (1823), ii, 195; Pigot, *Nat. Com. Dir.* (1828–9), ii, 930.

6 *HP* 30 Dec. 1836.

7 *YH* 1 July 1843; 1 June 184; 1 Nov. 1845; ERAO, TA/13; ibid. PE/10/T. 120; Aldabella and Barnard, *Breweries,* 25.

8 Aldabella and Barnard, *Breweries,* 25; *YH* 5 Jan. 1850.

9 *HP* 13 Mar., 12 June 1857.

10 Directories; *YH* 3 Feb. 1888.

11 Ross, *Driffield,* 186; Bulmer, *Dir. E Yorks.* (1892), 176.

12 OS Map 1:2,500, Yorks. CLXI. 12 (1893 edn).

Crown Brewery, it was taken over by John Smith's in 1897.[1] In 1901 J. W. Turner was, among other things, trading from the Market Place premises as a merchant in bottled ales and stouts.[2] Harland Lane was known as Brewhouse Lane in the mid 19th century.[3]

Howdon's Brewery Thomas Howdon, who had leased premises at River Head used for the wine and spirit, corn, timber, and coal trades in 1813,[4] was brewing and malting in Middle Street by 1822.[5] In 1845 he had maltings in Harland Lane and the brewery at no. 51 Middle Street South from where he farmed some 80 a.[6] Howdon (d. 1854) was assisted by his sons John (d. 1869) and William (d. 1878), respectively described in 1851 as maltster and brewer,[7] and they and William's executors later ran the business until *c.* 1880.[8]

Tindall's Brewery William J. Porter, licensee of the Sloop inn, afterwards the Langley Arms, River Head was brewing and malting there in the 1820s.[9] His successor, Thomas Tindall, who kept the inn from about 1830 to his death in 1865, also brewed there.[10] Besides the brewery at River Head, Tindall also had a malting in Wrangham Row, Providence Place in 1845,[11] and in 1849 he was described as a common brewer suggesting a concern of some size.[12] His other enterprises in 1851 included trading in corn and spirits.[13] The next licensee, Thomas Jefferson, also brewed there until 1879 when the Langley Arms Brewery was put up for sale.[14]

Hewsons' (Springfield) Brewery Matthew Hewson, keeper of the Blue Bell at River Head in 1851, was evidently also brewing there.[15] From the 1860s the tenancy of the inn was held by others, but Matthew Hewson (d. 1872), builder, and his son and successor George H. Hewson continued as brewers at River Head until at least 1879, despite the firm having been in liquidation in 1875.[16]

Albion Brewery Robert Brown, ran the Albion Brewery to the rear of no. 47 Middle Street North, *c.* 1856–59.[17] Brown, brewer, maltster and hop merchant, went bankrupt in 1859 and the brewery was taken over by Robert Hagyard by 1861 when he was employing two men.[18] The brewery had closed by 1870 when the building was adapted for the short lived school established by William Jarratt in opposition to the Board school in 1870. The building later became part of Shepherdson's cabinet works.[19]

Jessop's Brewery Edward Jessop, recorded as a Middle Street wine and spirit merchant in 1872, later also brewed and malted in Driffield. The Jubilee dinner in 1887 was said to have been enlivened by 'Mr Jessop's' gift of ale.[20] In 1891 he sold his business to a Market Weighton brewery, Simpson & Co.; the premises then comprised a wine merchant's shop, presumably that earlier described as in Middle Street but then identified as nos. 62–3 Market Place; the adjoining Tiger public house, and a malting in Wrangham Row, Providence Place. Simpsons was recorded in 1892 as a brewer and wine merchant of Market Place, but it is likely that production was transferred to Market Weighton or to Beverley.[21] In 1899 the Market Weighton firm, then Simpson & Heard, sold their property in Driffield, including the malt kiln and buildings in Wrangham's Row, to John Smith's of Tadcaster.[22]

Other 19th-century Breweries In 1840 C. J. Hannath was brewing in Middle Street North. His brewery with the Hall Garth site to the north was subsequently operated by Edward Fryer, brewer and maltster, until at least 1855.[23] Beer was being brewed at the Black Swan in Market Place in the 1840s; the brewhouse there was mentioned in 1841, and the landlord in 1846, Jefferson Storry, was also then recorded as a brewer and maltster.[24] James Lamplugh, landlord of the Tiger inn, Market Place, a brewer and maltster in 1846, had a malting in Chapel Lane, and in the 1860s was brewing in Kilham.[25] Another shortlived brewery was run in the early 1840s by Thomas H. and Joseph Nicholson, who were also coopers.[26]

1 RDB, 95/87/81 (1897).

2 Ibid. 165/112/97; OS Map 1:2,500, Yorks. CLXI. 12 (1910 edn); *Kelly's Dir. N & ER Yorks.* (1901), 468.

3 TNA, RG9/3608.

4 HUL, DDCV/41/1.

5 Pigot, *Nat. Com. Dir.* (1822), 607; White, *Dir. Hull & District* (1831), 247.

6 ERAO, TA/13; ibid. PE/10/T. 120; TNA, HO 107/2366.

7 TNA, HO 107/2366; Aldabella and Barnard, *Breweries*, 24.

8 TNA, RG9/3608; *YH* 21 Jan. 1854, 26 Oct. 1878; Petch, *Driffield Cemetery MIs*, 130; directories.

9 Baines, *Hist. Yorks.* (1823), ii. 195–6; ERAO, QDT/2/1.

10 ERAO, EB/1/144; White, *Dir. Hull & District* (1831), 247; TNA, HO107/2366; *DT* 5 Aug. 1865.

11 Ibid. TA/13; ibid. PE/10/T. 120.

12 RDB, GQ/326/338.

13 TNA, HO 107/2366.

14 Directories; *DT* 3 May 1879; RDB, LD/388/459.

15 ERAO, PE/10/T. 120; ibid. TA/13; TNA, HO 107/2366.

16 TNA, RG9/3608; *YH* 30 Sept. 1854; 13 Jan. 1872; 29 July 1875; Aldabella and Barnard, *Breweries*, 25–6.

17 White, *Dir. Hull & York* (1858), 660; Nicholson, *Capital of the Wolds*, 17–18; *YH* 3 Apr. 1852.

18 *YH* 5 Nov. 1859; TNA, RG9/3608.

19 Nicholson, *Capital of the Wolds*, 17–18.

20 Ross, *Driffield*, 35; Kelly, *Dir. N. & E.R.* (1889), 376.

21 RDB, 42/530/495; 48/270/251 (both 1891).

22 Ibid. 9/199/180; 9/219/198 (1899).

23 ERAO, PE/10/T. 120; ibid. TA/13.

24 Aldabella and Barnard, *Breweries*, 26.

25 ERAO, PE/10/T. 120; directories.

26 White, *Dir. N & ER Yorks* (1840), 205; HUL, DDSY/98/112; *YH* 2 Sept. 1843.

32. *Great Driffield: Former maltings, Skerne Road, 2011. Built for the corn merchant J. R. Mortimer in 1874, the maltings closed in 1962 and was converted to flats in 2004.*

Malting

In the early 19th century Driffield, being in 'good barley country', was said to be an ideal centre for malting, and it is likely that it had long been carried on there.[1] When John Johnson, gentlemen, died *c.* 1720 he had a kiln and malt worth the substantial sum of £111.[2] Joyce Sincleare was a maltster at Driffield in 1784, Edmund Maltby in 1789–91 and John Miller in 1792.[3] A new-erected malt kiln in Harland Lane for sale in 1800 may have been Blakeston's malting mentioned as being north of the lane in a deed relating to the Red Lion inn, and also that for sale or to let in 1810.[4]

There were seven malt kilns dotted around the town in 1845, four on the narrow lanes running east from Middle Street South and Market Place towards the beck.[5] Two were on Chapel Lane (King Street), one on Doctor Lane (Queen Street) and one on Wrangham's Row, Providence Place. The leading corn merchant James Harrison had a malt kiln associated with a large granary on the east side of the canal near Beechwood and the tanner Robert Skelton had a malt kiln on Eastgate North. The latter was later attached to Holtby's brewery, and was rebuilt by the lessee Daniel Byass, corn merchant.[6]

The most extensive maltings was that built to the designs of William Hawe by the corn merchant J. R. Mortimer on Skerne Road in 1874.[7] Mortimer was bankrupted in 1887, but the business continued, his brother Robert being recorded as the corn and manure merchant in 1889, when the Middle Street premises were also occupied by Mortimer & Wilton maltsters.[8] Under the management of J. R. Mortimer (d. 1911) and his son Edward, the malting side of the business, later Mortimer & Co. Ltd, became a substantial undertaking, with branches in Bridlington, Malton, and Scarborough.[9] The maltings were sold by Mortimer & Co. Ltd in 1928 to Gilstrap Earp & Co. Ltd of Newark (Notts.), and by that company in 1930 to W. J. Robson & Co. Ltd, then of Pontefract but later of Wakefield,[10] which produced malt in Driffield until the 1962. The premises were later used as a grain store after their sale

1 *YH* 8 May 1819.

2 BIA, precentorship wills, John Johnson, 1720.

3 *Bailey's Brit. Dir.* (1784), iii, 527; *Universal Brit. Dir.* (*c.* 1792), ii. 828; ERAO, PE 10/4.

4 *HP* 4 Feb. 1804; *Hull Rockingham* 27 Oct. 1810; RDB, CE/429/627.

5 ERAO, PE/10/T. 120; ibid. TA/13.

6 *YH* 24 July 1899. The remaining buildings having been used for The Rink entertainment centre were demolished 2010 and the Park surgery was built on the site. *DT* 16 Feb. 2011.

7 *DT* 13 June 1874; RDB, LH/153/213; 21/74/71 (1887); Aldabella and Barnard, *Breweries*, 27; Pevsner and Neave, *Yorks. ER.* 443; illus. at NMR (Swindon), Wailes 225/69 27/28. It is not correct that a malting and flour mill had been built on the site in 1840, nor that the work of the 1870s was a rebuilding: Aldabella and Barnard, *Breweries*, 27. Cf. OS Map 1:10,560, Yorks. CLXI (1855 edn); OS Map 1:2,500, Yorks. CLXI. 12 (1893 edn). Building may have been proposed in 1860, when the site was divided from other land and sold: RDB, HZ/306/385.

8 RDB, 21/73/70 (1887); Harrison, *Driffield*, 364; *Kelly's Dir. N & ER Yorks.* (1889), 376.

9 RDB, 98/227/222 (1898); 68/429/407 (1904); 220/539/473; *Kelly's Dir. N & ER Yorks.* (1901), 467; Harrison, *Driffield*, 364.

10 Mortimer & Co. seems, however, to have been kept as the trading name: *Kelly's Dir. N & ER Yorks.* (1937), 449.

to the millers E. B. Bradshaw & Sons Ltd in 1963;[1] as the works of A. P. Jennison, agricultural and general engineer, from 1974, and *c.* 2000 by a snooker club.[2] In 2004–5 the building was converted into flats.[3]

PAPER MAKING

Paper was being made in the parish by 1714, when a water-driven paper mill was mentioned.[4] It was probably this mill that was worked by William Long, paper maker, recorded at Great Driffield in 1717–19.[5] In 1736 Long or more probably his son, also William, bought a paper mill, of which he was then tenant, from Sir William St Quintin, Bt.[6] The mill stood close to the southern boundary of the parish almost a mile east of Bell Mill, on a 'by beck' off the main beck, the two streams defining 'Paper Mill Island' before rejoining downstream. The mill is shown, but not named, on the plan produced at inclosure in 1742 when William Long, paper maker, was awarded the 2-a. island and then bought 35 a. of adjoining ground from other proprietors.[7] There were two paper mills adjoining on the site in 1753, a second one having been 'lately erected' by Long. By this date Long had acquired Bell Mill where he made paper in addition to working the corn mill.[8] He insured a paper mill there in 1754, but had evidently gone bankrupt by 1758 when Chancery ordered the sale of his estates.[9]

Bell Mill and the two paper mills at Paper Mill Island, and Long's other property in Driffield, were eventually sold in 1761, to William Masterman of London, following another order by the Chancery court.[10] Long may have re-acquired the paper mill at Bell Mill in 1762 and soon afterwards rebuilt it, but the other two paper mills evidently became disused.[11] In 1766 they were marked as 'the old paper mill' on the map of the proposed route of the Driffield Navigation, and they were referred to in 1792 when Richard Arkwright bought them as part of the Skerne estate.[12] A building on the site of the mill in the 19th century was known as Mulberry Cottage, no doubt after a mulberry tree, or trees, growing there.[13] The cottage was described as 'more or less a ruin' in 1907 and had apparently gone three years later.[14]

William Long, senior and junior, were described as of Skerne, paper makers in 1768 and the following year they insured the paper mill at Bell Mill.[15] One of Long's apprentices at the paper mill ran away in 1765 and another was admitted to the Foundling Hospital, London 'in a very poor condition' in 1771.[16] The previous year Long, then said to be retiring, had advertised the paper mill to let, with two engines, two stuff chests, three iron presses and two coppers.[17] Two years later the mill, with one water wheel and the 'ground-work' for another water wheel, was for sale, and then again the following year, after the death of William Long, senior.[18] The mill was then bought by James Boddy, a paper maker of Pickering, and between 1779 and 1792 the owner and occupier of Bell Mills was another paper maker, Thomas Baxter.[19] Baxter was already working the mill in 1778 for at this date a local joiner had made him paper moulds, and later other work goods.[20] An apprentice at the paper mill ran away in 1783.[21] Bell Mills, then possibly only in use as a paper mill, was to let or sale by Baxter in 1790, and was bought in 1792 by Richard and William Porter and Joseph and Whittell Sheepshanks who built their textile manufactory there that year.[22] Paper making continued at Bell Mills, with references to paper makers Christopher Smith in 1792, Thomas Goor, 1798 and 1803, William Hartsgrove, 1799, and William Baker, 1801.[23] It had evidently ceased by 1807 when the old mill was no longer used for this purpose.[24]

Paper making was revived at Bell Mills when Lawrence Duxbury was recorded as a paper maker there in 1821 and again in 1823, but the following year the building adjoining the water corn mill was described as 'lately used as a paper mill'.[25]

1 Illus. at NMR (Swindon), Wailes 225/69 27/28.

2 RDB, 378/184/151; 422/33/30; 1303/384/340; 1884/146/126; 1884/147/127; Aldabella and Barnard, *Breweries*, 27; signs on building.

3 Local inf.

4 RDB, D/227/373.

5 Ibid. F/87/190; F/380/817.

6 Ibid. O/331/824; R/116/278–9; W/309/644. William Long, sen., was later a paper maker at Cottingham, where he purchased South Mill in 1719 and had rebuilt it as a paper mill (later Snuff Mill) by 1722. He had died by 1753: RDB, G/288/640; H/372/771; X/283/648. William Long, the son, married at Gt Driffield in 1730: ERAO, PE 10/3.

7 ERAO, IA. 41; RDB, B/153/42; R/116/279.

8 RDB, W/309/644; above, this section, milling.

9 A. H. Shorter, *Paper Mills and Paper Makers in England 1495–1800* (1957), 256; *Lond. Gaz.* 17 June 1758. In 1760 two of Long's apprentices ran away: *YC* 20 June 1760.

10 RDB, AD/204/454.

11 *YC* 13 July 1762; *General Evening Post* 28 Aug. 1773; HUL, DDSY/68/56.

12 HUL, DDX/16/250; RDB, AD/204/454; BR/34/53; HUL, DDX/16/250.

13 OS Map 1:10,560, Yorks. CLXI (1855 edn); OS Map 1:2,500, Yorks. CLXI. 12 (1893 edn).

14 Holderness, *Some Driffield Incidents*, 82; OS Map 1:2,500, Yorks. CLXI. 12 (1910 edn).

15 ERAO, DDMC/83/1; Shorter, *Paper Mills*, 256.

16 *YC* 13 Aug. 1765; ERAO, DDGR/42/21.

17 *YC* 20 May 1770.

18 Ibid. 21 Jan. 1772; *General Evening Post* 28 Aug. 1773.

19 RDB, AU/123/199; AU/124/200; BC/172/255; BQ/329/516; ERAO, QSF/322/C/3; *Bailey's Brit. Dir.* (1784), 3, 526.

20 Holderness, *Some Driffield Incidents*, 71.

21 *YC* 15 Apr. 1783.

22 Ibid. 27 Apr. 1790; RDB, BQ/329/516; below, this section, textiles.

23 *Universal Brit. Dir.* (*c.* 1792), ii. 828; RDB, BZ/193/300; Holderness, *Some Driffield Incidents*, 71.

24 *HP* 24 Feb. 1807.

25 Shorter, *Paper Mills*, 256; Baines, *Hist. Yorks.* (1823), ii. 197; *LM* 27 Mar. 1824.

LEATHER TRADES

With a good water supply, availability of hides and fleeces from the markets, fairs and local butchers and, following the opening of the canal, access to imported hides and oak bark, tanning was an obvious trade at Driffield as in all local market towns.[1] There were usually two or three tanners in Driffield parish, and their main customers were the many shoemakers and saddlers, and before the 19th century the glovers and breeches makers. Richard Simpson, working at Little Driffield as a glover, left his son his working knife and other tools in 1604.[2] Edward Lacup and John Dickson were glovers at Great Driffield in 1789; the latter was also a breeches maker.[3] There were four saddlers' shops in 1823 and six in 1851. Twelve men were employed in saddlery in 1851 and 16 in 1901. The numbers of shoemakers rose from 16 in 1823 to 20 in 1851, but the number employed there fell from 65 in 1851 to 40 in 1901.[4] Many of the boot and shoemakers worked alone but there were some large concerns such as that of Thomas Booth who employed nine men, three apprentices and four women in 1851, Thomas Wood with a staff of seven men in 1871 and William G. Purdon with six men and one woman in 1881.[5] In 1893 Purdon was turning out an average of 1,000 pairs of hand-sewn boots and shoes a year.[6]

Great Driffield

Tanners William Johnson, tanner, said to be of 'Driffield' *c.* 1748 may have had his yard in the town.[7] There were two tanners there in 1784, William Fox and Thomas Hall.[8] The latter, who was almost certainly the Thomas Hall, skinner, who died in 1798, probably had the tanyard in Great Driffield which in 1788 was said to have been occupied as such for 26 years.[9]

William Fox (d. 1794) tenanted a tannery, with bark house and drying house, on the south side of Bridge Street, between Middle Street North and the beck, when it was put up for sale by the owner Revd George Etherington in 1787.[10] Early the following year Fox purchased Nettleton Close, a commercial garden, on the west side of Eastgate North, reaching to the beck, and to the north of a lane later known as Laundry Lane, where he erected a house and tannery.[11] Following his death his widow Mary appears to have carried on the tannery, until her son William (b. 1785) was of an age to take over the business. In 1809 William Fox, tanner, married a daughter of the wealthy corn merchant, Richard Dunn.[12] Fox was acting as an agent for the sale of Dutch oak bark in 1819 and two years later he was ordered by the manor court to pay 1*s.* yearly for the privilege of damming the beck opposite his tanyard.[13] He lived in Paradise Cottage adjoining his tannery.[14] Fox was bankrupt in 1831, and the tannery comprising 75 pits, patent bark mill, bark chamber, bark house, drying chamber, leather houses and steam engine was sold to William Pickering of Sledmere, innkeeper.[15] Pickering, then tanner and maltster, died in 1835, and it was probably his tannery with malt kiln that was to let in 1838.[16] The Laundry Lane tannery and malt kiln, owned by Robert Skelton in 1845, was taken on for a brewery by Mary Holtby (née Skelton) *c.* 1850.[17]

Another tannery, said to be near the centre of Great Driffield and adjoining the beck, and possibly the one worked by Thomas Hall, was to let in 1818. Owned by John Reaston, builder, it had 30 tan pits, seven lime pits, two large drying sheds, three work houses, two large chambers for bark or leather and a bark mill.[18] The previous tenant may have been Richard Postgate, tanner, who went bankrupt in 1817.[19] The tanyard had also been used for fellmonging.

Jonathan Raylor, son of a Little Driffield tannery worker, had a small tannery in Shady Lane, later Victoria Road in 1872.[20] Raylor, whose occupation was given as fellmonger in 1881, was running the tannery with Thomas Raylor by 1879.[21] The business at no. 7 Shady Lane was expanded in the mid 1890s by the acquisition of other premises in York Road, perhaps the tannery at no. 5, just in Little Driffield township, which Robert Nicholson had in 1892.[22] The Raylors' operation, described as a fellmongery by 1901, was apparently closed about 1930.[23]

Fellmongers Twentieth-century fellmongers include T. W. Wilson who traded from the later 1920s until at least 1937, with premises at first in Church Street and York Road, and later in Little Driffield Road[24] and

1 Neave and Ellis, *Historical Atlas*, 80–1; ERAO, QSF/163/C/23.
2 BIA, precentorship wills, Richard Simpson, 1604 (will).
3 ERAO, PE 10/4.
4 Above, Tables 9 & 10.
5 TNA, HO 107/2366; TNA, RG10/4807; TNA, RG11/4793.
6 *Century's Progress*, 223.
7 ERAO, QSF/163/C/23.
8 *Bailey's Brit. Dir.* (1784), iii. 526.
9 *YC* 30 Sept. 1788. Hall was buried at Little Driffield. Benjamin Hall, tanner, who had a child baptised there in 1797, was probably a relative: ERAO, PE11/4.
10 *YC* 6 Feb., 18 Sept. 1787; ERAO, DDX17/15; ibid. MRD/18/4/1–26.
11 ERAO, DDX17/15; RDB, BM/370/610, CN/150/237–8; Barley, *Great and Little Driffield*, 20.
12 *YH* 5 Aug. 1809; above, this section, corn trade.
13 *YH* 20 Mar 1819; NYRO, ZDS/III/10.
14 NYRO, ZDS/III/10; Pigot, *Nat. Com. Dir.* (1822), 606; ibid. (1828-9), 931; Baines, *Hist. Yorks.* (1823), ii, 197; White, *Dir. Hull & District* (1831), 246.
15 RDB, EO/296/297.
16 *Lond. Gaz.* 8 Nov. 1831, 20 Dec. 1836; *Register of Electors for ER* (1834); *HA* 2 July 1838.
17 ERAO, TA/13; ibid. PE/10/T. 120; above, this section, brewing and malting.
18 *YH* 2 May, 21 Nov. 1818; 16 Jan. 1819.
19 Ibid. 24 May 1817.
20 *Post Office Dir. N & ER Yorks.* (1872), 354; TNA, RG11/4794.
21 TNA, RG11/4794; *Post Office Dir. N & ER Yorks.* (1879), 385.
22 OS Map 1:2,500, Yorks. CLXI. 11 (1893 edn); *Kelly's Dir. N & ER Yorks.* (1889), 376; Bulmer, *Dir. E Yorks.* (1892), 174.
23 Directories.
24 Ibid.

the Northern Butchers Hide & Skin Co. Ltd, established by 1933 and continuing in Providence Place in 1970.[1] It is not known what work was carried out by William Lawson & Sons, tanners from Skipton (WR) who bought the former laundry building in Laundry Lane in 1969.[2] The firm went into liquidation in 1979.[3]

Curriers Associated with the tanners were the curriers and leather cutters. In the late 18th and 19th century there was at least one independent currier working in the town, including Robert Blashell *c.* 1784–1807, Thomas Anfield 1828–49, and three generations of the Brown family.[4] Robert Brown of Exchange Street was recorded as a currier and leather cutter in 1851; the concern, later in Middle Street North, was carried on by George Brown in 1872, and later by Alfred Brown, described as a currier or leather merchant, until about 1910.[5]

Little Driffield

Tanners and Fellmongers Tanning and fellmongering were the main trades at Little Driffield from the 18th century until the mid 20th century. Elcanah Johnson, tanner, moved from Kilham to a tanyard at Little Driffield in 1735, and his wife was negotiating a loan to buy hides the following year.[6] A tanner, James Eddon, was there *c.* 1742.[7]

William Walker was a skinner and fellmonger at Little Driffield from *c.* 1800 until his death in 1845, when he was succeeded by John Walker (d. 1850).[8] The business was run from Springfield House to the north of the church at Little Driffield.[9] William Foster (1819–1908), farmer and innkeeper at the Langley Arms, took over the business by 1851, and had a tannery there by 1856.[10] The tannery was rebuilt to the designs of William Hawe in 1865.[11] Foster, who had a staff of 13 in 1871, was also a wool merchant and manufacturer of chemical manure.[12] By 1881 his son John T. Foster (d. 1897) was running the concern with 11 men.[13] By 1893 he was also manufacturing sheepskin rugs.[14] From 1901 his executors continued the firm solely as wool merchants. The business had been sold by 1918 to Robert J. Jefferson, wool merchant, who continued it until the mid 1930s.[15]

James Hutchinson (d. 1852), skinner and fellmonger, had a skinnery on the west side of the street at Little Driffield by 1834.[16] He was succeeded by his son John Hutchinson but by 1857 the business had been taken over by Francis Nicholson (d. 1894), fellmonger, who was also a tanner, leather glove maker, blood manure manufacturer and farmer by 1879.[17] He leased the tannery in 1870 from Viscount Downe but by 1889 was recorded only as a fellmonger.[18] His son Richard Nicholson, who is listed separately as a fellmonger in 1889–92, succeeded and worked until at least 1937.[19] He was followed by F. G. Nicholson, fellmonger, recorded in 1959.[20] The concern was apparently ended about 1960, when, following the pollution of the watercourse there, the UDC prohibited the fellmonger and knacker from rendering any more carcasses.[21]

Joseph Smith was a fellmonger at Little Driffield 1840–51, and he may have been related to the John Smith, tanner and fellmonger, there in 1871, probably an employee of William Foster.[22] George Blanchard, fellmonger, at Little Driffield in 1881, was a manufacturer of harvest and hedging gloves and sheepskin rugs there from the 1880s to his death in 1921.

TEXTILES

The preparation of fibres and the weaving of cloth were largely domestic activities or the province of small-scale artisans until the 19th century. Lawrence Preston, who had looms and a work house in Great Driffield in 1584, with quantities of linen and harden cloth, would have been typical of the local weavers.[23] In 1625 a Great Driffield farmer had hemp and harden 'at the webster', besides other hemp and flax undressed.[24] Hemp, grown locally in hemp garths in the late 17th–early 18th century, and rotted or retted, in ditches called hempdykes, was the main raw material for the coarse linen weavers who probably predominated.[25] Thomas Smith, linen weaver, died at Little Driffield in 1659.[26]

A woollen weaver, Richard Wilbert of Great Driffield,

1 ERAO, UDDR/1/1/44, Public Health Cttee, 26 May 1970; directories.

2 RDB, 1622/141/130; above, this section, brewing.

3 *Lond. Gaz.* 12 Apr. 1979, 4956.

4 *Bailey's Brit. Dir.* (1784), iii, 526; *Yorks. Poll Book* (1807), 166; Pigot, *Nat. Com. Dir.* (1828–9), ii, 931; *Slater's Royal Nat. Com. Dir. of Yorks. & Lincs.* (1849), 83.

5 Directories.

6 HUL, DDDU/11/153, 157–8.

7 ERAO, QSF/139/C/4.

8 Ibid. PE11/4; *Yorks. Poll Book* (1807), 168; directories; *YH* 7 June 1845; 13 Apr. 1850.

9 ERAO, TA/13; ibid. PE/10/T. 120.

10 TNA, HO 107/2366; Sheahan and Whellan, *Hist. York & ER.* ii. 504; directories.

11 *DT* 29 Apr. 1865.

12 TNA, RG10/4807; *Post Office Dir. N & ER Yorks.* (1872), 355; ibid. (1879), 386.

13 TNA, RG11/4794/64; MI Little Driffield churchyard to William and J. T. Foster.

14 *Kelly's Dir. N & ER Yorks.* (1893), 413.

15 Directories.

16 ERAO, TA/13; ibid. PE/10/T. 120; directories.

17 Directories.

18 NYRO, ZDS/IV/1/6/3.

19 RDB, 94/418/379 (1907); directories. Richard Nicholson was dead by 1943: BIA, Fac. 1943/35.

20 RDB, 1155/59/48.

21 ERAO, UDDR/1/8/55, Public Health Cttee, 5 May 1958; UDDR/1/8/57, Public Health Cttee, 23 May 1960.

22 Directories; TNA, RG10/4807.

23 BIA, precentorship wills, Lawrence Preston (Prustayne), 1584.

24 Ibid. John Dales, 1625.

25 HUL, DDMC/26/1a; RDB, B/153/42, H/658/1331; K/272/551. Hempdyke Heads, south-west of the town, were mentioned in 1742: ERAO, IA. 41.

26 ERAO, PE 10/1; Best, *Farming Bks*, ed. Woodward, 191.

left some of his working tools to his half-brother Stephen Wilbert when he died in 1624.[1] Wilbert's death and that of another Driffield weaver that year may have been why Henry Best of Elmswell chose to send his fine woollen yarn to weavers at Malton, 18 miles away, early in 1625.[2]

Locally-produced cloth was being finished by the later 16th century in the fulling mills built by Thomas Etherington around 1575 in or near Bull Crook on the southern boundary of Driffield, to the east of Bell Mill. Variously described as one or two 'walk' or fulling mills they were jointly owned by Thomas, William, George and Roland Etherington in 1578 when they were ordered to demolish the dam associated with the new mills, to restore the former course of the stream, and to compensate the tenant at Bell Mill for injury suffered by him. Their operations evidently continued, as the two fulling mills or a share of them were amongst the property left on death by Thomas Etherington in 1589, William Etherington in 1600 and Sir George Etherington in 1622. No later reference to the mills has been found but an allotment of land awarded at inclosure in 1742 included Walk Mill Lane.[3]

There was a cloth maker, Edward Nettleton, at Great Driffield in 1677 and a dyer, Richard Preston, in 1693.[4] Preston had a dye house, dyeing wares and tenters. It may have been his dye house shown on a 3-a. garth on the north side of what was known as Dye(house) Garth Lane, later Albion Street, on the inclosure plan of 1742. The dye works were presumably associated with Walk Mill, a fulling mill on the beck nearby, which probably also existed in 1742 but does not appear on the copy plan.[5] John Drinkrow who owned the Walk Mill was assessed for a 'dy hous' in 1768.[6] Amongst those awarded land in 1742 were two men called John Knaggs, probably father and son, who followed the occupations of flaxdresser and bleacher in 1742, and two weavers, Thomas Binnington at Great Driffield and John Binnington at Little Driffield.[7] William England was a flaxdresser *c.* 1758, and other weavers are recorded in the 1780s–90s.[8] In the 1790s a large textile factory was built to the south of the town at Bell Mills.

Worsted Yarn Mill, Bell Mills In 1792 Richard and William Porter of Great Driffield, described respectively as corn merchant and woollen draper, and Whittell and Joseph Sheepshanks, Leeds cloth merchants, bought Bell Mills in Skerne, then comprising a water corn mill, a paper mill, and a house.[9] Later that year the partners built a large worsted yarn mill there.[10] It was an 'extensive brick building', 108 ft long by 36 ft wide, of four stories each 10–12 ft high with a large warehouse in the roof; it was powered by a massive undershot wheel of cast iron.[11] The water wheel, 14ft 10 ins in diameter and 11ft 6 ins wide, could drive 32 spinning frames. In 1807 the mill contained 15 spinning frames, with six more under construction, of 56 spindles each; two drawing frames, two roving frames and a doubling and twisting frame.[12] When being built it was said that the mill would employ 'upwards of 400 persons', as did the nearby carpet manufactory at Wansford which no doubt the Porters and their partners hoped to emulate.[13] How successful the mill was, and how many were employed there is unknown. It was said that the workers, many of them women and girls, were brought to Driffield from the West Riding and Lancashire.[14] When the mill was for sale in 1807 it was stated that, because of the lack of rival factories, 'plenty of children may be hired at very low wages'.[15] Later in the 19th century older residents remembered the 'clatter of the iron-shod clogs of the operatives' as they left town to go to work early in the morning.[16] Six houses and six cottages were built near the mill for key workers.[17] As well as the mill there was a wool combers' shop for 20 combers and a dye house.[18]

Water-powered textile production on a large scale proved unable to compete with the steam-driven factories of the coal-rich West Riding,[19] and in 1802 the partnership between the Porters and the Sheepshanks was dissolved, although the partners evidently retained their joint ownership of the buildings.[20] Richard Porter (d. 1803) was bankrupt in 1803 and William Porter (d. by 1807) in 1804.[21]

1 BIA, precentorship wills, Richard Wilbert 1624 (will), 1625 (inventory).

2 ERAO, PE 10/1; Best, *Farming Bks*, ed. Woodward, 207.

3 Above, this section, milling.

4 ERAO, DDBD/16/1; BIA, precentorship wills, Richard Preston, 1693.

5 Above, this section, milling.

6 ERAO, DDX/17/15; DDX/1040/1.

7 RDB, B/153/42. John Knaggs, jun., weaver occurs in 1748 and 1755: HUL, DDMC/26/5–6. John Binnington, weaver, was buried at Gt Driffield in 1788: ERAO, PE/10/4.

8 ERAO, QSF/199/B/2; QSF/228/B/23; ibid. PE/10/4; RDB, BH/17/30.

9 RDB, BQ/329/516; above, this section, milling.

10 RDB, CM/135/219; *Universal Brit. Dir.* (*c.* 1792), ii. 827; Eden, *State of the Poor*, iii. 817. Datestone for 1792 on rebuilt premises. Illus. at HUL, DX/144/3 (A 5068/8; A 5069/17; A 5071/3).

11 *LM* 10 Oct. 1818; 27 Mar. 1824; Harrison, *Driffield*, 224; *BG* 4 Aug. 1977.

12 *HP* 24 Feb. 1807.

13 *Universal Brit. Dir.* (*c.* 1792), ii. 827.

14 Holderness, *Some Driffield Incidents*, 55.

15 *HP* 24 Feb. 1807.

16 Holderness, *Some Driffield Incidents*, 55.

17 *HP* 24 Feb. 1807.

18 Ibid.

19 Ross, *Driffield*, 98.

20 *Lond. Gaz.* 20 Oct. 1802.

21 *HP* 18, 25 Oct., 27 Dec. 1803; 10 Jan., 14 Aug. 1804; *Lond. Gaz.* 22 Nov. 1806; RDB, CM/135/219; CX/399/498; CX/400/499.

Flax Spinning Bell Mills were put up for sale in 1807, and seemingly purchased by Moxon and Carrick of Hull, and leased for five years from 1808 to Samuel Milbourn of Thorpe Bassett, gentleman who re-fitted the manufactory for flax spinning.[1] The next year Milbourn, described as a flax manufacturer, was indicted for assault on his bookkeeper. There had been a great expansion in flax growing with government subsidies during the French Revolutionary and Napoleonic wars. In 1803 a large quantity of flax burst into flames in the main street at Driffield and Walk Mill, Dye Garth Lane, was used as a flax works by 1810.[2] There were a number of flaxdressers in the town including William Jones who went bankrupt in 1807; his goods then included 'a quantity of checks, sheeting, shirting and linen cloths'.[3]

In 1812 a large factory near Driffield, clearly that at Bell Mills, was reported to be spinning and weaving linen or hemp to produce a coarse sacking.[4] The following year the mills were sold to Samuel Milburn.[5] His relative R. Snowball was occupying the premises in 1818–19 when the mills were, unsuccessfully, put up for sale. At that date the flax spinning mill had 18–24 spinning frames, seven to ten carders, two to three spreading frames and ten roving frames.[6] The occupier in 1823 was William Carrick, flaxdresser and spinner, who retired through ill-health the following year.[7] The premises, said to be in complete repair, with nine line and five tow frames and an 'entirely new cast iron wheel', along with the nearby corn mill, were then put up for sale, or let.[8] Soon afterwards the fittings of the flax mill were offered for sale. Following the purchase of Bell Mills by Richard Arkwright, the lord of Skerne manor, in 1825, the former textile mill was refitted as a corn mill.[9]

Other Textile Manufacture There were two worsted manufacturers, James Preston (d. 1822) and John Drury, a dyer, William Jackson, and two linen manufacturers, John Barnett and Thomas Bellshaw, in the 1820s.[10] There were usually two linen manufacturers up to 1851, with John Barnett followed by Joseph Barnett, and Thomas Bellshaw (who was at various times also recorded as a flax-dresser, sacking manufacturer, and ropemaker) succeeded by his son John Bellshaw, who had moved to Leeds before his death in 1853.[11] Joseph Barnett (d. 1869), was the last of the town's hand loom linen weavers, working two or more looms in the large kitchen of his house in Chapel Lane (King Street) until the mid-1860s.[12] He would hawk his finished cloth round the local villages and farms.[13] John Chapman, a sacking manufacturer employing a man and a boy in 1861, last appears as a waggon cover manufacturer in 1889.[14] Robert Hillerby wove carpets in a shop on Middle Street South in 1840.[15]

Of later textile manufacture nothing further is known of the Driffield & East Riding Knitting Factory that existed in Exchange Street in 1892, nor of the mill built later that year on Middle Street by Messrs Ross & Co. for flannelette weaving.[16] In 1922 John Beever & Son from Swan Bank Mills, Holmfirth (WR) set up a rug factory in Westgate that still existed in 1948; it produced hearth rugs.[17]

ROPEMAKING

Ropemakers were recorded at Great Driffield from the mid 17th century; initially they probably used locally grown hemp. Amongst ropers working in the town were William Byass in 1732, Thomas Burshill, 1795–8, John Downs, 1805, and Thomas Bossey, 1807.[18] Two ropers recorded in 1823 included Thomas Bellshaw (d. 1848) whose ropewalk was located on the east side of Beverley Lane, later St John's Road, in 1845.[19] From his successor, John Bellshaw,[20] the ropery may have passed to Robert Hogg, ropemaker of Beverley Lane in 1851,[21] and it was certainly the same which John Weatherill, maker of ropes and sheep nets, had by 1879.[22] He was employing one man and two boys in 1881.[23] Weatherill's walk, at no. 14, was still evident in 2006 as the entrance to a carpet warehouse. Weatherill was succeeded soon after 1905 by Walter Hammill,[24] who also worked in Wakefield. Hammill's ropewalk was later in Westgate, but was given up about 1930. The other ropemaker in 1823 was James Barclay of 'Middle Street'; his ropewalk was evidently to the east of the street, in Bandmaker, or Ropery, Lane, later Brook Street, until *c.* 1840.[25] Rope

1 *HP* 24 Feb. 1807; 15 Dec. 1818; ERAO, DDX/17/15.
2 *YC* 26 Dec. 1803; ERAO, PE/10/4 ibid. DDX/17/15; RDB, CH/398/647, CP/342/525.
3 *HP* 17 Mar. 1807; *YH* 20 June 1807.
4 Strickland, *Gen. View*, 282.
5 ERAO, DDX/17/15.
6 *LM* 10 Oct. 1818; *HP* 15 Dec. 1818; 12 Jan. 1819.
7 Baines, *Hist. Yorks.* (1823), ii, 197; *LM* 27 Mar. 1824.
8 *LM* 27 Mar. 1824.
9 Ibid. 24 July 1824; RDB, DY/19/23; above, this section, milling.
10 Pigot, *Nat. Com. Dir.* (1822), 606; ibid. (1828–9), 931; Baines, *Hist. Yorks.* (1823), ii, 197.
11 Directories; *YH* 8 Oct. 1853; 10 Feb. 1855.
12 Directories; Holderness, *Some Driffield Incidents*, 46–7; Nicholson, *Capital of the Yorks. Wolds*, 16–17.
13 Holderness, *Some Driffield Incidents*, 66.
14 TNA, RG9/3607; directories.
15 Nicholson, *Capital of the Yorks. Wolds*, 26–27; White, *Dir. ER Yorks* (1840), 205
16 *DT* 12 Mar., 31 Dec. 1892.
17 Ibid. 18 Nov. 1922; directories; Carr, *Driffield*, 19.
18 RDB, N/72/144; ERAO PE 10/4; *Yorks. Poll Book* (1807), 166.
19 ERAO, TA/13; ibid. PE/10/T. 120; RDB, FX/49/63; Baines, *Hist. Yorks.* (1823), ii. 197; *YH* 19 Feb. 1848.
20 White, *Dir. Hull & York* (1851), 605.
21 TNA, HO 107/2366.
22 *Post Office Dir. N & ER Yorks.* (1879),386.
23 TNA, RG11/4794/19.
24 ERAO, NV/1/107.
25 Baines, *Hist. Yorks.* (1823), ii. 197; Ross, *Driffield*, 81, 194; OS Map 1:10,560, Yorks. CLXI (1855 edn).

and sheep netting were made in Harper Street by Frederick Waites & Sons from 1915 until about 1980; the same concern were using the works as an ironmongery in 2011.[1] In the mid 20th century halters and stack nets were produced in Driffield by George Addy in Washington Street and his nephew Allan Addy in Westgate.[2] Ropes were also to be had from Joseph Laister, a Pocklington maker, who attended the cattle market.[3]

TIMBER AND ALLIED TRADES

Timber Merchants

Timber merchants were amongst the early traders to settle at Driffield once the canal had opened. The first were chiefly raff merchants, dealing largely in imported wood, much of it coming from the Baltic via Hull. There were large raff yards at River Head.[4] Timber was needed for fencing the inclosure allotments and for building the many new farmsteads and village houses on the Wolds as well as the houses, shops, and workshops in the rapidly expanding town. Edward Reaston, a timber merchant in 1784 was also a house carpenter.[5] There was little or no local timber to be had and in 1819 the timber and raff merchant William Stainton (d. 1858) acquired ash trees from near Wetherby (WR) some forty miles away.[6] The firm of Barnby & Stainton went bankrupt in 1823 when their stock consisted of 'deals, mahogany, wainscot, scantlings, slabs, oak, ash, elm and fir trees, several thousand felloes, spokes and naves for carriages, waggons, and carts. Dry wood of all kinds, used in making agricultural implements; post and rails, sheep bars, laths, etc.'.[7] William Stainton went on trading until the mid 1840s when he was succeeded by his son Thomas (d. 1859). The other main firm from *c.* 1840 to the mid 1860s was that of William Sterriker (d. 1862) and his son Thomas Atkinson Sterriker.[8] The latter was employing eight men and three boys in 1861.[9] The timber merchants' yards in the 1840s lay between Westgate and Middle Street North, and on the west side of Middle Street South, and there was another wood yard close to the railway station and a sawpit north of George Street.[10]

In the 1870s two timber merchants in or near Middle Street operated steam saw mills, one at Albion Mills run by first Matthew Blakeston who employed ten men and a boy in 1871, and then by Joseph Berry, and the other run by John Dunn.[11] By 1892 there were at least four steam-powered saw mills in Driffield, two in Middle Street North, one in George Street, and one at Cross Hill.[12] The timber merchants then obtained timber locally from the plantations formed by Sir Christopher Sykes and other landowners in the late 18th century.[13] In 1913 it was noted that many hundreds of tons of timber, especially larch, were consigned by rail from Driffield to the West Riding and elsewhere.[14]

The largest firms from the late 19th–early 20th century were those of John Taylor (d. 1912) and Henry Naylor, and their successors. Taylor's steam-powered saw mills, established in 1875,[15] were situated just north of Cross Hill, near the junction of Mill Street and Westgate.[16] The firm, then J. Taylor & Sons, moved in 1925 to large new premises on the south side of Mill Street on land purchased from Lord Downe in 1914 and part of the National school grounds acquired in 1922.[17] Following a division of the business in the late 1940s, Horace Taylor ran a sawmills on the Cross Hill site in opposition to his brother Harold who continued with J. Taylor & Sons (Timber) Ltd in Mill Street. The latter property was enlarged in the mid 20th century, but sawmilling ceased in 1989, and Taylors relocated to a small unit at Kelleythorpe on the industrial estate that had been developed by the firm's managing director, Derek Megginson.[18] Here Taylors specialised in the sale of fencing before closing down in 1997.[19]

Henry Naylor, as joiner and wheelwright, had taken over the business of his father-in-law Edward Moody, at the North End in 1869.[20] He described himself as an 'English and foreign timber merchant' in the 1890s and his sawmills, powered by gas-produced steam,[21] were situated on either side of Middle Street North, adjoining North Street.[22] There was a fire at Naylor's North End saw mill in 1925, and another in 1937 which all but destroyed the premises.[23] Part of the property was then bought by the county council for street improvement,[24] and later Sawyers Court was built on another part of the former mill.[25] Henry Naylor & Sons Ltd was evidently re-located after the fire to Eastgate North, where North End Sawmills was still run by the firm until the early 21st

1 *Yorks. Life* Sept. 1971, 49.
2 W. Simpkin, *Driffield and District Through 'The Times'* (2008), 228–9.
3 Directories; inf. from Donald Pudsey, Driffield, 2004.
4 *HP* 29 May 1804; *YH* 12 Dec. 1812.
5 *Bailey's Brit. Dir.* (1784), iii, 527; *Universal Brit. Dir.* (*c.* 1792), ii. 828.
6 *YH* 27 Mar. 1819; 29 May 1858.
7 Ibid. 14 June 1823.
8 Directories; *Driffield Monumental Inscriptions* (E Yorks. Family Hist. Soc., 1989), 17.
9 TNA, RG9/3607.
10 ERAO, TA/13; ibid. PE/10/T. 120.
11 Directories; TNA RG10/4807; above, this section, milling.
12 Bulmer, *Dir. E Yorks.* (1892), 178; *Kelly's Dir. N & ER Yorks.* (1893); 410–2; *Century's Progress*, 222.
13 *VCH Yorks. ER.* viii. 191–2.
14 *Borough Guide to Driffield* (1913), 16–17.
15 Ross, *Driffield*, 185.
16 *Driffield Souvenir Guide* (1972), 11.
17 *DT* 2 Jan. 1926.
18 RDB, 164/366/321; 565/16/11; 1826/585/484; OS Map 1:2,500, Yorks. CLXI. 12 (1893, 1910 edns); OS Map 1:10,560, TA 05 NW (1956 edn). Illus. at HUL, DX/144/3 (A 5069/21); inf. from Derek Megginson, Eastburn, 2011; above, this section, trade and industry, post-war.
19 Inf. from Derek Megginson, 2011.
20 *DT* 20 Nov. 1869.
21 ERAO, UDDR/1/1/1, p. 203.
22 RDB, 606/286/227.
23 *HT* 9 May 1925.
24 RDB 587/300/227.
25 Plaque on building.

century. Another member of the Naylor family, W. E. Naylor, began an electrically-powered saw mill in Queen Street in 1935, and by 2003 William E. Naylor & Son was a joinery and building concern, as well as a supplier of glass and pre-cast concrete components.[1] The firm built houses on the Mill Falls estate, where in 2004 it was developing Reina Drive.[2]

Basket Making

In 1823 James Mathers of Mill Street was recorded as a basket maker. The business had been moved to no. 55 Westgate by 1851, where it was later carried on by Mathers' sons, William and Thomas, until the early 1900s. Baskets were also being made by a cooper in 1851.[3] The willow for basket making was probably obtained from the willow yards located close to the southern boundary stream and Bell Mills in the 19th and early 20th century.[4]

Cabinet Making

Cabinet making was one of the more skilled crafts present in the expanding town from the late 18th century. There were two cabinet makers in 1792, and Septimus Dobson, who had carried on the trade, with that of upholsterer, 'for some time on a large scale' became bankrupt in 1814.[5] From the 1820s onwards there were usually six or seven cabinet makers, some combining this with general joinery and building.[6] By the end 19th century one firm, George Shepherdson & Co. Ltd, had expanded to become the town's main employer.

George Shepherdson & Co. Ltd The cabinet-making and building firm was founded by George Shepherdson (1793–1867) in 1818.[7] Shepherdson, who had married the granddaughter of William Porter of the Blue Bell, was based in Middle Street by 1823, probably at no. 46 Middle Street North, the property that he tenanted in 1845, and later owned.[8] As a builder George Shepherdson was one of the contractors for the new workhouse built on Middle Street North in 1837–8.[9] Shepherdson was declared bankrupt in 1842, but he did not cease trading and by 1861 he was employing six men and eight boys.[10] A serious fire gutted the workshop in 1862, and the same year the firm was taken over by Shepherdson's son, John Frank Shepherdson (1828–1913), under whose management it became much more than a successful small town business.[11] The numbers employed by the firm rose from 12 in 1881 to some 60 in 1892.[12] The following year George Shepherdson and Son, now a limited company, was said to have a workforce of about 100 'skilled and experienced cabinetmakers, in addition to commercial travellers, clerks, &c.', but the 250 employees claimed in 1901 may be an exaggeration.[13]

The success owed much to the association with the architect Temple Moore with whom the firm first worked on the remodelling and furnishing of Highfield, Driffield, for Harrison Holt in 1882. This evidently led to further contracts for building, restoration and refurnishing work at eight churches in the East and North Ridings for which Temple Moore was architect, and at least three others, up to 1894.[14] As well as the ecclesiastical work, which included the making of carved pulpits, screens, seats, pews, choir stalls, font covers, and reredoses, the firm undertook general house furnishing, fitted out shops, banks and offices and did a 'splendid wholesale trade with furniture dealers in all parts of the Kingdom'.[15] They were also the main contractors for the police station and court house built in Wansford Road in 1896–7.[16] The works, which used machinery powered by steam made in gas-fired boiler, was almost totally destroyed by fire in 1905.[17] It was rebuilt soon after on a smaller scale and the firm, then under the chairmanship of Dr A. T. Brand, was wound up voluntarily in 1908.[18]

Herbert, son of J. F. Shepherdson, took over the premises and had some 50 employees there in 1909.[19] The following year the whole business was said to have been removed to Stockport, Cheshire, but Herbert Shepherdson was still advertising his cabinet making business at no. 46 Middle Street North in January 1912.[20] The removal to Stockport probably took place soon afterwards and the firm of H. Shepherdson, craftsmen in wood, still existed there at the 'Driffield Works', Norwood Road in 1945.[21]

1 Directories; Naylor website, 2003.

2 Inf. from Mrs R. B. Leason, Driffield, 2004.

3 TNA, HO 107/2366; directories.

4 ERAO, TA/13; ibid. PE/10/T. 120; RDB, 13/335/312.

5 *YH* 19 Nov., 10 Dec. 1814; *HP* 28 Feb. 1815.

6 Directories.

7 Shepherdson letterhead at ERAO, PE/10/T. 136; Petch, *Driffield Cemetery MIs*, 36.

8 ERAO, PE/10/T. 120; ibid. TA/13; Holderness, *Some Driffield Incidents*, 44; Baines, *Hist. Yorks.* (1823), ii. 196; Bulmer, *Dir. E Yorks.* (1892), 174. The firm remained at this address until it closed.

9 ERAO, PUD/1/2/1, pp. 106, 125–6, 217.

10 *Lond. Gaz.* 30 Dec. 1842, 18; TNA, RG9/3608.

11 *HP* 19 Sept. 1862; Petch, *Driffield Cemetery MIs*, 36; *Century's Progress*, 221. J. F. Shepherdson and his son Joseph Shepherdson both worked as architects for Driffield Poor Law Union: ERAO, PUD/1/2/10, pp. 83, 123; plans for infirmary *c.* 1900 at ibid. PUD/1/4/1.

12 TNA, RG11/4793; *DT* 31 Dec. 1892.

13 *Century's Progress*, 221; *Kelly's Dir. N & ER Yorks.* (1901), 461.

14 Brandwood, *Temple Moore*, 39; *Century's Progress*, 221.

15 *Century's Progress*, 221; Directories.

16 Wood, *Policing from Wansford Road*, 2.

17 Shepherdson letterhead at ERAO, PE/10/T. 136; *DT* 27 Oct. 1988; Clubley, *Driffield*, pl. 17.

18 *Lond. Gaz.* 24 Apr. 1908, 3101.

19 Inf. from Mr E. Spehr, Hackham West, S. Australia, 2004; *Kelly's Dir. N & ER Yorks.* (1909), 491.

20 Inf. from Mr Spehr; *DT* 31 Dec. 1910; 21 Jan. 1912.

21 *Kelly's Dir. N & ER Yorks.* (1913), 511; *Kelly's Dir. Cheshire* (1914), 856; *Lond. Gaz.* 9 Nov. 1945, 5490; HUL, DDSY2/1/30/163.

METAL WORKING

The most numerous group among the metal workers in the 18th century were probably the blacksmiths and farriers, but the town also had a nail maker in 1777 and 1785–96.[1] Metal working was later said to have been encouraged in particular by the demand for agricultural implements and machinery.[2] Both demand and supply were stimulated from the 1850s by the agricultural show; in 1856 there were 50 stands of machinery.[3] By 1851 there were seven agricultural machine makers, millwrights, or engineers; three braziers or tinners; an iron and brass founder in Doctor Lane, and another nail maker, besides several smiths.[4] In terms of employment, founders and engineers numbered over forty, and there were about the same number of smiths and ironmongers.[5] The number of local machine makers fell in the early 20th century, presumably because of competition from national firms, but their place was taken to an extent soon afterwards by motor engineers, five concerns being recorded in 1925 and ten in 1937, besides another firm of motor body and coach builders.[6]

Foley Mark Foley was working as a blacksmith and maker of threshing machines and drills by 1822, and in 1851 he was employing six men at his Middle Street South works (no. 30).[7] He retired by 1857 and the business was taken over by his son George Moore Foley (1830–89) who employed 11 men in 1871. That year he advertised two and three horse reapers, weighing and winnowing machines, straw and turnip cutters and oil cake crushers.[8] George's son Arthur Foley (1863–1941), who succeeded in 1889, introduced an improved self-binder to the area, and later patented a corn drill.[9] The firm which had become Foley & Co., Ltd by 1905 had closed about 1910.[10]

Gibson Gibson's foundry established at River Head in 1826,[11] was moved to the junction of Middle and Bridge Streets by 1834.[12] Here Edward Gibson (*c.* 1801–86), iron and brass founder, machine maker, and ironmonger, employed four men in 1851, perhaps in addition to Gibson's two sons, Hutton and Samuel.[13] Gibson seems to have been succeeded by his elder son, (Edward) Hutton Gibson of no. 22 Middle Street North, and John Gibson of Bridge Street, both of whom were recorded as iron founders in 1889. Soon after the concern evidently passed to Samuel Henry Gibson (1863–1931) who moved the business to Westgate about 1895, and *c.* 1910 he retired and the foundry was taken over by John Wood.[14]

River Head Foundry Gibson's foundry at River Head was taken over by Thomas Lynoss by 1834, and then by William Graham, millwright and machine maker, by 1840.[15] Graham (d. 1849) was succeeded by his son Robert who in 1851 was employing eight men and an apprentice.[16] John Hodgson, an agricultural implement manufacturer and engineer, took over the River Head works from Robert Graham between 1857 and 1864.[17] By *c.* 1870 the foundry was operated by Peter Sibree (1842–1924), general and hydraulic engineer, who provided fittings for the new workhouse that year.[18] Sibree, who won awards for his hydraulic apparatus, was employing four men and ten boys in 1871.[19] He had given up the foundry by 1879.[20]

Harker John Harker (*c.* 1804–90) was working as millwright at Driffield by *c.* 1837. He worked on some of the larger mills in the area including Wansford mill.[21] By 1845 John Harker had a large machine-making works, incorporating an iron and brass foundry, to the west of Eastgate and north of the gas works.[22] He was employing two men and two boys in 1861, but the firm had closed by 1864.[23] Harker became engineer of the Driffield & East Riding Pure Linseed Cake Co. Ltd, probably from its establishment in 1861–2, and he patented improvements to a machine for making feed cake in 1867.[24]

1 RDB, AY/410/681; ERAO, PE/10/4. Two large lead figures of St John of Beverley and King Athelstan in Beverley minster have long been misattributed to a mythical foundry in Driffield in 1781: Barley, *Great and Little Driffield*, 33.
2 Bulmer, *Dir. E Yorks.* (1892), 165.
3 Above, soc. hist., Driffield agricultural show; Harrison, *Driffield*, 356–7.
4 White, *Dir. Hull & York* (1851), 600–5.
5 TNA, HO 107/2366.
6 *Kelly's Dir. N & ER Yorks.* (1925), 521–4; (1937), 446–50.
7 ERAO, PE/10/T. 120; ibid. TA/13; TNA, HO 107/2366; Pigot, *Nat. Com. Dir.* (1822), 606; Baines, *Hist. Yorks.* (1823), ii. 197.
8 Howorth, *Year Gone By*, 31.
9 *HT* 25 June 1938; *DT* 13 Dec. 1941. Woods were making corn drills to Foley's patent in 1912: *DT* 11 May 1912.
10 Directories; *HT* 25 June 1938.
11 Sheahan and Whellan, *Hist. York & ER.* ii. 498.
12 ERAO, TA/13; ibid. PE/10/T. 120; Pigot, *Nat. Com. Dir.* (1834), 713.
13 TNA, HO 107/2366; Ross, *Driffield*, 186.
14 Directories. In 1910 Hutton Gibson's property in Driffield included an 'empty' foundry in Bridge Street: ERAO, NV/1/107; below, this section, John Wood & Sons.
15 Directories. Probably the William Grime with premises on west side of River Head in 1845: ERAO, TA/13; ibid. PE/10/T. 120.
16 *YH* 16 Feb. 1849; TNA, HO 107/2366.
17 Directories.
18 ERAO, PUD/1/2/9, p. 371; *Kelly's Dir. N & ER Yorks.* (1872), 355.
19 TNA, RG10/4806; *DT* 2 Jan. 1875.
20 *Post Office Dir. N & ER Yorks.* (1879), 383–6.
21 Directories; HUL, DDSY/98/113; *HP* 30 July 1858; 16 July 1875; Sheahan and Whellan, *Hist. York & ER.* ii. 498; Allison, *ER Water-Mills*, 39; Petch, *Driffield Cemetery MIs*, 102; above, this section, corn milling.
22 ERAO, TA/13; ibid. PE/10/T. 120; White, *Dir. Hull & York* (1851), 604–5.
23 TNA, RG9/3607; *Slater's Royal Nat. Com. Dir. of Yorks.* (1864), 116–7.
24 *Lond. Gaz.* 19 Apr. 1867, 2381.

Johnson Samuel Johnson was making agricultural implements in Doctor Lane in 1848, and in 1861 he was employing 8 men and 8 boys there.[1] Johnson emigrated to Australia in 1870 and the foundry and all his moulds and patterns were acquired by Thomas Pickering.[2]

Pickering/Taylor In several cases, metal working was combined with ironmongery. Thomas Pickering (1818–78) was nephew and successor of Thomas Atkinson, ironmonger.[3] In 1851 as brazier, tinner and ironmonger, of Market Place, Pickering was employing five men and three apprentices. He was then the agent for an agricultural machinery manufacturer,[4] but in 1854 he opened his own foundry, the Albion (later Victoria) foundry at Cross Hill, chiefly to make implements.[5] In 1861 Pickering employed 15 men and 6 boys in the foundry, a further 2 men and a boy worked as tinsmiths and 2 men and 3 apprentices in the ironmongers' shop, and ten years later his workforce had expanded to 33 men and 7 boys.[6] The firm was much employed on the Sledmere estate where their fencing, cast-iron pumps and other work survive, and also many pumps around Driffield.[7] Pickering was succeeded in 1878 by his sons Charles G. (d. 1885) and Henry A. Pickering (d. 1886), and in 1889 Charles Taylor of Leeds ironfounder bought the business.[8] It was subsequently operated by Charles and Walter Taylor as C. H. Taylor & Son, later Taylors' (Driffield) Ltd.[9] Besides agricultural implements, Taylors' Victoria foundry on Cross Hill was producing stoves and grates in 1929. Production at the large works evidently ceased soon after 1964, and in 1972 the company sold the foundry.[10] It was bought by the UDC the following year, and much of the site was soon after cleared.[11] One building was later used for a market hall,[12] and since the mid 1990s another has been occupied as a licensed restaurant.[13]

Taylor's Sewing Machine Factory William Taylor (1840–1917), an actuary at Driffield Savings Bank patented a lock-stitch sewing machine for which he received a silver medal at the London Great Industrial Exhibition in 1866, and at exhibitions at Altona and Hamburg in 1869.[14] He filed several other sewing machine patents 1866–74, including ones for 'twisted loop' and 'cross-belt' sewing machines, the latter machine receiving a gold medal at the first African International Exhibition in Cape Town, South Africa in 1877. Taylor evidently set up a small factory to make his machines in the later 1860s; it was in Eastgate in 1871 when he employed six women as machinists.[15] By 1875 he was advertising nationally, with addresses in Driffield and Cheapside, London and depots in Hull and Wakefield.[16] He probably had help from his brother-in-law Peter Sibree at the River Head foundry. Although it is said that the company became insolvent in 1879, two years later Taylor was still manufacturing sewing machines on New Road, Driffield employing four men, one of whom, James Elvidge, is said to have purchased the business from him.[17] Taylor is also said to have made early bicycles and invented the cot with a drop-side, an automatic pole for lamplighting, washing machines and printing machines.[18]

John Wood & Sons Gibson's Westgate foundry was purchased by John Wood (1855–1937), who began making cast-iron ploughs at Bilsdale (NR) on the North Yorkshire Moors in 1874. The Bilsdale plough adapted for work on all types of land became popular over a wide area and Wood moved to Driffield in 1911 to be near a railway line and set up the Bilsdale Plough Works.[19] The firm was still manufacturing single furrow ploughs up to 1957 when the foundry closed.[20] The business which then dealt in agricultural implements, later specialising in garden machinery, was closed in 2005, when the site was re-developed for a supermarket.[21]

Mortimer and Robinson An agricultural engineering business was begun by 1905 by Mortimer and Robinson in works in Eastgate South. It was carried on after the First World War by Robinson alone, and later advertised itself also as an implement repairer's. It was closed after 1937.[22]

Richardson Percy Richardson, an apprentice steam engineer with Mortimer and Robinson, set up on his

1 TNA, HO 107/2366; RG9/3608; Sheahan and Whellan, *Hist. York & ER.* ii. 498; White, *Dir. Hull & York* (1851), 604.

2 *DT* 1 & 8 Oct. 1870; Howorth, *Year Gone By*, 37–8.

3 *HP* 13 May 1817; HUL, DDSY 98/114, 101/93.

4 TNA, HO 107/2366; White, *Dir. Hull & York* (1851), 602, 604.

5 Sheahan and Whellan, *Hist. York & ER.* ii. 498; Ross, *Driffield*, 182.

6 TNA, RG9 3607–8, R10/4807.

7 HUL, DDSY/93/114; Howorth, *Year Gone By*, 38.

8 Petch, *Driffield Cemetery MIs*, 101; *DT* 20 July 1889.

9 RDB, NM/31/48; 31/319/305 (1889); 77/310/300 (1895); 1826/585/484. Illus. at HUL, DX/144/3.

10 Watts, 'Industrial geography', 97.

11 ERAO, UDDR/1/1/46, Gen. Purposes Cttee, 6 Feb. 1973; ibid. NV/1/107; RDB, 1826/585/484; directories.

12 Above, this section, mkts and fairs.

13 ERAO, EYEY/1/4/8/3, Environment...Cttee, 24 July 1995.

14 *DT* 25 Sept. 1869, 1 Dec 1917; *HP* 10 June 1870.

15 TNA, RG10/4806; www.sewalot.com/taylorsewingmachine.htm

16 *Englishwoman's Domestic Magazine* 1 Jan 1875, 8.

17 TNA, RG11/4793. In June 1881 he was said to be out of business: *Lond. Gaz.* 24 June 1881, 3228.

18 www.sewalot.com/taylorsewingmachine.htm

19 Directories; *DT* 11 May 1912; M. Hartley and J. Ingilby, *Life and Tradition in the Moorlands of North-East Yorks.* (1972), 32–5. See page from firm's catalogue issued at Driffield *c.* 1920: ibid. 33.

20 Watts, 'Industrial geography', 97.

21 Directories; inf. from Mr M. Bentley, Driffield, 2006.

22 Directories.

own in Anderson Street in the 1910s. His motor and tractor engineering operation, re-located to Middle Street North by 1921, obtained the agency for Standard cars about that date, and later in the decade became the local Ford and Fordson dealer. In the 1950s the former coachworks of Pickering Bros. in Bridge Street were bought as a paint and repair shop, and later the business was extended to include industrial as well as agricultural and motor machinery, and branches were established beyond the town, in Hull and Sproatley.[1] The Driffield branch occupied a large modern garage in Westgate in 2004.

BRICKMAKING

The earliest reference to brickmaking in the parish was at Elmswell where Henry Best contracted with a Beverley brickmaker for 400,000 bricks in 1635.[2] A 'brick close' in Elmswell from about that date suggests that this was where they were made.[3] It was situated on the north side of the hamlet.[4]

There is good brickmaking clay to the north-east of Driffield town and a clay pit which had given a lane there its name by 1742[5] was almost certainly used for making bricks. In the 19th century bricks, tiles, and drainage pipes were made in works nearby. The location of the brick garth for which Richard Eggleston was assessed in 1768–72 is unknown, but it may have been the brick garth, recorded along with a brick kiln close, at the east end of Little Driffield in 1797 and later.[6]

Richard Porter, in 1784, and Isaac Milbourn, 1804–7, are the earliest known brickmakers at Driffield, and from the 1820s for almost a century there were two or three sizeable brick and tile works on the north side of Bridlington Road or east side of Scarborough Road.[7]

Waddingham (later Blanchard) Alexander Waddingham (d. 1850) was a brickmaker by 1823 and he had a brickyard on Bridlington Road, two fields west of the present cemetery, by 1845.[8] The yard was run in 1850–7 by Jane Waddingham, widow, who employed three men in 1851.[9] It had passed by 1864 to John Blanchard (1823–1901), whose family retained it until the death in 1924 of both Blanchard's son John and grandson Fred.[10] Blanchard made the bricks for Thixendale school in 1874 using specially made moulds.[11]

Pickering, later Clark William Pickering had a brickyard on Nafferton Lane (Bridlington Road) *c.* 1823–34, which was probably taken over by the builder William Clark (d. 1871) by the late 1830s.[12] In 1845 Clark had lime kilns off Scarborough Road.[13] He was succeeded for a short time as builder, brickmaker and lime burner by his son David B. Clark by 1869.[14]

Turner William Turner, son of William Turner (d. 1867) bookseller and wine merchant, had a brickyard by the early 1840s. It was probably that sited off Scarborough Road, directly east of Moot Hill, owned by William Turner, sen., in 1845 and tenanted by Moses Gage who was to serve 15 years as foreman in Turner's brickyard.[15] Turner sen. also owned a brickyard close on Bridlington Road in 1845 and tenanted another one there, with a brickyard.[16] The last which adjoined the site of the present cemetery was evidently the location for Turner's brickyard run successively by William Turner, jun. (1819–67), his widow Jane, who employed 15 men and 3 boys in 1871, and their son John William Turner (1851–88), and the latter's widow Emily, until the First World War.[17] J. W. Turner, who supplied large quantities of bricks to the Sledmere estate, employed 18 men at the yard in 1871.[18] In 1880 he was fined for employing two children aged seven and eight.[19]

Other Brickyards In addition to those noted above there were brickyard closes, possibly denoting former brickworks, owned by Henry Marshall and John Dickson, off Scarborough Road in 1845.[20] Here there were the later brickworks of Berry, Duggleby & Co. in the mid 1870s, Moses Gage, builder, *c.* 1892–1913, and William Leason & Son, builders, 1894–*c.* 1925.[21]

QUARRYING

There has been no large-scale commercial extraction in the parish, but chalk and gravel have been dug from several pits. One pit, in Spring Close, south of Driffield town, produced chalk for burning into lime before

1 *ER Farmers Jnl* 23 (1971), 13; *BG* 25 Aug. 1977; *DT* Jan. 2000 (millennium edn); directories; Clubley, *Driffield*, pl. 12.

2 Best, *Farming Bks*, ed. Woodward, 200.

3 Ibid. 30.

4 Ibid. 213; RDB, AN/196/12, see Best's allotment of 849 a.; below, Elmswell.

5 RDB, B/153/42.

6 ERAO DDX 1040/1–2; ibid. TA/13; ibid. PE/10/T. 120; NYRO, ZDS IV/1/6/1, 3; RDB, K/211/425; HM/74/71.

7 *Bailey's Brit. Dir.* (1784), iii, 527; *HP* 25 Sept. 1804; *Yorks. Poll Book* (1807), 167.

8 Directories; ERAO, TA/13; ibid. PE/10/T. 120; *YH* 16 Feb. 1850.

9 TNA, HO 107/2366.

10 Directories; Petch, *Driffield Cemetery MIs*, 64. Blanchard's later had a motor garage on the site: letter from C. J. Ketchell, 1975, in possession of D. Neave, 2010.

11 HUL, DDSY/101/92.

12 Directories; *HP* 31 July 1840, 10 Feb. 1871.

13 ERAO, TA/13; ibid. PE/10/T. 120.

14 *DT* 23 Oct. 1869; *Post Office Dir. N & ER Yorks.* (1872), 353.

15 ERAO, TA/13; ibid. PE/10/T. 120; *YH* 14 May 1859.

16 ERAO, TA/13; ibid. PE/10/T. 120.

17 Directories; Petch, *Driffield Cemetery MIs*, 100–1.

18 HUL, DDSY/101/85; 101/98; Howorth, *Year Gone By*, 37.

19 *HP*, 24 Sept. 1880.

20 ERAO, TA/13; ibid. PE/10/T. 120.

21 Directories; *DT* 17 Apr. 1875, 13 May 1876; *YH* 5 Dec. 1895; ERAO, NV/1/107. Gage's premises were bought by the builders, E. Hoggard & Sons, established in 1923: *DT* Jan. 2000 (millennium edn).

1724.[1] Its location suggests that the lime was needed for building, and in the 19th century several chalk pits and limekilns were worked in association with the brickworks on the north-east side of the town.[2] Chalk was used also by the UDC in its sewage works, and lime at the gas works.[3] Other chalk pits presumably produced lime for use on the heavier clay soils. The one exception to the small-scale operations occurred for a short period in the early 1980s, when gravel was dug near Kelleythorpe Farm for the by-pass.[4]

PRINTING

Several presses and binderies were operated in Driffield in the 19th century, mostly by booksellers and stationers who from the mid century also published three newspapers.[5] There were three printing works in Driffield in 2004, one belonging to a stationer, another producing the *Driffield Times*, and a third small concern; a fourth, Halstead's, had then recently been closed, and its site was being developed with houses as Beechlands.

The first recorded printer was John Etherington (d. 1808), druggist, bookseller and postmaster, who printed and published two songs with woodcut decorations, *c.* 1803.[6] Edward Creaser, who was apprenticed to Etherington in 1803, later recalled that during the Yorkshire election of 1807 there was so much printing to be done that they worked day and night for a fortnight.[7] Etherington was succeeded as postmaster and printer by Christopher Laybourne (d. 1831), clock and watchmaker, who printed Kilham Union Society Rules in 1809.[8] John Laybourne, probably Christopher's son, who printed a theatre bill at Driffield in 1820, was recorded as a printer in the town in 1823, but not in 1828 when Christopher occurs again.[9] The other printer and bookseller at this time was William Turner (d. 1867), also a wine merchant, who was succeeded *c.* 1851 by his son William, who continued as printer until his death in 1867.[10] On the death of Christopher Laybourne, his bookselling and printing business was evidently taken on by Benjamin Fawcett, a pioneer colour printer, who by the middle of the century was the town's main employer.[11]

33. *Benjamin Fawcett, colour printer, and wife, photographed* c. *1890, sitting in the garden of East Lodge, Eastgate, their home and location of the printing works from 1850.*

Benjamin Fawcett Fawcett was born 1808 at Bridlington where he was apprenticed to the printer William Forth.[12] He was a bookseller and printer in Middle Street, Driffield by 1831, probably in the house, shop, and printing office that he rented in 1845 from the Wesleyan trustees, the premises extending south-eastwards from the chapel to Middle Street North.[13] Fawcett was wood engraving by 1833, and produced his first known illustrated work in 1839, and the following year *Poetry about Birds* with hand-coloured woodcuts.[14] He subsequently became renowned for colour

1 RDB, H/729/1461; ERAO, IA. 41.

2 ERAO, TA/13; ibid. PE/10/T. 120; OS Map 1:10,560, Yorks. CLXI (1855 edn); Bulmer, *Dir. E Yorks.* (1892), 172, 176–7.

3 ERAO, UDDR/1/1/2, pp. 74, 158.

4 Humbs. CC *Mins* 1980–1, F 2904.

5 Below, soc. hist., newspapers.

6 BL, shelfmark 74/1870. c. 2(162) 'The pelican bonnet' and 'Nothing at all'; *YH* 23 May 1807. John Etherington's relationship to the Etherington gentry family of Driffield is unknown. He may have been the son of Christopher Etherington of York, bookseller, printer and publisher of the York Chronicle. R. Davies, *A Memoir of the York Press* (1868), 331–8.

7 J. Browne, *History of the Driffield Post Office*, undated newspaper cuttings in possession of C. J. Ketchell, 2000.

8 J. E. S. Walker, *Hull and ER Clocks* (1982), 77; ERAO, DDX/17/15.

9 T. Sheppard, *Evolution of the Drama in Hull and District* (1927), 197; Baines, *Hist. Yorks.* (1823), ii. 195; Pigot, *Nat. Com. Dir.* (1828–9), ii, 930.

10 Directories; Petch, *Driffield Cemetery MIs*, 100.

11 Walker, *Hull and ER Clocks*, 77; White, *Dir. Hull & District* (1831), 247.

12 Much of the following is based on M. C. F. Morris, *Benjamin Fawcett: Colour Printer and Engraver* (1925) and R. and A. McLean, *Benjamin Fawcett, Engraver and Colour Printer* (1988).

13 White, *Dir. Hull & District* (1831), 247; ERAO, PE/10/T. 120; ibid. TA/13. The buildings were demolished in the mid 20th century: *DT* Jan. 2000 (millennium edn).

14 McLean, *Fawcett*, 12.

illustrations, and many of the finest colour engravings were by the artist Alexander Frank Lydon (1837–1917) who worked for Fawcett for over thirty years from *c.* 1851, starting as an apprentice engraver.[1] Most important for the development of the firm was Fawcett's long collaboration with the Revd F. O. Morris, vicar of Nafferton 1844–54 and rector of Nunburnholme 1854–1893, for whom he printed a *Bible Natural History* (1849–50), then the hugely successful *History of British Birds* (1850–58) which was published in parts, ultimately making a six-volume set illustrated with some 360 coloured wood engravings. Over the next thirty years Fawcett printed a dozen similar works, published by Groombridge of London, mostly on natural history or topography, a number written by Morris such as his *Country Seats of the Noblemen and Gentlemen of Great Britain and Ireland*, illustrated by Lydon and issued in parts between 1864 and 1880. The monthly *Naturalist* magazine was also printed by Fawcett from the 1850s.

In 1850 Fawcett moved his family and the business to the larger premises of East Lodge and its outbuildings, at the southern end of Eastgate.[2] The printing works, which had eight hand presses, provided much work in Driffield. In 1851 about thirty men and women of the town were employed as printers, engravers, and colourers, and thirty years later 18 men, 15 girls and 9 boys, the young girls colouring monochrome engravings or re-touching colour prints.[3] What have been described as three of Fawcett's 'greatest masterpieces', *British Freshwater Fishes* (1879), *The Ruined Abbeys of Britain* (1882) and *Parrots in Captivity* (1884–7) were published at this time.[4]

The beginning of the decline of the firm is attributed to the collapse of the publishers Groombridge in the early 1880s, involving heavy losses for Fawcett. Soon after Lydon left the firm and went to London.[5] At the time of Fawcett's death in 1893 the firm was insolvent. His son Frank continued the printing business for a short time but early in 1895 all the machinery, type and fittings were sold by auction.[6]

East Lodge and the large grounds, extending back to Wansford Road, were bought in 1957 by East Yorkshire Printers Ltd, the proprietor of the *Driffield Times*, which then built another printing works there.[7] In 1989 the newspaper returned to premises in the centre of the town, and the Eastgate site was cleared later for development.[8] By 2003 it was occupied by a newly-built housing estate called Fawcett Gardens and a garden commemorating Benjamin Fawcett.[9]

POSTAL AND FINANCIAL SERVICES

Post Office

Before the opening of the canal letters for Driffield were brought once a fortnight from Kilham. In 1772 Henry Drinkrow entered into a bond with the Post Master General that resulted in letters being brought three times a week, and sent, via Malton.[10] A sub-post office was opened in the town about 1790. Its location was contested, presumably because of the benefits it would confer on the licensee. Several inhabitants, including the Revd George Etherington and Richard Porter, successfully petitioned for it to be kept by John Etherington (d. 1808), bookseller and stationer, rather than by the grocer/draper William Porter.[11] In 1800 a daily postal service from Malton to Driffield and Bridlington was introduced and in 1829 Driffield was approved as a post-town in its own right not a sub-post office of Beverley and Malton.[12]

The other early postmasters were Christopher Laybourne (d. 1831), clockmaker and printer, with an office in Middle Street, his daughter Catherine by 1840, in New Road/Exchange Street, then her husband Martin L. Domanski, a Polish refugee, from *c.* 1847, and Frank Dobson, jeweller and watchmaker, in Market Place, by 1851, and his son Frederick Frank Dobson (d. 1870).[13] The Post Office remained in Market Place, the address being specified as no. 8 in 1892, until about 1910, when new, purpose-built premises in Middle Street North were opened. A sub office close to the railway station, at no. 7 Middle Street South, was opened *c.* 1930.[14] In 2001 a new sorting office was opened on the industrial estate at Kelleythorpe[15] and the main post office in Driffield had been closed by 2004. The town was served by a post office in Market Place in 2010.

Banking

The Beverley Bank of Appleton, Machell & Smith, later Machell, Pease & Lidell, founded in 1793 is said to have opened a branch in Driffield in the 1790s with William Otley as agent until 1821 when the agency was withdrawn.[16] In 1812 Robert Simpson, draper became the

1 *DT* 21 Aug. 1883; Barley, *Great and Little Driffield*, 36; McLean, *Fawcett*, 17–18.
2 Illus. in Morris, *Fawcett*; opp. p. 86.
3 TNA, HO 107/2366; ibid. RG11/4793.
4 McLean, *Fawcett*, 22.
5 *DT* 21 Aug. 1883.
6 McLean, *Fawcett*, 23.
7 RDB, 1063/512/458; ERAO, UDDR/1/8/54, Building…Cttee, 7 Aug. 1957; UDDR/1/8/55, Building…Cttee, 9 Apr. 1958.
8 *DT* Jan. 2000 (millennium edn); below, soc. hist., newspapers.
9 *DT* 9, 16 Apr. 2003; *DP* 7 Feb., 14 Mar., 25 Apr. 2003.
10 Holderness, *Some Driffield Incidents*, 9.
11 HUL, DDSY/12/1; *Universal Brit. Dir.* (*c.* 1792), ii. 828; Holderness, Some *Driffield Incidents*, 4–6, 9–10; above, this section, printing.
12 *HA* 5 Apr. 1800; *HP* 22 Dec 1829.
13 Browne, *Driffield Post Office*; directories; *HP* 20 May 1870.
14 Directories.
15 Harrison, *Driffield*, 404.
16 ERAO, DDX/17/15.

agent for Bower & Co.'s East Riding Bank, represented in 2010 by the NatWest bank.[1] Also *c.* 1812 a branch of the Malton bank of Pease, Dunn & Pease was opened at Driffield with Milburn Allison, maltster and merchant as agent.[2] In 1820 it was taken over by the Malton & North Riding Bank of Hagues, Strickland & Allen which collapsed during the commercial crisis in 1826.[3]

Despite such setbacks the number of bank agencies increased. Branches were opened in Driffield by Harding & Co., Bridlington (now HSBC), in 1824, the York Union Banking Co. (now Barclays) in 1833, and Yorkshire Agricultural & Commercial Banking Co. by 1836.[4] The last a joint stock bank, crashed in 1842.[5]

In 1840 there were, including the savings bank established in 1831, five banks in Driffield.[6] The location of the offices of the early bank agents is obscured by the evident use of Market Place and Middle Street as alternative descriptions, but practically all were in or close to Market Place. Later in the mid century new bank premises were put up and full branches established under managers. About 1890 there were, with the Post Office Savings Bank, seven banks, all but one of them in Market Place.[7] Details of the history of the town's banks, existing in 2010, are given below.

Barclays Bank, originally York Union The York Union Banking Co. Ltd was founded in 1833, and that year opened a branch in Middle Street in Driffield, presumably in the house on the east side of Middle Street North which the company was renting in 1845.[8] A new bank in Market Place (no. 61) was built in 1861. Robert Galt manager from *c.* 1864, and a prominent figure in the town, absconded with cash in 1873.[9] In 1902 the York Union Banking Co. Ltd was amalgamated with Barclay & Co. Ltd, later Barclays Bank Ltd. John Dawnay, son of Hugh Richard Dawnay, Viscount Downe, lord of Driffield manor, served as a local director at the York office from 1905.[10]

HSBC, originally Harding & Co., later York City & County, Midland Bank Harding and Co., bankers of Bridlington opened a branch in 1824.[11] Called the Burlington (Bridlington) Bank in 1831, and the Burlington (Bridlington) and Driffield Bank by the 1850s,[12] it was managed by 1834 by George Forge, wine and spirit merchant, of Middle Street then Market Place, until his death in 1869.[13] His shop was on the west side of Market Place in 1845.[14] The bank was taken over in 1878 by the York City & County Banking Co. Ltd which had premises at no. 12 Market Place in 1892.[14] It was succeeded soon after 1905 by the London Joint Stock Bank Ltd, from about 1915 by the London Joint City & Midland Bank Ltd, and by the Midland Bank Ltd from the earlier 1920s. The branch was rebuilt by Midland Bank in 1922,[16] and it was taken over by HSBC in 1992.

34. *Great Driffield: Barclays Bank, Market Place, 2006. Built for the York Union Banking Company in 1861, designed by Edward Taylor of York.*

Lloyds TSB, originally Driffield Savings Bank, later Trustee Savings Bank and Lloyds In 1831 a branch of Hull Trustee Savings Bank was established at Driffield through the 'exertions' of J. B. La Marche.[17] The Revd Henry Jennings was secretary of the local initiating committee,[18] and Robert Simpson, a retired draper was appointed the bank agent. For the first 10 years the bank

1 Ibid.; below, NatWest.

2 ERAO, DDX/17/15; *YH* 1 Aug. 1818; 30 Dec. 1820; 10 Mar. 1827.

3 ERAO, DDX/17/15; *YH* 4 Sept. 1819; 30 Dec. 1820; *LM* 25 Feb. 1826; *HP* 28 Feb. 1826.

4 ERAO, DDX/17/15.

5 W. C. E. Hartley, *Banking in Yorks.* (1975), 73.

6 White, *Dir. N & ER Yorks* (1840), 205.

7 Ross, *Driffield*, 98–9.

8 ERAO, PE/10/T. 120; ibid. TA/13.

9 *HP* 6 June 1873.

10 Ibid. 237; J. Foster, *Pedigrees of Yorks.* iii, s.v. Dawnay.

11 ERAO, DDX/17/15.

12 Sheahan and Whellan, *Hist. York & ER.* ii. 498.

13 Directories; ERAO,DDX/17/15.

14 ERAO, TA/13; ibid. PE/10/T. 120.

15 Hartley, *Banking in Yorks.* 156; Bulmer, *Dir. E Yorks.* (1892), 175.

16 Pevsner and Neave, *Yorks. ER*, 442.

17 C. D. Hebden, *Trustee Savings Bank of Yorks. and Lincs.* (1981), 350.

18 ERAO, DDGR/44/29/29.

35. *Great Driffield: NatWest Bank, Market Place, 2006. Built as the National Provincial Bank in 1927.*

was conducted in a room in the Letters Inn (later Queen's Head), Middle Street.[1] In 1846 the bank then in Exchange Street was open only on Thursday afternoon.[2] Later it shared the court house built on the south side of Exchange Street in 1856 with the Mechanics' Institute.[3]

There were 1,237 depositors in 1853 and 1,764 in 1869 when considerable sums were paid in by farm servants at Martinmas.[4] The branch had a balance of £48,000 in 1864, when it became independent of the Hull bank.[5]

In 1886 new premises at no. 36 Market Place were bought for the independent Driffield Savings Bank.[6] Its supporters included the Elgeys, chemist and grocer; the industrialist Harrison Holt, Thomas Holtby, brewer, and the cabinet maker, J. F. Shepherdson.[7] The Driffield bank was amalgamated with the York County Savings Bank in 1911, and in 1975 became part of a larger grouping, the Trustee Savings Bank of Yorkshire and Lincoln. New premises in Middle Street South were obtained in the later 1920s.[9] After further amalgamation, the Trustee Savings Bank Group was merged in 1995 with Lloyds Bank to form the Lloyds TSB Group PLC, and the company operated the former Trustee Savings Bank branch, at no. 64 Middle Street South, as one of its two branches in Driffield.[9] The Middle Street branch was closed in 2006 and its business transferred to the Lloyds TSB branch in Market Place.[10] The building was subsequently demolished.

Lloyds Bank opened a branch at Driffield at no. 15 Market Place in 1963. Initially a 'clerk-in-charge' branch it became a full branch with its own manager in 1965.[11] It became the main Driffield branch of Lloyds TSB on the merger of the companies in 1995, and the sole branch from 2006.

NatWest, originally East Riding Bank (Westminster) and London & Yorkshire (National Provincial) The East Riding Bank, founded by Bower and others in Beverley

1 Ibid. DDX/17/15.
2 White, *Dir. Hull & York* (1846), 419.
3 RDB, NS/347/515; 193/39/37; *Kellys' Dir. N & ER Yorks.* (1872), 351.
4 *Driffield Observer* 21 Dec. 1853; *DT* 4 Dec. 1869; 15 Jan. 1870; 8 Dec. 1871.
5 *HP* 1 Apr. 1864.
6 RDB, 12/92/90 (1886). They may have been opened in 1887: Ross, *Driffield*, 91.
7 RDB, 12/465/439 (1899); 55/474/451 (1903); 233/165/130; *DT*, 5 Mar. 2003.
8 RDB, 386/316/268; Hebden, *Trustee Savings Bank*, 14, 63, 69, 124, 131; directories.
9 Lloyds/TSB website, 2003.
10 *DT* 12 July, 22 Sept. 2006.
11 Inf. from J. Mortlock, Archivist, Lloyds Bank, 2010.

in 1806,[1] had a branch in Driffield by 1812; Robert Dandy, draper, succeeded Robert Simpson as agent in 1818, and the bank recorded as in Middle Street or Market Place, may have been in his shop.[2] On Dandy's death in 1828 the agency was taken over by William Jarratt, who in 1845 was doing business from his house on the east side of Market Place.[3] In 1856 the house (later no. 51 Market Place) was rebuilt as a bank.[4] Beckett & Co. of Leeds bought the East Riding Bank in 1875, and in 1879 also took over the firm of Swann, Clough & Co. of York, the amalgamated banks subsequently forming the York and East Riding Bank. In 1920 that bank was amalgamated with the London, County, Westminster, & Parr's Bank Ltd, which was renamed Westminster Bank Ltd in 1923.[5]

A branch of London and Yorkshire Bank was opened at Driffield in 1875 with William Jarratt, formerly of the East Riding Bank, as manager.[6] The bank was based at no. 35 Market Place by 1886.[7] In 1903 the bank was amalgamated with the Union of London & Smiths' Bank, and in 1918 the latter bank was in turn merged with the National Provincial Bank of England to form the National Provincial & Union Bank of England, from 1924 the National Provincial Bank.[8] A new building was put up for the Driffield branch on a prominent site in Market Place (no. 29) in 1927.[9]

In 1968 the National Provincial Bank and the Westminster Bank merged to create the National Westminster Bank, now NatWest, the former National Provincial premises (now no. 28) being chosen for the new bank's Driffield branch.[10] The former Westminster Bank at no. 51 Market Place was disposed of and was a sports shop in 2010.

Yorkshire Bank, originally Yorkshire Penny Bank A penny savings bank was founded in 1860 by the curate Revd J. Skinner at the Mechanics' Institute. At the opening session the room was crowded with 'old and young' and a total of £12 10*s* 10*d* was received from 274 depositors; three weeks later there were 370 depositors.[11] It was presumably the same penny savings bank that was based in Exchange Street *c.* 1890.[12] It is unclear if it was a branch of, or inspired by, the bank founded in 1859 in the West Riding to provide the working classes with a means of saving, later called the Yorkshire Penny Bank. That philanthropic enterprise introduced school banks in 1874,[13] and a Yorkshire Penny Bank branch was operated at the National school from the late 19th century.[14] A branch of the Yorkshire Penny Bank Ltd was opened at no. 13 Market Place in the later 1920s.[15] In 1959 the Yorkshire Penny Bank became Yorkshire Bank Ltd, which in 1964 bought and rebuilt the Black Swan in Market Place for its Driffield branch. The premises opened in 1966 were still used by the bank in 2010.[16]

Building Societies

Mortgage facilities available from friendly societies from the beginning of the century[17] were expanded by the setting up of local building societies. Nothing further is known of the East Riding Building and Mutual Investment Society evidently established at Driffield in 1849.[18] The Driffield and East Riding Benefit Building Society, founded in 1865, had a much longer life.[19] At its first AGM in 1866, the president was Christopher Sykes, the vice-presidents E. H. Reynard of Sunderlandwick and the Revd. J. Davidson of Nafferton, and the honorary secretaries Robert Galt, manager of the York Union Bank, and the solicitor G. B. Tonge. The society had around 195 subscribers in its first year.[20] Amongst the early trustees or directors were Henry Angas, grocer, James Elgey, chemist, and W. G. Purdon, shoemaker. The society was based in Exchange Street by 1872 in the offices of the solicitor Frederick J. Brigham, who was then secretary, a post he retained for over thirty years. From *c.* 1920 W. H. Blakeston, solicitor, was the secretary, with whose firm the post and office remained, first at no. 18 Exchange Street and later at no. 51 Market Place.[21] In 1967 the society became the Driffield Building Society.[22] It was taken over by the Britannia Building Society in 1982 which subsequently ceased to keep an office in Driffield.[23]

1 T. E. Gregory, *Westminster Bank through a Century* (1936), ii. 136, facing p. 302.

2 ERAO, DDX/17/15; Pigot, *Nat. Com. Dir.* (1822), 606; Baines, *Hist. Yorks.* (1823), ii., 195; Pigot, *Nat. Com. Dir.* (1828–9), ii, 930.

3 ERAO, DDX/17/15; ERAO, TA/13; ibid. PE/10/T. 120.

4 Pevsner and Neave, *Yorks. ER.* 442; Ross, *Driffield*, 179.

5 Gregory, *Westminster Bank,* ii. 136–7.

6 *HP* 26 Feb 1875.

7 RDB, 12/92/90 (1886); 12/465/439 (1899).

8 H. Withers, *Nat. Provincial Bank 1833 to 1933* (1933), ix, 74, 79, 82, 90.

9 Datestone; Pevsner and Neave, *Yorks. ER.* 442; illus. at HUL, DX/144/3 (A 5069/1); photograph 1953 by Bob Allen at ERAO, PH/4/11.

10 NatWest website, 2003.

11 *HP* 6 Jan., 27 Jan. 1860, 16 May 1862.

12 Ross, *Driffield*, 91, 99.

13 Yorks. Bank website, 2005.

14 Ross, *Driffield*, 99; *Hull and East Riding Red Book* (1900), 214.

15 Directories; photograph 1953 by Bob Allen at ERAO, PH/4/11.

16 RDB, 1340/200/184; ERAO, UDDR/1/1/37, Building...Cttee, 14 Oct. 1963; Yorks. Bank website, 2003.

17 RDB, CF/198/304.

18 *HP* 9 Feb. 1849.

19 *DT* 6 Jan. 1900.

20 *HP* 16 Mar. 1866.

21 Directories; *Driffield Souvenir Guide* (1974), 67.

22 RDB, 224/512/432; 1742/118/98; directories.

23 Inf. from Mrs Sharp, Blakestons, solicitors, Driffield, 2006.

SOCIAL HISTORY

SOCIAL STRUCTURE

The distinctive character of a community comes from its social structure and pattern of landownership. Although the lord of Driffield manor had a large estate in Great and Little Driffield, he was non-resident and his holding had by the 13th century been divided between several tenant farmers. The rest of the Driffields was occupied mostly by freeholders of various kinds, although the 13th-century sources do also record a lower economic group, the some fifty tenants with little or no land, who presumably worked as labourers.[1]

The similarity in the circumstances of many of the inhabitants would seem to be confirmed by the hearth-tax returns of 1672. Great Driffield and Little Driffield then had together 159 households; of those 138 households, 87 per cent, had only a single hearth each, 15 other households had two hearths each. The remaining six, presumably belonging to the most affluent of the parishioners, had three or more hearths, and included one occupant with six hearths and another with as many as eleven.[2]

By the 18th century Driffield was very much a freeholder community allowing the town to expand rapidly once the canal was open. There were some 74 freeholders in the Driffields in 1730, over 130 by 1760 and 252 proprietors in 1845.[3] The fragmentation of property ownership continued in the later 19th and 20th century.

SOCIAL LEADERSHIP

Since the Middle Ages Driffield may have been a fairly homogenous community with no great gulf between any one social grouping and the next, but until the 20th century public office, greater wealth or extent of property ownership usually defined the elite, those who were the social and political leaders.

Medieval

In the absence of resident lords, an intermittent influence on the affairs of the parish in the Middle Ages was exercised by their officers who visited to hold courts. The record of the activities of the seigneurial officers, and of the reactions of the parishioners, is slight, and the one or two pieces of evidence come mostly from the mid 14th century, when Driffield was clearly experiencing a period of general discord and violence.[4] Thomas Burrell, steward of the countess of Pembroke, then lady of Driffield manor, appears on the record in 1347, when attempts were made to discover and arrest those who allegedly assaulted him and prevented his holding a court at Driffield.[5] Another Driffield officer was identified in the 1360s, when the abbot of St Mary's, York complained that Robert Claybrook of Great Driffield, the manorial bailiff, had taken his cattle, presumably from the abbey's farm at Elmswell; Claybrook evidently avoided proceedings, at least temporarily, by joining the king's forces in Ireland in 1363 and 1364.[6]

In the 14th and 15th century a number of resident families played a prominent role in local affairs. These include the Dring (Drenge) family who were involved in a series of violent incidents dating back to the 1320s, the causes of which remain unknown. In 1328 Henry Scrope and other notables were ordered by the Crown to enquire into the killings at Driffield of Thomas Dring and John Roos, and the following year Thomas's son John entered into a mutual bond with nine others, evidently in an attempt to keep the peace.[7] John Dring was recorded again in 1336, when the Crown granted him a year's immunity from legal actions, and in 1348 as owing money to the countess of Pembroke and engaged in a suit in Chancery.[8] The same or another John Dring was among those involved in a violent dispute with Robert Daniel of Beswick in 1358; in 1361 he was found to have killed a man in self-defence, and in 1367 he himself was killed in Driffield, it was alleged by a confederation of people from Driffield and elsewhere in the East Riding.[9] Those principally accused were later pardoned.[10] Dring's local enemies[11] included Richard Howsham of Elmswell, among those alleged in 1373 to have misused the property of St Mary's abbey, York, and shown violence to its servants at Elmswell and other places;[12] William Hill, a substantial proprietor in

1 Above, manors and estates, pattern of landholding.
2 TNA, E 179/205/504.
3 HUL, DDCV/42/1; above, manor and estates, pattern of landholding.
4 Below, this section, soc. leadership (medieval).
5 *Cal. Pat.* 1345–8, 320, 383; above, manors, Driffield.
6 *Cal. Pat.* 1361–4, 318, 428; 1364–7, 14, 157.
7 Ibid. 1327–30, 354; G. P. Brown, *Par. Ch. of All Saints* (1984), 7.
8 *Cal. Pat.* 1334–8, 222; *Cal. Close*, 1346–9, 487, 491.
9 *Cal. Pat.* 1358–61, 159; 1361–4, 148, 162; *Cal. Inq. Misc.* iii, p. 256.
10 *Cal. Fine R.* 1356–68, 354, 362; *Cal. Pat.* 1367–70, 90, 335, 394.
11 *Cal. Inq. Misc.* iii, p. 256.
12 *Cal. Pat.* 1370–4, 396–7.

Driffield and Kelleythorpe,[1] and the Rouths (Raufs) of Great Driffield.[2] Little is known of the Hill family although in the early 15th century John Hill of Driffield was named as a tax commissioner for the East Riding.[3]

The Rouths were resident in Driffield for over a century and gave their name to the manor of Routh Hall. William Routh had been allowed the privilege of his own confessor in 1350, and Thomas Routh had then both obtained the office of notary and, as a chaplain, been pardoned for the death of Richard Provost of Great Driffield.[4] The local significance of the Rouths and Drings is evident from the poll-tax record of 1377, the constables of Great and Little Driffield then being named as Thomas Routh and Thomas Dring.[5] John Routh, esquire, and his brother, Brian, were both of Great Driffield in the mid 15th century and in 1483 Brian Routh held Routh Hall manor.[6] In 1470 Brian Routh had been appointed a commissioner of array for the East Riding along with William Swillington, also of Great Driffield.[7]

It may have been the same William Swillington, or more probably his father, who was appointed a commissioner 'of walls and ditches' for the East Riding in 1446. He was the son of William Swillington, an illegitimate member of the family of Swillingtons of Swillington (WR) who had settled in Driffield in the late 14th century on his marriage to Margaret, daughter and heiress of John Dring.[8] In the 1430s Elizabeth Swillington, a disputed heiress of the senior branch of the Swillingtons was abducted with force from Driffield and imprisoned at Tattershall Castle (Lincs.) by another claimant Ralph, Lord Cromwell.[9] The arms of the Swillingtons and Rouths are on the tower of All Saints' church, Great Driffield, and on the north aisle where also are what appear to be the arms of the Arden (Ardern) family.[10]

The Ardens of Driffield and the Rouths were probably connected by marriage as they are both named in relation to the chantry founded in the church by John Tebbe in 1443.[11] Hugh Arden, who had an estate at Driffield in the early 1380s, and his descendants, who held the manor of Kelleythorpe up to 1543, were closely associated with the Percy family, earls of Northumberland.[12] In 1451–2 William Percy, youngest son of the earl, was prebendary of Driffield.[13] This was probably why local residents occasionally became involved in the periodic unrest that embroiled the Percies and their followers. The vicar of Great Driffield was among the 50 armed men linked to the earl of Northumberland who assembled at the Percy manor of Topcliffe in October 1453 during the disturbances in Yorkshire, between the Percies and the Nevilles, that were a prelude to the Wars of the Roses.[14]

The parish was disturbed in the early 1530s by the violent dispute between Sir William Percy, brother of the late earl of Northumberland, and Sir Robert Constable of Flamborough and Holme. A meeting of the justices in Driffield was said to have been disrupted by argument, and at Kelleythorpe, where Percy was lessee of John Arden, an attempt to detain Sir Robert's cattle and carts allegedly resulted in the beating of one of Percy's servants there.[15] John Arden, esquire, headed the 1524 subsidy list for Great and Little Driffield and Kelleythorpe. He was by far the wealthiest resident assessed at 26*s.* 8*d.*; the next wealthiest was William Gascoigne, gentleman, a descendant of the Swillingtons, assessed at 6*s.*[16]

1550–1770

By the mid 16th century a new family, the Etheringtons, was heading the tax list for Great and Little Driffield.[17] William Etherington, who was credited with a horse and harness in the 1539 muster roll, evidently acquired an estate in Great Driffield on his marriage to the heiress of Brian Skerne.[18] William Etherington and George Etherington, probably his son, served as bailiff of Driffield manor, either separately or jointly, before 1559, when the lord of Driffield, Sir Christopher Danby, granted them that office for their lives.[19] At his death in 1562 William Etherington, 'gentleman' of Great Driffield had at least 9 oxgangs of arable land and large flocks of sheep, and milling and corn dealing may have contributed importantly to his wealth. Reflective perhaps of his official status were the 'two coats of

1 *Cal. Inq. Misc.* iii, p. 236.

2 Above, manors and estates, Routh Hall.

3 *Cal. Fine R.* 1413–22, 88, 123.

4 *Cal. Papal Reg.* iii. 367, 372; *Cal. Pat.* 1348–50, 540. A William Provost had been pardoned earlier for a killing in return for service in France: *Cal. Pat.* 1338–40, 423; 1345–8, 555.

5 TNA, E 179/202/59, m. 24.

6 Above, manors and estates, Routh Hall.

7 *Cal. Pat. 1467–77*, 199.

8 A. J. Beanlands, *The Swillingtons of Swillington*, Thoresby Society Pubs. 15 (1909), 192, 210; above, manors and estates, Toley fee for later Swillingtons.

9 Nottingham Univ. Libr., Pa/L/2; T. Turville-Petre, 'The Persecution of Elizabeth Swillington by Ralph, Lord Cromwell', *Nottingham Medieval Studies* 42 (1998), 174–187.

10 Below, buildings, religious buildings.

11 Below, relig. hist., Middle Ages.

12 Below, Kelleythorpe.

13 Le Neve, *Fasti, 1300–1541, York*, 45.

14 R. A. Griffiths, 'Local rivalries and national politics: the Percies, the Nevilles and the Duke of Exeter 1452–3', *Speculum* 41 (Oct. 1968), 604. Peter Arden (Ardern), justice of Common Pleas, of the Driffield family was on two commissions of oyer and terminer set up in 1453 to investigate the unrest in Yorkshire; ibid, 594–6; above, manors and estates, Toley Fee.

15 TNA, STAC 2/22/162, printed in *Yorks. Star Chamber Proceedings*, iii (YAS Rec. Ser. 51), pp. 18–28. *DNB*, *s.v.* Constable.

16 TNA, E179/303/183; above, manors and estates, Driffield (Gascoigne).

17 TNA, E179/203/255.

18 TNA, E36/39; above, manors and estates, Driffield (Etherington).

19 TNA, C 142/157, no. 68.

plate', four steel caps, and other arms then found in his house.[1] William's son Thomas (d. 1589), who built up a large estate in the East and North Ridings, left personal property valued at almost £1,000, his sword, jewellery, cash, and clothing accounting for £117. Other signs of his wealth and status were the arms in the hall of his impressive house which included, besides the two coats of armour, equipment for eight horsemen; his plate of silver-goblets, bowls, salts, and spoons, valued in all at £20, and his direction that he be buried in his private pew, 'my ... closet', in Great Driffield church.[2] Thomas's eldest son George, later Sir George Etherington, was the highest tax payer at Driffield in 1600 and 1606–10, and his son Richard in 1625, but also prominent were members of the Spink and Silvester families.[3]

It was claimed that William Spink was a 'petty grocer' at Driffield who got his wealth 'by bargaining and taking of tithes to farm'.[4] He was a sub-lessee of the tithes of Driffield and he seemingly married well; his wife Margaret was probably a member of the Silvester family who were intermarried with the Etheringtons. Three of William and Margaret Spink's sons went to Cambridge University one of whom, Richard, is said to have been ordained; he died young in 1634 and like his father is commemorated by a monument in Great Driffield church.[5] On William's death in 1616 he left a great fortune, and his twelve-year old daughter, heiress of £500–£600, was abducted and forcibly married to Richard Dodson at Goodmanham.[6]

Other newcomers to the parish were the Bests at Elmswell and, of higher standing, the Cromptons.[7] Official opportunity presumably brought the Cromptons into the district, Elizabeth I's auditor, Thomas Crompton, acquiring Crown estates there in the 1590s. Two of his sons, Thomas and John, both knighted, inherited in turn the Skerne estate; the third Robert, a clerk in the alienation office, London, settled at Great Driffield by the 1620s.[8] The family's local connections were enlarged by Robert's marriage to Ceziah Strickland of Boynton, near Bridlington. The Cromptons were penalised for their adherence to the king, but nevertheless continued to be chief resident proprietors in Driffield in the later 17th century.[9] The widowed Ceziah Crompton (d. 1668) had the largest estate in Driffield in 1662, valued at £100, and her step-son Thomas Crompton the largest house, with 11 hearths, in 1672.[10] Thomas Crompton was a magistrate and in 1662, along with his brother-in-law and fellow magistrate, Sir Thomas Remington of Lund, he examined Isabel Binnington of Great Driffield who claimed to have been visited numerous times by the spirit of a man from London who had been murdered in her house 14 years earlier.[11]

The Crompton family's connection with Driffield had been severed by the end of the 17th century, but that of the Etheringtons, who for some reason were not on the tax lists in 1628 and 1641, but reappeared in 1664, continues into the 19th century.[12] William Etherington fought on the Royalist side in the Civil Wars and it may have been his widow, or more probably that of his cousin George Etherington, who was the Mrs Etherington with the second largest house, with six hearths, in Great Driffield in 1672.[13] The four-hearthed houses of John Etherington and Katherine Stork (d. 1679), daughter of Marmaduke Etherington, were the next largest.[14]

John Etherington, the head of the family, was a mercer living above his shop at Driffield on his death in 1720, but his eldest son Thomas was termed gentleman at the inclosure of Driffield's open fields in 1742, when he was awarded 430 a., an allotment second only to that of the non-resident lord of the manor, Richard Langley.[15] Thomas Etherington was therefore the most substantial resident freeholder, a position he enhanced by marrying Anne Stork, heiress of the next largest freehold, of 343 a., awarded to her brother Thomas Stork, gentleman. The only other resident accorded the title gentleman at inclosure was John Drinkrow. It was these two families, the Etheringtons and the Drinkrows, farmers and shopkeepers, along with the Grays, yeoman farmers, that were the leaders of Driffield society until the 1770s with, from mid-century, the proprietors of the three main inns.[16]

The Anglican church made little or no contribution. George Colebatch, vicar of Driffield, 1705–55, a substantial landowner in his own right and living in a grand house in Bridge Street, was reputedly a miser and a

1 BIA, precentorship wills, William Eddrinton, 1562 (inventory).

2 Ibid. Thomas Etherington, 1589 (will and inventory); TNA, E179/204/296.

3 TNA, E179/204/348, 371, 417.

4 C. C. Jones, *Recollections of Royalty* (1828), i. 207.

5 *Alumni Cantab. to 1751.*; below, relig. hist., 17th cent. (Anglicanism).

6 Jones, *Recollections*, i, 206–11.

7 For the Bests see below, Elmswell.

8 J. W. Clay (ed.), *Dugdale's Visitation of Yorkshire*, iii (1917), 419, 481; TNA, E179/205/453, 479.

9 Above, manors and estates, Driffield (Crompton).

10 YAS, MD335/Box 57; E179/205/504. Ceziah's sons Robert and Walter established minor landed families at Ruston Parva and Sunderlandwick respectively: Clay, *Dugdale's Visitation*, iii. 482.

11 *A strange and wonderfull discovery of a horrid and cruel murther* (1662).

12 TNA, E179/205/453, 467, 479. For the Etheringtons' descent see above, manors and estates, Driffield (Etherington).

13 J. W. Clay (ed.), *Yorks. Royalist Composition Papers*, iii (YAS Rec. Ser. 20), 206; TNA, E179/205/467, 504.

14 TNA, E179/205/504; ERAO, PE10/1.

15 BIA, precentorship wills, John Etherington, 1720; above, econ. hist., inclosure.

16 The list of those from Driffield petitioning in 1744 for a bridge between Sunderlandwick and Kelleythorpe is headed by Thomas Stork, Thomas Etherington, John Drinkrow and John Gray. ERAO, QSF/147/D/4; below, this section, inns and public houses.

recluse.[1] His successor, Francis Best, a member of county society, was non-resident except possibly on the occasions he attended the Driffield hunt.[2] Best however, was a trustee of the Beverley to Kendale House and Bainton Balk turnpike, and attended the first meeting of the Driffield Navigation commissioners.[3] The greatest support for the latter came from the lord of the manor and chief proprietor, Boynton Langley, who like his father, almost certainly the instigator of the inclosure of the open fields, evidently took a direct interest in the development of a town some 18 miles from their home. Langley subscribed £6,590 to the navigation, 43 per cent of the total sum. The Driffield residents who subscribed were Henry Drinkrow, grocer and builder of the Hunt Room, John Drinkrow, Thomas Gray, William Paul of Danesdale, who had bought George Colebatch's estate, William Porter of the Blue Bell and William Byass, owner of the Red Lion.[4]

1770–1870

The opening of the navigation transformed Driffield's social leadership, as much as it did its economy, with the arrival of the professionals, the attorneys and the medical men, and the corn, coal and timber merchants. Before the 1770s much of the legal work at Driffield was carried out by Marmaduke Prickett (1699–1765) and his son, also Marmaduke (d. 1809), who attended once a week from Kilham.[5] The first resident solicitor appears to have been Thomas Cator (d. 1824), who transferred his office from Malton (NR) in 1772, and three years later by marrying Mary, widow of Henry Drinkrow, he became part of the established society.[6] By 1782 the attorney William Conyers (d. 1796) had also re-located from Malton. His son and successor George Conyers (d. 1809) was clerk to the navigation commissioners, coroner for the East Riding from 1804, and captain of the Bainton and Driffield Volunteers.[7] There was usually a doctor resident at Driffield by the mid 18th century, for example the surgeon and apothecary George Cowart (d. 1767), son of a Beverley apothecary, who married Ann Drinkrow in 1759; they lived in a house in Middle Street with her brother Henry Drinkrow.[8] By the late 1780s the growing town had four apothecaries or surgeons.[9]

Of the leading corn merchants James Harrison, who founded the most successful firm, came from Malton, William and Richard Dunn were also newcomers, but Richard Porter was the son of the landlord of the Blue Bell. The merchants built up close links with the merchant communities at Hull and Wakefield, with sons often based there, thus broadening the outlook of the market town,[10] something that would have been contributed by those attracted to Driffield by its position in a 'fine sporting country', a selling point used in the local and national press.[11] These men of leisure included William Langley (d. 1791), brother of the squire, who spent most of the last year of his life lodging at the Red Lion, running up a bill of £210 with the landlord Alexander Mackintosh.[12] Others were Henry E. Rousby, former squire of Croome, who lived grandly at Driffield with a staff of six including cook and housekeeper, and five dogs, all individually named in his will, William Flint (d. 1832), author of a *Treatise on the Breeding, Training, and Management of Horses* and Captain William Rawson (d. 1850), a veteran of the battle of Waterloo, who retired to the town *c.* 1819 for some eight years to enjoy 'his favourite sports of shooting and angling'.[13]

Field sports may have lured the Hon. Philip Anstruther Leslie, son of Alexander, Lord Newark, to Driffield where he lived from *c.* 1793 until his death in 1801.[14] Leslie, whose first wife Frances (d. 1792) was the daughter of John Manners, marquess of Granby, married at Little Driffield in 1795, as his second wife, Harriet daughter of Vernon Southerne, dancing master.[15] His past connections gave Leslie a status in Driffield and he was chosen as chairman of the Agricultural Society in 1800 and appointed an officer in the Driffield Armed Association. He also allowed his name to head a list of local luminaries endorsing a patent medicine sold by the postmaster, printer and bookseller John Etherington.[16]

Etherington was probably not a member of the local landowning family whose head in the late 18th century was the Revd George Etherington (d. 1802), vicar of Collingham (WR), 'a gentleman of great literary science', who lived in the family house Westgate Hall.[17] The last of the family to live there was his son John Etherington, who had moved to Bridlington Quay by 1816 and died at Scarborough in 1820.[18]

1 ERAO, DDX/17/15.

2 Below this section, hunting.

3 ERAO, CSR/20/56.

4 HRO, DFP/748–9.

5 ERAO, DDX/17/15; *The Times* 11 June 1795. See F. F. Prickett, *The Pricketts of Allerthorpe* (1918).

6 *DT* 23 Apr. 1892.

7 ERAO, PE/10/4; *Browne's General Law List* (1782), [92]; *HP* 21 Jan. 1800; 10 Apr. 1804, 24 May, 12 July 1808; *YH* 30 Dec. 1809.

8 J. A. R. and M. E. Bickford, *ER Medical Men*, E Yorks. Family Hist. Soc. (2007), 34.

9 ERAO, PE10/4; *Bailey's Brit. Dir.* (1784), ii., 526–7; *Universal Brit. Dir.* (*c.* 1792), ii. 827.

10 Above, econ. hist., corn trade.

11 *The Times* 21 Oct 1792; 11 June 1795; *HP* 16 June 1807.

12 NYRO, ZDS/XVII/7.

13 TNA, PROB 11/1499; *Treatise on the Breeding, Training, and Management of Horses* (1815); ERAO, QSF/437/G/3; *HP* 29 Sept. 1807; *Gentleman's Magazine* Jan. 1832, 94; Oct. 1850, 438.

14 Col. Leslie, *Historical records of the family of Leslie* (1869), ii, 206–7; ERAO, PE10/4.

15 ERAO, PE11/6. A son was baptised Granby Leslie at Great Driffield in May 1794: ERAO, PE10/4.

16 *The Times* 9 Jan. 1799; *HP* 21 Jan., 15 Apr. 1800; below, this section, military organizations.

17 *YH* 8 Apr. 1820; above, econ. hist., printing.

18 *YH* 8 Apr. 1820; RDB, CZ/287/439; above, manors and estates, Driffield (Etherington).

In 1840 Westgate Hall was tenanted by Richard Shepherd (d. 1842), solicitor. By this date the lawyers and doctors were the established leaders of the small town society, and as elsewhere they were living in the grandest houses in the town.[1] The standing of Dr Washington Harrison (d. 1859) who built Hill Cottage, later the Old Vicarage, Washington Street, was demonstrated in 1836 when he was elected 25 to 7 against his nearest rival for the prestigious and lucrative post of the surgeon to the newly established poor law union.[2] The post of clerk to the union, for which there were 10 candidates, went to the solicitor Thomas Scotchburn, who received 34 votes to his opponent's 5 in the final poll. On Scotchburn's death in 1837 it was noted that Driffield had been deprived of one who for more than twenty years had 'employed his abilities, with great success, in public improvements'.[3] Latterly Scotchburn was in partnership with Richard Shepherd.[4] He was the founder and first secretary of the Driffield Agricultural Association, he established a cattle market, began the town's bone-crushing industry and campaigned for gas lighting in the streets.[5] Scotchburn's churchmanship is unknown but his fellow reformers, David Anderson, seedsman, and James Harrison, corn merchant, were Nonconformists.[6]

Nonconformists often took the lead in public affairs in the first half of the 19th century. The Anglican clergy who served Driffield at that time, the Revd Richard Allen and his nephew and successor George, were men of limited means and ability. By contrast the Nonconformist ministers generally found it easier to integrate with the largely Dissenting community. They included capable, educated men such as Henry Birch, an Independent minister who married a daughter of James Harrison, and the Baptist, James Normanton, who served as the second Registrar for the Driffield Registration District.[7] Normanton was brother-in-law of the refugee the Chevalier M. L. Domanski, late lieutenant in the Polish Army of Independence who was the town's postmaster and leading temperance advocate.[8]

Although the most active leaders of the local community in the mid-Victorian period tended to be Nonconformist and politically radical, it was the local landed gentry, firmly Anglican and Tory, to whom the townspeople still turned for social leadership. In the Driffield area those with most influence were the Sykes of Sledmere and the Reynards of Sunderlandwick whose patronage was important to the local shopkeepers and tradesmen. The Sykes with their 36,000-a. estate largely on the Wolds to the west and north-west of Driffield were of higher status than the Reynards, who had about 1,650 a. in the East Riding, nearly all in Sunderlandwick and Hutton Cranswick.[9] Sir Tatton Sykes (d. 1863) was a popular figure in the town, attending agricultural and sporting events, but it was his son Christopher, MP for the area, who served as a magistrate, a navigation commissioner and president of the Driffield Building Society.[10] The Reynards lived nearer and whilst the family was headed by Edward H. Reynard, from 1834 until his death in 1883, they played a significant part in town affairs.[11] Reynard was president of the Conservative Association and of the Flower, Poultry and Horticultural Society, vice-president of the Driffield Building Society, and chaired the Agricultural Society and meetings to build the Corn Exchange and establish the Volunteer Rifles.[12] He was a member of the Anglers' Club, attended the steeple-chases, exhibited flowers at the floral and horticultural show, supported the Mechanics' Institute and he and his family patronised balls, concerts and other entertainments in the town.[13] In 1870 Mrs Reynard was manager of Driffield Cottage Hospital with Miss Sykes of Sledmere.[14] With no magistrates drawn from Driffield residents until later in the century, the local bench was usually made up of Reynard and fellow gentry and clergy, such as Charles Grimston of Kilnwick Hall, John Grimston of Neswick Hall and the Revd G. T. Clare of Bainton and the Revd John Blanchard of Middleton on the Wolds.[15]

The last two were also honorary members of the Driffield Volunteer Rifle Company, the most socially fashionable body of which to be a member, or supporter, for a short time in the mid-Victorian town.[16] It was part of a nationwide popular middle-class movement in response to the perceived threat of a French invasion 1859–60.[17] From descriptions in the press the social aspect would seem to be more significant that the military. The Volunteers had an annual gala and were periodically entertained by the

1 Directories; below, buildings, domestic buildings.

2 *YH* 22 Oct. 1836.

3 *YH* 9 May 1818; 4 Nov. 1837; ERAO, DDX/17/15.

4 *HP* 22 May 1832; Pigot, *Nat. Com. Dir.* (1834), 711.

5 *HP* 13 Mar. 1835; above, econ. hist., agriculture after inclosure; cattle market; bone crushing.

6 Below, this section, Mechanics' Institute; local govt and politics; relig. hist., 1700 – *c.*1840.

7 Below, religious history, nonconformity.

8 *YH* 25 Sept. 1847; below, this section, temperance.

9 *VCH Yorks. ER.* viii. 23–8; J. T. Ward, *East Yorks. Landed Estates in the 19th Century* (E Yorks. Local Hist. Ser. 23, 1967), 64.

10 *HP* 21 Mar. 1856; 8 Apr., 8 July 1859; 3 Aug. 1860; 15 Apr. 1864, 15 Mar. 1866; below, local govt and politics.

11 J. J. Howard and F. A. Crisp (eds), *Visitation of England and Wales* (1897), v, 163–6.

12 *HP* 3 Feb. 1843; 23 Dec. 1859, 16 Mar. 1866, 11 Mar. 1870, 10 Nov. 1882; *YH* 24 Sept. 1853.

13 *HP* 26 Mar. 1841, 15 Dec. 1848; 4 May 1849; 21 Mar. 1856; 24 June 1859; 18 Mar, 30 Dec. 1870.

14 *HP* 16 Dec.1870.

15 *HP* 15 Oct. 1852; 12 June 1857; 4 Feb., 23 Dec. 1859; 2 Mar. 1860; 11 Mar. 1870.

16 Below, this section, military organizations.

17 P. Morton, 'A Military Irony: The Victorian Volunteer Movement', *RUSI Journal* 131 (Sept. 1986), 64.

36. *Great Driffield: Beechwood c. 1890. It incorporates on the left the former New White Hall of c. 1830, enlarged 1878–9 in the Queen Anne style by Temple Moore for the Revd Horace Newton.*

local gentry.[1] In 1861 they performed military exercises, and sang songs, accompanied by their band in front of the Reynards' invited guests on the lawn at Sunderlandwick Hall. There was lunch in a marquee and speeches followed by dancing. The corps made up of townsmen of 'great respectability', had the Reynards' son as a drummer in the band.[2] The officers included three solicitors, a surgeon, a corn merchant, a wholesale grocer and two farmers under the command of captain Edmund D. Conyers (d. 1863).[3] As well as being the town's leading solicitor Conyers was coroner for the East Riding and clerk to several bodies: the magistrates of Bainton Beacon, the poor law union, the commissioners of taxes, the Driffield Navigation Commissioners, the County Court and the burial board. He was also Superintendent Registrar of Births, Marriages and Deaths.[4] Conyers' lieutenant in the Volunteers was his brother-in-law Thomas Hopper (d. 1866), farmer, of Kelleythorpe.[5] Hopper, the first chairman of the Driffield & East Riding Pure Linseed Cake Co., had chaired the meeting to form the Agricultural Society whose annual shows brought thousands to the mid-Victorian town.[6]

1870–1914

The replacement of the earlier structures of parish, wapentake, and county by new local bodies of government and justice, that began with the poor law union, intensified in the 1870s and gave increased importance to the role of professionals and tradespeople in the social and political life of the town. The setting up of a school board in 1871 and the local board in 1874, elected by the ratepayers, led to a more intense politicisation of the community which conformed, with little or no deviation, to the standard Anglican/ Tory and Nonconformist/ Liberal divide.[7]

It was a time when the Nonconformist sects were at their most confident, their substantial membership was drawn from all sections of the community, including many from the families of professionals and leading tradesmen; they worshipped in impressive rebuilt chapels and provided there a range of social and educational activities. Their dominance however was challenged by the Anglican church which after having long laboured under a reactionary and ageing incumbent was transformed by the appointment in 1877 of the energetic and very wealthy Revd Horace Newton, who with his brothers owned a 23,500 a. shooting estate in Scotland.[8] On census night in 1891 Newton's household at Beechwood, the house he enlarged to the designs of his relative Temple Moore, consisted of himself, his wife, six daughters, a son, a brother-in-law and nine servants: cook, nurse, lady's maid, two housemaids, nursery maid, kitchen maid, scullery maid

1 *HP* 29 June, 28 Dec. 1860; 24 May, 14 June 1861; 13 June 1862.
2 *YH* 31 Aug. 1861.
3 *HP* 25 May 1860.
4 Ibid. 16 Oct. 1863.
5 *YH* 12 Dec. 1835; *HP* 25 May 1860, 23 Nov. 1866.
6 *HP* 4 Nov. 1853, 24 Jan. 1862.
7 Below, loc. govt and politics.
8 Below, relig. hist., 1840–1940 (Anglicanism); P. Gaskell, *Morvern Transformed* (1968), 160–2.

37. *Great Driffield: Highfield* c. *1910. Built in 1865, it was transformed into a half-timbered Elizabethan mansion by Temple Moore in 1881–7 for the industrialist Harrison Holt.*

and footman with a coachman living nearby.[1] The growing number of middle-class residents chiefly lived in the substantial houses put up from the 1870s in Beverley Road, close to the railway station, and in Beverley Street (later St John's Road) and Lockwood Street.[2] Here Newton built St John's church, a chapel of ease, first temporary but later permanent, that offered a more exclusive and probably more comfortable place of worship than the parish church. Certainly it attracted a congregation rivalling that of the older building in the early 20th century.[3]

Solicitors and doctors continued to be the key players in the community. James M. Jennings (d. 1896), coroner for the East Riding, in succession to his former partner E. D. Conyers, was the first chairman of both the school board and the local board. An Anglican, Jennings was the Conservative agent for the local constituency. His political rival for some twenty years was a fellow solicitor Luke White (d. 1920), a Nonconformist and Liberal, who also served on the school and local boards, was first chairman of the UDC and Liberal agent for the constituency before becoming the local MP.[4] Foremost amongst the local doctors was John Eames, Liberal and Congregationalist who was succeeded in his practice in 1882 by the American born Alexander T. Brand (d. 1934). A Conservative and a churchman, Brand, medical officer of Driffield workhouse and the Cottage Hospital, a surgeon-major in the local Volunteers, was a leading figure in the Freemasons' lodge and was one of the first residents to be appointed as a magistrate.[5]

Election to the guardians of the poor and the school and local board enabled many tradesmen and others to take on positions of leadership in the community, men such as James Elgey, grocer and chemist, William Scotchburn, draper, Henry D. Marshall, miller, William Bradshaw, gardener, and Thomas D. Whitaker, stamp distributor.[6] Women were prominent in church and chapel but they were excluded from public office, except that of poor law guardian, a position held from 1898 by Lady Margaret Bickersteth, wife of the clerk to the East Riding County Council.[7]

The Bickersteths lived at Beechwood by 1897, part of a group of more wealthy incomers who owned or rented the larger houses around the town in the later 19th–early 20th century. These included the Hungarian nobleman Count Gustav Batthyany (1828–1906) the son of Gusztáv, 5th Prince Batthyany-Strattmann, who was living at Grove Cottage, no. 1 Eastgate South, *c.* 1871–89,[8] and James Powell, who lived at Beechwood after the Bickersteths, and his son Henry, who lived at Southorpe Lodge, partners in Hammonds, a Hull department

1 TNA, RG12/3594.
2 Below, buildings, domestic buildings.
3 Below, relig. hist., 1840 to 1940 (Anglicanism).
4 Below, loc. govt and politics.
5 W. H. Scott, *N and E Ridings of Yorks. at the Opening of the Twentieth Century* (1903), 152–3. Brand wrote extensively on medical matters including an important work on the treatment of cancer: *British Medical Jnl*, 14 July 1934.
6 Below, loc. govt and politics.
7 *The Times* 24 Sep. 1932.
8 Inf. from S. Stokes, Bridlington Library, 2003.

store.[1] Henry Powell, a member of Driffield UDC and president of the Driffield Cricket Club, clearly made his home in the town, with easy rail access to Hull, so that he could pursue his favoured pursuits of shooting and fishing.[2] This may also have been the lure for Harrison Holt (d. 1931), a partner in the Hull seed-crushing firm of Willows, Holt & Willows, who after living for a short time on New Road purchased Millfield *c.* 1882 and had the architect Temple Moore transform it into the half-timbered Highfield.[3] Holt, who helped save the Driffield firm of F. C. Matthews and was its first chairman when it became a limited company in 1887, soon took on the leadership of Driffield society.[4] A major benefactor to the parish church he was appointed a magistrate and became president of the Charitable Society and of the Choral Society, and chairman of the Constitutional Club and the Recreation Ground Company.[5] To a large extent these prominent residents took the place of the local gentry whose continuing involvement in the town became most evident at the time of parliamentary elections.[6]

Since 1914

The First World War was a watershed for social leadership in the town. The break-up of the great estates saw the influence of landed families in further decline. Although the patronage of the Sykes and Reynard families remained significant for its tradesmen, socially the town became more self-sufficient. Initially leadership did continue to come from the residents of the larger houses, men such as Sir George A. Duncombe, Bt, cousin of the earl of Feversham, who tenanted Highfield by 1912 when Harrison Holt left to live at his other property at Kirkbymoorside (NR).[7] In 1922 Holt sold Highfield to Alfred W. Bean (1861–1944), formerly of Singapore, who was soon after appointed a magistrate and gave the town a new cottage hospital, named after him, in 1931.[8]

Solicitors retained many of the official posts between the wars but they appear to have had few of the social aspirations of their mid-Victorian predecessors. Herbert Brown (d. 1945), was, for instance, besides the clerk to the UDC 1911–41, a trustee of the Mechanics' Institute, the Congregational church, the Savings bank, and the Corn Exchange, while his partner William H. Blakeston (d. 1964), also a Mechanics' Institute trustee, had the clerkship of the water company.[9] The latter's brother, George M. Blakeston (d. 1964), an accountant, was the market keeper and assistant overseer and collector of rates.[10] The Blakestons were Wesleyan Methodists, and Lillian wife of W. H. Blakeston, who stood as a candidate for the County Council, presided over a Labour party gathering in 1929.[11] Another woman who rose to prominence was Amy Stather, wife of a draper, who became chairman of the UDC in 1937.[12]

Tradesmen become the dominant force in the town, men such as the builder Howard Leason, the timber merchants Harold J. Taylor and his brother and business rival, Horace Taylor and the miller J. B. Bradshaw. Harold Taylor, who was living at Beechwood by the mid 1930s, was chairman of the *Driffield Times*.[13] Although council membership became more diverse after the Second World War with long service from Eric T. Carr, head of the Church of England primary school and James Grinstead, shopkeeper, many of same families were councillors and led organizations into the later 20th century. Howard Leason was chairman of the UDC in 1953 and 1962, and Arthur Leason in 1971, (Francis) Alan Megginson (d. 2005), son-in-law of Harold Taylor was chairman in 1956 and 1965.[14] The developer of the Kelleythorpe Industrial Estate, so important to the town's economy in the early 21st century, was Derek Megginson, son of Alan.[15]

SOCIAL LIFE

Before the 18th Century

There is little information on the social life of the parish before the 18th century. For most of the population, work would have left little time for leisure pursuits in the modern sense. The main alternative focus, both before and after the Reformation, was provided by the Church. Besides attendance at its weekly services and occasional communion, both of which were obligatory, the Church provided the parishioner with the earliest

1 Scott, *N and E. Ridings*, 201.

2 Ibid.

3 Brandwood, *Temple Moore*, 21.

4 *YH* 26 Feb. 1887.

5 *Hull and ER Red Book 1900*, 214–5.

6 Below, local govt. and politics.

7 Duncombe, magistrate and deputy lieutenant for the East Riding, was a partner in Beckett's Bank and served as treasurer to the County Council and Driffield Poor Law Guardians and Rural District Council: Scott, *N and E Ridings*, 111; *Yorkshire Who's Who* (1912), 122.

8 *DT* 18 Mar. 1922; *The Times* 27 June 1944.

9 RDB, 193/39/37; 200/431/364; 227/457/384; 233/165/130; 762/477/399; *Driffield Souvenir Guide* (1974), 63; *Kelly's Dir. N & ER Yorks.* (1913), 515.

10 *Kelly's Dir. N & ER Yorks.* (1925) 518–9.

11 *DT* 28 Feb. 1931; below, loc. govt and politics.

12 Below, loc. govt and politics.

13 *Kelly's Dir. N & ER Yorks.* (1937), 446.

14 *Driffield Souvenir Guide* (1974), 63

15 Above, econ. hist., trade and industry (post-war).

known social grouping in the form of guilds, of which there were at least two in Great Driffield.[1] The religious, economic, and social lives of the parish came together also in the fairs, originally a four-day event in Eastertide but later distributed across the year, being held at Little Driffield on two feast days of St Mary (15 August and 8 September) and on Easter and Whit Mondays. The social side of the fairs involved music making and drinking beer or ale, and the Whitsun fair in particular became largely a pleasure fair.[2]

The calendar customs that lingered on into the mid 19th century, scrambling and bell ringing at New Year, plough plays on Plough Monday, and the ball games of Shrove Tuesday, are all likely to be pre-Reformation in origin as are activities such as 'riding the stang'.[3]

The 18th to early 19th Century

The changes that took place in the social life of Driffield in the 18th century chiefly involved visiting gentry, rather than the general population. By the 1730s gentlemen were regularly staying for the pleasure of fishing in the trout streams around the town. Other diversions came mid-century in the form of cock fighting, coursing and hunting. The expanding town became a modest social centre with a theatre, concerts, book club, and dancing school by the early 19th century For the rest of the inhabitants alehouses were the social venues and the Easter and Whitsun fairs were festive occasions, with entertainments and family gatherings, as were the Martinmas hirings.

The Victorian Town

The early Victorian period was a time of more rational entertainment and the beginning of organized sport. The Oddfellows, Foresters, Shepherds and other affiliated order friendly societies took over the Whitsun festivities with their feast days with parades, brass bands and sideshows. Rousing lectures were given at temperance meetings and visiting speakers provided enlightenment in the arts and sciences at the Mechanics' Institute. Concerts, balls and theatrical performances took place in the assembly room and the highlights of the year were the agricultural and floral and horticultural shows and the Volunteer band galas. In sport the gentry and others were drawn in by steeplechasing on the Wolds and the first cricket matches were played in the 1850s.

Mid-century formal education was extended with the rebuilding of the National school and the establishment of a school board in 1871. Church and chapels, rebuilt or restored, expanded their educational and social provision, engaging their members for much of the week. The temperance movement was provided with a meeting place and towards the end of the century inns and alehouses hosted the meetings of sports organizations. Cycling was followed by rugby, and these sports and cricket were accommodated at the recreation ground in 1893, with hockey added later, and tennis on courts elsewhere.

A high point so far as public celebration was concerned was probably the Jubilee of 1887. Though on a grand scale, the Jubilee programme conformed to the usual pattern of celebration observed on the earlier feast days of the friendly societies and on the day of the agricultural show. A revived Anglicanism provided bell-ringing and services in the parish church, one of them choral, and there was more music played by the band of the Rifle Volunteers which processed through the town with the Volunteers, the town's clergymen, the friendly societies, 'gentlemen of position', and the Jubilee committee. Another procession, of 2,000 Sunday school children, preceded tea parties in the various school-rooms, and there was more tea-drinking by up to 1,500 poor people in a marquee in King's Mill Road. The popular celebrations also included a dinner, for which one of Driffield's leading residents, Harrison Holt, gave an ox which was roasted in the field; the meal also included beer and, for teetotallers, ginger beer. 'More select' was the dinner served to 600–700 in the marquee. Sports were held on the field, and the day ended with the illumination of the town and a ball in the marquee.[4]

The 20th Century

Early in the century the key Victorian social organizations, friendly societies and temperance organizations, were in decline. There were some additions to the social scene, in the form of the cinemas and skating rinks, but they had relatively brief lives. Sports developed further in the 1920s with a golf course, two additional tennis clubs, one promoted by the Primitive Methodists, a newly-founded rugby union club, association football teams, and a rink opened for the craze of roller skating. At River Head the watermen had their own swimming club and gala. An amateur dramatic group and a choral society that flourished up to the Second World War were revived in the later 1940s.

The union of the various Methodist chapels between the wars and the decline of organized religion since saw the loss of many of the town's meeting places.[5] Both cinemas closed in the 1960s, but the next decade saw the founding of the male voice choir and the light opera company, both of which were active in 2010. Music and the arts were encouraged by folk music and dance festivals in the 1960s, and an annual carnival from 1980, which became a music festival in 1990. The successes have been the agricultural show, which, after a lapse in the earlier century, was revived, and is now the great social event of the year, and sport. Most sporting organizations flourished in the later 20th century. An

1 Below, relig. hist., Middle Ages.
2 Below, this section, fairs, feasts and galas.
3 Below, this section, customs.
4 Ross, *Driffield*, 32, 34–5.
5 Below, relig. hist., post-1940.

38. *Great Driffield: The custom of scrambling, 2005. A New Year tradition that was well established by the mid 19th century.*

indoor sports halls and a swimming pool were provided at a sports centre in 1979, with improved facilities in a grander leisure centre opened in 2009.

For a detailed account of individual social activities and sports see below.

CUSTOMS

Calendar Customs

There were a number of customs still practised at Driffield at fixed times in the year in the 19th and, in some cases, 20th century, but some were clearly going out of fashion by the early Victorian period.

New Year As in many other towns and villages it was the custom at Driffield to ring out the old year and ring in the new, and this was recorded there in 1842.[1] The antiquity of another New Year custom, scrambling, is uncertain although it was well established before the mid 19th century.[2] On New Year's Day crowds of children stood outside various shops and other premises in the town soliciting gifts of fruit, nuts, sweets and coins which were thrown out of an upstairs window in response to cheers and shouts. The numerous children would then scramble for them. Originally the children had shouted out a rhyme, but this had gone out of use by the 1930s.[3] Little support was given to scrambling by shopkeepers from the early 1970s and when the event failed to take place in 1995, the town council revived it along with a version of the old rhyme. Since 1996 scrambling has been held on 2 January, or the first working day after.[4]

Plough Monday Teams of 'plough boys' from local villages would perform their plough plays, with 'the twanging of wooden swords, and the rebounding of inflated bladders' around Driffield in early January seeking gifts from the inhabitants. This was recorded in 1841.[5]

Shrove Tuesday More popularly known as 'Ball Day' at Driffield when children had a half-holiday from school and played ball games in a local field or open space. The children each had their own ball and would see who could 'kep' or catch it most times without it falling to the ground.[6] In 1846 it was reported that nobody had turned out to throw a ball to prevent sickness in harvest 'according to the old superstition' nor had the new sexton remembered to ring the 'pancake-bell'.[7] However in 1859 children did once more seemingly catch balls and in the evening the town band played for country dances at Cross Hill.[8]

1 *HP* 7 Jan. 1842.

2 I. T. Ward, *New Year Scrambling at Driffield* (1995); *DT* 3 Jan. 1860, 6 Jan. 1900; *Driffield Town Guide* (2008), 47. Scrambling also took place at Hastings and Pudsey: *Sussex Archaeological Collections* 33 (1883), 238; *Notes & Queries* 5th ser. viii (1877), 504.

3 J. Nicholson, *Folk Lore of East Yorkshire* (1890), 21. The author John Nicholson was born at Great Driffield; Barley, *Great and Little Driffield*, 24.

4 *DP*, 20 Sept. 1995; *YP* 28 Dec. 1995; *Driffield Town Guide* (2008), 49–50; (2010), 37.

5 *HP* 22 Jan. 1841.

6 Barley, *Great and Little Driffield*, 24–6.

7 *HA* 27 Feb. 1846.

8 *HP* 18 Mar. 1859.

Royal Oak Day, 29 May The custom of 'mobbing' or throwing of eggs at those not wearing a sprig of oak leaves to celebrate the restoration of Charles II was said to have been little noticed in the town in 1849.[1]

Harvest The ringing of the harvest bell by the parish clerk, first noted as an ancient custom in 1841, was still practised at Driffield in the late 1930s.[2] The bell was rung 200 times daily, except Sundays, at five o'clock each morning and at seven in the evening over a period of four weeks, the 'harvest month', to let the harvesters know when to begin and end their work. By the 1930s the bell was rung at seven o'clock in the morning.[3]

November 5th Traditionally one of the main feast days in the East Riding, November 5th was celebrated at Driffield by the ringing of the church bells at intervals during the day with bonfires at night. In 1850 'disorderly young fellows' also fired squibs and firearms but the day was said to be unusually quite compared with the 'brilliant doings of former years'.[4]

Other Customs

Two incidents of 'riding the stang' or 'rough music', when the townspeople showed their displeasure at some action by another, were recorded at Driffield. In 1834 effigies of a shoemaker and his wife, who it was claimed had given false evidence against four men, were carried through the streets with banners and music before being burnt in the Market Place.[5] Similarly on three evenings in 1841 several hundred people carrying effigies to be burnt paraded the streets with flaming torches and blowing horns until finally stopped by the town's constables.[6]

FAIRS, FEASTS AND GALAS

The religious, economic, and social lives of the parish came together in the fairs, originally a four-day event in Eastertide but later distributed across the year, being held at Little Driffield on two feast days of St Mary (15 August and 8 September) and on Easter and Whit Mondays. In the early 17th century Henry Best noted that at both the Whit Monday and early September fairs a piper walked before the men from Nafferton and Lowthorpe who attended with clubs to keep 'good order and rule'.[7] This suggests that these fairs had a social side with music, merrymaking and much drinking. At fair time all the householders had the right to sell beer without licence, indicating the fact by hanging a green bush over the door.[8] The Whitsun fair in particular took on more of the features of a pleasure fair, with the amusements and disorder spreading into Great Driffield. When Charles Fothergill arrived there in early June 1805 he found to his 'sorrow' that it was the largest fair day of the year and the town was filled after dinner with 'pretty country girls and drunken louts' who disturbed his sleep.[9]

It was at Whitsun, probably because of the fair, that those living or working away traditionally returned to a family, or relative's or friend's home at Driffield for a celebratory meal and a short holiday.[10] In the early–mid 1840s, in addition to the pleasure fair, the various affiliated order friendly societies, Sunday schools and other institutions held their anniversaries, and Whit week with all its 'bustle and gaiety, with processions, banners, bells, and music' was termed the 'Carnival of Driffield' by the local paper.[11] By 1848 the pleasure fair and friendly societies were in decline; there were few amusements and at the Foresters' anniversary there was 'no procession, no music, no banners, no sermon, and no parading through the streets in fantastic dresses as on former occasions'.[12] There was a short-lived revival of the pleasure fair in the mid-1850s but from *c.* 1858 the focus of attention on Whit Monday was the annual evening gala organized by the Driffield Rifle Corps band, with dancing and old English sports.[13] The event, which attracted 1,500 people in 1861, was continued into the 1870s when cycle racing had been added to the entertainments.[14]

Throughout the second half of the 19th century the Martinmas hirings were far more important than Whitsun in the town's social calendar, for then Driffield formed 'the point of attraction, at which are collected all the rustic youth of both sexes, within a circle extending from 10 to 12 miles around'.[15] It was not only young farm workers who attended on hirings day, but also the farmers and their families. Thousands poured into the town, especially after the opening of the railway.[16] As well as the shops being full of goods to tempt the farm servants who had a year's wages in their pockets, there were stalls, side shows with animals and a 'choice selection of the tallest, smallest, and stoutest men and women' and other artistic and natural

1 Ibid. 1 June 1849.
2 Ibid. 10 Sept. 1841; *Driffield Observer* 1 Sept. 1855; *DT* 28 Aug. 1909; Barley, *Great and Little Driffield*, 26.
3 Barley, *Great and Little Driffield*, 26.
4 *HP* 8 Nov. 1850.
5 Ibid. 18 Apr. 1834.
6 Ibid. 1 Oct. 1841.
7 Best, *Farming Bks*, ed. Woodward, 118.
8 *YH* 22 Sept. 1906. The last of the 'bush' houses was closed in the 1860s: Ibid.
9 P. Romney (ed.), *The Diary of Charles Fothergill 1805* (YAS Rec. Ser. 142), 28–9.
10 *HP* 9 June 1843; 7 June 1844.
11 Ibid. 7 June 1844
12 *HA* 16 June 1848.
13 *HP* 13 June 1862; below, this section, music.
14 *HP* 24 May 1861; 2 June 1871.
15 *Yorks. Gazette* 18 Nov. 1854 quoted in Moses, 'Rustic and Rude', 158.
16 Above, econ. hist., hiring fairs.

curiosities, theatrical performances, roundabouts and above all the many public houses with dancing and other attractions.[1] At these times Driffield became 'a surging sea of drunkenness' as described by a policeman in 1858.[2] That year there was a riot at the hirings, and again in 1875, both events leading to local campaigns for their abolition.[3]

Local clergy, most notably the Revd F. O. Morris of Nafferton and the Revd J. Eddowes of Garton, campaigned against the hirings from the early 1850s, condemning the 'licentiousness of that degrading day'.[4] The curate of Driffield, Revd James Skinner, took more direct action in 1860 by engaging the Corn Exchange for a register office for female servants and serving tea and coffee.[5] In the following years various forms of rational entertainment were provided at the Corn Exchange, brass bands, balls and social teas, to counteract the attractions of the sideshows and the public house.[6] Only a small proportion of servants attended and there was no sign of any lasting impact on the nature of the amusements at the hirings which still had plenty of sideshows, swings and roundabouts in the 1920s.[7] The amusements were supplied by men such as William Shipley, steam roundabout proprietor of Middle Street North, and from *c.* 1919 the Corrigans of Hull.[8] The hirings ended in 1939.[9] Funfairs, originating in the earlier entertainments, have been held more recently.

The chief feature of the Driffield Carnival, begun in 1980 and initially successful, was a parade of floats entered by local businesses and others, but the event later declined as firms were closed or re-located outside the town; the carnival was eventually replaced *c.* 1990 by a town festival, featuring a large musical event in North End Park.[10]

MUSIC

Little is known of music-making in Driffield before the 19th century. A piper attended the fairs at Little Driffield in the early 17th century and the lord of the manor contributed to the cost of music at the fairs there in the late 18th century.[11]

Music may otherwise have been available mostly in the churches, and later in the Nonconformist chapels. The quantity there was probably limited (singing was 'introduced' at Little Driffield in 1832) and its quality is suggested by the 'discordant medley' said to have been produced by the choir and band at Great Driffield church in the early 19th century.[12] A probably important advance in music-making in the town was the building and re-building of organs in the churches and chapels which occurred later in the century.[13]

The military organizations formed from the late 18th century clearly influenced local musical life, one of the volunteer forces having its own band and march in the early 1800s.[14]

Nothing further is known of the 'Driffield Band' that performed at the Hunt Room along with a theatrical performance in 1820.[15] In 1828 the townspeople of Driffield subscribed £48 towards purchasing woodwind and brass instruments for a band of music 'to play on all public occasions in Driffield when thereunto requested and particularly on the annual festivals of the two Benefit Societies'.[16] In the 1830s–40s the band played at friendly society feast days in the town and local villages, coronation celebrations, steeplechases, the opening of the Hull to Bridlington railway, and the annual Little Driffield and Skerne music festivals.[17] William Clark (1794–1871), builder, 'the moving spirit in all musical matters in the town', was the leader of the band in the 1840s, and he was succeeded by his son David B. Clark (1828–77) by 1853.[18] Clark senior played the clarinet, violin and double bass and his son the violin.[19]

The band also performed as the Driffield Quadrille Band and as such played for balls in the town and when a music gallery was erected in the Mechanics' Institute in 1841 they volunteered to provide the musical entertainment for social events, meetings and lectures.[20] The Quadrille band was last mentioned in 1862, seemingly replaced by the Driffield Glee Band, a brass band that performed at local events in 1862–5.[21]

The first fully brass band in the town was that formed in 1849 by Mr Haughey, the organist at the parish church; it performed at the anniversaries of the Union and Foresters' friendly societies the following

1 *HP* 18 Nov. 1842; 20 Nov. 1857; *YH* 21 Nov. 1846; 17 Nov. 1849; Parrott, 'Decline of Hiring Fairs', 27–8.

2 Skinner, *Facts and Opinions*, 11.

3 *HP* 19 & 26 Nov. 1858; 20 Nov. 1875; *Bridlington Free Press* 25 Dec. 1875.

4 J. Eddowes, *Martinmas Musings; or, Thoughts about the Hiring Day* (1854), 10; see also F. O. Morris, *The Present System of Hiring Farm Servants in the ER of Yorks* (1854).

5 Skinner, *Facts and Opinions*, 25.

6 G. Moses, 'Reshaping Rural Culture? The Church of England and Hiring Fairs in the ER of Yorks. *c.* 1850–80', *Rural History* 13, i (2002), 73–4.

7 *YH* 15 Nov. 1875; Moses, *Rural Moral Reform*, 123–6; S. Caunce, 'ER Hiring Fairs', *Oral History* 3, ii (1975), 51.

8 *Kelly's Dir. N & ER Yorks.* (1901), 468; (1913), 517; Parrott, 'Decline of Hiring Fairs', 28; E. Corrigan, *Ups and Downs and Roundabouts* (1973).

9 E. Pontefract and M. Hartley, *Yorks. Tour* (1939), 67; Parrott, 'Decline of Hiring Fairs', 28.

10 Ibid.; inf. from Claire Binnington, Driffield Town Council, 2006.

11 Best, *Farming Bks*, ed. Woodward, 118; NYRO, ZDS/XVII/7.

12 Below, relig. hist., 1700 to *c.* 1840 (Anglicanism).

13 Ross, *Driffield*, 47, 74, 77.

14 Below, this section, military organizations.

15 T. Sheppard, *Evolution of the Drama in Hull and District* (1927), 196–7.

16 ERAO, PE10/T87.

17 *HP* 13 Sept 1831; 14 Feb 1840; 26 Mar. 1841, 7 Aug, 9 Oct, 1846; 21 May 1847; *HA* 21 June 1839; *DT* 28 Dec 1889.

18 *HP* 8 Jan. 1841; 30 Dec. 1853; 10 Feb. 1871.

19 *YH* 8 Aug. 1840; *HP* 6 Feb, 2 Apr 1852; 10 Feb 1871.

20 *HA* 30 Aug. 1839; *HP* 8 Oct 1841.

21 *HP* 7 Mar 1862; 3 July 1863; 15 July 1864; 22 July 1865; *Malton Messenger* 27 June 1863.

year.[1] Auckland's brass band recorded as playing in the town in 1856 may have been the forerunner of the Driffield amateur brass band established in 1857.[2] On the formation of the 8th Company (Driffield) East Yorkshire Rifle Volunteers in 1859 the Driffield brass band became the Volunteer band.[3] Also known as the Rifle Corps band it held an annual Whitsuntide Gala for a number of years which attracted large numbers to the town.[4] In 1865 the band severed its formal links with the Rifle Volunteers, and appeared as the Driffield Sax-Tuba Band before seemingly joining with the Glee Band to become Driffield United Brass band by 1867.[5] The United Brass Band continued the annual Whitsuntide galas.[6] The band was again linked formally with the Rifle Volunteers by 1874, and as the Volunteer band appears to have continued up to the early 20th century.[7] During the First World War members are said to have played in the band of the 2/5th Alexandra Princess of Wales Own Yorkshire Regiment.[8] Reformed as the Driffield Town Band after the war, it took part in the National Brass Band contest in London in 1928.[9] In 2004 the Driffield Silver Band, which then incorrectly traced its origins to the band established in 1828, had 35 members and performed at all major local events.[10]

There were other short-lived bands including the Union Fife and Drum Band made up of orphan boys from the workhouse in 1856, a Temperance band in 1875–6, the Driffield Musical Union band in 1876–91, and the Church Orchestral band in 1883–4.[11]

From the 1840s Driffield had a lively music scene with regular concerts by local and visiting performers. Initially they were held at the Mechanics' Institute and the assembly room at the Corn Exchange.[12] Here concerts were organized by the Philharmonic Society founded 1841 and still active over 20 years later.[13] A choral society existed in 1839 and 1857, and another with the same name founded *c.* 1893 lasted up to the Second World War.[14] Restarted after the war, it was linked to the Institute of Further Education in the 1970s and lasted up to the 1990s.[15] Driffield Male Voice Choir formed in 1971 was still flourishing in 2010 with some fifty members.[16]

The county council supported a festival of folk dance for several years in the 1960s, as well as a choral festival,[17] and about 1990 the district and town councils substituted a music festival in July, held chiefly in North End Park, for an earlier initiative, the Driffield Carnival.[18]

THEATRE

The earliest dramatic performances in the town appear to have been amateur productions that took place in the Hunt Room or in a barn on the corner of Beverley Road and Middle Street South at the beginning of the 19th century.[19] In 1801 a tragedy, Douglas, and a musical farce were performed in aid of the poor by a party of ladies and gentlemen including Christopher Laybourne and the 'young' Etheringtons. On this occasion the Hunt Room was fitted up as a theatre by the artist Benjamin Gale of Hull who painted the scenery.[20]

No professional actors are recorded before Joseph Smedley's company which appeared in the town for a short season for 22 years or more from *c.* 1807.[21] The company, which consisted chiefly of the manager's family, was Lincolnshire-based and usually had a summer season at Bridlington.[22] Smedley applied for a licence to open a theatre at Great Driffield in 1829 from 8 September to 1 November.[23] In 1820 another travelling company, that of Mr and Mrs G. Renaud, performed in the Hunt Room, a building referred to as the theatre or playhouse the following year when it was being used by the Primitive Methodists.[24]

Where the Gifford family, who were in the town for three weeks in September–October 1842, or Day and Thompson's 'numerous theatrical company', who stayed for two weeks in the following month, appeared is unknown.[25] Possibly it was in the galleried two-storey building behind the Buck Hotel, accessed by outside steps, that was used as a theatre before 1855.[26] Other

1 *HA* 30 Nov. 1849; 24 May, 12 July 1850.
2 *HP* 16 May 1856; *Driffield Observer* 1 June 1856; Ross, *Driffield*, 180.
3 *HP* 1 June 1860; R. W. S. Norfolk, *Militia, Yeomanry and Volunteer Forces of the ER 1689–1908* (E Yorks. Local Hist. Ser. 19, 1965), 56.
4 *HP* 24 May 1861; 13 June 1862.
5 Ibid. 1, 15 July 1865; 14 June 1867.
6 Ibid. 14 June 1867; 2 June 1871.
7 *DT* 18 July 1874; 22 June 1878; *HP* 3 Aug 1883.
8 Driffield Silver Band website (www.driffieldband.com); *Kelly's Dir. N & ER Yorks.* (1921), 498.
9 *DT* 4 Feb. 1922; www.driffieldband.com.
10 *Driffield Town Guide* (*c.* 2004), 10.
11 *Driffield Observer* 1 Mar., 1 Oct. 1856; *HP* 11 Feb. 1876, 22 Jan 1886; *DT* 29 May 1875; Sheppard, *Evolution*, 199; *Musical Times* 1 Feb 1883; *LM* 11 Dec 1884; *YH* 7 Mar. 1891.
12 *HP* 10 Dec 1841; 15 Dec 1848; 6 Feb 1852; 30 Dec 1853.
13 Ibid. 24 Dec. 1841; 20. Jan. 4 Mar.; 30 Dec 1842; 7 Nov. 1862; *HA* 13 Jan. 1843.
14 *HA* 25 Oct. 1839; *The Era* 18 Jan 1857; *YH* 26 Apr. 1893; *DT* 8 Nov. 1941.
15 *DT* 3 May 1947; Driffield town guides.
16 Inf. from Driffield Male Voice Choir website, 2010.
17 ER Educ. Cttee *Mins* 1961–2, 149; 1962–3, 99; 1963–4, 148; 1967–8, 119.
18 ERAO, EYEY/1/4/8/3, Environmental...Cttee, 14 Sept. 1992; inf. from Claire Binnington, Driffield Town Council, 2006.
19 ERAO, DDX/17/15.
20 *YH* 25 Apr., 9 May 1801; ERAO, DDX/17/15.
21 Howorth, *Driffield*, 50; *DNB*, *s.v.* Joseph Smedley.
22 Neave, *Port, Resort and Market Town*, 146.
23 Lincs. Archives Office LLHS/38/5.
24 Sheppard, *Evolution*, 196–7; H. B. Kendall *The Origin and History of the Primitive Methodist Church* (1906) ii. 94.
25 *HP* 7 & 10 Oct., 18 & 25 Nov. 1842.
26 Sheppard, *Evolution*, 198; Howorth, *Driffield*, 50; *HP* 29 Apr. 1853.

theatres were temporary such as the one erected by the comedian Harvey Teasdale in 1858.[1] Later most theatrical performances were in the assembly room at the Corn Exchange. Here Walter Shelley put on a short season of Shakespeare plays in 1863 and the first performance of a drama by H. Sydney Warwick and local writer Charles T. Holderness took place in 1893.[2]

Holderness was a founder of the Driffield Amateur Dramatic Club set up by 1883.[3] Later amateur groups have included the Driffield Amateur Dramatic Society in the 1930s, the Driffield Players, founded 1946 and still active in 1987 and the Driffield Light Opera Society which first performed in 1978 and changed its name to Driffield Musical Theatre in 2006.[4]

Driffield Town Theatre founded in 1985 brought professional theatre, music and dance to the town for over 20 years using the former town hall in Exchange Street.[5]

CINEMAS

Driffield formerly had two cinemas.[6] The Victoria Electric Picture Palace was opened in 1912[7] in Middle Street South. The building (no. 63a), at the junction with Queen Street, was conveyed in 1919 to the Driffield Victoria Theatre & Café Co. Ltd.[8] The cinema was apparently enlarged in 1929,[9] and it later had a façade with classical detailing and seated 552 patrons.[10] It closed in 1962, the building was sold, and soon afterwards a supermarket, was built on the site.[11] The second house, the Majestic cinema, at the junction of Middle Street North and Cranwell Road, opened in 1936.[12] It became a bingo hall in 1969, and it closed in February 1979 and was demolished soon after.[13] The site was later occupied by a public house.[14]

LIBRARIES

A select book club that drew its membership largely from the local clergy held its annual dinner at the Red Lion in 1822.[15] It was probably the same book society that was based at the shop of the stationer-bookseller William Turner in 1823.[16] Another bookseller, James C. Blakeston had a circulating library in 1851.[17]

Mechanics' Institute The library was a major element but had closed by 1951.[18]

Parochial Library A parochial library 'of useful and religious works in most kinds of pure literature ... intended for all classes' was set up by the curate the Revd James Skinner in 1860.[19] It had the financial support of Lady Sykes of Sledmere and her eldest son, Tatton.[20]

Constitutional Club The Conservative Working Men's Constitutional Club was said to have had a library of 7–8,000 volumes in 1893, but few users.[21]

County Library The present public library service in Driffield dates from 1930 when the county council opened a branch library in the council school.[22] The library was moved in 1931 to the Corn Exchange, where it was run by a joint committee of local volunteers and representatives of the county and urban district councils.[23] About 1936 the library had to be moved temporarily to the Congregational schoolroom in Exchange Street because of the loss of the Corn Exchange premises to the UDC.[24] In 1938 the county council bought several cottages at the junction of Cross Hill and St John's Road, demolished them, and built a new library, which was opened in 1939.[25] Plans for a new library were later dropped, and the Cross Hill building was extended instead.[26]

MUSEUMS

In 1878–9 the archaeologist and corn merchant J. R. Mortimer built a private museum in Lockwood Street (no. 25).[27] He had moved from his native Fimber, in Wetwang, some 7 miles away, into Driffield in 1869, and

1 Sheppard, *Evolution*, 198.
2 *HP* 30 Oct. 1863; *The Era* 25 Oct. 1863; *YH* 27 July 1893. Shelley had been manager of the Malton theatre: *Malton Messenger* 23 Oct. 1858.
3 Sheppard, *Evolution*, 199; *DT* 6 Jan., 14 Apr. 1883; *HP* 12 Dec. 1884; *YH* 17 May 1890.
4 *HT* 14 Apr. 1934; *DT* 26 Apr. 1947; *Driffield Town Guides*.
5 *Driffield Town Guide* (*c*. 2004), 16.
6 Following based on directories.
7 Harrison, *Driffield*, 406, where the location of the two cinemas is incorrect.
8 RDB, 202/515/441; *DT* 14 Jan. 1922.
9 Ibid. 341/473/378; 386/316/268.
10 ERAO, CCER/12/5/9.
11 Ibid. UDDR/1/1/36, Housing...Cttee, 7 May 1962; RDB, 1287/100/88; C. Ketchell (comp.), *Capital Tales: Stories from Driffield* (1989), 11.
12 *Cinema Miscellany in Yorkshire* (extract at Treasure House, Beverley, 2010.), 5; ERAO, UDDR/1/8/32, Highways...Cttee, 3 Feb. 1936; RDB, 1826/585/484.
13 ERAO, UDDR/1/1/43, Building...Cttee, 9 Apr. 1969; Ketchell, *Capital Tales*, 12.
14 Mavericks; inf. from Guy Stevens, Driffield, 2006.
15 ERAO, DDX/17/15.
16 Baines, *Hist. Yorks.* (1823), ii. 193, 195.
17 White, *Dir. Hull & York* (1851), 602.
18 Below, this section, Mechanics' Institute.
19 *HP* 28 Oct. 1859.
20 Ibid. 27 Jan. 1860.
21 *YH* 23 Feb. 1893, 22 Feb. 1894.
22 *DT* 18 Oct. 1930.
23 ER Educ. Cttee *Mins* 1931–2, 172–3.
24 Ibid. 1936–7, 47, 65, 139, 193, 232.
25 RDB, 597/54/45; ER Educ. Cttee *Mins* 1937–8, 227; 1938–9, 211; 1939–40, 198; datestone.
26 ER Educ. Cttee *Mins* 1972–3, 174; ERAO, EYEY/1/4/8/3, Environment...Cttee, 4 Apr. 1995; *DP* 10 Apr. 1996.
27 Following based on J. R. Mortimer, 'Notes on the history of the Driffield Museum of Antiquities and Geological Specimens', *Trans. Hull Scientific and Field Naturalists' Club* (1898), 135–141; Ross, *Driffield*, 84–5; Harrison, *Driffield*, 359–66; M. Giles, 'Collecting the Past, Constructing Identity', *Antiquaries Jnl* 86 (2006), 279–316; *DNB*, *s.v.* J. R. Mortimer

39. *J. R. Mortimer, photographed* c. *1905. The corn merchant and archaeologist settled in Driffield in 1869, and built a museum in Lockwood Street in 1878.*

had created a prosperous business there, dealing in corn, seed, and manure. He was also a renowned amateur archaeologist, who, over many years and with his brother Robert Mortimer of Fimber, assembled a large collection of geological and archaeological specimens, many recovered from the numerous barrows he dug in the district. The collection was kept in Mortimer's house at no. 34 Beverley Lane, now St John's Road, before its transfer to the new building. About 1890 there were reckoned to be 15,000 archaeological objects in all, coming from 300 barrows and more than 200 Anglo-Saxon graves, besides a sizeable collection of geological specimens. The museum was only occasionally open to the public, being intended principally for the use of Mortimer and his fellow scholars and enthusiasts. By Mortimer's death in 1911, his collection was estimated to have grown to *c.* 66,000 items. Under his will, it was sold in 1913 to Hull Corporation, which displayed it in the City Hall from *c.* 1930 until 1957, and subsequently in the Hull and East Riding museum in High Street.[1] The museum building in Driffield was sold in 1918 to the freemasons,[2] and was still a Masonic hall in 2010.

Mortimer's activities were continued in the 20th century by, among others, the butcher Cecil Grantham and his son Eric, whose archaeological collection, amassed since the early 1940s, was housed in a building behind their shop in North Street from the 1950s.[3] An attempt in the 1990s by East Yorkshire Borough Council and Driffield Town Council to re-establish a museum in the town attracted little support.[4]

NEWSPAPERS

Printing and publishing were largely in the hands of the town's booksellers and stationers. From the mid century the printer-booksellers also began to issue newspapers, at least one of which circulated far beyond Driffield. Their three titles were joined by a fourth *c.* 1880, but that paper only survived for a year or two, and two of the earlier publications were closed during the First World War. The surviving title, the *Driffield Times*, is still published, together with a sister publication, the *Driffield Post*, which was started and had a brief independent existence in the late 20th century. A short account of the Driffield newspapers follows.

The Driffield Observer Founded by the bookseller, printer and local historian Thomas Holderness (1823–1902) as the *Driffield Observer and Literary Journal* in 1853.[5] It was called the *Driffield Observer and East Riding Advertiser* from 1872 until its end in 1914.[6] Originally a four-page monthly publication, it was later enlarged to eight pages and published fortnightly.[7] It was published weekly on a Saturday by 1864, then on a Friday from the late 1870s.[8] Holderness was a Nonconformist, teetotaller and Liberal.[9]

The Driffield Times and General Advertiser A weekly, usually published on Thursday or Friday, the paper was founded in 1860 by George R. Jackson, a bookseller, stationer, and printer of Exchange Street.[10] Jackson, an Anglican and Conservative, the son of a tenant farmer on the Sledmere estate, had served his apprenticeship

1 *VCH Yorks. ER.* i. 425, 440.
2 RDB, 201/573/479; below, this section, freemasons.
3 ERAO, UDDR/1/8/54, Building...Cttee, 7 Aug.1957; *YAJ* 38 (1952–5), 446; *The Times* 7 Mar. 1970. The Granthams' collection was in storage elsewhere in Driffield in 2011. Inf. from P. Halkon, 2011.
4 *DP* 27 Jan. 1994, 10 Jan. 1996; *DT* 2 Sept. 1998.
5 Copies for 1853–6 in Local Studies Collection, Hull History Centre.
6 *Waterloo Dir. of English Newspapers and Periodicals 1800–1900* (1997), ii. 1540, 1542; directories.
7 *DT* 18 Jan. 1902.
8 *Slater's Royal Nat. Com. Dir. of Yorks.* (1864), 117; *Post Office Dir. N & ER Yorks.* (1879), 384.
9 *DT* 18 Jan. 1902.
10 Directories; *DT* 27 Oct. 1988.

with Thomas Holderness, the proprietor of the *Driffield Observer*.[1] The paper claimed to be neutral politically in 1918.[2] The paper long remained a family concern, together with the Filey weekly established by Jackson in 1865 and published until 1918, for many years from Driffield.[3] Jackson (d. 1893) was succeeded by his son Edward (d. 1903), and he by his brother-in-law, Edward Shepherdson, and other trustees of G. R. Jackson's will. A North Riding newspaper proprietor, Ernest Whittaker, bought the paper in 1934, and the Driffield Times Co. Ltd was formed in 1936. The title became simply *The Driffield Times* in 1937.[4] Local involvement remained, however, H. J. Taylor and his son-in-law Alan Megginson of the timber merchants Taylors serving on the board of the company.[5] Ownership changed several times in the later 20th century. East Yorkshire Printers Ltd was the proprietor by 1962, when the *Beverley Guardian* was added to the titles it published and printed in Driffield; its successor in 1984 was East Yorkshire Newspapers Ltd,[6] and by 2003 the *Driffield Times* belonged to Yorkshire Regional Newspapers Ltd, which was owned in turn by the Johnston Press. By a purchase of the later 1990s, the Johnston Press added the newly-founded *Driffield Post* to its titles; both of the Driffield weeklys were continued, the *Driffield Times* later appearing on Wednesday and the *Driffield Post* on Friday. The long ownership of the Jacksons was matched by the service of James Hart, who joined the *Driffield Times* in 1897, and was editor for many years in the 20th century.[7]

Soon after its start, the paper was printed by steam and widely distributed in the East Riding. The print works was put up in Exchange Street, in the 1860s, soon after the paper's foundation, and its high-arched entrance of rusticated stone with a king on the headstone remains. In 1959 that works was given up[8] and the *Times* was moved to the site of the former printing works of Benjamin Fawcett at East Lodge, between Eastgate South and Wansford Road.[9] The Exchange Street premises were then sold and added to the Bell Hotel, the entrance being filled in as part of the remodelling.[10] The paper moved to its current premises, a former warehouse off Mill Street, in 1989. Its sister papers, the *Driffield Post* and the *Beverley Guardian* are also produced there.[11]

40. *Great Driffield: Driffield Times office and printing works, Exchange Street, 2006. The printing works, built soon after the paper was founded in 1860, closed in 1959.*

The Driffield Express A weekly begun in 1871 by the printer and bookseller Henry Blakeston.[12] Editions appeared on Thursday and Saturday.[13] It became the *East and North Riding Chronicle and Driffield Express* late in 1873, and was the *East Riding Chronicle and Driffield Express* from the beginning of 1885 until its end in 1917.[14] By 1879 Tom Turner was the proprietor, his Express Company was at no. 19 Market Place in the 1890s.[15]

1 *DT* 20 May 1893, Jan. 2000 (millennium edn).
2 *Newspaper Press Directory* (1918), 129.
3 *VCH Yorks. ER.* ii. 145.
4 *Waterloo Dir. of English Newspapers*, ii. 1542.
5 Above, econ. hist., timber trade. It was perhaps the same H. J. Taylor who published a Bridlington paper between 1946 and 1954: *VCH Yorks. ER.* ii. 64.
6 *VCH Yorks. ER.* vi. 209.
7 *DT* Jan. 2000 (millennium edn); *Willings Press Guide* (2003).
8 RDB, 1004/245/213.
9 Above, econ. hist., printing.
10 Date said to be on headstone; inf. from Mr G. Riggs, Bell Hotel, 2004.
11 *Willings Press Guide* (2003); *DT*, Jan. 2000 (millennium edn).
12 *Kelly's Dir. N & ER Yorks.* (1872), 353.
13 Directories.
14 *Waterloo Dir. of English Newspapers*, ii. 1540.
15 Ross, *Driffield*, 99; directories.

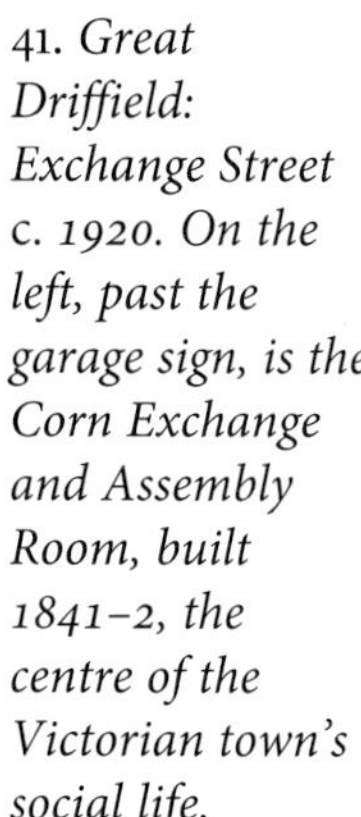

41. Great Driffield: Exchange Street c. 1920. On the left, past the garage sign, is the Corn Exchange and Assembly Room, built 1841–2, the centre of the Victorian town's social life.

Given gratis by the early 20th century it paid special attention to political matters, strongly advocating Conservative principles.[1] The *Driffield and Buckrose Mail* was later published from the same premises.[2]

The Driffield Freeman A radical weekly published on Thursday. It had only a brief existence, apparently having been begun in 1879 and last appearing in 1882.[3] The owner and editor, George Whiting, onetime schoolmaster and builder, was physically attacked by Dr Scotchburn annoyed by an article in the paper shortly before it closed.[4]

The Driffield and Buckrose Mail A weekly established in 1924, and belonged in 1929 to Scarborough Mercury Newspaper Co., and later to Scarborough & District Newspapers Ltd. It was published from the same premises at no. 19 Market Place as the then defunct *East Riding Chronicle and Driffield Express*, and appeared on Thursday or Friday. Publication ceased in 1943.[5]

Driffield Citizen and News East Yorkshire Newspapers Ltd, owner of the *Driffield Times*, also published a weekly paper called the *Driffield News* from 1986. In 1989 it became successively the *Driffield Citizen and News* and the *Driffield Citizen*. Publication evidently ceased in or soon after 1990.[6]

The Driffield and District Post Launched in 1991, and initially published on Wednesdays.[7] In the later years of the decade it was bought by the Johnston Press, the owner of the rival *Driffield Times*. The *Driffield Post* was thereafter published on Fridays and the *Driffield Times* on Wednesdays.

MECHANICS' INSTITUTE

In the early and mid Victorian period the Mechanics' Institute played a key role in bringing together the tradesmen, craftsmen and professionals of the rapidly expanding town. Here newcomers were quickly integrated with the established artisan and white collar workforce. It was the main place where influential members of the various churches and chapels, often political opponents, met in a united cause. Lectures were given on a wide range of subjects, avoiding party politics and religion, and there were concerts, balls and periodic public entertainments and an extensive library.

In 1837, following a request from certain young tradesmen for advice on forming a book club, the corn merchant James Harrison organized a meeting for the establishment of a Mechanics' Institute.[8] Harrison was appointed president and the Revd James Normanton, Baptist minister and Richard Jennings, solicitor, were appointed vice-presidents of a management committee. A donation of £20 was received from Marmaduke Langley, lord of the manor, who was made patron.[9] Other early supporters included David Anderson, seedsman, the Revd Henry Birch, Independent minister, and William Jarratt, bank manager who was treasurer for many years.[10] George Shepherdson, cabinet maker, T. D. Whitaker, accountant, John Browne, journalist

1 *Newspaper Press Directory* (1918), 129.
2 Below, this section.
3 *Morning Post* 24 Feb. 1879.
4 TNA, HO107/2366; RG9/3607; *YH* 1 July 1882.
5 HUL, DDSY/104/264; ERAO, PE/10/T. 64; directories; Yorks. Libraries and Information website, Newsplan database, 2006.
6 Newsplan database, 2006.
7 ERAO, newspaper clippings (31 May 1995, etc.).
8 *HA* 15 Dec. 1837; 22 Dec. 1858.
9 Ibid. 15 Dec. 1837.
10 *HA* 6 & 13 Jan. 1843; 21 Feb. 1845, 17 Sept. 1847; 27 Jan. 1854; 27 Jan. 1855.

and the Revd J. Cuzner, Baptist minister, all served as secretary and Samuel Stead (d. 1852), master of the National school, was the first librarian.[1] The strongest support was from Nonconformists but in 1868 when the president was Henry Angas, draper and grocer, an Independent, the secretaries were G. R. Jackson, editor and owner of the *Driffield Times*, and the artist Alexander F. Lydon, both Anglicans.[2] Lydon was connected with the Mechanics' Institute for over thirty years, serving as president for last eight years before he left Driffield in 1883.[3] The vice-presidents in his last year were the miller, H. D. Marshall and Luke White, solicitor and later MP, both Independents.[4]

The first meeting of the Driffield Mechanics' Institute and Literary Society was held in the Independent chapel but soon afterwards the former Wesleyan Methodist chapel on the east side of Westgate was obtained for premises.[5] When this building was required for other purposes the institute purchased the former court house on the south side of Exchange Street from Mary Conyers in 1865.[6]

During the first 21 years there were usually 15–20 lectures per session with audiences of 100–150, and frequently up to 200.[7] Many of the early lectures on arts, science, music, history and literature were given by local men, doctors, solicitors, leading tradesmen, Independent and Baptist ministers and, from the early 1850s, various Anglican clergy including the Revd Francis O. Morris of Nunburnholme, the Revd J. Eddowes of Garton and Revd J. Skinner, curate of Driffield.[8] Particularly popular were the chemical demonstrations by F. C. Matthews, jun., son of the local artificial manure manufacturer, and the numerous science lectures by J. D. Sollitt, headmaster of Hull Grammar School.[9] Among speakers from further afield most notable was the American writer Ralph Waldo Emerson who lectured on 'Napoleon' at Driffield in 1848.[10] Alfred Dickens, brother of Charles Dickens, lectured on architecture to the institute in 1853 when he was deputy engineer for the building of the Malton–Driffield railway.[11]

Other events organized by the institute included an exhibition of fine arts and natural curiosities held for nine weeks in the Corn Exchange in 1852, and a 'literary, artistic, scientific and musical conversazione' held over three days in 1862.[12] The latter was organized by group of the younger members; F. C. Matthews, jun., William Taylor, actuary and inventor, Thomas Holtby, brewer, G. B. Tonge, trainee solicitor and John Turner, printer, wine merchant and brickmaker. These five had volunteered to pay off the institute's debts and take over its management for three years when it had been threatened with closure.[13]

The institute's library, formed by donation, purchase, and the bequest of scientific works by F. B. Lockwood, increased from 843 books in 1847, to around 3,000 in 1862 and 5–6,000 volumes *c.* 1890, when works of fiction were most in demand.[14] Accommodation at the institute included a large reading room, open daily, provided with newspapers and periodicals.[15]

In the later 19th century lectures were few; there were only two in 1878 and probably none in 1880–1. Then the main activity was the series of Saturday evening musical, literary and theatrical entertainments of which there were 14 that winter with 119 different performers and attended by a total of just under 5,000 people.[16] The library and reading room remained popular into the early 20th century, but interest declined between the wars, and finally the Mechanics' Institute building was sold to the auctioneers Cook & Dee in 1951.[17]

TEMPERANCE

The temperance movement promoted by all the Nonconfomist denominations, and more latterly with the support of the Anglican church, was very active in Driffield from the late 1830s to the First World War. The periodic lectures and annual tea parties were popular events.

A Total Abstinence Society and a Temperance Society existed in the town in 1839, the latter formed that year.[18] Both organizations were still flourishing in 1870.[19] At first the Temperance Society was closely associated with the local 'tent' of the Independent Order of Rechabites, a temperance friendly society, and for a few years they held joint anniversary celebrations.[20]

The temperance movement was particularly popular

1 *Eastern Counties Herald* 23 Jan. 1851; *HA* 17 Jan. 1840; 27 Jan. 1854; *HP* 7 Jan. 1842; 26 Jan. 1849; 24 Dec. 1858; *YH* 16 Oct. 1852.

2 *HP* 17 Jan. 1868.

3 Ibid. 5 Jan. 1883.

4 Ibid. 6 Jan. 1882.

5 *HA* 15 Dec. 1837; ERAO, PE/10/T. 120; ibid. TA/13.

6 *HP* 29 Dec. 1865; 9 Feb. 1866; RDB, NS/347/515; 95/163/144 (1897); 193/39/37. The building was later called the Mechanics' Institute and Literary and Scientific Institution: Ross, *Driffield*, 85.

7 *HA* 22 Dec. 1858.

8 Reports in *HA* and *HP*.

9 *HA* 10 Jan. 1840; 12 Jan. 1844; 3 Mar. 1854; *HP* 25 Dec. 1857; 22 Feb. 1861.

10 *HA* 28 Jan. 1848.

11 Ibid. 1 Apr. 1853.

12 *HP* 7 Nov. 1862.

13 Ibid. 31 Jan. 1862.

14 *HA* 14 Jan. 1848; *HP* 31 Jan. 1862; Sheahan and Whellan, *Hist. York & ER.* ii. 500; *Kelly's Dir. N & ER Yorks.* (1872), 351; (1897), 440; Bulmer, *Dir. E Yorks.* (1892), 167;

15 *Kelly's Dir. N & ER Yorks.* (1872), 351; (1897), 440; Bulmer, *Dir. E Yorks.* (1892), 167.

16 ERAO, DDX/1039, minute books of the Driffield Mechanics' Institute 1866–1932.

17 *Hull Times* 3 Mar. 1934; *DT* 15 Feb. 1947; RDB, 900/311/263.

18 *YH* 30 Mar. 1839; *HA* 13 July 1849. The Driffield Teetotal Society that opened new rooms in 1841 may have been the same as the Total Abstinence Society: *HP* 20 Aug. 1841.

19 *HP* 4 Feb. 1870; *DT* 12 Nov. 1870.

20 *HA* 18 July 1839; *HP* 2 Aug. 1844; 7 Aug. 1846; below, this section, friendly societies.

in the 1840s and 50s. It was claimed that there were almost daily lectures on temperance at Driffield in the summer of 1841, and the Corn Exchange was crowded for the temperance festival in 1846. This was preceded by a procession through the town with banners and Driffield band, and the event had the added attraction of a female lecturer.[1] The postmaster, M. L. Domanski, a Polish refugee, was president of the Temperance Society and a popular lecturer in the late 1840s.[2]

A revival of the movement from the late 1860s was given impetus in 1872 when a lodge of the Independent Order of Good Templars, a temperance society, was opened in the town.[3] In 1874 the former Primitive Methodist chapel in Mill Street was bought by the Driffield Temperance Hall Co. Ltd for the use of the Good Templars and the Temperance Society.[4] The Temperance Hall with accommodation for 700 people became the venue for lectures and lodge meetings of the Templars, and many other public events.[5] Here were held the meetings for the week long mission in 1882 held by the Blue Ribbon Army, an Evangelistic temperance organization, when over 1,000 people took the pledge and 'donned the blue ribbon'.[6] The mission had the support of all the religious denominations in the town including the Anglican church, which since the arrival of the Revd Horace Newton as vicar had become actively involved in the temperance cause. In 1879 Newton leased a building which he fitted up as a coffee house, as an alternative to the public house, and by 1884 he had founded a branch of the Church of England Temperance Society and the following year hosted in the grounds of his home, Beechwood, a conference on the evils of beer in the harvest field.[7]

The Baptists were particularly active advocates of temperance. Their minister James Normanton had been one of the first to take the pledge at a meeting of the Total Abstinence Society in 1839, and the leading lay Baptist in the mid–later 19th century, T. D. Whitaker, was the first Chief Templar of the Good Templars' Lodge and first secretary of the Temperance Hall Co.[8] The Methodist chapels were equally dedicated, with the Wesleyans and Primitive Methodists filling all the official positions in the Temperance Society in 1867.[9] By the 1880s the Wesleyans had their own temperance society and branch of the Band of Hope, a juvenile temperance organization, and as late as 1931 the Primitive Methodists were hosting a conference on temperance.[10]

The temperance movement declined in the early 20th century, and in 1921 the Temperance Hall Co. was liquidated by William Wilson, the then secretary and a prominent Wesleyan Methodist; the premises, including the adjoining house with 'lodge' and committee rooms, were sold to a grocer, and were demolished in the later 20th century.[11] The Wilson family were long associated with temperance. Barbara Wilson kept a coffee house and temperance hotel in Middle Street South in the 1850s,[12] and Thomas Wilson, draper, was secretary of the Temperance Hall Co. by the late 1880s.[13] There were usually one or two temperance hotels in the town from the 1870s until *c.* 1930 and a cocoa rooms in 1892.[14]

FRIENDLY SOCIETIES

Working-class social groups included friendly societies.[15] Intended primarily to provide sickness, funeral, and other benefits for members from their common dues, the societies also had an important social function. Meetings were held regularly in a public house or other venue, and there were annual celebrations, involving a procession with music, a religious service, and a feast.

The first society in Driffield, the Union Friendly (or Benefit) Society, later Driffield Old Club, was founded in 1793 or 1794.[16] There were 110 members *c.* 1795, 233 by 1803,[17] and 451 in 1815. In 1831 the rules of the society were printed.[18] It was then led by a joiner, a chemist, a shoemaker, and a painter, with the clockmaker Christopher Laybourne as its clerk. More prominent residents - Richard Allen, the incumbent of Driffield,[19] Thomas Atkinson, ironmonger, the miller William Dickon, Thomas Dawson, corn merchant, and the farmer William Harrison – served the society as trustees. Members met monthly in the 'club room', in 1803 at the Blue Bell,[20] to pay over their dues. The feast was held on the second Monday in July.[21]

The Union society was joined *c.* 1823 by a second

1 *HP* 20 Aug. 1841; 7 Aug. 1846.

2 Ibid. 14 Apr., 9 June, 18 Aug. 1848.

3 *HP* 25 Jan. 1867; *YH* 2 Oct. 1893; G. P. Williams and G. T. Brake, *Drink in Great Britain 1900–79* (1980), 238–9; ER Yorks. District Lodge, Independent Order of Good Templars, *The Official Templar Guide to Hull and District*, no. 53, Feb. 1888.

4 *HP* 10 Apr. 1874.

5 Bulmer, *Dir. E Yorks.* (1892), 167; below, meeting rooms.

6 *HP* 6 Oct. 1882.

7 Ibid. 5 Dec. 1879; 8 Feb., 6 June 1884; 10 July 1885.

8 *YH* 30 Mar. 1839; *HP* 22 Sept. 1876; *DT* 18 July 1896.

9 *YH* 26 Jan. 1867

10 Ibid. 3 Nov. 1882; *DT* 7 Feb. 1931.

11 RDB, 239/213/188; 240/9/6; 242/437/332; photograph 1957 by Bob Allen at ERAO, PH/4/11.

12 TNA, HO 107/2366; White, *Dir. Hull & York* (1851), 601; *Slater's Royal Nat. Com. Dir. of Northern Counties* (1855), i, *Yorks.* 99.

13 *Kelly's Dir. N & ER Yorks.* (1889), 375, 377, and later directories.

14 Directories; *DT* 29 Nov. 1892.

15 Following based on D. Neave, *ER Friendly Soc.* (E Yorks. Local Hist. Ser. 41, 1988), 49–50, *and passim.*; see also D. Neave, *Mutual Aid in the Victorian Countryside 1830–1914* (1991), 25–8.

16 The rules were confirmed in 1795: F. M. Eden, *The State of the Poor* (London, 1797), iii. 818. The date 1793 seems to be the correct one, the society celebrating its 56th anniversary in 1849: *HA* 13 July 1849.

17 *Poor Law Abstract, 1804*, 588–9; Eden, *State of Poor*, iii. 818.

18 ERAO, QDC/2/29.

19 *Rep. Com. Eccl. Revenues*, 930–1.

20 RDB, CF/198/304.

21 ERAO, PE/10/T. 84, s.a. July 1828.

body, the Provident (Benefit) Society, or Driffield New Club.[1] The New Club's celebration, also including a sermon, took place the day after that of the Old Club.[2] The feast days of both were later enlivened by a town band formed partly for that purpose. By the earlier 1840s the Union Friendly Society had almost 400 members and funds of nearly £2,300, and the Provident Society about 80 members and some £940. Both declined later. The older society's membership, which had reached 600, was 141 in 1853 and 57 in 1867, when its funds amounted to only £569; the society in state of 'rapid decadence' in 1869 was dissolved the following year, its funeral paraphernalia and other goods being auctioned.[3] The Provident Society had been closed earlier, in 1854, when it had 61 members and £1,268.

The problems facing the early, local societies in the mid 19th century, of elderly memberships and difficult economic conditions, were added to by the establishment in the East Riding of branches of national affiliated order friendly societies. Despite the attractions of their elaborate ritual and dress, many of the affiliated branches also failed in the economically difficult years *c.* 1850. The Independent Order of Oddfellows, Manchester Unity, founded two lodges in Driffield in 1832[4] and 1838. The earlier lodge had 155 members in 1845 and 121 in 1850, and the later 86 and 49 respectively. The Ancient Order of Foresters opened three 'courts' in 1838, 1840 and 1842. The earliest, 'Court Alfred the Great', had 103 members by 1840, 224 and funds of just over £1,000 in 1890, and 349 members in 1915. The second court may have existed only briefly, and the third had a small membership. The anniversary celebrations of one or both Oddfellows' lodges were marred in 1840 by fighting, and perhaps for a similar reason the Foresters limited their anniversary celebrations in 1846 to a dinner in the Corn Exchange.

A group connected with the Primitive Methodist chapel established the Good Resolution tent of the Independent Order of Rechabites, a temperance body, in 1839 and a branch or gorsedd of the Ancient Order of Druids, was established in 1843.

There was a 'smash amongst the secret orders' at Driffield in 1850 when the two Oddfellows' lodges and one of the Foresters' courts were dissolved together with the Fold of Refuge lodge of the Loyal Order of Ancient Shepherds, which had existed since 1840.[5] The Tradesman's Free Gift, a sick and dividing fund which chiefly arose 'from the ashes of the two defunct Oddfellow's societies' in 1850, probably failed soon after.[6] The Rechabite tent and Druid gorsedd closed in 1864–5. Another local society, the Working Man's Friendly Society, established *c.* 1850 had 56 members and £104 by 1866 but was insolvent in 1874.

In the later 19th century and early 20th new societies were begun which lasted until the need for their existence was largely removed by national insurance schemes. Driffield Provident Benefit Society was founded in 1862; it had 85 members in 1870 and 80 in 1882.[7] The Garden of Eden lodge of the National United Order of Free Gardeners opened in 1869 with 37 members; it had 105 members six months later and 240 in 1882;[8] a British Workman branch had 40 members in 1882.[9] There was a United Ancient Order of Druids lodge founded in 1892, and branch of the Order of the Sons of Temperance in 1904.[10] The Provident Benefit Society, whose trustees in 1886 included a tradesman and shopkeepers of the town,[11] and the Sons of Temperance branch both had memberships in excess of 100 in 1910 but were closed in or soon after the First World War. The larger Gardeners' lodge had 506 members in 1912 but only 245 in 1924.[12] The Druid lodge, with *c.* 80 members in the 20th century, survived until the Second World War. The National Deposit Friendly Society had a district secretary in Driffield from the late 1920s, but it declined with the coming of the National Health Service in 1948.[13] Of all the friendly society branches established in Driffield from the mid 19th century, only that of the Foresters existed still in 1978.

The Driffield branch of a Primitive Methodist preachers' provident society was in fact established at North Frodingham in 1856, had a small membership, and was closed in 1873.[14]

FREEMASONS

In 1864 the Sykes Lodge of Freemasons was established at Driffield on the initiative of six men living in and near the town who were already members of Londesborough Lodge at Bridlington.[15] The lead figures were David Hornby, a Driffield solicitor and his brother Thomas, a farmer. Christopher Sykes, brother of Sir Tatton Sykes, Bt, of Sledmere, was chosen as 'Patron' of the lodge which was named after his family. Other prominent landowners, Lord Londesborough and Edward Horner Reynard of Sunderlandwick, were early members.

In the first 20 years (1864–1883) 122 members were admitted of which 41 were resident in Driffield. These local members included three farmers, two solicitors, two auctioneers, a surgeon, a bank manager and a

1 The 26th anniversary occurred in 1849: *HA* 13 July 1849.
2 ERAO, PE/10/T. 84, s.a. July 1832.
3 *DT* 17 July 1869; Ross, *Driffield*, 91.
4 The 17th anniversary was celebrated in 1849: *HA* 13 July 1849.
5 *HA* 14 June 1850; *HP* 5 Apr., 7, 14, 28 June 1850.
6 *HA* 18 July 1851.
7 TNA, FS 15/1501; *DT* 12 Feb. 1870; 6 Jan. 1883; Ross, *Driffield*, 91.
8 *HP* 7 May, 25 June 1869; *DT* 27 Nov. 1869; 6 Jan. 1883.
9 *DT* 6 Jan. 1883.
10 Neave, *ER Friendly Societies*, 50.
11 RDB, 10/17/17 (1886).
12 *HT* 26 Jan 1924.
13 Friendly Soc. Research Group, *Newsletter* no. 4 (Apr. 2000); directories.
14 *VCH Yorks. ER*. vii. 263.
15 This section is based on A. T. Brand, *The Sykes Lodge of Freemasons* (1919), the text online at www.driffield.org, 2010.

curate but the great majority were drawn from the tradesmen and shopkeepers of the town including four chemists, two corn merchants, two ironmongers, two coachbuilders, two hotel keepers, a timber merchant, a grocer, a draper, a wine merchant, a brewer, a corn miller, a provision dealer, a tobacconist, an earthen-ware dealer, a builder, a silversmith, a watchmaker, a hosier, as well as an insurance agent, a workhouse master, a railway inspector, a station master and the secretary of the Cake Mills. In 1892 the lodge was suspended for six months because of 'irregularity and unmasonic conduct on the part of one or two brethren'. A period of stagnation followed but from 1904 there was 'renewed vitality' and in 1915 membership had reached a peak of 100. That year a doctor, Alexander Brand, was the Worshipful Master, William Scotchburn, draper, Senior Warden, David Purdon, auctioneer, Treasurer, Thomas Conder, workhouse master, Secretary, Henry Shepherdson, cabinet maker, Senior Deacon, John T. Sokell, stationer, Junior Deacon, and John M. White, bank manager, Steward, all Driffield residents.

The first meeting of the lodge was held at the Bell Hotel at the end of November 1864. Four years later the former Baptist chapel on Chapel Lane was purchased by the Lodge, and after conversion was consecrated as the Masonic Hall at the beginning of 1871.[1] The hall was damaged by a bomb dropped from a Zeppelin in 1915. The meeting place of the lodge in 2010 in Lockwood Street, formerly the museum of the archaeologist J. R. Mortimer, was bought in 1918 for £600 and plans were drawn up for its conversion to the Masonic Hall later the next year.[2] The redundant hall in Chapel Lane was sold in 1921.[3]

MILITARY ORGANIZATIONS

From the late 18th century various volunteer military bodies were formed in and around Driffield, at first in response to the threat from revolutionary France. In 1796 the government formed the East Yorkshire Provisional Cavalry from horse owners selected by ballot, one of the five troops being based on Driffield; that force was, however, never active and was disbanded in 1799.[4] In the same period, the fear of invasion from the Yorkshire coast led to militia forces being stationed in Driffield, and waggons were kept ready in Middle Street to move women and children further inland.[5]

In 1798 the mutinies in the Royal Navy and a general nervousness about the effect of the example of France on the British working classes led to the formation of armed associations of reliable citizens, charged with the prevention of riots and looting in the event of an invasion. Driffield Armed Association had Henry Grimston then of nearby Sunderlandwick, as its captain commandant and the Driffield attorney Thomas Cator as first lieutenant. The Association comprised 120 men armed with muskets or pikes. Two officers of the association, the Hon. Philip Leslie and Richard Porter, fought a duel at the beginning of 1799.[6] That year the force became the Driffield Volunteers, or merged with another group with that name, exchanging blue coats for scarlet. From the area around his seat at Sledmere, some 6 miles from Driffield, Sir Christopher Sykes, Bt, also formed a cavalry troop of some forty volunteers in 1798. Both of those volunteer forces were disbanded in 1801, following the signing of the preliminaries for a peace treaty, which was eventually ratified at Amiens the following year.[7]

With the resumption of war with France in 1803, volunteer forces were again raised close to Driffield. John Grimston of Neswick, some 4 miles from Driffield, raised about 160 men who were formed into the two companies of the Bainton Beacon Volunteer Infantry. That force, alternatively said to comprise three companies of 60 men each, was encouraged by its own band and march. It was stationed at Bridlington in 1804, 1805, and 1807–8. In the last year it was commanded by Captain George Conyers, a Driffield attorney.[8] The Yorkshire Wolds Yeomanry Cavalry, with a strength of about 250, was similarly re-formed under Sir Mark M. Sykes, Bt. The reform of the militia in 1808 led to the rapid disappearance of both volunteer forces, some of the disbanded soldiers then transferring to the local militia.[9]

Volunteers were again used from the mid 19th century, when there were doubts about the efficacy of the militia and a worsening of relations with France. Driffield Volunteer Rifle Corps was formed in 1860, under the command of Captain Edmund Dade Conyers, solicitor, with his brother-in-law Thomas Hopper, farmer at Kelleythorpe, as lieutenant; it then had 44 members, 14 of them honorary.[10] The same year the corps, or company, was grouped with others as a battalion of the East Yorkshire Rifle Volunteers, and from 1883 it was a volunteer battalion of the East Yorkshire Regiment. The Driffield company was some one hundred strong about 1890. In that decade the volunteers formed a force which, under Major James Mortimer of Driffield, saw action in South Africa with the regulars of the regiment.[11] By Act of 1907, the

1 RDB, KY/300/397.
2 Ibid. 201/573/479.
3 Ibid. 229/199/179.
4 Following based on Norfolk, *Militia*, 17, 44.
5 Ross, *Driffield*, 91; *HA*, 4 Feb. 1797.
6 *The Times* 9 Jan 1799.
7 Ross, *Driffield*, 91; Norfolk, *Militia*, 19–21, 45, 47; *DT* 7 Aug. 2002.
8 *HP* 24 May 1808.
9 Ross, *Driffield*, 91; Norfolk, *Militia*, 24, 33, 49–50; Local Militia Act, 48 Geo. III, c. 111.
10 HUL, DDSY/12/2; *DT* 27 Oct. 1988; *HP* 23 Dec. 1859; 27 Jan., 25 May, 28 Dec. 1860; 14 June 1861; 5 Sept. 1862; 16 Oct. 1863.
11 Norfolk, *Militia*, 35–6, 38–9, 56; Ross, *Driffield*, 92; Howorth, *Impact of War*, 15–19; memorial stone to Lt.-Col. James Mortimer at recreation ground; *Kelly's Dir. N & ER Yorks.* (1897), 442. Photograph at ERAO, DDBD/16/15; cf. *Kelly's Dir. N & ER Yorks.* (1905), 480.

existing voluntary arrangements were abolished and replaced in 1908 by a new force, modelled on the regular army and administered in each riding by the Lord Lieutenant and an association.[1] The volunteers in Driffield had trained in premises on Cross Hill, but their successors were provided with a new base. The Territorial Force Association of the East Riding bought land to the east of Middle Street South with New Market Hall and another building in 1908, and the hall was subsequently used for a drill hall. An indoor, miniature rifle range was later added to the south of the hall.[2] The Driffield Territorial Force comprised two companies about 1910, one of them of cyclists, and was then part of the 5th Batallion Alexandra Princess of Wales Own Yorkshire regiment, and later of the Green Howards.[3] During the First World War the greater part of the battalion volunteered for service overseas under the command of Sir Mark Sykes, Bt, of Sledmere. When the battalion were eventually sent abroad in April 1915 it was under the command of Major James Mortimer and included some seventy men from Driffield.[4] Mortimer, then Lt Col, was killed on the Somme in 1916, his brother-in-law Capt. Frank Woodcock of Grove Cottage was killed the following day.[5]

In the later 20th century Territorial Army training was progressively removed from the town to the former airfield at Kelleythorpe.[6] In 1969 much of the land attached to the drill hall was sold to the UDC, but the drill hall itself and the rifle range were then retained for training cadets.[7] Those premises were also given up *c.* 1995, and then sold.[8] The former drill hall, which had evidently been remodelled since the late 19th century, was a wooden-clad, single-storeyed building used by a nursery school in 2006. The old shooting range to its south then housed a second-hand furniture dealership.

In 1970 the UDC let a building off Middle Street South, together with a plot of land to its rear to construct an indoor rifle range, part of its recent purchase from the Territorials, to the Driffield Rifle and Revolver Club,[9] and that club still occupied the premises in 2004. There was also another rifle range in Driffield, outdoors to the west of Skerne Road.[10]

It may have been the premises at Cross Hill used for training in the 19th century which were adopted as the headquarters of a squadron of the East Riding Yeomanry in the early 20th century; in 1913 the location was given as King's Mill Lane. By 1921 the squadron had been re-founded as an armoured car company, and moved to no. 4 'Railway Street'. It was evidently disbanded soon afterwards.[11]

Organizations in Driffield associated with the forces have included the Driffield & District Service Club Ltd, later part of the British Legion, and the Driffield Veterans; the former had a clubroom in Albion Street by 1925,[12] and the latter an unlocated hut, opened in 1950.[13] The outbuildings of Southorpe Lodge were used for the Pegasus club of the East Riding branch of the Parachute Regimental Association about 1970.[14]

DRIFFIELD SHOWS

Driffield Agricultural Show The Driffield Show, the town's main annual event in the early 21st century and, it is claimed, England's best one-day show, was established by the Driffield and East Riding Agricultural Society founded in 1853.[15]

One of the main objects of the society was to hold a show of livestock, crops, and machinery each July. The first show took place in 1854 in a field, variously described as beside King's Mill Road or off Shady Lane, now Victoria Road. Some 6,000 people of all classes were admitted by tickets priced from 3*d.* to 2*s.* 6*d.* each, and the sum so raised, amounting to almost £300, was distributed mostly in prizes.[16] The 1861 show was held on a Saturday, in fields off Shady Lane, and attracted some 7–8,000 people. Businesses were shut and a holiday enjoyed by many employees. The festivities extended to the town as a whole, and included a pleasure fair on Cross Hill, street photographers, a dinner in the Corn Exchange, and an evening ball. The success of the early shows was contributed to by the railway, many of the visitors arriving on specially laid on trains.[17] Later locations of the show were off St John's Road and, on the other side of the town, adjacent to Wansford Road and Bridlington Road.

There was no show in 1869 because of the Yorkshire Agricultural Society holding their show at Beverley.[18] Similarly in 1875 the Driffield show was cancelled to accommodate the three-day event of the Yorkshire Agricultural Society, which took place on a field between Little Driffield and Elmswell.[19] This was a great occasion for Driffield with nearly 27,000 people attending.[20]

There was no show again in 1883 when the Royal

1 Norfolk, *Militia*, 39–40.
2 RDB, 108/426/390; 1615/142/121; OS Map 1:2,500, Yorks. CLXI. 12 (1893 and later edns); directories. The earlier use of New Market Hall is not known: RDB, 48/111/109 (1902).
3 Directories.
4 Howorth, *Impact of War*, 41–50.
5 Ibid. 74–5.
6 Above, Kelleythorpe.
7 RDB, 1615/142/121; ERAO, UDDR/1/1/44, Gen. Purposes Cttee, 8 Sept. 1970.
8 Inf. from David Marley, Horsley & Dawson, Driffield, 2006.
9 ERAO, UDDR/1/1/44, Gen. Purposes Cttee, 7 Apr. & 26 May 1970. The relationship of this club to the apparently earlier Driffield & District Rifle Club is not known: ERAO, DDBD/16/17.
10 RDB, 33/235/220 (1901).
11 Directories.
12 Ibid.; OS Map 1:10,560, TA 05 NW (1956 edn).
13 *DT* 27 Oct. 1988.
14 RDB, 1658/318/276; 1838/39/39; ER CC *Mins* 1971–2, 128.
15 Milner, *Driffield Agricultural Soc.* 7–9; *Driffield Town Guide* (2008), 35.
16 *Farmers Magazine* 6 (1854), 149.
17 *DT* 4 July 2001.
18 *HP* 5 Mar. 1869.
19 Ross, *Driffield*, 32–3, 88–9; Harrison, *Driffield*, 358.
20 Milner, *Driffield Agricultural Soc.* 13–14.

42. *Kelleythorpe: Driffield Show, 2010. The one-day agricultural show founded in 1854 was first held on the permanent showground in Kelleythorpe a century later.*

and Great Yorkshire shows were combined at York. The agricultural depression must have contributed to the fall in attendances at the Driffield show to around 3,000 in the 1880s and in attempt to broaden its appeal the agricultural society added athletic and other sports, pony and donkey races, a gala and a ball at night. The visit of Prince Albert Victor in 1888 gave the event a boost, but the numbers attending continued to decline falling below 2,000 in the first decade of the 20th century.[1]

No shows were held during the First World War. On the eve of that conflict the society had become the Driffield Agricultural Society, and the secretaryship, earlier often held by a solicitor, was subsequently filled for many years by C. R. Kirby, the landlord of the Falcon inn and also secretary of the cricket club.[2] Shows, resumed in 1920, attracted once again 6–7,000 visitors, but the difficult economic conditions made them uneconomic, and they were abandoned in 1931. In 1937, after controversy between the committee and the members, new leaders were appointed, Sir Richard Sykes, Bt, taking the presidency and Peter Atkinson the office of secretary. A half-day show and evening entertainments were subsequently held annually on the recreation ground beside King's Mill Road until the outbreak of hostilities in 1939, in which year the gate had been almost 4,000. The Driffield show was begun again in 1946, and has since been held annually without interruption. About 17 a. at Kelleythorpe were bought in 1952,[3] and a permanent showground was opened there in 1953; more than 8,000 attended that show and the sports which followed it in the evening. The showground was enlarged with two purchases, both of 16 a., during the 1990s.[4] The one-day Driffield show now includes handicrafts and gardening, and much more, and is attended by over 22,000 people. Soon after its acquisition of the Kelleythorpe site, the society leased land to the local rugby club,[5] and, between shows, the society usually lets the exhibition area itself as pasture or for occasional events, often with a country connexion. Thus farm machinery was being auctioned there early in 2004, and later in the year large numbers were attracted to an annual rally of steam engines and vintage cars.[6]

Driffield Floral, Horticultural and Poultry Show Driffield Floral, Horticultural, and Poultry Society was founded and held its first show in 1852. The society was re-organized in 1853 with E. H. Reynard of Sunderlandwick as president and James Harrison as vice-president.[7] Between 1,500–2,000 attended the show that year and it was said that 'never did Driffield witness such an assemblage of the elite of the town and neighbourhood'.[8] The tenth annual exhibition was held in 1862 but the society probably folded soon afterwards.[9] Another Floral, Horticultural and Poultry Society was founded in 1872, and held its sixth and possibly last, exhibition in 1878.[10]

1 Ibid. 15–19; *YH* 21 July 1888.
2 Directories.
3 RDB, 928/124/114.
4 Inf. from Mr John Atkinson, Driffield, 2006.
5 Below, this section, rugby.
6 Advertisement at showground; *ER Gazette*, 19 Aug. 2004.
7 *YH* 25 June 1853; Sheahan and Whellan, *Hist. York & ER*. ii. 501.
8 *YH* 16 July 1853.
9 Ibid. 30 Aug. 1862.
10 Ibid. 6 July 1878.

SPORTS

Angling

The clear chalk streams of the parish with a plentiful supply of trout had become an attraction to sportsmen by the early 18th century. The streams were the preserve of the lords of the adjacent grounds. In Driffield the appurtenances of Routh Hall manor included fisheries in 1570,[1] and later all or much of the fishing belonged to the lord of Great Driffield manor. At inclosure in 1742, Richard Langley was expressly allowed a footway through all lands adjoining the beck in order to enjoy his fishing rights.[2] When the manorial estate was divided and sold in 1918 and 1919 some of the lots included fishing rights in the streams of Great and Little Driffield, including that running along the southern parish boundary called Driffield trout stream.[3] The division and sale of the earl of Londesborough's estate in Kelleythorpe in 1911 had similarly involved his fishing rights in another stretch of Driffield trout stream, and in Elmswell and Driffield becks.[4] Fishing rights were later reserved on the Elmswell estate, which in 1935 contained 4 a. of streams.[5]

Besides those belonging to the lords of Driffield, Kelleythorpe, and Elmswell manors, fishing rights in Great and Little Driffield were also claimed for one or both of the manors of Skerne and Wansford in the 17th century and later.[6] Such claims may have been meant to cover the fishing of Driffield's boundary stream from the opposite bank, and perhaps also any ambiguities introduced by changes in the course of that stream. When the Skerne estate was offered for sale in the early 20th century, one of its attractions was the 'celebrated Driffield Trout Stream or West Beck' which skirted the property for almost 6 miles.[7]

In 1734 it was noted that it was the 'usual diversion of gentlemen' to spend two or three days angling at Driffield.[8] Guide books to Scarborough later in the century suggest that those who 'delight in fly fishing' should go to Driffield and advertisements, in national and local papers, for the sale or letting of larger properties in the town invariably refer to the celebrated trout streams.[9] Anglers would stay at the Red Lion inn where the landlord Alexander Mackintosh was 'well known as a skilful sportsman, in all departments of rural entertainment, with gun, dogs, nets, or fishing rods'.[10] Mackintosh who settled in Driffield *c.* 1774 was initially landlord of the Nag's Head, and then of the Red Lion to 1800.[11] After giving up the inn he continued to live nearby to render 'every assistance to Noblemen and Gentlemen who resort thither for the purpose of pursuing the pleasures of Angling'; he also supplied all kinds of fishing tackle.[12] In 1806 was published *The Driffield Angler* written by Mackintosh with the help of the Hon. Philip A. Leslie.[13] As well as giving information on fresh-water fishes, instructions on fly-fishing and extolling the virtues of the local streams the book deals with shooting, training of gun dogs and coursing with greyhounds. Three years later local gentry subscribed towards a pension for Mackintosh, then destitute and nearly blind.[14] He died in Driffield workhouse in 1829.[15]

Mackintosh's book no doubt encouraged more sportsmen to visit the town and it became necessary to introduce greater controls.[16] In the 1820s Richard Arkwright, the lord of Skerne manor, issued printed fishing licences for the May to October season bearing a plan of his part of the trout stream in Skerne and Driffield.[17] A more concerted management of the fishery was adopted soon afterwards, with the foundation in 1833 of Driffield Anglers' Club.[18] Membership was limited originally to 45, later reduced to 40, each of whom was to subscribe £5 a year for the preservation of the fishery and employment of a head keeper. Members were issued with a silver ticket, with which they could 'introduce' a friend. For allowing their 20 miles of trout streams to be managed by the club, the owners were to enjoy free fishing; complimentary tickets were thus issued to Marmaduke Langley, lord of Driffield manor, Sir Tatton Sykes, Bt, lord of Kirkburn manor, and Charles Arkwright, for Skerne.[19] An annual dinner was to be held at the Red Lion for the members, who initially included the duke of Leeds, the earl of Mexborough, Lord Middleton, E. H. Reynard, lord of Sunderlandwick manor, and the Revd Francis Best, lord

1 *Yorks. Fines*, i. 382.

2 RDB, B/153/42; H/391/806.

3 Ibid. 188/425/393; 188/459/424; 192/489/431.

4 Ibid. 135/36/34; 135/95/85; 136/106/92.

5 Ibid. 430/505/409; 525/516/405.

6 TNA, CP 25(2)/613/1653 Trin. no. 2; CP 25(2)/756/24–5 Chas II Hil. [no. 35]; CP 25(2)/1258/33–34 Geo. II Trin. no. 618.

7 ERAO, DDLO/Box 80A.

8 *Journey from London to Scarborough* (1734), 27.

9 J. Schofield, *Guide to Scarborough and its Environs* (*c.* 1787), 129; J. Schofield, *The Scarborough Guide* (1796), 27–8; *Universal Brit. Dir.* (*c.* 1792), ii. 827; *The Times* 21 Oct. 1792, 11 June 1795; *HP* 27 Dec. 1803; 2 Oct. 1810.

10 Schofield, *Scarborough Guide* (1796), 27.

11 ERAO, QDT/2/3/32-40; ibid. DDGR/38/90.

12 *HP* 23 Dec. 1800.

13 A. G. Credland, 'Alexander Mackintosh (1742–1829) a forgotten sportsman and author of *The Driffield Angler*', *E Yorks. Historian* 6 (2005), 98–9. An edition of the book published 1821 has the title *The Modern Fisher or Driffield Angler*: ibid. For Leslie see above, this section, soc. leadership (1770–1870).

14 ERAO, DDGR 38/90.

15 Credland, 'Mackintosh', 27.

16 *Gentleman's Magazine* July 1805, 596; S. Oliver, 'Angling Recollections of Yorkshire', *New Sporting Magazine* (Sept. 1834), 302; *HP* 28 July 1837.

17 ERAO, CSR/31/6.

18 Following based on ERAO, DDX/659/1; Sheahan and Whellan, *Hist. York & ER.* ii. 501; Ross, *Driffield*, 90; *HP* 28 July 1837, 23 Apr. 1841.

19 White, *Dir. E & NR Yorks.* (1840), 210, 213.

of Elmswell. There were a number of clergy members including the Revd F. Chaloner who in 1843 caught 200 trout in five days.[1]

By the mid 1850s the Blue Bell Hotel had superseded the Red Lion as the club's headquarters.[2] Premises were later rented for a clubhouse. It was probably the anglers' club which, as 'Driffield Fishing Club', was renting a cottage in Skerne from Lord Londesborough in 1884,[3] and certainly the club occupied a cottage in Little Driffield, presumably Trout Stream Cottage at the southern end of the village street, as the tenant of Lord Downe in the early 20th century.[4] The Little Driffield premises were later abandoned for a cottage on the Poundsworth Mill site, in Hutton Cranswick, where trout hatcheries had been made by the mid 20th century.[5] The club still flourished in 2010, with a waiting list for membership.

There was later fishing in the canal. Part of that waterway had been stocked with trout by 1991, when the fishery was managed by Tony Harrison of Whinhill Lock and Trout Farm. He maintained that the restoration of the canal then under way was damaging his fishery.[6] From 2003 the Hull & District Anglers' Association was regulating fly fishing in the canal, and in particular protecting the brown trout there.[7]

Hunting

The earliest reference to hunting in the parish may be the grant made by the Crown in 1384 to the then prebendary of Driffield, allowing him, for life and while holding that office, free warren, or exclusive rights of hunting, in the demesne land comprising his prebend.[8]

Accommodation for the hunting season was to let at Driffield in 1768, and the following year the Driffield hunt was first mentioned.[9] It was a hunt club with around fifty members by 1772 comprising many of the leading gentry of the East Riding, some clergy and Hull merchants.[10] They met periodically for several days during the hunting season, with packs of hounds provided by members.[11] As well as having its own uniform, of a red coat and white waistcoat, both with silver buttons, and a velvet cap, the club had a Hunt Room, built in 1771 on land belonging to Henry Drinkrow adjacent to the Red Lion inn.[12] The club also had its own song which in 1771 consisted of 48 humorous verses all but six describing in turn each of its members including the Revd Francis Best, curate of Driffield, rector of South Dalton, and heir to the Elmswell estate.[13] Captain Langley, presumably Boynton Langley or his son Richard, successively lords of Driffield manor was elected a member in 1772.[14] Attendance at the club meetings was costly; Robert C. Broadley, from a Hull merchant gentry family, spent £5 in 1770, of which over half was on dinners and suppers, and Sir Christopher Sykes spent over £10 at each of two meetings in 1772.[15]

The hunt club was in financial difficulties through non-payment of subscriptions by 1786, when it appears to have closed, at least temporarily. No more meetings are recorded until 1792 when the club was revived with the support of Sir Christopher Sykes who considered that the main benefit of hunting was the way that it gathered together the 'gentlemen of the County'.[16] The club then met, with minor breaks, usually once a month in the hunting season until 1806–7 when there were two week-long meetings with hunting for three or four days on the Wolds and Holderness 'within reach of Driffield' with Richard Watt's and Sir Mark Masterman Sykes's foxhounds.[17] Then the club appears to have been in abeyance and some members joined a short lived hunt club at Beverley 1808–11.[18] In 1809 the owner of the Hunt Room at Driffield believed the club had moved to Beverley and asked the trustees if they would release the room to him.[19] The Driffield club did have at least one more meeting in 1811 before it was wound up.[20] The Hunt Room was used for a dancing school in 1811 and registered as a place of worship for Dissenters in 1818 was demolished in 1825.[21]

Stags were hunted by the members during the club meetings in 1804 and 1807, and there were also harriers at the latter date.[22] Driffield harriers were recorded again in 1817.[23] Two years later Edmund P. Turton, MP for Hedon, established a pack of harriers at Driffield.[24]

Nothing is known of the Driffield beagle hunt of which A. A. MacIlwaine of Kelleythorpe was master in 1922.[25]

1 *YH* 6 May 1843.
2 The duke of Leeds continued to occupy 'his old comfortable quarters' at the Red Lion: *HP* 1 May 1857.
3 RDB, NW/171/238.
4 OS Map 1:2,500, Yorks. CLXI. 11 (1893 edn); RDB, 94/418/379 (1907); 190/395/336.
5 OS Map 1:10,560, TA 05 NW (1956 edn); OS Map 1:10,000, TA 05 NW (1970 edn).
6 *DT* 14 Nov. 1991; *DP* 14 Nov. 1991.
7 Noticeboard.
8 TNA, C 53/160, no. 20.
9 I. M. Middleton, 'An investigation into early English fox hunting with an account of hunting with hounds in the East Riding of Yorkshire 1700–1850' (Hull MPhil thesis, 1995), 119.
10 Ibid. 120–1.
11 Ibid. 125.
12 Ibid. 127; ERAO, DDX/17/15.
13 ERAO, DDGR/38/31.
14 HUL, DDBM/33/35.
15 Middleton, 'Foxhunting', 125.
16 HUL, DDSY (3) vol. 9, 83–4.
17 *YH* 4 Oct. 1806, 28 Feb. 1807; *HP* 24 Feb. 1807.
18 Middleton, 'Foxhunting', 130–1.
19 ERAO, DDGR/43/29.
20 Middleton, 'Foxhunting', 130.
21 ERAO, DDGR/43/29/6; DDGR/43/31/16; ibid. DDX/17/15; BIA, DMH. Reg. 1, p. 75; below, this section, meeting rooms.
22 *YH* 4 Oct. 1806; 28 Feb., 17 Nov. 1807.
23 Ibid. 22 Nov. 1817.
24 YAS, DD/147/360.
25 *DT* 15 Apr. 1922.

Coursing Hare coursing took place on the Wolds near Driffield in the early 19th century.[1] Driffield Coursing Club described as recently formed in January 1922 existed until the Second World War. The club's greyhound coursing meetings, amongst the most important in the north of England, were held at different venues on the Wolds and Holderness.[2]

Horse Racing

Steeplechasing began at Driffield in 1839 probably on the initiative of Edward Reynard of Sunderlandwick who had ridden in the first steeplechase at York in 1835.[3] The Driffield steeplechases were run on the edge of the Wolds and held annually 1839–42.[4] They were revived again in 1848 but cancelled the next year for lack of entries.[5] With the backing of Lord Londesborough the steeplechases were run annually from 1853 until 1859 when they were finally abandoned.[6] The course for the second steeplechase in 1840 started in a field near the windmill at North End and covered 4 miles over 60 fences and ending in a field nearly opposite the start.[7] The ground to the north of Slaysdale Farm was called Horse Race Leys in 1845.[8]

The races had the support of farmers, merchants, clergy and local gentry, including the Sykes and Reynard families, and were particularly popular in the 1850s when thousands attended.[9] In 1859 a local paper condemned the races as dangerous and 'a scene of riot and drunkenness, reflecting little credit on the town'.[10] Most of the horses entered were locally owned and the very first race at Driffield was won by a horse called Peter Simple that came second in the Grand National in 1846.[11]

Cricket

There were several cricket teams playing in Driffield in the mid–late 19th century. A cricket club recorded in 1850 was a predecessor of the Driffield Cricket Club that existed from 1854 to 1884.[12] A local draper's apprentice Richard Daft (1835–1900), who went on to captain Nottinghamshire county club and play for the All England Eleven, is said to have been instrumental in founding the club.[13] Amongst the earliest players were F. C. Matthews, son of the chemical fertilizer manufacturer, and the artist A. F. Lydon.[14]

The Victoria Cricket Club, founded by 1858, was still playing in the 1870s, when the town had numerous short-lived teams, including the Rising Star, White Star and Union Jack clubs.[15] In 1874 Henry Marshall, miller of King's Mill, established a cricket club 'solely for young men connected with the Congregational Sunday School'.[16]

Marshall's Cricket Club rivalled and outlived the older-established Driffield club which was 'transformed' into the Driffield Church Bible Class XI in 1884.[17] The church team, which like Marshall's eventually widened their membership, played their matches at Beechwood, the home of the vicar, Canon Newton, until he retired in 1892.[18] In November 1892 it was agreed to amalgamate the two clubs to form the Driffield Town Cricket Club as part of a new Athletic Association which included cycling and football.[19] Early the next year Marshall's club decided to continue independently which they did until the death of Henry Marshall in 1910.[20]

James Mortimer, a corn merchant and son of the archaeologist J. R. Mortimer, was the first secretary of the Driffield Town club, and J. T. ('Jack') Brown (1869–1904) the first captain.[21] Brown, who became a prominent Yorkshire county and England cricketer, was born in Driffield, the son of the landlord of the Grapes inn. By the age of 16 he was playing for the church team and soon afterwards joined Marshall's club.[22]

In the early 1920s the Driffield Town club won the Hull & East Riding Cup successively for three years.[23] There were other teams in the town between the wars including Taylor's Cricket Club, under the presidency of the timber merchant Horace Taylor, and a Driffield Friday team.[24] Driffield Town club had five adult teams in 2009, the first eleven playing in the Yorkshire Premier League.[25]

The actual location of the early cricket pitches is uncertain although the Driffield club, from 1869 to 1884, and Marshall's club, from 1874, played on grounds

1 A. Mackintosh, The *Modern Fisher or Driffield Angler* (1821), 32.

2 *DT* 28 Jan. 1922; 6 Feb. 1926; *The Times* 31 Dec. 1931; 26–7 Oct. 1934; 17–8 Oct. 1935; 15 Oct. 1936; 14 Oct. 1937; 13–14 Oct. 1938.

3 *HA* 6 Feb., 13 Mar. 1835; 1 Apr. 1839.

4 *Bell's Life* 22 Mar. 1840; 28 Mar. 1841; *HP* 26 Mar. 1841; 11 Mar. 1842.

5 *Bell's Life* 12 Mar. 1848; *HP* 9 Feb. 1849.

6 *Bell's Life* 5 Nov. 1854; 16 Mar. 1856; *HP* 18 Mar., 1 Apr. 1853; 6 July 1856; 4,11 Mar. 1859; *Racing Times* 5 Apr. 1853; 18 Mar. 1857; 22 Feb. 1858, 21 Mar., 4 Apr. 1859.

7 *Bell's Life* 22 Mar. 1840.

8 See under Henry Broadley in ERAO, PE/10/T. 120; ibid. TA/13

9 *HP* 1 Apr. 1853; 21 Mar. 1856.

10 Ibid. 4 Mar. 1859.

11 J. Fairfax-Blakeborough, *Northern Turf History* (1949), ii. 76.

12 *HP* 6 July 1855; *Driffield Observer* 1 Nov. 1856; P. Howorth, *E Yorks. Cricket 1778–1914* (1995), 45, 50.

13 Ibid, 45; www.cricinfo.com (Richard Daft).

14 Howorth, *E Yorks. Cricket*, 46; *HP* 6 July 1855; 16, 30 July, 15 Oct. 1858, 16 June, 15 Sept. 1865.

15 *HP* 16 July 1858; Howorth, *E Yorks. Cricket*, 52.

16 Ibid. 50; *HP* 9 Jan. 1880; 3 Apr. 1885; *DT* 9 Apr. 1910.

17 *HP* 3 Apr. 1885; *DT* 31 May 1890.

18 Howorth, *E Yorks. Cricket*, 50, 52, 54.

19 *LM* 16, 23 Apr. 1892.

20 Howorth, *E. Yorks. Cricket*, 52; *DT* 10 Apr. 1909.

21 *LM* 16 Apr. 1892.

22 Howorth, *E Yorks. Cricket*, 116–121; www.cricinfo.com (Jack Brown)

23 *HT* 19 Jan 1924.

24 *Hull Times* 5 May 1934; *DT* 13 Mar. 1943.

25 Inf. from Driffield Town Cricket Club 2009.

either side of King's Mill Road.[1] Driffield Town Cricket Club used the former Church Bible Class ground at Beechwood in 1892–3 before moving to the newly opened recreation ground on King's Mill Road in 1894.[2] The club purchased the ground from Lord Downe in 1918, and it was still the club's base in 2009.[3]

Rugby

Driffield Town Football Club, evidently in existence by 1884, was playing under rugby rules in 1886.[4] It was probably the same club of which the Yorkshire county cricketer J. T. Brown was vice-captain 1891–2, and captain in 1893.[5] As the Driffield Rugby Football Club it successfully competed for the Hull and District Rugby Union Cup in 1899–1900.[6] It is unclear if references to a rugby club in the early decades of the 20th century are to this club or the rugby league club that played on the recreation ground in King's Mill Road for some 30 years from *c.* 1908.[7]

There were both union and league teams at the beginning of 1926, but later that year a meeting was held at the Cross Keys that led to the formation of the Driffield Rugby Union Football Club that was still flourishing in 2010.[8] The club rented pitches until the 1950s. Its first ground, off St John's Road, was succeeded after the Second World War by four others, before use of part of the Driffield Agricultural Society's showground at Kelleythorpe was offered to the club in 1952. The pitch was not ready to be played on permanently until the 1956–7 season.[9] A building on the former airfield was used for changing until one formerly housing a RAF cinema and Roman Catholic chapel there was bought in 1958 converted, and opened as a clubhouse in 1960.[10] Nine acres of the former airfield land earmarked for industrial development at Kelleythorpe was purchased in 1977 from Derek Megginson and laid out with two further pitches.[11] There was a growth of interest in the club and the single team was increased to three during the 1960s, and by the 1980s there were five senior squads, and junior rugby was developed by the club and at the secondary school. A field of over 6 a. directly north of the clubhouse was purchased in 1994 and was laid out the following year for rugby and, briefly, cricket. The pitch on the showground was given up in 1998, but in an agreement over access with the Driffield Agricultural Society two full-sized pitches and two junior pitches were laid out in 1999 on the society's car park fields. A two-storey clubhouse, built on the site of the old one, partly with a Lottery grant from Sport England, was opened in 2002.[12] The club then boasted a membership of more than 650, and in 2004 the large numbers of townspeople supporting the Sunday morning games of the seniors and juniors was said to affect church attendance locally.[13]

Rugby league was also revived in Driffield, and it was Driffield Rugby League Club which improved the facilities for its own and other sports on the council's recreation ground on Allotment(s) Lane in the 1990s.[14]

Other Sports

Football Association football, soccer, has been overshadowed by the popularity of rugby football at Driffield. Little is known of the Driffield Town association football club which twice played a Driffield grammar school side in 1894, or of the club formed by members of the Church Institute in 1899.[15] There was an association football club in the town throughout the 1920s–30s and a Driffield & District Football League by 1924.[16] Among local concerns with their own teams were the millers, E. B. Bradshaw & Sons Ltd.[17] There were two football clubs in 1949 and one in 1969.[18] The Driffield Mariners football club, associated with the Mariners Arms public house, played successfully in the Hull Sunday League in the early 21st century.

During the 20th century football pitches were made in North End Park and at the west end of Little Driffield, but otherwise facilities were slight until, at the end of the century, council land in the north-east of Driffield was developed as a recreation ground for football and other sports.[19] Little Driffield had a football club in the 1930s–40s.[20]

Hockey A hockey club was started in 1899 with men and women on the committee; they played on the new recreation ground on King's Mill Road.[21] The

1 Howorth, *E. Yorks. Cricket*, 47–8, 50.
2 Ibid. 54–5.
3 Howorth, *Impact of War*, 116.
4 *HP* 20 June 1884; *DT* 30 Jan. 1886.
5 *YH* 15 Jan, 2 Sept. 1891, 17 Aug. 1893; above, this section, cricket. The club played in crimson vests and blue shorts in 1894: *YH* 20 Aug. 1894.
6 *ER Chronicle and Driffield Express* 29 Sept 1894; *LM* 14 June 1899; *DT* 6 Jan. 1900; *YH* 3 Sept. 1900.
7 C. Atkinson, *Driffield Rugby Union Football Club 1926–2001: A Brief History* (2002), 3, 7; *DT* 21 Jan. 1922; 13 Apr. 1929; 26 Apr. 1947; HT 26 Jan. 1924.
8 *DT* 20 Feb., 8 May 1926.
9 Atkinson, *Driffield Rugby*, 1, 17–18.
10 Ibid. 23; RDB, 1124/223/195.
11 Atkinson, *Driffield Rugby*, 51; *HDM* 3 Aug. 1977; inf. from D. Megginson, 2011.
12 Atkinson, *Driffield Rugby*, 67, 72, 74–5, 77.
13 Inf. from Mr D. Longbottom, Driffield, 2004.
14 Below, this section, sports grounds.
15 *YH* 26 Feb., 2 Apr. 1894; 9 Sept. 1899; *DT* 6 Jan. 1900.
16 *DT* 31 Dec. 1921, 21 Jan. 1922; *HT* 9 Aug. 1924; *Kelly's Dir. N & ER Yorks.* (1929), 485; (1933), 455; *DT* Jan. 2000 (millennium edn).
17 *DT* 15 June 1994.
18 *Driffield Official Guide* (1949), 23; *Driffield Town Guide* (1969), 29.
19 Below, this section, sports grounds.
20 *HT* 15 Sept. 1934; *DT* 14 June 1947.
21 *YH* 26 Jan. 1899.

hockey club existing in 2010 was founded in 1909.[1] It apparently had a continuous existence with only minor interruptions in wartime. There are references to clubs for men and women in the 1920s.[2] The location of the pitch used by the club for some twenty years from *c.* 1927 has not been identified, but from the late 1940s hockey was played again on the recreation ground.[3] In the early 21st century the hockey club was based at the sports centre and from 2009 at the leisure centre.[4]

Tennis There was a lawn tennis club by 1884 and courts were laid out beside Bridlington Road in the 1890s.[5] Croquet was also played there, either from the outset or soon afterwards.[6] A second club was founded by the Primitive Methodist chapel in 1922 with a ground on Wansford Road.[7] In 1925 a tennis club was begun at the recreation ground on King's Mill Road; it still existed in 2010 along with the original lawn tennis club with its courts off Bridlington Road.[8]

Badminton A badminton club functioned from the later 1920s.[9] There were two badminton clubs from the mid 1950s, in the early 1970s they met weekly at Driffield School.[10] In 2010 the Driffield Badminton Group met at the leisure centre.[11]

Golf Driffield Golf Club was founded in 1923, its first course being laid out off Meadow Road, on the eastern side of the town.[12] In 1934 the club was moved to Sunderlandwick, just across the Driffield boundary in Hutton Cranswick parish. Part of the parkland of Sunderlandwick Hall, then the seat of the Reynard family but later owned by the Hull industrialist, Sir Thomas Ferens, was then used for an 18-hole course and a wooden clubhouse.[13] Because land was needed for agriculture the links were reduced to a 9-hole course in the Second World War, but in the early 1980s the course was restored to its former size and the clubhouse replaced by a brick building. The success of those changes made it necessary to extend the clubhouse in 2001, and in 2005 there was a membership of some 2,700.

Cycling Bicycles were introduced into Driffield in the summer of 1869 and the following year cycle races were held on the streets of the town.[14] A bicycle club was formed in 1879 and a cinder track was laid out encircling the cricket field where annual races were held for at least the next four years.[15] The bicycle club was last mentioned in 1886, and the following year the Driffield Cycling Club was formed with headquarters at the Cocoa House, no. 32 Market Place.[16] Forty cyclists joined at the first outdoor meeting and the president was Thomas Durrans who had a cycle depot at no. 25 Middle Street South.[17] Because of the popularity of the sport a cycle track was laid out on the new recreation ground in King's Mill Road.[18] The cycling club, which had 50 members in 1893 and 41 in 1902, was meeting in the Keys Hotel, Market Place, about 1910, but evidently did not survive the First World War.[19]

Swimming The town had a swimming bath as early as the 1890s. That bath was located near the junction of Eastgate North and Cranwell Street; it was operated by the cabinet maker Charles Dawson, and may have had a short existence.[20] Apparently about 1930 a swimming club was begun, its chief supporters including members of the Spencer family, and by 1933 another open-air swimming pool had been made by Albert Spencer, then also chairman of the UDC. His pool was rented for the local schools, and in 1952 the UDC was urged unsuccessfully to buy it.[21] The pool was evidently closed, and its site, off Eastgate South, was later that decade developed as Nayfield Close.[22] Another pool was provided for school pupils on the secondary school site by the Driffield Swimming Pool Association with help from the LEA in or soon after 1963.[23] It was later part of Driffield sports centre, off Manorfield Road, opened in 1979, which in turn was replaced by a large pool at the new leisure centre on the adjoining site in 2009.[24]

The Driffield Watermen's Swimming Club for keel owners and their families existed at River Head from

1 HUL, DDSY2/1/11/348, 352; Driffield Hockey Club website, 2009 (www.bsgphotos.co.uk/dhc).

2 *DT* 4 Feb. 1922; *Kelly's Dir. N & ER Yorks.* (1929) 485; (1933), 455.

3 *DT* 20 Sept. 1947; *Driffield Official Guide* (1949), 23; (1961), 15; *Driffield Souvenir Guide* (1974), 18

4 *Driffield Town Guide* (2008), 69; (2010), 73.

5 *HP* 29 Aug. 1884; *DT* 6 Jan. 1900; RDB, 298/285/238; directories.

6 Directories.

7 *DT* 21 Jan., 24 June 1922.

8 *Driffield Town Guide* (2004), 42; ibid. (2010), 73.

9 Directories.

10 Town guides.

11 *Driffield Town Guide* (2010), 73.

12 Following based on Driffield Golf Club website, 2005 (www.driffieldgolfclub.co.uk)

13 *HT* 12 May 1934.

14 *HP* 20 May, 10 June 1870; *DT* 25 June 1870.

15 *HP* 25 July 1879; 23 July 1880; 19 Aug. 1882; 3 Aug., 7 Sept. 1883.

16 *HP* 5 Sept. 1886; Simpkin, *Driffield and District*, 166–7.

17 Simpkin, *Driffield and District*, 166–7; *Kelly's Dir. N & ER Yorks.* (1889), 375.

18 *YH* 28 Aug. 1893.

19 Simpkin, *Driffield and District*, 175–7; Directories; *Borough Guide to Driffield*, *c.* 1913, 22.

20 Bulmer, *Dir. E Yorks.* (1892), 172; *Kelly's Dir. N & ER Yorks.* (1893), 410. The baths in Cranwell Street began as a public baths not swimming baths: *DT* 15 Apr. 1865.

21 ER Educ. Cttee *Mins* 1933–4, 77; 1948–9, 68, 140; 1952–3, 123; *Kelly's Dir. N & ER Yorks.* (1929), 485; (1933), 451, 455.

22 ERAO, UDDR/1/8/51, Building...Cttee, 8 Feb. 1955; UDDR/1/8/53, Housing...Cttee, 7 Aug. 1956.

23 Below, this section, Driffield County Secondary School.

24 *HDM* 13 Jan. 2009.

about 1905 until the Second World War, with an annual swimming gala.[1]

Sports Grounds and Facilities

There were several sports clubs in the town that wanted a permanent ground by 1893 when 11 a. on King's Mill Road was leased from Lady Downe for the purpose, and Driffield Recreation Ground Co. Ltd formed to provide and manage the ground.[2] The company's directors included Harrison Holt and Luke White, and James Mortimer and W. A. Brown were its secretaries. The recreation ground was to include cricket and football pitches, tennis courts, and a cycling track, but was also to be used generally for the recreation of children, and part of the site was to continue to be available for the agricultural show. When the ground was opened at the end of 1893 there was provision for cricket, cycling and rugby.[3] In 1918 when Driffield Athletic Club Ltd bought the freehold from Lord Downe, the occupier of the ground was given as Driffield (Town) Cricket Club.[4] In 1994, when a sports hall was built on the recreation ground, the existing or proposed facilities included pitches for both rugby and football.[5] The rugby union ground was at Kelleythorpe in 2010.[6]

In the later 20th century playing fields were created on council land in the north-east of Driffield. In 1974 recently-vacated ground was let for the making of a possibly temporary football pitch.[7] Another piece of council land on Allotment(s) Lane had been used for 'many years' for football and other sports by 1993, when the council planned to double the area of the recreation ground there to some 13 a. A request was then made to the council by Driffield Rugby League Club for a long lease to develop the very limited facilities of the ground for the playing of rugby and other sports.

Sport was encouraged about 1930 by the Driffield School Sports Association,[8] and after the Second World War by the local authorities. In 1960 the county council as LEA held the County Youth Sports at Driffield,[9] and the sports facilities at the new secondary school, which included a swimming pool,[10] were later developed as a resource for the town as a whole. From or by 1991 the sports hall built in the school grounds was thus run by a joint management committee composed of nominees of Humberside County Council and East Yorkshire Borough Council, respectively the LEA and the district council. Called Driffield Sports Centre, it included a fitness suite by 1994 and sunbeds in 1995.[11] It was later refitted and enlarged, and in 2005 the centre, open to the general public in the evenings and all day out of the school terms, was also offering a sauna, an artificial football pitch, meeting rooms, and a bar.[12] The sports centre was replaced by a new leisure centre in 2009.

INNS AND PUBLIC HOUSES

Public houses and inns were the chief meeting places and commercial centres in the Georgian and early Victorian town; their yards served as market places, and as stations for coaches and the many carriers serving the town's hinterland, and their rooms were used for a range of social and other events. The proliferation of public houses reflected the growth of the town. Driffield town had about ten licensed houses and a few beer sellers in the 1740s and 1750s; about five houses in the 1760s and 1770s, and, presumably stimulated by the growth in trade along the canal, ten houses again by 1793.[13] The growth of the town in the early 19th century saw an increase in the number of licensed houses, to 22 in the 1820s, and a similar number at the end of the century.[14]

There were usually two or three chief inns where important public meetings, major social gatherings and official business, such as inquests, took place. In the mid 18th century the Nag's Head was considered the chief inn, but this position was challenged by the Red Lion, the headquarters of the visiting sportsmen, and the Blue Bell, associated with the corn merchants. All three in turn hosted the early meetings of the Driffield Navigation Commissioners and in 1771 the turnpike trustees requested the landlords of the Nag's Head and the Red Lion to take down their respective signposts, no doubt hanging over the road, and place the signs against their houses.[15]

With the development of the town and its trade the two premises on Middle Street North, the Nag's Head and Red Lion, were superseded by the Blue Bell or Bell and the larger public houses in the Market Place, the Buck and the Cross Keys, as the venue for the more prestigious gatherings by the mid 19th century.

Little Driffield, where beer was sold also by villagers

1 *DT* 5 Aug. 1922, 20 Mar. 1943; Clubley, *Driffield*, pls. 73–4. Perhaps Driffield Watermen's Sports Club that existed in 1909. HUL, DDSY2/1/11/377.

2 NYRO, ZDS IV/10/4/9 (lease 24 Feb. 1893); Following based on account from the *ER Chronicle and Driffield Express* at ERAO, DDX/659/7.

3 *DT* 30 Dec. 1893.

4 RDB, 188/494/454; 188/495/455; 190/397/337; ERAO, NV/1/107.

5 ERAO, EYEY/1/4/8/3, Environmental…Cttee, 22 Mar. 1993; 21 Mar., 18 July 1994; *DT* 5 Aug. 1982; 22 Sept. 1994; *DP* 13 Oct. 1994.

6 Above, rugby.

7 ERAO, UDDR/1/1/47, Building…Cttee, 7 Aug. 1973; Gen. Purposes Cttee, 15 Jan. 1974.

8 *Kelly's Dir. N & ER Yorks.* (1929), 485; (1933), 455.

9 ER Educ. Cttee *Mins* 1959–60, 209.

10 Below, this section, Driffield County Secondary School.

11 ERAO, EYEY/1/4/8/2, Environmental…Cttee, 8 Apr., 29 July 1991; EYEY/1/4/8/3, Environmental…Cttee, 21 Nov. 1994; 10 Jan. 1995.

12 Driffield Sports Centre website, 2005.

13 ERAO, QDT/2/3.

14 Ibid. QDT/2/1; YML, F3/3/37; F2/3/3/71, directories.

15 *YC* 3 Apr., 7 Aug., 28 Aug. 1781; ERAO. TTBM/1.

43. *Great Driffield: Market Place from the north-west, c. 1910. A busy market day with the Bell Hotel on the left.*

during the fairs without licence, under the sign of a green bush,[1] had about six public houses in the 1740s and earlier 1750s but only three or so later in the century, and a single house was recorded *c.* 1790.[2] The village later had two or three houses.[3]

The later decline in local brewing in the face of competition from large regional concerns was associated with, and perhaps largely achieved by, the acquisition by the large breweries of local public houses. The chief purchaser was John Smith's Tadcaster Brewery Co. Ltd, which as early as 1890 bought the Golden Fleece, subsequently the Cricketers' Arms.[4] In 1897 the company bought four public houses from Thomas Holtby of Eastgate brewery; Westgate brewery with two licenced houses from Emily Turner, and from W. O. Jarratt the Falcon inn and the market house, comprising bars kept by the licensee of the Falcon and auction rooms.[5] In 1899 Simpson & Heard, brewers of Market Weighton, sold Smith's their recently-acquired estate in Driffield, comprising a wine merchant's shop, two public houses, and a malting.[6] The Nag's Head, added to the Tadcaster brewery's estate in 1903, was closed soon afterwards, and two of its other acquisitions, the Queen's Head and the White Horse, were shut about 1910 and 1915 respectively.[7] Other breweries from outside Driffield which obtained public houses there included Hull Brewery Co. Ltd; it had two beerhouses by 1888[8] and at least five houses in 1910. The Little Red Lion, seems to have passed soon after 1910 to Scarborough & Whitby Breweries Co. Ltd, and to have been closed about 1915.[9] A Grimsby brewery, Hewitt Bros, bought the Bay Horse in 1897.[10] The Bell Hotel belonged in 1910 to a Malton spirit merchant, while a Malton brewery had the neighbouring Black Swan.[11] The few houses remaining may then have been independent of the larger concerns but their owners also lived outside Driffield, at Malton and Bridlington. A century later the town still had some twenty drinking places. Perhaps more so than formerly, most of the public houses also offered food; some provided games or live entertainment, and several fulfilled their traditional role as venues for clubs. The public houses were then free houses, but John Smith's remained an important supplier of beer to the town; other northern breweries involved including Theakstons of Masham and the independent Cheshire brewer Burtonwood, which had bought two of the houses. The public houses proper had also been joined by a few licensed social clubs and pubs catering for young people. The latter had a particular importance for the social and economic character of the town, attracting taxi firms and fast-food outlets to the immediate vicinity.

1 Sheahan and Whellan, *Hist. York & ER.* ii. 503; *Kelly's Dir. N & ER Yorks.* (1872), 351.
2 ERAO, QDT/2/3.
3 Directories.
4 RDB, 35/122/116 (1890).
5 Ibid. 94/16/16; 95/87/81; 95/163/144 (all 1897) etc.
6 Ibid. 42/530/495 (1891); 9/199/180; 9/219/198 (1899).
7 Ibid. 48/270/251 (1891); 55/494/470 (1903).
8 RDB, 25/209/203 (1888).
9 ERAO, NV/1/107.
10 RDB, 95/461/426 (1897).
11 ERAO, NV/1/107.

Great Driffield: Principal Inns

The following gazetteer is based, unless otherwise indicated on alehouse licence lists,[1] and trade directories.

Bell, or Blue Bell, Market Place The Bell, or Blue Bell, was built by William Porter on the site of a cottage he bought in 1746; Porter then described as a carpenter was an innholder by 1758, and later a coal merchant.[2] The first meeting of the navigation commissioners was held at 'the house of William Porter, known by the sign of the Blue Bell' in 1767.[3] The tenancy was taken on by Robert Daniel, late butler to Sir Griffith Boynton of Burton Agnes, in 1783.[4]

Ten years later John Dobson, then tenant, described also as a brewer, bought the premises from William Porter's son Richard.[5] Dobson was succeeded by 1822 by Samuel Witty (d. *c.* 1832), son of licensee of the Red Lion, and then his widow Elizabeth Witty who had the licence until *c.* 1865.[6] Robert Kirby (d. 1869) a former landlord of the Falcon, followed by his widow Ann, and later her trustees then ran the Bell until the end of the century.[7] A later proprietor, W. J. Isherwood, who in 1913 was landlord of both the Bell and the Keys, sold the hotel to David Mill (d. 1942) in 1924.[8] In 2010 it was a Best Western hotel.

The Bell became the town's premier inn during the 19th century. A coaching inn where corn merchants and farmers congregated, both inside and outside, on market day, it was the favoured location for auctions and inquests.[9] It had an assembly room where concerts were held and major gatherings of the townspeople took place in the 1830s–40s.[10] The inn was the meeting place for the town's first friendly society in 1803 and later for an Oddfellows lodge.[11] The first Driffield Farmers Club was founded there in 1851, and the later one met there in 1889.[12]

It remained the hotel of the farming community throughout the 20th century although the corn market held here and at the Keys Hotel closed in 1940.[13] The nearby livestock market was closed in 2001, but the auction rooms nearby continued to flourish and attract trade to the hotel, which played an important role in the social and economic life of the town in 2010. Groups meeting there then included the Driffield Lions.

Black Swan, 44 Market Place Situated on the east side of Market Place the house was trading by 1823. It was licensed in the liberty of St Peter.[14] Never formally classed as an inn, it did have stabling for 20 horses and during the 1830s–40s it was one of the main meeting places in the town.[15] Inquests were held, and meetings of the guardians of the poor law union in 1837 and an Oddfellows' lodge 1839–48.[16] The inn, which belonged in the 20th century to the Malton brewer, Russell & Wrangham Ltd, was closed in 1964 and sold to Yorkshire Bank Ltd who built a bank on the site.[17]

Buck, (Old), Market Place The Buck was kept in 1792 by Christopher Walker.[18] Before 1825 it was sometimes called the Old Buck to distinguish it from the other Buck in Middle Street. A commercial and coaching inn it had a large public room, the scene of inquests, auctions and popular concerts.[19] The Buck was the meeting place and venue for the annual dinners of Court Alfred of the Ancient Order of Foresters, the Union Society and the Tradesmen's Association in the 1840s, and the Farmers Club, the rugby club and Driffield Harriers in the 1890s.[20] The sporting credentials of the inn had been established in 1871 when a large billiard room holding 100 people was added.[21] The Buck was associated with the Holtbys' Eastgate brewery until 1897, when it was sold to John Smith's of Tadcaster.[22]

Cross Keys or Keys, 20 Market Place The house, recorded in the 1820s, was kept by a farmer in 1851.[23] It became established as one of the town's chief inns after it was rebuilt *c.* 1859 when Christopher Hopper became landlord.[24] Then usually known as the Keys, it became a posting house, hosting auctions and inquests and

1 ERAO, QDT/2/1, 3.

2 RDB, S/344/827; AA/31/49; BC/98/146; BI/65/97; BQ/286/438.

3 Ross, *Driffield*, 104; Harrison, *Driffield*, 211.

4 *YC* 16 Dec 1783.

5 RDB, BQ/286/438; BR/430/696 ; *Universal Brit. Dir.* (*c.* 1792), ii. 828.

6 When sold in 1871 the inn was owned by Thomas Dawson, miller and corn merchant: Howorth, *Year Gone By*, 41.

7 TNA, RG9/3607; *YH* 6 Oct. 1866; *HP* 12 Feb 1869.

8 RDB, 644/79/69.

9 e.g. *HP* 27 Dec. 1803; 20 June 1826; 16 Jan. 1874; *YH* 28 Dec. 1844; 9 Oct. 1868, 1 Sept. 1888.

10 *HP* 21 Dec. 1830; 8 Oct. 1841; 12 Aug. 1842.

11 RDB, CF/198/304; *HP* 2 July 1843; above, this section, friendly societies.

12 *YH* 19 Apr. 1851; 5 Jan, 1889.

13 Atkinson, *Winds of Change*, 173.

14 YML, F2/3/3/71.

15 *DT* 15 Nov. 1963, at HUL, DDX/16/126. It had a club room by 1845: ERAO, TA/13; ibid. PE/10/T. 120.

16 ERAO, PUD/1/2/1, p. 91; *YH* 25 May 1839; 20 Mar 1841; 24 Jan. 1846; 17 June 1848.

17 ERAO, NV/1/107; ibid. UDDR/1/1/37, Building…Cttee, 14 Oct. 1963; RDB, 1340/200/184; *DT*, 15 Nov. 1963 (illus.).

18 *Universal Brit. Dir.* (*c.* 1792), ii. 828.

19 *YH* 19 Feb. 1841; 23 Apr. 1864; 3 Nov. 1880, 23 Jan. 1892, 15 Sept. 1895.

20 *YH* 21 May 1842, 24 Jan. 1846, 17 June 1848; 17 Oct. 1891; 20 Aug. 1894; 8 Feb., 23 Apr. 1895; 14 June 1899; *HP* 14 July 1848.

21 *YH* 1 Apr. 1871.

22 RDB, 94/16/16 (1897).

23 TNA, HO 107/2366.

24 Ibid.; D. Neave, 'Buildings of Great Driffield' Report for North Wolds Borough Council, Mar. 1977, [15–16]. Later the hotel was owned by the Pickering family, ironmongers and founders based on the adjoining site: RDB, NM/31/48.

44. *Great Driffield: Market Place looking north,* c. *1910. On the right, the Black Swan, closed in 1964, and soon afterwards replaced by the Yorkshire Bank.*

developing strong farming and sporting connections.[1] Here were held a dinner for tenants on the Sledmere estate to celebrate the marriage of Sir Tatton Sykes in 1874, and the early meetings of the Farmers' Club, from 1885, and the Improved Leicester Sheep Breeders' Association from 1893.[2] The corn market was held at the Keys and Bell Hotels up to 1940.[3] In the early 20th century the local cycling club met at the Keys, and later the rugby union club was based there.[4]

In the 1970s the building was altered and renamed the Highwayman, then the Ferret and Sprout, and by 1992 the Original Keys. By 2003 the house had been acquired by the independent Cheshire brewery, Burtonwood.

Falcon, formerly the Dog and Duck, 57 Market Place The Dog and Duck was recorded in 1791.[5] John Collier had the tenancy by 1831. The freehold was bought in 1844 by William Jarratt, who rebuilt the house and developed the ground behind it as a cattle market. His new building, renamed the Falcon by 1848,[6] continued to be tenanted by the Colliers until *c.* 1860. The house was used for inquests and the publican organized athletic sports in 1871 and pigeon shooting in 1880.[7] It was the headquarters of the Conservatives in the 1868 election.[8] In 1897 W. O. Jarratt sold the Falcon to John Smith's brewery of Tadcaster, together with the nearby market house.[9] C. R. Kirby, licensee in 1937, was the secretary of the Driffield Agricultural Society and honorary secretary of the cricket club.[10]

Nag's Head, 49 Middle Street North This was the chief inn of the town when it was kept by John Harland who built a cockpit there in 1761.[11] Arthur Young gave a favourable report of his stay there in 1768.[12] Standing on the west side of the street, south of the junction with Harland Lane, the inn was later kept by Alexander Mackintosh, and then the Etheringtons[13] until at least 1826, and in the mid 19th century by the Hoppers.

1 *HP* 18 Dec. 1868; *YH* 24 Dec. 1881; 8 Jan. 1891.
2 Ross, *Driffield*, 89; *YH* 24 July 1874; 4 May 1889; 8 Jan. 1891; 10 Mar. 1893; 19 Jan. 1895.
3 Atkinson, *Winds of Change*, 173.
4 *Kelly's Dir. N & ER Yorks.* (1913), 516; Driffield RUFC website, 2003.
5 *Universal Brit. Dir.* (*c.* 1792), ii. 828.
6 RDB, FZ/303/358; *1st Rep. Royal Com. Mkt Rights and Tolls*, Vol. II (Parl. Papers, 1888 [C. 5550-I], liii), p. 261.
7 *YH* 12 May 1849; 3 Apr. 1869; 1 Apr. 1871; 1 Dec. 1880; 1 Jan. 1889.
8 Wood, *Policing from Wansford Road*, 70.
9 RDB, 95/163/144 (1897).
10 *Kelly's Dir. N & ER Yorks.* (1937), 447–8.
11 *YC* 9 June 1761.
12 Young, *Six Months Tour*, iv, 589.
13 RDB, BZ/381/609; CE/53/86.

It was part of the estate of a Beverley brewery by the 1890s, and in 1903 became a John Smith's house.[1] In 1897 its attractions included a concert room, open nightly; stabling, and accommodation for cyclists. The inn seems to have been closed in or soon after 1905, and by 1909 was occupied by Dobsons, painters and decorators, who still had it in 2010. 'Dobsons rooms' used as a meeting place in the 1930s can perhaps be identified with the earlier concert room.[2]

Red Lion, 57 Middle Street North William Byass, roper, was the tenant of a cottage called the Red Lion in 1732,[3] almost certainly the inn he held in 1742.[4] In 1770 William Ballans took over the inn from Byass.[5] Named again in 1771,[6] the Red Lion stands on the west side of Middle Street North at the junction with Church Lane.[7] It was licensed in the liberty of St Peter.[8]

From the mid 18th to the mid 19th century the house was at the heart of the town's life. It was a coaching inn and housed the local excise office; meetings held there in the 1830s included those of the guardians of the poor law union, the navigation commissioners, the opponents of a new turnpike Act, and the court to revise voters lists; the house was the venue for inquests and the manorial and pie-powder courts, and the possible location of the town's lock-up, and auctions took place there.[9] The vicarial tithes were collected at the Red Lion, and, presumably for that reason, the church's copies of the tithe award records, later lost, were apparently kept there.[10]

In particular the Red Lion was closely associated with field sports. It was noted in 1800 that 'several noblemen and people of fashion, who pursue the amusement of angling, resort to this inn; and a monthly meeting of gentlemen, who attend the Driffield Hunt, during the sporting season, is held there'.[11] The Hunt Room built 1771 was adjacent to the inn and Alexander Mackintosh, the 'best fisherman in the north country', was landlord from the late 1780s.[12] The Driffield Anglers' Club, founded 1833, met there until 1853 when the annual dinner was moved to the Bell Hotel, signifying a drop in status for the Red Lion.[13] Part of the inn, including the sizeable Long Room and Music Room, was for sale in 1870.[14]

The house belonged to Darley's Brewery in 1885, then Hull Brewery in 1910 and later to its successor, Mansfield Brewery.[15] As the Charles Dickens, it was sold in the 1990s, refurbished, and re-opened under the old name in 1997, offering meals and accommodation.[16]

Little Driffield

Langley, later Downe, Arms By 1834 the Fosters, farmers and fellmongers at Little Driffield, also kept a public house. It was called the Langley Arms until the 1850s and soon afterwards became the Downe Arms. The house, on the south side of the main road and west of the village street,[17] was trading still in the late 20th century but had been closed by 2004.

Rose and Crown An alehouse recorded from 1765 kept by Thomas Wardell and named as the Rose and Crown in 1822 when held by Elizabeth Wardell. Standing in the east end of the village, on the north side of the main road,[18] it was trading still in 2004.

Wheatsheaf A house called the Wheatsheaf was licensed in the 1820s, but not recorded after 1828–9. It may have stood on the west side of the village street, where by 1855 an unnamed public house had been rebuilt as a private house.[19]

MEETING ROOMS

Hunt Room In 1771 the Driffield Hunt built a Hunt Room on land adjacent to the Red Lion inn on Middle Street North.[20] As well as for the hunt dinners the 'Great Hunt Room' was used for meetings of the agricultural society and the navigation commissioners in the 1790s and a theatrical performance in 1801 and annual dinners after the annual show of cattle 1801–3.[21] In the years 1810–17 Vernon Southerne conducted a dancing school in the Hunt Room and it was used for balls, concerts, theatrical entertainments and as a place of worship by the Primitive Methodists.[22] The building was demolished in 1825.[23]

1 Ibid. 48/270/251 (1891); 55/494/470 (1903).
2 *Kelly's Dir. N & ER Yorks.* (1909), 496; 1933, 455, 458; (1937), 450.
3 RDB, N/72/144.
4 Ibid. B/153/42; ERAO, IA. 41.
5 *YC* 15 May 1770. The Red Lion was to let again in 1781: *YC* 16 Jan. 1781.
6 MacMahon, *Roads and Turnpike Trusts*, 58.
7 RDB, CE/429/627; TNA, HO 107/2366.
8 YML, F2/3/3/15, 71.
9 ERAO, PE/10/T. 84, s.a. Mar. 1830; ERAO, PUD/1/2/1, pp. 1, 77; HUL, DDCV/41/1; *HP* 13 Dec. 1803; 23 June, 2 Sept. 1837; 27 June 1845; 4 July 1851; *YH* 9 May 1863; 20 Aug. 1887; Wood, *Policing from Wansford Road*, 1.
10 ERAO, PE/10/T. 71; PE/10/T. 84, s.a. Oct. 1828.
11 *HP* 23 Dec. 1800.
12 Rutland, J. H. Manners, Duke of, *Jnl of a Tour to the Northern Parts of Great Britain* (1813), 63; above, this section, angling & hunting.
13 *HP* 23 Apr. 1852; *YH* 30 Apr. 1853.
14 *DT* 23 Apr. 1870.
15 *YH* 30 Mar. 1882; 14 Apr. 1885; ERAO, NV/1/107.
16 *DT* 3 Dec. 1997.
17 RDB, 190/395/336; OS Map 1/2,500: Yorks. CLXI. 11 (1893 edn).
18 OS Map 1/2,500: Yorks. CLXI. 11 (1893 edn).
19 RDB, HL/158/170.
20 Above, this section, hunting.
21 *HA*, 2 May 1795; *YH* 30 May 1801; 20 Aug 1803; HUL, DDX/60/3; above, this section, theatre.
22 ERAO, DDGR/43/31/16; ibid. DDX/17/15; BIA, DMH. Reg. 1, p. 75; TNA, RG 31/5, no. 3231; *HP* 12 July 1814, 22 July 1817; above, this section, theatre; below, relig. hist. 1700–*c.* 1840 (nonconformity).
23 ERAO, DDX/17/15.

The Corn Exchange and Assembly Room was built on the north side of New Road, subsequently Exchange Street, in 1841–2 with money raised by the sale of shares. The building did not attract farmers from the Bell Hotel and their traditional pitches in Market Place but it did subsequently provide the town with its chief meeting place. Including two large rooms and with room for up to 450 persons, it was used for assemblies, public meetings, theatricals, concerts, and lectures.[1] During the first thirty years of its existence the average annual income of the Corn Exchange Co. was only £21, it paid a dividend once in 1864 and by 1872 it was £30 in debt.[2] In 1920 the Corn Exchange was sold by the trustees to William Shipley, traction machine proprietor.[3] Part of the premises was used for the public library from 1931, and in 1935 the UDC bought the building for a town hall.[4] The hall, much used for dances in the mid century, passed at the abolition of the UDC in 1974 to the succeeding North Wolds District Council, later East Yorkshire Borough Council. In the 1980s the borough council leased the building to the proprietor of the Bell Hotel, who remodelled it as a function room and health club.[5]

Temperance Hall A former Primitive Methodist chapel in Mill Street was acquired by the Driffield Temperance Hall Co., for use as a temperance hall in 1874.[6] The large meeting place which was used for many public events accommodated 700 persons.[7] It was closed and sold to a grocer in 1921.[8] The building had been demolished by 2004, when its site was empty.

New Market Building, 70 Middle Street South There was a public hall in the New Market Building, built 1886.[9]

EDUCATION

Public education in Driffield before 1870 was provided largely by Church and Nonconformist congregations, or by private entrepreneurs. The earliest known school in Driffield was being held in 1764. It was run by a master chosen by the inhabitants to teach reading, writing, and arithmetic in return for fees, and was attended by about forty children.[10] The same or another school was kept in the early 1790s by William Johnson, schoolmaster, perhaps in Doctor Lane, later Queen Street.[11] A few days before his death in 1814 Johnson, 'celebrated as a skilful teacher of navigation', paraded the streets of the town on a cart with his coffin in the form of a seaman's chest.[12]

By 1818 there were four day schools in Driffield, the largest being the National school, associated with the Church of England. The other day schools comprised one with 40 pupils, 'mostly of respectable parents', and two 'common day schools' with a total of 36 pupils.[13] A school-house garden to the east of Beverley Lane, mentioned in 1805, may have belonged to one of those schools.[14] In 1823, besides the National school, six others were recorded, two of them ladies' boarding schools.[15] Several new schools were opened later and by 1833 the town had 12. The National school was then attended by 102 boys and girls. The other 11 schools were all smaller, one having only 16 pupils and the average being apparently about 30; in all, 366 children, 172 boys and 194 girls, were taught in the non-National schools, all at their parents' expense.[16] The locations of some of the private schools were recorded in 1845,[17] and in 1851 seven governesses were at work in homes in the town and the lesser settlements.[18]

Private schools continued to flourish in the later 19th century. In 1872 a boarding and day school for boys, the forerunner of the grammar school; a girls' boarding school; a commercial school, and three other schools were recorded, and two music teachers then also found employment in the town.[19] The improvements made to public education presumably played a part in the decline of the private schools: Bourne House day and boarding school was closed in the early 1900s, and the boys' grammar school in 1911.[20] By 1921 only the girls' school kept in Manor House, Albion Street, remained, and that was closed in the mid 1930s.[21] Music teachers

1 RDB, FW/179/179; Sheahan and Whellan, *Hist. York & ER.* ii. 501–2; Ross, *Driffield*, 87; *Kelly's Dir. N & ER Yorks.* (1872), 351; Bulmer, *Dir. E Yorks.* (1892), 167; *HP* 12 June 1874.
2 ERAO, DDX/17/15.
3 RDB, 200/431/364; 205/562/493.
4 Below, loc. govt and politics; above, this section, libraries.
5 Inf. from Claire Binnington, Driffield Town Council, 2005.
6 *HP* 22 Sept. 1876.
7 Bulmer, *Dir. E Yorks.* (1892), 167.
8 RDB, 239/213/188; 240/9/6; 242/437/332.
9 *YH* 13 July 1886; *Hull and ER Red Book 1900*, 215.
10 *Drummond's Visit.* i, p. 139.
11 HUL, DDMC/26/21; ibid. 57/1; *Universal Brit. Dir.* (*c.* 1792), ii. 828.
12 *HP* 3 May 1814; *New Monthly Magazine* June 1814, 499.
13 *Educ. of Poor Digest*, 1079.
14 RDB, CH/301/480.
15 Baines, *Hist. Yorks.* (1823), ii. 195.
16 *Educ. Enq. Abstract*, 1083.
17 ERAO, TA/13; ibid. PE/10/T. 120.
18 TNA, HO 107/2366.
19 *Kelly's Dir. N & ER Yorks.* (1872), 353–5.
20 Below, this section, principal private schools.
21 *Kelly's Dir. N & ER Yorks.* (1921), 502; (1933), 456.

45. *Great Driffield: Primitive Methodist Sunday School pupils and teachers photographed in 1928.*

and the like seem to have been less affected by the changes, and in 1929 Driffield had two music teachers, a piano teacher, and an elocution coach.[1]

The contribution made to education by religious bodies was largely through Sunday schools. The Church Sunday school was said to have been established in 1796.[2] Schools provided by the Independents, later Congregationalists, in 1806 and the Wesleyan Methodists in 1812 had 130 and 80 pupils respectively in 1818.[3] A Primitive Methodist school was opened in 1829, and 268 children were being taught free in the three Dissenting Sunday schools by 1833.[4] In 1834 and 1854 respectively the Baptists and the Wesleyan reformers started more schools. The provision was, moreover, improved by the building of new premises. In the 1860s new schools, each accommodating *c.* 400 children, were built by the Congregationalists and the Wesleyan Methodists.[5] In all, some 2,000 Sunday scholars were said to have processed through the town in 1880 in celebration of the centenary of the Sunday school movement. The Dissenting congregations supported a day school, the short-lived British school, in the mid 1840s.[6] The Primitive Methodists provided a day school in their schoolroom in Mill Street in the mid century,[7] and from the late 19th century another day school was run by the Roman Catholics.[8] At Little Driffield a Church Sunday school built in 1845 became a day school for the smaller settlements in the following decade.[9]

The supply of elementary education in the town was found to be insufficient about 1870, and, under the Act of that year, a school board was formed for Great Driffield parish in 1871.[10] Enquiries revealed that the town then had eight or nine schools. The largest, and only 'public' school, was the National school, said to accommodate 389 boys, girls, and infants. A second school connected with the Church of England was for *c.* 60 girls, and there were seven other schools, attended by 140 or so boys and girls, and all regarded as too small. It was estimated that there were in all 953 children in need of elementary education in 1871, but that there were then only 381 places available in schools recognized as efficient. The newly-created board proposed to supply the lacking 572 school places by building a new school.[11] William Jarratt then attempted to meet the insufficiency of places and to prevent the provision of a Board school, by fitting up an old

1 Ibid. (1929), 484–7.
2 Following based on Ross, *Driffield*, 184.
3 Ibid. 69; *Educ. of Poor Digest*, 1079.
4 *Educ. Enq. Abstract*, 1083.
5 Below, relig. hist., 1840 to 1940 (prot. nonconf.).
6 *HP* 12 Feb. 1847.
7 ERAO, SB/14/1, p. 21; *Returns relating to Elem. Educ.* 474–5.
8 Bulmer, *Dir. E Yorks.* (1892), 166, 175.
9 Below, this section.
10 *Lond. Gaz.* 10 Feb. 1871, p. 486; J. J. Clarke, *Hist of Local Govt of UK* (1955), 57.
11 ERAO, SB/14/1, pp. 16, 18–21; *Returns relating to Elem. Educ.* 474–5.

brewery building in Brewhouse Lane, later Harland Lane, as a school. Jarratt was an officer of the National school, and, although his school was proposed as a public undenominational school for 208 pupils, it was in fact used briefly by the boys of the National school.[1] The Board school itself was begun in temporary accommodation before the buildings were put up in 1873–4.[2] In 1893 the Board school had 578 pupils (221 boys, 179 girls and 178 infants) and the National school 509 pupils (158 boys, 198 girls and 153 infants).[3]

The school board came to an end in 1903 when under the 1902 Education Act its responsibilities passed to the county council.[4] The former Board school, thereafter called in turn the Council or County school, and the National school, later the Church of England school, were subsequently the chief schools of the town.[5] Following the Second World War and the election of a reforming Labour government, education in Driffield was reorganized, secondary education being introduced in temporary premises in 1947 and transferred to new schools in the mid 1950s, and primary schooling being rationalized soon afterwards, the Church school becoming the town's school for infants and the County school that for juniors. Another infants' school with 180 places was opened in the north-east of the town in 1984.

In 2004 the LEA also supported the care of the youngest through its Early Years Team, which operated from the Driffield & Wolds Children's Centre in New Road, and, besides the schools provided by the local authority, there were then in Driffield three commercially-operated nursery schools.

Secondary Education Secondary schooling for the town and its district was begun in 1947 in temporary accommodation at the County school on Bridlington Road, and new schools built for the boys and girls were occupied in the mid 1950s. The schools were later amalgamated and extended, and the comprehensive system was adopted in 1973.[6]

Vocational, Further, and Technical Education Although the county council decided against providing central schools at Driffield in the 1920s,[7] it did in other ways use the town as a regional centre for delivering and expanding education. Cookery classes for girls from schools in the Driffield area were begun in the town by the council in or soon after 1905. They were perhaps held in the teacher training centre at Bourne House, Queen Street, which was established at the same time, and, on its closure in 1910, the cookery classes also ceased because of a loss of premises.[8] A new building for infants, opened at the Council school in 1914, included rooms where girls from that and other schools in the district were to be instructed in cookery, laundering, and other housework.[9] As the Driffield domestic subjects centre, it was later attended by children from as far away as Leconfield.[10] Handicraft classes for teachers were also held in the 1920s,[11] and the centre was presumably the venue used for classes in cooking for evacuees which were put on for Women's Institute members in 1939.[12]

Adult education was fostered by the Mechanics' Institute, established in 1837,[13] and the various religious denominations. The Wesleyan Reformers had a night school for the free instruction of apprentices in the 'elements of English education' with 50 pupils in 1855, the Primitive Methodists established a mutual improvement society in 1877 and Congregationalists a similar organization the following year.[14] The vicar or his assistants also attempted evening classes for adults intermittently from 1859; then held at the National school, they were acknowledged to have failed by 1884.[15] By that date the Anglican church was centring its adult education activities on the Church Institute formed in 1877.[16]

From the later 1890s the school board, in association with the county council, provided evening classes at the Board school in subjects including shorthand and French,[17] and a local committee was also organizing University extension lectures in 1903.[18] Another important source of adult education has been the Workers' Educational Association which has had a branch in Driffield since 1920, and which more recently worked in association with the University of Hull.[19] The WEA/University of Hull class taught there by Maurice Barley in the late 1930s produced a useful history of the town.[20]

Evening classes were again provided in Driffield by

1 ERAO, SB/14/1, p. 17; Aldabella and Barnard, *Breweries*, 25; *Rep. of Educ. Cttee of Council, 1872–3* (Parl. Papers, 1873 [C. 812], xxiv), p. 513; *1873–4* (Parl. Papers, 1874 [C. 1019-I], xviii), p. 435. The school in Harland Lane was mentioned again, as disused, in 1878: ERAO, PE/10/T. 59, s.a. Dec. 1878.
2 ERAO, SB/14/1, pp. 125–6, 162.
3 *DT* 4 Nov. 1893.
4 Clarke, *Local Govt*, 72, 163; ERAO, SB/14/5, p. 174.
5 For this and the following, see below, this section.
6 Below, this section.
7 ER Educ. Cttee *Mins* 1920–1, 2.
8 Ibid. 1905–6, 12; 1908–9, 274–5; 1910–11, 139, 216; below, this section, teacher training.
9 ER Educ. Cttee *Mins* 1912–13, 239; 1913–14, 19–20; 1914–15, 73, 213.
10 Ibid. 1920–1, 19.
11 Ibid. 1924–5, 154, 197.
12 Ibid. 1939–40, 69.
13 Below, this section, Mechanics' Institute.
14 *HP* 19 Jan. 1855; 9 Jan. 1880; Ross, *Driffield*, 91.
15 *HP* 28 Oct. 1859; ERAO, SL/29/1, p. 63; BIA, V. 1865/Ret. 1, no. 142; V. 1868/Ret. 1, no. 133; V. 1877/Ret. 1, no. 133; V. 1884/Ret. 1.
16 *HP* 18 Jan. 1878; 21 Nov. 1879; Ross, *Driffield*, 90.
17 ERAO, SB/14/4, pp. 125, 136, 157, 164.
18 ER Educ. Cttee *Mins* 1903–4, 32, 197; 1907–8, 203.
19 W. E. Styler (ed.), *Adult Education in E Yorks. 1875–1960* (1965), 19; Harrison, *Driffield*, 409.
20 Barley, *Great and Little Driffield*.

the county council from about 1940.[1] The evening school was provided with accommodation when the boys' secondary school was built in the 1950s, and was subsequently called Driffield Institute of Further Education or Driffield Technical Institute. About 1960 it included an engineering shop and a domestic studies room.[2] A new building for the institute was put up on the school site in the mid 1960s. The premises then included an agricultural science laboratory, and in 1965 the LEA appointed a lecturer in farm machinery, largely to work at Driffield.[3] The institute was later reorganized as an annexe of East Yorkshire College of Further Education, and the accommodation was enlarged about 1980.[4] It was presumably no longer used in 1999, when it was proposed to add the accommodation to the school.[5] Thereafter students were catered for on the college's other sites in Bridlington. In 2004, however, continuing education was being fostered in Driffield by the provision of learning centres run by the LEA and local colleges in a shop in the main street and at Driffield Business Centre, Skerne Road.[6]

Besides that of the Methodists in George Street, youth clubs in Driffield encouraged by the county council in the 1940s and 1950s included one evidently operated in association with the evening institute.[7] In the early 1960s the council appointed a full-time youth leader, and later in the decade a youth service annexe for 200 was built at the secondary school.[8]

Teacher Training In the early 20th century the county council also used Driffield as a regional centre for training its teachers to meet the higher standards then being demanded by central government. The need for such training had been recognized by Driffield school board in 1896.[9] In 1904 Saturday classes for pupil teachers and probationers from as far as Market Weighton were begun in the National school, with 57 in attendance, and classes leading to certification were added later that year.[10] The following year it was concluded that the Saturday classes had been useful in meeting the minimum requirements of the Board of Education, but that the division of training between the Saturday staff and the head teachers of the schools in which the pupils worked was 'an arrangement which has not been found to work with perfect smoothness ... in all cases'. The county council had by then already begun to offer scholarships to intending pupil teachers, from 14 to 16 years old, to enable them to attend secondary schools; for their subsequent training, and the instruction of other apprenticed teachers, a half-week centre at Driffield was then established at Bourne House in Queen Street. The work of the training centre was expanded in 1906, when its principal organized Saturday classes in the National school for the untrained women helpers known as supplementary teachers.[11] The pupil teacher system was given up by the LEA in 1910 in favour of training in secondary schools and colleges, and the Driffield centre was then closed.[12] The LEA later encouraged teachers to improve their skills by grants, such as those made to the local branch of the Educational Handwork Association and its members in 1914,[13] and running special courses at Driffield, like those in handiwork and horticulture.[14]

SCHOOLS

Public Schools

National School A National school was established in Driffield in 1816, and in 1818 it was the largest of the town's schools, with 107 pupils during the week and '40 more' on Sundays. It was supported partly by subscription and partly by the fees of 2*s.* a quarter paid for each pupil.[15] In 1819 it was proposed to build a new school building on a site given by the lady of the manor, Dorothy Langley, who also donated £50, but it is not clear whether that plan was carried out.[16] The National school was said to be in Mill Street in 1823,[17] and it still adjoined that street in 1845, but then fronted onto Cross Hill.[18] In 1833 the National school had 82 boys and 20 girls on its books.[19] The small building was conveyed by the lord of the manor, W. H. Dawnay, Viscount Downe, to the incumbent of the parish church and the churchwardens in 1853, together with ½ a.,[20] and the 'old school' was demolished and a new one built further back from Cross Hill in 1854, the cost being met by subscription and a government grant. The new school, comprising a large schoolroom divided between the boys and the girls and a rear classroom, was designed by Cuthbert Brodrick of Hull, together with the adjacent master's house; all is in the Gothic style and of red brick with

1 ER Educ. Cttee *Mins* 1941–2, 77; 1942–3, 82; 1943–4, 69; 1950–1, 45; 1955–6, 182.
2 Ibid. 1955–6, 216; 1956–7, 93; 1959–60, 141, 209, 213.
3 Ibid. 1963–4, 42; 1965–6, 21, 123.
4 Humbs. CC *Mins* 1981–2, E 267.
5 ERYC *Mins* (1998–9), Educ....Cttee, 1466; Policy...Cttee, 3015.
6 *ERG*, 5 Aug. 2004.
7 ER Educ. Cttee *Mins* 1943–4, 5, 22, 71; 1952–3, 50; 1955–6, 182; 1958–9, 42.
8 Ibid. 1960–1, 39; 1962–3, 32–3; 1963–4, 32, 39; 1964–5, 30.
9 ERAO, SB/14/4, p. 141.
10 ER Educ. Cttee *Mins* 1903–4, 301, 303; 1904–5, 19–20, 177.
11 Bourne House was then wrongly located as in King Street: ER Educ. Cttee *Mins* 1905–6, 4–6, 185, 253–4; 1906–7, 10.
12 Ibid. 1909–10, 111–12, 184–6; 1910–11, 20.
13 Ibid. 1914–15, 11.
14 Ibid. 1936–7, 94; 1941–2, 77.
15 Baines, *Hist. Yorks.* (1823), ii. 193; *Educ. of Poor Digest*, 1079; *DT* 22 Apr. 1922.
16 *HP* 25 May 1819; *Educ. of Poor Digest*, 1079.
17 Baines, *Hist. Yorks.* (1823), ii. 195.
18 ERAO, TA/13; ibid. PE/10/T. 120. Also undated site plan for new school at ibid. SGP/28; OS Map 1:10,560, Yorks. CLXI (1855 edn).
19 *Educ. Enq. Abstract*, 1083.
20 RDB, HA/391/432.

stone dressings.[1] The school's annual income *c.* 1855 was apparently £94, of which almost £60 came from subscribers; the remainder was contributed by the approximately 80 boy and 40 girl pupils, each of whom evidently paid school pence of 1½*d.* a week.[2] From 1856–7 the school also received grants from central government, which in 1860–1 amounted to some £520.[3]

The supporters of the National school were probably also responsible for the infants' school established in 1836 and held elsewhere in the town.[4] A new infants' school was built in 1839 on Doctor Lane (later Queen Street) and maintained subsequently by subscribers.[5] The school was attended by 60 infants in 1865.[6] It was replaced soon afterwards by a new infants' school, also designed by Brodrick, and built to the south of the newly built National school on land given by Viscountess Downe. The new school was opened in 1867, and had 80 pupils the following year.[7] It was usually regarded thereafter as a department of the National school, rather than a separate school.

By the later 1860s the number of older pupils at the National school had grown markedly. About 300 boys and girls were then enrolled, almost a third of them over 10 years old,[8] and in 1869 both the boys' and the girls' departments were overcrowded. Accommodation at the infants' school was then used to relieve the congestion.[9] In 1871 the National school was said to accommodate 312 children but then had some 370 in attendance.[10] In an attempt to meet the accommodation requirements of central government's Education Committee, the boys were removed from the overcrowded school to a new school made by the conversion of a building in Harland Lane. The school log book has entries for November 1871 referring to the 'last day in the infants' school' and 124 boys being marched from that building to the 'new school'. After a year or so, however, the Harland Lane building was abandoned and the boys returned to Cross Hill.[11]

The response to the overcrowding at the National schools may have been quickened by the arrival of energetic vicars in 1877 and 1892,[12] and in the late 19th and early 20th century the school buildings were much enlarged and the departments reorganized. At unknown date between 1876 and 1893, the infants' school became the boys' school, and the boys' and girls' school was given over to the teaching of the girls and infants.[13]

The enlargement of the earlier school building, then still occupied by the boys and girls, was evidently being considered in or about 1868 but at least part of that project came to nothing.[14] However, a classroom was added to the girls' department in or shortly before 1878,[15] and in 1894 the building was enlarged with another rear classroom, for infants, designed by the local architect Joseph Shepherdson.[16] The accommodation for girls was increased also soon afterwards.[17] By 1920 the school had five classrooms for the girls and the same number for the infants.[18] The other building, the infants' school of 1866, provided only one room, the schoolroom, until 1876; a classroom added then[19] is said to have been designed by J. F. Shepherdson.[20] By the early 1900s the then boys' school had two classrooms; in 1903 a third was built to designs by Joseph Shepherdson, and by 1920 the schoolroom had been divided to make another three classrooms.[21] The improvements to the Church school were assisted by the lord of the manor, Viscount Downe, who conveyed several pieces of ground for the school in the early 20th century.[22] Nonetheless, the accommodation was judged insufficient by the Board of Education in 1925, and as a result there were further alterations and additions later in that decade. The boys' department was duly remodelled in 1928 and the girls' and infants' building in 1929; the latter phase included the building of another classroom for the girls, and the transfer of an existing girls' classroom to the infants.[23]

The accommodation provided at the National, later Church, school reflected the growth of its premises. In the 1880s the combined capacity of all departments rose

1 ERAO, SGP/28; TNA, ED 7/135, no. 65; BIA, Ch. Ret. i; Sheahan and Whellan, *Hist. York & ER.* ii. 500; D. Linstrum, *Towers and Colonnades: the architecture of Cuthbert Brodrick* (1999), 103.

2 The arithmetic in the source is confused: TNA, ED 7/135, no. 65.

3 *Mins of Educ. Cttee of Council, 1856–7* (Parl. Papers, 1857 Sess. 2 [2237], xxxiii), p. 185; *Rep. of Educ. Cttee of Council, 1860–1* (Parl. Papers, 1861 [2828], xlix), p. 744.

4 White, *Dir. E.R Yorks* (1840), 202.

5 *Yorks. Gazette* 6 July 1839; White, *Dir. Hull & York* (1846), 418; HUL, DDSY/23/257; Sheahan and Whellan, *Hist. York & ER.* ii. 500.

6 BIA, V. 1865/Ret. 1, no 142.

7 ERAO, SGP/28; ibid. SL/29/1, p. 83; BIA, V. 1868/Ret. 1, no. 133.

8 Ibid. V. 1865/Ret. 1, no 142; V. 1868/Ret. 1, no. 133; *1st Rep. Com. on Employment of Children, Young Persons, and Women in Agric., App. Pt II* (Parl. Papers, 1867–8 [4068-I], xvii), p. 381.

9 ERAO, SL/29/1, p. 146.

10 Ibid. SB/14/1, p. 16; *Returns relating to Elem. Educ.* 474–5.

11 ERAO, SL/29/1, p. 212; *Rep. of Educ. Cttee of Council, 1872–3* (Parl. Papers, 1873 [C. 812], xxiv), p. 513; *1873–4* (Parl. Papers, 1874 [C. 1019-I], xviii), p. 435.

12 Below, relig. hist., 1840–1940 (Anglicanism).

13 ERAO, SL/29/1, p. 279; plan of 1893 at PE/10/T. 114.

14 Plan by Joseph Wright of Hull, and related, dated plan at ERAO, SGP/28.

15 Ibid. SL/29/3, p. 226.

16 Plan of 1893 at ERAO, PE/10/T. 114; *Kelly's Dir. N & ER Yorks.* (1897), 443. Also ERAO, PE/10/T. 112.

17 ERAO, SB/14/4, pp. 112, 132.

18 Ibid. PE/10/T. 114.

19 Ibid. SL/29/1, pp. 276, 279, 290; plans of 1865 and 1903 at respectively ibid. SGP/28 and PE/10/T. 113.

20 Pevsner and Neave, *Yorks. ER.* 441.

21 Plans of 1903 and 1920 at ERAO, PE/10/T. 113; ER Educ. Cttee *Mins* 1903–4, 208; *Kelly's Dir. N & ER Yorks.* (1905), 481.

22 RDB, 62/136/129 (1904); 165/94/80; 169/441/364.

23 ER Educ. Cttee *Mins* 1925–6, 183–5; 1928–9, 172, 215; 1929–30, 116, 160, 210. Also ERAO, PE/10/T. 113–114.

from 536 to 606 places;[1] in 1895 there were 655 places, 281 of them for boys, 195 for girls, and 179 for infants,[2] and by 1908 the school could accommodate 762 pupils, 321 of them boys, 262 girls, and 179 infants. The capacity of the school was later re-evaluated downwards, presumably because of a corresponding rise in the standard of accommodation required, falling to 663 places by 1911 and 572 by 1932.[3]

Actual attendances differed from enrolled numbers, and, in a district heavily involved with agriculture, were subject to fluctuation as children were withdrawn for field work or to attend local events like the Nafferton club feast. When the alternatives to school were too strong, a holiday was observed, as, for instance, in the case of the hirings in November,[4] and there were also occasional unscheduled closures because of outbreaks of diseases like measles.[5] Average attendance at the National, or Church, school was 230 in 1872–3,[6] 388 in 1893, 468 in 1897, and 570 in 1905.[7] Later about 500 children were usually present until the First World War but in the 1920s and 1930s numbers fell to some 400.[8]

Besides the improvements made to the buildings, the facilities at the Church school were also improved in the mid 20th century by the renting of part of the nearby recreation ground,[9] and the provision of school meals by Driffield UDC from 1943. The canteen was successively at the Church Institute, the skating rink, and, for most of the 1950s, in the Methodist schoolroom;[10] finally, about 1960, a canteen was provided at the school.[11]

The school was reorganized several times in the mid 20th century. In 1947 juniors from the County school were added to those already at Cross Hill to release accommodation at Bridlington Road for secondary schooling, then being established in Driffield,[12] and in 1950 the boys' and girls' departments at Cross Hill were amalgamated as Driffield Church of England junior school.[13] The use of the County school by seniors came to an end with the opening in the mid 1950s of the new secondary schools,[14] and primary provision in the town was duly rationalized in 1957; the Church junior and infants' schools then became the infants' school for the town and the County school its junior school.[15] Following that change, there were plans to remodel the existing buildings at Cross Hill or to build a new infants' school on another site,[16] but neither project was effected, and instead temporary classrooms were installed to cope with the rising numbers.[17] Eventually the existing school buildings were remodelled and extended. The new building, opened in 2001, provided a new entrance, school hall, and offices, besides connecting the two older buildings.[18] In January 2006 there were 254 pupils on the roll.[19]

British School A non-denominational British school, supported by the Independents, Baptists and the Wesleyan and Primitive Methodists had been opened in Eastgate by 1846.[20] The school was in financial difficulties the following year when the master's salary was reduced from about £70 to about £50 and the services of the female teacher were dispensed with.[21] It was last recorded in 1849.[22]

Board, later Council, School A school board was formed for Great Driffield parish in 1871,[23] and soon afterwards a school was begun in rented Sunday schools, boys being accommodated in Wesleyan Methodist premises and girls and infants by the Congregationalists. In 1872 the Board school, comprising both departments, cost some £350 to run, the largest outgoings being the salaries of the master and mistress. Expenditure was met mostly from local rates, the only other source of income being the school pence of the 150 boys and 100 girls at the school, each of whom paid 2*d*. a week, producing in all some £95 a year.[24] Soon afterwards, however, the school began to be supported by grants from central government, £152 being received in grants in 1873–4, for instance.[25] The rented accommodation was replaced by the Board school, built in 1873–4 in the junction of Wansford Road and Bridlington Road.[26] Designed by H. J. Paull of Manchester, the red and brown-brick buildings

1 *Rep. of Educ. Cttee of Council, 1881–2* (Parl. Papers, 1882 [C. 3312-I], xxiii), p. 773; *1885–6* (Parl. Papers, 1886 [C. 4849-I], xxiv), p. 616.

2 ERAO, SB/14/4, p. 78.

3 *Bd of Educ., List 21* (HMSO, 1908 and later edns), copy at BL (pressmark BS 10/48).

4 ERAO, SL/29/1, pp. 64, 67, 70, 78, etc.

5 ER Educ. Cttee *Mins* 1908–9, 37; 1914–15, 54.

6 *Rep. of Educ. Cttee of Council, 1872–3* (Parl. Papers, 1873 [C. 812], xxiv), p. 513.

7 *Kelly's Dir. N & ER Yorks.* (1893), 408; (1897), 443; (1905), 481.

8 *Bd of Educ., List 21.*

9 ER Educ. Cttee *Mins* 1939–40, 167; 1954–5, 143.

10 Ibid. 1943–4, 8, 19; 1949–50, 91; 1951–2, 180, 197; *Kelly's Dir. N & ER Yorks.* (1937), 447.

11 ER Educ. Cttee *Mins* 1959–60, 25, 35.

12 Ibid. 1946–7, 202–3.

13 Ibid. 1949–50, 266; 1954–5, 149; 1955–6, 151.

14 Below, this section, Driffield County Secondary School.

15 ER Educ. Cttee *Mins* 1956–7, 211; 1957–8, 66.

16 Ibid. 1957–8, 168, 234; 1964–5, 64; 1971–2, 170–1.

17 Ibid. 1956–7, 212; 1967–8, 37.

18 *HDM* 26 May 2001.

19 Inf. from the headteacher, Driffield CE infant school.

20 White, *Dir. Hull & York* (1846), 418; *HP* 12 Feb. 1847.

21 *HP* 12 Feb. 1847.

22 *Slater's Royal Nat. Com. Dir. of Yorks. & Lincs.* (1849), 83.

23 *Lond. Gaz.* 10 Feb. 1871, p. 486; Fig. 46.

24 TNA, ED 7/135, no. 64; inf. from Mr E. Spehr, Hackman West, S. Australia, 2004.

25 *Rep. of Educ. Cttee of Council, 1872–3* (Parl. Papers, 1873 [C. 812], xxiv), p. 513; *1873–4* (Parl. Papers, 1874 [C.1019-I], xviii), p. 435.

26 OS Map 1:2,500, Yorks. CLXI. 12 (1890 edn).

46. *Great Driffield: Board school, Wansford Road, c. 1910. Designed by H. J. Paull of Manchester, when built in 1873–4 it had accommodation for 700 pupils.*

incorporated a master's house. The school was built for 250 boys, 250 girls, and 200 infants,[1] but by the 1880s it was reckoned to accommodate only about 560 children. The school was altered and enlarged in 1896 to designs by Joseph Shepherdson.[2] There were said to be about 600 pupils on the books in 1892, and average attendance in the late 19th century ranged from *c.* 300 to almost 500.[3] Between 1906 and 1938 there were usually about 400 at the school.[4]

In 1903 the management of the school passed, under the 1902 Education Act, from the board to the East Riding County Council.[5] Measles caused the school to be closed in 1904; in 1912 an outbreak of diphtheria prevented 465 pupils from attending the Council school, and in 1910 and 1914 measles closed the infants' department.[6] The council added a classroom for boys in 1908,[7] and opened a detached building for the infants in 1914, those changes increasing accommodation at the school from 590 to 620 places,[8] besides providing, in the infants' building, rooms for the domestic instruction of girls from other schools in the Driffield area.[9] A room for manual instruction for boys was provided about 1930.[10] The council also enlarged the site with ¾ a. for a school garden and addition to the playing field in 1912;[11] with a rented playing field from 1936,[12] and by the purchase of some 2 a. in 1941.[13] Meals provided by Driffield UDC from 1943 were taken in a room converted to a canteen[14] until in 1947 a new canteen and temporary classrooms were put up on the recently-purchased land.[15]

The County school was reorganized in 1947 in connection with the introduction of secondary schooling to Driffield: the juniors were then moved out to the Church school at Cross Hill to release temporary accommodation for secondary pupils at Bridlington Road.[16] In 1950 the senior boys and girls were amalgamated under one headteacher as Driffield County Secondary School, and the rest of the school was renamed Driffield County Infants' School.[17] Following the withdrawal of the senior pupils to their new schools in the mid 1950s,[18] the primary schools in Driffield were rationalized; in 1957 the Church junior and infants' schools became the infants' school of the town and the County school its junior school.[19]

The Bridlington Road premises were further enlarged and remodelled to cope with increasing numbers in the later 20th century. The prefabricated rooms provided in the 1940s,[20] were supplemented by

1 ERAO, SB/14/1, pp. 66, 81, 125–6, 162; SB/14/6, s.a. 1872.

2 Ibid. SB/14/4, pp. 82, 107, 112, 133; OS Map 1:2,500, Yorks. CLXI. 12 (1893, 1910 edns).

3 *Rep. of Educ. Cttee of Council, 1879–80* (Parl. Papers, 1880 [C. 2562-I], xxii), p. 725; *1885–6* (Parl. Papers, 1886 [C. 4849-I], xxiv), p. 616; Bulmer, *Dir. E Yorks.* (1892), 167; *Kelly's Dir. N & ER Yorks.* (1893), 408; (1897), 443; (1901), 463.

4 *Bd of Educ., List 21.*

5 ERAO, SB/14/5, p. 174.

6 ERAO, UDDR/1/8/1, Sanitary...Cttee, 24 Oct. 1904; ER Educ. Cttee *Mins* 1910–11, 240; 1911–12, 311; 1914–15, 54.

7 ER Educ. Cttee *Mins* 1907–8, 166–7; 1908–9, 51, 148.

8 *Bd of Educ., List 21.*

9 TNA, ED 7/135, no. 64; ER Educ. Cttee *Mins* 1912–13, 164–5, 239, 328; 1914–15, 73, 238.

10 ER Educ. Cttee *Mins* 1930–1, 39, 157; 1931–2, 191.

11 RDB, 149/120/110; ER Educ. Cttee *Mins* 1912–13, 60.

12 ER Educ. Cttee *Mins* 1939–40, 93.

13 RDB, 648/207/166.

14 ER Educ. Cttee *Mins* 1943–4, 8, 19.

15 RDB, 926/240/200; ER Educ. Cttee *Mins* 1947–8, 94.

16 ER Educ. Cttee *Mins* 1946–7, 202–3.

17 Ibid. 1949–50, 266; 1950–1, 40.

18 Below, this section, Driffield County Secondary School.

19 ER Educ. Cttee *Mins* 1956–7, 211; 1957–8, 66.

20 Ibid. 1959–60, 14.

another two temporary classrooms in 1971,[1] and accommodation for the 4th year had been made from the former infants' building shortly before that.[2] The site was also enlarged, in 1962 just over an acre being added to the playing field and playground, and some 2 a. more being bought in the early 1970s.[3] It was then suggested that the junior school be remodelled and a new infants' school built next door, but those proposals were not effected.[4] There were about 420 pupils by 1994, and three mobile classrooms had to be installed in that decade to cope with the rapid increase in numbers. Between 2001 and 2004 the junior school was redeveloped and enlarged at a cost of some £2½ millions. The mobile accommodation and pre-fabricated buildings were then replaced by new blocks, comprising 13 classrooms and a school hall, music room, staffroom, and canteen; the former hall was converted into two more classrooms; the recently-vacated magistrates' court next door was linked to the new buildings and remodelled to provide library and computing facilities, and other facilities for art, drama, cookery, and physical education have also been added. The number of pupils was stable in the first years of the 21st century, at about 600.[5]

Northfield Infants' School In 1972 proposals made for primary school provision in Driffield included one for a new infant and junior school for 280 pupils to be built in the Northfield Avenue area, and a site of some 6 a. was selected for that purpose in the early 1970s.[6] When the school was opened finally in 1984, it was for infants alone, and had 180 places.[7] Falling numbers resulted in the infants' school having only 127 pupils of four to seven years old in December 2005.[8]

Driffield County Secondary School The UDC had asked the county council as the LEA for a senior school in Driffield in 1937,[9] but nothing was done until secondary education was introduced nationally following the Second World War. In 1947 temporary accommodation for secondary pupils from Driffield and the neighbouring villages was created by transferring the juniors from the County school on Bridlington Road to the Church school at Cross Hill.[10] From 1949 a room in the fire station was also used for teaching senior pupils.[11] The site for a secondary school and county college, of about 45 a., was bought in 1949 and 1950,[12] and also in 1950 Driffield County Secondary School was created by the amalgamation under one headteacher of the senior classes of boys and girls at the County school.[13] Additional classrooms for the secondary school were put up in or soon after 1953.[14]

New, separately-managed schools, one for the boys and the other for girls, were opened respectively in 1955 and 1957 on the large site on the south side of Bridlington Road.[15] Besides children from Driffield, the secondary schools took pupils from the parishes of Fridaythorpe, Sledmere, Weaverthorpe, and Wetwang,[16] and entry was widened later to include other parishes in the vicinity of the town.[17] D. R. Dukes, headmaster from 1950 of the mixed secondary school and later of the boys' school, retired at the end of 1963, whereupon the two secondary schools were amalgamated under a single headteacher, and in September 1964 it became co-educational.[18] The school buildings, which incorporated the technical institute, were enlarged in the 1960s,[19] and by 1966 there were places for 900 pupils of 11 to 16 years old. Further building was done in two phases in the earlier 1970s to create a comprehensive school with 1,200 places for pupils up to 18 years old. The school became comprehensive, and was renamed Driffield School, in 1973.[20] By 1994 it had 1,500 pupils.[21] The school was considerably developed about 2000. A new learning resources centre was made by conversion in 1996; a year or two later buildings on the school site, formerly used for further education but then no longer required for that purpose, were acquired for school use, and in 2003–4 technology and computer blocks were opened. In January 2006 Driffield School had 1,946 on the roll.[22]

A swimming pool for primary and secondary school pupils had been provided on the site by the Driffield Swimming Pool Association with help from the LEA in or soon after 1963,[23] and the sports hall there was later developed for joint use with adults.[24] This was replaced in 2009 by the Driffield Leisure Centre with sports hall and swimming pool for use by the secondary school

1 Ibid. 1970–1, 223.
2 Ibid. 1965–6, 167; 1967–8, 40.
3 Ibid. 1962–3, 42; 1963–4, 114; 1972–3, 95.
4 Ibid. 1971–2, 170–1.
5 *DT* 31 July 2002; *DP* 14 Mar. 2003; 16 Jan. 2004; inf. from the headteacher, Driffield Junior School, 2006.
6 ER Educ. Cttee *Mins* 1971–2, 170–1; 1972–3, 94.
7 *DT* 19 Jan. 1984.
8 Inf. from the headteacher, 2005.
9 ER Educ. Cttee *Mins* 1937–8, 201.
10 Ibid. 1946–7, 202–3.
11 ER CC *Mins* 1949–50, 48; ER Educ. Cttee *Mins* 1951–2, 40.
12 RDB, 828/588/485; 847/380/320; 861/392/329; ER Educ. Cttee *Mins* 1948–9, 45.
13 ER Educ. Cttee *Mins* 1949–50, 266; 1950–1, 40.
14 Ibid. 1952–3, 200; 1953–4, 51.
15 Ibid. 1953–4, 48; 1955–6, 108, 122; 1957–8, 146; inf. from Driffield School, 2006.
16 ER Educ. Cttee *Mins* 1955–6, 151.
17 Ibid. 1962–3, 60.
18 Ibid. 1950–1, 40; 1962–3, 132, 177; 1963–4, 24, 129; inf. from Driffield School, 2006.
19 ER Educ. Cttee *Mins* 1960–1, 128, 160; 1962–3, 75; 1963–4, 35; 1964–5, 109.
20 Ibid. 1967–8, 74, 106; 1970–1, 149–50; 1971–2, 33, 227; 1972–3, 130, 196.
21 *DP* 14 Apr. 1994.
22 ERYC *Mins* 1998–9, Educ....Cttee, 1466; Policy...Cttee, 3015; inf. from Driffield School, 2006.
23 ER Educ. Cttee *Mins* 1963–4, 85–6.
24 Above, this section, sports.

47. Great Driffield: Former mission room and school, Stone Lodge, Eastgate North, 2006. Built as a room for Anglican services and a day school for the north end of the town c. 1865.

during term time. The school site also included social work premises and the registrar's office,[1] and in 1997 the LEA designated land at the school for an arts centre, which was duly opened late in 2005.[2]

Primitive Methodist Day School The school kept by Enoch Sellers in the schoolroom belonging to the Primitive Methodists in Mill Street for some ten years from the mid 1840s was almost certainly associated with the adjoining chapel.[3] The day school held in the Primitive Methodist schoolroom, attended by 36 boys and girls in 1871, was then deemed inefficient by the local board. It was presumably closed soon afterwards.[4]

Anglican Mission School In 1865 some seventy children attended the Church Sunday school and about fifty more a 'Ragged' Sunday school, both maintained by subscribers.[5] Premises for the latter were evidently built in the north of the town, 'the worst part of Driffield', and opened by 1867. The 'new, mission school', or 'ragged school', was then also a day school, 'intended for … children of bad parents' and attended by on average 40 pupils, chiefly girls of six years and above.[6] Standing at the top of Eastgate North, it was still held in 1871,[7] but probably did not survive the opening soon afterwards of the Board school. From the beginning, the building was also used for Anglican worship, and that mission activity and the Sunday school continued after the loss of the day school.[8] The building, now known as Stone Lodge, continued to be used as a school into the second half of the 20th century.[9]

Roman Catholic School A Roman Catholic school had been begun by 1887.[10] It occupied premises in Westgate, adjoining the presbytery, probably one or more cottages which were later replaced by a piggery.[11] There were about 30 pupils in 1892,[12] but the school seems to have been closed soon afterwards.

King's Mill School In the early 1960s the county council, as a local health authority, built a training centre in Driffield for 50 children with severe learning difficulties, the facility including accommodation for 15 of them. Its site, off Victoria Road, was chosen partly because of its proximity to the council's infant welfare clinic.[13] The centre began to be used in December 1963,

1 *DP* 14 Apr.1994.

2 ERYC *Mins* 1996–7, Educ.…Cttee, 421; inf. from Driffield School, 2006.

3 ERAO, PE10/T120; White, *Dir. Hull & York* (1846), 418; White, *Dir. Hull & York* (1851), 601; *Slater's Royal Nat. Com. Dir. of Northern Counties* (1855), i. 96.

4 ERAO, SB 14/1, p. 21; Howorth, *Year Gone By*, 17.

5 BIA, V. 1865/Ret. 1, no. 142.

6 Ibid. V. 1868/Ret. 1, no. 133; ibid. LDS. 1867/2; *1st Rep. Com. on Employment of Children*, p. 381.

7 ERAO, SB/14/1, pp. 18, 20; Fig. 47.

8 Below, relig. hist., 1840 to 1940 (Anglicanism).

9 Howorth, *Year Gone By*, 17.

10 ERAO, SB/14/3, p. 233.

11 Inf. from Diocesan Archivist, Middlesbrough, 2006.

12 Bulmer, *Dir. E Yorks.* (1892), 166, 175.

13 RDB, 1214/338/301; ER CC *Mins* 1960–1, 146–7.

48. *Great Driffield: Driffield Grammar school, Church Street* c. *1890. A private school built in 1865, it closed* c. *1919 when it became an infant welfare centre.*

and was opened fully early in 1964. Another classroom was added after a year or two,[1] and in 1970 the centre accommodated 68 pupils up to the age of 16, and had room for 20 weekly boarders. By the Education (Handicapped Children) Act of that year, the unit became a special school in 1971; it was named King's Mill Special School in 1973.[2] The facilities at the school were then and later improved. Funds raised locally were used to add a pool in 1971; a nursery assessment centre, funded by Horace Taylor's charity, was opened in 1978, and in 2005 a former laundry room was remodelled as an additional classroom cum art studio. Serving a wide catchment area, King's Mill School had 90 pupils in 2006.[3]

Principal Private Schools 1800–1900

During the 19th century there were about fifty different private schools set up in Driffield, of which about twenty were boarding schools, seven for boys and thirteen for girls. The latter were often set up by widows or two or three unmarried sisters. Private schools frequently had a short life but the following made a more lasting contribution.

Driffield Academy (Earle's) In 1808 the Revd John Earle opened a boarding school for boys called the Driffield Academy.[4] The pupils, most of them under 12 years old, were taught Classics and other subjects for inclusive fees of *c.* £25 a year, land surveying and ornamental planting being available at £2 extra. The school, situated in Bridge Street, had 31 pupils in 1813.[5] In 1830 Earle moved the school to Watton where he was the incumbent.[6] Two of Earle's daughters opened a girls' boarding school at Driffield in 1829, which lasted for a few years.[7]

Forge's Richard Forge ran a day and boarding school for boys from the late 1820s until his death in 1856.[8] Initially in Doctor Lane, the school was moved to the west side of Middle Street South by 1840.[9] There were 13 pupils in 1851.[10] The house, schoolroom and playground were sold in 1862 for the building of the Baptist chapel.[11]

Driffield Grammar School (Monument House), 28 Church Street. The school for boys which was eventually called Driffield Grammar School was established by James

1 ER CC *Mins* 1963–4, 269; 1966–7, 150–1.
2 ER Educ. Cttee *Mins* 1970–1, 167–9; 1971–2, 151; 1972–3, 141, 170–1.
3 Inf. from King's Mill School, 2006.
4 *YH* 3 Sept. 1808; *HP* 20 Dec. 1808.
5 *HA*, 23 June 1810; *HP* 21 Dec. 1813; Pigot, *Nat. Com. Dir.* (1822), 606; Baines, *Hist. Yorks.* (1823), ii. 195.
6 *HP* 20 Apr. 1830, 24 June 1836.
7 Ibid. 26 May 1829, 20 Apr. 1830; 28 June 1831.
8 Pigot, *Nat. Com. Dir.* (1828–9), ii. 930; *HP* 25 Apr. 1856.
9 Pigot, *Nat. Com. Dir.* (1834), 711; White, *Dir. ER Yorks* (1840), 204; ERAO, TA/13; PE/10/T. 120.
10 TNA, HO 107/2366.
11 *YH* 3 May 1856; ERAO, EB/1/125, 138

Firth on Beverley Lane, later St John's Road, by 1864.[1] The following year Firth had a purpose built boarding school erected on the corner of Church Street and Shady Lane, later Victoria Road.[2] Designed by William Hawe it was originally known as Monument House.[3]

There were 35 boarders at the school in 1871, many of them the sons of farmers.[4] Firth married the sister of Revd William Mitchell the Independent minister and his pupils attended the Independent chapel.[5] This close link with the chapel was continued by the next head, the Revd Richard Bryer, an Independent minister, who probably succeeded by 1875.[6] Bryer, who had two assistant masters and eleven boarders in 1881, was followed as head *c.* 1888 by James P. Edwards, who may have been the first to have termed it a grammar school.[7] Then came an Anglican clergyman, Revd Thomas Duckett, 1891–2, who in turn was succeeded by one of his assistant masters, Robert E. E. Whitaker.[8] Another Anglican priest, Revd Kerchever Tillyard (1864–1947), educated at Cambridge and for six years assistant master at Ludlow grammar school, took on the school in 1898.[9]

In the early 20th century the county council sent intending pupil teachers on scholarships to Driffield Grammar School, and supported the school with a grant.[10] In 1919 Mr Tillyard offered the premises 'lately used for his school' to the county council, which bought them for a secondary school but promptly appropriated them instead for health purposes.[11] About 1920 the closure of the boys' school and one for girls (Ash Lea) was bemoaned as a 'very great loss to the Church' in the town and district.[12]

Conyers On the death of George Conyers, solicitor, in 1810 his widow Elizabeth opened a girls' boarding school in Middle Street.[13] The school still existed in 1834, at which date an Ann Conyers, possibly Elizabeth's daughter, had a boarding school on New Road that lasted into the later 1840s.[14]

Bourne House, Doctor Lane, later Queen Street In 1845 Elizabeth Boyes had a school for girls in Doctor Lane, leased from William Reaston.[15] By 1855 the school was being run by Eliza and Georgiana Reaston, who with their sister Jane had moved to Exchange Street by 1861 where they kept a boarding school until the early 1880s. The school in Doctor Lane, then called Bourne House, had been taken over before 1861 by Anne and Catherine Ross, sisters of the Driffield historian Frederick Ross, and aunts of the journalist Charles T. Holderness.[16] Anne Ross had previously run a boarding school on Exchange Street in the 1840s, and then with her sisters Harriet and Maria, another school on Middle Street North.[17] Bourne House school was closed on the death of Anne Ross in 1904.[18] The premises were used briefly as a teacher training centre by the LEA between 1905 and 1910.[19]

Manor House Manor House, or Old Manor House, at the junction of Eastgate and Albion Street, was being used for a girls' day and boarding school by 1892 with Miss Clara E. Wilkinson as principal.[20] It was taken over by the sisters Ada M. and Annie L. Manson by 1909 who ran the school until it closed *c.* 1935.[21]

Ash Lea Collegiate School A girls' school was being kept at Ash Lea, Mill Street by Matilda Weatherill, successively in turn with each of her younger sisters Honor, Catherine and Rachel, from *c.* 1895.[22] It was described as an 'excellent girls' boarding school with Church teaching'. It was closed following the death of Matilda in 1920.[23]

Schools in Little Driffield

Little Driffield Church of England School In 1845 the lord of the manor allowed a piece of common land on the north side of the main road at the west end of the village[24] to be used by subscribers to build a Sunday

1 *Slater's Royal Nat. Com. Dir. of Yorks.* (1864), 114.

2 OS Map 1:2,500, Yorks. CLXI. 12 (1893 edn).

3 *BG* 22 Oct. 1864; *DT* 29 July 1869; *Kelly's Dir. N & ER Yorks.* (1872), 354. Illus. at ERAO, DDX/498/1.

4 TNA, R10/4807.

5 *DT* 5 Apr. 1919.

6 *Post Office Dir. N & ER Yorks.* (1879), 384; TNA, RG11/4794. In 1881 James Firth was a commercial traveller at Bradford: TNA, RG11/4446.

7 TNA, RG11/4794; *Slater's Dir. of N & ER Yorks.* (1887), 62; *Kelly's Dir. N & ER Yorks.* (1889), 375.

8 TNA, RG 12/3955; Bulmer, *Dir. E Yorks.* (1892), 172; *Kelly's Dir. N & ER Yorks.* (1897), 447.

9 RDB, 202/500/428; *Alumni Cantab. 1752–1900*; *Kelly's Dir. N & ER Yorks.* (1901), 465–6; (1913), 516; TNA, RG 13/4519

10 ER Educ. Cttee *Mins* 1905–6, 108, 120, 178; 1906–7, 8; 1911–12, 126.

11 RDB, 202/500/428; ER Educ. Cttee *Mins* 1919–20, 85–6.

12 BIA, V. 1912–22/Ret.; below, this section (Ash Lea).

13 *HP* 27 June 1815; Baines, *Hist. Yorks.* (1823), ii. 195.

14 Pigot, *Nat. Com. Dir.* (1834), 711; White, *Dir. Hull & York* (1846), 418.

15 ERAO, TA/13; ibid. PE/10/T. 120; OS Map 1:2,500, Yorks. CLXI. 12 (1910 edn).

16 TNA, RG9/3607; RG10/4806; RG11/4793.

17 White, *Dir. Hull & York* (1846), 418; White, *Dir. Hull & York* (1851), 601; *Slater's Royal Nat. Com. Dir. of Northern Counties* (1855), i. 96; TNA, HO 107/2366; ERAO, TA/13; PE/10/T. 120.

18 *Kelly's Dir. N & ER Yorks.* (1872), 354; (1901), 467; Bulmer, *Dir. E Yorks.* (1892), 174; TNA, RG13/4519; ER Educ. Cttee *Mins* 1905–6, 5.

19 Above, this section, teacher training.

20 Bulmer, *Dir. E Yorks.* (1892), 175; TNA, RG13/4519.

21 *Kelly's Dir. N & ER Yorks.* (1905), 486; (1909), 497; (1933), 456; *DT* 7 June 1947.

22 Directories; Petch, *Driffield Cemetery MIs*, 122. The Weatherills were the daughters of the village schoolmaster at Birdsall: TNA, RG10/4823, RG11/4810. Catherine Weatherill married the Revd W. R. Sharrock, vicar of Driffield in 1915. *Alumni Cantab.1752–1900.*

23 BIA, V. 1912–22/Ret.; ER Educ. Cttee *Mins* 1915–16, 17.

24 OS Map 1:2,500, Yorks. CLXI. 11 (1893 edn).

school.[1] About 1855 it began also to be operated as a day school serving the townships of Little Driffield and Elmswell with Kelleythorpe. There were 40 pupils in 1868,[2] and in 1871, when there was reckoned to be space for only 34 children, it was attended by 19 boys and 39 girls.[3] The building was enlarged that year from a voluntary rate to meet the requirements of central government's Education Committee, and in the late 19th and earlier 20th century the school was usually reckoned to have places for 50 children. In 1879 there were 21 boys, 23 girls, and 31 infants on the roll, but average attendance was about 45 then; only 17 in 1893, and *c.* 30 in the early 1900s.[4] The school had to be closed because of influenza in 1910 and measles in 1913,[5] and the building may have been improved in consequence in 1913 or soon afterwards.[6] By 1918–19 there were usually 42 pupils in the school, and average attendance thereafter rose to 52 in 1926–7, before falling back to 34 in 1937–8.[7]

The management was informal until 1878, when the subscribers appointed a committee comprising the vicar, his assistant curate, the churchwardens, and two others. In 1878–9 the school was funded by subscriptions of £26 and by school pence, charged at the rate of 2*d.* a week for pupils over three years old and 1*d.* a week for the under-threes, and bringing in just over £19. Most of the income was then spent on the salary of the mistress.[8] Additional support in the form of grants from central government was received from 1881–2, when they amounted to £18.[9] After the name and boundary changes of 1885, the school was called Elmswell with Little Driffield Church of England school.[10] In 1915 W. R. Sharrock, vicar of Little Driffield, and the other managers conveyed the building and an adjoining plot of land to the York Diocesan Trustees.[11] The school was closed in 1948, the pupils going instead to schools in Great Driffield.[12] The building continued to be used for the Sunday school but in 1959 it was sold,[13] and has since been demolished.

Girls' School A day school for girls was begun in Little Driffield in 1829, and in 1833 had 12 pupils, all taught at their parents' expense.[14] It may have existed still in 1865, when the village was said to have two schools in all.[15] Miss F. M. Nikal, a schoolmistress of Little Driffield who published a history of France in Driffield in 1870,[16] may have run or been employed at the girls' school. No more is known of the school.

RELIGIOUS HISTORY

Two churches recorded in the extensive manor of Driffield in 1086 may have been at Great and Little Driffield, but this is not certain.[17] There is evidence of a church at Little Driffield before the Conquest, but nothing convincing with regard to the church at Great Driffield.[18] Little Driffield church was evidently built before Great Driffield and has long been considered the mother church of the parish.[19] Architectural features suggest that the present building dates from the 11th or 12th century,[20] but a church had almost certainly stood there before that. Fragments of a cross dating from the late 9th or 10th century survive in the church,[21] and Aldfrith, king of the Northumbrians, who died in Driffield in 705 AD,[22] has for long been thought to be buried there. An edition of the writings of the 16th-century topographer John Leland with later additions records Aldfrith's burial as well as death in Driffield, and, in the small church at Little Driffield, his renowned tomb with a Latin inscription. Aldfrith was by the 18th century being recorded as Alfred,[23] and, among many confusions, was the belief that King Alfred of Wessex (d. 899 AD) lay in Little Driffield rather than in Winchester. Local gentlemen who investigated the site in 1784 claimed to have found a stone coffin and other remains, but that was contradicted after a further, fruitless search in 1807 by the then curate.[24] The

1 Following based on TNA, ED 7/135, no. 45.
2 BIA, V. 1868/Ret. 1, no. 133.
3 *Returns relating to Elem. Educ.* 474–5.
4 *Kelly's Dir. N & ER Yorks.* (1893), 408; *Bd of Educ., List 21.*
5 ER Educ. Cttee *Mins* 1910–11, 47; 1913–14, 56.
6 Ibid. 1913–14, 253.
7 *Bd of Educ., List 21.*
8 TNA, ED 7/135, no. 45.
9 *Rep. of Educ. Cttee of Council, 1881–2* (Parl. Papers, 1882 [C. 3312-I], xxiii), p. 773.
10 ER Educ. Cttee *Mins* 1913–14, 56.
11 RDB, 172/352/303.
12 ER Educ. Cttee *Mins* 1946–7, 203; 1947–8, 168.
13 ERAO, PE/10/T. 161, s.a. 29 Apr. 1958, 16 Sept. 1960.
14 *Educ. Enq. Abstract*, 1083.
15 BIA, V. 1865/Ret. 1, no. 142a.
16 Ross, *Driffield*, 140.
17 *VCH Yorks.* ii. 197; above, vol. intro., early settlement.
18 Below, buildings, relig. buildings; above, vol. intro., early settlement. Blocks of masonry with a crude roll moulding, built into the inner wall of the tower of All Saints' church, have traditionally been said to have come from a pre-Conquest building. G. P. Brown, *Parish Church of All Saints, Great Driffield* (1984), 3.
19 L. Butler (ed.), *The Yorks. Church Notes of Sir Stephen Glynne, 1825–1874* (YAS Rec. Ser. 159), 192.
20 Below, buildings, relig. buildings.
21 *YAJ* 21 (1911), 261–2; *VCH Yorks.* ii. 114, 131; Lang, *Corpus of Anglo-Saxon Sculpture,* iii. 179.
22 Above, vol. intro., early settlement.
23 J. Leland, *De Rebus Britannicis Collectanae* (1774), ii. 515; iii. 278, 296; iv. 34.
24 *Notes & Queries* 1st ser. xii. 320–1; Baines, *Hist. Yorks.* (1823), ii. 194.

49. *Great Driffield: All Saints' church tower from Church Street c. 1900.*

supposed royal burial was commemorated before the rebuilding in 1807 by a painted inscription, and subsequently by a marble tablet to 'Alfred, King of Northumberland'.[1] An image later kept in the church, and attributed to the unknown St Eldred, may have been an earlier manifestation of a long tradition concerning the antiquity of the building and its connexion with an Anglo-Saxon notable.[2]

Driffield church was one of several mother churches of great royal manors in Yorkshire given by Henry I to Archbishop Gerard and York minster *c.* 1107. These churches were of some consequence, described as having dependent chapels, tithes and lands. The king ordered that they were to retain these parishes as in the time of King Edward the Confessor, the chapels and tithes that were due to them even in sokelands which had been granted away to royal barons.[3]

It seems likely that the Driffield church referred to in these grants was Little Driffield and that it was of considerable value. In 1107 or soon afterwards Archbishop Gerard used Driffield and its appurtenances to endow one of the canonries in York minster, henceforth known as the prebend of Driffield; in 1291 Pope Nicholas's assessment put the annual income of that prebend at £100.[4] Although the prebend included half the manor of Haxby (NR),[5] and half the chapel there was occasionally reputed to belong to Driffield parish,[6] it seems likely that the bulk of the prebendal revenues came from the historic endowments of the church.

At some stage after these grants but well before the mid 14th century, Little Driffield was superseded by Great Driffield as the chief church of the parish.[7] Little Driffield became a chapelry serving the townships of Little Driffield, Elmswell and Kelleythorpe.[8] It retained its burial ground in which Sir James Freville, lord of the manor of Kelleythorpe (d. 1286), requested to be

1 Bulmer, *Dir. E Yorks.* (1892), 169; tablet in chancel. By the late 19th century the mythology had been developed further. The life and death of the king had been elaborated to include a sister, the prioress of an otherwise unknown house at Little Driffield, the remains of which were said to exist near the church: *Kelly's Dir. N & ER Yorks.* (1889), 372. Also Ross, *Driffield*, 7–11.

2 *Test. Ebor.* iv, p. 137 n. An alternative explanation is that the name was a form of Ailred, the 12th-century abbot of Rievaulx, who was the object of a cult in Yorkshire: D. H. Farmer, *Oxford Dictionary of Saints* (1978), 7.

3 *EYC.* i, pp. 333–6.

4 Ibid. ii, p. 123; *VCH Yorks.* iii. 13; above, Great and Little Driffield, early settlement; manors and estates: rectory.

5 *Miscellanea*, iv (YAS Rec. Ser. 94), 27.

6 *VCH Yorks. NR.* ii. 138.

7 Below, this section, Middle Ages: Great Driffield.

8 ERAO, PE 11/1.

buried.[1] There seem also to have been one or two chapels in Great Driffield and another at Elmswell, but these unlike Little Driffield did not have parochial status.[2]

The chapelry of Little Driffield had been formed into an ecclesiastical parish by 1579, from which date registers of baptisms, marriages and burials survive.[3] There is no evidence, however, that the churches of Great and Little Driffield ever had separate incumbents. They were served together by a single priest from the 14th century.[4] Following the establishment of the prebend, a vicarage seems to have been ordained. Although no deed has been found, there was certainly a vicar by 1330.[5] From the late 17th century, the jointly held livings of Great and Little Driffield were usually regarded as one, under the title of Driffields Ambo. It was termed a curacy or vicarage until the income was augmented in the 1770s, and subsequently a perpetual curacy.[6] The livings were still perpetual curacies in the 1840s,[7] but since augmentation in the mid 19th century the benefice has been regarded as one or two vicarages. It has been recorded variously as Great Driffield vicarage with the annexed perpetual curacy of Little Driffield;[8] as Driffields Ambo vicarage,[9] and as the separate but united vicarages of Great Driffield and Little Driffield.[10] The combined parishes were known in the 20th century as Great Driffield with Little Driffield parish.[11]

The medieval church of Little Driffield, which had an image of the Virgin in its chancel by 1505,[12] was dedicated to St Mary by 1286 and so remained until at least 1700.[13] The church, however, was recorded as dedicated to St Peter in the mid 19th century, and thereafter to one or other of these two saints, until the later 20th century when the earlier attribution prevailed.[14] The parish church of Great Driffield was dedicated to All Saints by 1558.[15]

From the 12th century, the patron of the living was first the prebendary of Driffield, and, from 1484, the precentor of York minster, to whose office the prebend was then annexed.[16] Vicars were usually presented by the prebendaries, but in 1582 a turn was exercised by the lessee of the prebendary's rectorial estate.[17] Under the Cathedrals Act of 1840, the patronage passed from the prebendary to the archbishop of York.[18] The prebendaries of Driffield and later the precentors of York exercised a peculiar jurisdiction in the Driffield parishes, until the abolition of the liberty of St Peter in 1838.[19]

RELIGIOUS LIFE

MIDDLE AGES

Relatively little is known about the religious life of either of Driffield's churches throughout the whole of the Middle Ages.

Great Driffield

The building evidence of the church indicates two periods of activity and growth: about 1200 and in the mid 15th and early 16th century.[20] The patrons of the earlier enlargement are not known, but the work on the showy west tower and to the north aisle in the latter period seems to have been funded chiefly by the larger proprietors of the parish, who placed their arms on the new work.

The most prominent arms, now partially obscured by the clock face, appear to be those of the Scrope family, probably commemorating John, Lord Scrope who held the main manor *c.* 1425–55.[21] Elsewhere on the west front are the arms of the Swillingtons and the Rouths, the leading resident landowning families in the mid 15th century, and what are said to be the arms of

1 Cambridge, Fitzwilliam Museum MS 329, f. 109.

2 Below, this section, Middle Ages; below, Elmswell.

3 ERAO, PE 11/1.

4 BIA, Fac. 1960/2/26; *Cal. S.P. Dom. 1654*, p. 226; N. A. H. Lawrance, *Fasti Parochiales*, iii (YAS Rec. Ser. 129), 20–2; BIA, TA. 36M.

5 Below, this section, Middle Ages (Great Driffield).

6 Ibid. TER. J. Driffield 1693–1868; RDB, B/153/42; I/310/689; below, this section, 1700 to *c.* 1840: Anglicanism.

7 ERAO, PE/10/T. 120; BIA, TA. 36M.

8 *Lond. Gaz.* 1 Aug. 1856, pp. 2656–7.

9 TNA, HO 107/2366.

10 *Lond. Gaz.* 13 May 1904, p. 3099.

11 BIA, Fac. Bk. 11, p. 176; *Lond. Gaz.* 10 May 1907, p. 3207.

12 Ross, *Driffield*, 51.

13 Cambridge, Fitzwilliam Museum MS 329, f. 109; BIA, Bp. Dio. 3, ER, p. 102; Ross, *Driffield*, 51.

14 BIA, Ch. Ret. i; *Yorks. Worship Returns 1851*, i. 91; RDB, 1707/266/225; directories; noticeboard at church, 2004. Perhaps in error, *Crockford* (2004–5) has St Peter.

15 BIA, precentorship wills, Edward Warde, 1558, where burial in the 'churchearth of All Hallowes' was requested.

16 Le Neve, *Fasti, 1541–1857, York*, 33.

17 RDB, H/348/720; Lawrance, *Fasti Parochiales*, iii. 20–2; *Herring's Visit.* i. p. 223; *Rep. Com. Eccles. Revenues*, 930–1.

18 3 & 4 Vic. c. 113; BIA, CD. 583; *Crockford* (2004–5).

19 Below, local government, before the 19th century: manorial admin.

20 Below, buildings, relig. buildings.

21 Burke, *General Armory*, 908. The arms bearing *a bend* here identified as belonging to the Scropes have for long been attributed to the Hotham family, as have those of the Rouths, *on a bend cotised three mullets pierced* and have been associated with a legend that the tower was built by a Hotham as absolution from a vow: C. V. Collier and H. Lawrance, 'Ancient Heraldry in the Deanery of Dickering', *YAJ* 25 (1920), 77–8. The Hothams who were the lords of Kelleythorpe 1327– *c.* 1370 belonged to a junior branch settled at Bonby (Lincs.) Their arms differed being those that the Hotham family of South Dalton have used since the 17th century: P. Saltmarshe, *History and Chartulary of the Hothams of Scorborough* (1914) 9, 229. They had no direct interest in Driffield parish in the 15th century.

St Mary's abbey, York, the lord of Elmswell manor, and Robert Rolleston, prebendary and rector of Driffield, 1436–51, and provost of Beverley.[1] The label stops of the west window of the north aisle have the arms of the Rouths and Swillingtons, the latter impaled with what may be the arms of the Arden or Beeston family.[2] In 1666 Dugdale recorded the arms of the Beeston, Swillington, Routh and Mallory families in the windows of the north aisle.[3]

The chancel roof was said to be defective in 1416, and again in 1473.[4] This probably led to the rebuilding of the chancel which was undertaken by the rector *c.* 1505.[5] The work was evidently not finished by 1510 when a complaint was made that the prebend had not made his stalls in the choir nor provided a sufficient 'resting place' for the clergy.[6] Following the transfer of the rectory of Driffield church to York minster in the 12th century, a vicarage seems to have been ordained, though no deed has been found. The status of the first known priests at Driffield is uncertain. In 1275 Driffield was in the charge of a 'parish priest', and two other priests then mentioned may also have worked there;[7] another parish priest of Driffield was recorded in 1303.[8] The first known vicar, Haldan of Driffield, was presented in 1330.[9] He exchanged the benefice in 1351 but for some reason then went into exile. Then followed the long and eventful incumbency of John son of William Smith of Great Driffield, from 1353 until his death in 1391. John was licensed to be absent in 1355 to recover from an assault; in the 1360s and 1370s he was punished by the Church authorities for immorality, and in 1365 he acknowledged before the chapter of York that he should personally serve Little Driffield 'chapel' or else provide a chaplain to do the duty there. John Barrow, vicar from 1391, passed the benefice by exchange to Matthew Barrow in 1418, and after his death in 1432 there was a similar successive tenure by two members of the Waplington family until the 1450s.[10] In addition to the vicar John Smith there was a chantry chaplain and two other chaplains serving Great Driffield in 1473 and a parochial chaplain, Richard Kirkby, for Little Driffield with Elmswell.[11] The unnamed priest officiating in 1489 was called a curate, which may mean that the vicar sometimes, as later, employed a deputy to serve the cure.[12] In addition to the vicar, a chaplain and chantry priest at Great Driffield and two chaplains at Little Driffield, in 1510, a certain Cuthbert Rogg, an unbeneficed priest, was resident there to the annoyance of the parishioners.[13] Six clergy were recorded as serving Driffield in 1525–6, the vicar, four chaplains and a chantry priest.[14]

The chantry was founded in or soon after 1443 by John Tebbe of Great Driffield to support a chaplain who was to say mass daily for the king, and for Tebbe and his wife Joan, Peter Arden and his wife Katherine, and William Routh and his late wife Margaret. The following year the chantry was endowed with two houses and 7 oxgangs in the township.[15] It was held at the altar of St Nicholas and St Mary the Virgin, and was later called St Mary's or occasionally St Nicholas's chantry.[16] The patronage of the chantry belonged to the lords of Driffield, the Lords Scrope of Masham presenting the chaplain in the later 15th and early 16th century, and their heirs, the Danbys, subsequently.[17] Thomas Lutton had the nomination in the mid 1530s, and then sold it to George Swillington.[18] The altar was perhaps at the east end of the south aisle, where a pillared, ogee-headed piscina remains. In the 1450s and early 1460s the chantry chaplain was Thomas Waplington, a former vicar of Driffield.[19] The relatively undemanding office of chantry chaplain was well-paid compared with that of the vicar, in 1525–6 the chaplain receiving £5 a year as against a value of some £9 in all for the vicarage.[20]

Another chantry foundation may have been the chapel of St Helen (Ellen) in Driffield. Its location is not more precisely recorded, but it was perhaps the chapel which obviously existed in the south of the township; evidence of Christian burial has been found there[21] and land to the east of Skerne Road was later called Chapel Nook.[22] It was probably built in the 1290s, indulgences for those aiding the chapel being offered in 1291 and 1297, and confirmed in 1301.[23] It was perhaps served by Thomas Spouse who occurred as a chantry chaplain in Driffield in 1432.[24] The chapel's endowment may have comprised only the building itself and a little land.[25]

In the Middle Ages the parish church's religious and

1 Brown, *All Saints*, 2; *DT* 6 Nov. 1880; R. T. W. McDermid, *Beverley Minster Fasti* (YAS Rec. Ser. 149), 107–8.

2 The arms bearing three buckles below the parapet on the south front of the tower, and quartered with those of Swillington on the west front have not been identified.

3 Brown, *All Saints*, 8.

4 *York Fabric Rolls* (Surtees Soc. 35, 1859), 249, 256.

5 Below, buildings, relig. buildings.

6 *York Fabric Rolls*, 264.

7 *Reg. Giffard*, p. 280.

8 *Reg. Corbridge*, i, p. 187.

9 The details of incumbents are based on Lawrance, *Fasti*, iii. 20–1.

10 John Barrow of Driffield, deacon, probably another member of the family, was presented for adultery in 1440: J. S. Purvis, *A Medieval Act Book* (1943), 23.

11 YML, L2 (3) c, f. 25v–26. Kirkby was charged with adultery in 1474: Purvis, *Medieval Act Book*, 28.

12 BIA, Reg. 23, f. 61, printed in *Test. Ebor.* iii, p. 355.

13 YML, L2 (3)c , f. 121; P. Marshall, *The Face of the Pastoral Ministry in the ER, 1525–1595* (1995), 6.

14 'ER Clergy in 1525–6', *YAJ* 24 (1917), 65, 70, 78.

15 *Cal. Pat.* 1441–6, 172, 265.

16 YML, H 2/3, f. 117; *Cal. Pat.* 1575–8, 366; Ross, *Driffield*, 51.

17 Lawrance, *Fasti*, iii. 99.

18 *Yorks. Fines*, i. 73.

19 Lawrance, *Fasti*, iii. 98.

20 'ER Clergy in 1525–6', 70.

21 Loughlin and Miller, *Survey*, 90.

22 Thomas Stork's allotment of 4 a. 2 r. 6 p.: RDB, B/153/42; ERAO, IA. 41.

23 *Reg. Corbridge*, i, p. 8.

24 Lawrance, *Fasti*, iii. 98 n.

25 Below, this section, Reformation.

50. *Little Driffield: St Mary's church from the south west, 2011.*

social functions were extended by parishioners' guilds, of which there were at least two in Great Driffield by 1463, those dedicated to the Trinity and to St Mary.[1] Pious members of the laity in Driffield may also have included a hermit, for land called 'Heremytecroft' was mentioned there in 1383.[2] Aside from the parish church and the chapel or chapels, religious influences seem to have been few in Great Driffield in the Middle Ages. In 1291 a Franciscan friar from the house in Beverley preached in Driffield in support of the Crusade by order of the archbishop.[3] A few religious houses also had estates in the township, but, apart from York minster's rectorial holding, there is no indication that any were large, or that any outposts were established in Driffield.[4]

Little Driffield

Although originally probably the mother church of the parish and housing a tomb believed to be King Aldfrith's, by the 16th century the church was considered small.[5] There is evidence that it had a medieval burial ground, in the form of eleven grave slabs with incised crosses which have been built into the present fabric of the church; they date mostly from the 13th and 14th centuries.[6]

The chancel roof was in need of repair in 1416 and 1473 and it was letting in rain in 'diverse places' in 1519 when the 'steeple' was broken as was glass in the chancel window.[7]

At an unknown date, but before the later 16th century, the grounds of Little Driffield, Elmswell, and Kelleythorpe were formed into a parish or chapelry with its own registers for baptisms, marriages and burials.[8]

REFORMATION

As there was little monastic land in Driffield parish, except at Elmswell, the closure of the religious houses at the Reformation would have had only limited direct effect on the residents of the chief settlement. Almost certainly of greater significance there was the suppression of the chantries and guilds in 1548 under the Act of the previous year.[9] The former estate of St Mary's chantry was let subsequently by the Crown,[10] and was eventually sold in 1607 to George Ward and Robert Morgan. It then comprised the former chantry house, six others, 7½ oxgangs, and other land in Driffield, all let

1 YML, L2 (4) 305v. The two guilds are recorded again in 1528: *Test. Ebor.* v, p. 132 n.

2 *Cal. Close*, 1381–5, 589.

3 *Hist. Papers and Letters from the Northern Reg.* ed. J. Raine (Rolls Ser. 61), 93–5.

4 Above, manors and estates, rectory *and* estates of relig. houses.

5 Above, this section, intro.

6 J. R. Earnshaw, 'Medieval Grave Slabs from the Bridlington District', *YAJ* 42 (1967–70), 336–42, illus.

7 *York Fabric Rolls*, 249, 256; YML, L2 (3) c, f. 184v.

8 ERAO, PE/11/1, s.a. 1600; BIA, D/C. CP. 1608/4; RDB, K/211/425; TNA, C 54/434, no. 72.

9 1 Edw. VI, c. 14.

10 TNA, C 66/1446, mm. 42–4; *Cal. Pat.* 1575–8, p. 366.

for £7 8*s*. a year.[1] The last chantry priest, Thomas Mainprice, then fifty years old, was continuing to be paid the £5 net value as a pension in 1548, but probably died soon afterwards.[2] The other foundations seem to have been much less significant. St Helen's chapel was evidently also suppressed as a chantry, and in 1563 the Crown granted the building and a garden in Driffield, the whole valued at only 1*s*. a year, to John Strowbridge and John Nettleton as concealed premises.[3] The small endowment of Holy Trinity guild, comprising two cottages and a little arable land in Great Driffield, rented for nearly 6*s*. a year, similarly passed to the Crown at its suppression, and in 1553 was granted to Christopher Estoft and Thomas Dolman. Besides the endowed foundations, a small sum of cash given or left to the church for occasional observances for the dead was also confiscated by the Crown at the suppression.[4] The effect of those changes on the religious life of the town is hard to judge, for although the services of a chantry priest had been lost there were still four priests serving Great and Little Driffield in 1550.[5]

Fundamental changes in the appearance of churches and in the services held in them were also ordered by the radical ministers of Edward VI, though less than full compliance was frequent, and in the case of Driffield it may have been felt necessary to replace the serving vicar with more committed protestants. Robert Barker, vicar from 1541, has been identified with one of that name, late prior of Byland abbey, who after the dissolution of the priory in November 1538 may have served in the household of Thomas Butler at Nunnington (NR).[6] Barker was said to have died by 1549, when he was succeeded at Driffield by John Gilby, who was followed by Robert Ringrose the following year.[7] Barker's death would seem, however, to have been a fiction, and he resumed his ministry under the Roman Catholic Queen Mary. In 1558, as vicar, he subscribed the orthodox Catholic will of Robert Grundall of Great Driffield who left his soul to 'the mercy of God praying the most blessed Virgin Mary, mother of our Saviour Jesus Christ, and all the holy company of Heaven to pray for me'.[8] Barker continued as vicar under the more liberal protestant regime of the Elizabethan Church and died in office towards the end of 1581.[9] He was said to be allowing Latin in services in 1565, and, unsurprisingly, Catholic practices and vestments remained in use in the church in the 1570s.[10] On his death Barker had a library of around 150 books, all composed before 1500 and mostly theological works with no hint of the 'new learning' or Reformation Protestantism. The books, which may have originally come from the library of Byland abbey, were left in the care of Edward Nettleton of Elmswell and John Nettleton, possibly the recusant of that name from Hutton Cranswick who was known as a collector of manuscripts from former monastic libraries.[11]

The earlier veneration of the Trinity – evident from the guild – seems also to have continued into the late 16th century, two of the church's bells being made in 1593 with that dedication.[12] Roman Catholicism was not, however, strong in Driffield later. Against the evidence of religious conservatism, there is, moreover, one suggestion that protestantism may have been positively welcomed by some in the town; in 1563, when Robert Jackson was suspected of adultery, it was recalled that he had earlier been in trouble 'for such words as he had spoken in Queen Mary's time', presumably against the restoration of Roman Catholicism.[13]

SEVENTEENTH CENTURY

Anglicanism

The joint living of Great and Little Driffield had been relatively poorly paid at the Reformation, and remained so until the 18th century. The value of the living in the 16th century is problematic. Two valuations were recorded in 1535, one of £7 10*s*. 2*d*. net a year for Driffield 'vicarage' and the other, of £5 3*s*. 5*d*. net, for Great Driffield; the lower figure presumably omitted the vicarial income from the parish of Little Driffield.[14] A slightly higher value for the joint living is suggested by the survey of clergy incomes in 1525–6. The vicarage was then supporting two clerks, the previous incumbent who had resigned in 1523 but was taking £4 13*s*. 4*d*. of the annual income as a pension and his successor who had only £4 a year.[15] A net value of £8 or £9 a year placed Driffield in the middle rank of livings in the rural deanery of Harthill, above the poorest, valued at £4 a year, like Warter and Market Weighton, but below parishes like Hutton Cranswick and South Dalton, where the incumbents enjoyed incomes of £15, and much inferior to the richest livings of Bainton and Cottingham, valued at £36 and £107 respectively.[16] By the mid 17th century the two churches, and 200 families, were being served by Ralph Mason for an income of about £16 a

1 TNA, C 66/1747, mm. 25 sqq.

2 C. J. Kitching, 'Chantries of ER of Yorks. at the Dissolution in 1548', *YAJ* 44 (1972), 185.

3 *Cal. Pat.* 1563–6, p. 52.

4 Ibid. 1553, 254, 256; Kitching, 'Chantries', 185, 190, 194.

5 YML, L.2(3)c, 227v–228.

6 C. Cross, 'A Medieval Yorkshire Library', *Northern History* 25 (1989), 282.

7 Lawrance, *Fasti*, iii. 22; YML, L.2(3)c, 227v–228.

8 BIA, precentorship wills, Thomas Morton, Robert Grundall, 1558.

9 BIA, CP. G. 1097; Lawrance, *Fasti*, iii. 22.

10 H. Aveling, *Post Reformation Catholicism in E Yorks., 1558–1790* (E Yorks. Local Hist. Ser. 11, 1960), 13, 60.

11 Cross, 'Medieval Yorkshire Library', 281–2.

12 Boulter, 'Ch. Bells', 219.

13 BIA, CP. G. 1097.

14 *Valor Eccl.* (Rec. Com.), v. 142.

15 'ER Clergy in 1525–6', 65, 70; Lawrance, *Fasti*, iii. 22.

16 *Valor Eccl.* v. 140–2.

year.[1] He was excused payment of the clerical subsidy in 1638 because of his poverty,[2] and later benefited from the attempt made during the Interregnum to remedy some of the financial inequalities in the Church. In 1646 he was granted an augmentation of £12 a year from the £62 annual rent paid by the lessee of the rectory to Parliament, which had confiscated the estates and rents of the precentor-rector.[3]

The stipend of the incumbent of the two Driffields was composed almost entirely of tithes and offerings from his parishioners which had evidently been assigned to him at unknown date. By the earlier 17th century some of the tithes were paid not in kind but by compound money rents, Henry Best of Elmswell then settling the small tithes and offerings he owed Ralph Mason, 'vicar', for 15*s*. a year.[4] Detailed information about the incumbent's portion was given later in the 18th-century glebe terriers. He was entitled to all the small tithes, except for those of wool and lambs which belonged to the rector's share in the churches.[5] Various other dues, probably in origin compositions for tithes, were also collected. At Easter, an annual payment of 3*s*. 4*d*. was taken for each mill or kiln in the parishes, and 1*d*. for a (market) garden, while on 1 January each house had to render a hen or 6*d*.; as later described, the last obligation was restricted to houses with common rights, and was settled by a rent of 8*d*. The Easter offering itself was a charge of 2*d*. on each adult parishioner. Those sources of income were supplemented by incidental ones like the incumbent's fees for weddings and burials.[6] The vicarage houses of the two parishes and their sites seem to have been the only glebe. That at Little Driffield was said in 1615 to have been allowed to fall into great decay by Robert Greenhaugh, vicar,[7] and neither the house nor its site were mentioned later among the property of the combined living. By that date the incumbent was probably living in Great Driffield in the vicarage house on the south side of Church Lane, but between 1649 and 1693 that house was demolished; thereafter its small site constituted the only glebe. No replacement house seems to have been provided, those serving the Driffield churches presumably living in their own or rented accommodation.[8]

The joint cure may have been neglected by Robert Greenhaugh, vicar from 1602 until his resignation in 1615.[9] It was later held by puritans, Valentine Mason serving as vicar from 1615 to 1623, and Ralph Mason (no relation), from 1625 until his death in 1666.[10] Henry Best, who had brought several puritan books with him when he moved to Elmswell from Essex in 1617, lent a protestant work, an abridgement of Foxe's *Acts and Monuments*, to Ralph Mason in 1633.[11] The vicar evidently took little interest in the upkeep of the chancels of the two churches which had seating in decay and were in need of 'beautifying' in 1636.[12] About 1650 poorly-paid Mason claimed that he had to provide two services in both Great and Little Driffield churches each Sunday,[13] and, perhaps not surprisingly, he was then said by the Parliamentary commissioners to preach in the two churches 'after his fashion'.[14] During the Commonwealth period Mason, whose diligence and political and moral worthiness was certified by his neighbours, was chosen as the civil 'register' for Little Driffield and Elmswell, but at Great Driffield the people chose George England.[15] Mason was re-instated as vicar by 1658, but was absent from his cure in 1662.[16]

The incumbent in 1666 was perhaps William Shaw, clerk, who then instituted proceedings against the churchwardens of Great Driffield.[17] Later in the century the quality of the ministers serving the Driffields caused further discord. In 1675 the curate, Gerrard Didsbrough, was suspended by the ecclesiastical authorities for scandalous but unspecified faults.[18] Of William Dickinson, curate of Driffield in the earlier 1680s, it was alleged that he conducted clandestine marriages, one of them in a house in the town about ten o'clock at night; allowed penances to be done privately in return for cash, and was a drunkard, a swearer, and a frequenter of Driffield's inns.[19]

Little is heard of the 17th-century congregations but there were evidently a handful of people connected with the church in one way or another who were affluent enough to be commemorated there. At Great Driffield members of the Spink family, then or earlier lessees of the rectory, were remembered formerly by tombs in the chancel.[20] The monuments representing

1 Lamb. Pal. Libr., COMM. XIIa/17/326, 488. *Cal. S.P. Dom. 1654*, p. 226 has just over £13 a year.

2 R. A. Marchant, *Puritans and Ch. Cts in the Dioc. of York, 1560–1642* (1960), 262.

3 *Cal. S.P. Dom. 1654*, pp. 226–7.

4 Best, *Farming Bks*, ed. Woodward, 182–3, 196.

5 BIA, TA. 36M; RDB, B/153/42.

6 BIA, TER. J. Driffield 1716, [1743], 1809.

7 Ibid. V. 1615/CB. 1, f. 192v.; Lawrance, *Fasti*, iii. 22.

8 Lamb. Pal. Libr., COMM. XIIa/17/488; BIA, TER. J. Driffield 1693; RDB, AG/302/579; 95/87/81 (1897).

9 Lawrance, *Fasti*, iii. 22.

10 A descendant of Valentine, the Revd Wm Mason (d. 1797), was a poet whose preferments included the prebend of Driffield in York minster: ERAO, PE/10/2; Marchant, *Puritans and Ch. Cts*, 262–3; *DNB*, *s.v.* Wm. Mason; Ross, *Driffield*, 139; Lawrance, *Fasti*, iii. 22.

11 Best, *Farming Bks*, ed. Woodward, pp. lviii, lxi, 161–3, 183, 185, 196, 249.

12 J. S. Purvis, *The Condition of Yorks. Church Fabrics 1300–1800* (1958), 19.

13 *Cal. S.P. Dom. 1654*, p. 226.

14 Lamb. Pal. Libr., COMM. XIIa/17/326. The transcription in *TERAS* 2 (1894), 26–7 is misleading in merging details from another parish with those of Driffield.

15 *Cal. S.P. Dom. 1654*, p. 226; ERAO, PE10/1; PE11/1.

16 ERAO, PE11/1; Marchant, *Puritans and Ch. Cts*, 262.

17 BIA, D/C. CP. 1666/15.

18 Ibid. 1675/7.

19 Ibid. CP. H. 3836.

20 Above, manors and estates, rectory.

the Revd Richard Spink (d. 1634) and William Spink, both kneeling were later broken up, the figures being reduced to busts and mounted in the nave until 1904, when they were moved to their present positions in the north aisle.[1] Members of another prominent family, Mary Etherington (d. 1690) and husband Richard Etherington (d. 1696), are commemorated, also in the chancel, by a gravestone with incised arms.[2]

Nonconformity

There were eight recusants at Driffield in 1607 including Thomasin Gale, widow, a member of a Roman Catholic gentry family from Wilberfoss.[3] The three who refused to take communion in 1615 and those involved in three secret baptisms in 1633 were probably also Catholics.[4]

From the 1650s there was a significant following for the Society of Friends in Driffield and area. The ready acceptance of radical Quaker beliefs in the locality may owe something to the writings and preaching of Paul Best, an early English advocate of Socinianism or Unitarianism, who died at Great Driffield in 1657 after some ten years residence there or nearby. Best, the elder brother of Henry Best of Elmswell, served as a soldier on the continent in the 1620s-30s coming into contact with anti-Trinitarian Socinianism in Poland and Transylvania. On his return to England, where he served in the Parliamentary forces, he was soon actively promoting his new faith for which he was imprisoned and eventually condemned to death. Released from prison in 1647 he retired to Driffield. Best's anti-Trinitarian theology was not out of step with Quaker beliefs and his major work *Mysteries Revealed* (1647) had the approval of at least one writer from that sect in the 1650s.[5]

Quakerism was introduced into the area by George Fox and William Dewsbury who held meetings in villages near Driffield in 1652.[6] It was at one of these meetings at North Frodingham that Thomas Thompson, a farm worker from Brigham, was converted and he began preaching 'repentance to the people'.[7] Towards the end of 1652 Thompson went to Driffield parish church, presumably during service time, and there it is claimed he said he was Christ.[8] It was not long before there was significant group of Quakers in Great Driffield including Thomas Nicholson, Thomas England and Richard Pearson who in 1657–61 refused to pay the sums demanded for the repair of the parish church.[9] England and Pearson, along with the latter's son Robert and daughter Isabel, were imprisoned for three months in York Castle for attending a Quaker meeting at Skerne in 1661.[10] During this time the elder Pearson's wife and another son, probably Thomas, were fined for non-attendance at church.[11] Thomas Pearson was charged in 1669, with Robert Etherington, Silvester Simpson and James Blackburn, for absence from church, and presented at the Visitation court in 1675 for not paying the church rate.[12] Etherington and the Ann Etherington of Great Driffield admonished by the Quaker monthly meeting for 'departing from the truth' by marrying in an Anglican church in 1669 may have been members of the prominent local family.[13] Other Driffield Quakers included James Blackburn and Ann Couper who were married at a Quaker meeting at Cottam in 1666.[14] No Quaker meetings for worship are recorded at Great Driffield, but regular meetings took place at Elmswell 1671–83 and at Skerne 1694–1716.[15] These meetings may have been attended from Great Driffield but there is no definite record of Quakers there after the 1670s. Francis Buskin, Robert Hick, and Richard Marshall presented for non-payment of the church rate at Driffield in 1688 have not been identified as Quakers and may have belonged to another Dissenting sect.[16]

1700–*c.* 1840

Anglicanism

The earlier attempt to divert monies from the rectory to the poor living[17] was resumed about 1700. The then rector, Dr James Fall, precentor of York and prebendary of Driffield from 1692 to his death in 1711,[18] augmented the living with £2 a year paid out of the rectorial tithes.[19] In 1706, after the augmentation had been made, the two Driffields were said to be worth £17 a year.[20] From the 1710s a small income was also received from Francis Ellis's charity in return for preaching one or two

1 ERAO, PE/10/T. 59, s.a. Dec. 1880; BIA, Fac. 1904/8. *DT* 13 Nov. 1880; Ross, *Driffield*, 50–1 confuses the history of the figures by almost certainly repeating a much earlier account, thereby giving the impression that the 'tombs' existed still in the late 19th century.

2 Ross, *Driffield*, 132.

3 Aveling, *Post Reformation Catholicism*, 59–60.

4 Ibid. 60.

5 *DNB*, *s.v.* Paul Best.

6 N. Penney (ed.) *"The First Publishers of Truth"* (1907), 293–4; T. Thompson, *An Encouragement Early to Seek the Lord and be Faithful to Him in An Account of the Life and Services of that Ancient Servant of God Thomas Thompson* (1708), 16–17.

7 Thompson, *Encouragement Early*, 17–18.

8 Howorth, *Driffield*, 17.

9 ERAO, DDQR/16; BIA, D/C. CP. 1662/8; D/C. Cit . (Teile file 1).

10 J. Besse, *A Collection of the Sufferings of the People called Quakers* (1753), ii, 100. Thomas England married Mary Todd at a Friends meeting at Kilham in 1662: TNA. R6/1119.

11 Besse, *Sufferings*, ii, 111.

12 *Depositions from York Castle* (Surtees Soc. 10), 167; BIA, D/C. CP. 1675/3.

13 ERAO, DDQR/12.

14 TNA, R6/1119.

15 ERAO, DDQR/12.

16 BIA, D/C. CP. 1688/10.

17 Above, this section, 17th cent.

18 Le Neve, *Fasti, 1541–1857, York*, 10.

19 BIA, TER. J. Driffield 1716, [1726]. By lease of 1825 the rector charged the tenant of the rectory farm with payment of the £2: ibid. CC. P./Dri. 10, Dri. 11.

20 Ibid. Bp. Dio. 3, ER, p. 102.

sermons a year in Great Driffield church. In 1726 the total value of the combined living was some £21.[1] The living of Great Driffield in particular was augmented with £200 of Bounty money by lot in 1772.[2] By the 1820s the challenge of Nonconformity and other reasons, presumably including the growth of the town, led to further steps being taken to revive the mission of the Established Church in Driffield. The curacy of Little Driffield was augmented by lot in 1821 with a Parliamentary grant of £400, and in 1825 the rector, Edward Rice, precentor of York, gave £200, which prompted a matching grant of £300 from parliament.[3] The combined income of the curacies of Great Driffield and Little Driffield averaged £154 a year net about 1830.[4]

Tithes remained the chief source of the incumbent's income but a small landed estate was formed for the living during the period. At inclosure in 1742 the common pasturage rights belonging to the site of the demolished vicarage house were extinguished in return for 4 a. awarded to the incumbent.[5] The augmentation obtained in 1772 had been used to buy 9 a. more by 1781, when the land was adding £6 15*s*. to the annual income of the living,[6] and the augmentations of the 1820s were similarly spent mostly on the purchase of another 7 a. in Driffield.[7]

The Driffield cures were, not surprisingly in view of their poor funding, held with others, and part of the service was delegated to assistants in return for a share of the income. George Colebatch, curate or vicar for many years from 1705, also held the neighbouring living of Wetwang with Fimber, and that of Sledmere.[8] Francis Best, curate of Driffield from 1755, was also rector of South Dalton, and resident there, 9 miles from the town. Best's duty at Driffield was done, for half of the income there, by an assistant curate, Christopher Seymour, who for want of a house boarded with one of the farmers. Seymour augmented his meagre livelihood by serving Wetwang church and its chapel of Fimber with the Driffields, a combination of cures which was by then traditional. The combination of churches and the use of poorly-paid assistants probably go some way to explain the low level of religious activity by the Anglicans in the 18th century. In 1764 Seymour provided a single service with a sermon each Sunday at 'Driffield', and quarterly celebrations of communion there. There were then said to be over 250 communicants in the parish, but less than a third of those, 'upwards of 70', had received the previous Easter. Those services were probably held in the parish church at Great Driffield, and there is no mention of any provision in Little Driffield church.[9]

Richard Allen, a schoolmaster at Sledmere when he was ordained deacon at York in 1784 and appointed to the vicarage of Wharram Percy in 1787, was acting as curate at Driffield in 1792 six years before he was admitted as perpetual curate there in 1798.[10] By 1818 Allen was assisted by a curate, to whom he allowed roughly a third of the income of the living.[11] Much of the duty was then done by the curate, William Biggs, termed the officiating minister, possibly because of Allen's age.[12] By 1828 the duty at the parish church was evidently done largely by the then assistant curate, Allen's nephew, George Allen, when Richard Allen recorded that he had preached at Great Driffield for the first time in 10 years because of his nephew's illness. About sixty parishioners then communicated at Great Driffield, and in 1832 the incumbent reckoned the congregation there 'very respectable'.[13] Richard Allen's share in services consisted mainly of reading prayers in the parish church and officiating at Little Driffield, where he lived. Services there comprised chiefly prayers, with occasional quarterly celebrations of communion and the rare sermon. Congregational singing was introduced at both churches in 1832 apparently to good effect.[14] Richard Allen's long ministry was ended by his death aged 74 in 1833; George Allen then succeeded him.[15]

Some idea of the religious experience at Great Driffield in the earlier 19th century can be had from glebe terriers and other sources. The church had by then been 'churchwardenized', and that process, generally unsympathetic to the character of the medieval building, was continued in the early 1800s, when some of the windows were enlarged and the nave ceiled.[16] One medieval fitting did, however, survive the alterations into the 19th century, the wooden chancel screen.[17] Seating in the nave may have been poor and, with the increasing numbers in the town, was increasingly insufficient. The wealthier inhabitants had by the early 18th century made their own arrangements by building several large pews: that of the Cromptons, accommodating about twenty people, stood in the north-east corner adjoining the minister's seat and the

1 Ibid. TER. J. Driffield [1726]; HUL, DDMC/99/1.
2 Hodgson, *QAB*, p. cccxlv.
3 BIA, TER. J. Driffield 1825; Hodgson, *QAB*, pp. cciv, cccxlvii.
4 *Rep. Com. Eccles. Revenues*, 930–1.
5 BIA, TER. J. Driffield 1764, 1770; RDB, B/153/42.
6 BIA, TER. J. Driffield 1781; Hodgson, *QAB*, p. cccxlv.
7 BIA, TER. J. Driffield 1849.
8 Ibid. CC. P./Dri. 10, Dri. 1; *Herring's Visit.* i, p. 223; iii, pp. 251–2. He died in 1755: ERAO, PE/10/3.
9 *Drummond's Visit.* i, pp.129–30, 139–40.
10 PE10/ 4; Letter to D. Neave from N. Gurney, Borthwick Institute, 1972; *Universal Brit. Dir.* (*c.* 1792), ii. 827.
11 *Rep. Com. Eccles. Revenues*, 930–1.
12 *Educ. of Poor Digest*, 1079.
13 ERAO, DDX904/1/1–3.
14 Ibid. DDX904/1/3, entries for 22 Jan. and 1 July 1832.
15 Memorial to Richard Allen in Little Driffield ch.; BIA, V. 1865/Ret. 1, no. 142; ibid. Fac. Bk. 6, pp. 1086–7.
16 BIA, D/C. Fac. 1805/5; below, buildings, relig. buildings.
17 As at Little Driffield, the chancel screen is said to have been taken down in 1737, but, in fact, seems to have been retained until the late 19th-century restoration: Ross, *Driffield*, 56; Butler, *Yorks. Church Notes*, 192–3; A. Vallence, 'Roods, Screens and Lofts of the ER', *YAJ* 24 (1917), 127.

Stork family's pew, while another pew, for a dozen worshippers, was situated 'opposite', presumably adjoining the south aisle.[1] Oak stalls were used by the rest of the congregation, until, as part of the early 19th century 'improvements' they were replaced by pews, later described as 'ugly [and] high-backed',[2] and condemned because of the rents charged for their use which excluded the poorest parishioners.[3] More pews were fitted by subscription in 1841, perhaps adding to the free seating.[4] The church was clearly plainly appointed in other ways. The pulpit, a three-decker 'unshapely structure of plain deal', stood in the centre of the chancel screen.[5] Boards hung around the nave,[6] displaying the Royal Arms and religious texts like the Creed, provided most of the decoration, though by the mid 18th century the chancel had its fine twelve-branched brass chandelier.[7] There was a single communion service of silver, comprising a flagon given by Francis Ellis in 1720, and chalice and paten given or made in 1775.[8] Opinions about the church in the earlier 19th century varied, the interior being commended for its 'great neatness and regularity' in 1827, but the church as a whole being said to have a 'very antique appearance' *c.* 1840.[9]

The musical content of services at Great Driffield was delivered largely by the church choir accompanied by wind instruments and a bass viol, in all said to produce 'a somewhat discordant medley'.[10] The choir and musicians presumably performed from the gallery at the west end of the nave,[11] and it was there, under the tower arch, that an organ was installed by 1827.[12] A rare event in the church was the confirmation in 1841 of 299 young women and 163 young men by the archbishop of York.[13]

Church and chapel came together in support of the Bible Society, a branch of which founded at Driffield in 1815 was re-founded in 1828, and a branch of the Religious Tract Society, established by 1831.[14]

Nonconformity

Despite the lack of services in the parish church, and their probable absence altogether at times at Little Driffield, there was no recorded dissent from the Church of England before the later 18th century.[15] As elsewhere in the East Riding support for the Society of Friends had evaporated and in 1764 there were said to be no Dissenting families of any kind in Driffield parish.[16] Soon all was to change as migrants already members of Dissenting congregations elsewhere moved into the growing town following the opening of the canal. A Methodist Society was evidently formed by 1771 and the following year John Wesley preached in the town, a Baptist congregation was established in 1786 and Independents were meeting there around 1800. Soon all these Dissenting groups had purpose built meeting houses or chapels. Thomas Gray by his will made in 1817 left £40 each to the Baptist, Independent and Wesleyan Methodist towards paying off the debts on their chapels.[17] They were joined by the Primitive Methodists in 1820 and Nonconformity became the dominant force in the religious, social and political life of the expanding town.

Methodists

Wesleyan Methodist Registrations of the house of Thomas Baron in 1771 and a 'new preaching house' in 1777 were almost certainly for the same Methodist congregation.[18] A new chapel was built by 1793 on part of John Gray's garden on the east side of Westgate.[19] It was recorded as the 'newly-erected Methodist meeting house' in 1797, and its galleried interior is believed to have accommodated 400 worshippers.[20] That building was replaced in 1828 by a new larger chapel put up nearby, between Middle Street North and Westgate.[21] The galleried building had pews for 500 and free accommodation for a further 300 and alongside two preacher's houses.[22]

In 1787 the Driffield society had 29 members, 15 men and 14 women, and over the next two decades membership fluctuated between 25 and 40. Amongst the class leaders in the 1780s-90s were William Johnson, breeches maker, fellmonger and brewer, William Ushaw, corn and coal merchant, and John Reaston, tailor.[23] They were joined in 1794 by David Holtby of Little Driffield, who converted during a religious revival that year, and by David Anderson, seed

1 BIA, CP. I. 694.

2 Ibid. D/C. Fac. 1805/5; Ross, *Driffield*, 47.

3 Below, this section, 1840 to 1940 (Anglicanism).

4 BIA, Ch. Ret. i; ERAO, PE/10/T. 99, s.a. 1841.

5 ERAO, DDX/17/15; Brown, *All Saints*, 5; Ross, *Driffield*, 47.

6 BIA, D/C. Fac. 1805/5.

7 Ibid. TER. J. Driffield 1764, 1809, etc. Two other lights, with five branches, were added later: ERAO, PE/10/T. 71.

8 Copy 1777 terrier at HUL, DDCV/41/3; BIA, TER. J. Driffield 1809.

9 Butler, *Yorks. Church Notes*, 193; G. Lawton, *Collectio Rerum Ecclesiasticarum de Dioecesi Eboracensi* (1840), 295.

10 Ross, *Driffield*, 47.

11 Butler, *Yorks. Church Notes*, 193.

12 Ross, *Driffield*, 47; Butler, *Yorks. Church Notes*, 193; also ERAO, PE/10/T. 99, s.a. 1828.

13 *HP* 1 Oct. 1841.

14 *YH* 25 Feb. 1815; *HP* 10 June 1842; White, *Dir. Hull & District* (1831), 245.

15 Above, this section, 17th cent.

16 *Drummond's Visit.* i, p. 139.

17 ERAO, DDX 17/15.

18 Thomas Baron was mentioned in both: TNA, RG 31/5, nos. 323, 473.

19 ERAO, DDX/17/15. The site is now the entrance to the Methodist Church car park from Westgate.

20 BIA, Fac. Bk. 3, p. 289; RDB, FI/271/257; Ross, *Driffield*, 73, 83. Perhaps the same was the 'new' Methodist chapel registered in 1802.

21 TNA, RG 31/5, no. 4137; ERAO, TA/13; ibid. PE/10/T. 120. The old chapel was then used for the Mechanics' Institute and Methodist Sunday school. It later became Stott's carriage works and was demolished by the 1960: DDX/17/15; OS maps.

22 *Wesleyan Methodist Magazine* July 1829, 474.

23 ERAO, MRP/1/7; MRQ/1/36.

merchant, in 1799.[1] The latter (d. 1849) became the most influential Wesleyan Methodist in the town.[2] Other early class leaders were George Huddleston, bookseller and stationer, and William Fox, tanner, in 1816 and James Harrison, corn factor, in 1817.[3] Harrison apparently left the Methodists around 1820 and soon afterwards he registered a Dissenting meeting place at River Head.[4]

Driffield chapel having been successively in York, Pocklington and Bridlington circuits became in 1809 the head of a new circuit comprising places in the western part of the Wolds.[5] Membership at Driffield rose from 52 in 1806 to a peak of 140 in 1815. The arrival of Primitive Methodists in 1820 led to a sharp fall to 80 members in 1827, but rose again to 120 in 1833.[6]

Primitive Methodist Primitive Methodism reached Hull in 1819, and in the autumn of that year Samuel Laister, was sent on a mission to the Yorkshire Wolds. He was no doubt the 'aggressive' Primitive Methodist preacher from Hull who spoke on Cross Hill, Driffield to a 'curious crowd'.[7] A Primitive Methodist Society was established in the town by 1820 with Thomas Wood (d. 1881), a young shoemaker recently arrived from Warter, as the first class leader.[8] Weekly meetings were held in Westgate, and the former Hunt Room, then used as a theatre, was rented for Sunday services.[9] Here William Clowes, one of the founders of the Connexion, preached in 1821.[10] Driffield was placed in the Hull circuit and a minister was sent to organize the society. A chapel was built on Mill Street in 1821–2, financed by a loan from William Byass, a retired farmer, which he changed to a gift before his death.[11] A Sunday school was put up in 1828, and a gallery added in 1840.[12] The first trustees included two shoemakers, two bakers, a carpenter, a tailor, a blacksmith, a worsted manufacturer, two farmers and two labourers.[13]

A Primitive Methodist preacher appeared at Little Driffield in 1823 and it is said that the first meetings took place in a stable with an 'entrance against a manure heap'.[14] A house in Little Driffield, licensed for unidentified protestant Dissenters in 1828, was for Primitive Methodists.[15] By 1830 the Primitive Methodists from the area were holding annual camp meetings at the village.[16] Attendance at Little Driffield Anglican church was affected by a camp meeting in 1830 and by an 'irregular assembly of Ranters' in 1832.[17]

In 1837 Driffield became the head of a large circuit comprising 50 preaching places including Bridlington, until 1857, and Hornsea, until 1861.[18] At this time the circuit also had a mission at Glasgow, Scotland.[19] A great revival took place in the circuit in 1841–2, adding 300 to those attending the chapel in Driffield.[20]

Particular Baptist

The Particular Baptist church in Driffield was begun in the 1780s.[21] Some members of the Baptist chapel at Bridlington were said to have moved to Driffield about 1785, and around the same date William Wrightson, a member of the Salthouse Lane Baptist congregation in Hull, who was undertaking missionary work at Hutton Cranswick, was invited to preach at Driffield. Meetings began in an old brew house and in April 1786 ten people were baptised by Joseph Gawkrodger of Bridlington in Poundsworth Mill stream. The miller at Poundsworth, or Red, Mill, George Dawson, was recorded later as a founder member of the Driffield church.[22] A house in the town registered for Dissenting worship in 1786 was evidently for the Baptists.[23] Wrightson became the first pastor and in 1788 a chapel was built beside the beck, at the end of a lane off Middle Street South, later Chapel Lane and now King Street. The chapel was built on land bought with three cottages;[24] another plot was used for the adjoining burial ground, and by the mid 19th century five cottages stood on the rest of the ground.[25] The first trustees included Francis Brown of

1 *HP* 9 Jan. 1846; ERAO, MRQ 1/36.

2 Below, loc. govt and politics, politics.

3 ERAO, MRD/1/5/1.

4 TNA, RG 31/5, no. 3419; no. 3493. There were other secessionists such as the group of Methodists who registered the house of Henry Robinson, shoemaker, for worship in 1810: BIA, Fac. Bk. 3, p. 544.

5 ERAO, MRP/1/7; MRQ/1/36; MRD/1/5/1.

6 ERAO, MRQ/1/36; MRD/1/5/1.

7 H. B. Kendall, *Origins and History of the Primitive Methodist Church*, ii (1906), 93.

8 Ibid. 93–4; H. Woodcock, *Piety Among the Peasantry* (1889), 43.

9 Ross, *Driffield*, 76.

10 Kendall, *Origins*, 94; Woodcock, *Piety*, 84.

11 *Primitive Methodist Magazine* (1857), 11; ERAO, DDX/17/15; BIA, DMH. Reg. 1, p. 378. RDB, DO/33/33; DO/34/34; *Yorks. Worship Returns 1851*, i. 91; OS Map 1:10,560, Yorks. CLXI (1855 edn); *Lond. Gaz.* 1 Mar. 1850, p. 655.

12 The schoolroom or meeting house registered for worship in 1843 was perhaps that belonging to the Primitive Methodist chapel: ERAO, DDX/17/15; BIA, DMH. 1843/1; TNA, RG 31/5, no. 4557. Cf. RDB, DO/34/34.

13 ERAO, DDX/17/15; Woodcock, *Piety*, 88.

14 Woodcock, *Piety*, 125–6.

15 TNA, RG 31/5, no. 4145.

16 ERAO, DDX904/1/2; *HP* 9 June 1848.

17 ERAO, DDX/904/1/2, s.a. May 1830; DDX/904/1/3, s.a. June 1832.

18 Kendall, *Origins*, 96; Woodcock, *Piety*, 85.

19 Woodcock, *Piety*, 85–6; ERAO, MRD/2/4/1.

20 Woodcock, *Piety*, 87.

21 Following based on *DT* 6 Nov. 1886; *Baptists of Yorks.* (Yorks. Baptist Assoc., 1912), 69, 206–7; Ross, *Driffield*, 70–2.

22 ERAO, EB/1/113.

23 TNA, RG 31/5, no. 671. Thomas Bursell (Burshill) the younger and elder then supported the request for registration, and a Thomas Bursell was named again when the chapel was registered in 1788: ibid. no. 725; Ross, *Driffield*, 186.

24 ERAO, EB/1/113.

25 TNA, RG 31/5, no. 725; RDB, GS/107/100; D. and S. Neave, *ER Chapels and Meeting Houses* (1990), 8 (illus.); OS Map 1:10,560, Yorks. CLXI (1855 edn). The chapel was later mistakenly dated 1790: *Yorks. Worship Returns 1851*, i. 90.

51. *Great Driffield: Former Baptist chapel and burial ground, King Street* c. *1980, built for a Particular Baptist congregation in 1788. Closed in 1862 it became in succession a freemasons' lodge, a Conservative Club and WRVS hall.*

Kelleythorpe, Thomas Burshill, roper, John Thirwell, bricklayer, and George Dawson.[1]

Wrightson is said to have served as minister until his resignation in 1797, following differences with his congregation. No pastor was then appointed for some years, and the congregation was served by temporary preachers, among them Wrightson again, who, as a Baptist minister of Great Driffield, was involved in the purchase of a house in New Road, later Exchange Street, presumably for a manse, in 1805.[2] Eventually, in 1814, another pastor James Normanton, was appointed. He married a daughter of Christopher Laybourne, post master, and was elected Registrar for the Driffield Registration District in 1841.[3] During his ministry, which lasted until 1846, the church prospered, and its premises were enlarged with a vestry cum schoolroom in 1835. Thereafter changes of minister were frequent, and the church was troubled by dissension over its property. In 1848 the heir of a former trustee was claiming rents, which were also being withheld by tenants; the chapel had had to be forcibly re-possessed after occupation by one faction, and allusion was made to a 'disgraceful busybody' and to the immorality of the minister.

Independents

The Independent church was formed at Driffield in 1800 made up of worshippers from other Independent congregations who had moved to the town. They first met in a barn belonging to Thomas Burshill, rope-maker, in Middle Street South, then in a chamber above the workshop of George White, cabinet maker, in New Road, later Exchange Street.[4] This was probably the house in New Road registered for Independents in 1801.[5] The following year the congregation built Providence chapel, at a cost of £440, on the south side of that street. It was dedicated in 1803.[6] The accommodation was enlarged with galleries in 1819, and in 1846 a school was added behind the chapel.[7] A small burial ground adjoining was closed in 1865.[8] The early leaders of the congregation were James Pinder, clog maker, and George White and George Shepherdson, both cabinet makers.[9]

1840–1940

A broad view of religious life in the parish in the mid 19th century can be obtained from the worship census returns of 1851 (Table 13).[10] Taking the congregations at the best attended Sunday service in each place of worship, it is clear how poorly the Established Church was doing relative to the Nonconformist chapels, and how far both Church and Chapel were from reaching the entire population of the parish. On Census Sunday, the most popular services in the two Anglican churches were attended in all by about 490 people, roughly 11.5

1 ERAO, EB1/113–4.

2 RDB, CK/33/53. The minister in 1851 lived in Exchange Street: *Yorks. Worship Returns 1851*, i. 90.

3 *HP* 11 Jan. 1831; 1 Jan. 1841.

4 *DT* 23 Nov. 1901.

5 BIA, Fac. Bk. 3, p. 277.

6 The chapel was said to have been built in 1802 and was registered in 1803: BIA, Fac. Bk. 3, pp. 325–6; RDB, CP/172/260; *Yorks. Worship Returns 1851*, i. 90; www.d-c-c.org.uk .

7 ERAO, TA/13; ibid. PE/10/T. 120; J. G. Miall, *Congregationalism in Yorks.* (1868), 256.

8 *DT* 2 Dec. 1865.

9 Ibid. 23 Nov. 1891.

10 *Yorks. Worship Returns 1851*, i. 90–1.

	Seating (Free)	Morning	Afternoon	Evening	Total Attendances	%
Great Driffield						
Anglican	605	310		153	463	19.5
	(195)	(SS 130)			(SS 130)	
Wesleyan Methodist	620	180	130	360	670	28.5
	(214)	(SS 86)			(SS 86)	
Primitive Methodist	450	30	280	330	640	27
	(110)		(SS 40)		(SS 40)	
Baptist	220	72		120	192	8
	(50)	(SS 36)	(SS 36)		(SS 72)	
Independent (Congregational)	350	160		230	390	16.5
	(50)	(SS 59)			(SS 59)	
Total	2,245	752	410	1,193	2,355	100
	(619)	(SS 311)	(SS 76)		(SS 377)	
Little Driffield						
Anglican	97		35 (SS 18)		35 (SS 18)	
	(30)					
Primitive Meth.	(30)			30 Av	30	
Elmswell Primitive Meth.				30	30	

SS = Sunday School
Source: *Yorks. Worship Returns 1851*, i. 90–1.

Table 13. *Driffield Parish: Religious Census 1851*

per cent of the population of the parish.[1] Some 1,100 people or 26 per cent of the parishioners then went to the most frequented services in the Nonconformist chapels. Even if all of those attending other services were additional worshippers, rather than people attending for a second time, there was clearly also a considerable proportion of the population who attended neither church nor chapel regularly in the mid century. This was despite the fact that some employers actively 'encouraged' their workers to attend a place of worship. When Isaac Watson, a servant on Mrs Harrison's farm on Driffield Wold, was fined by local magistrates, two of the three being Anglican clergymen, with refusing to attend church on Sunday having been requested to do so by his mistress, there was a national outcry.[2] It reached the popular press and the marquis of Townshend wrote to the Home Secretary and leave was given to introduce a bill in the House of Commons 'for the abolition of fines for non-attendance at a place of divine worship on Sunday'.[3]

Anglicanism

The Established Church was reformed and reinvigorated in Driffield in the mid and late 19th century. The finances of the living were modernised in the 1840s by tithe awards, under which money rents were formally substituted for the compositions by then being paid instead of tithes. From 1845 the perpetual curate's tithes in Great and Little Driffield were thus commuted for rent charges totalling £100 a year,[4] and in Elmswell and Kelleythorpe for rents amounting to £27 15*s*. a year.[5] The financial inequalities of the Church were addressed in the Cathedrals Act of 1840, by which the property given originally to support local churches but later for the most part diverted, with those churches, to cathedrals was to be transferred to a central Church fund

1 Above, vol. intro., population.
2 *HP* 12 Aug., 9 Sept. 1864.
3 Ibid. 9 Sept. 1864; 3 Mar. 1865.
4 A rough, annotated copy of the award, and its plan, respectively at ERAO, PE/10/T. 120 and TA/13, have been used in this and other sections. The apportionment and plan is also at BIA, TA. 869VL.
5 BIA, TA. 36M; ERAO, DX/100.

52. *Great Driffield: Congregation leaving All Saints' church after a service c. 1910.*

administered by commissioners.[1] In Driffield's case, the then precentor of York released the rectory to the Ecclesiastical Commissioners in 1853, taking instead an annuity for life.[2] The net income of the Driffields was £216 a year about that date, of which tithe rents accounted for £110, the glebe £85, and fees most of the rest.[3] Soon afterwards the income of the joint living of Great and Little Driffield was increased from the Common Fund: £12 a year was granted in 1856 to meet a gift of £400 from the precentor, and a further £20 a year was added when the precentor's annuity ceased at his death in 1862.[4] Another grant was paid out of the Common Fund from 1865, the £180 a year comprising £60 for the vicar and £120 as a stipend for an assistant curate.[5] By 1884 the net value of the living was almost £368 a year, excluding the £120 received for an assistant curate.[6] The incumbent's income was augmented with £25 a year in 1904, and about that date the Ecclesiastical Commissioners, partly in response to a £500 benefaction, made further provision for assistant curates.[7]

In the mid 19th century the incumbent of Driffields Ambo was living in a house at Little Driffield, probably his own or rented,[8] which remains as the Old Vicarage, York Road. In the 1860s the Ecclesiastical Commissioners attempted to remedy the continued lack of a parsonage house for the joint living, then comprising Great Driffield vicarage and the perpetual curacy of Little Driffield. The sum of £35 a year was paid to the living from the Common Fund from 1865; the following year the Commissioners agreed to pay up to £103 of any mortgage costs, and another grant from the Common Fund, of £1,400, was made in 1867.[9] No house was obtained, however, and the sum of £1,400 for many years merely generated extra income for the living.[10] The tenure of the Driffields by vicars with private means probably accounts for the delay in supplying a parsonage house. Horace Newton, vicar 1877–92, described later as a 'fabulously wealthy clergyman', lived in a large private house called Beechwood, which soon after he arrived in the parish he had had enlarged to designs by Temple Moore.[11] Newton's successor, W. R. Sharrock, had a house in Driffield by 1893, presumably that in Downe Street, earlier called Hill Cottage and Chestnut Villa, which was certainly the vicarage house by 1909; evidently leased at first, it was purchased by Sharrock in 1914.[12] A house in Beverley Road (no. 20) was left to the living by Richard Davison (d. 1901)[13] for a vicarage house, but was never so used, and in 1922 it was

1 3 & 4 Vic. c. 113.

2 *Lond. Gaz.* 14 June 1853, pp. 1650–1.

3 *Yorks. Worship Returns 1851*, i. 90. Most of the glebe was sold in the 1920s: RDB, 237/137/112; 237/602/496; 325/557/444.

4 BIA, TER. J. Driffield 1857, 1865; *Lond. Gaz.* 1 Aug. 1856, pp. 2656–7; Le Neve, *Fasti, 1541–1857, York*, 11.

5 *Lond. Gaz.* 11 May 1866, pp. 2880–4; letter of 1866 at ERAO, PE/10/T. 73.

6 BIA, V. 1884/Ret. 1.

7 Letters of 1903 and 1904 at ERAO, PE/10/T. 73; *Lond. Gaz.* 13 May 1904, p. 3099; 10 May 1907, p. 3207.

8 TNA, HO 107/2366; BIA, V. 1868/Ret. 1, no. 133.

9 Letters of 1866 and 1867 at ERAO, PE/10/T. 73; *Lond. Gaz.* 13 Apr. 1866, pp. 2375–6; 11 May 1866, p. 2894; 1 Mar. 1867, p. 1480.

10 BIA, V. 1884/Ret. 1.

11 Newton and two brothers owned 34,000 a. of Argyllshire: *DT* 20 Jan. 1983; Brandwood, *Temple Moore*, 14, 19–20, 212; *Kelly's Dir. N & ER Yorks.* (1889), 374; (1897), 440.

12 BIA, NPH. 1922/2; ERAO, TA/13; *Kelly's Dir. N & ER Yorks.* (1893), 409; OS Map 1:2,500, CLXI. 12 (1893 and 1910 edns).

13 Memorial window in Great Driffield church.

sold[1] and Sharrock's house in Downe Street, with *c.* 1 a. of grounds, was bought for the living.[2]

Despite the financial reforms, improvement in the church life of the parishes may have been slowed by the long incumbency of George Allen (1791–1881), who held the Driffields from 1833 until 1876.[3] He was remembered as 'an aged vicar, of slender talents and a stammering tongue'.[4] Nevertheless, small changes continued to be made to improve the quality of the services in the churches. By the late 1850s Allen was employing assistant curates for Great Driffield and his other living of Kirkburn, and only performed the duty at Little Driffield, where he lived.[5] The provision there was meagre. One service and a school were held each Sunday, the former for a congregation of thirty-five on Census Day in 1851, and about sixty in the 1860s. Communion was celebrated just four times a year, with usually about fifteen receiving.[6] At Great Driffield there were two Sunday services and a Sunday school by 1851, when the morning congregation numbered 310 at the census.[7] In 1865 the assistant curate serving the parish church preached three sermons a week, and on Sundays attracted 'almost different congregations' averaging 450 in the morning and 350 in the evening. Communion was then monthly with usually about 30 people receiving. The curate seems also to have served as chaplain at the workhouse.[8] The poorer part of his congregations in the parish church was said to be increasing in 1865 but accommodation was difficult on account of the 'unrighteous and unchristian pew system', introduced *c.* 1805;[9] in 1851 only 195 of the 605 seats in the church were free. One lady had a padlock placed on her pew door and refused to admit anyone.[10]

It was the socially-minded young graduate assistant curates rather than the incumbent who began to transform the standing of the Anglican church in the town. James Skinner, assistant curate 1858–62, best known for his campaign against the 'evils' of the annual hirings, started a parochial library and penny savings bank, supported the Mechanics' Institute and served as honorary chaplain of the Volunteer Rifles.[11] His successor Robert Nares, assistant curate 1862–70, who continued to campaign for improvements at the hirings, was outspoken in his responses to the archbishop's visitation queries in 1865.[12] In them he 'told the plain unvarnished truth' in 'the interest of the Church' rather than his 'own selfishness'. He complained of the 'long established and well organised Dissent' in the town, 'the laxity of church discipline' and the lack of clerical help, the last because of the age and inactivity of the vicar. The evening school that he ran was 'sadly hindered' by the lack of suitable accommodation, and he was 'virtually excluded' from the National school, from which no more than a tenth of the day scholars attended the church Sunday school which he gathered together 'with the help of some ladies'.[13] It was Nares who set up the mission hall at North End. Here in Eastgate North, close to Moot Hill, he was running a second Church Sunday school, the 'Ragged' school, in 1865,[14] and the main function of the new building was evidently to house and perhaps develop that school. In 1867, when the newly-opened mission or ragged school was operating as a day school, Nares obtained a licence to hold services other than communion there.[15]

Much of the regeneration of Church life in Driffield occurred in the late 19th and early 20th century, under the leadership of George Allen's successors, Horace Newton, vicar 1877–92, and W. R. Sharrock, vicar 1892–1940.[16] The Ecclesiastical Commissioners had provided for the employment of one assistant curate when they augmented the vicarage in the 1860s,[17] and another grant, sums raised locally, and further grants out of the Common Fund enabled two or three to be employed by Newton[18] and Sharrock.[98] About 1880 the vicar bought the house next to the church, no. 58 Middle Street North, for the accommodation of the assistant clergy, and it was subsequently occupied by one or more of the assistant curates.[20] Assistant clergy also lived elsewhere in the town in the late 19th and earlier 20th century.[21]

1 RDB, 246/127/109; ERAO, NCH/39/2; ibid. PE/10/T. 100, s.a. 1940.

2 BIA, NPH. 1922/2; RDB, 254/567/493.

3 The extended ministries of Richard and George Allen were, nevertheless, commemorated by a window in 1895: BIA, V. 1865/Ret. 1, no. 142a; ibid. Fac. Bk. 6, pp. 1086–7; *Kelly's Dir. N & ER Yorks.* (1937), 443.

4 Woodcock, *Piety*, 95; *HP* 2 Dec. 1881.

5 BIA, V. 1865/Ret. 1, no. 142a; TNA, HO 107/2366.

6 BIA, V. 1865/Ret. 1, no. 142a; V. 1868/Ret. 1, no. 133; V. 1871/Ret. 1, no. 135; *Yorks. Worship Returns 1851*, i. 91.

7 *Yorks. Worship Returns 1851*, i. 90.

8 BIA, V. 1865/Ret. 1, no. 142; V. 1868/Ret. 1, no. 133; V. 1871/Ret. 1, no. 135.

9 Ross, *Driffield*, 47, 56–7.

10 *HP* 28 Aug. 1874.

11 Ibid. 24 Dec. 1858; 28 Oct, 9 Dec. 1859; 27 Jan, 25 May 1860; 16 May 1862.

12 *Alumni Cantab. 1752–1900*; Moses, *Rural Moral Reform*, 185; *HP* 18 Nov 1870; BIA, V. 1865/Ret. 1, no. 142.

13 BIA, V. 1865/Ret. 1, no. 142; *Yorks. Worship Returns 1851*, i. 90.

14 BIA, V. 1865/Ret. 1, no. 142.

15 BIA, LDS. 1867/2; ibid. V. 1871/Ret. 1, no. 135; *1st Rep. Com. on Employment of Children, Young Persons, and Women in Agric., App. Pt. II* (Parl. Papers, 1867–8 [4068-I], xvii), p. 381; above, soc. hist., educ.

16 BIA, Fac. 1953/2/12; *Alumni Cantab.1752–1900*; *DT*, 20 Jan. 1983. Photograph of Sharrock in *DT* 30 Oct. 1980. On his death Sharrock was 'the oldest beneficed clergyman in England': *The Times* 25 Mar. 1940.

17 *Lond. Gaz.* 11 May 1866, pp. 2880–4.

18 BIA, V. 1877/Ret. 1, no 133; V. 1884/Ret. 1; Bulmer, *Dir. E Yorks.* (1892), 170.

19 RDB, 172/352/303; BIA, V. 1900/Ret. 1, no. 148; ERAO, PE10/T.224; letter of 1903 at ERAO, PE/10/T. 73; *Lond. Gaz.* 10 May 1907, p. 3207.

20 ERAO, PE/10/T. 59, s.a. Jan. 1881; RDB, 88/446/427 (1897); *Kelly's Dir. N & ER Yorks.* (1889), 374; (1913), 514; *Crockford* (1980–2), 369.

21 Directories.

53. *Great Driffield: St John's Anglican church, St John's Road c. 1910. Built to serve the middle-class community at the south end of the town, it replaced a temporary mission hall in 1900, and closed in the 1960s.*

Church restoration and worship The most pressing need, after probable past neglect and faced with the rebuilding of the Nonconformist chapels then under way, was almost certainly the restoration of the two churches. Both buildings, said to be in good repair in 1865 and 'sufficient' in 1868, were found by the new incumbent to be decayed in 1877.[1] Moves towards restoring the parish church had in fact been begun in 1874, and it was largely rebuilt and enlarged by George Gilbert Scott the younger and his assistant Temple Moore between 1878 and 1881, over £2,000 of the £12,000 spent being contributed by the vicar, Horace Newton.[2] The restored building was then said to accommodate 758 people, and later to seat about 650.[3] About 1900 more seating was provided below the tower, and further embellishment was carried out in the 1900s by Temple Moore.[4] At Little Driffield the church had been rebuilt on a smaller scale in 1807.[5] It underwent a partial restoration in 1863 when it was given a 'much more neat and ecclesiastical appearance' with new pulpit, reading desk, choir stalls, communion rail and altar.[6] The church was largely rebuilt between 1888–90, to designs by Temple Moore and again paid for in part by Newton; the church subsequently seated 136.[7]

One of the earliest of Newton's initiatives was evidently the provision of decent service of communion plate at Little Driffield.[8] Aside from their quality, the number of services was also increased in both churches: at Little Driffield the small congregation had two Sunday services and monthly celebrations of communion by 1884, while in the parish church communion was fortnightly by 1877, weekly from 1884, and more frequent still about 1920.[9]

Accommodation and services were added to further by the building of a mission hall at the south end of the town. In the late 1870s a temporary, wooden building was put up at the end of Lockwood Street by the vicar, Horace Newton, and other subscribers for the holding of services during the restoration of the parish church. Designed by Temple Moore and seating some 450 people, it was subsequently kept as a mission church or hall dedicated to St John (the Evangelist), being opened in 1881.[10] Newton duly leased the premises to his successor, and in 1895 the church was partly rebuilt, and a licence obtained for the vicar or his assistants to take

1 BIA, V. 1865/Ret. 1, nos. 142, 142a; V. 1868/Ret. 1, no. 133; V. 1877/Ret. 1, no. 133.

2 Below, buildings, relig. buildings.

3 BIA, Fac. 1878/26; ERAO, PE/10/T. 59, s.a. Oct. 1874, May 1878; Bulmer, *Dir. E Yorks.* (1892), 166; Brown, *All Saints*, 9.

4 BIA, Fac. 1899/7; Pevsner and Neave, *Yorks. ER.* 440.

5 BIA, Fac. 1960/2/26; Baines, *Hist. Yorks.* (1823), ii. 194.

6 *HP* 11 Sept. 1863.

7 BIA, Fac. 1960/2/26; Bulmer, *Dir. E Yorks.* (1892), 168; *Kelly's Dir. N & ER Yorks.* (1893), 407; Pevsner and Neave, *Yorks. ER.* 597.

8 ERAO, PE/10/T. 71; *Yorks. Ch. Plate*, i. 240.

9 BIA, V. 1877/Ret. 1, no. 133; V. 1884/Ret. 1; V. 1912–22/Ret.

10 Ibid. V. 1894/Ret. 2; ERAO, PE/10/T. 59, s.a. March *and* May 1878; Ross, *Driffield*, 184; Pevsner and Neave, *Yorks. ER.* 95; Brandwood, *Temple Moore*, 212. The full dedication appears in the later baptism register: ERAO, PE/10/accession 1197.

all services there apart from marriages.[1] It was replaced in 1899–1900 by a new, brick church with 400 seats, all free.[2] Morning and evening services were provided in the mission church on Sundays by 1893, and evening prayer on weekdays as well by 1897.[3] A licensed lay reader was taking one of the services in 1894, which then and later included a regular Sunday service for children. About 1920 the Sunday services at St John's drew congregations of up to 250 people; communion was then celebrated fortnightly.[4]

Worship in the mission school at North End lapsed in 1871, and the day school failed at about the same date,[5] but religious activity was soon resumed there, possibly as a result of a missionary week led by a visiting clergyman and attended by the archbishop of York in the autumn of 1875.[6] By 1877 a Sunday service was being held in the 'mission room', and communion was then celebrated there weekly. In 1900 a Sunday school and a Sunday evening service conducted by lay workers were being held in North End mission room. About 1920 the room was reckoned to accommodate 100, and the evening service was then attended usually by some 80 people.[7]

Several other places were mentioned as locations for services from the late 19th century. The incumbent or his assistant usually served as chaplain at the workhouse; in 1894 an evening service with a sermon was provided there, frequently or always by the lay reader. About 1920 an afternoon service usually attended by some seventy people was held in the workhouse chapel, and communion was being celebrated there in 1931. Services were also conducted in and after 1894 at Wold House Farm, over two miles from the town. Four laymen supplied a service with sermon there, held in 1900 on Sunday afternoons.[8] Another mission room was established about that date in Doctor Lane, later Queen Street. A morning service with a usual congregation of 20 was held there *c.* 1920, and the room was still used for worship in 1931.[9]

In the late 19th and early 20th century particular attention was paid to the social life of the churches. Newton founded the Church Institute, with regular lectures, secular and religious, soon after his arrival in 1877, and set up a temperance Coffee House elsewhere in the town two years later.[10] Sharrock greatly expanded the churches activities and organizations which he publicised through the parish magazine, the *Driffield Church Monthly*, which he began soon after his arrival in 1892.[11] By the end of the century the church ran a lending library, a clothing club, a penny bank, a boys' gymnasium, a Sunday school sick club, Young Men's Friendly Society, Church Lads' Brigade, mothers' meetings, as well as the Sunday schools and Band of Hope and adult temperance meetings.[12] The vicar then had the help of three assistant clergy as well as paid and many unpaid lay workers. There were 38 Sunday school teachers, 28 female district visitors, 20 sidesmen and a parochial church council of 44 in 1893–4, and the church choir comprised 45 men and 42 women in 1896–7.[13]

Much of the weekday activity presumably took place in the Church or Parish Room, built next to the church in or soon before 1894.[14] In 1910 new premises were obtained: the Church Institute then built on the site of several cottages in Church Lane subsequently provided, besides the gymnasium, reading and games rooms, and a rifle range. Membership numbered 163 by 1921,[15] and the premises were enlarged *c.* 1940.[16]

The success or otherwise of the Church's efforts in the later 19th century is difficult to assess. In terms of the Church's own measure, of average attendance at services and numbers of communicants, there was apparently little increase in effectiveness. Congregations at single services in the parish church seem to have remained much the same between the 1860s and 1930s, but the total number of churchgoers in the parish had certainly been increased by the opening of new places of worship. The best congregations at Great and Little Driffield had totalled some 350 in 1851. In the early 1920s 300 went to the parish church on Sunday mornings, 250 to St John's, 30 to Little Driffield, and 20 to Queen Street mission, while later services at North End mission and the workhouse usually attracted 80 and 70 respectively. The Evangelical churchmanship of Newton meant that there was no special emphasis put on the communion service. During his incumbency the number taking communion at Easter fell from 21 in 1879 to only 12 ten years later. All changed with the arrival of Sharrock who started a

1 ERAO, PE/10/T. 71, 135; *Kelly's Dir. N & ER Yorks.* (1897), 440.

2 BIA, CD. 583; ibid. Fac. 1960/2/26; RDB, 27/473/446 (1900); ERAO, PE/10/T. 136; *Kelly's Dir. N & ER Yorks.* (1901), 461; OS Map 1:2,500, Yorks. CLXI. 12 (1893, 1910 edns); illus. at HUL, DX/144/3 (A 5071/6); ERAO, PE/10/T. 194.

3 *Kelly's Dir. N & ER Yorks.* (1893), 408; (1897), 442; (1909), 493.

4 BIA, V. 1894/Ret. 2; V. 1900/Ret. 1, no. 148; V. 1912–22/Ret.

5 Ibid. LDS. 1867/2; ibid. V. 1871/Ret. 1, no. 135; *1st Rep. Com. on Employment of Children, Young Persons, and Women in Agric., App. Pt. II* (Parl. Papers, 1867–8 [4068-I], xvii), p. 381; above, soc. hist., educ.

6 Ross, *Driffield*, 183.

7 BIA, V. 1877/Ret. 1, no. 133; V. 1900/Ret. 1, no. 148; V. 1912–22/Ret.

8 Ibid. V. 1865/Ret. 1, no. 142; V. 1868/Ret. 1, no. 133; V. 1884/Ret. 1; V. 1894/Ret. 2; V. 1900/Ret. 1, no. 148; V. 1912–22/Ret.; V. 1931/Ret.; OS Map 1:10,560, Yorks. CLXI (1855 edn).

9 BIA, V. 1912–22/Ret.; V. 1931/Ret. Photographs of the 'schoolroom' or mission room are at ERAO, DDX/498/1.

10 *HP* 5 Dec. 1879; Ross, *Driffield*, 90, 183.

11 It was begun by 1893: *Kelly's Dir. N & ER Yorks.* (1893), 408. Bound copies of the magazine run from January 1894 until the end of 1966: ERAO, PE/10/T. 162–90.

12 BIA, V. 1900/Ret. 1, no. 148; *Driffield Church Monthly* (1898).

13 ERAO, PE10/T224.

14 BIA, V. 1894/Ret. 2; RDB, 88/446/427 (1897).

15 RDB, 119/350/315; *Kelly's Dir. N & ER Yorks.* (1913), 511; (1921), 497.

16 RDB, 626/418/324; ERAO, PE/10/T. 80, 111, 158.

communicants' guild which had 401 names on it in 1893–4.[1] The number of communicants on Easter Day rose from 14 in 1892 to 311 in 1902, when there were three communion services.[2] There were 425 communicants on Easter Day in 1912 and 540 in 1931, but the numbers of communicants at monthly services rarely exceeded 40 and at weekday services was usually less than 10.[3]

Prominent Anglicans in the later 19th century included Thomas Holtby, brewer, George R. Jackson, proprietor and publisher of the *Driffield Times*, Henry Botterill, George B. Tonge, and William Wigmore, solicitors, John W. Turner, wine merchant and brickmaker, Henry B. Pearson, bank manager, Alfred Scotchburn, doctor, William Scotchburn, draper, George W. Harrison, corn merchant, Richard Hornby, farmer, Alexander F. Lydon, artist, and Harrison Holt, Hull seed-crusher and Driffield resident.[4] Richard Davison (d. 1901), the secretary of the Driffield & East Riding Pure Linseed Cake Co., a churchwarden for nine years, was a major subscriber to the building of St John's church and donated several stained glass windows to the parish church.[5]

The 20th century In Driffield, as elsewhere, the influence of religion was greatly reduced during the 20th century. Canon Sharrock attributed many of his problems to the First World War. Most fit men had been sent into battle; some 130 parishioners had been killed, and one of the consequences was the lack of assistants, both curates and lay workers. A growth in religious indifference and a decline in the 'never high' moral standards of many parishioners he attributed to the billeting of soldiers in the town from 1914. About 1920 some of the youth groups were in abeyance for lack of funds and leaders, and a parochial library had had to be given up for lack of interest.[6] In 1931 Sharrock reported that, for the first time in his ministry in Driffield, he was without a paid woman worker; he was then assisted only by one curate and a licensed Church Army captain, who undertook most of the pastoral visits. The Church men's society was 'like a dead fire', and evangelism and debate about the prayer book were causing contention in the community. On the other hand, the Church Institute, open each day from 8 a.m. to 10 p.m., and the gymnasium both continued to flourish; the *Church Monthly* was still being produced and distributed to about 1,000 homes,[7] and both St John's church and North End mission room were apparently still being used for worship in 1937.[8] Early in the Second World War the senior curate, Rev. T. E. Warner, gave up his commission as a chaplain in the RAF and effectively his priesthood, to become an air gunner in the RAF, much to the dismay of the archbishop of York.[9]

Protestant Nonconformity

The religious census conducted in 1851 makes clear the extent to which the Nonconformity had become the dominant religious influence in the parish. Even individually the larger chapels seem to have equalled the contribution being made by the Anglicans. On Census Sunday the Wesleyan Methodist and Primitive Methodist chapels each attracted congregations in the mid 300s, similar to the combined total for the Anglican churches, while the best attendances at the Independent and Baptist chapels were 230 and 120 respectively; with usually 30 Primitive Methodists at Little Driffield and the same at Elmswell. Over a quarter of the population attended the most popular Nonconformist services. In 1865 the curate serving the parish church believed that three-quarters of the population were Nonconformist, and the more precisely stated ratio of Dissenters to total worshippers was believed to be the same in 1877.[10] Membership figures for all the Nonconformist denominations and their Sunday schools were given in a local newspaper in 1883.[11]

Nonconformity was manifestly at its strongest in the mid and late 19th century. Methodism and the Independents (Congregational) prospered most and new sects made little impact. Residents were said to be annoyed in 1850–1 by the 'insane and periodic ravings of a so-called Mormon elder' who received some support from the 'vilest characters'.[12] The Mormons and 'the Campbelites' had established meetings in houses in the town by 1865, but nothing further is known of them.[13]

The Wesleyan Methodists suffered a minor set back in the 1850s when controversy at the national level resulted in secession and the creation of the new Methodist Reform Church; locally, the Wesleyan Methodists were said to have lost members and in consequence to have accumulated debts.[14] On the other hand, the new congregation balanced the Wesleyans' loss, and, in the earlier 1860s, gave the town another chapel, the relatively modest Wesleyan Reform Union building. Shortly before, the rebuilding or replacement of the older chapels, on a large scale and at considerable

1 ERAO, PE10/T224.
2 Ibid. PE10/45, 57.
3 Ibid. PE10/45, 48.
4 *DT* 6 Nov. 1880, 23 Apr. 1892; *HP* 6 Apr. 1883.
5 *DT* 29 Apr. 1892; 7 Dec. 1901; RDB, 18/372/352 (1887); BIA, Fac. 1899/11, 1902B/15.
6 BIA, V. 1912–22/Ret.; ibid. Fac. 1919B/30.
7 Ibid. V. 1931/Ret.
8 *Kelly's Dir. N & ER Yorks.* (1937), 445, 447.
9 *The Times* 12 July 1940.
10 BIA, V. 1865/Ret. 1, no. 142; V. 1877/Ret. 1, no. 133.
11 *DT* 6 Jan. 1883; Table 14. The Anglican church had 400 children in its Sunday school.
12 *HP* 7 June 1850, 12 Sept. 1851. Robert B. Thompson (1811–41), an early leader in the Church of Jesus Christ and the Latter Day Saints and official church historian, was born at Great Driffield: A. Jenson, *Latter-Day Saints Biographical Encyclopedia* (1901), i. 253
13 BIA. V. 1865/Ret. 1, no. 142.
14 Ross, *Driffield*, 73.

Denomination	*Church Membership*	*Sunday School Membership*
Wesleyan Methodist	430	250
Primitive Methodist	310	435
Methodist Free	80	70
Congregational	145	313
Baptist	56	115

Source: *Driffield Times*, 6 Jan. 1883.

Table 14. *Great Driffield: Nonconformist Church Membership 1883*

cost, was begun. Perhaps because of the dissension which had undermined the church in the 1840s, and possibly led to the withdrawal of at least one of its leading members, the Baptists led the rebuilding in 1862, followed by the Independents in 1866–7, then the Primitive Methodists in 1873 and finally the Wesleyan Methodists in 1879–80.

It was at this point that the Dissenting congregations faced a number of challenges; firstly from a re-invigorated Anglican church. During 1879 Driffield witnessed an active crusade by the Anglicans when, through the 'wealth, youth, ability, the charm of bachelor curates, the influence of active ladies, [and] the almost unbounded generosity of the vicar', several tradesmen left the chapels and went to the church.[1] Then came the invasion of the United Christian Army and the Salvation Army in the early 1880s which met with some success, albeit temporary, drawing away 'the class of hearers' from whom the Primitive Methodist chapel usually recruited its membership.[2] The arrival of a Roman Catholic priest in 1882 and the building of a Catholic church four years later is unlikely to have hit Nonconformist congregations directly, except in uniting them in opposition to the arrival of a church headed by what one biased former resident termed 'that detestable scourge of humanity – the Pope of Rome'.[3]

The Nonconformist congregations and, from the 1870s, the Anglican church, openly supported each other. For example in 1850 the Independent and Primitive Methodist ministers gave addresses at the annual services for Wesleyan missions, and the Independent and Wesleyan ministers jointly addressed a meeting of the Bible Society.[4] The Baptist, Independent and Primitive Methodist ministers were present at the laying of the foundation stone of the Wesleyan Reform chapel in 1863.[5] Representatives of all five Nonconformist denominations were present at a meeting pressing for the closing of public houses on Sunday, which was chaired by the vicar in 1882, and the vicar and the solicitor James M. Jennings, an active Anglican, provided the flowers for the 'winter garden' held to reduce the debt on the Primitive Methodist chapel in 1884.[6]

Eleven Nonconformist ministers resided in 1894, besides the Roman Catholic priest, the two or three Salvation Army captains usually stationed in Driffield, and two 'Christian Mission Evangelists'. Eight of the ministers were Wesleyan or Primitive Methodists serving the extensive circuits.[7] The country parishes were evangelised by Dissenters from Driffield, with large numbers going out each week, a practice that the vicar evidently thought worth copying in 1894.[8] The vicar of Sledmere however, condemned Driffield as a 'hot bed of schism' which poured out a supply of ministers who visited the cottages and influenced 'church-people to join their sect and attend their meetings'.[9]

Methodists

Wesleyan Methodist In 1851 the Wesleyan chapel had 620 seats, of which 214 were free. Its congregation was then said to average 180 in the morning, 130 in the afternoon, and 400 in the evening, and those numbers were recorded on Census Sunday that year, except for the evening service which attracted 360. The Sunday school was attended by 86 children.[10] It was held in the old chapel, which was also shared for a while by the Mechanics' Institute; in 1867 the old chapel was sold, a nearby plot bought, and a new school put up.[11]

The Wesleyan chapel, remodelled and enlarged by 200 seats in 1862 to designs by William Hawe, was rebuilt in 1879–80 to designs of H. J. Paull at a cost of almost £7,000. The new chapel was lit by gas and said to accommodate over 1,000 persons; the premises also included a schoolroom for 400 children, put up in 1867,[12] a band room, and a vestry.[13]

The chapel premises were later enlarged by purchases on Westgate. Two cottages, nos. 53–4, were bought in 1921, and have been remodelled as one house.[14] The adjoining properties, the first chapel, then or lately used as a coachbuilder's workshop, and a building called the widows' rooms were purchased

1 Woodcock, *Piety*, 95.
2 ERAO, MRD/2/4/3.
3 Ross, *Driffield*, 186.
4 *HP* 14 June 1850.
5 Ibid. 25 Sept. 1863.
6 Ibid. 21 Apr. 1882; 12 Dec. 1884.
7 BIA, V. 1894/Ret 2.
8 Ibid.
9 Ibid.
10 *Yorks. Worship Returns 1851*, i. 90.
11 ERAO, EB/1/144; DDX/17/15; RDB, KA/284/384; KA/285/385–6; 304/202/162; Ross, *Driffield*, 181; above, soc. hist., Mechanics' Institute.
12 RDB, KA/284/384; 304/202/162.
13 ONS (Birkdale), Worship Reg. no. 25094; Bulmer, *Dir. E Yorks.* (1892), 166; Ross, *Driffield*, 74, 183; *Lond. Gaz.* 16 July 1880, p. 4003; *HP* 25 July 1879; Neave, *ER Chapels*, 24 (illus.), 50, 65.
14 RDB, 228/74/61; 861/449/378.

respectively in 1925 and 1962;[1] both sites have been cleared and used for car parking.

In the 1870s Driffield Wesleyan circuit comprised 26 preaching places with a fluctuating membership that rose from 855 in 1873 to peak of 1118 in 1876.[2] Many more regularly attended the services. There were 34 lay preachers in the circuit in 1877, of which 18 lived in Driffield.[3] William Cant, sometime before 1900, founded a charity to help the Wesleyan trustees defray the cost of hiring horses for local preachers serving the circuit.[4] Three or four ministers served the circuit from the mid 19th century. Two houses for ministers were built in New Road *c.* 1850.[5] Those houses were replaced in the late 1920s, no. 15 Lockwood Street being bought for the superintendent minister in 1928, and nos. 31–2 New Road sold in 1929 and 1930.[6]

The Wesleyan Methodists have been led by many of the town's leading businessmen. Prominent Wesleyans in the mid and later 19th century included the machine makers Mark and G. M. Foley; the brewer Thomas Tindall; the grocers R. J. and G. R. Wrangham and Robert and G. W. Lance; the miller R. T. Kirby of Bell Mills; the tailor and draper Francis Dry, and the timber merchants Matthew Blakeston and William Stainton, besides several farmers from the vicinity.[7] Not all were so well off; for example Joseph Barnett (d. 1869), the last of the town's hand-loom weavers, was superintendent of the Sunday school for many years.[8] The trustees of the Wesleyan chapel in the 1920s included three timber merchants, Horace Taylor and Henry and John Naylor; Thomas Wilson, a coal merchant; E. B. and J. B. Bradshaw of Bell Mills; the printer Leonard Sokell; G. M. and W. H. Blakeston, respectively accountant and solicitor, and William Wilson, the temperance draper.[9] Both the Blakestons and the Bradshaws continued to be prominent in the affairs of the re-unified Methodist church in the later 20th century.[10]

Primitive Methodist The Primitive Methodist chapel had 450 seats, 110 of them free, and standing room for about 130 people in 1851. On Census Sunday that year, the morning service was attended by 30 people, the one in the afternoon by 280, and the evening service by 330, and a Sunday school was held for 40 children.[11] There were 225 children in the Sunday school that year.[12] The numbers attending the chapel and school caused both to be enlarged. The walls of the chapel were raised in 1856 and additional windows and a new gallery inserted.[13] The school was enlarged in 1864 and the chapel walls heightened again in 1865.[14] The chapel was licensed for marriages in 1850 and a dozen years later it was said that for every one marriage solemnised in the parish church there were four in the Primitive Methodist chapel.[15]

In 1873–4 a new chapel was built in George Street, the first chapel subsequently being used as a temperance hall.[16] The impressive new building seated 1,000 people; other premises on the site included eleven schoolrooms and classrooms, and the total cost was £5,000.[17] Within its first decade the congregation of the new chapel was said to have doubled.[18] Membership at 168 in 1862, with 450 hearers, reached a peak of 321 in 1881, with 750 hearers and 430 in the Sunday school.[19] By the late 1880s membership had fallen to 251, much affected earlier in the decade by the 'operations' of the Salvation Army and United Christian Army. At least one lay preacher joining the Salvationists.[20]

The George Street chapel headed what at one time was the most numerous country circuit in the Primitive Methodist connexion.[21] By the late 19th century the circuit had 1,500 members, and some 30 village branches, as well as a mission room in North Street.[22] The circuit was served by four ministers in the later 19th century, and in the earlier 20th century by three, all resident in Driffield.[23] Ministers at Driffield in the later 19th century included Henry Woodcock, author of *Piety Among the Peasantry: being Sketches of Primitive Methodism on the Yorkshire Wolds* (1889) and other books, and Charles Kendall (1881–2), who whilst at the chapel served as President of the Primitive Methodist

1 Ibid. 304/202/162; 1275/251/226.

2 *HP* 27 July 1883.

3 Copy of Driffield Wesleyan Circuit Plan, 1877 in possession of D. Neave, 2010.

4 ERAO, NCH/39/1.

5 RDB, GQ/326/338; TNA, HO 107/2366. For earlier houses for ministers near the chapel, see under 'Wesleyan trustees' in ERAO, PE/10/T. 120; ibid. TA/13.

6 RDB, 366/253/201; 394/525/411; 405/177/147.

7 Ibid. FI/271/257; IX/17/24; KA/284/384; NZ/396/568; 50/449/412 (1892); ERAO, EB/1/144; directories; *Wesleyan Methodist Magazine* 19 (July 1873), 670–2 (Robert Lance).

8 Nicholson, *Capital of the Yorks. Wolds*, 16–17.

9 RDB, 240/9/6; 242/437/332; 366/253/201.

10 Ibid. 861/449/378; 1352/5/5; 1401/436/390; *DT* 24 June 1993.

11 *Yorks. Worship Returns 1851*, i. 91.

12 ERAO, MRD/2/4/1.

13 *Driffield Observer* 1 Oct. 1856.

14 ONS (Birkdale), Worship Reg. no. 16855; RDB, IW/236/327; Ross, *Driffield*, 77; Neave, *ER Chapels*, 50; ERAO, DDX/17/15.

15 *HP* 25 Jan. 1850; Woodcock, *Piety*, 91.

16 Below, soc. hist., temperance.

17 RDB, LF/118/156; Bulmer, *Dir. E Yorks.* (1892), 167. Illus. at HUL, DX/144/3 (A 5068/28), and in Neave, *ER Chapels*, 69 and Harrison, *Driffield*, facing p. 113. The new chapel was registered in 1874: ONS (Birkdale), Worship Reg. no. 21959; *Lond. Gaz.* 13 Oct. 1874, pp. 4689–90.

18 Ross, *Driffield*, 77.

19 ERAO, MRD/2/4/2–3.

20 Ibid. MRD/2/4/3.

21 J. S. Werner, *The Primitive Methodist Connexion: Its Background and Early History* (1984), 107.

22 Ross, *Driffield*, 190; Bulmer, *Dir. E Yorks.* (1892), 167. It was presumably that mission room which later was said to accommodate 100 people: BIA, V. 1912–22/Ret.

23 BIA, V. 1912–22/Ret.; V. 1931/Ret.; Bulmer, *Dir. E Yorks.* 170.

Conference.[1] His successor at Driffield, Richard Harrison, was chairman of Driffield School Board in 1883.[2] In 1851 the superintendent, Thomas Ratcliffe, and another minister were living in Middle Street South, and another two ministers lodged with a grocer in Westgate.[3] Two houses in Lockwood Street (nos. 17–18) were apparently bought in the 1876, and in 1892 they were occupied by the superintendent and another minister; the other two ministers then lived in George Street, presumably in rented accommodation.[4] Another house, no. 10 George Street, was bought in 1925,[5] and in 1937 no. 2 Carlton Villas, Lockwood Street, was left by Clara Miller to the George Street congregation, by then united with the Wesleyan Methodists, for a minister's house.[6]

Membership of the George Street chapel declined from 257 in 1901, to 214 in 1910 and 186 in 1921.[7] The chapel still claimed 450 adherents in 1931.[8]

In 1932 the Primitive Methodist Church united with those of the Wesleyan Methodists and the United Methodists to form one Methodist Church, though in Driffield, as elsewhere, some Primitive Methodists stood aside from the union.[9]

William Nipe, grocer and corn dealer, Joseph Booth, brewer, Edward Moody and Thomas Foster, joiners, Thomas Wood, shoemaker, Matthew Collinson, farmer, and one or two labourers were prominent in the congregation in the mid 19th century.[10] Thomas Jackson (d. 1863), grocer, 'of portly build, and awesome bearing' was society and circuit steward and Sunday school superintendent for many years; he was followed by Isaac Miller, blacksmith.[11] In 1908 the trustees included James Reed and John Dossor, wholesale grocers, George Verity, draper, David Railton, coal merchant, and Alfred Longbottom, aerated water manufacturer.[12] Samuel Henry Gibson, the ironfounder, a bank manager, Walter Hives, and a number of railway workers were amongst the trustees in 1920.[13]

At Little Driffield the building being used for Primitive Methodist services in 1851, perhaps the earlier house, had free seating for 30 people and standing room for 20 more, and on average 30 people attended the Sunday evening service provided there.[14] The community evidently prospered, in 1861 registering for worship a building in Little Driffield, then occupied by John Foster, and in 1878 building themselves a chapel to accommodate 200 people.[15] The chapel stood on land given by Lord Londesborough at the west end of the village, on the south side of the main road.[16] Membership of the chapel ranged from 24 to 34 in the 1880s–90s with 50–60 attenders.[17] There were 25 adherents in 1931.[18]

Primitive Methodist (Continuing) A group of local Primitive Methodists separated from the rest of the congregation at Methodist union in the 1932.[19] A warehouse in Westgate was converted into the Bourne Primitive Methodist (Continuing) chapel and opened in 1933 and registered in 1936.[20] The trustees in 1934 included Frederick Pickering and George Everett (d. 1951), respectively a shoemaker and a grocer of the town, besides other members of the congregation from Hutton Cranswick, North Frodingham, Beswick, and Lockington.[21]

Wesleyan Reform, later United Methodist Free Church A Wesleyan Reform congregation was formed at Driffield in 1853 as a result of the expulsion of a local preacher, Peter Cowen (d. 1876), from the Wesleyan Methodist chapel for preaching to Wesleyan Reformers at Bridlington.[22] By the end of 1853 the Wesleyan Reformers had taken part of the Corn Exchange as a place of worship and the next year they opened a small chapel in Harland Lane.[23] In 1863 two of the founders, Cowen, a letter carrier, and James Wilson, grocer and draper, purchased land in Bridge Street to build a chapel which was opened the following year.[24] Built at a cost of £700 the chapel, which had 200 sittings, was designed by Charles E. Taylor, the 20-year old son of Richard Taylor, manager of the Driffield branch of the York Union Bank who was another founder member of the

1 Ross, *Driffield*, 78; F. Ross, *Celebrities of the Yorks. Wolds* (1878), 177–8; *HP* 12 May 1882. Charles Kendall was the father of H. B. Kendall, author of the *History of the Primitive Methodist Church*, 2 vols.

2 *HP* 6 Apr. 1883.

3 TNA, HO 107/2366; *Yorks. Worship Returns 1851*, i. 91.

4 RDB, 103/51/39; Woodcock, *Piety*, 95; Bulmer, *Dir. E Yorks.* (1892), 170.

5 RDB, 301/639/491.

6 Ibid. 576/89/72; 584/116/91.

7 ERAO, MRD/2/5/24, 53, 100.

8 Ibid. MRD/2/4/14.

9 Below, this section, Primitive Methodist (Continuing).

10 RDB, IH/164/198; IW/236/327; LF/118/156; *Kelly's Dir. N & ER Yorks.* (1872), 354; ERAO, MRD/2/6/1.

11 Woodcock, *Piety*, 90, 94; *Primitive Methodist Sunday School, George Street, Driffield 1828–1928 Souvenir* (1928), [10]; E Yorks. Family Hist. Soc., *Driffield MIs*, 13.

12 RDB, 657/62/58; directories.

13 RDB, 712/456/388.

14 TNA, HO 107/2366 [Middle Street]; *Yorks. Worship Returns 1851*, i. 91.

15 ONS (Birkdale), Worship Reg. nos. 12622, 24365; *HP* 31 May 1878; Woodcock, *Piety*, 126.

16 OS Map 1:2,500, Yorks. CLXI. 11 (1893 edn); RDB, 162/313/256; 301/639/491.

17 ERAO, MRD/2/4/3–4.

18 Ibid. MRD/2/4/14.

19 Above, this section, Primitive Methodist.

20 *HT* 29 July 1933; ONS (Birkdale), Worship Reg. no. 57102.

21 RDB, 490/218/171; *Kelly's Dir. N & ER Yorks.* (1933), 456–7.

22 *HP* 6 June 1851; 4 Mar. 1853; ERAO, MRD/28/8/2.

23 *HP* 4 Nov 1853, 2 June 1854. The latter, then described as a former foundry, was used later by the Salvation Army: below, this section.

24 ERAO, MRD/18/4/14; RDB, IM/323/430.

congregation.[1] The Taylors were key supporters of the Bridge Street chapel. Another son, William Taylor (d. 1917), sewing machine manufacturer, was a lay preacher there and Sunday school superintendent, and William's daughter Hilda Taylor was a trustee and chapel treasurer in 1931.[2]

The Wesleyan Reform congregation amalgamated with the United Methodist Free Church in 1869 and the first resident minister was appointed.[3] The chapel was enlarged and refitted in 1889, and later accommodated 400 people.[4] Membership was always limited; it ranged from 32 in 1864 to 80 in 1883 and 42 in 1931 but from the beginning there was a flourishing Sunday school with 90 members in 1864 and 70 in 1883.[5] Supporters were largely drawn from the families of lesser tradesmen and the trustees in 1921 included a shoemaker, a tailor, a cabinet maker, a confectioner, a gas fitter, a warehouseman, a labourer, a cartman, a gardener, a housekeeper and the female assistant actuary of the Savings Bank.[6]

In 1907 the United Methodist Free Churches joined with other offshoots of Wesleyan Methodism to form the United Methodist Church, which in turn joined with the Wesleyans and Primitive Methodists as the Methodist Church in 1932. The Bridge Street chapel continued in use by the new body until it was closed in 1959 and sold to the Scouts Association.[7]

Particular Baptist

In 1851 the Baptist chapel had 220 seats, 50 of them free, and standing room for a further 30. The congregation was then said to average 130, and on Census Sunday 72 attended the morning service, 120 in the evening, and there were 36 children at the Sunday school.[8]

A new chapel, designed by William Hawe, was built on the west side of Middle Street South in 1861–2.[9] The chapel, largely paid for Miss Mary Drinkrow, a member of the congregation, cost about £1,500 and was registered for worship in 1864.[10] The large stuccoed building was refronted in red brick with Whitby stone dressings to the designs of J. F. Shepherdson in 1884, when three classrooms were added to the schoolroom.[11] It subsequently seated 300, and had room for 150 children in the Sunday school.[12] Despite such developments there was a significant drop in support at this time. The number of members fell from 56 in 1883 to 46 in 1886 and the number of Sunday scholars fell from 115 to 77 Sunday scholars.[13]

The former chapel and the cottages in the later King Street had been sold in the 1870s, the old chapel and vestry being bought in 1872 for a freemasons' lodge,[14] and so used until *c.* 1920.[15] The building was later the Conservative Club, before being sold to the WVS, later the WRVS, in 1963. It was afterwards known as Cass Hall.[16] The burial ground was sold to the WRVS in 1967; it still contained 15 gravestones in 2010.[17]

There may have been a manse in Exchange Street from 1805.[18] A new manse, no. 19 Lockwood Street, was built in 1876,[19] but in 1892 the Baptist minister was living in New Road.[20] Trustees appointed in 1850 included Thomas D. Whitaker, accountant and tax collector, the leading Baptist in the town in the later 19th century and Henry Angas, grocer and draper, who had moved to the Independents by 1869.[21] The latter's father Caleb Angas, farmer and agricultural writer, worshipped at the church.[22]

Independent, later Congregational

In 1851 the Driffield chapel had 350 seats, 50 of them free, and on Census Sunday that year 160 people attended the morning service, 230 that in the evening, and there were 59 children in Sunday school. Much building work was done in the 1860s at a cost of some £3–4,000. A new Sunday school for 450 children was built on the north side of Exchange Street in 1862,[23] and in 1866–7 Zion Providence chapel was rebuilt to seat 500 people. The building was later known as the Congregational church.[24] There seems to have been no

1 *HP* 25 Sept 1863; TNA, HO107/2366; ONS (Birkdale), Worship Reg. no. 16151.

2 *DT* 1 Dec 1917; HRO, DCW/490; website: www.sewalot.com/taylorsewingmachine.

3 *DT* 28 Aug., 4 Sept. 1869; HRO DCW/490. The chapel was re-registered as a United Methodist Free Church in 1874: ONS (Birkdale), Worship Reg. no. 21806; *Lond. Gaz.* 5 June 1874, p. 2912.

4 BIA, V. 1912–22/Ret.; Bulmer, *Dir. E Yorks.* (1892), 167; Neave, *ER Chapels*, 14 (illus.), 50.

5 ONS (Birkdale), Worship Reg. no. 16151; *DT*, 6 Jan. 1883; HRO, DCW/490.

6 RDB, IM/323/430; 6/149/129 (1898); 232/200/164; 750/199/163. The last was Hilda Taylor.

7 ERAO, MRD/18/2/2, MRD/18/4/26.

8 *Yorks. Worship Returns 1851*, i. 90.

9 ERAO, EB/1/138; *HP* 11 Oct. 1861; 6 June 1862.

10 ONS (Birkdale), Worship Reg. no. 16465; *Lond. Gaz.* 13 Jan. 1865, p. 170; *Baptists of Yorks.* 207.

11 *The British Architect*, 3 Oct. 1884; *HP* 3 Oct 1884.

12 Ross, *Driffield*, 71–2, 185; Bulmer, *Dir. E Yorks.* (1892), 166; Neave, *ER Chapels*, 50; OS Map 1:2,500, Yorks. CLXI. 12 (1893, 1910 edns).

13 *DT* 6 June 1883; 6 Nov. 1886.

14 RDB, KY/300/397; LG/26/35; ERAO, EB/1/156–7, 168.

15 Above, soc. hist., freemasons.

16 ERAO, UDDR/1/1/37, Housing...Cttee, 2 Mar. 1964; RDB, 1335/516/472; 1486/594/382; name and date 1987 in glazing of door.

17 ERAO, EB1/168/1; Petch, *Driffield Cemetery MIs*, 153, 156.

18 Above, this section, 1700 to *c.* 1840 (Particular Baptist).

19 ERAO, EB/1/147, 168; ibid. NV/1/107; *Baptists of Yorks.* 207.

20 Bulmer, *Dir. E Yorks.* (1892), 170.

21 ERAO, EB/1/113, 128, 138, 147, 165; RDB, GS/107/100; *DT* 6 Nov. 1886; below, this section, 1840 to 1940 (Independent).

22 *DNB*, *s.v.* Caleb Angas; Petch, *Driffield Cemetery MIs*, 156.

23 *HP* 16 Oct. 1863; RDB, 92/129/120 (1897); Bulmer, *Dir. E Yorks.* (1892), 166; Miall, *Congregationalism*, 256; Ross; OS Map 1:2,500, Yorks. CLXI. 12 (1893, 1910 edns).

24 ONS (Birkdale), Worship Reg. no. 18038; Bulmer, *Dir. E Yorks.* (1892), 166; Miall, *Congregationalism*, 256; *Lond. Gaz.* 9 Aug. 1867, p. 4421; Neave, *ER Chapels*, 50, 65 (illus.).

54. *Great Driffield: Providence Congregational church, Exchange Street* c. *1980. Built 1866–7, replacing a chapel of* c. *1800.*

manse in the mid 19th century, the minister living in his mother-in-law Elizabeth Harrison's house in Middle Street South in 1851,[1] but one was built in 1889 on the corner of The Avenue and Bridlington Road.[2] The work of the congregation beyond the town was probably continued in the later 19th century, and in 1915 North Frodingham chapel and its affiliated chapels became part of the Driffield pastorate.[3] The Congregational church in Driffield was confident enough to consider building another school in the early 20th century but that plan was later abandoned.[4]

The first trustees had been mostly regional Independent ministers or prominent co-religionists of Hull, but by the mid century, besides the minister, five of those appointed were from Driffield, among them George Shepherdson, builder and cabinet maker, and Henry Angas, grocer and draper, formerly a leading Baptist.[5] The Shepherdsons' connection with the Exchange Street church was a long one. George's son William built the organ in the old chapel in 1847,[6] he and his two sons George and Joseph served successively as organists for over 60 years.[7] John F. Shepherdson was for a time a member of the congregation but in later life was said to have held himself aloof from sectarianism.[8] Joseph Shepherdson, architect, was a Congregational trustee in 1904.[9] Other prominent members have included Henry. D. Marshall, miller, one of the deacons; William Bradshaw, gardener, superintendent of the Sunday school; Matthew Boak, photographer; Peter Sibree, engineer; Sir Luke White, MP and solicitor, Herbert Brown, solicitor and Dr Eames and his family.[10] Leading ministers included Henry Birch, 1842–56, a supporter of the Mechanics' Institute and author of several books, some printed in Driffield, William Mitchell, 1856–72, and R. F. Bracey, 1885–1917, who helped build it into the most influential congregation in the town.[11]

Other Protestant Nonconformists

Society of Friends A Quaker meeting was held in the Wesleyan Sunday school in November 1869, but it is not known if this became a more regular event.[12]

Salvation Army The Salvation Army arrived in the town in October 1881 when a certain Major Thompson established a barracks in the club room at the Red Lion.[13] The venture which was subjected to interference from local 'roughs' was short-lived and was abandoned the following month.[14]

In 1884 the Army returned and took over the old foundry in Harland Lane, formerly used by the Wesleyan Reformers, for weekday use, and the assembly room in the Corn Exchange for Sunday services.[15] They used the Temperance Hall in Mill Street from 1889; but this had been given up by 1896.[16] The Army is not mentioned in directories at this time but

1 TNA, HO 107/2366.

2 RDB, 26/343/304 (1888); Bulmer, *Dir. E Yorks.* (1892), 166.

3 *VCH Yorks. ER.* vii. 268.

4 RDB, 64/18/17 (1904); 140/466/422; 227/457/384.

5 Ibid. IB/323/412.

6 Sheahan and Whellan, *Hist. York & ER.* ii. 499.

7 *Nonconformist Musical Jnl*, Jan. 1891, 7.

8 *DT* 14 Dec. 1901.

9 RDB, 63/47/45 (1904). Relationships from E. Spehr, Hackham West, S. Australia, 2004.

10 RDB, GS/107/100; KM/266/357; 26/343/304; 26/344/305 (1888); 63/47/45 (1904); 717/549/466; 753/284/235. *HP* 16 Sept. 1881; *DT* 23 Nov 1901.

11 Miall, *Congregationalism*, 256; *DT* 23 Nov. 1901; Ross, *Driffield*, 69, 179; inf. from Mr E. Spehr, Hackman West, S. Australia, 2004; e.g. H. Birch, *Princes against People; or, The Fall of Hungary* (1853) printed by J. C. Blakeston, Driffield.

12 *HP* 13 Nov. 1869.

13 Ibid. 28 Oct. 1881.

14 *Eastern Morning News* 14 Apr. 1882.

15 *HP* 25 Apr., 2 May, 18 July 1884; ONS (Birkdale), Worship Reg. no. 28025.

16 ONS (Birkdale), Worship Reg. nos. 28099, 31332.

they had a barracks in the town in 1894.[1] Premises in Church Street were registered in 1900 but these were given up by 1910, and where or whether the Army operated for the next few years is not known.[2] In 1925 services were being held in Mill Street, possibly in the Temperance Hall, and that year a hall in Empire Buildings, Middle Street North was registered for the Army's use.[3] That hall was replaced in 1931 by a new building, the Citadel in Eastgate South.[4]

United Christian Army This Evangelical organization, founded in the West Riding in 1880 with its base in Goole, had a branch in Driffield by 1882 when a mission hall in Church Street and the Temperance Hall in Mill Street were registered for the worship of its members.[5] Driffield became one of the United Christian Army's main centres, and its fourth anniversary was celebrated there at a great public meeting in the Temperance Hall in September 1884. On the platform were representatives of nearly all the sects in the town including the Anglicans, Independents, Baptists and Wesleyan Methodists.[6] When the Army had its half-yearly conference at Driffield in January 1885, the Independent and United Methodist chapels were made available for its use and at the public meeting the vicar, Horace Newton, took the chair and spoke of the good work the Army had done in the town.[7]

In July 1885 a split occurred in the United Christian Army over the actions of the leader the Revd William Garner, and Mr Watts, the evangelist based in Driffield, seceded from the sect and took with him a large following of the members. Garner sent down another evangelist, Mr Machin, to secure possession of the hall in Church Street, which he did by breaking down the door. The police were called in to deal with the tumult that followed. On the following Sunday the Army and the secessionists each held outdoor services accompanied by a brass band. Mr Watts attracted a large crowd which stood quietly aside as the 'soldiers' led by Mr Machin 'filed past singing and trumpeting forth the words and music'. There was great support for Watts in the town and the owner of the hall in Church Street confirmed him as tenant.[8] Nothing further is known of the United Christian Army or the secessionists; they were not recorded in the 1889 directory or afterwards.[9] The Temperance Hall had ceased to be used by 1896 and the mission hall was de-registered in 1900, perhaps becoming for a few years the barracks of the Salvation Army instead.[10]

Plymouth Brethren A congregation of Plymouth Brethren were worshipping in rooms in Chapel Lane, later King Street, with two services on a Sunday by 1901.[11] They still met there in 1910, but were not recorded again until 1931 when they had a place of worship for some 500 people.[12] This was probably Emmanuel Hall, at River Head, mentioned in 1933.[13] The hall recorded in the 1940s, probably made from the outbuildings of the nearby Southorpe Lodge, was being used by a military club in 1970.[14]

Roman Catholicism

Roman Catholicism, which seems to have played little part in the religious life of the parish after the Reformation,[15] was revived in the late 19th century. A Catholic priest was appointed to serve Driffield by December 1882 and early the following year 'eight or nine' persons were confirmed by the Bishop of

55. *Great Driffield: Apse of the Roman Catholic church of Our Lady and St Edward, Westgate, 2006. The church was built in 1885–6.*

1 BIA, V. 1894/Ret. 2.
2 ONS (Birkdale), Worship Reg. no. 37948; directories.
3 ONS (Birkdale), Worship Reg. no. 50024; directories.
4 ONS (Birkdale), Worship Reg. no. 53180; *DT* 7 Feb., 4 July 1931.
5 *HP* 23 June 1882, 15 June 1883; ONS (Birkdale), Worship Reg. no. 26092.
6 *HP* 3 Oct. 1884.
7 Ibid. 16 Jan. 1885.
8 Ibid. 10, 17 July 1885.
9 Directories.
10 ONS (Birkdale), Worship Reg. 26142; above, this section, Salvation Army.
11 *Kelly's Dir. N & ER Yorks.* (1901), 463.
12 ERAO, NV/1/107; BIA, V. 1931/Ret.
13 *Kelly's Dir. N & ER Yorks.* (1933), 453.
14 RDB, 751/463/380; above, soc. hist., military organizations.
15 BIA, Bp. Dio. 3, ER, p. 102; above, this section, 17th cent. (nonconf.)

Middlesbrough in the Corn Exchange, then being used for Roman Catholic services, in the presence of Lord and Lady Herries of Everingham and Lady (Christina Anne Jessica) Sykes of Sledmere.[1] Lady Sykes, who with her son Mark had converted to Roman Catholicism in November 1882, is said to have encouraged the founding of the mission at Driffield.[2] In 1883 Westgate House was bought for a presbytery and a church was built in the grounds in 1886.[3] Dedicated to Our Lady and St Edward, accommodating 200 people, it cost £2,000 and was paid for by Lady Herries of Everingham.[4] By 1892 the priest was providing morning and evening services on Sundays, and a school in the afternoon, and a day school was then being held, perhaps in some adjacent cottages. Father Maurice O'Regan, parish priest from 1908 to his death in 1958, except for five years in the 1930s, was popular through his 'keen interest in town affairs and field sports'.[5] A new presbytery was built in 1926.[6]

AFTER 1940

Anglicanism

The ending in 1940 of Canon Sharrock's ministry, with his death at the age of 98 years,[7] began a period of change and experimentation in the religious life of the parish church, due also probably to relatively frequent changes of incumbent.[8] The long-established Low Church tradition at Driffield was first modified by an increased emphasis on the sacraments and ritual. As early as 1930 Canon Sharrock had denied a complaint about the Romanization of services,[9] but the High Church tendency was evident at the parish church later. The chancel north aisle was being used as a chapel dedicated to the Virgin Mary by 1943, when a processional cross was also introduced, and in 1961 an aumbry was made in the Lady chapel and the sacrament began to be reserved there.[10] Other influences were introduced in the 1980s. The modern liturgy was then adopted for most services in the parish church, and evensong in particular reflected the Charismatic movement. The less sacramental approach was accompanied also by the development of religious activity outside the church building, in the homes of parishioners,[11] offsetting to some extent the closure of St John's church in the 1960s[12] and the mission room or school by 1970.[13] Also closed and sold in the early 1960s was the Church Institute, the proceeds being applied to the maintenance of the Church room,[14] and in 1967 the vicarage house in Downe Street was disposed of, except for part of the grounds which about that date was used to build a smaller vicarage house.[15] One reflection of the less institutional Anglicanism of the late century was the claim made in 1982 that over £4,000 worth of Christian literature had been sold in the church in a two and a half year period.[16]

In the late 20th century the vicar was helped by an honorary curate, and an assistant curate was employed in the late 1990s.[17] The living was vacant in 2004, when a slightly reduced number of services was being supplied by local priests and readers. An evening service and two celebrations of communion were then being provided each Sunday in the parish church, while at Little Driffield communion was fortnightly and there was a morning service every fifth Sunday. At Great Driffield a communion was also celebrated during the week, but other weekday services were then in abeyance. Some services at All Saints included contemporary music played by young musicians, but at St Mary's, Little Driffield, worship was much more traditional, with the 1662 Prayer Book in use and musical accompaniment limited to the organ. Overall, the Church membership was said at the beginning of the 21st century to include representatives of several branches of Anglicanism, including the local Evangelical tradition of the late 19th and earlier 20th century, and the later Anglo-Catholic and Charismatic emphases. In 2004 there were 224 on the electoral roll at All Saints and 43 at St Mary's; attendances on Sundays were usually about 110 and 40 respectively. Church organizations then included the Mothers' Union and the Sunday school.[18]

Nonconformity

Nonconformity also contracted, changed, and to an extent renewed itself in the mid 20th century. Chapel attendance was said to have declined following the First World War,[19] and the importance of the chapels was almost certainly reduced by amalgamation and closure, subsequent to the union in 1932 of the main Methodist churches. That coming together, a reversal of the earlier proliferation of congregations by secession, did, however, itself generate another small congregation in

1 J. A. Barry, *A Hundred Years at Our Lady and St Edward's* (*c*.1986) [1]; *HP* 9 Feb. 1883.
2 C. S. Sykes, *The Big House* (2004), 191–2.
3 *HP* 27 Apr. 1883; *YH* 16 Nov. 1886.
4 *YH* 16 Nov. 1886; BIA, V. 1912–22/Ret.
5 Barry, *Hundred Years* [2].
6 Ibid.
7 ERAO, PE/10/T. 100, s.a. 1940.
8 Driffield clergy list, copy at ERAO.
9 ERAO, PE/10/T. 100.
10 BIA, Fac. Bk. 12, p. 293; ibid. Fac. 1943/40; Fac. 1961/2/25.
11 Brown, *All Saints*, 10.
12 BIA, CD. 583; ibid. OC. 825. The baptisms register and that of services suggest that St John's was little used after 1950: ERAO, PE/10/accession 1197; PE/10/T. 133.
13 ERAO, PE/10/T. 198; OS Map 1:10,000, TA 05 NW (1970 edn).
14 ERAO, PE/10/T. 150.
15 RDB, 1492/384/353; BIA, MGA. 1966/8.
16 *DT* 29 Apr. 1982.
17 *Crockford* (1980–2), 369; (1998–9), 121, 398.
18 Noticeboards at churches; notice sheet for Great and Little Driffield churches, July-Aug. 2004; inf. from Mr D. Longbottom, Driffield, 2004.
19 BIA, V. 1912–22/Ret.

Driffield, a group of continuing Primitive Methodists. The largest of the chapels in the union, the former Wesleyan chapel, became the new Methodist church, and two Primitive Methodist chapels and that of the United Methodists were later closed and converted to other uses. Another chapel, that of the Baptists, had also been closed by 1960, leaving, of the older denominations, only the Methodists and Congregationalists, and the small Continuing Primitive Methodist congregation. Perhaps in part because of their relative numbers in the declining congregations, women members became slightly more prominent in the running of the churches in the 20th century. In 1912 the trustees of the Congregational church had all been men, but in the mid 1940s five women were appointed together with an equal number of men, and similarly eight of the thirty-eight trustees of the re-unified Methodist church in 1964 were women.[1]

There was, however, some activity and growth as well as contraction and closure. The Salvation Army continued its work in the town from its new base, the Citadel in Eastgate, and several Evangelical groups established themselves in Driffield in the later 20th century. The most successful of the new congregations was that which built the small Elim Pentecostal church in Wansford Road in 1951.[2]

Methodist The union of the Methodist churches in 1932 may have had little immediate effect on the Methodist bodies in Driffield which for years afterwards maintained separate chapels.[3] One exception seems to have been the small Primitive Methodist chapel at Little Driffield, which was perhaps closed soon after the unification and certainly was sold in 1937;[4] the building was demolished for the building of Chapel House *c.* 2000.[5] The largest of the town chapels, that of the former Wesleyan Methodists, known by 1950 as Trinity Methodist church,[6] was eventually adopted as the new, united Methodist church; the other chapels closed, and much Methodist property in the town sold. The chapel of the Primitive Methodists in George Street was closed between 1950 and 1964, when the building was de-registered and sold;[7] during its subsequent remodelling for commercial use the façade, already bereft of its turrets,[8] was replaced.[9] In 2004 the former chapel was occupied as a carpet showroom. The former United Methodist chapel in Bridge Street was closed in 1959 and sold to the Scout Association and in 2010 it housed an advertising agency.[10] The ministers' accommodation was also rationalized in the mid century, the house in George Street belonging to the former Primitive Methodists being sold in 1962,[11] and Eastlea, Beverley Road, bought for the Methodist minister, evidently in 1964.[12]

At the beginning of the 21st century Driffield Methodist church had a congregation of about eighty,[13] for whom two services and a meeting of the junior church were provided each Sunday.[14] The Methodist manse was by then in King's Mill Road.[15]

Primitive Methodism (Continuing) The plain chapel of the Continuing Methodists was still used in 2005, when its two Sunday services were attended by some fifteen to twenty worshippers, and led by a pastor from Hull.[16]

Baptist Like the other congregations, that of the Baptists shrank in the 20th century, and their chapel in Driffield had been closed by 1960, when the premises were sold for development as a shop.[17]

Congregational The Congregational church was in decline in the 1930s and closure was contemplated in 1942. It continued without a minister for six years, but had revived somewhat by the 1960s.[18] The minister's house, now The Old Manse, was sold in 1946, and replaced the next year by a modern house, no. 56 Manorfield Road,[19] and the Congregational Sunday school had been closed by 1950.[20] The latter building was occupied as flats and by an advice centre in 2004. The Congregational church itself was then an Evangelical body, staffed by two ministers. Morning worship was provided each Sunday in the church, and there were also fortnightly meetings of the Women's Guild there, but much of the ministry was conducted elsewhere. Fortnightly meetings were thus held in members' homes for Bible study, and the church was also involved with the local Alpha course which was promoted on the church's website. In 2010 the Congregational church had 12 members and 18 adherents, five years earlier the church was attended regularly by about 25 people.[21]

1 RDB, 717/549/466; 753/284/235; 1352/5/5.
2 Below, this section.
3 *Kelly's Dir. N & ER Yorks.* (1937), 445.
4 RDB, 574/12/11.
5 *DT* 5 Aug. 1998 (illus.).
6 RDB, 861/449/378.
7 ONS (Birkdale), Worship Reg. no. 21959; RDB, 1366/250/232; *DT*, 27 Oct. 1988.
8 Harrison, *Driffield*, facing p. 113.
9 ERAO, UDDR/1/1/38, Building...Cttee, 7 July 1964; 2 Feb. 1965; Neave, *ER Chapels*, 50, 69.
10 ERAO, MRD/18/2/2, MRD/18/4/26; *HDM* 1 Apr. 1977.
11 RDB, 1278/62/58.
12 Ibid. 1401/436/390.
13 Inf. from the Revd Ian Jones, Driffield, 2005.
14 Noticeboard at church, 2003.
15 Inf. from Mr D. Longbottom, Driffield, 2004.
16 Inf. from the Revd Ian Jones, Driffield, 2005.
17 ERAO, EB/1/138.
18 Driffield Congregational Church website (www.d-c-c.org.uk), 2010
19 RDB, 738/387/324; 768/341/291.
20 Inf. from Driffield & District Access Group, Market House, 2004. The schoolroom was used in the mid 1940s by the WVS: ER CC *Mins* 1945–6, 254.
21 Driffield Congregational Church website, 2010; inf. from the Revd Ian Jones, Driffield, 2005.

Salvation Army The Salvation Army continued its work into the 21st century but in or by 2000 closed its base, the Citadel,[1] which stood disused in 2003. The Army was then holding two services each Sunday in the small Elim Pentecostal church in Wansford Road,[2] and the following year the Roman Catholic church was used for an Army service.[3] A house church had been established at no. 125 The Mount by 2005, when about twenty-five members were worshipping there.[4]

Elim Pentecostal Church (Driffield Christian Fellowship) Evangelicals opened a small, newly-built church at no. 35a Wansford Road as the Elim Foursquare Gospel Pentecostal church in 1951.[5] Later the congregation used the town hall instead or as well as the Wansford Road building.[6] By 2003 the Salvation Army were holding two Sunday services in the church, which was then known as the Driffield Christian Fellowship chapel.[7] In 2005 membership of the Elim church stood at about fifty but congregations often numbered eighty or more. Two Sunday services were then held, usually at the community centre in Mill Street but once a month at Driffield School instead.[8] In 2010 the Sunday meetings were usually in the Performing Arts Building at Driffield School.[9]

Christian Brethren A building in George Street called the Gospel Hall was used for worship by the Christian Brethren from 1952, but it had been closed by 1981.[10]

Jehovah's Witnesses The sect opened Kingdom Hall at no. 66 Middle Street North in 1957.[11] No more is known of it.

River Church The River Church, an independent Evangelical body formed about 2000 by secession from the Kingdom Faith Ministeries, acquired the former foundry on Cross Hill for its worship. In 2005 its congregation was put at between 35 and 40.[12]

Roman Catholicism

After the Second World War the Roman Catholic church had a sizeable congregation drawn from Driffield and surrounding area. There were 157 parishioners at Mass on the 4th Sunday of Lent in 1959.[13] A parish hall was erected in the early 1960s and it became the centre of much weekday activity.[14] In the early 21st century there was a thriving branch of the Catholic Women's League and an active Parish and Social Commitee, and congregations were increasing.[15]

LOCAL GOVERNMENT AND POLITICS

BEFORE THE 19TH CENTURY

The local government of Driffield and its neighbourhood was for long chiefly the concern of the various manorial courts. Much of each court's time was taken up with the regulation of the main economic activity of the area, agriculture, and with the related matter of drainage. In the case of Driffield's court, the acquisition of a market and fairs, and later of some industry, also added rudimentary responsibilities for public health and fair trading. On the other hand, the high proportion of land in Driffield and its neighbourhood held by freeholders seems to have made the courts of little significance in the local land market.

The manorial courts also acquired jurisdiction over matters belonging to the king or to his representative in the county, the sheriff. The franchise exercised most often by manorial courts was that of administering an ancient system of peacekeeping called the frankpledge.[16]

Alongside the manorial courts, the district had another focus for local government, the church and its territory, the parish.[17] Nothing is known of the activities of parish meetings or vestries in the parish or parishes of Driffield in the Middle Ages. As later, their core activity would have been maintaining the fabric and services of the churches, and laying a rate on the parishioners for those purposes. The probable unimportance of parochial administration relative to

1 ONS (Birkdale), Worship Reg. no. 53180.
2 Below, this section.
3 Notice in Little Driffield church, 2004.
4 Inf. from the Revd Ian Jones, Driffield, 2005.
5 ONS (Birkdale), Worship Reg. no. 63017.
6 ERAO, UDDR/1/1/47, Gen. Purposes Cttee, 30 Oct. 1973.
7 Notice at church.
8 Inf. from the pastor, the Revd Arthur Wood, Driffield, 2005.
9 www.driffield-christian-fellowship.org.uk
10 ONS (Birkdale), Worship Reg. no. 63535.
11 Ibid. no. 66149.
12 Inf. from the Revd Ian Jones, Driffield, 2005.
13 R. Carson, *The First 100 Years: A history of the Diocese of Middlesbrough 1878-1978* (1978), 277.
14 Barry, *Hundred Years* [2].
15 *DT* 31 Dec. 2008.
16 Below, this section, manorial admin.
17 Clarke, *Local Govt*, 8–9.

that of Great Driffield's manorial court is suggested by the appointment in the latter of constables for the parishes of Great and Little Driffield.

From the 16th century legislators enhanced the power of the parish by choosing it as the body to deal with several aspects of local government, including the maintenance of roads and the problem of poverty.[1] In fact, the growth in the scope of parish government was probably rather less than might appear from the Acts. For instance, despite the powers of supervision allowed to the parish meeting under the Highway Act of 1555, the customary obligation on parishioners to keep local roads in repair was enforced later in Driffield manor court. On the other hand, from the middle of the 16th century baptisms, marriages, and burials in Great and Little Driffield parishes were recorded in registers with some thoroughness. However, apart from the registers and some churchwardens' accounts from the 1720s, there are few records of parochial administration before the 19th century.

The choice of the parish as the government's preferred organ of local government was accompanied, earlier and later, by other changes which tended to reduce the role of the manor court. As a law and order measure, frankpledge had been rendered irrelevant finally by the introduction in the 14th century of justices of the peace,[2] and their powers in local administration and justice were later further developed. Similarly, inclosure in the 18th century, which replaced a communal system of agriculture with one of private enterprise, very largely did away with the need for a manorial court as an economic organizer and enforcer.

MANORIAL ADMINISTRATION AND COURTS

The inhabitants of Driffield obtained a measure of freedom from the administration of the king's officers in 1201, when King John let the town and most of the manor of Driffield to the tenants at an increased compound rent of £72 a year net.[3] There is no evidence that any privileges amounting to borough status were gained, but the use in the 1220s of the term 'borough' to refer to Driffield and its dependencies outside the parish was probably of some significance.[4]

Little is known of the government of the manor later in the Middle Ages. What evidence there is then and later suggests that its court, held for absentee lords on a manor largely populated by freeholders, was generally of limited importance. The jurisdiction of the court would seem to have been enlarged in the early 13th century by the king's ownership of Driffield, and the recognition on that account of its court as a royal court, capable of hearing disputes concerning freehold land. In 1218–19 a suit about a freeholding in Kilham was thus claimed to belong to Driffield court, and the sheriff was then ordered to summon that body to examine the matter.[5] A few years later the royal justices similarly referred a suit over land in Driffield back to the manor because it was part of the royal demesne.[6]

The 13th-century court was also responsible for maintaining law and order on the manor, a task probably fulfilled largely through the ancient frankpledge system;[7] oversight of the frankpledge on the manor was certainly later part of the court's jurisdiction.[8] The frankpledge was reviewed regularly at particular sessions of the manor court, and it may have been in one of those leet sessions in the early 13th century that Thomas Mifrancays accused another man of killing his sister. The case was anyway later transmitted through the regional court for Harthill wapentake to the royal justices sitting in York. When Thomas's sureties, two Driffield men, failed to bring him to court, the bailiff or serjeant (*serviens*) of William de Forz, count of Aumale and then the lord of Driffield, was ordered to arrest him.[9] Besides the frankpledge, other royal rights of justice were claimed by later lords of the manor, after its cession by the Crown. About 1280 John de Balliol, lord of Driffield, was thus claiming the related franchises of hanging thieves caught on the manor (*infangenethef*) and having a gallows. His claim was challenged by the Crown, on the grounds that those liberties had not been specified in its earlier grant of the manor to Balliol's predecessors.[10] The power to judge a thief was, nevertheless, mentioned as belonging to Driffield court in 1290.[11]

The court at Driffield was mentioned again in 1304, when the manor was once again in the king's hands.[12] It was then held every three weeks,[13] but some of the tenants may have attended much less frequently. The cottagers at Little Driffield had been said a few years before to have owed suit to the lord's court only three times a year, although they had to attend additionally when summoned by the lord or to judge a thief. Perhaps significantly, the profits of the court then added relatively little to the manorial income.[14]

Later references to the administration of Driffield manor are few. The steward of the court was said to

1 Ibid. 27–8, 52.
2 Ibid. 21.
3 *Rot. Chart.* (Rec. Com.), 85; There are references to the king's *ministri* in 1107, two of whom are named. *EYC* I, 333–6.
4 *Bk of Fees*, i. 356. Cf. ibid. ii. 1354.
5 *Rolls of the Justices in Eyre for Yorks.* ed. D. M. Stenton (Selden Soc. 66), pp. 48–9, 59.
6 *Cur. Reg. R.* xi, p. 439.
7 Below, this section, police.
8 RDB, H/391/806; HUL, DDCV/42/4.
9 *Rolls of Justices in Eyre*, pp. 305–6, 327.
10 *Yorks. Hund. and Quo Warr. R.* (YAS Rec. Ser. 151), 211–12; H. S. Bennett, *Life on the English Manor* (1937), 196.
11 Below, next para.
12 Above, manors & estates, Driffield manor.
13 *Abbrev. Plac.* (Rec. Com.), 250.
14 *Yorks. Inq.* ii, p. 96.

have been assaulted while holding a court at Driffield in 1347, and the office of bailiff was recorded in the 1360s and 1559.[1]

Insignificant profits may account in part for the evident lack of care in keeping its records. Already in 1638 the lord of the manor was claiming that no court records existed,[2] and the court rolls do not seem to have survived. However, there are many subsidiary papers dating from the 1730s to 1825, which shed light upon the modern court.[3]

By the 18th century the court usually met annually in April, evidently under the stewardship of a local lawyer.[4] The court's executive officer was the bailiff, and a second bailiff was sometimes employed by the steward,[5] and two or three affeerors were appointed to set fines in the court. The court's business was varied, comprising oversight of tenurial arrangements on the manor; regulation of agriculture and drainage in the two Driffields, and of the district's commercial life, and the old duty of maintaining law and order, which was fulfilled in part by the regular appointment of two constables for Great Driffield and one for Little Driffield. Tenants of the manor, both freeholders and lessees, were admitted and sworn in the court, and it was there that attempts were made to prevent the unlicensed sub-letting of holdings. The supervision of farming and drainage was in the hands of four bylawmen and four or five grip/drain-searchers, often the same individuals, and one or two pinders. There was presumably less to do after inclosure in 1742, but with much of land left open pastoral offences continued to provide the bylawmen and the pinder with work into the 19th century.[6] The supervision of the watercourses in particular may have been concerned largely, and increasingly, with the town beck. In 1740 a fine was laid for the washing of 'puddings', or entrails, there [7] and in the 1820s the court licensed a Driffield tanner to dam the stream near his premises.[8]

The commercial life of the town, particularly the retailing of bread and ale, had probably long been regulated by the lord, and that aspect of his court's activity almost certainly grew as its rural work lessened during the 18th century. One or two aletasters/market searchers were appointed in the 18th century, and more officers were added in the early 19th century, reflective of the revival of the market.[9] Among the new posts were those of up to four inspectors of weights and measures and three market searchers; the offices were usually held by the same individuals, two of whom were also constables of Great Driffield. Ale-tasting seems, on the other hand, to have declined in importance, that office being combined in the 19th century with those of bailiff and pinder. Other mercantile posts added then included two leather searchers. Commercial dealing in the town was facilitated, moreover, by the court leet's function as a place where small debts – sums up to £2 – could be recovered.[10] This was still happening once a year in 1840, when the court met on Easter Tuesday; the steward presided as 'judge', a jury was formed from the respectable inhabitants, and the lessee of the tolls and town's crier acted as bailiff.[11]

Thomas Etherington held the lease of Courthouse Close in 1589, and the unlocated court house was mentioned again in 1723,[12] but by the early 19th century courts were being held in the house of William, and later of Mary, Witty, the Red Lion inn, Middle Street.[13] The inn was also the venue for courts of pie-powder held on the days of the manorial fairs at Little Driffield.[14] The court leet was still held in 1840.

Tenants on the rectorial manor of Driffield had to attend its court in the late 13th century, and sessions were evidently still being held by the prebendary in the mid 17th century.[15] The court probably lapsed soon afterwards, and *c.* 1700 the tenants owed money rents but no suit of court.[16] It was said in 1779 that there had formerly been reckoned to be 40 houses in the two Driffields belonging to St Peter's liberty and the prebend of Driffield, and that the current prebendary had the right (implicitly not then being exercised) to hold a court there.[17] Those parts of the two Driffields that were within the liberty of St Peter's still acknowledged the liberty's jurisdiction up to its abolition in 1838.[18] Three years earlier four Driffield alehouses, including the Red Lion and the Black Swan, had been licensed at the brewster sessions held at York for the liberty.[19]

1 *Cal. Pat.* 1345–8, 320; 1361–4, 428; 1364–7, 157; TNA, C 142/157, no. 68.

2 TNA, C 3/399/161.

3 Call rolls 1730–1817 (HUL, DDCV/42/1); papers, including by-laws, 1733–1817 (ibid. DDCV/42/2); presentments 1733–1818 (ibid. DDCV/42/3); papers 1733–52 (ibid. DDCV/42/4); by-laws 1769 (ibid. DDCV/42/9); verdict papers, presentments 1818–25 (NYRO, ZDS/III/10/1/1–9).

4 John Conyers from Malton was steward from the 1730s to 1765; his son William Conyers, then of Driffield, in 1792 (*Universal Brit. Dir.* (*c.* 1792), ii. 827) and in the early 19th century John Lockwood.

5 HUL, DDCV/42/4, s.a. 1733, 1735; DDCV/42/7.

6 Above, econ. hist., agric. (inclosure).

7 HUL, DDCV/42/4, s.a. 1740; J. Wright, *English Dialect Dict.* (1923), iv. 636.

8 NYRO, ZDS/III/10/1/5.

9 Above, econ. hist., mkts and fairs.

10 Pigot, *Yorks. Dir.* (1828–9), 929.

11 *HP* 1 May 1840.

12 BIA, precentorship wills, Thomas Etherington, 1589 (will); RDB, H/392/807.

13 Baines, *Hist. Yorks.* (1823), ii. 196.

14 Above, econ. hist., mkts and fairs.

15 Lamb. Pal. Libr., COMM. XIIa/17/487–8; *Miscellanea*, iv. 27.

16 BIA, Bp. Dio. 3, ER, p. 102.

17 ERAO, DDGR/42/29/10.

18 A. Leake, *The Liberty of St Peter of York 1800–38* (1990), 2, 31–2.

19 YML, F2/3/3/71.

The prebendary also had spiritual and testamentary jurisdiction over all parishioners, enabling him to regulate their sexual and marital behaviour; enforce the payment of tithes and other Church dues, and to prove wills and oversee the administration of testamentary estates. That jurisdiction, belonging to the diocese before being assigned to him with his landed estate, was exercised through the court of the precentor and prebendary in York, contentious cases being heard in the court of the dean and chapter.[1]

A manor of Great Driffield held in the 17th century by the Cromptons may have included a court with view of frankpledge, but no more is known of it.[2]

PARISH GOVERNMENT

The earliest records of parochial administration to survive are the registers recording baptisms, marriages, and burials, which begin in 1556 for Great Driffield and 1579 for Little Driffield.[3] The officer responsible for keeping the registers and doing the parish's other secretarial work was the parish clerk. Separate clerks for Great and Little Driffield are recorded intermittently from 1473 to 1550.[4] In 1595 old inhabitants testified to the election of the parish clerk in the parish church by the parishioners or the majority of them over the preceding half century. That custom seems to have been under challenge from the church authorities in the later 16th century, however. In the 1580s diocesan pressure was exerted successfully on the electors, and when that clerk died, in or about 1595, the vicar refused the choice of the parish, and another man held office briefly without election.[5] The clerk was paid for his work in several ways: he took fees from individual parishioners, for instance at their weddings, and received an annual sum of 7*d.* from each house and 5*d.* from each cottage, and two sheaves of corn from each oxgang at harvest. In the 1720s part of the church rate was also spent on the writing of the registers.[6] Although the corn renders and payments from houses continued to be recorded in the glebe terriers, the former due was almost certainly extinguished at inclosure in 1742, and possibly also the latter, in return for a 3-a. allotment then awarded to the clerk.[7] The land, at Amen Corner on Spellowgate, was evidently rented for £9 a year in the 1880s, that income being divided equally between the churchwardens of Great and Little Driffield churches. The same sum was paid to the clerk as a salary, presumably for serving both churches.[8] The field was later vested in the parochial church council and the York Diocesan Board of Finance which together sold the land in 1971.[9]

The registers apart, virtually no records of parochial government before the 19th century have survived locally. Exceptional are the accounts of John Leason and Robert Carter, churchwardens in 1727 and 1728, which, having been challenged successfully by other parishioners, remain among the records of that dispute.[10] The two rates laid had amounted to almost £69, and a few pounds more than that had been spent, much apparently on building works and glazing. Other expenditure was concerned with the running of the church, or churches, payments being recorded for new bell ropes; for bread and wine; for mending the clock, and for bell ringing, washing, cleaning, and heating. Sums had also been spent on administrative and festive occasions, like the perambulation of the parish boundaries and the ringing supper. Some charity had been dispensed, bread and ale being given to several individuals, and a dozen people being relieved because of their losses by fire, in one case evidently started by lightning. The dispute gives an interesting glimpse into the administrative life in the mid 18th century, as well as illustrating some of the social tensions in the town. In 1729 a meeting to read and sign the accounts had been held in the church porch but objections were then registered by John Stork and for John Boyes. Subsequently, without formal adjournment and in Leason's alehouse, Leason, Thomas Harrison, and Richard Porter persuaded some parishioners to sign the accounts, but others refused. The account book, kept by Richard Harrison, the parish clerk, was later requested by Boyes and Stork, who allegedly detached the 1727–8 record.

Poor Relief

The relief of poverty had to a large extent been the concern of the Church or for private charity in the Middle Ages. After the Reformation, and the loss of religious corporations supporting the poor, that obligation was transferred to the parish by legislation concerned as much with social control as charity. The appointment of two overseers of the poor, to collect and distribute alms, was enacted in 1551–2, and in the 1560s it was made compulsory for parishioners to contribute towards the relief of the poor. A general oversight of the care of the poor belonged also to the

1 Lamb. Pal. Libr., COMM. XIIa/17/485; Purvis, *Medieval Act Book*; S. Brown, *The Medieval Courts of York Minster Peculiar* (1984); C. I. A. Ritchie, *Ecclesiastical Cts of York* (1956), 33 *et seq.*; above, manors and estates, rectory.

2 TNA, CP 25(2)/754/20 Chas II Mich. [20 from end].

3 For Great Driffield marriages and burials are missing for some years *c.* 1600, and the record of marriages is deficient again in the 1690s: ERAO, PE/10/1–4, 16–17, etc. Little Driffield registers. ibid. PE/11/1–4, 6, etc. An incomplete series of transcripts of the registers, beginning in the 17th century, also survives: BIA, Prec. PRT.

4 YML, L2(3)c Visitation book 1472–1550.

5 BIA, D/C. CP. 1595/8; Brown, *All Saints*, 13 has a list of parish clerks from the mid 17th to the early 20th cent.

6 BIA, D/C. CP. 1730/1.

7 RDB, B/153/42; BIA, TER. J. Driffield 1764, etc.

8 ERAO, PE/10/T. 71; ibid. PE 10/T. 88, s.a. 1887, 1892–3.

9 RDB, 1707/266/225.

10 BIA, D/C. CP. 1730/1.

justices of the peace and their appointee, the High Constable of the Bainton Beacon division of Harthill wapentake.[1]

The efforts of the parish were supplemented by local customs and more formal charity. In Elmswell in the 17th century a handful of inferior wool was allowed to the poor when the sheep were clipped, preference being given to those from that place, and women and children were allowed to glean during the corn harvest there. The customary allowances were small concessions, however, and most of the labourers in Elmswell were said in the 17th century to depend upon parochial poor relief. In the Driffields the gleaning[2] and grazing rights enjoyed by the poor were almost certainly reduced by inclosure in 1742, though probably not immediately. The pasturage of the balks, claimed in the 17th century to be communal,[3] was evidently disputed again following inclosure, and in 1769 the tethering of cattle on the 'land ends' was reserved to the owners of the adjacent land.[4] A by-law of 1781 forbidding the keeping of horses, pigs, geese, and sheep in the lanes did allow the jury of the manor court to except animals belonging to the poor of the parishes, however, and a 1783 by-law was made similarly in part to protect the gleaning rights of the poor by barring pigs and cattle from the harvested closes for four days after harvest. Gleaning by the poor was referred to again in 1800, when people from other parishes were said to be gleaning in the Driffields.[5]

In Great Driffield the poor also received by custom two bushels (a *mett*) of wheat on Good Friday from the rectory; in a particularly difficult year, 1623, the rector's lessee was presented for ignoring the custom but then evidently agreed with the overseers to comply by paying 3*s*. 4*d*. a month instead.[6] Another benefit was the 1*s*. from each marriage fee usually given by the incumbent of Driffield in the 18th century.[7]

More formal were the charities set up to help the poor. In 1615 a Driffield yeoman, Harbert Hanley, left £2 to the churchwardens of Great Driffield for a stock for the poor of the town but no more is known of it.[8] Francis Ellis (d. by 1712), an East India official, or a relative Matthew Ellis left money to be invested for the relief of the poor, while in 1714 Walter Crompton devised £1 a year from land in Hutton Cranswick for distribution to poor widows and widowers of Driffield parish.[9] Besides the charities, the poor were helped by single donations, like that of the wealthy Thomas Etherington, who left 10*s*. to the 'poor folks in Driffield' in 1589,[10] and the gifts recorded in the churchwardens' accounts of the 1720s.[11]

The help available from the parish and private individuals was almost certainly small and intermittent, and many of the elderly with limited means probably relied mostly on working relatives. Elizabeth Holmes, a labourer's widow, may have been more formal than others in the arrangements she made in the 17th century with her kinsman, the Driffield labourer Peter Leppington: he was to provide her with board and lodging, 'washing and wringing', and all necessities, and was to bury her and settle her debts, all without charge, in return for all her goods at her death.[12]

The cost of the poor to the parish rose markedly in the later 18th century and the early 19th, in part because of the price inflation accompanying the French wars which pushed some parishioners into poverty, while at the same time making their relief more expensive.[13] In Great Driffield spending on the poor increased in real terms over the period, reflecting but outstripping inflation.[14] The net expenditure in the town was almost £22 in 1760–1 but from the mid 1770s to the early 1790s about £100 a year was usual. Standing at £245 by 1802–3 and more than £400 in the 1810s, the cost continued to escalate to £861 in 1819–20, remained at that level in the 1820s, and then increased again to over £1,000 in 1830–1. Outside the town, in the rural parts of the parish, the increases were at a more modest rate, but again represented real rises in expenditure on the poor. In Little Driffield poor relief cost £6 in 1775–6; £11 in the 1780s; £22 in 1802–3; an average of £55 between 1815 and 1821, and later about £45. The relative burden of looking after the poor is clear from the figures returned for 1812–13: of almost £920 raised by rates in Great Driffield, £485 was spent on the poor; £359 on the church, the roads, and county expenses, and £72 on the militia. As the costs rose, so did the attempts to avoid responsibility for the poor of other parishes or for the children of errant fathers with means. In 1772–3 eight vagrant families were removed from Driffield to their native places;[15] in 1802–3 relief had had to be given to 203 vagrants and others not belonging to Great Driffield township, and in the 1810s its officers spent an average of £55 a year on law suits to limit such liabilities. The number and nature of the poor, and the way in which they were relieved, is indicated by statistics

1 Clarke, *Local Govt*, 18, 24–5, 27–8.
2 BIA, D/C. CP. 1601/5.
3 Above, econ. hist., agric. before inclosure.
4 HUL, DDCV/42/9. 5 Ibid. DDCV/42/2, s.a. 1781, 1783, 1800.
6 BIA, V. 1623/CB. 1, f. 200.
7 Ibid. TER. J. Driffield 1716, 1764.
8 Ibid. precentorship wills, Harbert Hanley, 1615 (will).
9 Below, this section, charities.
10 BIA, precentorship wills, Thomas Etherington, 1589 (will).
11 BIA, D/C. CP. 1730/1.
12 Ibid. precentorship wills, Eliz. Holmes (Howmes), 1634.
13 N. Mitchelson, *Old Poor Law in E Yorks.* (E Yorks. Loc. Hist Ser. 2, 1953), 5.
14 Following based on *Abstract of Returns relative to Expense of Poor* (Parl. Papers, 1803–4 (175), xiii), pp. 588–9; ibid. *1813–15* (Parl. Papers, 1818 (82), xix), pp. 518–19; *Poor Rate Returns, 1816–21* (Parl. Papers, 1822 (556), v), p. 196; *1825–9* (Parl. Papers, 1830–1 (83), xi), p. 227; *1830–4* (Parl. Papers, 1835 (444), xlvii), p. 220; Eden, *State of the Poor*, iii. 819.
15 Harrison, *Driffield*, 176.

collected in the early 19th century. In 1802–3 the town supported 82 poor people, most of them on outdoor relief, that is relieved at home rather than in the poorhouse: outdoor relief was given to 64 permanently and 10 occasionally, and only 8 were maintained in the poorhouse. In Little Driffield 5 were relieved permanently and 1 occasionally, all of them outside the poorhouse. Of those 92 people, 54 were children under 15 years old, disabled, or elderly. About 1815 the town was relieving almost 70 people, with just 5 or 6 of them in the poorhouse; Little Driffield then had 6 poor.

It was apparently the first of Great Driffield's workhouses which was built in the 1770s. That workhouse or poorhouse was put up in 1777 to the east of Beverley Lane, later St John's Road, close to the pinfold.[1] In 1813 the management of the workhouse was held to be unsatisfactory, and a new superintendent, Mary Laybourn, was consequently engaged; besides coals, she was to receive wages and goods worth 4*s.* a week, 3*s.* 6*d.* a week for each inmate, and £1 more for each mother she nursed.[2] That workhouse was replaced by a house in Middle Street North in 1838, and in 1839 the buildings on Pinfold Hill were sold.[3] Other publicly-provided housing for the poor were the two cottages built on waste land at the top of Eastgate North. They were probably the 'small houses for paupers' which the parish was considering building in 1832.[4] Those cottages were demolished after 1910.[5]

FROM THE 19TH CENTURY

Local government was transformed in the 19th century. In response to the rising costs of relieving the poor and the evident inadequacy of much local administration, an Act of 1819 enabled ratepayers to elect a body of local officers, known collectively as a select vestry, to deal with poor relief and other matters, the oversight of the justices being continued but limited where such select vestries were set up.[6] The need for change was evident in Driffield. In 1810 the parish accounts were said to be 'irregularly kept and produced without dates, and many omissions and neglects overloooked injurious to the interests of the parishioners', and in 1813 the management of the workhouse caused concern.[7] Some improvements may have been made before the select vestry was established: vestry minute books survive from about 1810, and there are churchwardens' accounts for Great Driffield from 1818.[8] The select vestry included Little Driffield, and had as its chief officers four overseers of the poor, four constables, four surveyors of highways, one for Little Driffield, and two churchwardens. Apart from the churchwardens, the officers were appointed by the magistrates from lists of candidates presented annually following election by the ratepayers.[9] Besides those long-established parochial officers, new appointments were made of men to collect the local rates and to manage more closely the relief of the poor and the maintenance of the parish's roads. Christopher Laybourne, clockmaker and the vestry clerk, was thus also made the assistant overseer of the poor and collector of the parish rates for the church, the poor, and roads in 1822, while John Meek in 1832 held the office of assistant overseer with that of assistant surveyor of highways.[10] From the 1840s a rate was also laid for lighting and watching and 12 inspectors appointed, a nuisance removal committee of 12 ratepayers was established in 1855, and early in the 1860s a burial board was constituted.[11]

Though parochial administration through the select vestry continued for many years, it was changed and much restricted during the 19th century by the creation of related bodies with either wider or more specific remits. In 1868, after several such developments, the most contentious element of parochial funding was removed, when, following discord in many places, including Driffield,[12] the compulsory church rates, charged on all parishioners, Anglican or not, were abolished by Gladstone's government;[13] subsequently the parish churches were supported by their congregations.[14]

The first of the parish's obligations to be transformed was that of relieving the poor.

1 RDB, AU/369/599; AY/410/681; AZ/136/201; CH/301/480; Eden, *State of Poor*, iii. 819; *DT* 18 Feb. 1998.

2 ERAO, PE/10/T. 99.

3 Ibid. PUD/1/2/2, p. 31; RDB, FM/29/31; below, this section, Driffield poor law union.

4 ERAO, PE/10/T. 99, s.a. 1832, 1856; ibid. TA/13; ibid. PE/10/T. 120.

5 Ibid. NV/1/107.

6 Clarke, *Local Govt*, 33.

7 Above, this section, parish govt (poor relief).

8 ERAO, PE/10/T. 87–8, 99–100. The opening entries in the first vestry volume begin in 1806 but are only random notes; the record of vestry, later parish church meetings, continues to the mid 20th century, but its value for local government is slight after the establishment of the local board in 1873.

9 Ibid. PE/10/T. 99, s.a. 1833, 1837, 1842, 1866; M. A. Crowther, *The Workhouse System 1834–1929* (1981), 11.

10 ERAO, PE/10/T. 99, s.a. 1806, 1822, 1832.

11 Ibid. s.a. 1843, 1844, 1855; below, this section, public services (burial).

12 The Independent minister, the Revd William Mitchell, and a member of that church, Henry Angas, challenged the church rate in 1861: ERAO, PE/10/T. 99; Miall, *Congregationalism*, 256.

13 E. L. Woodward, *The Age of Reform, 1815–70* (1938), 492; Ross, *Driffield*, 180.

14 ERAO, PE/10/T. 99, s.a. 1868; letter of 1869 in ibid. PE/10/T. 88; *DT* 30 Oct. 1869.

56. Great Driffield: Former Union Workhouse, Middle Street North, 2006. The five-bay building had an entrance hall and office on the ground floor. The garage behind occupies more of the workhouse built 1837–8.

DRIFFIELD POOR LAW UNION

The business of housing and otherwise supporting the poor was removed from the parish to a regional authority, the poor law union, which combined the poor and the resources of many townships. In 1836 Great Driffield, Little Driffield, and Elmswell with Kelleythorpe townships, civil areas which together comprised the ecclesiastical parish of Driffield, were thus combined with 40 other neighbouring townships for the purposes of administering the poor laws; as the largest place and fairly centrally situated, Driffield became the head of the union. The total area, of 165 square miles, extended some six or seven miles east, west, and south of the town, and about ten miles to the north, and crossed older wapentake and divisional boundaries; the population of the union in 1851 was over 18,000.[1] Each constituent parish or township continued to bear the cost of its own poor but expenditure on buildings and the salaries of union officers was met by the ratepayers of the union as a whole until 1865, when the whole charge was placed on the union. The board of guardians managing the union, directed to varying extent by a succession of central government bodies,[2] held its meetings at the workhouse until 1898, when the Mechanics' Institute was hired for them instead.[3]

Driffield Poor Law Union responded quickly to the new arrangements, securing a large site extending westwards from Middle Street North to Westgate and building a new workhouse for about 200 people there in 1837–8,[4] replacing earlier houses in Driffield, Nafferton, Foston, and presumably other places.[5] The union workhouses were intended to reduce the numbers being relieved by offering shelter and work instead of outdoor-relief, but in both cases of a kind calculated to dissuade all but the desperate from accepting.[6] In the case of the Driffield house, able-bodied paupers were to be employed breaking stone, the rate being set in 1838 at a ton a day each.[7] Most of those in the house were, however, too young, too old, or too sick to work, in 1853 the 64 inmates comprising 38 children, 15 women, and 11 men, for instance,[8] and the house's function as a refuge and hospital was almost certainly of greater significance than as a place of work. The building was enlarged with an infirmary in 1853 and a block for women in or soon after 1856, and eight doctors were then employed by the union for its indoor and outdoor

1 *3rd Rep. Poor Law Com.* 167–8; Sheahan and Whellan, *Hist. York & ER.* ii. 502; Fig. 15.

2 Crowther, *Workhouse System 1834–1929*, [note on terminology], 23, 51.

3 ERAO, PUD/1/2/18, p. 170. The union records preserved in the East Riding archives at Beverley include the minute books from 1836 to 1930 (ERAO, PUD/1/2/1–27).

4 Ibid. PUD/1/2/1, pp. 101, 106, 217, 251; PUD/1/2/5, p. 198; plan of 1856 at PUD/1/4/1. OS Map 1:10,560, Yorks. CLXI (1855 edn); below, buildings; Fig. 56.

5 ERAO, PUD/1/2/1, p. 286; *VCH Yorks. ER.* ii. 186.

6 Crowther, *Workhouse System*, 41 *and passim.*

7 ERAO, PUD/1/2/1, p. 185.

8 Ibid. PUD/1/2/5, p. 198.

57. *Great Driffield: Union Workhouse, Bridlington Road c. 1910. The new, large workhouse was built next to the cemetery on the eastern edge of the town in 1866–8.*

poor.[1] Pauper children were sent to the National school in 1837, but from the 1850s a master and a mistress were appointed to teach them at the workhouse.[2]

The premises in Middle Street were replaced by a new workhouse for about 180, built on a 7-a. site beside Bridlington Road from 1866; the buildings had evidently been completed by 1868,[3] when the former workhouse was sold, in a manner disapproved of by the poor law board, to the ironfounder Edward Gibson.[4] Layouts involving several smaller buildings more suited to the various groups of inmates were favoured instead of the earlier single building by the 1860s and 1870s, when the second wave of workhouse building was under way nationally,[5] and the Bridlington Road development was evidently of that kind. In 1866 the workhouse was to include, apart from the 'main building', an entrance block, and a dining hall and kitchens,[6] and in 1869, soon after its completion, the workhouse was enlarged by the addition of a six-bayed isolation block for patients with fevers and infectious diseases.[7] There was also a separate infirmary at the workhouse, where 16 patients, about half of them bed-ridden, and one woman in the labour ward were being cared for in 1898;[8] the accommodation was then regarded as inadequate but plans to replace or enlarge it had little effect until 1910–11, when the existing building was extended.[9] Soon afterwards, by order from central government, guardians were ordered to employ a trained nurse in workhouse infirmaries.[10]

By 1870 the workhouse was reckoned to have room for 215 inmates, with accommodation for 7 more in each of the vagrant wards, male and female.[11] Accommodation or occupation in the early 20th century was between 169 and 200.[12]

As nationally, there was much unemployment and poverty in the parish in the 1880s, in part due to bad harvests, and again *c.* 1920.[13] During bad years, the help afforded by the union, both outdoor and in the workhouse, was supplemented by the continuing philanthropic tradition. Driffield Soup Committee was thus supplying over two hundred families in 1831.[14] Subscribers also provided medical care for those outside the workhouse, and in the 1860s collections for the poor in the parish church included one for a clothing club,[15] probably the same as the clothing society that had 160 members in 1842.[16] Sermons were

1 Sheahan and Whellan, *Hist. York & ER.* ii. 502.

2 ERAO, PUD/1/2/1, pp. 131, 178; PUD/1/2/5, p. 5; PUD/1/2/6, p. 197; PUD/1/2/10, p. 204.

3 Ibid. PUD/1/2/9, pp. 17, 120–1, 148, 164, 371; specification of 1867 at ibid. PUD/1/4/1; RDB, IX/180/246. The building dates 1867 and 1868 are given in Bulmer, *Dir. E Yorks.* (1892), 168 and *Kelly's Dir. N & ER Yorks.* (1889), 373 respectively; Fig. 57.

4 ERAO, PUD/1/2/9, pp. 405, 413; RDB, KH/187/214.

5 Crowther, *Workhouse System*, 62.

6 ERAO, PUD/1/2/9, p. 164.

7 Ibid. PUD/1/2/10, pp. 83, 123, 150–1, 222; plan of 1869 at ibid. PUD/1/4/1.

8 Ibid. PUD/1/2/18, p. 152.

9 Ibid. PUD/1/2/17, pp. 106, 125, 133, 441; PUD/1/2/22, pp. 155, 244, 300; plans (1896 and n.d.) at ERAO, PUD/1/4/1; *Kelly's Dir. N & ER Yorks.* (1913), 513; OS Map 1/2,500, Yorks. CLXI. 12 (1893 and 1910 edns).

10 Crowther, *Workhouse System*, 87.

11 ERAO, PUD/1/2/10, p. 223.

12 *Kelly's Dir. N & ER Yorks.* (1901), 463; (1905), 480; (1909), 493; (1913), 513.

13 BIA, V. 1884/Ret. 1; V. 1912–22/Ret.; *DT* 27 Oct. 1988.

14 ERAO, DDGR/44/29/27.

15 BIA, V. 1865/Ret. 1, no. 142; V. 1868/Ret. 1, no. 133; Ross, *Driffield*, 90.

16 *HP* 25 Nov. 1842.

regularly preached on behalf of the clothing club which in 1892–3 had 400 members in Great Driffield and 35 in Little Driffield.[1] The churchwardens' account for 1879–80 records expenditure of £18 on the poor; £10 on an invalid kitchen, and a subscription of £11 to the Cottage Hospital.[2] Some of the needy and old also benefited from the several charities established in the 19th and 20th centuries, most of them to provide free or subsidised housing.[3]

Action by the Liberal government in the early 20th century also began to alleviate poverty and lessen at least some of the need for assistance from the guardians. A restricted non-contributory old age pension was introduced in 1908, a health and unemployment insurance scheme for some workers in 1911, and other legislation provided protection for the able-bodied poor.[4]

Conditions for those in the workhouse were also improved. The guardians were forbidden by the Local Government Board from housing children over the age of three in the workhouse permanently after 1915, and were bound to provide alternative accommodation for them.[5] At Driffield the guardians bought houses in Victoria Road and Bridge Street in 1915, and duly established children's homes there.[6] Along with the loss of the young and any able-bodied poor, who were then assisted outside the house, and the improvements in accommodation and medical services, came a change of name, from workhouse to poor law institution. Subsequently, the institution had two main functions: housing poor inmates – vagrants, unmarried mothers, and the elderly, and providing a hospital service which was increasingly accessed by others than the poorest.[7] Under the Local Government Act of 1929, boards of poor law guardians were abolished in 1930, and their functions and property transferred to county councils.[8]

LOCAL BOARD, LATER URBAN DISTRICT COUNCIL

In the mid 19th century the attention of central government turned also to the question of public health. An Act of 1848 allowed local boards of health to be established in towns to supervise sanitary matters; subject to the approval of the General Board of Health, the boards had power to rate and to issue by-laws. By the Public Health Act of 1872, the system was made compulsory, the poor law board becoming the sanitary authority in rural areas and improvement commissioners or local boards in towns.[9] In 1873, following a petition by ratepayers of Great Driffield, the relatively unregulated sanitation of the town was duly placed under the supervision of a local board of health.[10] Under the Local Government Act of 1894, Great Driffield civil parish, formerly township, became an urban district, and the 12 members of the local board were re-constituted as the urban district council.[11] The chief responsibilities of the UDC were the maintenance and cleaning of the roads and streets; the provision of a sewerage system and other sanitary services; the lighting of the town, and, after 1897, the making and supply of gas.[12]

In 1935 a new, smaller urban district and civil parish of Driffield was created from Great Driffield urban district and civil parish and parts of the civil parishes of Elmswell with Little Driffield and Skerne; the remainder of Great Driffield was then added to Nafferton civil parish in the rural district of Driffield.[13] The urban district and its council were done away with as part of the re-organization of local government in 1974.[14]

UDC meetings were held in the Mechanics' Institute reading room in Exchange Street until 1935, when the council bought the former Corn Exchange for a town hall from the executors of William Shipley.[15]

The local board inherited from its predecessor, the vestry, a yard on the north side of York Road, which by 1892 was being used in part for the fire service.[16] It was enlarged in 1896 by the board's successor, the UDC.[17] On the abolition of the UDC in 1974, the yard passed to the district council, and evidently remained in use until 1990, when East Yorkshire Borough Council decided it was unneeded.[18] In or soon after 1993 the site was sold to a housing association for development with affordable homes, as part of a housing partnership scheme,[19] and Westlands Mews was put up there soon afterwards. The UDC also had offices in a building in Eastgate South; after re-organization in 1974, they were used by the county council's highways department before apparently being given up.[20]

1 Ibid. 1 Dec. 1856; *DT* 11 Dec. 1869; ERAO, PE/10/T. 88.
2 ERAO, PE/10/T. 88.
3 Below, this section, charities.
4 Crowther, *Workhouse System*, 84–5.
5 Ibid. 86.
6 RDB, 167/550/470; 167/551/471; directories; below, this section, children's homes.
7 Crowther, *Workhouse System*, 3, 87, 95.
8 Clarke, *Local Govt*, 95–6; Crowther, *Workhouse System*, 109.
9 Clarke, *Local Govt*, 48, 50, 55.
10 Great Driffield board minute books from 1880 are at ERAO, LBDR/1–3; below, this section, politics (small town politics).
11 *Lond. Gaz.* 2 Jan. 1874, p. 3; Bulmer, *Dir. E Yorks.* (1892), 165; Clarke, *Local Govt*, 71, 112–13.
12 ERAO, UDDR/1/1/1, p. 128; UDDR/1/1/2, p. 221–2.
13 *Census*, 1931 (pt ii); Fig. 3.
14 Below, this section, district councils.
15 *Kelly's Dir. N & ER Yorks.* (1897), 440; RDB, 534/147/128; 541/69/54; 644/79/69; ER Educ. Cttee *Mins* 1936–7, 47, 139; OS Map 1/10,000: TA 05 NW (1970 edn).
16 OS Map 1/2,500: Yorks. CLXI. 12 (1893 edn).
17 RDB, 81/216/205 (1896); ERAO, UDDR/1/1/1, p. 90.
18 ERAO, EYEY/1/4/8/2, Housing...Cttee, 15 Oct. 1990; *DT* 22 May 1986.
19 ERAO, EYEY/1/4/8/3, Environmental...Cttee, 13 Sept. 1993.
20 ERAO, EYEY/1/4/10/1, Housing Cttee, 5 Sept. 1978; Humbs. CC *Mins* 1976–7, D 46.

SCHOOL BOARD

Public schooling before the mid 19th century was provided mostly by denominational bodies, whose efforts then began to be assisted by grants from central government. Under the Elementary Education Act of 1870, school districts were created, and, where the existing schools were insufficient, ratepayers were empowered to elect a school board to provide additional schools; the board's activities were to be funded by an increase in the local rate for the poor. A school board for Driffield town was formed in 1871,[1] and operated until 1903, when, under the Education Act of the previous year, it was abolished and its duties transferred to the East Riding County Council.[2]

DISTRICT COUNCILS

As outlined above, by the Public Health Act of 1872 the boards of poor law guardians were made responsible for sanitary matters in rural areas, and they remained the sanitary authority until the passing of the Local Government Act of 1894. The sanitary districts then became rural districts governed by elected councillors, who also served as local representatives on the poor law boards. Besides its responsibility for public health, the RDC was also made the local highway authority.[3]

As rural places in Driffield Poor Law Union, Little Driffield, Elmswell, and Kelleythorpe, comprising two townships until 1885, and thereafter the single civil parish of Elmswell with Little Driffield, were included in Driffield sanitary district. From 1894 they were part of the succeeding administrative area, Driffield rural district. The boundaries of the rural and urban districts of Driffield were altered in 1935.[4] At the re-organization of local government in 1974, under the Local Government Act of 1972 and subsequent statutory instruments, Driffield urban district and its council were abolished, and the area, co-terminous with Driffield civil parish, was added to the rural districts of Driffield and Pocklington and the borough and most of the rural district of Bridlington, the whole being named North Wolds district and forming part of the new county of Humberside.[5] North Wolds district, later borough, had its name changed to East Yorkshire borough in 1981.[6] The district authority was abolished in 1996, and Driffield parish, together with the other parts of the ancient ecclesiastical parish – in Great and Little Driffield, Elmswell, and Kelleythorpe – then lying in the civil parishes of Kirkburn, Garton, and Nafferton, became part of the new East Riding unitary area which replaced Humberside.[7]

Like the UDC, that for the rural district met in the reading room of the Mechanics' Institute in the early 20th century.[8] In 1932 the rural district council bought a house formerly called Ash Lea but then West Garth at the junction of Mill Street and Victoria Road for its offices and meetings.[9] The premises later passed to the successor authorities, in 1974 to North Wolds District Council, later East Yorkshire Borough Council, which held some of its meetings there,[10] and in 1996 to the East Riding of Yorkshire Council, which retained it for offices.[11]

TOWN COUNCIL

Following the abolition of the UDC in 1974, ratepayers in Driffield voted for a parish council in 1978, and one was eventually obtained in 1981. The parish council of 13 members immediately renamed itself Driffield Town Council, and its chairman was subsequently called mayor.[12]

Housed at first in the district council offices at West Garth,[13] the town council had few powers beyond the management of the allotments and playgrounds.[14] In 1986 it was trying to involve itself in East Yorkshire Borough Council's management of the market,[15] and in the years preceding the abolition of the borough council and the creation of a new East Riding unitary authority in 1996 the town council again sought to enlarge its powers and independence.[16] Its clerk became full-time in 1993,[17] and the following year the council's membership of 13 was increased to 16, largely on account of the town's growth.[18] When the district council built a community centre in the grounds of West Garth in 1994, the town council was given office space there, but in 1998 that was replaced by purpose-built accommodation, then added to the centre by the town council.[19] Also in 1998 the council opened a works depot in a former pumping station on North Street, leased from the Environment Agency.[20]

1 *Lond. Gaz.* 10 Feb. 1871, p. 486; below, this section, politics (small town politics).

2 Above, soc. hist., education. The records of the board are at ERAO, SB/14/1–24.

3 Clarke, *Local Govt*, 50, 70–1. The records of Driffield rural sanitary authority from 1881 are at ERAO, RSDR/1–4, and those of the rural district council from 1894 at ibid. RDDR/1–4.

4 Above, vol. intro., area.

5 20–21 Eliz. II c. 70; S.I. 1972/2039; 1973/551.

6 North Wolds Borough Council Mins 1973–4, 4–7; 1980–1, 360; *Census*, 1991.

7 Humberside (Structural Change) Order 1995, copy at ERAO.

8 *Kelly's Dir. N & ER Yorks.* (1909), 491.

9 RDB, 446/325/261.

10 e.g., ERAO, EYEY/1/4/10/1, Housing Cttee, 20 July 1974.

11 *HDM* 2 Jan. 1998.

12 ERAO, CCHU/10/MIS. 231; *HDM* 12 Mar., 23 Apr. 1981; *DT* 27 July 1978.

13 *HDM* 2 Jan. 1998.

14 *YP* 19 Mar. 1996.

15 ERAO, EYEY/1/4/8/2, Housing...Cttee, 14 July 1986.

16 *DP* 14 Feb. 1996.

17 *DT* 28 Jan. 1993; inf. from Claire Binnington, Driffeld Town Council, 2006.

18 *HDM* 12 Mar. 1981; *DP* 28 July 1994.

19 *DT* 28 Jan. 1993; *DP* 14 Feb. 1996; *HDM*, 2 Jan., 13 Feb., 27 July 1998; inf. from Claire Binnington, Driffeld Town Council, 2006.

20 *HDM* 9 June 1997; *DT* 29 July 1998.

The town council's attempts to enlarge its remit were resisted by other authorities and individuals, often successfully. In the mid 1990s the town and district councils tried in vain to interest the townspeople in establishing a museum in Driffield.[1] Early in 1997 there was friction over the running of the cemetery and the provision of other services between the town council and the new East Riding of Yorkshire Council, which had retained control of those functions.[2] The following year the council tried to increase its influence by having the boundaries of Driffield parish revised to include Kelleythorpe, with its agricultural showground and industrial estate; that proposal was resisted successfully, notably by the other parishes involved, Garton and Kirkburn.[3] The town council did, however, succeed in twinning the town with St Affrique (France) in 1998,[4] and in 2001 it obtained some control over the town's market from the East Riding of Yorkshire Council.[5]

PUBLIC SERVICES

ROADS AND BRIDGES

By custom a parish was bound to keep its highways in repair, a duty which was, in theory, discharged by parishioners labouring on the roads for a day or so a year. Two constables were ordered to be appointed in each hundred, or wapentake, in the late 13th century, and then given some responsibility for local roads, and the Highway Act of 1555 allowed the parish meeting to elect two surveyors of highways, but the effect of those measures on Driffield's roads is not known. Almost certainly more effective was the supervision which the justices of the peace exercised from the late 17th century; they were then given the power to appoint the parochial surveyors, and to lay rates on proprietors for repairing the roads, in place of the old labour due. The inspection of bridges in particular became a duty of the High Constable, who was appointed by the justices sitting in quarter sessions.[6] Since part of Driffield parish lay within the liberty of St Peter's, York, local officers, like the constables, were subject also to the supervision of the sessions of the peace held for the liberty until 1838, as well as the petty and quarter sessions for the rest of the East Riding.[7]

There is in the case of Driffield parish little evidence about how the roads were maintained before the 18th century. Much of the work would seem to have been done under the old system of day works, and managed not by parish officers but through the manor court; it was certainly there that failures to perform day works on the roads were fined in the 18th century.[8] On occasion local roads were repaired also at the expense of individuals like Thomas Etherington (d. 1589), who left money for that purpose as an act of charity.[9] The materials for mending the roads were obtained locally for the most part: at inclosure in 1742 a gravel pit to the south of the town was expressly set aside for road repairs; in the north of the town there was then a lane named from a stone pit there,[10] and there were later gravel pits beside Bell Mill Lane and Eastgate.[11] Stone was however also brought from further afield. A note dated 1806 in a parish book thus laid down the rates for fetching cobbles from Barmston beach; carriage of 1½ ton of cobbles by a parishioner with a full team of horses discharged one day work, while hired hauliers were to receive 6*s.* for each ton transported.[12] Later the UDC imported stone by rail, and used tar and ashes from its gasworks on the roads.[13]

The state of the local roads in the earlier 18th century can only be guessed at. By then the justices were rating the parishioners for the more important of the local roads, and presumably appointing and supervising surveyors of highways. The rate approved for the repair of Driffield's highways in 1737 was very low at a penny in the pound, but that may reflect the parsimony of the local JPs or of the ratepayers rather than the good state of the parish's roads.[14] That the upkeep of the roads by the parish under the supervision of the justices was insufficient is suggested by the turnpiking later of one of the parish's more important routes. As was done frequently elsewhere, the road connecting Driffield to Beverley was removed from the control of the justices by Act of 1766, and committed instead to commercial operators for them to improve, in return for tolls charged on traffic; that arrangement remained in place until 1881. It was perhaps with turnpiking in prospect that in 1765 the justices built a new brick and stone bridge over the boundary stream separating Kelleythorpe and Sunderlandwick,[15] and the Beverley road was improved further on the Kelleythorpe/Great Driffield boundary

1 Above, soc. hist., museums.
2 *DT* 15 Jan. 1997.
3 *HDM* 2 Oct. 1998.
4 *DT* 11 Nov. 1998.
5 Above, econ. hist., mkts and fairs.
6 Clarke, *Local Govt*, 18–19, 21, 52–3.
7 ERAO, DDGR/42/29/10; Leak, *Liberty of St Peter*, 12–19.
8 HUL, DDCV/42/4, s.a. 1733, 1752.
9 BIA, precentorship wills, Thomas Etherington, 1589 (will).
10 RDB, B/153/42 [roads]; ERAO, IA. 41. The former quarry, although built over, remains very evident beside the lane, now called Windmill Hill.
11 ERAO, TA/13; ibid. PE/10/T. 120; OS Map 1:10,560, Yorks. CLXI (1855 edn).
12 ERAO, PE/10/T. 99.
13 Ibid. UDDR/1/1/1, pp. 27, 211, 220; UDDR/1/1/2, pp. 90, 149.
14 MacMahon, *Roads and Turnpike Trusts*, 11.
15 ERAO, QAB/1/1.

in the early 19th century, when a ford in Driffield Beck was replaced by a bridge; the name of the ford, or wath, Alamanwath, thought to have been Anglo-Scandinavian and meaning 'all men's ford', was retained, as Hallimanwath, for the bridge.[1]

Before the turnpike road was returned to public control in the late 19th century, the basis of a modern system of repairing the highways had been laid down by further legislation. By the Highway Act of 1835, the labour requirement on parishioners was abolished, and highway rates substituted, and later in the century the upkeep of main roads and bridges was committed to the new county councils.[2] In fact, the county authority was slow to assume direct responsibility for its roads, and in the late 19th century it paid the UDC £114 a year to maintain the main roads for it. Five roads were then proposed by the UDC for designation as main roads – that to Little Driffield, Bridlington Road, Wansford Road, Scarborough Road, and Skerne Road.[3] The East Riding County Council later became more involved with its roads, and established a highways depot in Driffield. By 1939 it was situated on land rented from Driffield RDC on the west side of Wansford Road,[4] but in the mid 1940s it was removed to River Head.[5] A warehouse was bought there and the premises otherwise extended by the succeeding county council in the later 1970s.[6]

The number of chief roads maintained by the county council increased gradually during the 20th century as lesser routes were improved by the UDC and RDC, and then adopted as county roads. As well as repairing them, in the mid 20th century the county council also improved its roads.[7] Hallimanwath Bridge, which carries the road from Beverley (A164) into the parish over Driffield Beck,[8] was altered to include a timber footbridge in or about 1936, and the council further improved the road and bridge there about 1970.[9] Other bridge and carriageway operations were carried out in Skerne Road: in or soon after 1958 Clough Bridge was almost doubled in width, and in the early 1970s work was done on the bridge at Bell Mills.[10] The road from Driffield to Wansford and Skipsea (B1249) was made safer about 1935 but its course was changed more radically in the 1960s, when a new, straight stretch was constructed near Whin Hill Farm.[11] Also improved were the roads to Market Weighton (A163)[12] and that to York and Malton (A166). The latter road, known in Elmswell by the 17th century as Garton Gate, or Road,[13] was evidently diverted near the hamlet, perhaps at inclosure in 1771. The former course across Cow Pasture remained, however,[14] and in the 1960s it was revived to straighten the road.[15] The county council's improvements, like those of the UDC,[16] were frequently concerned with making the junctions of its roads safer. In the case of the Beverley road, the junction with Skerne Road was widened about 1930, with a contribution from the UDC, and that with Middle Street South in the early 1970s, several cottages being removed for the latter work.[17] A traffic island was added at the junction of the Beverley and Market Weighton roads (A163–4), south of the town, in 1962, and that junction was further improved in the 1970s.[18]

Lesser roads and bridges remained the responsibility of the more local bodies. It was thus the select vestry which in 1826 rebuilt Cow Bridge between Little Driffield and Kelleythorpe;[19] which established a works depot at North End in 1855, and which *c.* 1870 was paving the streets of the town.[20] The duty later passed to the vestry's successors, the local board of health and the UDC, while the responsibilities of the lesser townships were assumed by the rural sanitary authority, later the rural district council.[21] After the UDC was abolished in 1974, its functions with regard to local roads passed to the succeeding district council, but in 1996 the shared responsibilities were united in the East Riding unitary authority.[22]

For their part, the local board and later the UDC also improved the town streets, as well as maintaining them. Thus Eastgate South was widened at its junction with Albion and Harper Streets *c.* 1900.[23] Work done on the Cross Hill area in the mid 1920s similarly involved the improvement of the junctions of Cross Hill with Mill

1 OS Map 1:10,560, Yorks. CLXI (1855 edn); MacMahon, *Roads and Turnpike Trusts*, 29–30, 59, 66–7; Ross, *Driffield*, 192–3.

2 Clarke, *Local Govt*, 68–9.

3 ERAO, UDDR/1/1/1, pp. 23, 129, etc.; UDDR/1/1/2, pp. 65–6.

4 ER CC *Mins* 1939–40, 383–4. The RDC had bought it in 1906: RDB, 87/2/2.

5 RDB, 751/463/380; ER CC *Mins* 1945–6, 207; 1946–7, 199; 1949–50, 554; 1950–1, 360; 1952–3, 68; 1971–2, 139.

6 Humbs. CC *Mins* 1976–7, E 1703; G 1358; 1977–8, D 326.

7 ER CC *Mins* 1930–1, 321–2; 1931–2, 171; 1932–3, 138, 231.

8 See under roads in RDB, B/153/42; A. Bryant, *Map of ER Yorks.* (1829); OS Map 1:10,560, Yorks. CLXI (1855 edn).

9 OS Map 1:2,500, Yorks. CLXI. 16 (1893 edn); RDB, 549/246/195; 1636/141/102; 1642/293/265; 1731/100/77.

10 RDB, 1124/40/35; ER CC *Mins* 1956–7, 162; 1970–1, 431.

11 RDB, 496/109/79; 1292/65/55; 1311/286/262; ER CC *Mins* 1960–1, 130–1; OS Map 1:25,000, TA 05 (1953 edn).

12 RDB, 1114/425/381.

13 Best, *Farming Bks*, ed. Woodward, 19.

14 RDB, AN/196/12; photograph of an 1815 map, in the possession of Professor D. M. Woodward, Beverley, in 2003, and reproduced in Best, *Farming Bks*, ed. Woodward, 213; T. Jefferys, *Map of Yorks.* (1775); OS Map 1:10,560, SE 95 NE (1956 edn).

15 RDB, 1442/88/85; 1759/495/416; OS Map 1:2,500, Yorks. CLXI. 7, 11 (1910 edn).

16 Below, this section.

17 RDB, 419/249/203; 1771/564/450; 1815/493/412; ER CC *Mins* 1930–1, 297.

18 ER CC *Mins* 1962–3, 228; 1963–4, 18; 1972–3, 388.

19 Ibid. PE/10/T. 99; OS Map 1:10,560, Yorks. CLXI (1855 edn).

20 ERAO, PE/10/T. 99, s.a. 1855, *c.* 1870.

21 Clarke, *Local Govt*, 53, 71.

22 Above, this section, district councils.

23 RDB, 67/493/459 (1894); ERAO, UDDR/1/1/1, p. 236; UDDR/1/1/2, pp. 237, 241.

Street and of Mill Street with Victoria Road.[1] Albion Street, which now carries traffic away from the main street, was itself widened in the 1960s, and the manorial rights were then bought largely to facilitate further changes to Cross Hill.[2] About the same date, the UDC, which had previously expressed concern about the safety of the railway crossings, secured the replacement of that in Eastgate South by a footbridge,[3] and in the 1970s work was done to the nearby junction of Eastgate South with River Head.[4]

The division of responsibility for roads between the county and local authorities required co-operation to make the system work well, notably in Driffield town, where some of the streets were also county roads. In 1930, for instance, the county council agreed to pay the UDC for the cleaning and watering of those Driffield streets which formed part of the main roads at the rate of £30 a mile,[5] and in 1943 the county council acceded to a request from the UDC for 'cats eye' studs on county roads in the urban district.[6] All the road authorities had, moreover, to grapple with the problems caused by a growing volume of motor traffic in general, and of holiday traffic to and from the coast in particular.[7] Gradually attempts were made to control traffic visiting the town, or attempting to pass through it. Vehicle-operated traffic lights installed at the junction of Exchange Street and Market Place in 1932 were duly followed from 1945 by parking controls on the busiest streets and by a one-way system begun in the mid 1960s.[8] The more radical solution of a by-pass was considered from the 1930s but was only achieved 50 years later. In the interim, the UDC began to encourage vehicles out of the streets by providing car parks. In 1957 and 1959 a car park was laid out on land bought by the council in Eastgate South and Galloway Lane, to the east of the main street, and arrangements were then made for ex-servicemen to staff it.[9] More car parking was provided on the site of a former foundry on Cross Hill in the 1970s, and in the mid 1990s a market hall there was removed and the car park cum market site was once again remodelled.[10]

The largest road project undertaken by the county council, in conjunction with national government, was the construction between 1980 and 1982 of a by-pass for Driffield.[11] The road was intended in particular to relieve the town of summertime traffic to Bridlington, and had been planned as early as 1934. The following year the route eventually built, around the west and north of Driffield town, was rejected by the county council.[12] When the project was revived, after the war, the by-pass was planned to run around the south of Driffield, passing also through Kirkburn and Skerne parishes before joining Bridlington Road to the east of the town.[13] In 1963, however, the western and northern route of Great Driffield was substituted, and that project was later elaborated to include a link road diverting traffic from York Road in Little Driffield around the north of that village.[14]

WATER SUPPLY

Driffield and the other settlements depended for their water on streams, springs, and wells until the late 19th century. One of the town wells may be commemorated in the street name Cranwell, in the 16th century also recorded as Crandwell.[15] In 1856 water was said to be plentiful and its quality excellent,[16] but that was not the case later. Doubts about the purity of the supply were expressed by the Local Government Board in 1872 but parish officers, fearful that a local board might be set up and that expenditure on local services would rise sharply in consequence, countered robustly. Almost the entire water supply was said to come from deep wells unaffected by the admittedly polluted town beck, and the only action thought necessary was the sinking of a few more wells by proprietors, certainly not the expensive provision by the parish of a waterworks.[17] There was further concern about the quality of the supply in 1880, when deeper bore holes were called for.[18] The provision of a waterworks for the district caused controversy between the local board and a group of entrepreneurs who obtained incorporation as Driffield Water Co. Ltd under the Driffield & District Water Act of 1882.[19] The following year the local board's alternative scheme was abandoned when the Local Government Board refused to support an application for permission to borrow money, and the ratepayers

1 RDB, 314/14/7; 283/100/85.

2 ERAO, UDDR/1/1/37, Housing ...Cttee, 20 May 1963; UDDR/1/1/38, Gen. Purposes Cttee, 6 Dec. 1964; RDB, 1388/16/16.

3 ERAO, UDDR/1/1/39, Housing...Cttee, 2 Aug. 1965.

4 RDB, 1875/285/232.

5 ER CC *Mins* 1930–1, 31–2.

6 Ibid. 1943–4, 11.

7 Ibid. 1946–7, 199.

8 Ibid. 1932–3, 17, 139; 1945–6, 142; 1964–5, 160–1.

9 ERAO, UDDR/1/8/48, Building...Cttee, 29 Jan. 1952; UDDR/1/8/54, Housing...Cttee, 1 Apr. 1957; Building...Cttee, 3 Dec. 1957; UDDR/1/8/56, Housing...Cttee, 5 Oct. 1959; RDB, 1051/126/115; 1154/211/193.

10 ERAO, UDDR/1/1/46, Housing...Cttee, 1 Jan. 1973; EYEY/1/4/8/3, Environment...Cttee, 4 Apr. 1995.

11 Humbs. CC *Mins* 1980–1, F. 2495, 2778; *HDM* 9 Oct. 1980; 28 May 1982.

12 ER CC *Mins* 1934–5, 258, 376–7.

13 ERAO, CCER/1/4/2/18, Highways Cttee, 26 June 1950; 1 Jan. 1951; *DT* 15 Feb. 1947.

14 ER CC *Mins* 1962–3, 349; 1972–3, 304; 1973–4, 240–1, 243; Humbs. CC *Mins* 1981–2, J. 235; *HDM* 31 Aug. 1977; 30 Mar. 1978.

15 BIA, CP. G. 1097.

16 Sheahan and Whellan, *Hist. York & ER.* ii. 498. Ross, *Driffield*, 89.

17 ERAO, PE/10/T. 99, s.a. 1872; printed report of vestry meeting at ibid. DDX/659/3.

18 *DT* 27 Oct. 1988.

19 45–6 Vic. c. 150 (Local); *HP* 16 Dec. 1881, 5 May, 14 July, 18 Aug., 24 Nov. 1882.

then blocked any further opposition to the company's proposal.[1] The water company bought 2 a. for a reservoir in the north-west of Great Driffield, beside Spellowgate, in 1883,[2] and a pumping station built there was opened in 1884. The reservoir, fed by springs and a deep well, had a capacity of 397,000 gallons.[3] In 1914 the company bought another well, next to the beck on the south side of North Street, and later built a pumping station there.[4] The North Street station was enlarged in 1921; the site of the waterworks by 3 a. in 1947,[5] and in 1955 a second, covered, reservoir was made at Maiden's Grave on Driffield Wold, close to the northern boundary of the former parish.[6]

Under the Water Acts of 1945 and 1948, central government was allowed to create water boards, and to arrange for the transfer to them of the operations of existing suppliers.[7] Reorganization in East Yorkshire took some time. In 1957 Driffield Water Co. was considering transferring its undertaking to Driffield RDC, but that did not happen. Finally, in response to an application by Driffield UDC, Driffield RDC, and the other local authorities of the region, an order was made in 1961 constituting a joint board, the East Yorkshire (Wolds Area) Water Board, and transferring to it the water operations of the councils and of the Driffield Water Co.; the board came into existence in 1962.[8] Work done by the board included the provision of mains water to houses in Kelleythorpe about 1970.[9] At local government reorganization in 1974, the water board was subsumed in a larger regional body, the Yorkshire Water Authority, which then also took over the local authorities' responsibilities for sewage services. In 1976 the former board's office at Easterfield House in New Road was closed and the work transferred to Hull.[10] Soon after its creation in 1974, Yorkshire Water Authority sunk a borehole and built a small works on Elmswell Wold.[11] Despite the extra capacity obtained in the mid century, however, population growth and low rainfall caused concern later about the amount of water being taken from the streams.[12] The pumping station in North Street had ceased to be used and belonged to the Environment Agency by 1997, when the building was leased to the town council for a works depot.[13]

SEWERAGE

Oversight of the watercourses of the parish belonged to the manorial courts, and, from the 16th century, also to a body with a wider jurisdiction, the Court of Sewers for the East Parts of the East Riding.[14] Situated away from the marshy areas of the riding, Driffield attracted little of the Court's attention though.[15] The town and the lesser settlements were nonetheless prone to occasional flooding by storm water draining off the Wolds, and by the later 19th century even parish officers were admitting that sewerage was a difficult problem.[16] After one such inundation, in 1872,[17] the poor law guardians, as the rural sanitary authority, proposed improvements to the drainage system, but they were disliked in the town, and led to the formation of a separate sanitary authority for the urban area, the local board, in 1873.[18] In 1879–80 the new authority installed a new drainage system for the town at a cost of some £10,000. The project, designed by engineers of Hull, included an outfall works and filtration area, for which 7 a. beside the canal to the south of the town was purchased.[19] The improved system could not cope, however, with flash flooding from the Wolds, and Driffield was inundated again several times in the late 19th and early 20th century.[20]

The growth of the town and the development of the airfield later burdened the system, and in or shortly before 1948 the County Medical Officer of Health found the treatment works unsatisfactory and Driffield canal polluted as a result. In response the UDC proposed to rebuild the sewage works to meet the needs of some 12,000 people, of which it was estimated 7,700 would live in the town, 1,000 on the airfield, and 3,000 in neighbouring villages in Driffield Rural District.[21] Schemes for the new works and the replacement for some of the town's sewers were submitted in 1950, and much of the work had been completed by 1957. The new sewage works was in operation by 1958.[22] The work was funded jointly by the UDC and Hull Corporation,

1 *HP* 9 & 16 Mar. 1883; Ross, *Driffield*, 184–5; *1st Rep. Royal Com. Mkt Rights and Tolls*, Vol. II (Parl. Papers, 1888 [C. 5550-I], liii), p. 264.

2 RDB, NR/360/517.

3 Ross, *Driffield*, 31; E. Aylwin and R. C. Ward, *Development and Utilisation of Water Supplies in the ER of Yorks.* (1969), 26; Bulmer, *Dir. E Yorks.* (1892), 165.

4 RDB, 162/429/358; *HDM*, 9 June 1997. Driffield Water Order, 1948 at ERAO, DDX/237/41.

5 RDB, 240/7/5; 762/477/399.

6 OS Map 1:10,000, TA 06 SW (1983 edn); inf. from Mr B. Baxter, Yorkshire Water, Bradford, 2006.

7 Clarke, *Local Govt*, 123.

8 ERAO, UDDR/1/8/54, Public Health Cttee, 6 Aug. 1957; ER CC *Mins* 1961–2, 189, 287.

9 ER CC *Mins* 1969–70, 149.

10 *HDM*, 4 May 1977; ER CC *Mins* 1971–2, 281–2.

11 Inf. from Yorkshire Water, 2006.

12 *DT* 9 Jan. 1992.

13 *HDM* 9 June 1997.

14 Above, this section, manorial admin.; J. A. Sheppard, *The Draining of the Hull Valley* (E Yorks. Local Hist. Ser. 8, 1958), 4.

15 ERAO, CSR/4/215.

16 Ibid. DDX/659/3.

17 Ross, *Driffield*, 182.

18 Above, this section, local board.

19 ERAO, NV/1/107; Ross, *Driffield*, 31; OS Map 1:2,500, Yorks. CLXI. 12 (1910 edn).

20 *BG* 11 May 1978; *DT*, 27 Oct. 1988; Ross, *Driffield*, 186. The flood of 20 May 1910 was much photographed: Clubley, *Driffield*, pls. 43–7, 62

21 ERAO, UDDR/1/8/45, Public Health...Cttee, 11 Nov. 1948; ER CC *Mins* 1948–9, 170, 344.

22 ERAO, DDX/237/41.

58. *Great Driffield: Cemetery lodge, Bridlington Road, 2011. The seven-acre cemetery was consecrated in 1865.*

which intended to extract water downstream;[1] as part of its operation, the corporation opened a new filtration plant beside the River Hull in Watton parish in 1960.[2] A sewerage scheme for Little Driffield, including the building of a pumping station there, was carried out about 1960.[3] At local government reorganization in 1974, responsibility for sewerage was transferred from the local councils to a new regional body concerned also with the supply of water, the Yorkshire Water Authority,[4] later Yorkshire Water. By 1991 the sewerage system in Driffield was being severely tested by the rapid growth of the town. There were then said to be nearly 1,000 homes awaiting planning permission, and by 1994 another water body, the National Rivers Authority, was calling for a halt to large-scale building in Driffield until a projected new sewage plant was built.[5] In 1997–8 Yorkshire Water, in conjunction with the National Rivers Authority, laid a new main sewer through the town to the waste treatment works, which were then also renewed.[6]

BURIAL

Burial powers in Great Driffield belonged to the parish and to some of the Nonconformist chapels until the mid 19th century. Great Driffield churchyard, for long the chief burial place in the town, was enlarged by about ½ a. by conveyance of 1843 and consecration of 1845.[7] The insufficiency of those arrangements for burial in the growing town led to the formation in 1863 of a new body, a nine-member burial board for Great Driffield, which bought 7 a. beside Bridlington Road for a cemetery in 1864.[8] One third was then laid out for use by Nonconformists, and a like area for Anglican burials, which was duly consecrated in 1865. Buildings put up included a mortuary chapel on each of the two graveyards.[9] The rest of the land was left undeveloped.[10] The provision of a cemetery allowed burial to be ended in the parish church and its yard; in the Independent chapel, and at the Baptist burial ground in 1866.[11] The powers of the board passed in 1896 to Driffield UDC,

1 Ibid. UDDR/1/8/47, Public Health Cttee, 31 Mar. 1950; UDDR/1/8/54, Public Health Cttee, 4 Nov. 1957.

2 *VCH Yorks. ER.* i. 282, 373.

3 ERAO, UDDR/1/8/54, Public Health Cttee, 20 Dec. 1957; RDB, 1155/59/48.

4 Above, this section, water supply.

5 *HDM* 6 Feb. 1991; *DP* 29 Sept. 1994.

6 *YP* 9 Aug. 1996; *DT* 1 Mar. 1995; 5 Feb. 1997; *HDM* 24 June 1998.

7 BIA, CD. 206; RDB, DQ/429/52.

8 ERAO, PE/10/T. 99, s.a. 1863; *HP* 20 Mar. 1863; *DT* 9 Apr. 1864.

9 Photograph 1953 by Bob Allen, at ERAO, PH/4/11.

10 RDB, IS/211/292; BIA, CD. 356; Pevsner and Neave, *Yorks. ER.* 441. The unused portion had been laid out by 1909: OS Map 1:2,500, Yorks. CLXI. 12 (1893 and 1910 edns).

11 *Lond. Gaz.* 27 Mar. 1866, p. 2040.

and later to that body's successors.[1] Land bought in 1911 for the future extension northwards of the cemetery[2] was eventually used for that purpose in 1957[3] and 1975.[4] In 2001 the authority then responsible, the East Riding of Yorkshire Council, and Driffield Town Council were considering restoring one of the chapels, which had recently been taken out of use.[5]

In Little Driffield burial continued in the churchyard, which was enlarged with land given in 1893 and consecrated in 1895,[6] and extended again in 1965.[7]

GAS SUPPLY

The streets of the town were lit by the Driffield Gas Light Co., which was formed in 1835 following a poll of ratepayers, after strong opposition from the farmers.[8] The gasworks, put up by John Malam,[9] stood in the junction of Exchange Street and Eastgate North, which was known there as Gas House Street in the 1840s.[10] The site was extended by purchase in 1883 and 1892, and in 1897 the company and its works were acquired by the UDC.[11] The works were improved *c.* 1900; new mains then laid in the town, and in the 1920s the site was enlarged.[12] Under the Gas Act of 1948, the gasworks were transferred the following year from the council to the North Eastern Gas Board.[13] Street lighting was changed from gas to electricity in 1951.[14] The gasworks were evidently closed in or soon after 1957, when mains were laid to supply Driffield with gas from works in Bridlington; the latter were themselves discontinued in 1968 following the introduction of natural gas from the North Sea.[15] The site of Driffield gasworks has since been cleared.

ELECTRICITY SUPPLY

Electricity was generated and used from the 1880s in commercial concerns like Bell Mills,[16] but a more general application of the new technology may have been discouraged by the UDC, which ran the gasworks from 1897. The following year the Driffield solicitor W. H. Jennings, attempted, without success, to form a company to light the town electrically, and a later approach from the Northern Counties Electrical Supply Co. was rebuffed by the council.[17] As a source of light and power, electricity only became generally available in Driffield about 1930, when the Buckrose Light & Power Co. Ltd set up in the town. In 1931 the company bought nos. 20–1 Middle Street South and land extending back along Lockwood Street, and subsequently had a substation and a regional office there; in that year a substation was evidently also built in the north of the town, off Bridge Street. The chief premises were enlarged in 1938, when garages and workshops were added in Lockwood Street,[18] and again, as Electricity Buildings, in the mid 1940s.[19] Buckrose Light & Power Co. Ltd may have been succeeded briefly, in or after 1947, by another company, before electricity supply was nationalized in 1948.[20] Electricity was adopted generally as a source of power soon afterwards. The streets of the town were lit electrically from 1951, and about that date, too, the UDC and the Yorkshire Electricity Board extended lighting beyond the town, along York Road and into Little Driffield.[21] Many substations were also added to supply electricity to the new, post-war housing estates, both public and private.[22] In or soon after 1952 a large electricity depot was established beside Skerne Road, and a year or two later an electricity station for the town and its surroundings was put up on the Wansford Road.[23] The depot has been given up but the Wansford Road works was operated still by YEB in the early 21st century.[24]

The premises of the electricity company in Middle Street South were sold in 1991 and subsequently occupied by a dealer in garden machinery.[25]

FIRE SERVICE

'A new and beautiful fire engine, long wanted in Driffield', was purchased for use in the town and neighbourhood in 1840 with money raised by public subscription. Made by Tilley of London, the engine cost about £140. It was managed by the watch committee, and chargeable to their rate.[26] The service was continued by the succeeding authorities, the local board and Driffield

1 ERAO, NV/1/107; ibid. UDDR/1/1/1, p. 109; BIA, CD. 891.

2 RDB, 135/37/35; ER CC *Mins* 1911–12, 218–19.

3 BIA, CD. 850; ERAO, UDDR/1/8/54, Gen. Purposes Cttee 2 Apr. 1957.

4 BIA, CD. 891.

5 *DT* 18 Apr. 2001.

6 BIA, CD. Add. 1895/2. A resolution was passed restricting burials to parishioners in 1862: *HP* 5 Dec. 1862.

7 RDB, 1421/49/44.

8 *HP* 13 & 27 Mar., 24 Apr. 1835.

9 Sheahan and Whellan, *Hist. York & ER.* ii. 497–8; Ross, *Driffield*, 87. Malam was then also manager of a Hull lighting company: *VCH Yorks. ER.* i. 373.

10 ERAO, TA/13; ibid. PE/10/T. 120; RDB, FX/68/91; OS Map 1:10,560, Yorks. CLXI (1855 edn).

11 RDB, NQ/381/496; 55/100/96 (1892); 58/141/135 (1893); 92/129/120 (1897).

12 Ibid. 323/569/461; ERAO, UDDR/1/1/2, pp. 25, 120, 150, 155.

13 RDB, 1061/263/235.

14 ERAO, UDDR/1/8/47, Housing...Cttee, 8 Aug. 1950.

15 *VCH Yorks. ER.* ii. 64.

16 Above, econ. hist., milling.

17 ERAO, UDDR/1/1/2, pp. 38, 184, 186; *Kelly's Dir. N. & ER Yorks.* (1897), 446.

18 ERAO, UDDR/1/8/35, Highways...Cttee, 4 July 1938; *Kelly's Dir. N & ER Yorks.* (1933), 454.

19 RDB, 422/603/488; 430/575/463; 730/179/150.

20 Ibid. 743/215/180; Clarke, *Local Govt*, 59; local inf.

21 ERAO, UDDR/1/8/47, Housing...Cttee, 8 Aug., 4 Sept., 4 Dec. 1950.

22 Ibid. UDDR/1/8/50, Housing...Cttee, 4 Aug., 7 Sept. 1953; RDB, 743/215/180; 854/223/181; 1239/98/92, etc.

23 RDB, 917/517/462; 996/259/231; OS Map 1:10,000, TA 05 NW (1970 edn).

24 Local inf.

25 Inf. from Rodger Bentley Power Equipment Ltd, 2006.

26 *HP* 20 Nov. 1840; ERAO, PE/10/T. 99, s.a. 1856.

UDC.[1] The brigade of occasional firemen comprised a captain, or superintendent,[2] and six firemen in 1893; ten officers in the early 1900s, but after the First World War only eight. The engine was evidently kept in the authority's yard in York Road, close to the junction with Spellowgate,[3] but, from *c.* 1900, the fire service also had premises in Exchange Street.[4] The brigade assisted at fires in the district, going to Cowlam, Great Kelk, and Frodingham Bridge, all about five miles away, in 1899, for instance, and incurring costs which the council did its best to recoup.[5] The force fought a serious fire at King's Mill with its engine, which was horse drawn and manually operated, in 1906, and there were very destructive fires also in 1905 and 1911, respectively at Shepherdson's furniture factory in Harland Lane and at the seat of the Sykes family, Sledmere House.[6] Perhaps partly in response to those events, Driffield urban and rural district councils in 1912 combined to provide a joint fire brigade with a motor fire engine.[7] Aldred Bros & Co., motor engineers of Middle Street South, was appointed in 1920 to maintain and drive the engine.[8] A new engine was obtained in 1929, and the old one was subsequently housed at Stephenson's garage, later Williamson's, also in Middle Street South.[9] By the 1930s the Exchange Street premises were also being used to station ambulances.[10]

The fire service was integrated into the National Fire Service during the Second World War,[11] and evidently then a new fire station was established close to the junction of Scarborough Road and Bridlington Road. The NFS station comprised four buildings, some or all of them wooden huts.[12] Responsibility for the fire service was transferred to the East Riding County Council in 1948, in 1974 passed to its successor, Humberside County Council, and after the replacement of that authority in 1996 belonged to Humberside Fire Authority.[13] In the early 1960s the county council built on the enlarged site of the wartime facility a new fire station, comprising three vehicle bays, two garages, and a drill tower.[14] The firemen, earlier summoned to action by the hooter on the steam laundry and then by a siren at the police station,[15] were warned from the 1960s by an automatic system operated from the fire service headquarters in Beverley.[16]

In the 1950s and 1960s volunteers of the Auxiliary Fire Service were accommodated at Driffield fire station.[17]

TELEPHONE SERVICE

A Government telegraph office was set up at Driffield post office at the beginning of 1870 with wires connecting it to a room at the railway station.[18] A telephone service may have been introduced about 1900, when the UDC was considering applying for a telephone exchange licence.[19] By 1905 there was a call office at the post office and a branch of the National Telephone Co. was established in the town.[20] The company was presumably taken over by the Post Office in 1912,[21] and the exchange in George Street by 1929, then probably in the post office in Middle Street North until an automatic exchange was built in Middle Street South in or soon after 1937.[22] It remained in 2003, when it was operated by British Telecom. Another supplier, Kingston Communications PLC, was proposing in 2000 to convert redundant police garages in Wansford Road into a hi-tech telephone exchange.[23]

HEALTH SERVICES

Rudimentary measures of public health were undertaken before the 19th century by Driffield's manor court,[24] but the growing numbers made such regulation insufficient, and a local board of health was substituted in 1874 and replaced by the UDC in 1894.[25] Officers employed by the latter body included, besides a medical officer, an inspector of 'nuisances', dairies, canal boats, and lodging houses.[26] The threats to public health revealed in the minutes of the UDC's Sanitary and Sewerage Committee include overcrowding and the continuing misuse of the beck, in 1904 being dirtied by the watering and cleaning of cattle and horses in Bridge Street. The health of the town was by then being regularly monitored by the medical officer. The most common infectious diseases seem then to have been scarlet fever, erysipelas, measles, and typhus,[27] and in some years scarlet fever, diphtheria, and measles

1 Following based on directories. 2 ERAO, UDDR/1/1/1, p. 14.

3 OS Map 1:2,500, Yorks. CLXI. 12 (1893 edn).

4 ERAO, UDDR/1/1/2, pp. 115–16.

5 Ibid. UDDR/1/1/2, pp. 80, 93, 105.

6 Ibid. UDDR/1/8/8, Highways...Cttee, 6 June 1911; *DT* 22 May 1986 (illus.); Wood, *Policing from Wansford Road*, 77–8 (illus.).

7 ERAO, UDDR/1/8/8, Highways...Cttee, 5 Feb. 1912; UDDR/1/8/9, Fire Brigade Cttee, 19 June 1912.

8 Herbert Aldred, the proprietor, also served as chairman of the UDC, and Alfred Aldred was a firemen: ERAO, UDDR/1/4/1, pp. 186–7, 349; directories; *DT* 12 June 1986. Illus. of tender at HUL, DX/144/3; *DT* 29 May 1986.

9 ERAO, UDDR/1/4/1, pp. 364, 371; *DT* 12 June 1986.

10 Below, this section, ambulance service.

11 ERAO, UDDR/1/4/2, 25 Sept. 1941; 25 Oct. 1945.

12 RDB, 828/588/485; ER CC *Mins* 1950–1, 466.

13 ER CC *Mins* 1947–8, 186, 354; 1973–4, 172.

14 ER Educ. Cttee *Mins* 1959–60, 49; ER CC *Mins* 1959–60, 81; 1960–1, 166–7; 1961–2, 199; OS Map 1:10,000, TA 05 NW (1970 edn); Wood, *Policing*, 82.

15 ERAO, UDDR/1/4/1, p. 162; UDDR/1/4/2, 25 Oct. 1945.

16 Wood, *Policing*, 81.

17 ER CC *Mins* 1949–50, 497; 1968–9, 52–3.

18 *DT* 27 Nov. 1869; ERAO, UDDR/1/1/1, pp. 192, 194; NV/1/107.

19 ERAO, UDDR/1/1/2, p. 210.

20 Ibid. NV/1/107; *Kelly's Dir. N & ER Yorks.* (1905), 479, 484.

21 *VCH Yorks. ER.* ii. 66, 146.

22 *Kelly's Dir. N & ER Yorks.* (1929), 485; ibid. (1933), 455; ERAO, UDDR/1/8/34, Highways...Cttee, 13 Sept. 1937.

23 *HDM* 15 Aug. 2000. 24 Above, this section, manorial admin.

25 Above, this section, local board.

26 ERAO, UDDR/1/1/1, pp. 8, 127.

27 Monthly reports of Medical Officer of Health in ERAO, UDDR/1/8/1, Sanitary... Cttee minutes.

59. *Great Driffield: Alfred Bean Hospital, Bridlington Road, 1950s. Opened in 1931, the original building was incorporated in an enlarged hospital opened in 1990.*

reached epidemic proportions. From 1916, however, the UDC had recourse to the infectious diseases hospital then built in Driffield for the East Riding hospital district by the county council.[1]

The early history of medical treatment in the parish is not known. For a doctor or surgeon, it was almost certainly necessary, before the mid 18th century, to send to one of the larger centres in the region. In 1591 Stephen Dawson thus sent his neighbour to Beverley to fetch the surgeon Kydd for a consultation.[2] By the late 18th century there were usually three or four apothecaries or surgeons in the town.[3]

For those unable to pay the full cost of an apothecary or a doctor, medical services were provided by philanthropic bodies from the early 19th century, and after 1836 the poor law union was bound to supply basic health care to the poor and elderly in its charge.[4] The quasi-hospital and old people's home which the poor law institution had become by the earlier 20th century was then transferred, with the other responsibilities of the poor law board, to the county council, which was already providing maternity, dental, and welfare services in Driffield, besides having the isolation hospital there. After the creation of the NHS in 1948, the county's hospitals were taken over by the Leeds Regional Hospital Board, with day-to-day administration being delegated to the East Riding Group Hospital Management Committee.[5] At reorganization in 1974 the Yorkshire Regional Health Authority replaced the board, and a new subordinate body was created, the Humberside Area Health Authority, with responsibility for new health districts, of which that of Beverley covered Driffield.[6] Further re-structuring in the earlier 1980s changed the Humberside authority to the East Yorkshire Health Authority, which closed two of the three hospitals at Driffield and opened a new community hospital.[7] From 1994 the new facility was managed by the East Yorkshire Community Healthcare NHS Trust within the new and larger Northern and Yorkshire health region.[8]

Dispensary

A dispensary had been established in the town by 1823.[9] In 1854 advice and medicines were given to 491 poor people from the town and some ten miles around, and some 35 were then attending the doctor's Wednesday morning surgery.[10] The dispensary was perhaps later subsumed in another charitable venture, the Cottage Hospital.

Cottage, later Alfred Bean, Hospital

A hospital for the working classes was begun in 1867 by a committee of ladies including Miss Mary Sykes of Sledmere and Mrs Reynard of Driffield.[11] The foundation trustees were, however, all men, including Sir Tatton Sykes, Bt, and the Revd R. H. Foord.[12] The hospital was supported largely by subscriptions and operated at first

1 Below, this section, Northfield Hospital.
2 BIA, D/C. CP. 1590/5.
3 Above, soc. hist., soc. leadership.
4 Above, this section, Driffield poor law union.
5 *Hosp. Yr Bk* (1949–50), 9, 98, 106.
6 *Hosp. and Health Services Yr Bk* (1976), 5, 68.
7 Ibid. (1984), 5, 75; below, this section.
8 *IHSM Health Services Yr Bk* (1995), 13/100.
9 Baines, *Hist. Yorks.* (1823), ii. 193.
10 HUL, DDSQ(3)/23/7.
11 Following based on Harrison, *Driffield*, 311–12.
12 Plaque in hospital, 2005.

in a loaned house, variously described as in Eastgate[1] and Brook Street; payments from in-patients of 1*s.* 6*d.* a week contributed relatively little towards the costs. A nurse, supervised by one of the town's doctors, ran the hospital, which had six beds and a dispensary for medicines. Before 1871, when the first premises were lost, 45 in-patients and 59 out-patients were treated in one year. A new, eight-bed hospital was built on Bridlington Road in 1872 by public subscription and opened the following year. [2] In 1886 an accident ward was added at the expense of Richard Holtby of Nafferton, who also left £1,000 to the hospital. About 50–60 people a year were treated there later,[3] from about 1930 the patients including children with tonsil and adenoid problems treated by arrangement with the local education authority.[4]

The hospital was replaced by a new building, also on Bridlington Road and given in 1931 by Alfred W. Bean of Highfield. Its management committee then comprised two solicitors, H. W. Rennison and W. H. Blakeston, the timber merchant Horace Taylor, J. B. Bradshaw, miller, R. T. Holtby of the brewing family, and Robert Campbell, presumably the Elmswell landowner.[5] The former Cottage Hospital, by then called Ten Gables, was sold in 1932;[6] it was so called still in 2004, when it was a private nursing home. In 2006 the building was occupied as a house.

The Alfred Bean Hospital, which had 18 beds, an operating theatre, and X-ray apparatus, was extended in 1935,[7] and *c.* 1950 there were 21 beds.[8] It was later run with the neighbouring hospital, the East Riding General.[9] When that was closed in 1990 and demolished in 1992, the Alfred Bean ward was saved after campaigning by the Driffield Hospitals Defence League.[10]

The new Alfred Bean Hospital was opened in 1990.[11] A community hospital, it comprised a ward with 21 beds, a day hospital, an out-patients' department, and various clinics.[12] A cancer unit was added in 1994.[13] In 2006 the hospital comprised a minor injuries centre, a GP ward, and the outpatients' department staffed by visiting consultants.[14]

East Riding General Hospital

The poor law union was responsible for much of the medical care of the poor in its area, which was divided for the purpose into eight districts; a local doctor was appointed to each district as its medical officer, and in addition a Driffield practitioner supervised care in the workhouse.[15] Developments at the workhouse during the 19th century increased its medical and caring functions, and by the early 20th century the union's buildings on Bridlington Road were being used, almost exclusively, as a hospital and a home for old people and the mentally handicapped. The county council took over the medical services and other functions of the poor law board in 1930.[16] Soon afterwards a new master and matron were appointed to run the former workhouse, by then called the public assistance institution, and the children's homes in the town, and the medical officer was confirmed in his post, with the stipulation that the sick wards were to be visited daily. Besides nurses, other staff at the institution then included a laundress, an engineer, a seamstress, and a teacher for the mentally-handicapped patients.[17] Medical departments there included a maternity ward, and hospital and isolation blocks.[18]

At the beginning of the Second World War, the institution was enlarged to form an emergency hospital. In 1939 the Ministry of Health leased some 2 a. behind the former workhouse from the county council, and put up a 'temporary hospital' comprising ten hutted wards, each of 30 beds, and an operating block.[19] The isolation block of the institution was also converted into accommodation for some of the additional nurses; others lived in the requisitioned no. 4 The Terrace nearby.[20] The existing and new buildings were opened as Driffield Base Hospital, largely for service personnel, civilian casualties, and prisoners, in 1940.[21] The hospital was managed by a sub-committee of the county's Public Assistance Committee, and run by the promoted former matron of the institution and a resident medical officer. Its staff was helped domestically by some of the institution's residents, employed for a small wage.[22]

After the war the hospital buildings were released to the county council which set about converting them into a Public Assistance Hospital to accommodate homeless or chronically sick people from the former workhouses at Bridlington, Howden, Patrington, and Pocklington, all then scheduled for closure in whole or

1 Ross, *Driffield*, 34.
2 RDB, 55/474/451 (1903).
3 Bulmer, *Dir. E Yorks.* (1892), 167; *Kelly's Dir. N & ER Yorks.* (1893), 406; (1897), 441; (1921), 497.
4 ER Educ. Cttee *Mins* 1929–30, 167.
5 RDB, 462/554/446.
6 Ibid. 450/196/154.
7 *Kelly's Dir. N & ER Yorks.* (1933), 451; (1937), 443; *DT* 27 Oct. 1988.
8 *Hosp. Yr Bk* (1949–50), 106; Fig. 59.
9 *Hosp. Yr Bk* (1964), 68. Plans of the two hospitals *c.* 1985 at NMR (Swindon), NBR 102111.
10 NMR (Swindon), NBR 102111; *DT* 20 Mar. 1986; *HDM* 22 Dec. 1994; *DP* 3 July 1998; OS Map 1:10,000, TA 05 NW (1970 edn).
11 It was presumably the official date, 15 January 1991, that was recorded on the plaque in the entrance in 2006.
12 *DT* 20 Mar. 1986; 8 Feb., 22 Nov. 1990.
13 *HDM* 22 Dec. 1994.
14 Inf. from Alfred Bean Hospital.
15 Sheahan and Whellan, *Hist. York & ER.* ii. 502; *Kelly's Dir. N & ER Yorks.* (1889), 373.
16 Above, this section, Driffield poor law union.
17 ER CC *Mins* 1931–2, 225–7, 343, 345, 452–3.
18 Ibid. 1934–5, 283; 1935–6, 166; 1942–3, 19.
19 RDB, 629/410/299; ER CC *Mins* 1939–40, 276, 428; *DT* 22 Nov. 1990.
20 ER CC *Mins* 1940–1, 182, 271; 1946–7, 236.
21 Ibid. 1940–1, 52; *DT* 22 Nov. 1990; RAF air photograph, run 53, no. 3028.
22 ER CC *Mins* 1939–40, 566; 1940–1, 51, 182.

in part.[1] In 1946 the wartime additions and the former institution became Driffield County Hospital. The employees of the emergency hospital, comprising a medical staff of 25 and about 80 other workers, were retained, and an establishment of almost 200 then approved for the new hospital, which was intended to provide 294 beds for patients in the huts and the old isolation block, and accommodation for 115 homeless residents. Changes to the buildings included the remodelling of the former workhouse infirmary as a nurses' home.[2]

The council's plans were probably informed by the likelihood of a further, general change in health provision. Also in 1946 the Act which would create the National Health Service, and remove the hospital from the council's control, passed through parliament. On the effective date, in 1948, the Leeds Regional Hospital Board and its East Riding Group Hospital Management Committee became responsible for the Driffield hospitals.[3] From 1948 the Driffield hospital was known as the East Riding General Hospital, except for the former workhouse, later named Wolds House, which accommodated the elderly until 1969.[4] About the date of reorganization in 1948, a new eight-bed maternity ward was opened at the hospital to replace the county council's maternity home in Church Street,[5] and it was also enlarged by the effective incorporation in the mid century of the neighbouring Alfred Bean Hospital.[6] The capacity of the East Riding General fluctuated downwards in the later 20th century, from some 280 beds about 1950 to 236 in 1974, evidently including those in the Alfred Bean Hospital, and 111 in 1986.[7]

Those housed in the former workhouse at Driffield included some mentally ill and handicapped patients. There had been 32 such admissions in 1917, and 52 were accommodated in 1934. By then those patients were beginning to be transferred to the recently-opened institution of the East Riding and York Joint Board for the Mentally Defective at Brandesburton; a few with mental problems remained at Driffield during the Second World War, when Brandesburton Hospital was requisitioned by the military, but they were moved to Brandesburton after it re-opened.[8] The succeeding East Riding General Hospital maintained the connection with mental illness, however, facilities there including a clinic for psychiatric out-patients.[9]

The East Riding General Hospital was closed in 1990, and demolished in 1992.[10] Much of the large site was soon after used for a housing estate.[11]

Northfield Hospital

Under the Isolation Hospitals Acts of 1883 and 1901, the county council in 1912 established a hospital district in the East Riding and a committee to run it, arrangements which were confirmed by the Local Government Board the following year.[12] The district comprised at first the areas of 15 of the 23 sanitary authorities in the East Riding, but was later enlarged.[13] It was decided to establish an isolation hospital in the centre of the district, and in 1914 the committee duly bought 5 a. on the east side of Scarborough Road at Driffield as its site.[14] The location of the hospital was opposed by Harrison Holt and Colonel Duncombe, respectively owner and tenant of Highfield, the grounds of which house were said to extend to within twenty yards of the proposed hospital, and another prospective neighbour, David Holtby of The Mount, Scarborough Road, threatened to leave the town. The committee, nevertheless, resisted the pressure to re-site the facility on the workhouse site in Bridlington Road.[15] A 'temporary' hospital of wood and asbestos was put up and opened in 1916, by which date cases of typhus in Driffield had had to be treated in the isolation block of the workhouse and at the Cottage Hospital.[16] Early in 1918 the hospital had 16 patients suffering from diphtheria and scarlet fever, most of them from Driffield town.[17] In 1919 and 1920 a former military hut and the buildings of a Hull hospital, of wood and asbestos, were bought to enlarge the 10-bed hospital, which subsequently comprised five wards and an enlarged administration block and could accommodate 42 patients.[18]

The hospital was managed by a medical superintendent and, as his assistant, by a Driffield doctor, and in 1922 the nursing staff comprised a matron and three nurses. At busy times private nurses had to be engaged to supplement the efforts of the permanent staff. The duties of the matron then included keeping fowls on the large site and supplying eggs to the hospital.[19] Many suffering

1 *VCH Yorks. ER.* ii. 67; v. 101.

2 ER CC *Mins* 1945–6, 309–10; 1946–7, 53–4, 139–42, 186.

3 ERAO, UDDR/1/8/58, Gen. Purposes Cttee, 23 Mar. 1961; UDDR/1/1/39, Finance Cttee, 13 Sept. 1965; ER CC *Mins* 1949–50, 81–2; Clarke, *Local Govt*, 97.

4 *DP* July 1998 (illus.); *DT* 20 Mar. 1986; 15 Sept. 1988; OS Map 1:10,000, TA 05 NW (1970 edn).

5 ER CC *Mins* 1946–7, 218, 386; 1947–8, 330.

6 *Hosp. Yr Bk* (1964), 68. Plans of the two hospitals *c.* 1985 at NMR (Swindon), NBR 102111.

7 *Hosp. Yr Bk* (1949–50), 106; *Hosp. and Health Services Yr Bk* (1976), 68; (1988), 69.

8 ER CC *Mins* 1946–7, 100; 1947–8, 200; *VCH Yorks. ER.* vii. 247.

9 *Hosp. Yr Bk* (1964), 68.

10 *DP* 3 July 1998.

11 *DT* 20 Mar. 1986; 2 Jan. 1993.

12 RDB, 402/394/340; ER Hosp. Cttee *Mins* 1913–25, 1–2. (Minutes at ERAO, CCER/1/5/21.)

13 ER Hosp. Cttee *Mins* 1925–34, 96–7.

14 Ibid. 1913–25, 3, 6; RDB, 166/330/275.

15 ER Hosp. Cttee *Mins* 1913–25, 22–3; *Kelly's Dir. N & ER Yorks.* (1913), 514.

16 ER Hosp. Cttee *Mins* 1913–25, 47–50, 52–3, 61.

17 Ibid. 111–12.

18 Ibid. 130, 136, 144, 156, 162, 257.

19 Ibid. 53, 175, 207; ER Hosp. Cttee *Mins* 1934–9, 135.

from scarlet fever were admitted in 1924, and in 1927 an epidemic of diphtheria inflated the number of patients treated; 74 were cared for in 1923, 147 the following year,[1] and 164 in 1927.[2] Difficulties were compounded in 1928 by a fire which destroyed the administration block and most of the wards, and reduced the accommodation to some ten beds. By then the East Riding hospital district had been enlarged to include Beverley borough,[3] and had a total population of 108,000, and it was thus proposed to rebuild the hospital for 60 patients.

The new, brick-built hospital, comprising three ward blocks, administrative building, laundry block, and porter's lodge, to designs by Bernard Stamford, the county architect, was put up from 1929; the site was enlarged by 3 a. in 1930,[4] and the following year the hospital was fully operational. The staff establishment then comprised seven nurses, five domestics, an engineer, and a gardener/ambulance driver.[5] An outbreak of typhus at Malton in 1932 and scarlet fever the following year tested the hospital, and some patients had to be sent instead to the isolation hospital at Howden.[6] In 1935 the prospect of the further enlargement of the hospital district led to another ward block for 24 patients being proposed, but that seems not to have been built.[7] Annual admissions in the later 1930s usually exceeded 200, and in 1936 and 1939 totalled some 360.[8]

In 1939 the committee was dissolved by order of the Minister of Health, and its property and functions transferred to the county council.[9]

By the mid 1940s the Driffield hospital had an establishment of almost forty staff but was under used, and arrangements were consequently made for infectious diseases to be treated instead in the facilities of neighbouring authorities, like Hull Corporation. As part of the new scheme, approved in 1948, the former isolation hospital at Driffield became the chief TB hospital in the riding, with 60–70 beds and a nursing establishment of 18. The management of the county sanatorium, soon afterwards called Northfield Sanatorium,[10] was then united with that of the county council's other hospital in Driffield at the former workhouse.[11] With the introduction of the National Health Service, also in 1948, the county hospitals were transferred to Leeds Regional Hospital Board, which in 1961 was considering making Northfield into a general hospital for the neighbourhood with 56 beds, and closing the other two hospitals in Driffield.[12] Variously described later as a chest, geriatric, and long-stay hospital, it had 78 beds in the 1960s and 1970s, and 58 in 1980.[13] Northfield Hospital was eventually closed by the East Yorkshire Health Authority in or soon after 1986, in anticipation of the building of a new community hospital.[14] All but the administration block was then demolished, and much of the site has been used for housing.[15] The main building, the administration block, was later sold for use as Northfield Manor Nursing Home.[16]

Infant Welfare Centre and Maternity Home

Under the Maternity and Child Welfare Act of 1918, the county council was obliged to provide some maternity and child welfare services.[17] By 1919 it had provided a few midwives in the riding, one of them based in Driffield, and it then set about meeting its responsibilities more fully by establishing an infant welfare centre in Driffield. The former grammar school premises at the junction of Church Street and Victoria Road were bought in 1919 and adapted for the centre, which was opened in 1920.[18] The welfare clinic was held on alternate Wednesdays, and from 1928 orthopaedic clinics were also held there.[19] From the outset a room in the building was also dedicated for use as a dental clinic for schools.[20] The accommodation for the clinics was improved about 1950, following the closure of the maternity home which had shared the premises at no. 28 Church Street. After the introduction of the NHS in 1948, the orthopaedic clinic at Church Street was provided by the hospital authority, and it may have been there also that the health authority held its Driffield school eye clinic.[21] A permanent dental surgery was provided in the 1960s,[22] and, as Driffield Health Services Clinic, the former welfare clinic was operated until at least 1973.[23]

1 ER Hosp. Cttee *Mins* 1913–25, 270–1, 276–7.
2 Ibid. 1925–34, 76–7, 96–7.
3 *VCH Yorks. ER.* vi. 230.
4 Illus. at NMR (Swindon), NBR 102113.
5 Ibid. 95–8; 123–4; 179–80, 191; RDB, 402/394/340.
6 ER Hosp. Cttee *Mins* 1925–34, 253, 285, 287.
7 Ibid. 1934–9, 54–5, 67, 72.
8 Ibid. 158; ER CC *Mins* 1939–40, 550.
9 ER Hosp. Cttee *Mins* 1934–9, 143, 152
10 *Hosp. Yr Bk* (1949–50), 106; OS Map 1:25,000, TA 05 (1953 edn).
11 ER CC *Mins* 1941–2, 188; 1945–6, 308; 1946–7, 339; 1947–8, 20, 82, 195, 333–4; *VCH Yorks. ER.* iv. 67.
12 ERAO, UDDR/1/8/45, Public Health...Cttee, 7 Mar. 1949; UDDR/1/8/58, Gen. Purposes Cttee, 23 Mar. 1961.
13 RDB, 1570/243/202; *Hosp. Yr Bk* (1964), 68; *Hosp. and Health Services Yr Bk* (1973), 71; (1976), 68; (1982), 69.
14 *DT* 20 Mar. 1986.
15 Illus. in *DT* Jan. 2000 (millennium edn).
16 NMR (Swindon), NBR 102113.
17 Clarke, *Local Govt*, 185.
18 RDB, 202/500/428; ER CC *Mins* 1919–20, 277–8, 280; 1920–1, 207; ER Educ. Cttee *Mins* 1919–20, 85–6, 148.
19 ER CC *Mins* 1920–1, 333; 1927–8, 383–4; ER Educ. Cttee *Mins* 1931–2, 58, 216; 1943–4, 48.
20 ER Educ. Cttee *Mins* 1919–20, 131, 148; 1920–1, 46.
21 ER CC *Mins* 1947–8, 330–1; 1948–9, 28; 1950–1, 56–7; *Hosp. Yr Bk* (1949–50), 107; (1964), 69; *Hosp. and Health Services Yr Bk* (1973), 72.
22 ER Educ. Cttee *Mins* 1963–4, 70; 1967–8, 22; ER CC *Mins* 1963–4, 385.
23 ER CC *Mins* 1972–3, 404.

Another part of the former grammar school was equipped as a maternity home for difficult confinements, and also opened in 1920.[1] The Driffield midwife had shortly before been transferred to Norton, and when it opened the maternity home was committed to the superintendant health visitor. In 1925, however, the Ministry of Health, which partly funded the home, insisted that a resident midwife be appointed to allow the chief health visitor to attend to her other duties, and from 1930 there was a second resident nurse-midwife at the home; from 1939 the maternity home was run by a matron.[2] The home was also funded from a maintenance charge on the patients,[3] the numbers of whom rose from about 40 in the later 1920s to 121 in 1934 and 219, the highest figure to date, in 1938.[4] The maternity home was discontinued after the Second World War when another one was provided at the County Hospital.[5] Part of the premises at no. 28 Church Street were later used to improve the welfare clinic there; the rest was made into flats for county health workers and office accommodation.[6] In 2006 the premises were empty and for sale and later demolished.

Girls' Hostel

In 1921 representatives of the Church, the county council, the local poor law boards, and others set up a branch of a diocesan organization dedicated to the protection and rescue of women, and helping unmarried mothers; it was known as the East Riding Association for Purity and Social Welfare from 1923, and as the East Riding branch of the York Diocesan Association for Moral Welfare by 1935.[7] A house, no. 2 Downe Street, was bought and equipped as a hostel in 1922–3, and about 1935 replaced by the larger no. 31 New Road. This hostel seems to have been given up *c.* 1960.[8]

Ambulance Service

The police provided a rudimentary ambulance service until the end of the Second World War. A purpose-built carriage was used from 1911, when it was given by the young Congregationalists; it was kept in a garage in Exchange Street, evidently that used also by the fire brigade.[9] At the coming of the NHS in 1948, responsibility for providing an ambulance service was transferred from the police to the county council,[10] which nevertheless used the police station garages in Wansford Road until a new ambulance station built in Victoria Road was opened in 1964.[11] The ambulance service was later organized regionally and in 2010 the Driffield station was part of the Yorkshire Ambulance Service.

RESIDENTIAL CARE

Children's Homes The responsibility for housing children passed, with the other functions of the poor law guardians, to the county council in 1930. The following year the homes inherited from the guardians comprised two for boys, Brockville (no. 7) Bridge Street and no. 43 Victoria Road, with 12 and 9 boys respectively, and a home lived in by 9 girls, at no. 42 Victoria Road.[12] The council then increased the provision for boys by buying Northern House, on the east side of Scarborough Road.[13] A lack of numbers caused Brockville to be closed in 1938,[14] and in 1957 the council closed the homes in Victoria Road.[15]

Brook Cottage community home was built by the county council on the site of Brook Cottages, Beckside, in the early 1970s.[16] For disturbed or handicapped children, the home was opened in or soon after 1974, replacing Northern House.[17] The latter was subsequently used by the education service as a residential centre until *c.* 2000; Northern House had been sold and re-occupied as a private house by 2006.[18] The Beckside home had probably been closed by 2001, when the successor authority, the ERYC, was proposing to sell land there,[19] and it stood empty in 2004.

Homes for the Elderly Under the 1948 National Assistance Act, the accommodation and care of those needy elderly people not requiring nursing was continued as the duty of the county council. In 1952 the council was supporting 63 such cases in the former workhouse, then part of the East Riding General Hospital.[20] Despite the building of another home, The Limes, in the town,[21] the council continued to maintain residents in the hospital, their accommodation being given the name Wolds House in 1956.[22] The following year 60 people lived in Wolds House.[23] It was closed in 1969.[24]

1 Ibid. 1920–1, 42, 457; ER Educ. Cttee *Mins* 1919–20, 148.
2 ER CC *Mins* 1919–20, 281; 1920–1, 457; 1921–2, 226; 1924-5, 370; 1930–1, 339, 341; 1939–40, 245.
3 Ibid. 1920–1, 207; 1938–9, 557; 1944–5, 197.
4 Ibid. 1927–8, 383–4; 1934–5, 386; 1938–9, 550.
5 Above, this section, ER Gen. Hosp.
6 ER CC *Mins* 1947–8, 330–1; 1948–9, 28; 1949–50, 516; 1959–60, 281.
7 Following based on ERAO, PE/10/T. 128–9; directories.
8 ER CC *Mins* 1949–50, 27; 1952–3, 388; 1956–7, 349.
9 Above, this section, fire service.
10 ERAO, UDDR/1/8/45, Public Health…Cttee, 7 Mar. 1949.
11 RDB, 1214/338/301; ER CC *Mins* 1961–2, 182; 1963–4, 268; Wood, *Policing*, 73–6 (illus.).
12 ER CC *Mins* 1930–1, 492.
13 RDB, 423/516/429; ERAO, UDDR/1/8/35, Highways…Cttee, 4 July 1938; ER CC *Mins* 1938–9, 84; directories.
14 RDB, 628/555/452; ER CC *Mins* 1938–9, 84; 1939–40, 436.
15 RDB, 1077/373/343; ER CC *Mins* 1955–6, 464.
16 ERAO, UDDR/1/1/46, Gen. Purposes Cttee, 7 Nov. 1972; RDB, 1829/464/405; 1833/509/435; 1863/326/274, etc.
17 Humbs. CC *Mins* 1974–5, C. 161; E. 257; F. 1197.
18 Ibid. 1975–6, B. 491; H. 944; inf. from King's Mill School, 2006.
19 *HDM* 2 Feb. 2001.
20 ER CC *Mins* 1952–3, 103, 105.
21 Below, this section.
22 ER CC *Mins* 1956–7, 222, 327.
23 Ibid. 1957–8, 14.
24 Ibid. 1968–9, 178.

60. *Great Driffield: Former Police Station, Eastgate North, 2011. Built 1843–4 as a lock-up with three cells and a house for the police superintendent of Bainton Beacon petty sessional division.*

As early as 1946, council policy had been to provide 'hostels of a "country house" type' for needy people not requiring nursing.[1] With assistance from the Ministry of Health, the council eventually provided The Limes, a purpose-built home for the elderly, on the east side of Scarborough Road, in the mid 1950s.[2] In 1957 The Limes had 38 residents.[3] As part of the national policy of privatising residential care, the home was sold in 1998.[4] In 2006 it had 51 rooms.[5] By arrangement with the health authority and later the county council, The Limes was also used from the 1990s to deliver day-care services, until then provided at the East Riding General Hospital. The day centre was moved *c.* 2005 to the community centre in Mill Street.[6]

In 1970 the county council bought Woodlands Hotel, formerly Souththorpe Lodge, demolished that building, and in 1971 built another home for *c.* 45 elderly people.[7] The management of the home, Woodlands, was later taken over by Humberside Independent Care Association, which about 1995 bought it from the county council. The home had 56 rooms in 2006.[8]

Millside Nursing Home About 1995 a nursing home was built in Riverside Close for people with severe learning and physical difficulties, hitherto cared for in hospitals then being closed. The home was put up and operated privately until the East Riding of Yorkshire Council and the health authority took it over, in or about 2003. In 2006 the small facility was home to 14 people.[9]

POLICE AND COURT SERVICES

Police

The earliest known system for ensuring public order and bringing wrongdoers to justice was the frankpledge system. As the name suggests, the system applied to freeholders, the conduct of the unfree tenantry being the responsibility of their respective lords. Freeholders were formed into associations of ten men, one of whom was responsible for the good behaviour of the group and for action being taken against crime in the locality. The system was supervised by a local court, that of the hundred, which in Driffield's case may have been held on a mound in the north-east of Elmswell.[10] Later in the Middle Ages, as was often the case, responsibility for the frankpledge system passed as a franchise, or liberty, to the various manor courts of the parish.[11]

About 1300 the system was augmented by the employment of constables. A statute of the late 13th

1 Ibid. 1946–7, 54.
2 RDB, 987/19/15; ER CC *Mins* 1954–5, 303; 1955–6, 201, 400, 427–8.
3 ER CC *Mins* 1957–8, 14.
4 ERYC *Mins* 1996–7, Council 123; 1997–8, Social Services Cttee 289; inf. from The Limes, 2006.
5 Nursing Homes Directory website, 2006.
6 Humbs. CC *Mins* 1990–1, 7169; inf. from The Limes, 2006.
7 RDB, 1658/318/276; ER CC *Mins* 1969–70, 115; 1970–1, 19–20; 1971–2, 125, 216, 241.
8 Inf. from Woodlands, 2006; Nursing Homes Directory website, 2006.
9 Inf. from Millside, 2006.
10 *VCH Yorks. ER*. iii. 130.
11 Clarke, *Local Govt*, 7–8; above, this section, manorial admin.

century ordered the appointment of two constables in each district, and from 1328 every parish had to appoint a constable.[1]

In Driffield parish there was a close connection between policing and the head manor court. The constables for Great and Little Driffield were appointed in the manor court, presumably because of its leet jurisdiction, that is, the privilege of overseeing the local frankpledge arrangements. The court apparently sat at the Red Lion inn in Middle Street North, and there is said to have been a lock-up in that inn's outhouses.[2]

Little is known of the parish's part in policing. It had its own lock-up at the workhouse near Cross Hill, and when those buildings were sold in the late 1830s it was proposed to use some of the proceeds in building a new lock-up; it is not known whether that was done.[3] There were also stocks and a pillory, the latter said to have been last used in 1808.[4] The stocks, which were portable, apparently stood in Market Place in the early 1800s,[5] and on Cross Hill in 1822. They stood in the Market Place when their use was revived in 1851.[6] They were later kept at the police station in Eastgate North; after that building's replacement in 1896–7 outside the new court house in Wansford Road, and from the 1970s at Driffield School.[7]

Supervision of the activities of local courts and constables devolved upon the justices of the peace, whose introduction as royal agents of justice and administration in the 14th century led to a decline in the importance of the king's earlier local representative, the sheriff. The justices sat in plenary sessions for the whole riding, the quarter sessions, and more frequently and locally in petty sessions held for particular parts of the East Riding. An executive officer later appointed for each petty sessional area was the High or Chief Constable; his specific duties came to include the licensing of ale-houses; dealing with diseases of livestock; the checking of weights and measures, and a variety of other matters even less related to policing.[8]

The modern county police force had its beginnings in Acts of the mid 19th century. Under the Parish Constables Act of 1842, the East Riding magistrates provided lock-ups in the petty sessional divisions, and appointed salaried superintending constables to take charge of them and the parish constables.[9] As the chief place in the petty sessional division of Bainton Beacon, Driffield was chosen as the site for the superintendent constable's house and station. Put up in 1843–4 in Eastgate North, between New Road and Washington Street, it included two or three cells.[10] The parish constables continued to be unpaid, part-time policemen, but the 1842 Act regulated their appointment and function: they were thus no longer to be appointed in courts leet but were to be chosen by the justices in petty sessions from lists of suitable candidates provided by the parish overseers. From the 1840s four parish constables were duly appointed for Driffield from candidates proposed by the select vestry, which also employed watching and lighting inspectors for the town.[11] The town evidently had a paid perpetual constable who carried the duties of the parish constables; for many years it was Joseph Dandy (d. 1852), who had been a sergeant in the Driffield Armed Association, the Driffield Volunteers and the local militia.[12]

More radical change resulted from the County and Borough Police Act of 1856, which ordered a paid constabulary to be established, but promised partial funding from central government to augment the local police rate. The East Riding force came into existence the following year.[13] In Bainton Beacon division, the initial force comprised the superintendent, based at Driffield, and six other officers, two of them also stationed in Driffield.[14] The quality of the policing remained low in the mid century, however. In 1847, for instance, an early superintendent at Driffield and one of his parish constables were sent for trial at the quarter sessions on theft charges, and the superintendent at Driffield from 1857 was guilty of many misdemeanors before his retirement in 1871.[15] Later changes to the policing of the riding included the substitution of a joint management committee of JPS and county councillors for the JPs alone in 1889.[16]

The county force continued to use Driffield's first police station for the rest of the century.[17] In 1896–7 new premises were put up in Wansford Road comprising a police station, with four cells and, once again, a house for the superintendent constable, and a court house.[18] The Eastgate building was probably used later to house police officers, and was eventually sold by the county council in 1956;[19] it remains as a private house. On the eve of the First World War the number of policemen attached to the Driffield station stood at fourteen,

1 Clarke, *Local Govt*, 18–19.

2 Wood, *Policing*, 1; above, this section, manorial admin.

3 ERAO, PE/10/T. 99, s.a. 1838; ibid. PUD/1/2/2, p. 31.

4 J. Nicholson, 'The Stocks in E Yorks.', *TERAS* iii (1895), 42–4.

5 Ross, *Driffield*, 91.

6 *HP* 29 Aug. 1851.

7 *DT* 18 Feb. 1998; OS Map 1:2,500, Yorks. CLXI. 12 (1910 edn); Wood, *Policing*, 4–5 (illus.).

8 Clarke, *Local Govt*, 18, 20–1; Clarke, *Country Coppers*, 9–10.

9 5 & 6 Vic. c. 109; Clarke, *Country Coppers*, 12, 108.

10 RDB, FX/68/91; *HP* 12 Jan. 1844; Sheahan and Whellan, *Hist. York & ER.* ii. 502; Wood, *Policing*, 1; OS Map 1:10,560, Yorks. CLXI (1855 edn); Fig. 60.

11 ERAO, PE/10/T. 99, s.a. 1842, 1844, 1866. The office of parish constable was formally ended in 1872: Clarke, *Local Govt*, 52.

12 *HP* 17 Oct. 1834; *YH* 28 Aug. 1852.

12 19 & 20 Vic. c. 69; Clarke, *Local Govt*, 52, 228–9; Wood, *Policing*, 118.

14 Clarke, *Country Coppers*, 19.

15 Ibid. 13, 23–4.

16 Clarke, *Local Govt*, 69; Clarke, *Country Coppers*, 38.

17 Bulmer, *Dir. E Yorks.* (1892), 167;

18 RDB, 80/323/300 (1896); *Kelly's Dir. N & ER Yorks.* (1897), 441; datestone; Wood, *Policing*, 2–3; below, buildings; Fig. 61.

19 RDB, 1027/554/480.

61. *Great Driffield: Court House, Wansford Road, 2011. Built in 1896 with adjoining police station it was the magistrates' court for Bainton Beacon until 2001.*

comprising the superintendent, a sergeant, and twelve constables; four of the constables policed the town while the other eight patrolled the rural parts of the division. During the conflict the depleted police force was supplemented from the East Yorkshire Volunteers, and the hooter at the steam laundry was employed to warn of air raids.[1]

The police force was reorganized later into progressively larger groupings. About 1920 the Buckrose division was thus added to that of Bainton, the superintendent at Driffield being made responsible also for Norton and the lesser stations in Buckrose, and the new police area being renamed in consequence the Driffield division. Further reorganization, in 1947, made Driffield a substation of Pocklington; subsequently the superintendent was based at Pocklington and the Driffield force was led by an inspector.[2] Soon afterwards, in the 1950s, Driffield was merged with Bridlington to form a new division of Buckrose. The East Riding of Yorkshire Constabulary was replaced finally in 1968 by the York & North East Yorkshire Police Authority, composed of the forces of the North and East Ridings and the city of York, and with a headquarters in Northallerton. That arrangement was revised at local government reorganization in 1974, when much of the former East Riding Constabulary was added to Hull Corporation's force and police from north Lincolnshire to create an authority to serve the new county of Humberside.[3] The court house in Wansford Road was closed in 2001,[4] but Humberside police continues to operate from the police station there.

Courts

In 1827 Driffield inhabitants petitioned for the town to become the magistrates' meeting place, instead of the New Inn at Bainton, 6 miles away.[5] A temporary change had been made by 1840, when the petty sessions were being held weekly in the new workhouse in Driffield.[6] The town's Corn Exchange was built with a room for the magistrates in 1842,[7] and subsequently the petty sessions for the Bainton Beacon division of Harthill wapentake were held at Bainton and Driffield on alternate fortnights.[8] In October 1858 it was decided to hold the fortnightly petty sessions only at Driffield because it had 'long been felt an inconvenience to have to attend at Bainton New Inn'.[9]

From the 1840s another court began to sit in the town. By Act of 1846, new branch courts of the county court, popularly known as small debts courts, were created to deal with civil suits involving sums of £20 or less occurring in districts made by dividing each county. The new court was presided over by a judge, and had a staff including one or more bailiffs, a treasurer, and a clerk. A county court district based

1 Wood, *Policing*, 32, 37–8.
2 Clarke, *Country Coppers*, 57; Wood, *Policing*, 48, 111.
3 RDB, 1828/374/287; Clarke, *Country Coppers*, 95, 106; Wood, *Policing*, 108.
4 Below, this section.
5 Letter of 21 Mar. 1827 at HUL, DDBM/32/13; Ross, *Driffield*, 87.
6 White, *Dir. E & NR Yorks.* (1840), 201.
7 RDB, FW/179/179; specification at ERAO, PUD/1/4/1.
8 White, *Dir. Hull & York* (1846), 416; Sheahan and Whellan, *Hist. York & ER.* ii, 495, 501–2; ERAO, PE/10/T. 99, s.a. 1850.
9 *HP* 8 Oct. 1858.

upon Driffield was duly formed in 1847.[1] The county court had to be held at least monthly,[2] and the Driffield court later sat at that interval in the Corn Exchange.[3]

A new court house in Exchange Street was built in 1856 by E. D. Conyers, whose official posts included the clerkship of both the petty sessions and the county court.[4] His building was later shared by the Mechanics' Institute and a savings bank. By the 1890s, when £20 a year was being paid for the court accommodation there, the local magistrates were meeting in petty session every fortnight; county court sessions had conversely become less frequent, with meetings at two-monthly intervals.[5]

A new court house was built with the police station in Wansford Road in 1896–7, and the petty sessions and the county court proceedings were subsequently held there. Mostly minor matters were dealt with by the courts - cases of drunkenness and disorderly conduct; assaults, and debts, including non-payment of local government rates.[6] The police court was renamed the magistrates' court in the 1950s, and in the 1980s prosecution was transferred from the police to the Crown Prosecution Service.[7] The court at Driffield was closed in 2001, after which local cases were heard in the magistrates' courts at Bridlington or Beverley.[8] The redundant court building was later added to the adjacent school.[9]

In 1862 Driffield's role in local law and order was augmented when, after petitioning by the justices of Yorkshire, a coroner's court was established in the town to serve the East Riding district, comprising much of the East and part of the North Riding.[10] The office of coroner for the East Riding was held by a succession of Driffield lawyers, George Conyers serving from 1804 to 1809, and his son, Edmund Dade Conyers, from 1826 until his death in 1863. Conyers was succeeded in the office by his partner J. M. Jennings (d. 1896). Appointment by then belonged to the Yorkshire county councils, and the Yorkshire Joint Committee which duly selected Luke White as East Riding coroner who served until his disgrace in 1919.[11] Another Exchange Street solicitor, Thomas Holtby, held the office 1919–47.[12]

HOUSING

By the early 20th century housing in the town was in short supply,[13] and some of the existing stock was evidently insalubrious and overcrowded. In 1904, for instance, the UDC, whose officers included a building surveyor, condemned as the home of a family of twelve a two-bedroomed cottage in Providence Place.[14] There was said to be a need for 20–30 houses in the town in 1919 but the UDC took no action.[15] It was only after considerable local agitation and the intervention of the Ministry of Health that Driffield UDC began to improve the town's housing.[16] In February 1934 houses in Queen Street, Harland Lane, and Eastgate South, as well as some in Paradise Row, also in Eastgate South, and Promise Square, were defined as clearance areas,[17] and before the outbreak of the Second World War the council had built 48 houses, mostly on part of the authority's allotments to the east of Scarborough Road.[18] The new road made there had been named Eastfield Road by 1938.[19] The first instalment, of 12 houses, with their design amended by the Ministry to include a bathroom, were put up by the Driffield builder Messrs. A. Leason & Sons in 1935 and 1936.[20] A hot water system was provided when the second group of houses were built soon afterwards.[21] In 1936 and 1937 the first tenants were moved into the new houses from soon-to-be demolished houses in Harland Lane, Paradise Row, Promise Square, and Providence Place.[22] Apart from the Scarborough Road development, the UDC's pre-war housing also included five bungalows, put up in Gibson Street in 1938.[23]

Development after the Second World War

The attempt to provide sufficient and decent housing for rent was delayed by the war and the shortages which followed it, but the council began to build again soon after the conflict ended, and by the mid 1950s it was housing 750 people in some 180 council houses.[24] Further building and a few purchases had increased the number of council dwellings in the town to 290 by

1 *HP* 9 Apr., 24 May 1847.

2 County Courts (England) Act, 9 & 10 Vic. c. 95; *Lond. Gaz.* 10 Mar. 1847, pp. 990–1017.

3 Sheahan and Whellan, *Hist. York & ER.* ii. 501–2.

4 White, *Dir. Hull & York* (1851), 601.

5 RDB, 193/39/37; Bulmer, *Dir. E Yorks.* (1892), 167; Wood, *Policing*, 2.

6 RDB, 80/323/300 (1896); directories; Wood, *Policing*, 2–3, 6–8.

7 *DT* Jan. 2000 (millennium edn).

8 Notice at court building, 2003; *HDM* 17 Jan. 2002.

9 Above, soc. hist., educ. (Board school); Fig. 61.

10 *Lond. Gaz.* 29 Apr. 1862, pp. 2217–20.

11 Ross, *Driffield*, 195; below, politics.

12 *The Times* 16 Dec. 1947.

13 BIA, V. 1912–22/Ret.

14 ERAO, UDDR/1/8/1, Sanitary ... Cttee, 4 July 1904; UDDR/1/1/1, p. 24.

15 *HT* 29 May 1919

16 Ibid. 19 Dec. 1931; 14 Oct., 16 Dec. 1933; 17 Feb., 14 Apr., 15 Dec. 1934; 16 Nov. 1935; ERAO, UDDR/1/8/33, Public Health...Cttee, 1 Oct. 1936.

17 ERAO, UDDR/1/8/30, Housing Cttee, 19 Feb. 1934.

18 Ibid. UDDR/1/8/31, Public Health...Cttee, 11 Feb. 1935; UDDR/1/8/32, Burial, Allotments...Cttee, 3 Sept. 1935; *Driffield Official Guide* (1949), 18; below, this section, allotment gardens.

19 ERAO, UDDR/1/8/35, Public Health ...Cttee, 10 Oct. 1938.

20 Ibid. UDDR/1/8/32, Public Health...Cttee, 29 May, 12 July 1935; 13 Jan., 9 Mar. 1936.

21 Ibid. 6 Jan. 1936.

22 Ibid. 9 Mar. 1936; UDDR/1/8/33, Public Health...Cttee, 11 May, 2 June 1936; 4 Jan. 1937.

23 Ibid. UDDR/1/8/34, Public Health...Cttee, 21 Feb., 7 Mar. 1938; UDDR/1/8/35, Public Health...Cttee, 4 *and* 25 July 1938; UDDR/1/8/36, Public Health...Cttee, 11 Dec. 1939; RDB, 598/217/174.

24 ERAO, UDDR/1/8/51, Housing...Cttee, 5 Apr. 1954; UDDR/1/8/52, Housing...Cttee, 6 Mar. 1956.

62. *Great Driffield: Kirby Homes of Rest, Bridlington Road, 2006. Founded in 1932 by W. L. Kirby, miller, the son of a former owner of Bell Mills, and built the following year.*

1972,[1] and to some 470 by the end of the century. Some of the housing provided by the UDC and the district councils which succeeded it was sold to the tenants in the late 20th century. In 2001 Driffield civil parish had 4,954 dwellings, of which 366 were rented from the then housing authority, the East Riding of Yorkshire Council; owner-occupations accounted for 4,007 properties, and the 581 remaining were rented from private landlords.[2]

Scarborough Road Estate In 1939 the Scarborough Road site had been enlarged by the purchase of almost 7 a. lying to the north of Eastfield Road, between Allotments Lane and Brickyard Lane,[3] and it was there that the UDC resumed building in 1946 or 1947,[4] Brickyard Lane being improved as Northfield Road.[5] More houses, in Northfield Crescent, were occupied in 1949.[6] A further 4 a. was then bought for housing,[7] and between 1952 and 1954 another forty houses were put up in a continuation of Northfield Road and a cul-de-sac called Northfield Avenue.[8] More land was bought in 1958,[9] and between 1960 and 1962 Messrs D. Naylor & Son of Driffield built some 40 houses for the council along the new Star Hill Road,[10] which was completed with another 20 houses in 1968 and 1969.[11]

There was further building on the council allotments off Scarborough Road from the late 1970s. Fifty homes, a mixture of houses, bungalows, and flats, were then put up in Eastfield Road and new streets called Southfield Road and Southfield Close,[12] and 16 more bungalows for the elderly were added *c.* 1990.[13]

Deira Court In the late 1960s the UDC in association with the county council provided sheltered housing for the elderly. The site, on the east side of Scarborough Road, was bought in 1967,[14] and Deira Court, comprising 41 flats and 5 bungalows, completed in 1969.[15]

1 Ibid. UDDR/1/1/45, Housing...Cttee, 7 Feb. 1972.
2 East Riding of Yorkshire Council, parish profiles, derived from the Office for National Statistics, Census 2001. A copy of the profiles was kept in Beverley Public Library in 2006.
3 RDB, 618/583/403.
4 ERAO, UDDR/1/8/43, Public Health...Cttee, 1 July 1946; UDDR/1/8/44, Public Health...Cttee, 3 Nov. 1947.
5 Ibid. UDDR/1/8/43, Public Health...Cttee, 9 Sept. 1946; UDDR/1/8/44, Public Health ...Cttee, 1 Mar. 1948; RDB, 630/496/410; 738/66/58.
6 ERAO, UDDR/1/8/46, Housing...Cttee, 7 June, 7 Nov. 1949.
7 RDB, 838/19/18.
8 ERAO, UDDR/1/8/47, Housing...Cttee, 8 Aug. 1950; UDDR/1/8/48, Housing...Cttee, 7 Jan. 1952; UDDR/1/8/49, Housing ...Cttee, 5 Aug. 1952; UDDR/1/8/50, Housing...Cttee, 6 July 1953.
9 RDB, 1109/321/288.
10 ERAO, UDDR/1/8/57, Housing...Cttee, 26 May 1960; UDDR/1/8/58, Housing...Cttee, 4 Sept., 2 Oct. 1961; UDDR/1/1/36, Housing...Cttee, 2 July 1962.
11 Ibid. UDDR/1/1/41, Housing...Cttee, 2 Oct. 1967; UDDR/1/1/42, Housing...Cttee, 7 Oct. 1968; UDDR/1/1/43, Housing...Cttee, 7 July, 2 Sept. 1969.
12 ERAO, EYEY/1/4/10/1, Housing Cttee, 30 Sept. 1975; 14 Mar. 1978; 4 Sept. 1979; 5 May 1981; ibid. EYEY/1/4/8/1, Housing...Cttee, 29 Nov. 1982.
13 Ibid. EYEY/1/4/8/2, Housing...Cttee, 1 June, 2 Nov. 1987; 11 Apr. 1988.
14 RDB, 1494/293/264; 1494/295/265.
15 ERAO, UDDR/1/1/39, Housing...Cttee, 4 Oct., 1 Dec. 1965; 3 Jan. 1966; UDDR/1/1/41, Housing ...Cttee, 2 Oct. 1967; UDDR/1/1/42, Housing...Cttee, 2 Dec. 1968; UDDR/1/1/43, Housing...Cttee, 14 July 1969.

The Close In the 1960s the UDC planned a 'grouped dwellings scheme' of old people's flats with accommodation for a warden; it was then allotted funds for that purpose by the county council, but it was only in 1974 that its successor, North Wolds District Council, bought the site, of some 5 a. in the junction of Scarborough and Bridlington Roads, adjoining an old people's home, The Limes, and the recently completed Deira Court.[1] The new estate, which had been put up by 1978, eventually comprised a mixture of flats, bungalows and houses, most of the *c.* 75 dwellings standing loosely built in The Close, with smaller groups in Paddock Court, Limes Walk, and Eastholme Close.[2]

Washington Street and Smaller Projects Besides the larger housing projects, the councils have also developed sites in the town, sometimes in connection with their duty to clear unsatisfactory private housing. In 1957 four flats were built on the site of Paradise Row, in Eastgate South,[3] and later land nearby was used for eight houses called Galloway Court. As late as 1964 the UDC was ordering the British Railways Board as the owner of St John's Place to convert the earth closets there to water,[4] and action to remove the worst housing seems to have been given fresh impetus by local government re-organization in 1974. The new North Wolds District Council closed houses in the town, and designated St John's Place, as well as terraces in Washington Street, Eastgate North, Westgate, and Providence Place, for clearance.[5] The council duly rebuilt Washington Street with some forty dwellings, mostly flats, about 1980.[6] Smaller-scale infilling with council houses has included old people's bungalows built on land acquired with Primrose Cottage, Eastgate North, in 1958,[7] and, also in the north of the town, Park Court.

Alongside its building operations, the councils have worked to improve private housing in Driffield, in partnership with national government. From the 1960s the UDC thus administered a system of improvement grants designed to encourage house owners to provide basic amenities and modernize their properties,[8] and later there were also schemes to modernize the older of the council houses.[9] The new district authority which succeeded the UDC also attempted to increase the housing stock for needy groups by collaborations with a housing association and a self-build project, but such initiatives seem to have been unproductive.[10]

ALLOTMENT GARDENS

The first allotments were the ¼-a. plots that the Ancient Order of Foresters let to members from a few acres of land near the town in 1850.[11] The scheme, which did not last long, was revived in 1853 by four leading townsmen, Thomas Atkinson, Henry Angas, William Turner, and Robert Tonge, who leased some 32 a. in three or four fields in on Beverley Road for allotment gardens for the 'industrial classes'. The land was divided into ¼-a. plots and sub-let that year to about 75 tenants, including the poor law union for the use of the old men and children in the workhouse. The tenants of the gardens, popularly-known as the 'diggings', were also encouraged with a gift of lime. Apart from the food produced to feed poor families and for them to sell, the allotments were then said to be morally and socially beneficial by promoting habits of industry, providing useful and profitable employment for the leisure hours of working men, and removing 'labourers from the street corners and the alehouses'.[12] These allotments were lost in 1892–3 when the holders were given notice to quit.[13]

By this time there were other allotments, some probably on land offered to the local board by Lord Londesborough and Lady Downe in 1888, following the Allotments Act.[14] Around 1900 there were three sets of allotments in the north of the town, two lying south of York Road and one on the west side of Eastgate North, and a fourth set at the south end of the town, adjoining Albion Street.[15] More permanent arrangements were made by Driffield UDC in 1912, on 44 a. to the east of Scarborough Road bought the previous year.[16] Those gardens were supplemented by others on land requisitioned by the council in 1917 and 1919, and soon afterwards the council met the increased demand for plots by reducing the size of some of them. During the Second World War, the council once again requisitioned land for allotments.[17] By the mid century the allotment gardens mostly lay on the outskirts of the town. Besides those near Scarborough Road, there were

1 ER CC *Mins* 1967–8, 228; 1968–9, 199; ERAO, EYEY/1/4/10/1, Housing Cttee, 31 Dec. 1974; 11 Feb. 1975.

2 *DT* 6 July 1978.

3 RDB, 401/523/443; 494/342/265; 965/279/251; 971/24/24; 1066/179/160; ERAO, UDDR/1/8/52, Housing...Cttee, 4 July 1955; UDDR/1/8/54, Housing...Cttee, 1 July 1957.

4 ERAO, UDDR/1/1/38, Public Health Cttee, 14 Dec. 1964.

5 Ibid. EYEY/1/4/10/1, Housing Cttee, 11 Feb., 18 Nov. 1975; 5 July 1977; 14 Nov. 1978.

6 Ibid. 13 Feb., 4 Sept. 1979.

7 Ibid. UDDR/1/8/54, Housing...Cttee, 10 Feb. 1958; UDDR/1/8/56, Housing...Cttee, 25 May 1959; UDDR/1/8/58, Housing...Cttee, 17 Apr. 1961; RDB, 1098/524/463.

8 ERAO, UDDR/1/1/37, Housing...Cttee, 3 Feb. 1964; UDDR/1/1/45, Housing...Cttee, 6 Mar. 1972.

9 Ibid. UDDR/1/1/45, Housing...Cttee, 4 Oct. 1971.

10 Ibid. EYEY/1/4/10/1, Housing Cttee, 1 July 1975; 16 June, 18 Nov. 1980; EYEY/1/4/8/2, Housing...Cttee, 2 Nov. 1987.

11 *HA* 13 Dec 1850.

12 K. J. Allison, 'The provision of allotment gardens in E Yorks', *Northern Hist.* 37 (2000), 275–6; *HP* 28 Jan. 1853, 13 July 1855 ; *HA* 6 May 1853; White, *Dir. Hull & York* (1851), 600–01, 604, 606.

13 *DT* 22 Apr. 1893.

14 *YH* 18 Feb. 1888.

15 OS Map 1:2,500, Yorks. CLXI. 12 (1893 and 1910 edns).

16 RDB, 135/37/35; ERAO, UDDR/1/1/1, p. 52; ER CC *Mins* 1911–12, 218–19.

17 Allison, 'Allotment gardens', 283, 285–7, 289.

then gardens on the west side of Spellowgate; to the east of Wansford Road, and west of Skerne Road. Of the earlier gardens within the town, only those to the north of Church Street remained then.[1] Land adjoining the drill hall was also said to have been used for gardens in the mid century.[2]

The Scarborough Road allotments had been reduced in the 1930s by the building of council houses,[3] and in the later 20th century the area given over to allotment gardens generally shrank further. On the Scarborough Road site, some 15 a. of allotments remained beside Allotment(s) Lane until the mid 1970s, when they were closed by North Wolds District Council for more house building. Replacement gardens then made on another part of the 44 a. bought in 1911, to the east of the cemetery,[4] were run in 2006 by Driffield Town Council; the site then comprised 116 plots and car parking.[5] When the Skerne Road allotments were closed about 1970, there were only two plotholders, one of whom was subsequently accommodated on land at the UDC's sewage works.[6] The Wansford Road gardens largely disappeared *c.* 2000 under the private housing of the New Walk estate.[7] Allotments remain, however, on the large Spellowgate site, which is leased for the purpose and is privately operated.[8]

Allotment gardens had been made at Little Driffield, on the Elmswell estate of the earl of Londesborough, by the late 19th century. The 8-a. plot, lying alongside the northern back lane of the village, was shared among cottagers for rents amounting to £15 a year in 1905, and that use continued until at least 1931, and possibly into the 1950s.[9] Part of the site was occupied in 2004 as the village football field.

PARKS

North End Park In 1922 Mr and Mrs R. Holtby of Elmswell gave the Hall Garth site to the UDC as a playground for the children of Driffield.[10] It was later improved as North End Park, some work being done in the later 1940s.[11] The UDC bought land from the executors of R. T. Holtby to enlarge the park in 1967.[12] It was later managed by the town council, which in 1999 created an area for skateboarding there;[13] in 2004 there was also a football pitch and a children's playground.

Part of the park was used for a garden of remembrance commemorating local war dead. Driffield Social Committee put up a shelter there incorporating a Second World War memorial in or about 1951.[14] In the early 1990s the surrounding ground was landscaped by the East Riding of Yorkshire Council, the WRVS, and subscribers, and in 1993 a stone was added there honouring the members of the local Bomber Command stations, including that at Driffield, who lost their lives between 1942 and 1945.[15] The park, also called Hall Garth Recreation Ground, was further improved *c.* 2000, when it comprised some 1.8 ha.[16]

Millennium Green At the instigation of the town council, and with help from the Countryside Commission (later Agency) and the National Lottery, land at King's Mill was bought in 1999 for a town green and to mark the millennium.[17]

CHARITIES

18TH-CENTURY CHARITIES

Ellis Francis Ellis, governor and merchant of Fort St George, Madras (now Chennai), India, left £100 for Driffield church, just over half of which was used to buy 1½ oxgang in Wetwang in 1711 or 1712. The net income from the land was to be divided into halves, one part being paid to the incumbent for a sermon on Good Friday, and the other used to defray the costs of the churchwardens.[18] From 1764 the incumbent's duty was recorded as the provision of two sermons a year in Great Driffield church.[19] The land, then let for £3 10*s.* a year,[20] was exchanged for 26 a. at the inclosure of Wetwang in 1806.[21] The holding was let for £38 in 1897,[22] but was evidently sold later, and in 2006 nothing was known of the charity.[23]

1 OS Map 1:10,560, TA 05 NW (1956 edn); OS Map 1:10,000, TA 05 NW (1970 edn); RAF air photographs, run 53, no. 3030; run 79, no. 4130.

2 Inf. from Christine Malpas, Driffield, 2006.

3 ERAO, UDDR/1/8/31, Public Health...Cttee, 11 Feb. 1935; UDDR/1/8/32, Burial, Allotments...Cttee, 3 Sept. 1935.

4 Ibid. EYEY/1/4/10/1, Housing Cttee, 30 Sept. 1975.

5 Inf. from Claire Binnington, Driffield Town Council, 2006.

6 ERAO, UDDR/1/1/44, Gen. Purposes Cttee, 8 Sept. 1970; UDDR/1/1/45, GPC, 6 Apr., 7 July 1971. For earlier gardens there, see ERAO, UDDR/1/1/1, p. 142.

7 Some allotments remained there in 2004. *DT* 3 Dec. 1981; 5 Aug. 1982.

8 Inf. from Claire Binnington, Driffield Town Council, 2006.

9 RDB, 73/365/331 (1905); 425/332/270; OS Map 1:2,500, Yorks. CLXI. 11 (1893 edn); OS Map 1:10,560, TA 05 NW (1956 edn).

10 RDB, 253/391/332; *DT* 4 Mar. 1922

11 Concrete bridge dated 1946.

12 RDB, 1524/426/381.

13 ERYC *Mins* (1998–9), Educ....Cttee, 1457.

14 ERAO, UDDR/1/8/47, Housing...Cttee, 5 Feb. 1951.

15 *DP* 9 Sept. 1993.

16 Noticeboard, 2006; ERYC website, parks, 2004.

17 *DP* 24 Dec. 1996; *HDM* 9 Jan., 18 May 1999; noticeboard; Countryside Agency website, 2004.

18 Draft, and possibly defective, deed at HUL, DDMC/99/1; BIA, TER. J. Driffield 1716, [1726].

19 BIA, TER. J. Driffield 1764.

20 *Drummond's Visit.* i, p. 139.

21 BIA, TER. J. Driffield 1809.

22 ERAO, PE/10/T. 71.

23 Inf. from Mr D. Longbottom, Driffield, 2006.

It seems that either the unspent part of Francis Ellis's bequest was diverted to the relief of the poor or that another, similar charity was created by the bequest of a Matthew Ellis, presumably a relative of Francis. The real or supposed charity of Matthew Ellis comprised a gift of £100, the interest on which was to be used each year to relieve poor persons chosen by the overseer. The poor's charity was lost in the 1790s, when the holder of the money became insolvent.[1]

Crompton Walter Crompton by will proved in 1714 left £1 a year from land at Sunderlandwick, in Hutton Cranswick, for distribution to poor widows and widowers of Driffield parish. His charity was still active in 1823,[2] but no more is known of it.

LATER CHARITIES

Westgate Almshouses John Gray of Great Driffield (d. 1798) built almshouses on the east side of Westgate, immediately north of the new Methodist chapel,[3] to house seven poor, elderly men or women of the town not in receipt of poor relief; the cottages were to be occupied rent-free, but the beneficiaries were to keep them in repair. Gray left the trust to a relative, but the almshouses were later the responsibility of the overseers of the poor, and were given to widows.[4] In 1851 the cottages were administered by unspecified 'trustees' and occupied by five poor women.[5] The almshouses, or widows' rooms, were transferred later from the overseers to the UDC. The building was condemned in 1957, sold in 1962 to the Methodist church, and has been demolished.[6]

Church Rest Houses In 1910 W. R. Sharrock, vicar of Driffield, bought 14 cottages in and to the south of Church Lane.[7] Those premises were mostly demolished and in 1913 twelve new cottages were built on the site but facing Westgate. The next year Sharrock conveyed the new houses and the two remaining to trustees as a memorial to his wife, Elizabeth Anna Sharrock (d. 1913).[8] The newly-built cottages were to be used as almshouses, called the (Memorial) Church Rest Houses, and maintained from the rents from the older houses. The almshouses were for occupation by the elderly rent free, with the possible exception of the central cottage, which might be allotted to a nurse caring for the other residents. The endowment was later enlarged by the bequest of some £2,300 left by Canon Sharrock (d. 1940)[9] for the maintenance of the almshouses and the provision of occasional allowances to the occupiers. By the 1960s tenants were being charged a small sum towards repairs. The houses were modernized in the 1970s.[10] In 2003 the Church Rest Houses charity had a gross annual income of some £10,000.[11]

Railway Cottages The North-Eastern Railway Cottage Homes & Benefit Fund, established to provide homes for railwaymen invalided in the Great War and later also for other disabled employees, built two cottages in Wansford Road in 1930.[12] The cottages were managed by the Railway Housing Association & Benefit Fund in 2006.[13]

Kirby Homes of Rest By a deed of 1932 a charity was created by W. L. Kirby, a local miller, and the following year almshouses were built in Bridlington Road.[14] The Railway Housing Association & Benefit Fund, which also had accommodation for disabled people in Wansford Road, took over the almshouses about 1982, and modernised them the following year. In 2006 the charity ran the Kirby Homes as sheltered housing for disabled people over 55 years old, employing a non-resident warden to assist the tenants.[15]

Dunning G. B. Dunning (d. 1938) left nos. 32–3 Scarborough Road in trust for letting at low rents to elderly married couples.[16] Charity Commission Schemes were obtained in 1978 and later, and by 2003, when the gross annual income was almost £6,000, the houses were let on weekly tenancies to people over 50 year in need of various kinds.[17]

Etherington and La Marche The Etherington and La Marche charity was founded by deed of 1870 and will of Jane Holden (née La Marche), proved in 1871. She left almost £7,000 stock for needy Anglican clergymen, merchants, and their families living in Great Driffield and Hull. The annual income was £280 net in 1964; £700 about 1980; just over £1,000 in 1996–7, but only about £400 by 2003–4, the last two gross sums. It was used mostly to help retired clergymen *c.* 1980, but in the early 21st century was being allowed to accumulate.[18]

1 *9th Rep. Com. Char.* 746.
2 Ibid. 745–6.
3 RDB, 304/202/162.
4 ERAO, DDX/17/15; Ross, *Driffield*, 83.
5 ERAO, TA/13; ibid. PE/10/T. 120; TNA, HO 107/2366.
6 ERAO, UDDR/1/8/54, Gen. Purposes Cttee, 7 May 1957; UDDR/1/8/57, Gen. Purposes Cttee, 6 Dec. 1960; UDDR/1/8/58, Gen. Purposes Cttee, 23 Mar. 1961; RDB, 1275/251/226.
7 Following based on ERAO, PE/10/T. 111.
8 Window in Great Driffield ch.
9 BIA, Fac. 1953/2/12.
10 ERAO, PE/10/T. 96, 159.
11 Char. Com. central register, 2004.
12 *Humbs. Dir. of Char.* (Humbs. CC, Beverley, *c.* 1980), 120; datestone.
13 Inf. from the charity, Bank Top House, Garbutt Square, Darlington.
14 Review of Char. *Rep.*, 143; *Kelly's Dir. N & ER Yorks.* (1937), 443; Fig. 62.
15 Inf. from the charity, Bank Top House, Garbutt Square, Darlington, and the warden, 2006.
16 RDB, 634/423/330; ERAO, NCH/39/3.
17 Char. Com. central register, 2004.
18 *VCH Yorks. ER.* i. 338; *Humbs. Dir. of Char.* 38, 47; Review of Char. *Rep.* 118; Char. Com. central register, 2004; above, manors and estate, Driffield (Etherington).

Horace Taylor By will proved in 1974, the timber merchant Horace Taylor left land for the benefit of the residents of Driffield, the rents from which could be distributed as cash grants to the needy; spent on providing medical help, or otherwise used to support worthy causes.[1] In 1999, when the permitted objects included helping certain youth clubs, the gross income was £20,000.[2]

Driffield Charitable Society Founded in 1882, the vicar, the Revd Horace Newton, was the first chairman and the miller H. D. Marshall, a Congregationalist, was the secretary, a post he held until his death in 1910.[3] In 1884–5 the society distributed 100 bags of coal, given by Harrison Holt, and over 5,500 pints of soup funded by Thomas Holtby, brewer, Canon Newton and W. O. Jarratt.[4]

The Charitable Society was registered as a charity in 1964 for the benefit of the residents of Driffield. The charity was later said 'to enable those who desire to help the suffering to do so in such a manner that they are not encouraging idleness'. About 1980 the small income, variously put at some £10 or £20, was being given to a community organization. In the late 1990s the gross income was less than £50 a year, and there was no expenditure.[5] It ceased to exist and was removed from the Charity Commissions register in 2005.[6]

POLITICS

National and local politics played a significant part in Driffield life through much of the 19th and 20th century. The semi-industrial and commercial character of the rapidly expanding town with its sizeable freeholder community, along with a strong Nonconformist presence, meant that Driffield's political complexion contrasted with that of its purely agricultural and great landowner dominated hinterland. In the later 19th century the way the town voted was seen to be crucial in determining the result in parliamentary elections for the Buckrose constituency.

Before the mid 19th century the main evidence of political affiliation is provided by the poll books produced for parliamentary elections. Driffield was in the vast Yorkshire constituency until 1832, then in the much smaller East Riding constituency, both returning two MPs, but with few contested elections. After a by-election in 1742, when 32 Driffield freeholders voted for Cholmley Turner, the successful Whig candidate, and 5 for the Tory, George Fox, there were only three contests before the introduction of the Secret Ballot Act in 1872.[7]

The first was the celebrated 1807 Yorkshire election when voting took place over 15 days in the Castle Yard at York. The three candidates were William Wilberforce, Independent Tory, Hon. Henry Lascelles, Tory, and Lord Milton, Whig.[8]

The strong support for Milton from Driffield residents, two-thirds of them voting for him, was unusual for the East Riding. A similar number voted for the popular local candidate Wilberforce, but less than a third, probably die-hard Tories, cast one of their two votes for Lascelles. This contrasted with the town's rural hinterland and the East Riding as a whole where the support for Wilberforce outstripped that for the other two candidates.[9] Some influence in favour of Milton may have been exerted on Driffield residents by

Place of residence	*No of voters*	*Wilberforce*		*Lascelles*		*Milton*	
Great and Little Driffield	69	46	67%	20	29%	45	65%
Rural hinterland*	231	186	81%	88	38%	105	45%
East Riding	3,556	2,754	77%	1,771	50%	1,313	37%
Yorkshire	22,363	11,806	53%	10,990	49%	11,177	50%

Source: Yorks. Poll Book (1807).
* 42 townships later included in Driffield Poor Law Union area. (White, *Dir. Hull & York* (1851), 598.)

Table 15. *Yorkshire Election 1807: Driffield and East Riding*

1 *Humbs. Dir. of Char.* 48, 128; Review of Char. *Rep.* 143; inf. from the charity, 2006.
2 *Char. Com. central register, 2004.*
3 *HP* 13 Apr. 1883.
4 Ibid. 17 Apr. 1885.
5 *Char. Com. central register, 2004; Humbs. Dir. of Char.* 144; Review of Char. *Rep.* 142–3.
6 www.charitycommission.gov.uk
7 *Yorks. Poll Book* (1742).
8 E. A. Smith, 'The Yorks. Elections of 1806 and 1807: a study in electoral management', *Northern History* 2 (1967), 62–90.
9 Table 15; *Yorks. Poll Book* (1807).

Place of residence	*No of voters*	*Bethell*		*Broadley*		*Thompson*	
Great and Little Driffield	119	56	47%	45	38%	66	55%
Driffield District	606	411	68%	333	55%	254	42%
East Riding	6,204	3,592	58%	3,257	52.5%	2,985	48%

Source: ER Poll Book (1837): Driffield District.

Table 16. *East Riding Election 1837: Driffield and East Riding*

the lord of manor and major landowner, Richard Langley, who from the voting pattern of the villages on his estates in the North Riding seems to have been a Whig supporter.[1] The other prominent landowners, the Etheringtons, were Milton supporters. George Etherington and his brother-in-law, John B. La Marche, both resident in Hull, plumped for Milton, and Henry Etherington, then a merchant in Dantzig, split his votes between Wilberforce and Milton.[2] Twenty-two Driffield residents split their votes between Wilberforce and Milton, and 23 plumped for Milton.[3] Amongst the latter were George Conyers, the town's leading solicitor and David Anderson, a prominent Wesleyan Methodist.

David Anderson (1768–1849), a nurseryman and seedsman, was the most politically active resident in the early nineteenth century.[4] On his death it was noted that he 'took especial interest in all the great political questions of the day. He was decidedly liberal in his opinions, and an ardent advocate for the abolition of the restrictions on commerce, for an extension of the representative system, the propagation of peace principles, and the civil and religious liberty of the subject.'[5] Anderson took a lead in all the 'progressive' movements of the times regularly drawing up petitions from the town at his own expense. These included the petition from protestant Dissenters of Great Driffield for the repeal of the Test and Corporation Acts that was presented by Lord Milton to the House of Commons in 1827, and at least a further eight petitions from the town presented there in 1830–34 dealing with, amongst other topics, the abolition of slavery, the repeal of assessed taxes, better observance of the Sabbath, and in favour of reform.[6] There was much popular support in Driffield for parliamentary reform. The news of the king's dissolution of Parliament following the defeat of the first Reform Bill in 1831 was greeted with great rejoicings in the town, and when the second bill was passed by the Commons there was a display of fireworks and the town band paraded the streets until late.[7] Concern over their possible rejection of the bill led to a petition in its favour being sent from Driffield to the House of Lords.[8] The defeat of the bill, the later resignation of the Whig government, and the attempt by the duke of Wellington to form a Tory government were not well received in the town. On 16 May 1832 the vicar, Richard Allen, recorded in his diary that there had been 'an ignorant rabble parading the streets of Driffield Magna preceded by a Band of Music and an Effigy which was ultimately committed to the flames'.[9] The following month, with the Whigs returned to office and the third Reform Bill rapidly passed, the vicar commented 'What folly are the Sons of Ignorance guilty of in rejoicing at the passing of the Reform Act, without waiting to see what effects it will produce.'[10]

The Reform Act did not greatly increase the number of Driffield residents eligible to vote in proportion to the rise in population, but it did create the new smaller East Riding constituency, the first election for which took place in 1837. The candidates, all East Riding landowners, were two Tories, Richard Bethell of Rise, chairman of the East Riding Quarter Sessions, and Henry Broadley of Welton, and a Whig, Paul Thompson from Escrick, near York.

Once again the Whig candidate had the most support at Driffield but came bottom of the poll overall. For the Tories Bethell a popular figure clearly had the advantage over Broadley despite, or because, the latter owned over 500 a. at Driffield. Amongst those who voted for the two Tories were the vicar, Revd George Allen, Washington Harrison and Joshua Horwood, surgeons, William Jarratt, bank manager, and Matthew Turner, Broadley's tenant at Danesdale.[11] Those who plumped for the Whig candidate included active supporters of

1 *Yorks. Poll Book* (1807), 297–300, 306, 315. Langley appears not to have voted.

2 *Yorks. Poll Book* (1807), 445, 447, 462. On his death La Marche was described as a 'reformer': *HA* 26 July 1839.

3 *Yorks. Poll Book* (1807), 166–8.

61 V. Tonks, *The Andersons: The history of a Kilham family 1772–1880* (1986), 16–17; *HP* 5 Mar. 1805.

5 *HP* 6 Jan. 1849.

6 *HP* 29 May 1827; 24 *Parl. Deb.* 2nd ser. 596, 672; 1 *Parl. Deb.* 3rd. Ser. 200; 3 *Parl. Deb.* 3rd ser. 857; 10 *Parl. Deb.* 3rd ser. 20; 16 *Parl. Deb.* 3rd ser. 284; 22 *Parl. Deb.* 3rd ser. 431.

7 Howorth, *Driffield*, 56–7.

8 12 *Parl. Deb.* 3rd ser. 106; Howorth, *Driffield*, 57.

9 ERAO, DDX/904/1/3; Howorth, *Driffield*, 57. The effigy was likely to be of the duke of Wellington: *HP* 29 May 1832.

10 ERAO, DDX/904/1/3.

11 *ER Poll Book* (1837); White, *Dir. ER Yorks* (1840), 204–6.

Place of residence	*No of voters*	*Sykes*		*Broadley*		*Haworth*	
Great and Little Driffield	234	148	63%	66	28%	144	62%
Driffield District	870	694	80%	494	57%	290	33%
East Riding	8,363	6,297	75%	5,591	67%	2,601	31%

Source: ER Poll Book (1868).

Table 17. *East Riding Election 1868: Driffield and East Riding*

reform, the ironmonger Thomas Atkinson who a year earlier had attended a dinner at York for the radical Daniel O'Connor, Thomas Scotchburn, solicitor, David Anderson, the Revd James Normanton, Baptist minister, and Caleb Angas, farmer, then living at Neswick, near Bainton.[1] The last three were soon to become active locally in the Anti-Corn Law movement.

A lecturer, probably from the Anti-Corn Law League, spoke in the Market Place in Driffield in 1839, and support for and against the repeal of the Corn Laws divided the community over the next few years.[2] In 1840 Anderson secured around 300 signatures on a petition from the town calling for the repeal of the Corn Laws presented to the House of Commons and the following year Normanton attended an Anti-Corn Law gathering at Manchester.[3] Following the bad winter of 1841–2 when it was claimed that 'the labouring poor, the artisan and the small tradesmen' were 'in greater distress than ever known in these parts' there was increased agitation in the town in favour of the repeal of the 'obnoxious corn and provision laws'.[4] A second petition with over 600 signatures was sent to parliament, an effigy of the prime minister, Peel, was burnt in the Market Place, and around 500 attended a lecture by Mr Falvey from the Anti-Corn Law League.[5] Attempts by the local landowners, corn factors and some farmers to secure support for the Corn Laws met with less success. They too presented petitions, and held a gathering in the Corn Exchange, attended by Sir Tatton Sykes, Bt, E. H. Reynard of Sunderlandwick and other landed gentry.[6] The corn merchant James Harrison read a paper on the fallacies of Free Trade to the Driffield Farmers' Club in 1851 which was published by his son 30 years later.[7] Not all the local landed gentry and farmers were in favour of the Corn Laws and early opponents were John Grimston of Neswick and his main tenant farmer, Caleb Angas (d. 1860), 'an unflinching advocate of civil and religious liberty' who wrote many letters to the *Sun* newspaper, the main organ of the free-trade movement.[8]

There was some, probably shortlived, Chartist activity at Driffield late in 1841 when, in response to visiting lecturers, a local group was formed that proposed joining the National Charter League.[9] Similarly in May 1848 there was a Chartist meeting in the Market Place and local Chartists drew up a petition calling for reform.[10] The town had become more politicised and most unusually in 1849 there was a contest for the election of the two guardians of the poor. The event 'excited a good deal of interest' with two of the four candidates, Caleb Angas, now resident in Driffield, and William Harrison, farmer, issuing cards in the Whig colour, orange, on which they proclaimed to be 'the Friends of the Poor'. Harrison easily topped the poll but Angas came bottom.[11]

As the most prominent Liberal supporter in the town, Angas's son, Henry Angas, a wholesale grocer, played a key role in the 1868 parliamentary election. The candidates were Christopher Sykes, brother of Sir Tatton Sykes, Bt, of Sledmere, and William H. Harrison Broadley of Welton, a Driffield landowner, for the Conservatives and Lt Col. Benjamin Haworth of Cottingham for the Liberals.

Although it would appear that support in Driffield was evenly divided between Sykes and Haworth, many voted for Sykes out of deference rather than political affiliation. If the 61 votes split between the Conservative candidates and the Liberal are deducted from the Conservative total then their true share of the vote was only 38 per cent.[12] Only the most ardent party supporters appear to have voted for Broadley, as had been the case with his uncle some 30 years earlier. The election was held at Martinmas and the large numbers of farm servants roaming the streets of Driffield joined with many of the townspeople 'of the rougher sort' to form a riotous mob, ostensibly in support of the Liberal

1 *YH* 26 Sept. 1835; 9 Apr. 1836; *ER Poll Book* (1837).
2 *Yorks. Gazette* 29 June 1839.
3 *HP* 24 Apr.1840; 53 *Parl. Deb.* 3rd ser. 352; *Report of the Conference of Ministers of All Denominations on the Corn Laws* (1841), 12.
4 Howorth, *Driffield*, 66.
5 Ibid. *Driffield*, 66–7.
6 22 *Parl. Deb.* 3rd ser. 431; 72 *Parl. Deb.* 3rd ser. 1104; 76 *Parl. Deb.* 3rd ser. 692; Howorth, *Driffield*, 67.
7 J. Harrison, *The Fallacies of Free Trade* (1881).
8 *DNB*, *s.v.* Caleb Angas; *HP* 17 Feb. 1860.
9 *The Northern Star* 6, 13 Nov. 1841.
10 *HA* 19 May, 2 June 1848.
11 Ibid. 13 Apr. 1849.
12 *ER Poll Book* (1868) 43–9.

candidate. Nearly every square of glass was broken in the town centre, and the Reynards of Sunderlandwick Hall, Conservative supporters, were allegedly attacked in their carriage. The unrest was only put down when police were brought in from York, Beverley and elsewhere.[1]

Over the next few years labour unrest was a feature of Driffield life. Early in 1872 there was a strike followed by a lock-out of workers at the linseed cake mill, then under the chairmanship of the bank manager William Jarratt.[2] At the same time a large meeting of farm workers, brickyard labourers and others was held at the Black Swan, when it was resolved to stand out for higher wages.[3] The following year representatives from the Lincoln and Neighbouring Counties Labour League held meetings in Driffield and surrounding villages, ending with a great gathering of labourers on Cross Hill.[4] A similar event occurred at the Corn Exchange in 1874 when William Banks, general secretary of the Labour League, spoke.[5] A branch of Joseph Arch's Agricultural Labourers League was formed in 1876 and 62 members enrolled, but there was evidently no lasting local trade union movement at this time.[6]

SMALL TOWN POLITICS

Local political life entered a new phase in the early 1870s with the establishment of a school board and a local board with members elected by the ratepayers. It was the large Nonconformist element in the town that pressed for the establishment of a school board, the motion being proposed by Thomas D. Whitaker, Baptist, and seconded by Henry D. Marshall, Congregationalist, at a public meeting in January 1871.[7] The election of the first board, which had all 'the bustle and excitement ... of a borough election on a small scale', was fought on sectarian rather than party political lines. Over 80 per cent of the 1,150 ratepayers voted and those elected were George R. Wrangham, wholesale grocer, representing the Wesleyan Methodists, James M. Jennings, solicitor, an Anglican but standing as an independent, Thomas D. Whitaker, stamp distributor, nominated by the Primitive Methodists with the support of the Baptists, William Jarratt, bank agent, representing the Anglicans, and William Bradshaw, gardener and Congregationalist, standing as a candidate for the working men.[8] Jennings, who was elected chairman, and Jarratt were Conservatives, the rest Liberals.[9] Jarratt's motive in getting elected was to stop a board school being established; he wanted the National school, of which he was a manager, to be extended or found additional premises which he offered to do.[10] When his plans were not supported Jarratt absented himself from the school board, and eventually he was excluded for non-attendance.[11] The school board, increased to seven members in 1877 was re-elected every three years.[12] The majority of members were Nonconformist, including a Primitive Methodist minister in 1877 and 1883.[13] There were 10 candidates for the board in 1886 all of whom were 'Liberals and Dissenters'.[14]

In 1873 the unsatisfactory sanitary state of Driffield and the deficient and impure water supply, the wish to avoid what was considered a costly a drainage scheme proposed by the board of guardians, and the desire to get the matter into their own hands led the ratepayers to apply to have a local board under the provisions of the Local Government Act.[15] The application was approved and the election for the first board was held in March 1874. There were 29 candidates for the 12 places, and of those elected six were Liberals, including Henry Angas, Thomas D. Whitaker, and Drs Eames and Wood and at least five Conservatives, including James Elgey, who was top of the poll, and James M. Jennings who came second.[16] With an election for a third of the board every year its membership was always changing as was the balance of power, although the Liberals were usually dominant, as was the case with the UDC which succeeded the local board in 1894.[17]

The dominance of the Liberals in the town was underlined by the election of two representatives to the new East Riding County Council in 1889 which 'had all the appearance of a Parliamentary struggle'. Luke White, solicitor, the Liberal agent, and William Bradshaw, chairman of the Liberal Association defeated the Conservatives, James Elgey, chemist, and Thomas Holtby, brewer.[18] Holtby was said to have been nominated by the publicans and therefore opposed by the strong temperance movement.[19] The Liberals usually held the two seats up to the First World War.[20]

LATE VICTORIAN POLITICAL LEADERS

Many townsmen held public office in the late Victorian period, but certain individuals stand out because of the

1 *DT* 27 Nov. 1868; *HP* 23 Dec. 1868; Wood, *Policing*, 70–1.
2 *HT* 24 Feb. 1872; Howorth, *Year Gone By*, 31–3.
3 *HT* 24 Feb 1872.
4 *YH* 8 Feb. 1873; *HP* 22 Aug. 1873.
5 *HP* 6 Nov. 1874.
6 Ross, *Driffield*, 90.
7 *HP* 20 Jan. 1871. Whitaker was secretary of the Driffield branch of the National Education League: *Report of the 3rd Annual Meeting of Members of the National Education League 17–18 Oct. 1871* (1871), 206.
8 *HP* 10 Mar 1871.
9 *ER Poll Book* (1868), 45–9; *HP* 26 Aug. 1870.
10 Howorth, *Year Gone By*, 55, 111–2.
11 *HP* 10 Jan. 1873.
12 Ibid. 2 Mar. 1877.
13 Ibid. 2 Mar. 1877; 16 Feb., 11 May 1883.
14 Ibid. 19, 26 Feb. 1886.
15 Ibid. 26 Sept., 10 Oct. 1873; 20 Mar. 1874.
16 Ibid. 20 Mar. 1874.
17 Ibid. 6 Apr. 1883; *DT* 9 Apr. 1898; *Hull and ER Red Book 1900*, 211.
18 *BG* 19 Jan. 1889.
19 J. P. B. Dunbabin, 'Expectations of the new County Councils and their realization', *Historical Jnl* 8 (1965), 368.
20 *Hull and ER Red Book 1900*,189.

length and prominence of their involvement in local government. There was a clear correlation between religious and political affiliations – all the Conservatives appear to have been Anglicans and all the Liberals Nonconformists. The nominal leadership of the Driffield Conservatives usually lay with the Reynards, the landed family seated at Sunderlandwick, just over the town's southern boundary, and sometimes further afield with the Sykes family at Sledmere.[1] Within the town, James M. Jennings, solicitor, was the leading Conservative for more than 30 years up to his death in 1896. He was successively Conservative agent for the East Riding and Buckrose constituencies, and in 1880 he called a meeting to form a Conservative Association for the East Riding.[2] The son of an Anglican clergyman, Jennings held many public offices, including coroner for the East Riding, clerk to the magistrates of Bainton Beacon division, and to the Income Tax Commissioners, Driffield Navigation, the burial board, Waterworks Co. and Corn Exchange Co..[3] An 'intelligent and humane man', he was liberal in outlook and commended for his tactful handling of his fellow members when elected first chairman of the school board and the local board.[4] William Jarratt (d. 1875), bank manager and chairman of the Driffield Pure Linseed & Cake Co., Anglican and Tory, was a very different character and gave Jennings much trouble as a member of the first school board.[5] Similarly, his son William Otley Jarratt (d. 1896), solicitor, clerk of the poor law guardians and also chairman of Driffield Pure Linseed Cake Co., sided with the anti-drainage camp against Jennings when a member of the local board.[6]

Amongst more supportive fellow Conservatives was James Elgey (d. 1900), chemist and grocer, a director of the Driffield & East Riding Pure Linseed Cake Co., vice-president of the Savings Bank, and a member of the burial board and of the committee of the Driffield Benefit Building Society.[7] Elgey, a sidesman at All Saints' church, came top of the poll at the election for the first local board, of which he was chairman more than once.[8] He was a member of the first UDC serving as chairman 1895–6.[9] William Scotchburn (d. 1917), draper, chairman of the UDC for eight years 1900-08, had split his votes between Sykes and the Liberal Haworth in the 1868 election, but later became a staunch Tory.[10] An Anglican, he was vice-president of the Working Men's Constitutional Club, manager of the National school, member of the burial board, director of the Recreation Ground Co., Driffield Water Co. and Gas Light Co.[11] Scotchburn was a long serving member of the local board, first elected in 1878.[12] He was said not to have welcomed his son's marriage to the daughter of Luke White, and when White stood as Liberal candidate for Buckrose in 1900, Scotchburn nominated his rival.[13] The first local woman to hold public office was probably Lady Margaret Bickersteth of Beechwood, Driffield, who was elected as a poor law guardian in 1898.[14] An Anglican and Conservative, she was the wife of John J. Bickersteth, Clerk to East Riding County Council, and daughter of the 4th earl of Ashburnham.[15]

The leading Liberals, made up of tradesmen, industrialists, craftsmen and a sprinkling of professionals were almost all practising Nonconformists, men like Thomas D. Whitaker (d. 1896), stamp distributor and accountant, a deacon at the Baptist church and an original committee member of the Liberal Association. Whitaker was active in the Mechanics' Institute from its early days, becoming vice-president, and he played a leading role in securing a school board of which he was a member, intermittently, for a number of years, as he was of the local board. A strong advocate of temperance, Whitaker was chairman of the Temperance Hall Co. Ltd from its foundation and the first Chief Templar of the 'Hope of Driffield' Lodge of Good Templars.[16] Although Liberals were drawn from each of the town's Dissenting congregations, the Congregationalists appear to have been the most openly party political. It was in the Congregational school room that the Liberal Association was founded in 1881. The first president, Dr John D. Eames, was a church member, as were William Bradshaw, Henry D. Marshall and Luke White, all of whom were elected to the first committee.[17] William Bradshaw (d. 1907), gardener, superintendent of the Congregational Sunday school, was a member of the first school board, and was elected to the local board in 1876, and to the new East Riding County Council in 1889 and served as a member of the UDC from its formation in 1894 until his death.[18] Henry D. Marshall (d. 1910), miller at King's Mill, for 30 years a deacon at the Congregational church was vice-president of both the Driffield and the Buckrose Constituency Liberal Associations. He was a

1 *HP* 26 Aug 1870; 10 Nov. 1882.
2 Ibid. 3 May 1880.
3 *DT* 4 July 1896.
4 *HP* 10 Mar., 12 May 187; 20, 27 Mar. 1874; P. Howorth, *From White House to Workhouse: Luke White 1845–1920* (1998), 15–16.
5 *HP* 24 Jan. 1862; 10 Mar., 8, 22 Dec. 1872; 10 Mar. 1873; 19 Jan. 1875; *ER Poll Book 1868*, 44.
6 *HP* 6 Nov. 1863; 1 Apr. 1881; 14 Apr., 4 Aug. 1882.
7 *ER Poll Book 1868*, 44; *HP* 24 Jan. 1862; 20 Mar. 1863; 14 Mar. 1873; *DT* 13 Jan., 6 Oct. 1900.
8 *HP* 20 Mar. 1874; 14 Apr. 1881; 6, 27 Apr. 1883.
9 *Driffield Souvenir Guide* (1974), 63.
10 *DT* 12 May 1917; *ER Poll Book* (1868), 46.
11 *DT* 23 Apr. 1892; 12 May 1917.
12 *HP* 13 Apr. 1877; 12 Apr. 1878; 6 Apr. 1883; *DT* 17 May 1917.
13 *DT* 13 Jan., 6 Oct. 1900; Howorth, *From White House*, 70.
14 *DT* 9 Mar. 1898; *Hull and ER Red Book 1900*, 188, 211–2.
15 *The Times* 24 Sep. 1932.
16 *HP* 7 Jan. 1841; 3 Feb., 10 Mar. 1871; 20 Mar. 1874; 2 Mar. 1877; 12 Apr. 1878; 25 Nov 1881; 6 Apr. 1883; 26 Feb. 1886; *DT* 9 Apr., 25 June 1892; 18 July 1896.
17 *HP* 25 Nov. 1881.
18 Ibid. 10 Mar. 1870; 14 Apr. 1876; 16 Aug., 25 Nov. 1881; directories; Petch, *Driffield Cemetery MIs*, 157.

member of the local board 1875–84, but much of his time was spent in other voluntary work as treasurer, vice-president and president of the Mechanics' Institute, and vice-president of the Congregational Mutual Improvement Society and of the town's Choral Society. Marshall was president of the Driffield Free Church Council, a trustee of the Savings Bank and Cottage Hospital, a director of the Temperance Hall Co., and honorary secretary of the Driffield Charitable Society from its formation. He ran a Young Men's Class at the Congregational church in connection with which he started Marshall's Cricket Club in 1874.[1] Joel Dossor, partner in the wholesale grocery firm of Lance & Co., who served as organist at the Primitive Methodist chapel for 27 years, was president of the Liberal Association at his death in 1913.[2]

Luke White (d. 1920), the most prominent politician to emerge from Victorian Driffield, was in the early days of his political career when he joined the committee of the Liberal Association. Born in 1845, into a labourer's family at Naburn, near York, White left school at 14 and the following year he was taken on as clerk in the offices of Robert Dale, a York solicitor. He moved to Driffield in 1866 as managing clerk to George Hodgson, solicitor, the local Tory agent, and in 1871 he was accepted as an articled clerk. Soon after White had qualified as a solicitor in 1874, Hodgson died, and he took over the firm. At first White attended the Primitive Methodist chapel, but he and his wife soon moved to the Congregational church.[3] He was secretary of the Mechanics' Institute in 1870 and later vice-president.[4] White entered local politics when he was elected to the local board in 1875, claiming to be 'free from all party feeling and acting solely for the ratepayers'. He was soon in conflict with fellow board members, both Liberals such as T. D. Whitaker and Dr Eames, and the chairman, James M. Jennings, over the expense of a drainage system proposed. White opposed the scheme, and when more likeminded members were elected in 1877 he was made chairman. He served as chairman again in 1882, and when he stood for re-election in 1884, in opposition to 'present excessive rates' he came top of the poll.[5] White was also intermittently a member of the school board, having been first elected in 1877.[6] As candidate for Driffield South he was elected to the first East Riding County Council in 1889, becoming an alderman in 1892, and he was the first chairman of the Driffield UDC in 1894, and then again in 1897–9.[7] White resigned his position in the county council when he was appointed County

63. *Sir Luke White MP, photographed c. 1890. A popular MP whose photograph is said to have been displayed in many homes in the Buckrose constituency.*

Coroner in 1896, and his seat on the UDC in 1900 when he stood successfully as Liberal candidate for the Buckrose constituency.[8]

PARLIAMENTARY ELECTIONS 1880–1910

It was through acting as Liberal agent for the northern part of the East Riding constituency at the 1880 election that White became closely involved with party politics in a wider sphere.[9] It was the first election contested for the East Riding constituency since 1868 and the first since the Secret Ballot Act. The sitting members, the Conservatives, Christopher Sykes and W. Harrison-Broadley, the latter with a recently enlarged estate in Driffield, defeated the Liberal, Henry L. Wood, second son of Lord Halifax. The result was not well received in Driffield where all the windows of the Cross Keys, the Conservatives headquarters, were smashed.[10] The Liberal vote was higher than expected and both parties were spurred on to improve their local organization. A

1 *HP* 16 Apr. 1875; 12 Apr. 1878; 25 Nov. 1881, 16 Jan. 1885; *DT* 9 Apr. 1910.
2 *DT* 18 Jan. 1913.
3 Howorth, *From White House*, 9–13.
4 *DT* 15 Jan. 1870; *HP* 6 Jan. 1882.
5 Howorth, *From White House*, 15–18, 24; *HP*, 16 Apr. 1875; 11 May 1877; 3 Nov. 1882.
6 *HP* 2 Mar. 1877; 5 Mar. 1880; 26 Feb. 1886.
7 *BG* 19 Jan 1889; 21 Aug. 1920; *Driffield Souvenir Guide* (1974), 63.
8 Howorth, *From White House*, 35–9.
9 Ibid. 30.
10 Ibid. 30–1.

Conservative Association was formed at Driffield in 1880 and a Liberal Association the following year.[1]

Under the Third Reform Act 1884–5, which gave the vote to agricultural labourers, the East Riding was divided into three single-member constituencies. Driffield was at the centre of the new Buckrose constituency and the place selected for the declaration of the poll.[2] In the 1885 election Christopher Sykes was re-adopted as Conservative candidate with James M. Jennings as agent, and James Cousins of Allerton Park, near Leeds was chosen as the Liberal candidate with Luke White as agent. Sykes won but with a majority of only 296.[3] Later the following year there was another election and this time Sykes lost to the Liberal W. A. McArthur by one vote. Sykes appealed and he was eventually awarded the election by 11 votes.[4] Sykes 'defeat' was attributed to the 'strong radical element' that prevailed in Driffield and the other towns and large open villages of the district.

In an attempt to build support the Conservatives founded a Working Men's Constitutional Club and a branch of the Sykes Habitation of the Primrose League.[5] The membership of the Constitutional Club with rooms in Market Place rose from 117 in 1886 to 362 in 1888.[6] The club room had a billiard table and library by 1892; the former was probably more popular than the latter for only 44 members borrowed books in 1893.[7] A purpose built Liberal Club was opened on Exchange Street in 1888.[8]

The retirement of Christopher Sykes, whose election had owed much to his family's standing in the district, and his replacement by an outsider, F. W. Fison, as Conservative candidate, gave the Liberals the opening they needed and their candidate Angus Holden secured a 652 majority at the 1892 election.[9] On the eve of the poll a brass band followed by a crowd numbering some 2,000 processed around the town finishing up at Cross Hill where they were addressed by Holden.[10] A similar number gathered outside the Corn Exchange for the declaration.[11]

Holden was returned with a much reduced majority in 1895, and when he announced three years later that he would not be seeking re-election the local Liberal Association approached Luke White to be their candidate and he accepted.[12] White had masterminded Holden's elections and had cultivated the local community, attending chapel anniversaries, club feasts and other social occasions, but despite his popularity he only defeated the Conservative candidate, E. C. Meysey-Thompson, by 91 votes in the 1900 election.[13] Driffield was proud of White's achievement and a few days later at the Free Churches harvest festival in the Congregational church 'a laurel wreath suspended by white ribbon' was hung over the pew where 'the newly elected MP has sat for a number of years'.[14] Alongside a landslide victory for the Liberals nationally White increased his majority to 1,602 at the 1906 election and was knighted in 1908.[15]

White's parliamentary seat was threatened in 1908 when Mark Sykes, eldest son of Sir Tatton Sykes, Bt, agreed to stand as Conservative candidate for Buckrose in the next election.[16] In addition to Sykes's candidacy the political scene was becoming more diverse with the growth of the Labour movement and growing support for votes for women. Suffragettes held political meetings in Driffield in 1908 and the following year there was a local branch of the National Union of Women's Suffrage Societies with Dora Mortimer, the daughter of John R. Mortimer, corn merchant and archaeologist, as secretary.[17] A petition that the branch organized calling for the enfranchisement of women was quickly signed by Sir Luke White and his colleague and agent Herbert Brown, as well as the Revd R. Bracey, Congregational minister, and at least two active Conservatives, William Scotchburn and Henry Wray.[18] The more militant Women's Social and Political Union held meetings in the town in 1910; amongst the speakers was Mary Phillips, the longest serving suffragette prisoner.[19]

Aware of Sir Luke White's popularity Mark Sykes put much effort into cultivating the constituency throughout 1909, attending friendly society feast days, setting up rifle clubs and giving presents of game to all the local press.[20] He was faced by the actions of the Revd Henry Woodcock, a popular Primitve Methodist minister at Driffield who put out an appeal to the labourers of Buckrose to vote Liberal, and the Driffield and District Free Church Council that recommended 'all Free Churchmen, Temperance Workers, and advocates of Democratic Government' to use their 'vote and influence to secure the triumphant re-election of Sir

1 Ross, *Driffield*, 183–4; *HP* 25 Nov. 1881.
2 Neave and Ellis (eds), *Historical Atlas*, 139.
3 Howorth, *From White House*, 32–3, 41.
4 F. W. S. Craig, *British Parliamentary Election Results 1885–1918* (1974), 424.
5 *VCH Yorks. ER.* viii. 45; *YH* 25 Jan. 1889; *DT* 7 May 1892; *ER Chronicle and Driffield Express* 29 Sept. 1894.
6 *YH* 25 Jan 1889.
7 Ibid. 22 Jan. 1892, 23 Feb. 1893.
8 *British Architect* 2 Mar. 1888.
9 Craig, *Election Results 1885–1918*, 424.
10 *DT* 16 July 1892.
11 Ibid. 23 July 1892.
12 Howorth, *From White House*, 49, 51.
13 Ibid. 54–5.
14 *DT* 20 Oct. 1900.
15 Howorth, *From White House*, 59, 61.
16 Ibid. 66.
17 *DT* 19 Sept. 1908; HUL, DDSY(2) 1/12.
18 *DT* 25 Dec 1909.
19 *DT* 10 Dec 1910; *DNB*, *s.v.* Mary Elizabeth Phillips. See also P. Howorth, *The Impact of War: Driffield and the Wolds 1914–1919* (2002), 11–12.
20 HUL, DDSY(2)1/12 DDSY(2)/2/3.

Luke White'.[1] One of Sykes' correspondents described Buckrose as 'a real Radical and Nonconformist district', within which the Conservative agent described north Driffield as 'very bad'.[2]

There were two parliamentary elections in 1910. White was returned in January with a greatly reduced majority of 218 on a 92 per cent turnout, and in December with a majority of 232 on a lower turnout. The cost of these elections, and the expenses of being a MP, which he remained throughout the First World War, brought about Sir Luke White's downfall. He fell ill at the end of 1917 and was admitted to an asylum early the next year. It was then discovered that he had embezzled over £25,000 from 61 individual clients and 22 trust estates. White was too ill to stand trial and he died in Driffield workhouse in 1920.[3]

DRIFFIELD POLITICS BETWEEN THE WARS

Sir Luke White had a big personal following in Driffield, and his fall from grace had its repercussions on the local Liberal Party. Charles Smith, grocer, who had been an active Liberal since at least 1892, serving as secretary of the Buckrose Liberal Association, and as a member of the local board, UDC and county council, and chairman of Bainton Beacon magistrates' bench, went over to the Unionist Party on the death of White 'as he always said he would'.[4] At the General Election in 1918 there was no Conservative candidate for Buckrose but Algernon Moreing, a mining engineer, stood as a Coalition Liberal and was returned with a 6,134 majority on a low turnout, with an Independent Labour candidate second and an Asquith supporting Liberal third.[5] The Labour candidate George Dawson, a railway worker from Middle Street, Driffield, received 3,176 votes. As secretary of the local branch of the Agricultural Labourers and Rural Workers Union Dawson had organized a farm workers' strike a few months earlier.[6] The union, renamed the National Union of Agricultural Workers, was well supported in Driffield into the 1920s. It organized a series of marches through the town in 1919 and three years later the local branch oversaw a strike that was not sanctioned by the head office.[7] In March 1922 some 600 striking farm workers marched from the railway station to the skating rink for a meeting and later that year local members dissatisfied with the NUAW had discussions with the Northern Counties Landworkers League.[8] The Driffield district was the only area of 'real union strength' amongst agricultural workers in the East Riding in the early 20th century.[9]

There was no Labour candidate for Buckrose at the next three general elections when it was a straight fight between Liberal and Conservative, with the latter successfully represented by Admiral Sir Guy Gaunt.[10] He was opposed in 1922 and 1923 by Thomas Fenby, a Nonconformist blacksmith from Bridlington who had a strong local following.[11] Fenby reduced the Conservative majority to 601 in the 1922 election which was disastrous nationally for the Liberals when they came third behind Labour for the first time.[12] The following year Fenby reduced the majority to 214, but gave up the candidacy in 1924 when he was returned for East Bradford.[13] A scandal led to Gaunt's resignation in 1926 and in the consequent by-election Albert N. Braithwaite was returned for the Conservatives, retaining the seat until 1945.[14] He was opposed by Liberal and Labour at the by-election and in 1929, and on both occasions the Labour candidate lost his deposit but the Liberals came second with more than 40 per cent of the vote.[15] Labour support within the constituency was probably at its strongest at Driffield. Here Mrs Lilian Blakeston, wife of a local solicitor, a poor law guardian and former secretary of the National Union of Women's Suffrage Societies presided over a meeting in support of the Labour candidate, and the uproar caused by a large 'Socialist' element during Braithwaite's post-election speech led to rumours that the town had become 'subservient' to the 'Red flag'.[16] In 1931 Braithwaite was returned unopposed, the Liberal candidate having withdrawn, as elsewhere, to demonstrate support of the National Government.[17] Four years later Braithwaite gained his highest ever majority, but his Liberal opponent did surprisingly well receiving 45 per cent of the votes cast when nationally his party received only 6 per cent.[18] Despite the rapid decline in support nationally for the Liberal party it remained significant in Driffield and area.

The Liberals formed the largest group on Driffield UDC between the wars. At least seven of the twelve councillors were Liberals in 1920–1 and eight in

1 *Bridlington Free Press* 17 Dec. 1909; *DT* 1 Jan. 1910; HUL, DDSY(2)1/12.

2 HUL, DDSY(2) 1/12, 15.

3 Howorth, *From White House*, 68–9, 74–5, 77.

4 *DT* 9 Apr., 25 June 1892; 5, 12 Mar. 1898; 11 Dec. 1926.

5 F. W. S. Craig, *British Parliamentary Election Results 1918–49* (1977), 504.

6 Howorth, *Impact of War*, 103–4, 115–6; Caunce, 'Twentieth-Century Farm Servants', 164.

7 Howorth, *Impact of War*, 120; ERAO, DDX 831/1/1.

8 *DT* 18 Feb, 4, 11, 25 Mar., 15 Apr., 29 July 1922; ERAO DDX831/1/2.

9 Caunce, 'ER Hiring Fairs', 51.

10 Craig, *Election Results 1918–49*, 504.

11 Neave, *Port, Resort and Market Town*, 265–6.

12 M. Pearce and G. Stewart, *British Political History 1867–1995* (1996), 225.

13 Neave, *Port, Resort and Market Town*, 265.

14 Craig, *Election Results 1918–49*, 504.

15 Ibid.

16 E. Crawford, *The Women's Suffrage Movement* (2001), 175; *DT* 1 June 1929; 28 Feb. 1931; *HT* 8 June 1929.

17 Craig, *Election Results 1918-49*, 504; Pearce and Stewart, *British Political History*, 404.

18 Craig, *Election Results 1918-49*, 504; Pearce and Stewart, *British Political History*, 413.

1928–9.[1] There were ten candidates for four seats on the council in 1927. The leading Liberal Albert Spencer (d. 1940), county councillor, JP and provision merchant, president of the Rugby Club, Watermen's Swimming Club and Town Band, easily came top of the poll with 1,173 votes.[2] Another Liberal Samuel H. Gibson, JP, a long serving member of the UDC and former county councillor, Primitive Methodist, and reputedly the largest property owner in the town, came second with 563 votes.[3] Third with 544 votes was Harold J. Taylor (d. 1966), timber merchant, the most prominent Conservative on the council to which he was first elected in 1919.[4] Amongst those defeated were Amy Stather, vice-president of the Liberal Association, the first woman candidate, and Harry Watt, a Labour councillor who had been returned unopposed three years earlier.[5] Watt was a former Liberal as was Walter Smith, railway shunter, another Labour councillor who was chairman of the UDC in 1928.[6]

There was now considerable Conservative following in the town and Harold J. Taylor defeated the Liberal Howard Leason, builder, for the county council seat of Driffield North in 1928 and 1931.[7] Leason, first elected to the UDC in 1916, came top of the poll in 1929, and also returned was Amy Stather, as the first woman councillor.[8] In 1937 she served as chairman, the only woman to hold this position during the 80 years existence of the council.[9]

DRIFFIELD POLITICS AFTER 1945

Buckrose was unusual in that there was no Labour candidate at the immediate post-war election in 1945, and the sitting Conservative Sir A. N. Braithwaite was defeated by the Liberal G. Wadsworth who had a majority of 950.[10] Nationally only 12 Liberal MPs were returned and Buckrose was the only constituency where a sitting member lost to a Liberal.[11] Labour had little success in more local elections, all seven of their candidates standing in the UDC election in 1946 failed to be returned and the following year the four identifiable Labour candidates, including the long-serving Walter Smith, chairman 1940–2, came bottom of the poll.[12] All but the Labour candidates stood as independents in the post-war UDC elections although some had identifiable political affiliations. Eric T. Carr, headmaster of the Church of England school, who came top of the poll was a Conservative, as was F. Alan Megginson, who came third in 1947.[13] Megginson, secretary of the Conservative Association, was one of the directors of the *Driffield Times* of which his father-in-law H. J. Taylor was chairman.[14] The Liberal, Howard Leason, who sat on the council for over 40 years, was fifth in the poll in 1947.[15] The previous year he had been elected as county councillor for Driffield North.[16]

Driffield lost its key role in parliamentary elections when it was decided to move the declaration of the poll to Bridlington in 1945, and then to locate the town towards the western edge of a new Bridlington constituency for the 1950 election.[17] Wadsworth stood in the new constituency at the 1950 election but was defeated by the Conservative, the Hon. Richard Wood, son of Lord Halifax, a major landowner in the western part of the East Riding. From that date Driffield has been represented by a Conservative MP, whilst changing boundaries and names have placed it in the constituencies of Howden, 1955-83, Bridlington, 1983-97, and East Yorkshire from 1997.[18] As the largest settlement in the Howden constituency Driffield was the scene of big eve of the poll election meetings until 1983.[19]

In the 1950s–60s the elections for the Driffield UDC were not fought openly on party political lines, and on at least two occasions the candidates were returned unopposed.[20] Party labels were introduced at a by-election in 1970 when Jim Kirkwood, Secretary of the Driffield and District Trades Council, standing as a Labour candidate, was returned. At the following election in 1971 there were five Labour candidates, the only ones signifying their political allegiance, and they came bottom of the poll.[21] Although not standing under a party banner the two leading figures, and two of the longest serving members on the UDC were Eric T. Carr, Conservative, and James F. Grinstead, Liberal, who were also the town's two representatives on the East Riding County Council for a few years before its demise in 1974.[22] Grinstead, who was chairman of the local Liberal Association and the Driffield Branch of the Workers' Educational Association, ran a combined wallpaper and gramophone shop in Market Place.[23]

1 *Kelly's Dir. N & ER Yorks* (1921), 498; (1929), 481; *DT* 29 Apr., 11, 18 Nov. 1922; 14 Feb., 10 Oct. 1931.
2 *HDM* 5 Apr. 1927.
3 *DT* 11 Mar. 1922, 10 Oct. 1931; *HDM* 5 Apr. 1927.
4 *HDM* 5 Apr. 1927; Petch, *Driffield Cemetery MIs*, 105.
5 *HDM* 5 Apr. 1927.
6 *DT* 29 Apr. 1922; 8 May 1926; *HDM* 5 Apr. 1927.
7 *DT* 28 Feb., 14 Mar. 1931.
8 Ibid. 30 Mar. 1929.
9 *Driffield Souvenir Guide* (1974), 63.
10 Craig, *Election Results 1918–49*, 504.
11 *DT* 3 May 1947.
12 Ibid. 6 Apr. 1946; 23 Mar. 1947; *Driffield Souvenir Guide* (1974), 63.
13 *DT* 6 Apr. 1946; 23 Mar. 1947; *Driffield Souvenir Guide* (1974), 54.
14 *DT* 23 Mar., 23 Aug. 1947.
15 Ibid. 23 Mar. 1947.
16 *DT* 6 Apr. 1946. Leason was elected a County Alderman in 1953: *Driffield Souvenir Guide* (1974), 54.
17 *DT* 8 Aug. 1945; Neave and Ellis, *Historical Atlas*, 139.
18 Neave and Ellis, *Historical Atlas*, 139.
19 P. Bryan, *Wool, War and Westminster* (1993), 208.
20 *Driffield Souvenir Guide* (1972), 50–1.
21 Ibid. 51–2.
22 *Driffield Souvenir Guide* (1974), 51, 54.
23 Ibid. 31, 72; pers. inf.

The UDC ceased to function from 1 April 1974, when Driffield became part of the District (later Borough) Council of North Wolds (later East Yorkshire). Driffield divided into two wards, had five seats on the North Wolds District Council, and at the first election Grinstead was elected head of the poll for the North ward, and Carr for the South ward.[1] Carr was also elected, with 68 per cent of the vote, as the town's first representative on Humberside County Council. He was opposed by Mrs M. H. O'Mullane, secretary of Driffield Labour Party.[2] In the early 1980s Driffield returned the only Liberal on the County Council, Philip Redshaw, who also represented the town on East Yorkshire Borough Council.[3]

After much lobbying Driffield won the right to have a town council, for which the first elections were held in 1981.[4] By the late 1990s the council was said to be Labour-controlled and in 2010 the sixteen members included six Labour, one Liberal Democrat and nine Independents, and local interests, rather than part considerations, were said to determine policy.[5] This contrasted with the three representatives of the Driffield and Rural Ward on the East Riding of Yorkshire Council who were all Conservatives.[6]

BUILDINGS

Visually the centre of Driffield retains much of the character of a late Victorian or Edwardian market town. The majority of the buildings, largely of brick with pantile or slate roofs, date from between the opening of the canal in 1770 and the First World War. Shops, some with their original fronts, numerous inns, banks and offices, mostly of the 19th century, are concentrated on Market Place and Middle Street South, whilst houses ranging from Georgian mansions to modest Victorian terraces, interspersed with commercial premises, and the occasional Nonconformist chapel, line Middle Street North, Bridge Street and Exchange Street with its extension New Road.

There is much Victoran housing: working-class and artisan terraces dominate Eastgate, Westgate and the lesser side streets with more select middle-class detached and semi-detached villas to the south on Beverley Road, St John's Road and Lockwood Street, the so-called 'West End' of Driffield. Most of the grandest 19th-century houses, built by gentry, industrialists and succesful tradesemen, remain on the edges of the town, but the grounds of some have been encroached upon by the large scale housing estates, private and local authority, which from the mid 20th century made a major impact on the character and economy of Driffield.

Little is left of the town's industrial past, except at River Head, with the canal, warehouses, cranes and former steam mill. Elsewhere the larger Victorian industrial buildings that were once scattered through the centre of the town have been cleared away, and replaced by industrial estates on the periphery.

BUILDING MATERIALS

Until the mid 18th century most of Driffield's population would have lived in small, single-storeyed cottages with mud or clay walls, thatched roofs and earth floors. The construction of mud walls and thatching was described in the 17th century by Henry Best, and several cottages of this description survived at Elmswell in the late 19th century.[7] Part of a similar mud and thatch cottage and a mud-walled outbuilding, on the site of Stone Lodge at the north end of Eastgate, are shown on a photograph of the 1850s.[8] There were said to be only three tiled buildings in Great Driffield *c.* 1770.[9] A row of thatched buildings in Middle Street was destroyed by fire in 1803 and three thatched cottages were demolished in the town in 1859.[10]

The more substantial houses, such as that of Thomas Etherington (d. 1589) described below, would have been timber-framed. The first recorded use of brick in the parish was by Henry Best at Elmswell who had bricks made there in 1635, almost certainly for building the Old Hall.[11] Bricks were probably made in Great Driffield by the mid 18th century and there were substantial brick and tile works to the east of the town by the early 19th century.[12] From 1770 bricks along with tiles, slate and timber for building were imported via the canal and from the mid 19th century via the railway.

1 *Driffield Souvenir Guide* (1974), 51.
2 Ibid. 31, 54.
3 *DT* 21 Jan. 1982.
4 *HDM* 12 Mar. 1981.
5 Inf. from Claire Binnington, Clerk to Driffield Town Council, 2010.
6 Inf. from East Riding of Yorkshire Council, 2010.
7 Best, *Farming Bks*, ed. Woodward, 63–4, 112, 144–8, 150–5; ERAO, DDX/498/1; HUL, DDMC/26/22; Fig. 81.
8 Clubley, *Driffield*, pl. 40.
9 ERAO, DDX/17/15.
10 *HA* 26 Dec. 1803; *HP* 29 July 1859.
11 Below, Elmswell.
12 Above, econ. hist., brickmaking.

RELIGIOUS BUILDINGS

Although there were possibly churches at both Great and Little Driffield before the Conquest,[1] the surviving fabric at All Saints' and St Mary's indicates post-Conquest rebuilding. Both places seem to have had two-cell buildings with west towers. At Little Driffield later medieval additions were restricted to aisles and the upper stages on the tower, but the 12th-century All Saints' developed as a characteristic medieval town church with extensive additions including a prominent west tower. All Saints' church was generally kept decent before the 19th century, while St Mary's was first reduced in size and then poorly rebuilt in the early 1800s. Perhaps significantly, the three bells which Little Driffield church had in 1552,[2] had by the 19th century been reduced to one.[3] Lora Dawnay (d. 1812), Viscountess Downe and mother of Marmaduke Langley, the lord of Driffield manor, was commemorated, however, in the church of Little Driffield, rather than the town church, so assumptions about the smaller building's status should be guarded. In the later 19th century a wealthy and energetic vicar caused both churches to be renewed. Great Driffield church was expensively restored by an architect sympathetic to its predominantly Perpendicular aesthetic, while at Little Driffield the same taste for the late Gothic, combined with the growing interest in church archaeology, led to the transformation of the rustic early 19th-century building into a 14th-century style church, and the preservation and incorporation of stonework documenting the earlier history of the building.

Driffield's only other Anglican church, dedicated to St John and built on Lockwood Street in 1899–1900, has been demolished. Like the Roman Catholic church of 1885–6, it was designed in the Romanesque style then fashionable because it was adaptable and economical to build. The brick-built St John's church, by Hicks & Charlewood of Newcastle-upon-Tyne, though towerless and quite small with only some 400 seats, had a complex plan of chancel with aisle, and nave with aisles and transepts, south vestry, and west porch.[4] The simpler Roman Catholic church of Our Lady and St Edward has only chancel with an apsidal end towards Westgate and nave with tall gabled bellcote at the west end and a south vestry connecting to the later presbytery. The interior has two broad Norman-style arches. The church was designed by a Yorkshire architect, Edward Simpson of Manningham (WR), and built of hard red brick with yellow terracotta decoration.[5]

Some of Driffield's Nonconformist congregations were actively investing in comfortable new buildings before the Anglicans responded to the need to improve their churches. The only indication of the scale of the earlier chapels is provided by the former Baptist chapel in King Street. Built in the late 1780s in the local vernacular tradition, possibly by John Thirlwell, bricklayer of Driffield and a Baptist trustee, its religious purpose is distinguished only by an arched doorway and windows, the latter positioned to light a west pulpit and an east gallery, which has been converted into an upper room.[6] The Independents' Providence chapel of *c.* 1800 may also have been built by a local craftsman and member of the congregation, one George White, 'house carpenter of Great Driffield'.[7] In 1866–7 Providence chapel was rebuilt on a larger scale. The Gothic style then generally favoured by the denomination was adopted, but it was rendered in a more elaborate Italian manner, using polychrome brick and stone, to designs by the architect, H. J. Paull of Manchester, who shortly before had produced Millfield House for a prominent member of the congregation, and later designed other buildings in the town.[8] The Methodists were particularly active. All three congregations of Methodists built new chapels in the later 19th century, and both that in Bridge Street, designed by the Driffield-born C. E. Taylor for the United Methodist Free Church in 1863–4 and the centrally-sited Wesleyan chapel of 1879–80, again by H. J. Paull, have classical façades, though there the resemblance ends. The former building, box-like and put up for just £700, has simple details executed in white brick, the Wesleyan chapel, on which some £7,000 was spent, a grand façade in brick and ashlar with an applied temple front canted out to form an imposing two-storeyed portico. The United Methodist chapel fronts onto the street while the Wesleyan building stands well back on a large site, and the contrasts between the internal arrangements and fittings were equally striking. The Primitive Methodist building in George Street, designed in 1873 by Joseph Wright of Hull, was almost as large and

1 Above, relig. hist., [introd.].

2 *Inventories of Ch. Goods* (Surtees Soc. 97), 76.

3 BIA, TER. J. Driffield 1857; Boulter, 'Ch. Bells', 219.

4 BIA, CD. 583; ERAO, PE/10/T. 136; *Kelly's Dir. N & ER Yorks.* (1901), 461; OS Map 1:2,500, Yorks. CLXI. 12 (1910 edn). The contractor was William Leason & Son: *British Builder*, 19 Oct. 1900, 286. Illus. at HUL, DX/144/3 (A5071/6); ERAO, PE/10/T. 194.

5 Ross, *Driffield*, 79; Fig. 55.

6 ERAO, EB/1/113; C. Stell, *Inventory of Nonconformist Chapels and Meeting-houses in N of Eng.* (1994), 194; Fig. 51.

7 RDB, CP/172/260; BIA, Fac. Bk. 3, pp. 277, 325–6.

8 Above, relig. hist., 1840 to 1940 & post-1940 for this and rest of para; Fig. 54.

64. *Great Driffield: Former United Methodist Free Church chapel, Bridge Street, 2006. Designed by Driffield-born architect C. E. Taylor, it opened in 1864 and closed in 1959.*

expensive as the Wesleyans' chapel, and had a similarly grand façade, two-storeyed and gabled in the Romanesque style and flanked by towers topped by tall pyramidal slate roofs with gabled dormer windows. By 1964 the re-united Methodists were using only the central Wesleyan chapel which later had its portico enclosed by unsympathetic glazed screens. The façade of the Primitive Methodists' chapel was removed after 1964, and the former United Methodist chapel discreetly altered for office use after 1977. The second chapel of the Baptists, put up in Middle Street South to designs by the local architect William Hawe in 1861–2, was closed in the mid 20th century and subsequently demolished.

Both Anglicans and Nonconformists had, as was usual in the 19th century, chapels at the cemetery in Bridlington Road. The stone lodge and the chapels, designed by Pritchett & Sons of Darlington (Durham) and built in 1864–5, followed a standard Decorated Gothic pattern. The chapels, Anglican to the west, Nonconformist to the east, have had their spires removed.[1]

ALL SAINTS, GREAT DRIFFIELD

The church stands in a large yard on the western valley side above the town beck and Bridge and Middle Streets. It is mostly faced in limestone ashlar and much of the fabric is now 19th- and 20th-century in character, including the nave roof slates.[2] The richly decorated top stage of its tall west tower forms a landmark, rising above the town and dominating the rest of the church, which has a chancel with north aisle, vestry, and organ chamber, and an aisled and clerestoried nave with south porch.

The church built after the Conquest seems to have had a west tower, the foundations of which have been identified below the present one, apparently showing signs of fire damage.[3] The nave was probably tall and aiseless, lit mainly by small, high, round-headed windows, the positions of which may well be marked by the present clerestorey windows. A corbel table above them may replace a similar feature of the early building. The church was aggrandized during the late 12th century and perhaps into the early 13th. The earliest evidence is the font which has shafts with waterleaf capitals characteristic of *c.* 1180.[4] Aisles were added about 1200, a date suggested by the use on the aisle doorways of decoration and mouldings characteristic of the transition to the Early English style. The four-bayed arcades have round arches and circular piers; there is dogtooth on the north doorway, and keeled mouldings and dogtooth on the elaborate south doorway. The chancel seems also to have been rebuilt during that period: carved stones kept in the church might have come from a chancel arch,[5] and the priest's door on the south side of the chancel is decorated with stiff leaf and palmette, much recut in the 19th century. There was a similar doorway on the north side of the chancel.[6]

The church was remodelled again later in the Middle Ages. In the 14th century the arches of both chancel and tower were re-constructed as larger openings and the south aisle was altered, and probably widened, to judge from the evidence of its handsome Decorated windows.[7] The most splendid work was done in the mid 15th century when the tower was largely rebuilt and heightened to 100 ft. Said to be 'one of the finest in the county',[8] it is of three stages with large belfry openings and prominent buttresses, decorated with crocketed, ogee-headed niches and rising to panelled battlements

1 Pevsner and Neave, *Yorks. ER*, 441; above, loc. govt, public services (burial).

3 For the materials, see BIA, Fac. 1878/26.

4 *DT* 6 Nov. 1880; Ross, *Driffield*

5 Pevsner and Neave, *Yorks. ER*, 440.

6 Stones and notes in chancel north aisle, 2004.

7 Sheahan and Whellan, *Hist. York & ER*. ii. 499.

8 For the church before restoration, see Butler, *Yorks. Church Notes*, 192–3; Sheahan and Whellan, *Hist. York & ER*. ii. 499. Drawing of *c.* 1818 in Butler, ibid. 192; illus. of church from the south-east *c.* 1840, at All Saints, Driffield, 2010; Fig. 65.

8 Butler, *Yorks. Church Notes*, 192–3.

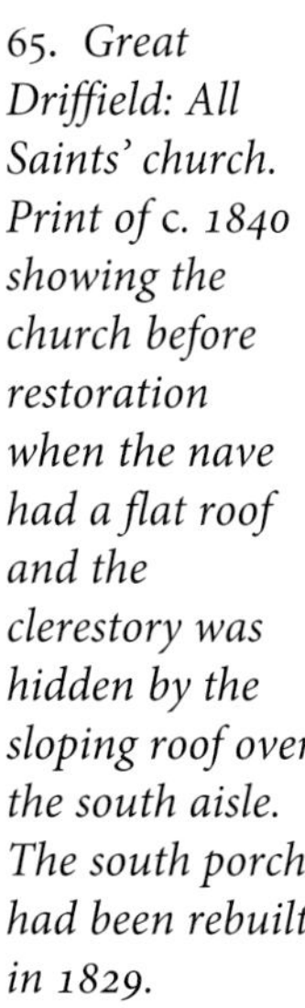

65. Great Driffield: All Saints' church. Print of c. 1840 showing the church before restoration when the nave had a flat roof and the clerestory was hidden by the sloping roof over the south aisle. The south porch had been rebuilt in 1829.

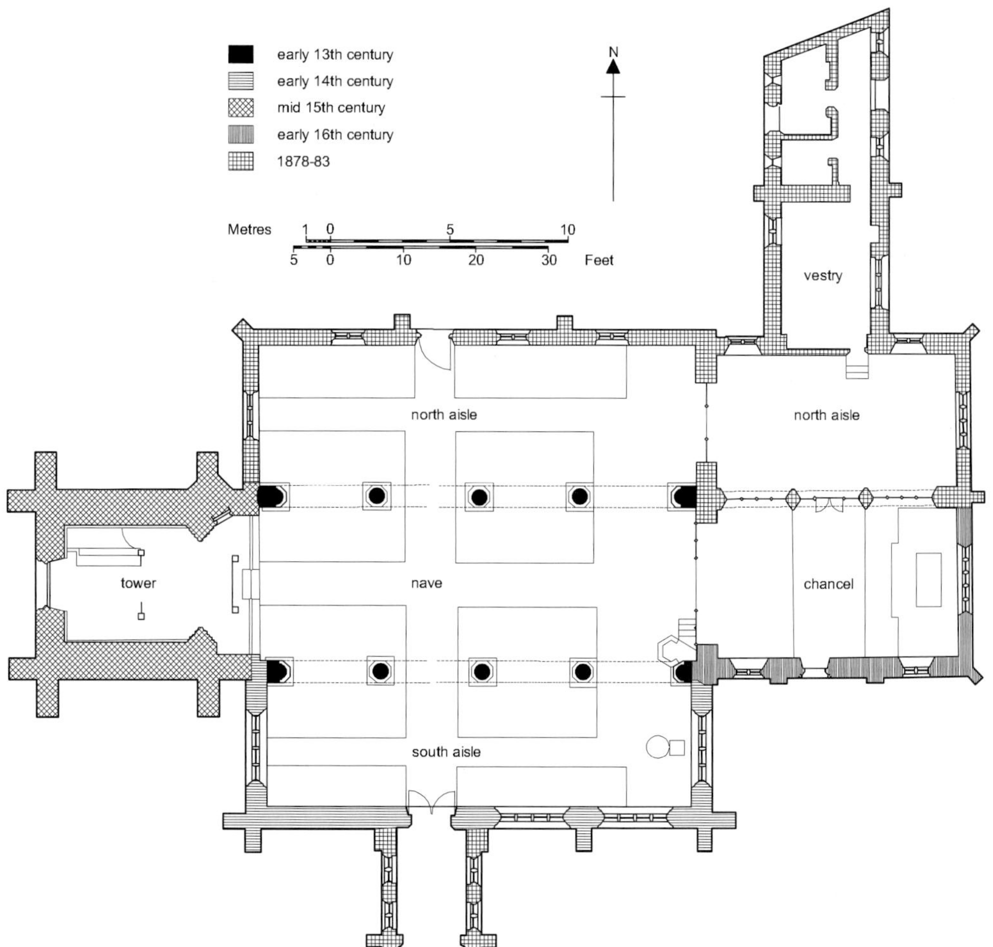

66. Great Driffield: All Saints' church, ground plan c. 2000.

67. *Great Driffield: All Saints' church, interior looking east, 2006. The rood screen was designed by Temple Moore and made by Shepherdsons of Driffield in 1904.*

and large crowning pinnacles. The western façade, which has a large window and a doorway, both set within ogee arches, emphasized the approach and the view from the west. The arms of several local proprietors carved on the tower and on the north aisle presumably record their support for the building work then undertaken.[1]

The chancel was reconstructed *c.* 1500: the rector, the prebendary of Driffield, was excused from paying tax in 1505 because of his expenditure in 'rebuilding' the chancel.[2] It is wide but not particularly grand, the windows being two-light and square-headed except for the east window which fills much of that wall. The north aisle must also have been rewindowed about that time, possibly the 'church works' for which Robert Swillington of London, draper, left 10*s.* in 1520.[3]

Thereafter little major work seems to have been done for several decades, and indeed in the early 17th century the chancel was neglected by the rectorial lessee.[4] At an unknown date the gabled roofs of the nave and the south aisle were reconstructed, the nave being given a flat, low roof and the aisle a sloping cover obscuring the clerestory windows, which were consequently blocked up on that side.[5] More alteration and refitting was undertaken in the early and mid 19th century, but traces of that work were almost entirely removed by the later restoration. The church was re-pewed in 1807 and about this time a singing gallery was put under the tower arch where an organ was placed in 1829.[6] At the latter date the south porch was rebuilt as a stuccoed, windowless structure and in 1834 a new clock was put in the church tower made by James Harrison of Hull.[7] A vestry was added to the north side of the church in 1841,[8] the chancel arch may have been rebuilt *c.* 1850,[9] and in 1864 funds raised by public subscription were spent on the surviving memorial window for the Prince Consort in the south aisle, the work being entrusted to a local glazier, George Baron.[10]

Restoration In 1874 full restoration of the church was proposed which the architect G. E. Street estimated would cost around £4,600.[11] No action was taken until after the appointment of Horace Newton as vicar in 1877 when Sir George Gilbert Scott was asked to

1 Above, relig. hist., Middle Ages.

2 *Cal. Fine R.* 1485–1509, pp. 362–4.

3 J. W. Clay (ed.) *N Country Wills* (Surtees Soc. 116), 276.

4 BIA, V. 1623/CB. 1, f. 200.

5 Print of church *c.* 1840, at All Saints, 2004. For a photographic view of the church before restoration, see Clubley, *Driffield*, pl. 48.

6 ERAO, DDX/17/15.

7 Ibid. PE/10/T. 99, s.a. 1828; ERAO, DDX/17/15; Sheahan and Whellan, *Hist. York & ER.* ii. 499; illus. of church *c.* 1840, at All Saints, 2004; *DT* 6 Nov. 1880; Ross, *Driffield*, 4.

8 BIA, Ch. Ret. i; ERAO, PE/10/T. 99, s.a. 1841. John Browne states that the vestry was added in 1844: ERAO, DDX/17/15.

9 Ross, *Driffield*, 47, 55.

10 White, *Dir. Hull & York* (1851), 605; *Kelly's Dir. N & ER Yorks.* (1889), 371.

11 *British Architect* 16 Oct. 1874; ERAO, PE/10/T. 59, s.a. Feb. 1875.

prepare a further report and estimate.[1] Scott died the following year and his son, George Gilbert Scott jun., was appointed architect for the restoration. His assistant, Temple Moore, was engaged to Newton's niece.[2] Scott valued the predominantly late Gothic style of Great Driffield church, and re-used all of its medieval tracery in his restoration, which was the largest such job of his mature career.[3] Between 1878 and 1880, at a cost of over £12,000, the restoration was achieved due largely to the largesse and energy of the vicar.[4] The chancel, the north aisle to the nave, and south porch were reconstructed, the aisle being widened by 5ft to match the south aisle, and the recently-built vestry on the north side of the chancel was replaced by a vestry, an upper organ chamber, and the chancel north aisle, the last connected to the chancel by a three-bayed arcade and all in a 15th- or 16th-century style to match the chancel.[5] The roofs, covered with Collyweston slate, were returned to their former designs and the south clerestory was re-instated. 'Unsatisfactory and heavy' pinnacles are said to have been added to the tower.[6] The restored building, which was lit by gas,[7] accommodated 758 people, and was later said to seat about 650.[8] The rebuilt vestry was soon deemed insufficient, and so at the vicar's expense was linked by a cloister to the neighbouring house which was then bought to accommodate the assistant clergy.[9] The cloister was designed by Temple Moore, and may have been built by 1883.[10]

Woodwork, including new roofs, pulpit, and pews, were designed by Scott and supplied by James Elwell, the Beverley woodcarver.[11] Other fittings were added gradually. The base of the tower was fitted out and additional seats provided there to designs by the Driffield architect, Joseph Shepherdson, in or soon after 1899.[12] Oak screens, enclosing the chancel from its north aisle and the nave, and a carved retable, were designed by Temple Moore between 1904 and 1906 and made by Shepherdsons of Driffield. They were given to the church by Harrison Holt of Highfield.[13] The stained glass in the east window and in the north chapel of 1895, in the south aisle, 1899, and the west window of the north aisle, 1905, are by H. Victor Milner, the rest of the north aisle windows of 1910 and the south porch windows of 1914 and 1936 are by Burlison and Grylls.[14] A late 12th–13th-century carving in stone of a bishop, set into the outside of the east wall of the vestry, was moved from above the east window of the south aisle to the vestry *c.* 1880.[15] The thoroughly comprehensive restoration also saw the addition by Mallaby of Masham of three new bells to the existing three,[16] and the replacement of the church clock.[17] Moore's firm continued to be involved with Great Driffield church, designing panelling for the chancel in 1928,[18] and restoring the tower in 1936–7, under the direction of Leslie Moore at a cost of nearly £1,100, raised jointly by the church and the UDC.[19] Further work on the tower was done in 1963–4,[20] and *c.* 1970 a gallery was built once again below the tower for the organ, which was then restored and enlarged from the instrument hitherto at St John's.[21]

ST MARY, LITTLE DRIFFIELD

The small, mainly 19th-century church, built of square blocks of dressed, coursed limestone and with Westmorland slate roof covering,[22] has a short chancel, a long nave embracing the east side of a tower, and north porch to the nave. Documentary evidence allows the church to have been built before 1066, and earlier origins still are suggested by fragments of a cross with interlace decoration dating from *c.* 900 AD, one loose and the other built into the north wall of the nave.[23] Fabric of the 11th century or the 12th survives in the tower; in the east and south walls of the nave; in the chancel; and as pieces of stonework, chevron-patterned in the porch. Most clearly of early date, probably 11th-

1 *DT* 6 Nov. 1880; ERAO, PE/10/T. 59, s.a. Sept. & Nov. 1877.

2 Printed restoration account in vestry book at ERAO, PE/10/T. 99; *Kelly's Dir. N & ER Yorks.* (1897), 440; Brandwood, *Temple Moore*, 12.

3 G. Stamp, *An Architect of Promise: George Gilbert Scott Junior ... and the late Gothic Revival* (2002), 228–9, 376.

4 Ross, *Driffield*, 58–9

5 ERAO, PE/10/T. 59, s.a. May 1878, Apr. & Dec. 1880; Jan. 1881; Lamb. Pal. Libr., ICBS 08335.

6 ERAO, PE/10/T. 59, s.a. Jan. 1880; Brown, *All Saints*, 1.

7 *DT* 15 Jan. 1949; illus. at HUL, DX/144/3 (A 5071/22).

8 The church was officially re-opened on All Saints' Day (1 Nov.) 1880. *DT* 6 Nov. 1880; BIA, Fac. 1878/26; Ross, *Driffield*, 58–9; *Kelly's Dir. N & ER Yorks.* (1889), 371; Brown, *All Saints*, 9.

9 ERAO, PE/10/T. 59, s.a. Dec. 1880, Jan. 1881, Feb. 1883; above, relig. hist., 1840 to 1940 (Anglicanism).

10 Undated plans of alterations at ERAO, PE/10/T. 63; Brandwood, *Temple Moore*, 212.

11 ERAO, PE/10/T. 59, s.a. May 1878, Nov. 1878; Brown, *All Saints*, 5–6.

12 BIA, Fac. 1899/7. The work may have been delayed by several years: ERAO, PE 10/T. 88, s.a. 1905–6, 1907.

13 BIA, Fac. 1904/8; 1905/56; 1906/11; ibid. Fac. Bk. 11, p. 351; tablet in church; *British Architect* 11 Nov. 1904, 362; Brandwood, *Temple Moore*, 228, 230, pl. 146. Remnants of the medieval screen are said to have been given to Londesborough church in 1909: Brown, *All Saints*, 5.

14 BIA, Fac. 1895/1, 1899/11, 1910/32, 1936/1/6.

15 Ibid. Fac. 1960/2/26; Pevsner and Neave, *Yorks. ER.* 440; illus. of church *c.* 1840, at All Saints, 2004; Ross, *Driffield*, 44.

16 BIA, TER. J. Driffield 1764, etc.; ERAO, PE/10/T. 59, s.a. Apr., June 1880; Boulter, 'Ch. Bells', 219; Ross, *Driffield*, 47, 58–9. The peal of six bells was restored and re-hung in 1998: *DP* 16 June 2000.

17 BIA, TER. J. Driffield 1764, etc.; Ross, *Driffield*, 47, 59.

18 BIA, Fac. 1928/2/9.

19 Ibid. Fac. Bk. 11, p. 614; ERAO, PE/10/T. 64, 100, s.a. 1936 & 1937.

20 Brown, *All Saints*, 10.

21 ERAO, PE/10/T. 213; BIA, Fac. 1968/1/46; Brown, *All Saints*, 3, 6, 10; *DT* 14 Mar. 2001.

22 For the materials, see BIA, Fac. 1888/10.

23 Above, relig. hist., Middle Ages (Little Driffield).

68. *Little Driffield: St Mary's church, interior looking west, 2006. Norman tower arch and simple Jacobean-style pews by Temple Moore* c. *1890.*

century, is the base of the tower, which has a round-headed arch of two orders to the nave and resting on imposts; there are similar imposts on the tower side of the arch. The western imposts have been carved at some time with human masks and the base of the jambs have spurs. Because of 19th rebuilding much of the evidence for the earlier church has gone although it appears to have had north and south aisles. The antiquary William Stukeley noted on a visit in 1740 that it had 'been a large church with two rows of arches, but the side walls are now removed, and built under those arches'.[1] Pier bases and capitals from the north aisle have been built into the north wall and porch, and the south doorway has a pointed arch with pellets in the moulding of *c.* 1200. A plain, two-light window in the tower may also be 13th century. In the 14th century the tower was heightened,[2] and the chancel arch reconstructed, suggesting that the chancel may also have been remodelled then, although its present appearance results largely from the later restoration.

Little is known of later changes until the 19th century. The screen dividing the chancel from the nave is said to have been removed in 1737,[3] and by 1807 the aisle had also been demolished. Much of the chancel and nave was rebuilt in 1807, the foundations of a more extensive building, presumably including the footings of the demolished aisles, being revealed in the process.[4] The rebuilt church was later described as a 'hideous, low-backed deformity' and as small with 'wretched conventicle windows'.[5] Accommodation was increased by 30 seats in the early 1860s, when new pews and other fittings were installed by subscription, and later the nave accommodated about 100 adults and almost 40 children.[6]

The church was restored in 1889–90, to designs by Temple Moore.[7] The cost of some £1,500 was borne by the vicar, Horace Newton, and other subscribers. The chancel arch, the east gable of the nave, and the upper part of the tower were rebuilt incorporating old stonework; modern brickwork in the chancel's south

1 *The Family Memoirs of the Rev. William Stukeley*, iii (Surtees Soc. 80) 382–3.

2 Butler, *Yorks. Church Notes*, 277.

3 Vallence, 'Rood, Screens and Lofts', 127; Ross, *Driffield*, 56.

4 The date of rebuilding was later given, probably in error, as 1809. Baines, *Hist. Yorks.* (1823), ii. 194; Sheahan and Whellan, *Hist. York & ER.* ii (1856), 503–4; Bulmer, *Dir. E Yorks.* (1892), 168.

5 Butler, *Yorks. Church Notes*, 277; Bulmer, *Dir. E Yorks.* (1892), 168.

6 BIA, Ch. Ret. i; ibid. Fac. 1888/10; Ross, *Driffield*, 56.

7 BIA, Fac. 1888/10; Lamb. Pal. Libr., ICBS 09248; Bulmer, *Dir. E Yorks.* (1892), 168; *Kelly's Dir. N & ER Yorks.* (1889), 372; (1893), 407; (1897), 441. The project had been considered earlier in 1882: Brandwood, *Temple Moore*, 20, 217.

wall was replaced with stone, and in the nave the south doorway was blocked and a new entrance with a porch made on the north side. The 'wretched' windows – mostly, including the east window, large and pointed with Y-traceried glazing – were re-made, and one or two new windows added, all in 14th-century style. Old tracery was re-used in the porch window. Also restored was the chancel door which had earlier been blocked up. All the roofs were renewed, and the floor, which had been raised at the earlier rebuilding, was taken back to its old level. Re-fitting included the installation of simple pews in the nave. The 18th-century pulpit was introduced from Pocklington church at restoration *c.* 1890,[1] as were evidently the late 19th-century light fittings.

Parts of 11 grave slabs of the 12th–14th century with incised cross details are built into the outside walls of the church. One may be from the tomb of Sir James Freville of Kelleythorpe who was buried here in 1286.[2]

PUBLIC BUILDINGS

The Victorian town acquired a number of public buildings starting with the Union Workhouse built in 1837–8.[3] The contractors and designers were George Shepherdson and William Clark of Driffield.[4] It was closed in 1868 and sold to an ironfounder but a surprising amount of the building survives, including the former workhouse office and entrance range on Middle Street North (no. 62), brick and slate with Tuscan porch and stuccoed band, and to the rear a considerable part of the shell of the barn-like workhouse.

The next two public buildings erected, the former Corn Exchange, Exchange Street, 1841–2,[5] and the former police station, Eastgate North, 1843–4, were designed by Henry F. Lockwood, then of Hull.[6] The Corn Exchange had a pedimented classical stone façade with a central entrance flanked by columns and Corinthian pilasters until it was given the present dull front when it became the town hall in 1935.[7] The police station, now a private house (no. 37 Eastgate North), is unaltered externally. The middle bay, of the three-bay brick building, projects and rises above the other two and has pilasters to the corners, a round-arched doorway and a hipped roof with overhanging eaves.

Lockwood's former pupil, Cuthbert Brodrick of Hull, designed the National school (Driffield Church of England Infant School) and adjoining master's house on Cross Hill, built 1854. As befitted a Church school it is in a simple Gothic style, of brick with stone dressings, with paired lancet windows and projecting entrance porches with corner buttresses and pointed-arched openings. The house is more Tudor-style. The later Board school (Driffield Junior School) by Henry J. Paull of Manchester, the favoured architect of town's Nonconformists, is plainer and more classical. Built 1873–4 the most distinctive feature of the many gabled, brown-brick and slate-roofed single-storeyed school are the decorative cast-iron tops to the ventilation stacks.[8] It was built on the corner of Wansford Road and Bridlington Road on the eastern edge of the town, the favoured location of the later 19th-century public buildings following the opening of the cemetery on Bridlington Road in 1865.

The new 'almost palatial' Union Workhouse, demolished in the 1990s, was built next to the cemetery 1866–8. John E. Oates of Halifax (WR) was the chosen architect but additional wards were designed in 1869 by John F. Shepherdson of the Driffield cabinet-making firm.[9] Shepherdson also designed a ward added in 1884 to the Cottage Hospital (now Ten Gables), Bridlington Road.[10] This brick and slate building with gabled dormers and a gable to the projecting central bay, erected in 1872, was by the prolific architect William Hawe (1822–97), who was based for a few years in Driffield. He designed numerous domestic and commercial buildings in East Yorkshire including the chapel-like museum that J. R. Mortimer erected in Lockwood Street, Driffield in 1878 to house his archaeological finds.[11]

The police station built on Wansford Road in 1896–7, to replace the one in Eastgate North, and the adjoining former court house, were designed by Alfred Beaumont, the East Riding County Council surveyor.[12] Of hard brick with stone details the police station has two-storey bays and round-arched doorways. The more decorative court house has a shaped gable with a small

1 Bulmer, *Dir. E Yorks.* (1892), 168.

2 Earnshaw, 'Medieval Grave Slabs', 336–7. A thumbnail sketch of Freville's tomb made in the mid-C15 shows a grave slab with what looks like an incised cross: Cambridge, Fitzwilliam Museum, MS 329, f. 109; see J.M. Luxford, 'Thys Ys To Remembre': Thomas Anlaby's Illustrations of Lost Medieval Tombs', *Church Monuments* xx (2005), 36–7.

3 For more detail on the public buildings and their development see relevant sections above.

4 ERAO, PUD/1/2/1, pp. 101, 106, 217, 251; plan of 1856 at PUD/1/4/1; Fig. 56.

5 RDB, FW/179/179; *HA* 10 June 1841; Sheahan and Whellan, *Hist. York & ER.* ii. 501–2; Fig. 41.

6 RDB, FX/68/91; *HP* 12 Jan. 1844; Sheahan and Whellan, *Hist. York & ER.* ii. 502; Fig. 60.

7 Pevsner and Neave, *Yorks. ER*, 442–3.

8 D. Neave, 'The Buildings of Great Driffield', unpublished report for Borough of North Wolds, 1977; Fig. 46.

9 ERAO, PUD/1/2/10, pp. 83, 123; Ross, *Driffield*, 82; Fig. 57.

10 Neave, 'Buildings of Great Driffield', [11].

11 Pevsner and Neave, *Yorks. ER*, 92–3.

12 Wood, *Policing*, 2–4; Fig. 61.

triangular pediment and triangular pediments to the windows flanking the entrance.

The county architect, Bernard Stamford, designed the Northfield Hospital, built off Scarborough Road from 1929, closed in 1986 and since demolished except for the former administration block. Now used as a nursing home, it is an E-shaped Neo-Georgian brick building of two storeys and attic, with a seven-bayed centre range and side wings of two bays.[1] Elcock & Sutcliffe, a practice specialising in hospital buildings, were responsible for the Alfred Bean Hospital, Bridlington Road of 1930–1. Originally comprising a two-storeyed administration block with side wings of one storey containing the wards and operating theatre, the building forms the core of the enlarged hospital opened in 1990.[2] Next door, and far more lively, are the Kirby Homes, almshouses built in 1933 to a design Frank Tranmer of Harrogate (WR).[3] A two-storeyed crescent shaped range of brown brick and stone with mullioned windows, full-height bays and shaped gables over the entrances.

DOMESTIC BUILDINGS

BEFORE 1770

Although no pre-18th century domestic buildings survive something of their character is revealed by probate inventories. The house of Thomas Etherington (d. 1589), almost certainly the grandest in Great Driffield, conformed to a medieval pattern. It was evidently composed largely of ground-floor rooms, among them a hall, dining parlour, and three lodging parlours. First floor rooms included the 'great chamber', an adjoining bedroom, and probably Etherington's study, and over the great chamber was a garret room. The complex was completed by ground-floor service rooms, like the kitchen and the buttery, and by the farm buildings.[4] Lesser houses seem usually to have consisted of two principal rooms on the ground floor; the parlour, which from its contents was used by the chief members of the household for sleeping and perhaps also eating, and a general living room for cooking, eating and other purposes, often called the 'house', sometimes 'forehouse'.[5] The dwelling of Robert Hardy (d. 1604), a prosperous farmer with more than 7 oxgangs of land, was probably typical of many houses in the parish in the 17th century. The parlour contained his bed and other items and the 'house' a variety of cooking utensils, a table, a chair, and other seating, besides agricultural equipment. There was at least one upstairs room, but it was used as a storeroom rather than as a bedroom.[6] The house of John Knaggs (d. 1695) was much the same although he had in addition a 'backer end' where corn, some of it awaiting thrashing, was stored.[7]

The rectory and vicarage houses, although relatively large with three ground-floor rooms and chambers above, were evidently of the common, traditional construction with straw-thatched roofs in 1649,[8] and the hearth-tax returns of 1672 make clear the modest, and presumably traditional, nature of most of the housing then in the parish.[9]

Despite Driffield's developing as a social and trading centre there was evidently little change in the domestic buildings by the 1760; they were still chiefly mud and thatched cottages and even the walls of the yards and gardens were made of the 'white muck from the roads'.[10] The only surviving single-storey cottage in the town, no. 27 Westgate, possibly of the mid 18th century, is brick-built but the end gables are higher than its pantiled roof, suggesting it was originally thatched. The three tiled houses said to have existed *c.* 1770 have been identified as the demolished Etherington manor house on Westgate,[11] the much altered Red Lion in Middle Street North, and no. 17 Bridge Street (Bridge House).[12] The latter, which was altered externally *c.* 1900, has earlier brickwork to the rear elevation and internally panelling and a staircase of the early–mid 18th century.[13] Leason House, no. 6 Church Lane, also has a staircase and other internal fittings of this date.[14]

1770–1900

Driffield was transformed by the construction of the navigation, opened in 1770, and over the next 70 years at least 600 houses and cottages were erected, all brick built and roofed in pantile or slate.[15] The grandest houses were built not only for the merchants, professionals and leading tradesmen, but also those who went to Driffield for sport. In 1791 a 'sporting box or cottage orné' at the south end of the town was offered for sale in *The Times*,[16] and in 1806 one of the attractions of a newly-built house was said to be its proximity to the West Beck Fishery.[17] Old White Hall (now extended as the Riverhead Nursing Home), on

1 NMR (Swindon), NBR 102113.
2 Fig. 59.
3 *DT* 31 Oct. 1933; Fig. 62.
4 BIA, precentorship wills, Thomas Etherington, 1589 (inventory).
5 Ibid. precentorship wills.
6 Ibid. Robert Hardy, 1604 (inventory).
7 Ibid. John Knaggs, 1695 (inventory).
8 Lamb. Pal. Libr., COMM. XIIa/17/482, 488.
9 Above, soc. hist., social structure.
10 ERAO, DDX/17/15.
11 The Roman Catholic presbytery was built on part of the site.
12 ERAO, DDX/17/15; ERAO, TA/13; ibid. PE/10/T. 120.
13 Neave, 'Buildings of Great Driffield', [10].
14 English Heritage Listed Building online database.
15 Neave, 'Buildings of Great Driffield', [2].
16 *The Times* 20 Oct. 1791; 11 June 1795.
17 *YH* 17 May 1806.

69. *Great Driffield: No, 27 Westgate, 2006. A mid 18th-century single-storey brick and pantile cottage, probably originally thatched.*

the east side of the canal, was owned in the late 18th century by Thomas Legard, a member of a local gentry family. Advertised as a 'sporting villa', it was sold in 1800 to John Wilson, a Hull merchant,[1] who rebuilt a 'great part' of the present large rendered five-bay house with a hipped slate roof.[2]

William Porter, the corn merchant, innkeeper and promoter of the canal, built Grove Cottage, to the east of River Head in the late 18th century. His house may have been the three bay end-stack block in the centre of the present building which was greatly extended in the 1870s when it was the home of a Hungarian nobleman, Count Batthyany.[3] To the west of River Head stood Southorpe Lodge, described as 'newly erected' on 1806; the Woodlands residential home is now on the site.[4] Also gone is East Lodge, Eastgate South, of a similar date but smaller.[5] Rose Garth (formerly Rose Villa), an early 19th-century grey brick house built for a member of the Boyes family, still stands to the north of Beverley Road and New White Hall, a cream brick and slate roofed villa of *c.* 1830, is incorporated in Beechwood and the Beeches, set in wooded grounds to the east of the canal.[6]

Other Regency villas were built further north on or close to New Road which was laid out *c.* 1800.[7] At the east end of the road is Easterfield House built for Dr Francis Forge *c.* 1820, an attractive three-bay house flanked by curved screen walls with niches. Similar but a little more stylish with its curved Ionic porch, is the cream brick villa, Sunnycroft, which Driffield iron-monger, Thomas Atkinson, built for himself on Bridlington Road in 1826.[8] Plainer, except for another Ionic porch, is the Old Vicarage (formerly Hill Cottage) nearby on Downe Street, the home of a doctor in the early–mid 19th century. Doctors, and solicitors, also lived on Middle Street North the east side of which, below the parish church, was lined with large houses. Burnside, no. 25, of the 1820s, is the most substantial to survive. Of three bays, red brick with a hipped slate roof, it has a stuccoed band and matching single-storey, one-bay, wings.[9] More modest are nos. 22 and 58 Middle Street North, both of *c.* 1820; the former has a Regency reeded doorcase with lion's head corner pieces. Around the corner on Bridge Street, no. 21, another house long occupied by doctors, is probably late 18th century. It has a pilastered doorcase with segmental pediment and decorative fanlight.

Other early–mid 19th century middle class and artisan housing was built on New Road where there is a series of terraced detached and semi-detached houses.

1 RDB, CB/347/554.
2 *HP* 29 Jan. 1805.
3 Above, soc. hist., soc. leadership.
4 RDB, CK/569/922; Scott, *N and ER Yorks.*, 47 (illus.).
5 Clubley, *Driffield*, pl. 19.
6 ERAO, TA/13; ibid. PE/10/T. 120; OS Map 1:10,560, Yorks. CLXI (1855 edn).
7 Above, Gt and L Driffield intro., develop. (18th–21st c.).
8 Neave, 'Buildings of Great Driffield', [10, 20.]; Figs 11 & 70.
9 The adjoining no. 24 was enlarged and rebuilt for Dr Eames by John F. Shepherdson in 1875: *DT* 1 May 1875.

70. Great Driffield: Sunnycroft, Bridlington Road, 2006. Built by Thomas Atkinson, ironmonger and builder, for himself in 1826.

The least altered are nos. 31–2, a tall three-storey pair on the corner of Scarborough Road. They date from the late 1840s as do another contrasting three storey pair, nos. 17–18 Albion Street.

Of the 254 dwellings that were erected between between 1833 and 1848, 27 were associated with shops, 47 were houses and 180 (71 per cent) were cottages, mostly two-up, two-down, and in terraces along Eastgate, Westgate and the minor streets running east from Middle Street South.[1] Some of these brick and pantile terraces survive on Eastgate, Westgate and Adelphi Street; good examples include Lora Cottages, Eastgate North and Marine Row, Eastgate South, both dated 1842.[2] Few cottages have retained their doors and windows unaltered. A rare example is no. 14 Eastgate South which still had its 16-paned hung-sash windows in 2010. Further north along the same street no. 35 has a good early 19th-century doorcase and the adjoining pair of cottages (nos. 36–7) have slightly canted shallow brick bays, typical of Driffield in the 1830s–40s. The least altered example is no. 96 Middle Street South, a single-bay cottage with a timber hung-sash bay window on a brick base with hung-sash window to the first floor. Nearby nos. 90–1, larger commercial properties, have the same bays to the first and second floors, as does no. 56 Market Place originally part of the adjoining Falcon inn, built in the 1840s.[3]

The second great phase of house building was in the 1860s–70s when terraces with larger bay windows and small front gardens were built along Church Street and

71. Great Driffield: Falcon inn, Market Place, 2006. Built by William Jarratt, bank manager and entrepreneur, in the mid 1840s. It has shallow projecting bays characteristic of Driffield buildings at that time.

1 ERAO, DDX/17/15.

2 The name and date on Lora Cottages have been erased.

3 RDB, FZ/303/358; Fig. 71.

72. Great Driffield: St John's Villa, St John's Road, 2006. The Driffield and Beverley architect William Hawe built the house for himself c. 1865.

Victoria Road, the latter more substantial with three or four rooms on the first floor. It was also when middle-class villas, detached and semi-detached were built on Downe Street, and on Beverley Road and St John's Road.[1] Beverley Road, re-aligned on the building of the railway, developed first with terraced housing on the south side at the west end, before much grander houses were built on the north side, towards the east end, in the 1870s. Amongst the most distinctive are the White House, no. 29, built 1872, of white brick with a three-storey tower porch and no. 28, built 1873, with overhanging eaves and an elaborate French classical doorcase. The latter house was designed by William Hawe who was probably responsible for Ash Grove, a stuccoed villa of the early 1860s, and the remodelled Bell Vue House, both on the south side of Beverley Road. On St John's Road Hawe built for himself St John's Villa, *c.* 1865, a particularly elaborate example of his favourite French classical style with a chateau-like tower at the rear.

Lockwood Street, laid out between Middle Street South and St John's Road in the early 1870s is lined with houses, chiefly semi-detached, of a 'superior class' as was intended. Lived in by tradesmen, lesser professionals, retired farmers, maiden ladies and Nonconformist ministers, the houses were built over a 30-year period, and exhibit a range of styles. Some have simple stuccoed facades with heavy window surrounds, others are of brown brick, with gables, decorative barge boards, and pointed windows with polychrome brick voussoirs, and some are Arts and Crafts influenced with mock-timber framing to the first storey. There are bay windows throughout some with delicate lace-like cornices.

Back on St John's Road, nos. 40–2, dated 1897, are Jacobethan in style, with tile-hung and timbered gables, stained glass, a balcony and oriel window. Similar, but built more than a decade later, are two large detached villas on King's Mill Road (nos. 21–2). On the same road nos. 8–13 (Alma Terrace), built *c.* 1880, are good examples of more standard late Victorian terrace housing. They have round-headed door and first-floor window surrounds with red and yellow brick voussoirs, and elaborate wooden cornices to the ground-floors bay windows. Similar terraces, although more restrained, were built *c.* 1890 on the north side of Bridge Street and nearby on the east side of Eastgate North. A little later, *c.* 1900, the builder George Leason transformed Chapel Lane, then renamed King Street, with terraces of pale brick houses with red brick details, rendered gables and some mock timber-framing.[2]

Amongst the larger later Victorian houses are nos. 28–30 New Road, a stuccoed three-storey terrace with

1 Neave, 'Buildings of Great Driffield' on which the rest of this para. is based.

2 *DT* 16 Oct. 1926.

rustication to the ground floor, and vermiculated rustication to the doorcases, and The Terrace, Bridlington Road of the late 1870s. Detached houses include the Manor House, Eastgate South, almost certainly by Hawe, plain but with a tall projecting tower porch with distinctive circular windows, and West Garth (formerly Ash Lea) on Mill Street. By far the grandest of the Victorian villas is Highfield (originally Millfield House), standing in extensive grounds at the north end of the town. Built in 1865, to the designs of the Henry Paull, for Henry Angas, a grocer, the house was considerably altered and enlarged in 1881–7 for Harrison Holt by Temple Moore, a relative by marriage. He transformed the rather dull building into a vast half-timbered, many gabled, faux Elizabethan manor house. The elaborate interior has plenty of plasterwork, panelling and stained glass.[1] Temple Moore had earlier considerably enlarged New White Hall, near the canal, into Beechwood for the wealthy Revd Horace Newton, his first major patron and the uncle of his future wife. In 1878–9 he had added a three-storey red brick and stucco wing to the house in the fashionable Queen Anne style.[2]

TWENTIETH-CENTURY HOUSING

Development slowed down in the early 20th century. A variety of largely semi-detached suburban-style houses displaying the typical Arts and Crafts derived features of rendering, mock-half timbering and long sloping gables were built on the east side of St John's Road, with more standard inter-war examples with semi-circular arched porches and half-timbered gables, on the south side of Beverley Road. More modest are the rendered houses on St John's Gardens, built with concrete blocks by the builder and architect J. W. Hepton in 1929.[3] There are other distinctive inter-war houses at the western end of King's Mill Road, facing the cricket ground, one in a vernacular style with a shaped gable, another retaining its sun-ray front door.

In the years just before Second World War and the 20 years after, much of the housing development was local authority in the standard style. Maurice Parkin of Bridlington and Horth & Andrews of Hull were architects for the earliest council houses, the latter firm designing those on Gibson Street in 1938.[4]

There were roughly 5,000 homes in Great Driffield in the early 21st century of which around 3,000 were built since *c.* 1950.[5] Much of this housing is less apparent than might be thought for the recent estates are on level ground behind houses earlier strung along the main routes into the town. The newer housing comprises detached and semi-detached houses, many bungalows, and some low blocks of flats. Differing levels of prosperity and aspiration are reflected in the building styles and lay-outs. The homely Mill Falls development consists largely of closely-built bungalows, but larger bungalows more spaciously arranged occupy the nearby King's Mill Park and King's Mill Close, and there is a group of 'superior, executive' homes at the southern end of Bracken Road, fronting onto Beverley Road. Such housing is also found in the northern streets, off Spellowgate. The estates are laid out in the usual late 20th-century way, with one or more sinuous roads serving many short, side, cul-de-sac streets, usually called 'garths' or 'closes'.

COMMERCIAL BUILDINGS

Driffield's role as a market town from the late 18th century is evident in the prominently sited banks, solicitors' offices and inns and public houses. Commercial development from the mid 19th century involved the appearance of many new small-scale properties along the main street, often designed to serve more than one purpose. By 1905 almost all of Market Place and Middle Street South was lined with shops, while Middle Street North was more varied with a mix of local shops and individually occupied houses at the south end, and less pleasant trades such as a sawmill and a blacksmith's at the north end. Professionals lived and worked in some of the Middle Street North houses, and Exchange Street seems to have been a favoured location for solicitors, auctioneers, accountants and other professional services.[6]

Large scale processing and manufacturing industries, most of which were related to the agricultural economy of the area, grew up along the streams that ran through the centre of the town and to the west and south, and harnessed water power or used it for processing or transport. The opening of the railways in 1846 and 1853 intensified the industrial character of the southern part of the town that began with the opening of the canal.

INNS AND PUBLIC HOUSES

Many inns were places of commerce as well as the focus of social life and the principal inns were located in Market Place, with the exception of the Red Lion and the Nag's Head. In Driffield farmers dealt in corn at the Bell Inn and Cross Keys long after the Corn Exchange

1 Brandwood, *Temple Moore*, 161 & pls. 166–7; *The Journal* Sept. 2009, 50–1; Fig. 37.

2 Brandwood, *Temple Moore*, 20, 159–60 & pl. 164; Fig. 36.

3 *HT* 18 Aug. 1929.

4 ERAO, UDDR/1/8/32, 34.

5 Modern infilling of the older streets and earlier building on the estates make the calculations approximate: *Register of Electors* (2004). In 2001 the number of dwellings was 5,155: Census 2001.

6 *Kelly's Dir. N & ER Yorks.* (1905), 479–86.

73. *Great Driffield: Bell Hotel, Market Place, 2011. Originally called the Blue Bell, it was reconstructed in the 1850s when it was given its present façade.*

had been built, and the Falcon had a role in the development of the cattle market. Some inns also had brewhouses attached. Unlike many of the commercial buildings, in particular shops, a number of public houses in the town still look more or less as they did when built. This is true of the early 19th-century Spread Eagle on Exchange Street, the Falcon, Market Place and the Mariners on Eastgate South of the 1840s, and the Royal Oak, Victoria Road of the 1860s.

The chief inns, the Red Lion, the Bell, the Cross Keys and the Buck, were rebuilt or modernised in the 1850s–60s. Only the Bell has retained its status to the present day. A mid 19th-century drawing shows it as a typical mid–late 18th century brick and pantile building of two storeys and attics, four bays wide with an off-centre arch leading to the yard behind. To the right of the arch was a small Palladian-style window.[1] The inn was remodelled in the 1850s, heightened to three storeys, stuccoed and a recessed entrance bay placed off centre with a Doric porch and balustrade balcony above. The latter was removed in the 1970s.[2] Incorporated into the hotel is a two-storey three bay building on the north side of Exchange Street. Of grey brick with blocked windows flanking a full-height rusticated archway, also blocked, with a carved king's head on the keystone, this was the first printing works of the *Driffield Times*, established in 1862.[3]

SHOPS AND OTHER COMMERCIAL BUILDINGS

The majority of the older shop premises appear to have been adapted from existing houses. Amongst the oldest are nos. 54–5 Market Place (Costello's), a late 18th-century brick house with dentilled cornice, tumbled gable and pantiled roof, and no. 43 Market Place (Post Office), similar but a little later in date. No early 19th century shopfronts survive; plate-glass windows were first used in the town in 1841 by William Metcalfe, a hatter and picture seller, at the north end of Market Place.[4]

In the mid to late 19th century the chief provision shops were Elgey's at the corner of Market Place and Mill Street, and Robinson's at nos. 52–3 Market Place.[5] The former, a large three-storey, five-bay mid-19th

1 Carr, *Driffield*, cover; Fig. 73.
2 Plans in possession of D. Neave, 2010.
3 Neave, 'Buildings of Great Driffield', [13].
4 *HP* 7 May 1841; ERAO, TA/13; ibid. PE/10/T. 120.
5 T. Sheppard (ed.), *Yorks. Past and Present* (1912), 248; above, econ. hist., trade and ind. (1851–1918); for illus. of Robinson's in early 19th century see title page of Holderness, *Some Driffield Incidents*.

74. *Great Driffield: Costello's, nos. 54–5 Market Place, 2006. A late-18th century brick and pantile building with tumbled gable and dentilled eaves cornice.*

75. (right) *Great Driffield: New Market Building, Middle Street South, 2006. Built as offices with public meeting room in 1886.*

century range was replaced by the National Provincial bank in 1927, but the latter, with extensive rear premises, survives behind the much altered facades of Johnsons and Currys.

The tall block combining offices and warehouse built for the wholesale grocer Robert Lance at no. 41 Market Place (Lounge Bar & Grill) in 1865–6 is more typical of larger towns. With a three-storey elaborate French classical stone front, it stands more than a storey higher than neighbouring properties and could be mistaken for a bank of the same period. It was designed by William Hawe who was also responsible in 1870 for the much altered pair of shops opposite, nos. 35–6 Market Place.[1]

Other late-19th century purpose-built shops further south on Middle Street South include nos. 46–50, a parade of five shops that conform to an established pattern of oriels above shop fronts, here with northern European style pilastered gables raised at either end. In the same style, but more successful, on the east side of the street is the New Market Building (no. 70), built as offices and a meeting room in 1886. It has terracotta

1 *DT* 25 Feb. 1865; 25 June 1870; Fig. 21.

76. Great Driffield: Market Place, east side, 2006. In the centre, the former East Riding Bank, built 1856 and designed by Cuthbert Brodrick; to the right, part of Robinson's East Riding House of Commerce established in the late 18th century.

panels and bands, pilasters, a shaped gable, an oriel window over an entrance archway, and decorative cast-iron down pipes. A terrace of late 19th-century shops and houses, nos. 37–40, on the west side of the street has a different character, of hard red brick with cream and blue brick details, with a decorative terracotta eaves cornice, and bold pedimented dormers. Further south a five-bayed block of paler brick, nos. 24–5, is more restrained and incorporates an entrance to a yard flanked by matching shopfronts with oriel windows above.

The southern part of Middle Street North became more commercial in the early 20th century when three of the larger houses were altered in 1910 by the architects Thorp & Turner of Goole to form the Post Office,[1] which stood empty in 2010, and Dobsons decorators converted the former Nag's Head inn giving it a pleasing Edwardian shop front.

Little change took place to the fabric of Middle Street South until the later 20th and early 21st century when there was much rebuilding of shops and other buildings involving the demolition of the 1930s Woolworth's store and the Trustee Savings Bank, and the introduction of larger premises by national retail chains.

BANKS AND OFFICES

Like shops many of the earliest banks and offices were in existing buildings alongside living quarters, but from the mid 19th century purpose-built accommodation was provided. In the 1820s the solicitor John Foster had his office at his home, no. 23 Exchange Street, a four-bay two-storey house of *c.* 1805 with 16-pane sash windows and two pedimented doorcases, one the clients' entrance.[2] Further east along the street the solicitor E. D. Conyers rebuilt his office in 1856, with a suite of rooms to accommodate the magistrates' and county court and other public meetings.[3] This plain stuccoed building with round-arched windows to the ground floor, later the Mechanics' Institute, was an auctioneer's premises in 2010. More showy are nos. 17 and 18 Exchange Street; the former, built as the Liberal Club in 1888 and designed by Joseph Shepherdson[4] has the doorcase and ground-floor windows flanked by granite columns which support carved Ancaster stone lintels, the latter, also of the late 19th century, is more restrained with wide plain ashlar surrounds to the round-headed openings of the door and windows.

1 *British Architect*, Sept. 1910, 184.

2 Baines, *Hist. Yorks.* (1823), ii, 195; ERAO, TA/13; ibid. PE/10/T. 120. Williamson's solicitors had their offices in no. 23 in 2010; Fig. 10.

3 *Post Office Dir. N & ER Yorks.* (1857), 1238.

4 *British Architect* 2 Mar 1882, vii.

The banks congregated in Market Place. Here purpose-built premises were erected in the classical style then favoured by banks as a means of inspiring confidence in their customers.[1] The first in 1856, for the East Riding Bank (later Westminster), no. 51 Market Place, was designed by the celebrated Hull architect Cuthbert Brodrick. He skilfully made the narrow three-bayed front look grander than its size might have warranted by limiting the composition to large arched openings, making the Greek details subservient to the whole, and using finely jointed stone.[2] The York Union Bank (later Barclays) followed in 1861 with a large five-bayed palazzo-style building at no. 61 Market Place. Its design, by a minor York architect Edward Taylor, is less inventive than Brodrick's though quality of execution is high.[3]

The large joint stock banks, amalgamations of many smaller more local concerns, that emerged in the 20th century asserted their new status with much larger and instantly recognisable buildings. In 1922 the Midland Bank, known for favouring conservative styles, commissioned a Neo-Georgian building, to replace their premises at no. 12 Market Place, from the York practice, Brierley & Rutherford.[4] Five years later the National Provincial Bank filled the corner of Market Place and Mill Street with a fine new building designed, like many of that bank's branches, in a domestic style. Modelled on an early 18th-century brick house it has a main doorway accentuated with a fine cartouche.[5] Opposite is the more modest premises built in 1964 by the newly-formed Yorkshire Bank on the site of the Black Swan.

INDUSTRIAL BUILDINGS

77. Great Driffield: Warehouses at River Head, 2011. Probably those built in the 1780s or 1790s by the navigation commissioners. Converted to flats.

Victorian Driffield was a minor industrial centre with numerous steam mills, maltings, breweries, sawmills and foundries spread throughout the town. Many industrial buildings were located in largely residential streets, but the greatest concentration was at the southern end, around River Head and the railway station, with bone mills, breweries, timber yards, grain warehouses and the vast cake mill. Further north on Eastgate were Matthew's large artificial manure works and the town's gasworks with a foundry adjoining. Off Middle Street North, just south of the parish church, there was a large brewery and nearby stood Shepherdson's extensive cabinet works. Not far away were two saw mills and the large Victoria foundry on Cross Hill. Everywhere there were tall chimneys, and smoke, smells and noise.

Little remained of these industrial buildings in 2011, or of the wind and water mills that formerly stood on the edge of the town

1 Above, econ. hist., banking.

2 *Driffield Observer* 1 Nov. 1856; Linstrum, *Towers and Colonnades*, 39 (illus.); Fig. 76.

3 *DT* 18 Aug. 1860; Pevsner and Neave, *Yorks. ER*, 442; Fig. 34.

4 Pevsner and Neave, *Yorks. ER*, 442.

5 Datestone; Pevsner and Neave, *Yorks. ER*, 442.

78. Great Driffield: Nos. 20–20A River Head, 2011. The house on the right is of the late 18th century, and that on the left of the early 19th century.

WATER MILLS

Some physical evidence survives of three water mills which probably occupied medieval sites on the Driffield Beck and the River Hull or West Beck.[1] Apart perhaps from the configuration of mill streams, leets and mill ponds, no remains predate the late 18th century. At Bell Mills the 18th-century former textile mill was burned down in 1949 and was replaced by a six-storeyed brick building in the 1950s. The miller's house, said to be new in 1774, was largely rebuilt in the late 19th century except for two north-eastern bays, each with three storeys of Yorkshire casements which have been incorporated into the rear range of the L plan. The late 19th-century façade is classical, symmetrical and two-storeyed with bay windows, porch, and in front contemporary cast-iron railings. Further south-west along the river are the scanty remnants of Poundsworth Mill, including the 19th-century miller's house and a small building that stood on the south side of a large foldyard. At King's Mill, the mill was destroyed by fire in 1906 and all that remain are former farm buildings, converted to housing, and the miller's house incorporated in a dwelling on the site.[2]

RIVER HEAD BUILDINGS

River, or Canal, Head retains much of its late Georgian and Victorian character with a range of buildings and other features associated with the navigation opened in 1770. Two of the five canal locks, Town and Whinhill, are within the parish, both restored, and at River Head there are two 19th-century wharf cranes.

The range of two and three-storey brick and pantile warehouses on the west side of the canal at River Head probably include those built between 1784 and 1799.[3] Part converted to flats, only the most southerly range remains in its original state with five bays of small windows and a bay of loading doors towards the canal. Another warehouse across the road has a datestone of 1877 with the initials J. G. for James Gidlow, soot merchant.[4] Of three storeys and attic with gable end and loading doors to the street, it is attached to a four-bayed house with a cart entrance giving access to the rear of the premises, used since the early 20th century by the corn merchant firm of James Mortimer Ltd.

On the east side of the canal is the impressive Riverhead Mill, a steam-powered mill built for grinding corn and crushing bones by the millwright and ironfounder John Harker in 1842 for James Harrison & Sons. The four-storeyed brick mill with pantiled roof and elaborate metal tie-plates is a single deep-plan range of nine by three bays at right-angles to the canal. There are loading doors on each floor and the attic storey so that loads could be hoisted directly to and from the barges. To the rear, running south parallel to the canal, is a two-storeyed range. Associated with the mill are the pair of three-bayed houses nos. 20–20A River Head, one late 18th century with pedimented doorcase with decorative fanlight and 16-paned sash windows, the other early 19th century, taller with lower-pitched roof and elongated 12-paned sashes. The older property might be the 'good family house' occupied by William Parkin, merchant, in 1807

1 Above, econ. hist., milling.
2 HRO, DBHT/9/740; Fig. 19.
3 Neave, 'Buildings of Great Driffield', [21]; Fig. 77.
4 ERAO, PUD/5/1/1; TNA, RG11/4793; Fig. 25.

79. *Great Driffield: Sugar mill, former linseed cake mill, Anderson Street, 1957. The manufacture of animal feed ceased at the mill in 1940, and from 1947 it was worked as a sugar mill, then sweet factory until* c. *1970. Largely demolished in the early 21st century.*

with granaries and timber yard adjoining the wharf or the 'large messuage' at Canal Head, advertised for sale by Isaac Milbourn the same year.[1] Either may refer instead to the three-bay house further west, no. 27 River Head.

RAILWAY BUILDINGS

Opened in 1846 the railway station, the handsome brick and slate-roofed stationmaster's house with overhanging eaves, and the crossing-keeper's cottages to the north and south were designed by G. T. Andrews of York. Alterations were carried out to the station in 1865 by Thomas Prosser, the railway company architect, who a year earlier had designed a warehouse there, possibly that on Beverley Road near the Skerne Road corner.[2]

CAKE MILLS AND ARTIFICIAL MANURE WORKS

The town's most extensive industrial complex was the Driffield & East Riding Pure Linseed Cake Co.'s steam-powered mill that lay to the east of River Head.[3] Built in 1861–2 it was designed by Joseph Wright of Hull, a former pupil of Cuthbert Brodrick, who is best known for his Nonconformist chapels.[4] The original elaborate brick and slate-roofed range was of nine bays, four-storeyed with attics, with lower three-bay wings. It faced north onto the railway line and sacks of linseed could be loaded from railway wagons via a hoist through the wide doorway above ground floor level. A single track branching off the main line ran into the yard to the south-east. A major extension with ornate domed clock tower was added to the south in 1870. The mill was partly destroyed by fire in 1887 and then rebuilt. Largely demolished in the early 21st century, only two derelict ranges of two storeys, five and eight bays long, fronting Anderson Street, survived in 2010.

Further north on Eastgate South are the remains of F. C. Matthews' artificial manure works and cake mill.[5] Established on this site *c.* 1850, the large four-storeyed steam mill has gone but a dark-red brick and slate two-storeyed warehouse or workshop, used by a builders' merchant, and houses for clerk and foreman, all of the 1860s–70s, remained in 2010.

1 *HP* 16 June, 3 Nov. 1807.
2 Pevsner and Neave, *Yorks. ER*, 443; *DT* 28 May 1864.
3 Above, econ. hist., seed crushing and animal feed.
4 Neave, *ER Chapels*, 68.
5 Above, econ. hist., bone crushing and manure manufacture; seed crushing and animal feed.

80. *Great Driffield: Cross Hill and Market Place from the air in 1925. In the foreground, the National school, and, centre right, the extensive Victoria Foundry established by Thomas Pickering in 1854.*

BREWERIES AND MALTINGS

No brewery buildings appear to survive and of the older malt kilns the only remnant is an early 19th-century building with a pointed arched opening on the north corner of Harland Lane and Middle Street North.[1]

The large maltings south-west of the railway station on Skerne Road built for J. R. Mortimer to the designs of William Hawe in 1874 has been successfully converted to flats.[2] V-shaped of three storeys and attics the thirteen and nine bay outer façades are interrupted by pilasters, and in the centre is of each façade is a tall projecting lucarne.

METAL WORKING

In the 1840s John Harker's foundry was on Eastgate North adjoining the gas works, bounded on the north by Cranwell Street and on the west by Driffield Beck.[3] Large decorative cast-iron tie-plates, similar to those on Riverhead Mill (Fig. 30), can be seen on the rear wall of the former foundry when viewed from Cranwell Bridge.

On the south side of Cross Hill are the remnants of the large Victoria foundry established in 1854. Much of the site was cleared in 1974 but a four-storeyed brick-built block of the later 19th century, with an open-fronted single-storeyed range adjoining to the east and a much altered two-storeyed wing to the west, stood in 2010.

FARMS

Most of the post-inclosure farmsteads remain although some of the smaller ones are no longer used for farming. One of the least altered is Field House Farm on Bridlington Road; here the late 18th –early 19th century brick and slate end-stack farmhouse still stands backing onto its contemporary foldyard. At the larger Wold House Farm, the original end-stack farmhouse of *c.* 1800 remains, L-shaped of brick and pantile, with later additions, but it had become the hind or foreman's house in the 1880s when the present, larger farmhouse was built nearby.[4] Similar changes took place at Great Kendale, and at Middlefield (Field House) and Danesdale where the original farmhouses were replaced in the 20th century. The early 19th-century foldyard was still used at Danesdale in 2010.

1 ERAO, TA/13; ibid. PE/10/T. 120.
2 *DT* 13 June 1874; Fig. 32.
3 ERAO, TA/13; ibid. PE/10/T. 120.
4 Date in roof woodwork: inf. from Mr R. W. Tennant, 2006.

OTHER GREAT DRIFFIELD TOWNSHIPS

ELMSWELL AND KELLEYTHORPE

In the mid 19th century the settlements of Elmswell, of 1,293 a., and Kelleythorpe, of 1,105 a., together formed the 2,398-a. township of Elmswell with Kelleythorpe in the parish of Driffield.[1] The township was a civil parish from 1866 until 1885 when it became part of Elmswell and Little Driffield civil parish.[2] Since 1935 Elmswell has been in Garton on the Wolds civil parish and Kelleythorpe in Kirkburn civil parish.[3] The settlements of Elmswell and Kelleythorpe are treated separately here.

ELMSWELL

SETTLEMENT

The buildings of the reduced hamlet of Elmswell stand at the southern end of its farmlands and about 1½ mile west of Great Driffield on gently shelving ground close to the springs and streams which attracted its early inhabitants.

Early Settlement

Early evidences of man in the neighbourhood of Elmswell include an embanked roadway extending eastwards down the valley of Garton slack towards the springs at Elmswell. It may have been made during or before the Iron Age, when it became the focus for many burials.[4] From Elmswell and Garton the roadway probably led eastwards over the Wolds and eventually down into the Vale of York, as it did later, and the early significance of the route is evident from its use as an important local boundary.[5]

There were at least five Bronze Age round barrows in Elmswell of which two survive located, possibly for ritual reasons, near a spring on the settlement site.[6] There is evidence of late Iron Age activity from the 1st century AD, with finds of coins and a plaque, that continues into the Romano-British period with the first conclusive proof of settlement found on the southern side of the beck in the 1930s.[7] Cobble and clay floors with post holes, some wall footing, and other finds led to the conclusion that huts, possibly of wattle and daub, may have occupied the site. The date of the settlement was indicated by pottery and coins of the 1st to 4th centuries, the former including decorated Samian and Parisian ware which along with some window glass suggest a site of reasonably high status.[8] Besides a hearth, several pits were discovered, and quantities of slag, some possibly connected to the making of pottery but the rest certainly derived from iron working. The need to impound stock may well have accounted for ditches bounding the site, which also sheltered two inhumation burials, while the querns, or hand mills for grinding corn, among the finds suggest, once again, the growing of cereals. Later excavation, fieldwalking, and aerial photography have extended the known area of the Romano-British settlement. Further east and on the other side of the beck, at Bramble Hill, pottery of the 3rd and 4th centuries, Roman coins, and more building remains were found. Some carved stonework there is believed to have been connected with religious

1 OS Map 1:10,560, Yorks. CXLIV, CLXI (1854–5 edn). The modern spelling of Elmswell, rather than Emswell as in the official civil parish name 1866–1935, is used throughout.

2 Youngs, *Guide to Local Administrative Units*, 541.

3 *Census*, 1931 (pt ii).

4 J. S. Dent, 'Roman Religious Remains from Elmswell', in J. Price and P. R. Wilson (eds), *Recent Research in Roman Yorks.* (1988), 89; Mortimer, *Forty Years' Researches*, 245; OS Map 1:25,000, SE 95 (1953 edn); above, vol. intro., early settlement.

5 Above, vol. intro., communications (roads); Mortimer, *Forty Years' Researches*, 245; OS Map 1:25,000, SE 95, TA 05 (1953 edn).

6 J. Bradley, *The Henry Best Estate, Elmswell: Assessment of archaeological potential*, Humber Archaeology Reports 56 (2002), 17–18.

7 Following based on illustrated reports: A. L. Congreve, *A Roman and Saxon Site at Elmswell, East Yorks. 1935–6* and *1937* (Hull Museum Publications 193 & 198, 1937 & 1938); P. Corder, *Excavations at Elmswell, E Yorks. 1938* (1940); Fig. 5.

8 Bradley, *Henry Best Estate*, 22.

81. *Elmswell: Mud and thatch cottages in the 1890s. Typical of housing in Driffield parish before the late 18th century.*

observances, perhaps, in view of the location, a water cult. Crop marks have also defined the early fields of Elmswell, and its drove roads feeding into the roadway in Garton slack to access the higher settlements.[1]

The withdrawal of the Roman forces may have had only a limited effect on the residents at Elmswell, who seem to have continued to live near the 'village' or to have re-occupied it after an interval. During both the 19th- and 20th-century investigations in Elmswell, discoveries included Anglo-Saxon pottery and other artefacts.[2] The argument for continuity of settlement would seem to be strengthened by some of that pottery, which dated from the 6th or 7th century and had a hybrid character reflecting both Romano-British and Anglo-Saxon models. It has also been argued that the iron-working skills of the established population at Elmswell may have encouraged the incomers to the site, thereby ensuring its survival. There is, however, evidence that the district as a whole was attracting immigrants, for whatever reasons, notably the large pagan and Christian cemeteries in the south of the neighbouring Garton, about a mile west of Elmswell, which have been dated to the 7th century.[3]

Medieval and Later Settlement

It is not known whether the present hamlet of Elmswell existed as part of the Romano-British settlement excavated to the south or whether it was founded later in the Middle Ages. Either way, there were presumably buildings on the site by the 11th century, when Elmswell was entered as a manor in the Domesday survey and soon afterwards given to St Mary's abbey, York.[4] Such archaeological investigation as there has been in the present hamlet has revealed only medieval foundations and pottery from the 13th or 14th century.[5] Nothing is known of the large, rectangular enclosure defined by earthworks which existed some distance from the hamlet, to the north of Sykes Lane.[6]

The name Elmswell, meaning 'Helm's spring', is Anglian, and was recorded from 1086 both as Helmeswell and Elmeswell; in 1598 the suffix 'upon the Wold' was added, perhaps to distinguish it from Hemswell (Lincs.). Other variants employed from the 16th century were Emswell, Hemswell, and Empswell, and the first was commonly used into the 20th century.[7]

The name Spellow, believed to mean 'speech mound', has been used at least since the 17th century for ground in the north-east of Elmswell, and it may have been there that the men of Driffield hundred assembled.[8]

Only vague indications of the size of the later medieval settlement are available, but it was almost certainly reduced over the succeeding centuries. In 1377, when almost 350 paid the poll tax in the two Driffields, 92 inhabitants were liable in Elmswell.[9] Twelve men were listed in the muster roll of 1539 and there were evidently about fifteen houses in Elmswell in the early 17th century.[10] Some nine houses were recorded in the mid century, all but two of them, presumably Elmswell

1 Ramm, *Parisi*, 120; Dent, 'Roman Religious Remains', 89–95; Loughlin and Miller, *Survey*, 98; Challis and Harding, *Later Prehistory*, i. 99; ii, fig. 37.

2 Ramm, *Parisi*, 134, 136.

3 *VCH Yorks. ER*. ii. 216; Loveluck, 'Anglo-Saxon Landscape', 39–40.

4 Below, Elmswell manor.

5 Loughlin and Miller, *Survey*, 98.

6 OS Map 1:2,500, Yorks. CLXI. 11 (1910 edn).

7 BIA, D/C. CP. 1608/4; *PN Yorks. ER* (EPNS), 154; *Census*, 1931 (pt. ii); *VCH Yorks*. ii. 320.

8 *PNER* (EPNS), 116; Best, *Farming Bks*, ed. Woodward, 202.

9 TNA, E 179/202/59, mm. 24, 33.

10 Best, *Farming Bks*, ed. Woodward, 216–17; *Yorks. Fines*, iv. 89.

Hall and West Hall, cottages.[1] By the early 19th century there were four farms,[2] the houses of which, with half a dozen cottages and farm buildings, stood loosely grouped on the rectangular site.[3] From the hamlet sunken lanes led northwards to Elmswell's main roads, those to Driffield, Garton, and Pocklington. The lane from the chief house, Elmswell, later Old, Hall, passed through a 3-a., funnel-shaped common where most of the springs which had attracted settlement rose.[4]

The contraction of the settlement seems to have occurred particularly along its eastern and possibly also its northern edge, and about 1850 foundations were noted in both of those locations, close to the main road.[5]

There was further change in the hamlet after the acquisition of the estate in 1844 by the Denisons, later Lords Londesborough, and they certainly added a new chief house there, the present Elmswell Hall. Nevertheless, the hamlet was described in the late 19th century as comprising largely of cottages, several of them still mud-built and thatched.[6] Just before the Second World War, when it was bought by the Mackrills, the estate was again run-down and part of it was subsequently occupied by the military. From about 1950 the family developed the estate, securing a piped water supply and mains electricity, and making many changes to the domestic and farm buildings.[7] Elmswell Hall was enlarged and refurbished in the 1960s; two other houses, Springwell Farm or House and Rose Cottage, then converted and modernised, and in the 1980s a 19th-century barn was made into a house.[8] Some buildings were demolished. These included five cottages to the south of the springs and east of the beck, which were removed in the 1960s and replaced by two houses built closer to the main road;[9] the sites of the demolished cottages were marked in 2004 by prominent earthworks. Since the mid 19th century the complex of buildings around Old Hall has also been gradually reduced,[10] and by 2004 besides Old Hall and Cherry Garth, there were some six houses on the old hamlet site.

Away from the hamlet, the inclosure of the commonable lands in 1771[11] had little effect in terms of new building for many years. A burial vault for Francis Best (d. 1779) and his widow Rosamond (d. 1787) was made about a mile north of Elmswell, and woodland called Spellow Clump planted around it,[12] but it was only under the Denisons, Lords Londesborough, that farmhouses began to be put up on former commonable land. A single-storeyed cottage, now much altered as Elmswell Lodge, was built beside the main road on the western boundary soon after 1841.[13] Elmswell Wold and Spellow Farms were added later, the former by 1861 and the latter by 1890.[14] Two cottages were added near Elmswell Wold Farm in the early 20th century.[15]

LANDOWNERSHIP

Elmswell Manor

A manor of Elmswell, comprising 9 or 10 carucates, was held in 1066 by Norman, but had passed to the king by 1086.[16] The manor may have been a sub-manor of Driffield, for the 10 carucates were later said to 'belong' to that manor.[17] Another 2 carucates held by the king in Elmswell presumably represented a berewick of Driffield manor.[18] The whole settlement of Elmswell was granted later in the 11th century by William II to St Mary's abbey, York,[19] and the township and manor of Elmswell remained part of St Mary's liberty[20] until the house's dissolution in 1539.[21] Much of Elmswell was held by the abbey's tenants about 1320, when the demesne, or home, farm, there seems to have comprised 3 carucates.[22] Most of those tenancies were evidently added later to the lord's holding, which comprised most of the settlement at inclosure in the 18th century.[23]

The whole estate at Elmswell, comprising both the demesne and the tenanted land, was let by the abbey in the 16th century. Shortly before 1536 a Lady Pickering held the manor, and in that year a new lease for 40 or 41 years was made to Ralph Buckton of Elmswell (d. 1540), his wife Margaret (d. 1545), and his son-in-law Robert

1 TNA, E 179/205/504; S. Neave, 'Rural settlement contraction in the ER of Yorks. *c.* 1660–1760' (Hull Univ. PhD thesis, 1990), 311; Best, *Farming Bks*, ed. Woodward, 130–1;

2 Baines, *Hist. Yorks.* (1823), ii. 202.

3 Based on a photograph of an 1815 map, in the possession of Professor D. M. Woodward, Beverley, 2003, and reproduced in his edition of Best's farming books (p. 213). Another map, of the same date but with differences of detail, is at BIA, CC. Pr. 11/3.

4 BIA, TA. 36M; OS Map 1:10,560, Yorks. CLXI (1855 edn); OS Map 1:2,500, Yorks. CLXI. 11 (1910 edn).

5 OS Map 1:10,560, Yorks. CLXI (1855 edn). For population figs. for Elmswell and Kelleythorpe 1801–81 see above, vol. intr., table 2.

6 Ross, *Driffield*, 109; Fig. 81.

7 Cf. OS Map 1:2,500, Yorks. CLXI. 11 (1910 edn); OS Map 1:10,000, SE 95 NE (1982 edn).

8 Inf. from H. Graham Mackrill, Elmswell, 2004.

9 Inf. from Mr Mackrill.

10 ERAO, DX/130; OS Map 1:2,500, Yorks. CLXI. 11 (1910 edn).

11 RDB, AN/196/12.

12 Mortimer, *Forty Years' Researches*, 264; J. Foster, *Pedigrees of Yorks.* iii, s.v. Best; Ross, *Driffield*, 55, 110–11; OS Map 1:10,560, Yorks. CLXI (1855 edn). This was presumably the burial ground of an acre mentioned in 1844: RDB, FZ/239/283.

13 ERAO, DX/130; OS Map 1:10,560, Yorks. CLXI (1855 edn).

14 TNA, RG 9/3608; *YH* 17 July 1890; OS Map 1:2,500, Yorks. CLXI. 3, 6–7 (1892–3 edn).

15 OS Map 1:2,500, CLXI. 3 (1910 edn).

16 *VCH Yorks.* ii. 287, 323.

17 Description of William II's charter to St Mary's abbey recorded in YAS, MD 161/c/j.

18 *VCH Yorks.* ii. 197, 320.

19 *EYC.* i, pp. 269–70.

20 *Feudal Aids*, vi. 204; *Cal. Pat.* 1313–17, 555; *Cal. Close*, 1422–9, 129.

21 *VCH Yorks.* iii. 111.

22 TNA, LR 11/51/732.

23 Below, this section.

Heneage.[1] After the Bucktons' deaths, Heneage evidently sub-let Elmswell. A Mr St Quintin held the estate briefly before John Hall and Alexander Dawson, and their assignee Dorothy Lakyn, widow, was the occupier in 1564.[2] In 1576 Heneage's son, Sir Thomas, obtained a renewal of the lease from the abbey's successor, the Crown, for 21 years at a rent of £29 7*s.* a year, but soon afterwards he transferred his interest to Edward Nettleton.[3] Nettleton was said to have been followed as lessee, both of Elmswell and the adjoining settlement of Kelleythorpe, by John Thwing.[4] Elmswell manor was sold by the Crown to Thomas Crompton and others in 1590, subject to the payment of the annual rent in perpetuity.[5]

Henry Best, a Yorkshireman working in London as a scrivener, bought the manor from Thomas Crompton and his wife Mary in 1597–8, and in 1598 he and his wife Ann resold it to his brother, James Best, of Hutton Cranswick, subsequently of Elmswell, (d. 1617).[6] It then included appurtenances in Great and Little Driffield and outside the parish.[7] In 1618 Best's son and heir, Paul Best, sold the manor to his brother Henry (d. 1645), and it thereafter descended from father to son, being held in turn by John Best[8] (d. 1669), Charles Best (d. 1719), Francis Best (d. 1779), the Revd Francis Best (d. 1802), and the Revd Francis Best (d. 1844).[9] The estate, which was then wholly occupied by tenants, included 9 carucates and 2 oxgangs in 1727; at the inclosure of Elmswell in 1771 Francis Best was awarded 967 a. there for his commonable lands, and in 1823 the holding was put at 1,140 a.[10] The heirs of Francis Best (d. 1844) were his nieces, Rosamond Best and Maria Hotham, then the wives respectively of Henry Robinson and W. B. Wainman.[11] In 1844 the Robinsons and Wainmans sold W. J. Denison the manor, together with a leasehold interest in the rectorial tithes there.[12] Denison (d. 1849) was succeeded by his nephew, Lord Albert Conyngham, who then changed his surname to Denison, was made Baron Londesborough in 1850, and died in 1860. He added some 60 a. in Great and Little Drifffield by purchase in 1855.[13] The estate descended subsequently to Lord Londesborough's son, W. H. F. Denison, who was created earl of Londesborough in 1887 and died in 1900, and grandson, W. F. H. Denison, earl of Londesborough.[14] The last sold the Elmswell estate in 1911.[15] It then comprised about 1,520 a., mostly in Elmswell and Little Driffield but also including some 70 a. in Cottam, in Langtoft. All but a few acres was bought by Robert Holtby whose family had tenanted Elmswell House since 1875.[16] In 1915 the 405-a. Elmswell Wold Farm, which included the land in Cottam, was sold to Hugh Campbell. The rest of the estate passed at Holtby's death in 1928 to his widow Gertrude as tenant for life.[17]

Several small sales were made in 1931,[18] but 1,051 a. remained for Mrs Holtby and the other trustees to sell to Marjorie Mackrill in 1939.[19] In 1962 Mrs Mackrill gave her sons Ian and Henry Graham Mackrill 621 a. of the Elmswell estate as joint tenants.[20] In 1984 Ian Mackrill divided his half share into quarters, one of which he then gave to his brother's daughter, Henrietta Fenton, and the other to nephews; the latter share was bought by H. G. Mackrill and his wife Pamela in 1995. The part of the Elmswell estate kept by Mrs Mackrill in 1962 was inherited at her death in 1985 by H. G. Mackrill; it comprised Spellow Farm, then of 351 a. In 1992 Mr Mackrill gave most of that farm to his daughter, Mrs Fenton, in trust. The Elmswell estate bought by Mrs Mackrill in 1939 thus belonged in 2002 to H.G. Mackrill, his wife, and their daughter.[21] H. G. Mackrill died in 2010.[22]

Most of 43 a. bought by the military in 1948 was later re-purchased,[23] and in 1966 H. G. Mackrill enlarged his estate further by buying 147 a. in Kelleythorpe.[24]

Chief houses The chief house on the manor in the mid 16th century may have been that occupied by William Lakyn, gentleman (d. 1563). Lakyn was evidently the main sub-tenant at Elmswell, and it was he who paid the Crown its rent for the manor. His house comprised four ground-floor rooms, besides a kitchen and a buttery, and three upper rooms. The rooms included the lord's and chapel chambers upstairs, and

1 *L&P Hen. VIII*, xiv (I), p. 310; *DNB*, *s.v.* Sir Thomas Heneage, where Buckton's estate is wrongly identified as Hemswell (Lincs.). Ralph and Margaret Buckton were buried in Little Driffield church: memorial in nave; *YAJ*, 14 (1898), 508; 25 (1920), 78; 27 (1924) 381.

2 BIA, D/C. CP. 1564/1.

3 TNA, C 66/1158, m. 20; C 66/1163, m. 10.

4 Best, *Farming Bks*, ed. Woodward, 217.

5 TNA, C 66/1345, mm. 9–13.

6 J. Foster, *Pedigrees of Yorks.* iii; Best, *Farming Bks*, ed. Woodward, pp. lvii, lxiv, 245, 257–8.

7 ERAO, DDHV/9/13; *Yorks. Fines*, iv. 89, 93.

8 ERAO, DDHV/9/17; Best, *Farming Bks*, ed. Woodward, 246–7; *DNB*, *s.v.* Paul Best.

9 J. Foster, *Pedigrees of Yorks.* iii.

10 RDB, K/211/425; AN/196/12; DO/352/400.

11 J. Foster, *Pedigrees of Yorks.* iii, s.vv. Best, Hotham & Norcliffe.

12 RDB, FZ/239/283; FZ/246/284. The sale was agreed before Francis Best's death: H. Best, *Rural Economy in Yorks.* ed. C. B. Robinson (Surtees. Soc. 33), 169.

13 RDB, GT/12/17; HG/302/380; HK/317/333.

14 *Complete Peerage*, s.v. Londesborough.

15 HRO, DBHT/9/767.

16 RDB, 73/365/331 (1905); 134/281/259; 135/110/92; *VCH Yorks. ER.* ii. 268; *YH* 24 July 1875.

17 RDB, 169/234/191; 417/565/457; 525/516/405.

18 Ibid. 426/481/367; 426/482/368, etc.

19 Ibid. 629/423/309; HRO, DBHT/9/1142.

20 RDB, 1327/61/55.

21 Inf. from H. Graham Mackrill, Elmswell, 2002.

22 *The Times* 30 Mar 2010 (Obituary).

23 RDB, 792/303/242; 1296/483/433; inf. from Mr Mackrill.

24 RDB, 1439/447/405.

82. *Elmswell: Old Hall* c. *1980. Built by Henry Best, probably in the late 1630s, of bricks made nearby. It was in a derelict state in 2010.*

the hall and Lakyn's own and two other parlours below.[1] Pieces of carved limestone, including door and window dressings, found near Old Hall, and a sculpted woman's head re-set in that house, are believed to have come from a 16th-century building of some quality, possibly from Lakyn's house.

Various building dates have been proposed for the new manor house, now called Old Hall,[2] but around 1640 would seem to be most likely based on architectural and documentary evidence. In 1635 Henry Best contracted with a Beverley brickmaker for 400,000 bricks, 29,000 of which had been paid for by the end of that year, and 240 pine boards were bought in Hull and boated to Elmswell in 1642.[3]

Old Hall, which is built of red bricks, stands on the western bank of one of the branches of Elmswell Beck. A linear house with an east-west orientation, it has two storeys with attics. The steeply-pitched roof is covered now with pantiles but may originally have been thatched.[4] The plan was simple, consisting of three rooms on each floor. The house was entered from the north through a small, two-storeyed, off-centre porch, was lit by low, brick-mullioned windows, and heated by hearths along the southern side of the house, where there are three large, integral chimney stacks.

The unusual features of the house – a main front facing north and the use of the southern wall for chimney stacks rather than ground-floor windows – may, it is thought, be made sense of if it faced an earlier building standing opposite it on the north side of a yard. In support of that theory, attention has been drawn to the similar, raised ground levels of the site of Old Hall and the area to its north, where, moreover, the ground is retained by a brick wall with an ashlar base.[5]

In 1669 the ground-floor accommodation of the Old Hall comprised a central hall, eastern parlour, and western kitchen, and presumably also the buttery recorded then. Above the principal rooms were three chambers and a small room in the upper part of the porch which was perhaps the 'chest' then mentioned. Finally, the attics were occupied by another three rooms,[6] one of those garret rooms perhaps being the 'folkes chamber' used by the regular and seasonal workers on the farm.[7] The upper parts of the house were reached by a stairway from the south-east corner of the hall.[8]

Henry Best also built or rebuilt at least one of the other farmhouses on the estate, that named New or West Hall in the 17th century.[9] West Hall is perhaps to be identified with a remodelled house at Elmswell which

1 Inventory printed in Best, *Farming Bks*, ed. Woodward, 229–32.

2 Best, *Farming Bks*, ed. Woodward, p. xlix.

3 Ibid. 116 n, 132, 200.

4 For detailed discussion and illustration of the house, see English Heritage, NMR, NBR 61449, which includes a building report of 1993 by Adam Menuge; Best, *Farming Bks*, ed. Woodward, pp. xlix–lii; plates I–III; Figs 82 & 83.

5 Menuge, 'Building report', 4–6.

6 Ibid.

7 Best, *Farming Bks*, ed. Woodward, 50.

8 Menuge, 'Building report', 9.

9 Ibid. 78–9, 130.

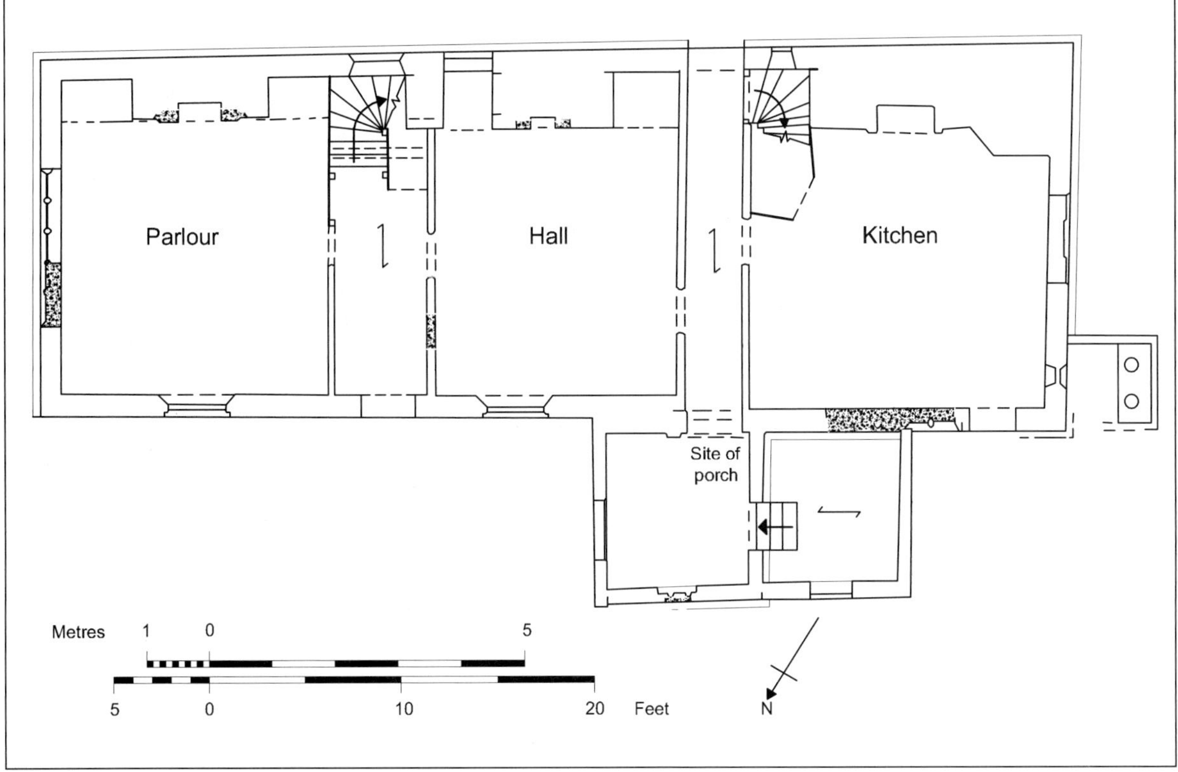

83. *Elmswell: Old Hall, ground plan.*

has brickwork of the 17th century and was called Hall Farm before the name was changed to Cherry Garth.[1]

It was evidently Old Hall which John Best's widow Sarah occupied in 1672, and for which she paid tax on nine hearths.[2] The Bests apparently ceased to live at Elmswell during the lifetime of Charles Best (d. 1719),[3] and tenants subsequently occupied the house, which was usually known as Old Hall after the building of Elmswell House (later Elmswell Hall).

The north side of the Old Hall was altered in the late 18th and early 19th century, datestones of 1656 being moved in the process. The porch was remodelled and its doorway blocked. To its east the old northern wall was rebuilt, slightly recessed, and was given sash windows and a new entrance door. The former porch was extended westwards by an outshot then or soon afterwards, and later by a lean-to scullery.[4] Inside the house, the hall was reduced by the making of a passageway from the new north entrance door to the existing southern stairway, and at the west end of that room another partitioned passageway was made, leading from the old porch to a new back door made in the south wall. The re-fenestration of the northern side of the house, and the internal remodelling of the Hall, resulted in the reduction and blocking up of original windows in the other walls, and 17th-century panelling in the parlour and the middle chamber was also altered to accommodate the changes.[5]

From 1965 the house stood empty and was allowed to fall into decay.[6] Despite a long battle to save the building it was roofless and in extreme disrepair in 2011, with much of the panelling lost.[7] Nearby a fragment of Old Hall's brick dovecot, also of the 17th-century, remained. A large barn also stood near the manor house until its demolition about 1860. The high-pitched, thatched roof was supported by wooden props, two of them dated 1607; the floor area, which was believed to have been reduced but still accommodated six loaded waggons, was 330 sq. yd.[8]

Elmswell House, later Hall, standing some 400 m. north-west of Old Hall, was built on a vacant site in 1856, for a Driffield solicitor, E. D. Conyers (d. 1863),

1 Inf. from Mr Mackrill, 2004.

2 She was also liable for another house, then empty, with seven hearths, perhaps West Hall: TNA, E 179/205/504.

3 J. Foster, *Pedigrees of Yorks.* iii, s.v. Best; Ross, *Driffield*, 127.

4 Illus. of north and south fronts in Best, *Rural Economy*, ed. Robinson, frontispiece.

5 Menuge, 'Building report', 8, 10, 12–15.

6 RDB, 525/516/405; 1427/126/109; Best, *Farming Bks*, ed. Woodward, p. lii; inf. from Mr Mackrill, 2004.

7 *YP* 17 July 2009.

8 Sheahan and Whellan, *Hist. York & ER.* ii. 504; Ross, *Driffield*, 109–10; illus. in Best, *Rural Economy*, ed. Robinson, facing p. 170.

84. *Elmswell: Elmswell House from sale particulars of 1939. Later renamed Elmswell Hall it was built for E. D. Conyers, Driffield solicitor and farmer, in 1856.*

who also farmed in Elmswell.[1] The house had some 5 a. of grounds in 1939.[2] It was requisitioned by the military authorities in 1941, but in 1950 the house and huts built in the grounds were released to the Mackrills. As Elmswell Hall it was given with about 3 a. to H. Graham Mackrill by his mother, Marjorie Mackrill, in 1962. He enlarged and refurbished the house to designs by John Blackmore, occupying it from 1963.[3] The small, Tudor-Gothic, country house built of white brick on a more or less rectangular plan, had service rooms occupying the northern range and principal rooms in the centre and south of the building. The mid 20th-century remodelling and restoration of the house involved its extension westwards.

ECONOMIC HISTORY

There is no indication that the iron working and pottery manufacture of the Romano-British period was pursued later.[4] With the exception of corn milling, the economy of Elmswell has been based solely on agriculture since the early Middle Ages. The farming of the township was particularly well documented in the 17th century.

Agriculture: the Middle Ages

It is clear from the few records there are for Elmswell in the Middle Ages that it was a small farming community largely concerned with the cultivation of corn. Much of its land probably lay, as later, in three open fields, the pattern perhaps like that in the Driffields, with eastern and western fields extending the full length of the township and an intervening shorter middle field to the north of the settlement. The chief farm was that of the lord of Elmswell, St Mary's abbey, York, which was run by its servants until the 15th century, when it was let instead. The rest of the township was held very largely by the abbey's tenants.

Like the rest of the parish, Elmswell was adversely affected by the aftermath of the Conquest. In 1086 there was reckoned to be land for five ploughs there but the manor was said to be waste.[5] Early farmers at Elmswell included Forne and Turgis, whose lands were granted by the lord of the manor, St Mary's abbey, York, *c.* 1200 respectively to Hugh son of William of Elmswell, Forne's great-nephew, and William son of Reginald of Elmswell. Those holdings were held freely, mostly or entirely for an annual money rent, though Hugh and his heirs were charged also with ploughing the abbey's demesne land twice a year. Similar freeholdings had been granted earlier to Alan and Reginald, both sons of a William of Elmswell.[6]

Some idea of the later economy of the settlement is provided by brief and not wholly legible accounts for 1320–2.[7] Much of Elmswell was then 'farmed', or rented out, by St Mary's abbey. The tenants – freeholders, bond tenants, and 'cottars', or smallholders – owed money

1 TNA, HO 107/2366; date on building; OS Map 1:10,560, Yorks. CLXI (1855 edn); OS Map 1:2,500, Yorks. CLXI. 11 (1910 edn); White, *Dir. Hull & York* (1851), 601. For Conyers, above, Gt and Little Driffield, soc. hist., soc. leadership (1770–1870).

2 RDB, 629/423/309.

3 Ibid. 1327/296/263; 1370/131/122.

4 Above, Elmswewll, early settlement.

5 *VCH Yorks.* ii. 287.

6 YAS, MD 161/c/j; *EYC.* i, p. 342. Elmswell freeholders occur as witnesses to abbey deeds in the 12th century, when Turgis the dispenser was also recorded: *EYC.* ii, p. 294; iv, pp. 119, 149, etc.

7 TNA, LR 11/51/732.

rents amounting to nearly £10 a year.[1] There was a variety of other obligations. Some tenants rendered also or instead corn rents, 60 quarters of wheat and 86 quarters of oats being received in 1320. Other renders included 'lake hens', or wildfowl, at Christmas, 34 from Elmswell and 4 from Driffield. Ploughing and other works were also owed to the abbey, all or most of them probably by the bond tenants, but many of those duties were then waived in return for additional money rents amounting to nearly 15*s*. a year. In both 1320 and 1321, however, the abbey did call on tenants to perform labour services worth 3*s*. 4*d*., comprising the reaping of the corn on 'Ockeldale' and its carriage to 'the water', possibly the River Hull or one of its tributary streams. An aid, a tax taken from the tenants by the lord, was charged at £3 6*s*. 8*d*. in 1320–1 and again in 1321–2; other small payments were due as 'recognitions', perhaps entry fines taken on a change of tenancy, and tenants had to grind their corn at the seigneurial mills, allowing part of the grain or flour – the *multura* – to be taken in payment.

The part of Elmswell not leased by the abbey, the home farm of Elmswell manor, apparently comprised 3 carucates. That estate was run by one or two officers of St Mary's abbey who accounted for the farming operations in 1320–2 as serjeants or servants (*servientes*) of Elmswell.[2] The farming was done largely by a staff comprising four ploughmen, eight or nine carters, and a swineherd. One or two boys were also employed, apparently occasionally. More importantly, specialist staff were drafted in at certain times: a bailiff was mentioned, but it is not clear whether he was permanently attached to Elmswell; harvesting was supervised by a reaper, and a smith was similarly called in to overhaul the farm's ploughs and other equipment. Most of the permanent and occasional staff received both allowances of food and cash stipends, the swineherd, for instance, being allowed annually almost 2 quarters of barley and a stipend of 9*d*. At busy times, the efforts of the staff and some of the tenants were augmented by labour paid for specific tasks, in 1320–1 nearly £3 being paid for the weeding, reaping, and threshing of the corn. In that year, too, the tenants had also been paid and given bread for lending a hand with the ploughing.

The farm at Elmswell was clearly largely concerned with the growing of corn. The harvest of 1320 produced 71 quarters of wheat, 67 quarters of barley, 66 quarters of oats, and 32 quarters of peas, from sowings respectively of 33 quarters, 21 quarters, 30 quarters, and 16 quarters. Apart from the draught animals, of which there were 14 in 1321, the chief livestock kept were pigs and birds of various kinds. The pigs numbered about 50, and there were some 30 geese, 17 ducks, and many pigeons. Later references to a Coney Garth close suggest that the abbey may at some other time have also had a rabbit warren in Elmswell or Little Driffield.[3] It is hard to believe that sheep were not also kept, but they were not mentioned in the source, perhaps because they were the responsibility of another official who answered for them elsewhere. Practically all of the corn rendered by the tenants was taken to the abbey in York, almost 150 quarters of wheat and oats being delivered there in 1320–1. The demesne produce was, on the other hand, mostly used on the farm. Of 71 quarters of wheat harvested and 7 quarters of tithe corn, only 19 were delivered to York and 4 more to 'Grimston' for the abbot; 30 were used for seed; almost 25 given in allowances to the staff, and most of the rest was made into bread for visitors from the abbey, for carters, and for the tenants helping with the ploughing. Other produce was fed to the stock, some 12 quarters of 75½ quarters of barley being consumed by the oxen, pigs, dogs, and pigeons; slightly more going to the staff in allowances, and only 8½ quarters reaching York. Besides the farm stock, oats were fed to the abbey's cart horses, to the mounts of official visitors, and to at least one horse carrying fish from the abbey's manor of Hornsea to York.

Both the demesne farm and those of the tenants were made up largely of land in the open fields and common grasslands, but little is known about the farmlands before the 17th century. Glimpses of the agricultural system are, however, to be had from notes on the proceedings of the manor court.[4] Waste ground called Greendikes was evidently the cause of tension between the lord and his tenants: in 1388 tenants were forbidden from turning their cattle there before the lord had put out his cattle and horses, on penalty of 3*s*. 4*d*. for each beast in default, while in 1391 another order was issued against tenants encroaching on Greendikes with their ploughs. Pasture may have been in short supply again about 1515, when a stint of 10 sheep for each oxgang held was in force, and when a farmer from Great Driffield rescued his sheep 'at night' from Elmswell's pound.

The demesne farm was evidently still being run by the abbey in the later 14th century,[5] but soon afterwards direct exploitation of the demesne was abandoned. In 1428 John Cottam, a Driffield mason, John Waterhouse, and John Cartwright, respectively farmers of Driffield and Elmswell, and William Otley of Driffield leased the manor of Elmswell and its demesne lands from the abbey for a six-year term.[6] A valuation of the manor of *c*. 1500 has the farm, or rent, of the demesne contributing nearly £7 of the annual value of some £32; the rents of tenants at will and a freeholder accounted

1 One farm appears among the cash receipts on the stock and grange account in 1320–1.

2 The source mentions a *serviens* at Burton Agnes, where the abbey also had an estate: *VCH Yorks. ER*. ii. 111.

3 RDB, K/211/425; Best, *Farming Bks*, ed. Woodward, 202.

4 YAS, MD 161/c/j.

5 *Cal. Papal Reg*. v. 2; *Cal. Pat*. 1370–4, 396–7. *Cal.Papal Reg*. viii. 351 would seem to be anachronistic.

6 YAS, MD 161/c/j.

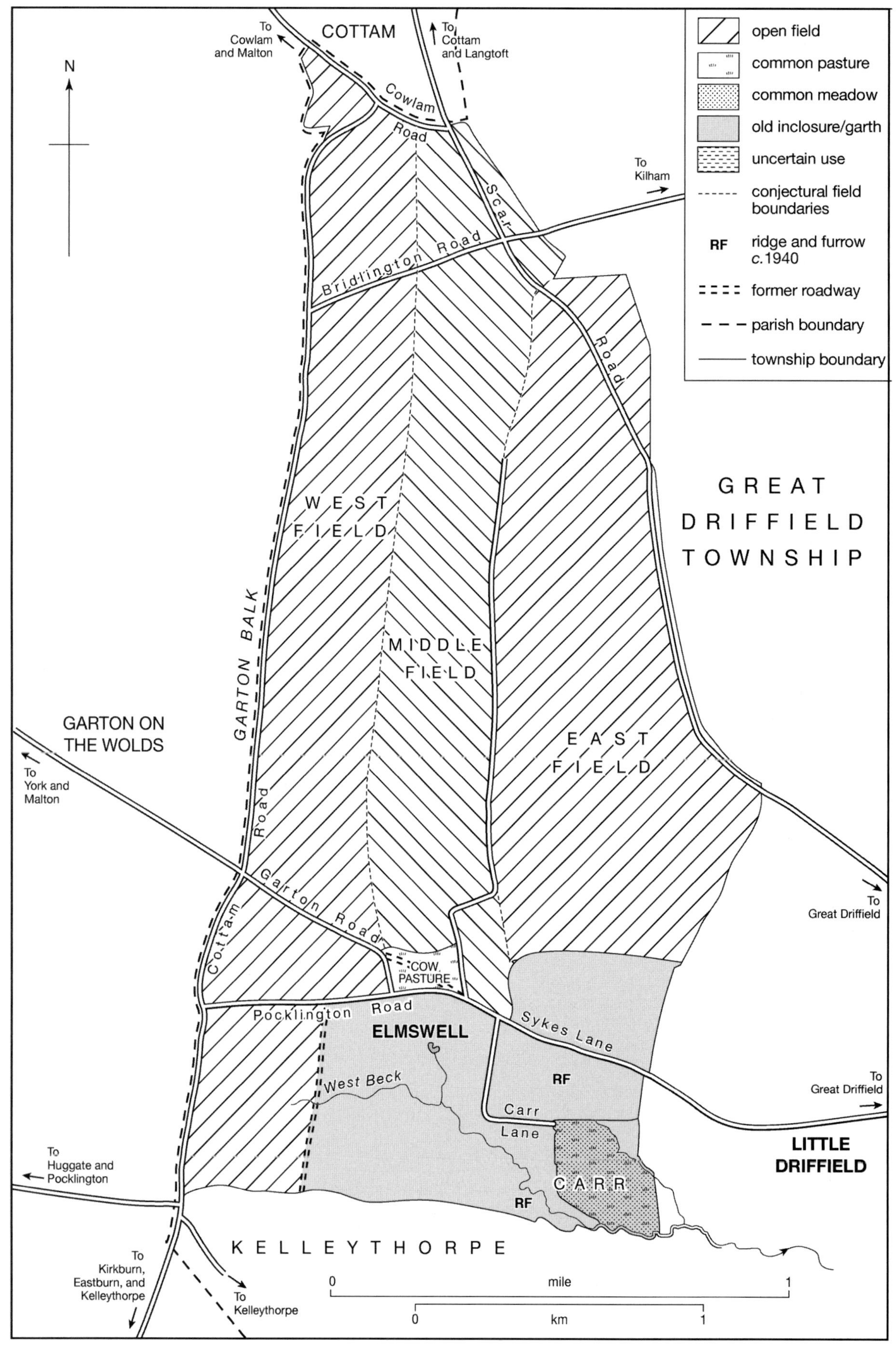

85. *Elmswell before inclosure.*

for practically all of the remaining value.[1] William Lakyn (d. 1563), who probably held the demesne farm, owed a money rent of £41 a year, corn rents worth at least £25, and was accountable to the lord for the live and dead stock on the farm.[2]

Agriculture: 1600–1800

The rural economy of Elmswell was described in detail in the 17th century in a renowned farming manual and a related memorandum book, both of which are almost certainly the work of Henry Best (d. 1645), lord of the manor of Elmswell.[3] The account which follows is based on those works.

Common lands and inclosure Elmswell had three open fields in the 17th and 18th centuries, East, West, and Middle Fields.[4] Most of Elmswell lay in those fields, West Field extending the full length of the township from the Cottam boundary in the north to that with Kelleythorpe in the south, a distance of 2 miles and a fall in altitude from over 80 m. above sea level to less than 30 m. The boundaries of the individual fields cannot be determined conclusively; at inclosure few, and in this respect unhelpful, allotments were made. On the other hand, the old divisions of the arable were evident in the sinuous boundaries of many of the modern closes, and a detailed map based on a survey of 1815 makes up for the apparent loss of the inclosure plan.[5] West Field certainly included the areas later called Mask Hills, Butts, and Little Closes; the western part of High Wold, and presumably also Garton Gate, Linton Wold, and half of Cinquefoil Wold. The probable composition of Middle Field was Kelder Gate, Clay Hill, the other half of Cinquefoil Wold, and its share of High Wold. A field road awarded at inclosure may follow part of Middle Field's eastern boundary. The lands of East Field lay north-east of the hamlet, also extending up the slope into High Wold.[6]

The large fields encompassed a variety of soil types as well as topography; around the hamlet clay and chalk gravel beds were covered by a strong, deep loam, but rising up the slope the loamy soils became progressively thinner and more chalky.[7] The fields were rendered more manageable by division into flatts, furlongs, or falls. Within the flatts lay the basic units of the open-field system, the lands, selions, or strips of individual farmers. In East Field, for example, Long Wandills (Wandales) flatt was composed of 12 lands, each of 2 a., in the 17th century.[8] The width of lands varied, a 'broad land' in Elmswell then being about 28 ft wide. Later, the width of a narrow land was put at some 12 ft and that of the possibly more numerous broad lands, then called 'ordinary' lands, at 27 ft, and one exceptionally broad land was 36 ft wide.[9] Some of the flatts belonged to a single proprietor, the lord of the manor. Judging from closes later marked as tithe-free, the demesne flatts occupied the westernmost parts of West and Middle Fields, where the lands ran north-south, but in East Field, where the lands lay east-west, the demesne flatts seem to have been the most northerly parts of each division.[10] Such regularity suggests that the demesne, and perhaps the other lands, had been long undisturbed or that that the fields had been re-ordered fairly recently in the 17th century.

Best reserved his best clay soils for the winter corns, wheat and rye, and those grounds alone were favoured with 'fold-mucking', manuring by folded sheep.[11] The poorest, high land was cultivated only intermittently, as an 'out-field'; Best reported that in or about 1641 only 'our in-field' was sown, and that there was consequently then no barley on the Wolds.[12] The out-field was presumably represented in the 19th century by the *c.* 400 a. of the township then categorized as 'plantation and waste land'.[13]

The other chief area of commonable land was the Carr, an area of gravely soil beside the southern boundary stream, which provided Elmswell with both meadowland and rough grazing. In the 17th century it contained 39 'lands' lying north-south and belonging to nine tenant-farmers of Elmswell in multiples of 2 to 11 lands; there seem also to have been another 5 lands, divided between three of the farms, in the north-east of the Carr, adjoining grassland called St Nicholas's Ings.[14] The lands in the Carr, which show that it had once been tilled, were still evident in aerial photographs of the mid 20th century.[15] Hay was taken from the lands, usually in early July,[16] and then between Michaelmas (29 September) and Lady Day (25 March) the Carr was used as a common pasture.[17] The pasturage in the Carr was rationed according to the number of lands held; the

1 ERAO, DDHV/9/7, printed in Best, *Rural Economy*, ed. Robinson, 166 n. For the date, compare the account of 1498–9 included in YAS, MD 161/c/j.

2 Best, *Farming Bks*, ed. Woodward, 229, 231–2.

3 Ibid. pp. xvii–xviii, and *passim*.

4 RDB, AN/196/12; Best, *Farming Bks*, ed. Woodward, 19, 45, 52.

5 Photograph in the possession of Professor D. M. Woodward, Beverley, 2003, reproduced in Best, *Farming Bks*, ed. Woodward, 213.

6 RDB, AN/196/12; photograph of 1815 map.

7 ERAO, DX/100, cited in Best, *Farming Bks*, ed. Woodward, p. xxiv.

8 Best, *Farming Bks*, ed. Woodward, 52.

9 Ibid. 18; Best, *Rural Economy*, ed. Robinson, p. 40 n.

10 Photograph of 1815 map. For tithes, see above, Gt and Little Driffield, manors and estates (rectory, tithes, Elmswell).

11 Ibid. 19, 49.

12 Ibid. 59.

13 Ibid. p. xxiv.

14 Ibid. 42–3, 212. An apparently partial schedule of the common recorded elsewhere details only 34½ lands: ibid. 133.

15 RAF air photographs, run 53, no. 3033; run 79, no. 4132.

16 Best, *Farming Bks*, ed. Woodward, 33, 42.

17 Ibid. 85.

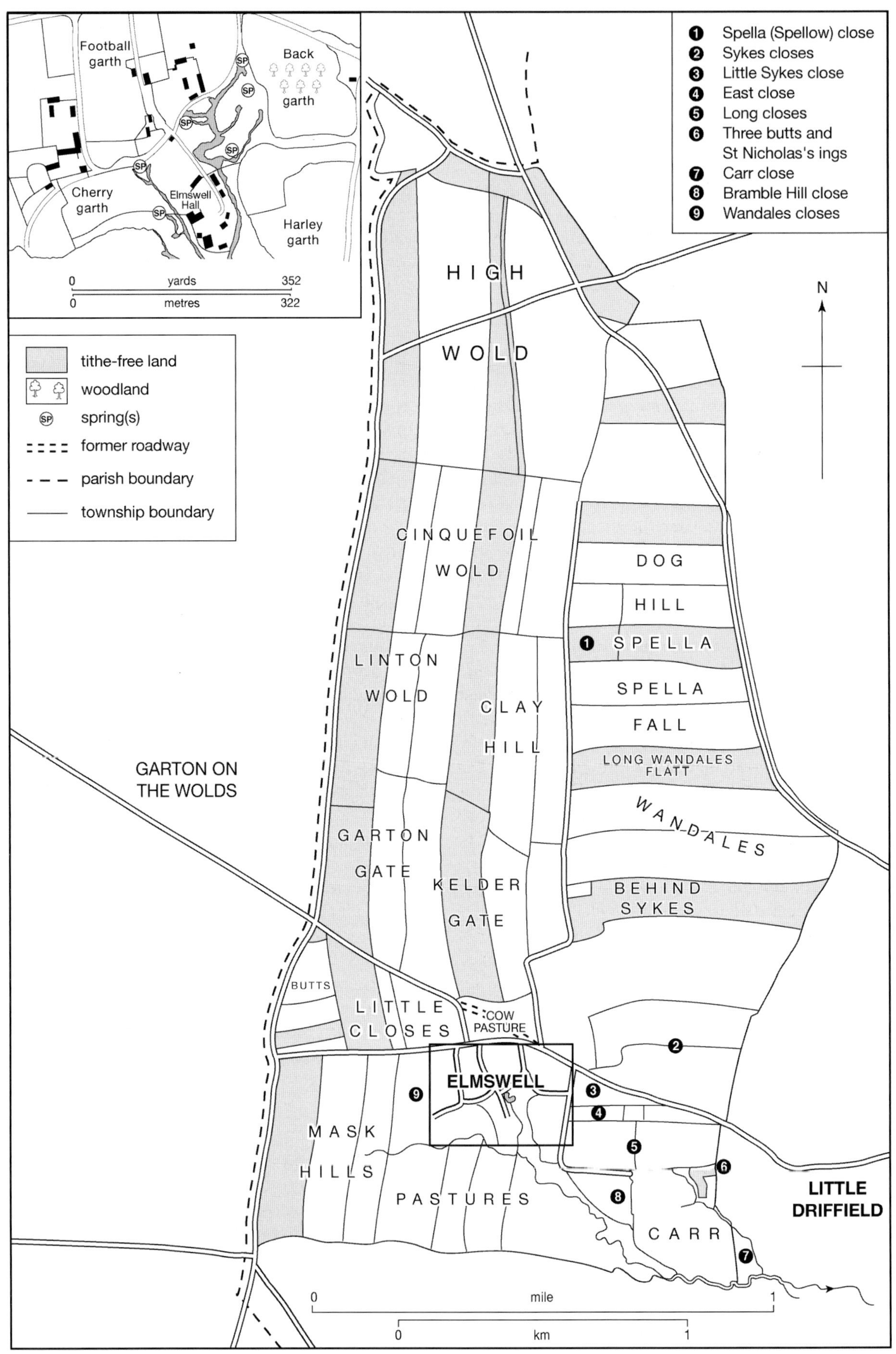

86. *Elmswell after inclosure in 1771 and settlement plan of 1815.*

stint for ewes was then five for each land held, but one of the farmers then enjoyed no rights because he lived outside Elmswell.[1]

There seems to have been a smaller common pasture on the north side of the hamlet; in 1631 the appurtenances of 10 oxgangs included, besides 5 lands in Elmswell Carr, the same in Elmswell Cow Pasture, and an 8-a. close called Cow Pasture was recorded later.[2] The pasture may have been used earlier in whole or in part as a brick field. Other common meadowland and grazing was provided by the field balks,[3] where oxen and horses might be tethered from St Helen's Day (3 May),[4] and earlier in the year the hamlet's lanes were grazed by ewes and lambs.[5]

The commonable lands seem to have been changed, and in some cases inclosed, by the 17th century. Reference then to 'lands', combined with later evidence of ridge and furrow,[6] show that the area to the east and south of the hamlet had once been tilled, perhaps as parts of East and West Fields. By the 17th century, however, some of that ground lay in demesne closes called Long, Sykes, and Carr Closes, and further north the 4-a. Spellow Close had evidently been taken from the demesne flatt of that name in East Field. Carr Close, located in the south-eastern corner of the township, contained six short lands.[7] Another part of the former tillage, in the Carr, was used as commonable grassland by the 17th century.[8] The date of those inclosures and changes of use are not known, but other former tillage, lying south of Elmswell, was clearly inclosed during the earlier 17th century. Best said that the lands in the pasture had been let for 2*s.* each about 1600 but that 'now being inclosed' they fetched some 9*s.*, and the pasture lands of another proprietor, Alice Edwards, had similarly risen in value from 2*s.* 6*d.* to 7*s.* a land.[9] The inclosed grounds were presumably later represented by the four closes called Pastures.[10] The inclosure was probably facilitated by exchanges which consolidated holdings in the grassland. In 1634 Best gave up two lands in the pasture to two proprietors for their 'Wandills', lying further north, on the west side of the hamlet.[11] The Wandills, or Wandales, were probably also parts of the common, the name sometimes denoting meadowland which was annually divided among the commoners for mowing in 'dales', or doles, measured with a standard rod, or 'wand'.[12] The Wandales acquired by Best were subsequently used as meadows and sheep pastures, under the various descriptions of North, South, and New Wandale Closes, and they later comprised 8 a.[13] Another indication of change was Best's reference to Carr Lane, commonly so called 'because it is now made the highway into the carr'.[14]

Commonable grassland, nevertheless, remained after the inclosures. In the winter of 1641 there was friction between Best and the other farmers over the use of the Carr in winter, and in particular about the foddering of sheep there, Best's sheep being then separated from the town sheep and fed hay 'on our own lands'. Another difference of opinion arose from the townsfolk's desire to restrict the pasture there in Spring to ewes with lambs and Best's policy of lambing in his own closes and feeding the rest of his flock on the common.[15] The continuation of the Carr as a common pasture is also suggested by the remark that the Carr was sometimes overcharged with sheep.[16] The lord's interest in the common was limited to a balk and odd pieces of land,[17] perhaps as a result of the exchanges made to effect inclosure. At final inclosure in 1771 the Carr contained only *c.* 30 a.[18]

The common lands, reduced by earlier inclosure, and probably further re-organized and consolidated by exchanges and purchases, were finally inclosed in 1771. There were then only two estates, and 'inclosure' was almost certainly a confirmation and a tidying up rather than anything else. The award made by commissioners appointed by the owners of Elmswell dealt with 1,053 a., including a few acres already inclosed but involved in exchanges. Francis Best received 967 a., and James Moyser's daughters and coheirs, Diana Strickland, Mary Tate, and Sarah Moyser, the remaining 87 a.[19]

The Demesne The demesne estate in Elmswell had altered little in size by the 17th century, when it was said to include 30 oxgangs, or 3 carucates and 6 oxgangs, of open-field land. The tithe-free status of the demesne[20] presumably accounts for the distinction between demesne and other land being adhered to into the 17th century, when the lord's farm and the demesne were clearly no longer the same things. Besides the demesne, Best then owned practically all of the settlement. He let

1 Ibid. 7.
2 Ibid. 199; photograph of 1815 map.
3 RDB, O/359/882.
4 Best, *Farming Bks*, ed. Woodward, 124.
5 Ibid. 13.
6 RAF air photographs, run 53, no. 3033; run 79, nos. 4132–3.
7 Best, *Farming Bks*, ed. Woodward, 42, 136, 202; RDB, AN/196/12; photograph of 1815 map.
8 Above, this section [carr].
9 Best, *Farming Bks*, ed. Woodward, pp. xxii, 135, 137. For Alice Edwards, see below, this section, Kelleythorpe manor.
10 Photograph of 1815 map.
11 Best, *Farming Bks*, ed. Woodward, 133. For another inclosure after an exchange, see ibid. 42–3.
12 Cf. *VCH Yorks. ER.* vii. 72, 176, 250, 393.
13 Best, *Farming Bks*, ed. Woodward, 40, 86; photograph of 1815 map. Another area, in East Field, was also called Wandales and may thus once have been used for meadow, but by the 17th century it was part of the tillage: ibid. 52.
14 Best, *Farming Bks*, ed. Woodward, 41.
15 Ibid. 77–8, 85.
16 Ibid. 87.
17 Ibid. 43.
18 RDB, AN/196/12.
19 Ibid. No inclosure plan is known.
20 Best, *Farming Bks*, ed. Woodward, 202.

some of his land in Elmswell,[1] but much of the land was added to the demesne proper to form a large-scale farming operation. About 1640 Best was farming three farms with the demesne, West Hall, West House, and Bonwick's Farm, the whole probably exceeding 7 carucates.[2]

The demesne grassland in Elmswell comprised some 50 a. of meadow closes, about 25 a. of pasture closes, and unquantified meadowland in the Carr and on the field balks.[3] Right of pasture for sheep on the wold of neighbouring Cottam also belonged to Elmswell manor, though from the 17th century it seems usually to have been let rather than used as part of the lord's farm. The intercommoning with proprietors in Cottam probably dated back to the Middle Ages, and the farming operations at Elmswell of St Mary's abbey. In 1623 Henry Best, as the abbey's successor as lord of Elmswell manor, claimed grazing for 300 sheep throughout the year over the 500-a. Monk Leys, later known apparently as Cottam Warren. The right was alternatively said in the earlier 17th century to be for 360 sheep. Later the pasturage at Cottam was let with one of the Elmswell farms; 400 sheep were then permitted to graze 319 a. of the former warren during the day, but had to be returned to Elmswell each night.[4]

The sufficiency, or otherwise, of the grassland is difficult to evaluate from Best's writings. What is clear is that they were used as part of a farming system which paid scant attention to the township boundary. Best regularly let hay in the Carr, often to farmers of Kirkburn, in 1630 taking £2 for the crop of the demesne lands there and part of one of the farm's lands, for instance.[5] A meadow close belonging to the demesne, the 4-a. Spellow Close, was similarly let to men of Eastburn, in Kirkburn, in 1628 for £4 10*s*., and in 1639 its winter grazing fetched about £2.[6] If Best sometimes sold hay and pasture, perhaps in response to a general scarcity and high prices, he, like other farmers of Elmswell, also frequently needed to purchase 'gates', or pasture rights, for his cattle in other townships. Calves were sent to summer pastures on the Wolds as far afield as Raisthorpe and Thixendale, in Wharram Percy parish, and West Lutton, all about ten miles from Elmswell. Other pastures used lay in the equally-distant Beeford and Skipsea, both in Holderness, and in the neighbouring places of Cottam, in Langtoft parish, and Kelleythorpe.[7]

The farming done on the enlarged demesne estate in the mid 17th century was mixed, but its chief object was almost certainly corn production. Five ploughs were employed 'constantly' on the 7 carucates *c*. 1640.[8] Corn was taken regularly to market from November onwards. Usually at least eight pack horses were used for the lengthy journeys, but carts were also employed occasionally, apparently with other farmers of the neighbourhood. The journey to Malton market, which was busy early, meant starting from Elmswell some four hours before dawn. The main markets were Malton, for wheat, maslin (a mixture of rye and wheat), and barley, and Beverley, where wheat, oats and barley were sold. Some barley was also sent to Pocklington, and wheat was sold by a sample taken by salters to Bridlington shippers, who then transported it to Newcastle-upon-Tyne and Sunderland. Sheep, which as fertilisers of the tillage played an important role in the arable farming, were the chief concern after corn. Much of the Farming Book was given over to the raising of sheep, though the significance of sheep husbandry in local farming is perhaps exaggerated by the probable loss of other parts of Best's text dealing with the other livestock.[9] Nonetheless, Best had 130 sheep and lambs in 1618; usually *c*. 250 in the 1620s, and 419 or 464 in 1642.[10]

The stock were moved often in search of grazing; from the Carr and the closes they were put onto the higher wold land in spring, and then folded on parts of the fallowed field over the summer and autumn, before being returned to the higher pasture for the winter. The Carr and closes were used for the younger sheep in winter, and, in the worst conditions, also for the sheep from the wold, the grazing then being supplemented with hay produced on the farm.[11]

The wool produced in Elmswell was usually sold on the farm, and then carried into the West Riding on pack horses throughout the summer, although in 1642 the purchaser was a Beverley man.[12] Sheep were sold regularly through the local fairs. Ewes and lambs sold well at the Little Driffield fairs at Easter and Whitsun, especially when Holderness men were in the market to stock their pastures, and fat sheep also had a good sale there and at the Cross Fair in Beverley at Ascensiontide. Rams sold also at Easter, and at the summer and autumn fairs at Little Driffield, while old ewes and young sheep in particular were sent to the last sheep fair of the year at Kilham on All Saints Day (1 November).[13]

The other aspects of Best's farming, as revealed in his writings by both firm information and suggestive general discursions, included dairying and the fattening of beef. Fourteen cows were being milked *c*. 1640, and in all 28 cattle were kept in 1642.[14] The livestock also included horses and pigs, 17 and 21 respectively being

1 Below, this section, other farms.
2 Best, *Farming Bks*, ed. Woodward, 130, 139, 202.
3 Ibid. 202–3.
4 RDB, FZ/239/283; *VCH Yorks. ER*. ii. 267–8; Best, *Farming Bks*, ed. Woodward, pp. xxxi, 203, 223.
5 Best, *Farming Bks*, ed. Woodward, 43, 134.
6 Ibid. 135, 202.
7 Ibid. 125, 168, 173–4.
8 Ibid. 139.
9 Ibid. p. xxi.
10 Ibid. 99–100, 164, 167, 174.
11 Ibid. 7, 13, 16, 18–19, 31, 75–82, 85–7, 99.
12 Ibid. 28, 32.
13 Ibid. 11–12, 32, 75, 117–20.
14 Ibid. 139, 150.

on the farm in 1669. Poultry and swans were kept,[1] the latter for market, and partridges may also have been raised at Elmswell. Bees were certainly kept there.[2]

Other farms A source which seems to mix old descriptions and rents with later, 17th-century information, suggests nonetheless that in the 16th century Elmswell had ten farms, besides the demesne holding.[3] Most of the farms by then belonged to the lord of the manor, whose estate had evidently been enlarged by the acquisition of properties formerly held by manorial tenants; there is no longer any evidence of unfree, service-owing tenancies,[4] and farms on the estate were then held by modern leases. Webster House Farm was let, for instance, for a three-year term in 1631, with 6 oxgangs at first and then with 10 oxgangs, at £2 a year for each oxgang.[5] After the demesne farm, of almost 4 carucates, the largest on the manor was that later named as West Hall Farm,[6] which had 2 carucates; two other farms had a carucate each; five had 6 oxgangs each, and a freeholder, the only one on the manor, had 2 or 4 oxgangs. Another 4 oxgangs in Elmswell, perhaps with no house, belonged to the lord of Kelleythorpe manor and were occupied by a tenant of his.[7] As well as the farms, there were a few smaller holdings, comprising cottages with a little land.

The farms in Elmswell had been re-organized by the mid 17th century. Notes on the settlement dated about 1625 and *c.* 1640 reveal the changes.[8] The number of tenanted farms had fallen from eight to five, some of the farmhouses evidently being downgraded to cottage holdings, and only one of the 6-oxgang farms remained. Conversely, West Hall Farm had been enlarged, and the farms of a carucate increased from two to three.

By 1727 there had evidently been further amalgamation and re-organization on the estate, which by then was wholly occupied by tenant farmers. Of the five farms on the manor, the 'demesne' farm and the earlier West Hall Farm were unchanged with 30 and 16 oxgangs respectively; the other farms comprised two with 12 oxgangs each and one of 4 oxgangs.[9] By 1778 there were apparently only four farms on the *c.* 970-a. estate.[10]

Agriculture: From the 18th century

Elmswell was a purely agricultural community throughout the 19th century. In 1841 the 38 inhabitants for whom an occupation was given included there were 5 farmers, 10 agricultural labourers, 14 male and 6 female farm servants who lived in, and a shepherd, a gamekeeper and a dressmaker.[11]

When the estate was put up for sale in 1843 it comprised 913 a. of arable land, 199 a. of pasture and 41 a. of woodland divided into five similar sized farms, averaging 230 a.[12] The old inclosed part of the township around the village was permanent grass land but it was considered 'hardly rich enough for cattle'.[13] The lower slopes of the Wolds were cultivated under a six-year rotation, a fallow year being succeeded by crops of wheat and beans, then by another fallow year, a wheat crop, and two years of seeds for grazing. On the highest land and thinnest soils the Northumberland five-course rotation was used, the sequence being oats, turnips, spring wheat and barley, and clover and grass mown or grazed in the final year.[14]

The farms were reduced to four by 1851; the largest, almost certainly based on what becomes the Old Hall, covered 617 a. It was tenanted by Richard Holtby who employed 14 men, 6 of whom lived in. The other farmers were Robert Hardy with 215 a. and Robert Botham with 110 a. The fourth farm, occupied by the hind or foreman to E. D. Conyers, the Driffield solicitor, covered 400 a., probably included land at Little Driffield.[15] By 1861 Conyers was living in the new-built Elmswell House and farming some 670 a. based on the hind's house, probably Home Farm. The stock sold from his farm following his death included 655 Leicester sheep, descended from leading local flocks, 48 cattle and 15 working horses.[16]

John S. Jordan (1840–95) who tenanted Elmswell House for about ten years from *c.* 1865, was farming 760 a. in 1871, not all in the township.[17] He became well known for his shorthorn cattle and Leicester sheep but he lost a lot of stock during the rinderpest outbreak in the mid 1860s.[18] Disease hit the township again at the end of the century with at least 12 outbreaks of anthrax amongst cattle and sheep there between 1893 and 1900. The farmers, Robert Holtby and Richard Hardy, and the authorities concerned were evidently unaware that the bacteria spores were soil-borne with a very long lifetime, and they repeatedly returned cattle to the infected fields.[19]

Cattle and sheep were important to the mixed

1 In 1598 Henry Best's sale to James Best had included a pair of swans on Elmswell and Driffield Becks: ERAO, DDHV/9/13.
2 Best, *Farming Bks*, ed. Woodward, 64–72, 114–15, 129–30, 244.
3 Ibid. 216–17.
4 Above, this section, agriculture (Middle Ages).
5 Best, *Farming Bks*, ed. Woodward, 199.
6 Ibid. 130–1.
7 Ibid.
8 ERAO, DDHV/75/49, printed in Best, *Farming Bks*, ed. Woodward, 218–19; ibid. 130–1.
9 RDB, K/211/425.
10 Ibid. AZ/281/459.
11 TNA, HO 107/1218/1.
12 *HP* 23 June 1843.
13 TNA, IR 18/11557.
14 Ibid.
15 TNA, HO 107/2366.
16 *YH* 13 Feb., 9 Apr. 1864; 4 Feb. 1865.
17 Ibid. 20 Mar. 1875.
18 Ibid. 26 Jan. 1895.
19 Ibid. 21, 28 Aug., 8 Nov., 16 Dec. 1893; 28 Apr., 28 June, 17 Aug., 20 Sept. 1894; 5 Mar. 1895; 19 May, 2 June 1896; 13 Sep., 31 July 1900.

Year	% of total area of crops and grass returned							Total	Number per 1000 acres				
	Wheat	Barley	Oats	Turnips	Other crops	Clover	Perm. grass	acres	Horses	Cattle	Sheep	Pigs	Poultry
1866	21	5	13	18	4	13	26	2,334	ND	50	1236	57	ND
1911*	12	16	16	13	2	16	25	2,569	43	139	922	87	ND
1941	14	20	11	13	3	15	25	1,968	27	157	1022	98	273

*Returns for 1911 also include Little Driffield ND No data
Source: 1866 TNA, MAF 68/77–8; 1911 TNA, MAF 68/2490; 1941 TNA, MAF 32/1057/5, ibid.1059/8

Table 18. *Elmswell and Kelleythorpe: Crops and Stock 1866–1941*

farming economy of Elmswell where a quarter of the township was permanent grass in the late 19th and early 20th century. The figures for crops and stock for Elmswell and Kelleythorpe in 1866 and 1911 are very similar to those for Great Driffield (Tables 6 & 18), reflecting the impact of the agricultural depression from the late 1870s. There was a marked decline in the acreage of wheat grown but a rise in barley and oats. The acreage of clover rose but that of turnips fell reflecting the decrease in number of sheep and increase in number of cattle. By 1941 the acreage of barley had risen further and wheat had recovered to some extent, but the acreage of oats had declined. The number of cattle and sheep had increased and as elsewhere the keeping of pigs and poultry on a more commercial scale had become more common.

A minor crop not recorded in the agricultural returns was watercress which was gathered from the clear chalk streams in the township for sending to the West Country and London markets. Men from Hull and Leeds were fined for gathering watercress illegally at Elmswell in 1870.[1]

The National Farm Survey carried out in 1941 provides information on individual farms during the early part of the Second World War. There were then three main farms at Elmswell: Home Farm, Springwell Farm, and Elmswell Wold Farm, and all were awarded the highest grade, A.[2]

Home Farm, with its land mainly around the low-lying village site, had the highest proportion of permanent grass. Springwell Farm, which also included the land of Spellow Farm, occupied the middle section of the township stretching on to the Wolds, and Wold Farm the highest ground. Barley was the main crop on each farm, occupying around 20 per cent of the land, with wheat equally important at Wold Farm. Stock were significant on each farm, with more cattle kept on the lower pastures and more sheep on the Wolds. Horses were still used on the farms, although each had one or two tractors.

Separate information is not available for Elmswell later in the 20th century, as the annual agricultural returns for the township were included in the parish of Garton on the Wolds, but it is likely that farming there

Elmswell farms	Acres	Wheat acres	Barley acres	Oats acres	Turnips acres	Clover acres	Perm. grass acres	Cattle	Sheep	Pigs	Poultry	Horses
Springwell	598	99	122	63	90	87	101	95	690	19	130	18
Wold	404	82	81	53	6	94	28	37	359	19	132	13
Home	366	45	68	35	40	62	107	76	302	56	255	14
Total	1,368	226	271	151	195	24	236	208	1,351	94	517	45

Source: TNA, MAF 32/1059/8

Table 19. *Elmswell Farms: Crops and Stock 1941*

1 *HP* 8, 22 Apr. 1870. 'Very fine water cresses' were said to grow at Elmswell in the 1850s: Sheahan and Whellan, *Hist. York & ER.* ii. 504.

2 TNA, MAF 32/1059/8.

would have followed the pattern at Great Driffield.[1] The changes that took place at Spellow Farm in the years 1958–99 recorded by the tenant Norman Kirkwood in his autobiography were not untypical.[2] Initially it was a mixed farm, covering 352 a. of which 43 a. were permanent pasture. Wheat and spring barley were grown for seed, there was a flock of 200 sheep and 150 beef cattle were kept for fattening. Turkey rearing was introduced around 1961, and there were some 20,000 turkeys on the farm by 1966, when they were given up in favour of egg production with 4,000 hens. By the end of the 1960s there was further change from sheep, cattle and hens to the rearing of 1,000 pigs for bacon. During the depression in farming in the late 1980s, pig rearing was abandoned and the farm became all arable. In 1995 the tenant gave up working the land himself and employed a contractor.

Milling

St Mary's abbey, York, had two mills at Elmswell in the early 1320s, one powered by water and then let for £1 13*s.* 4*d.* a year, and a windmill rented out for £1 6*s.* 8*d.*[3] A water mill was recorded again later, apparently *c.* 1500; then said to have been 'built by John Sharpe', perhaps meaning rebuilt, it was rented for 6*s.* a year.[4] The settlement seems still to have had two mills in the 1590s.[5]

SOCIAL HISTORY

Henry Best's writings shed much light on the social life of the small agricultural settlement in the early 17th century. He records folk remedies, courting and marriage customs and the key social events of the agricultural year, the harvest supper and the feast for the 'clippers' at the end of sheep shearing.[6] Football Garth mentioned by Best as a field name suggests this sport was played in the village.[7]

The annual feast, when 'rustic games and sports were kept up on the village green for nearly a week', was remembered in the mid 19th century as being very popular with the people of Driffield and area.[8] There was usually at least one cottage licensed as an alehouse at Elmswell in the mid–late 18th century, and a former public house, part fallen down, still stood in 1857.[9]

RELIGIOUS HISTORY

There was a chapel at Elmswell in the Middle Ages. Little is known of it. John Donnays, chaplain, who was presented in the manor court of Elmswell in 1383 for a drainage offence and poaching, may have served it, and land belonging to the chapel was mentioned in 1404, when it was apparently let to a tenant.[10] The village lay within the parish or chapelry of Little Driffield by 1473 and one of the two or more chaplains recorded there in the late 15th–early 16th century may have served the chapel at Elmswell.[11] A priest, Richard Holand, was said to be 'of Elmswell' in 1510.[12]

Foundations are said to have been found in the unlocated close later called Chapel Garth.[13] The chapel chamber recorded in what may have been the chief house in Elmswell in 1563 was presumably a private oratory, perhaps made originally for the resident and for visiting officers of St Mary's abbey in York.[14]

James Best of Elmswell (d. 1617) was probably a puritan. His son, Henry Best, brought several puritan books with him when he moved to Elmswell from Essex in 1617, and in 1633 he lent a protestant work, an abridgement of Foxe's *Acts and Monuments*, to the vicar, Ralph Mason.[15] Henry's brother Paul Best, who died at Great Driffield, in 1657 was imprisoned in the 1640s for anti-Trinitarian views and John Best (d. 1669), Henry's son, evidently held Nonconformist views for his last four children were not baptised until four years after his death.[16]

John Best may have been a Quaker, as were three of the appraisers of his inventory: Richard Pursglove of Swinkeld, Watton, Richard Towse of Garton and Christopher Towse of Elmswell.[17] Christopher Towse and his fellow villager, John Middleton, were fined for not attending church in 1661.[18] Elmswell was a Quaker meeting place 1671–83, with the meetings evidently held at the house of John Wilson. For allowing this Wilson had all his goods, valued at £24, distrained and sold in 1683.[19]

In 1851 thirty Primitive Methodists were worshipping in part of a house in Elmswell, perhaps that registered by protestant Dissenters in the 1821 or 1822.[20] It afforded

1 Above, Gt and Little Driffield, econ. hist., agric. (later 20th c.).
2 N. E. Kirkwood, *To Farm is to Live* (1999), 81–130.
3 TNA, LR 11/51/732.
4 ERAO, DDHV/9/7, printed in Best, *Rural Economy*, ed. Robinson, 166 n. Cf. YAS, MD 161/c/j for the dating.
5 *Yorks. Fines*, iv. 89.
6 Best, *Farming Bks*, ed. Woodward, 23, 98, 122–3, 200–1.
7 Ibid. 136; for later reference see RDB, K/211/425.
8 ERAO, DDX/128/33.
9 Ibid. QDT/2/3/1–17, 31–4, 36, 38, 40–2, 44, 46, 48; ibid. DDX/128/33.
10 YAS, MD 161/c/j.
11 YML, L2(3)c, ff. 26, 60, 121, 184
12 Ibid. f.121
13 RDB, O/359/882; Best, *Farming Bks*, ed. Woodward, 202; Ross, *Driffield*, 110.
14 Another room there was then called the lord's chamber: Best, *Farming Bks*, ed. Woodward, 229.
15 Best, *Farming Bks*, ed. Woodward, lviii, lxi, 161–3, 183, 185, 196, 249.
16 Above, Gt and Little Driffield, relig. hist. (17th cent., nonconformity); Best, *Farming Bks*, ed. Woodward, lxi–lxii.
17 Best, *Farming Bks*, ed. Woodward, 269; ERAO, DDQR/16; HUL, DQR/11/1.
18 ERAO, DDQR/16.
19 Ibid. Christopher Towse and Pursglove were amongst the dozen people attending the meeting that time.
20 TNA, RG 31/5, no. 3724; BIA, DMH. Reg. 1, pp. 373–4; *Yorks. Worship Returns 1851*, i. 91.

free accommodation for 60 people, but attendance was lower because of the small population and the nearness of Driffield; in consequence, although a service was provided each Sunday evening, there was a sermon only every other week. It was evidently the same building that was registered in 1861 but it had ceased to be used by 1896.[1]

LOCAL GOVERNMENT

Manorial Administration and Courts

In the Middle Ages the special privileges granted to or claimed by St Mary's abbey, York extended to its manor of Elmswell. In 1263 the officers of York were thus said to have infringed the liberties of St Mary's abbey by exacting tolls from the house's tenants, including those on the manor of Elmswell.[2] Another privilege was the seigneurial right to the game of the township, a right justified in the 1270s as part of the abbot's more extensive rights of chase in Yorkshire.[3] In 1383 the lord's warren, or right to game, in Elmswell was allegedly broken by a chaplain taking hares without licence.[4]

The abbey held courts on its manor at Elmswell, and the view of frankpledge or leet jurisdiction, was exercised at principal sessions of the manor court, the so-called sheriff's tourns, held twice a year and in the early 14th century presided over by one or two monks sent from the abbey.[5] No records of the various courts at Elmswell are known to have survived and knowledge of their proceedings depends on some brief notes made from the records kept at St Mary's abbey after its dissolution.[6] The manorial court was largely concerned with the agriculture and drainage of the township. In 1404 tenants of the neighbouring township of Garton were allegedly soaking flax and hemp in ditches in Elmswell, and claiming common rights there, and an order was duly made to counter any recurrences with arrests. The court also managed the abbey's relationship with its tenants, requiring succeeding freeholders to do homage and pay relief, or inheritance tax; enforcing attendance of free tenants at the court baron held for them, and in 1402 fining an unfree tenant for marrying 'outside the lordship', an action which might compromise the lord's rights over future generations and therefore required a compensatory payment. Later references to the court are slight. In the later 16th century a steward presided over it for a fee of £1 3*s.* 4*d.* a year,[7] and a list of fines imposed in the court in 1674 suggests that its main business continued to be the regulation of local agriculture.[8] View of frankpledge was recorded as an appurtenance of the manor in the late 18th century,[9] but by then the court had probably ceased to meet.

Township Administration

The township of Elmswell with Kelleythorpe had its own officers including a constable, recorded in the mid 17th century,[10] one or two surveyors of the highways in the late 18th–early 19th century and presumably overseers of the poor.[11]

At Elmswell in the 17th century certain labourers were said 'for the most part' to live on parish relief, and they were provided with accommodation in four cottages 'because of the use of them in time of harvest'.[12] There would have been few paupers in the township; only one was noted in 1815, but nevertheless the annual cost of caring for the poor there rose sharply from £9 in 1775–6 to an average of £27 in the early 19th century, £37 between 1816 and 1829, and £74 about 1830.[13]

KELLEYTHORPE

Kelleythorpe covering 1,105a. was part of the township of Elmswell with Kelleythorpe in the parish of Driffield in 1851.[14] It is a roughly triangular area of level 'shaley, chalk gravel land' lying mainly between the 15m. and 25m. contours and bounded on the north and north-east by the Elmswell, then Driffield, Beck, and on south-east by the Driffield Trout Stream.[15] A stream known as the Gipsey Race runs through the middle of the area from the higher ground to the north-west to join the Driffield Beck near Hallimanwath Bridge.[16] Gipsey Race occurs elsewhere in East Yorkshire as the name for a Wolds stream which rises only in wet seasons. 'Gipsey' is thought to be derived from the Anglian or Scandinavian words for yawning or gasping, and to convey the idea of a convulsive and intermittent activity; 'race' is a Scandinavian term for a watercourse.[17]

1 ONS (Birkdale), Worship Reg. no. 12623.
2 *Monastic Notes*, ii (YAS Rec. Ser. 81), 56–7.
3 *Yorks. Hund. & Quo Warr. R.* 78.
4 YAS, MD 161/c/j.
5 TNA, LR 11/51/732.
6 YAS, MD 161/c/j.
7 TNA, C 66/1158, m. 20; C 66/1345, mm. 9–13.
8 Best, *Farming Bks*, ed. Woodward, 227.
9 RDB, BD/422/691.
10 Best, *Farming Bks*, ed. Woodward, 171, 202; *Cal. S.P. Dom. Chas. II, Addenda 1660–85*, pp. 59–60.
11 ERAO, QSF/275/C/15; ibid. QSR/1/21/34; *HP* 9 Feb. 1849.
12 Best, *Farming Bks*, ed. Woodward, 217.
13 *Abstract of Returns relative to Expense of Poor* (Parl. Papers, 1803–4 (175), xiii), pp. 588–9; ibid. *1813–15* (Parl. Papers, 1818 (82), xix), pp. 518–19; *Poor Rate Returns, 1816–21* (Parl. Papers, 1822 (556), v), p. 196; *1825–9* (Parl. Papers, 1830–1 (83), xi), p. 227; *1830–4* (Parl. Papers, 1835 (444), xlvii), p. 220.
14 OS Map 1:10,560, Yorks. CXLIV, CLXI (1854–5 edn).
15 TNA, IR 18/11557.
16 OS Map 1:10,560, Yorks. CLXI (1855 edn).
17 *PN Yorks. ER* (EPNS), 4–5.

SETTLEMENT

Recorded in Domesday Book the small medieval settlement of Kelleythorpe presumably stood close to Kelleythorpe Farm, the chief and for long virtually the only remaining house.[1] The site, close to a number of springs, is about a mile south-west of Great Driffield town, on the southern side of the Gipsey Race. By the end of the 20th century much of Kelleythorpe was taken up by the former airfield and associated housing, a large industrial estate, the grounds of a rugby club and Driffield showground.

Early Settlement

Archaeological evidence, formerly plentiful in Kelleythorpe but now much reduced by excavation, farming, and the making of the railway and the airfield, indicates a history of settlement extending back to the early Bronze Age. Among the earliest evidences of human activity in Kelleythorpe are several round barrows excavated in the 19th century.[2] The most significant was How Hill, a conical shaped barrow that stood on the north side of the Gipsey Race, 300 metres west of Hallimanwath Bridge, until levelled for the Market Weighton railway in 1887. It had almost certainly been made during the Bronze Age for the person, clearly of high rank, who was buried there in a stone cist. Pins or rivets of bronze and gold and bronze dagger found with or near the skeleton have been dated to *c.* 1750–1600 BC.[3]

There was further activity at the end of the Iron Age and beginning of the Romano-British period. When the airfield was being developed in the 1930s fifty small grave mounds, similar to those at Danes' Graves in Great Driffield, were opened. Pottery suggested that the site was abandoned in the 2nd century AD.[4] Later excavation and examination of crop marks has increased the number of burials to about eighty and added contemporary sites, in all suggesting Iron-Age occupation across the centre of Kelleythorpe, from the earlier barrows in the west to a point about ½ mile south-west of Kelleythorpe Farm.[5]

As in other parts of Driffield, so in Kelleythorpe, there are early indications of Anglo-Saxon settlement.[6] The Bronze Age barrow containing the cist burial was used as a place of burial, apparently during the 6th and 7th centuries AD, for about fifty people, some of whom were clearly affluent. Anglo-Saxon goods discovered in the barrow included iron artefacts faced with solid silver appliqué work.[7] That at least some of the land in the west of Kelleythorpe occupied into the Roman period may have continued to be so used is suggested by the discovery of a small Anglo-Saxon cemetery near the western boundary, and by finds from that period made elsewhere in Kelleythorpe.[8] Further north, the occurrence of building foundations, a bronze brooch, spearheads of bronze and flint, and Anglo-Saxon pottery may indicate another site, possibly an outlier of the settlement at Elmswell, which had a long occupation.[9]

Medieval and Later Settlement

The place name Kelleythorpe is Scandinavian, and means Keling's village; it was recorded in Domesday Book as Calgestorp, and later in the Middle Ages as Kelingthorpe and Killingthorp.[10] Kelethorp and Kelithorp were used from the 13th century, and Kelleythorpe or Kellythrop commonly in the 17th.[11] The valued pastures of Kelleythorpe were called the greets, a local name referring to their gritty or gravely soils, and in the 18th and up to the mid 19th century the whole or part of Kelleythorpe was usually known as Driffield Greets.[12]

Kelleythorpe is a deserted medieval settlement that was probably always quite small. Six houses were recorded on Kelleythorpe manor in 1374, and 16 people there paid the poll tax in 1377.[13] By the 16th century there were probably only two farmhouses,[14] and in 1672 most of the 12 households recorded jointly for Kelleythorpe and Elmswell were in Elmswell; the only house which can then be located in Kelleythorpe had 5 hearths, and was probably the manor house.[15] There was evidently only one house there *c.* 1770.[16] Kelleythorpe Cottages on the Beverley road were built by the Denisons, Lords Londesborough, whose cipher they bear, apparently in the earlier 1850s.[17]

1 Below, Kelleythorpe manor.

2 Mortimer, *Forty Years' Researches,* 261–2, 271–84; Loughlin and Miller, *Survey*, 112.

3 Mortimer's barrow C38. Mortimer, *Forty Years' Researches*, 271–83; *HP* 7 Oct. 1870; *VCH Yorks.* i. 396–7; *YAJ* 41 (1963–6), 346, 349–50.

4 Corder, *Excavations at Elmswell*, 8; Sheppard, 'Excavations at Eastburn', 35–45; Philips, ' Iron Age Site', 183–91.

5 Finds discussed (under Eastburn and Driffield aerodrome) in Challis and Harding, *Later Prehistory*, i. 25, 69, 75, 87, 157, 170; ii, figs. 7–9, 38; Loughlin and Miller, *Survey*, 112–13.

6 Above, vol. intro., early settlement.

7 Mortimer barrow C 38. Mortimer, *Forty Years' Researches*, 271–83; Loveluck, 'Anglo-Saxon Landscape', 30, 34–6; Loughlin and Miller, *Survey*, 113.

8 Loughlin and Miller, *Survey*, 113; Congreve, *Roman and Saxon Site at Elmswell, 1935–6*, 5; Corder, *Excavations at Elmswell*, 8; Sheppard, 'Excavations at Eastburn', 35–45.

9 OS Map 1:2,500, Yorks. CLXI. 11 (1910 edn); Mortimer, *Forty Years' Researches*, 257; above, this section, Elmswell, early settlement.

10 Killingthorpe occurred as late as the 1820s: A. Bryant, *Map of ER Yorks.* (1829).

11 *PN Yorks. ER* (EPNS), 155; Best, *Farming Bks*, ed. Woodward, *passim*; E 179/205/504.

12 RDB, AZ/281/459; ERAO, CSR/31/37; Best, *Farming Bks*, ed. Woodward, 86, 125, 298; *HP* 9 Feb. 1849.

13 TNA, E 179/202/59, m. 32; *Cal. Inq. p.m.* xiv, p. 52.

14 Below, manors, Kelleythorpe.

15 TNA, E 179/205/504; Best, *Farming Bks*, ed. Woodward, 130–1.

16 T. Jefferys, *Map of Yorks.* (1775).

17 OS Map 1:10,560, Yorks. CLXI (1855 edn); OS Map 1:2,500, Yorks. CLXI. 16 (1893 edn); Sheahan and Whellan, *Hist. York & ER.* ii. 504.

87. *Kelleythorpe, Montgomery Square, RAF Driffield, in 2006. Housing for senior officers built in the later 1930s.*

Virtually all later building in Kelleythorpe was associated with the airfield and industrial estate there. The showground of the Driffield Agricultural Society and the clubhouse and pitches of the Driffield Rugby Union Club are in Kelleythorpe township and cover some 55 a.[1]

David Brown (1762–1832), son of Francis Brown of Kelleythorpe, became an East India Company chaplain, and his promotion of missionary work in Bengal led directly to the formation of the Church Missionary Society.[2]

Airfield

In 1917–19 a military airfield was made on a 240-a. site to the north-west of Kelleythorpe Farm. The land, 60 a. from Kelleythorpe and 180 a. from Eastburn, was requisitioned in 1916. Construction work was not completed until early 1919 but the airfield, then called Eastburn, was occupied by No. 2 School of Aerial Fighting of the Royal Flying Corps from October 1917. Renamed RAF Driffield in 1919 it only continued in use until the next year when the flying school was disbanded. The buildings which all stood in Eastburn township were demolished in 1925.[3]

The airfield was revived in the 1930s, when 225 a. of Kelleythorpe were bought for the purpose.[4] Five hangars, administrative buildings, and residential quarters were put up at Kelleythorpe between 1935 and 1937, and RAF Driffield was opened in 1936. After the outbreak of war it served as a bomber station. Attacked in 1940, with the loss of 12 planes and 13 personnel, it was reopened in 1941 when Canadian, New Zealand, and Australian air forces flew from it.[5] The airfield was closed in 1942 for the laying of concrete runways, and re-opened in 1944. Driffield was used as the RAF's first jet-flying training school from 1946; from 1955 as a fighter jet station, and from 1957 as a fighter weapons school. In 1958 it became a missile base manned by USAAF personnel, with four satellite stations elsewhere in the East Riding. The base was closed in 1963,[6] but Hawker Siddeley tested aircraft there in 1967–8. The Army took over the site in 1977; re-named it the Alamein Barracks; converted the former airfield into a driving circuit, and established a school of mechanical transport there. The site was then or soon afterwards reduced by the sale of land for an industrial estate,[7] and the former hangars were let as grain stores.[8] In 1992 the Army withdrew to Leconfield, and the following year the RAF reoccupied the station as a satellite of Staxton Wold radar station. Driffield's main function for the

1 Above, Gt and Little Driffield, soc. hist., Driffield shows; sports (rugby).

2 *DNB*, *s.v.* David Brown.

3 This and following paras. based chiefly on G. Simmons and B. Abraham, *Strong Foundations: Driffield's Aerodrome from 1917 to 2000* (2001).

4 Some 180 a. more there and in Elmswell were acquired later: above, this section, Elmswell manor; below Kelleythorpe manor.

5 A memorial stone for Bomber Command victims of the Second World War, put up in Driffield in 1993, came from Australia: *DP* 9 Sept. 1993.

6 ER Educ. Cttee, *Mins* 1963–4, 48.

7 Above, Gt and Little Driffield, econ. hist., trade and ind. (post-war).

8 *DP* 31 May 1995.

RAF was the accommodation of about a hundred service families, and residents later also included some of its personnel stationed at Leconfield.[1] The non-residential parts of the former airfield were used by the Territorial Army and the cadet branches of the Army and Air Force,[2] and the driving course was still employed by the Army Transport School. The RAF finally withdrew to Staxton in 1996, and the site, reduced by earlier sales to some 70 a., was unsuccessfully offered for sale.[3] In 2004 the buildings, apart from the houses and one or two of the administrative blocks occupied by the cadets, stood empty. Kelleythorpe industrial estate was then being extended over the former airfield, the rest of which continued to be used by the Army for driving instruction and other training. The hangars remained as grain stores.

Besides the communal accommodation on the airfield, a dozen houses for married officers, in a 'Queen Anne' style, were built around a large green called Montgomery Square, and leading off it twelve less grand houses were put up in Gott Close. By the 1950s two housing estates had also been put up on the south side of the Market Weighton road (A163), Ramsden Close also for married officers and the much larger, Auchinleck Close, with over 120 houses, for married airmen.[4] Some seventy houses were sold off in 1991.[5] Service personnel continued to live in Kelleythorpe after the closure of the station in 1996, but there were subsequently 50–100 unoccupied houses there.[6] The former service housing had all been sold to private buyers by 2006.[7]

LANDOWNERSHIP

Morcar's manor of Driffield included most of Kelleythorpe in 1066, tenants holding 3 carucates of sokeland and the earl having a dependent estate, or berewick, there, evidently assessed at 1½ carucate. In 1086 the holding of the king, Morcar's successor, in Kelleythorpe was reckoned at 4½ carucates in all.[8] In the later 13th century the lands at Kellythorpe belonging to Driffield manor were said to contain some 6 carucates.[9]

Kelleythorpe was held of the Crown and its successors, the Scropes, as a sub manor under Driffield for £4 a year.[10]

Kelleythorpe Manor

By 1182 the estate had descended to Thomas son of Ralph son of Wimund, who was mentioned until 1192–3 and probably also called Thomas of Kellythorpe.[11] It was presumably the same estate which Ralph of Kelleythorpe succeeded to about 1210.[12] He evidently died in the earlier 1220s, and in 1225 the Crown granted the keeping and marriage of Ralph's daughter and heir, a minor, together with the estate in Kelleythorpe, to Thomas de Blumvill (Blundvill).[13] The Blumvill interest passed before 1230 to Baldwin de Freville, who then had custody of the daughter and Kelleythorpe manor, comprising 5 carucates and 6 oxgangs. Soon afterwards the heir, not yet twelve, was married to Baldwin's brother, Roger de Freville,[14] and the estate subsequently descended in the Frevilles, apparently like their manor of Etton.[15] James de Freville held Kelleythorpe manor at his death in 1286 when he was buried at Little Driffield.[16] His daughter Joan married Roger Ughtred, who in 1322 was defending his possession of the estate against Robert de Lascy and his wife Ellen.[17] Other claimants may then have been Thomas de Freville and his son Nicholas, one of whom was later reckoned to have been lord of Kelleythorpe manor.[18] In 1327 the Lascys granted their manor of Kelleythorpe, perhaps meaning their claim to the estate, to John Hotham, bishop of Ely and Lord Chancellor, for their lives, in exchange for an estate from the bishop or his nephew, Sir John Hotham.[19] The Hothams seem to have obtained full possession of the manor by 1331, when the bishop conveyed it to his nephew and Sir John's heirs.[20] The same or another Sir John, as Sir John Hotham of Bonby (Lincs.), his son, also Sir John Hotham of Bonby, and the younger man's wife Ivetta were apparently dealing with the family's estates in 1344,[21] and after the younger Sir John's death in 1351 his widow Ivetta had a life estate in the Yorkshire lands, including Hotham and Kelleythorpe manors. The reversion on

1 *HDM* 25 Feb., 1 Mar. 1993; *DT* 5 Apr. 1995.
2 *DP* 31 May 1995.
3 Ibid. 3 July 1996; *DT* 3 Sept. 1997.
4 *Register of Electors* (2004); ER CC *Mins* 1955–6, 503; OS Map 1:10,000, TA 05 NW (1970 edn).
5 *DP* 21 June 1995; *HDM* 15 Oct. 1996.
6 *YP* 29 June 1996; *DP* 3 July 1996; *HDM* 15 Oct. 1996; 21 Aug. 1997.
7 Inf. from Claire Binnington, Driffield Town Council.
8 *VCH Yorks.* ii. 197, 320.
9 *Yorks. Inq.* i, p. 109; ii, p. 96.
10 TNA, C 142/51, no. 100; *Pipe R.* 1190 (PRS, N.S. i), 66; *Cal. Inq. p.m.* xiv, pp. 51–2.
11 *Pipe R.* 1182 (PRS 31), 35–6; 1190 (PRS, N.S. 1), 66; 1193 (PRS, N.S. 3), 65; *EYC.* i, p. 492.
12 *Pipe R.* 1211 (PRS, N.S. 28), 30.
13 Ibid. 1222 (PRS, N.S. 51), 147; *Ex e Rot. Fin.* (Rec. Com.), i. 135; *Mem. R.* 1231 (PRS, N.S. 11), 26. Custody and marriage had earlier in 1225 been granted to the king's cook: *Rot. Litt. Claus.* (Rec. Com.), ii. 36.
14 TNA, C 60/31 m. 2; *Ex e Rot. Fin.* i. 227–8; *Bk of Fees*, ii. 1354; *Cal. Lib.* 1226–40, 217.
15 *VCH Yorks. ER.* iv. 106;
16 ERAO, DDX1282/44/1 (microfilm of Anlaby cartulary Fitzwilliam Museum, Cambridge MS329).
17 *Abbrev. Plac.* (Rec. Com.), 341, where James's surname is given in error as Truul.
18 *Cal. Close*, 1385–9, 499.
19 Ibid. 1327–30, 207.
20 *Yorks. Fines, 1327–47*, pp. 40–1.
21 *Cal. Close*, 1343–6, 387–8. The pedigree in J. Foster, *Pedigrees of Yorks.* iii here seems unlikely.

Ivetta's death was settled in 1352 and 1356 on one of the older Sir John's daughters, Alice Hotham, and her prospective husband, (Sir) Hugh Despenser.[1] The Despensers obtained possession before the death in 1374 of Sir Hugh Despenser; the manor then comprised the lord's own holding, the demesne, of a carucate, and nearly 2 carucates of tenanted land. Sir Hugh was succeeded by his widow Alice (d. 1379), and then by his son (Sir) Hugh, who in 1388 conveyed the manor to Hugh Arden (Ardern) and others.[2]

Hugh Arden had bought a small estate in Driffield earlier in the 1380s.[3] The Ardens were evidently connections of the Percy family. Together with Henry Percy, earl of Northumberland, and others, Hugh Arden of Driffield was ordered in 1381 to make a proclamation in Scarborough against risings,[4] and he served in the 1390s as trustee and executor of Mary Percy, widow of John de Ros, Lord Ros. In 1439 Thomas Arden, esquire, confirmed land in Driffield to the next earl, also Henry Percy, and others.[5] In the earlier 16th century a brother of the earl of Northumberland, Sir William Percy, occupied the Ardens' lands in Kelleythorpe, as their lessee.[6]

Kelleythorpe manor may have been held by Thomas Arden as successor to William Arden of Kelleythorpe, esquire, who in 1435 was apparently buying land there from John Hill and his wife Alice.[7] A later tenant was perhaps Sir Peter Arden (d. 1467), a chief baron of the Exchequer, who left a vestment for Little Driffield church.[8] John Arden, who had the manor by 1509 and died in 1527, was succeeded by his widow Margaret and then by his son Ralph.[9] Ralph Arden sold the manor to Sir William Fairfax and his son Guy in 1543. They may have been acting for Robert Heneage of Lincoln, who had acquired the leasehold of Kelleythorpe shortly before[10] and in 1545 bought the manor from the Fairfaxes.[11] Robert Heneage's brother Sir Thomas Heneage was guardian of Ralph Arden *c.* 1530.[12] The Heneages were then also prominent as leaseholders in the neighbouring settlement of Elmswell.[13] Robert Heneage's son, Sir Thomas Heneage (d. 1595), and Thomas's wife Ann exchanged Kelleythorpe manor with the Crown in 1576.[14]

Kelleythorpe manor was let by the Crown to Thomas Crompton in 1592,[15] and in 1604 granted to Sir James Hay, later earl of Carlisle, his wife Honor, and their heirs.[16] The estate included land in Great and Little Driffield, and 6 oxgangs in Elmswell, in the 16th and 17th centuries.[17] Hay (d. 1636) was succeeded by his son, also James, earl of Carlisle, who in 1645 sold the estate, then with land in Sunderlandwick, in Hutton Cranswick, to Robert Scawen and others.[18] John Heron bought the manor from Scawen and the others in 1658,[19] and bequeathed it to his daughter Catherine, who married first Sir John Hotham, Bt, (d. 1691) and secondly John Moyser.[20] James Moyser, son of John by an earlier marriage, occupied Kelleythorpe from the early 18th century, before the deaths of his stepmother and father. He died in 1751.[21] For lack of male heirs, the estate passed in undivided sixths to the female line. In 1753 Elizabeth Moyser and Catherine Burton, daughters of John Moyser and Catherine Heron, sold their 2/6 to James Moyser's daughters, Mary and Sarah Moyser and Diana Strickland, and in 1761 William Gee, son of John and Catherine Moyser's daughter Constance, sold his 1/6 to James's daughters, who thereafter had undivided 1/3 shares. At the inclosure of Elmswell in 1771, Diana Strickland, Mary, then the wife of Bartholomew Tate, and Sarah Moyser were awarded 87 a. there.[22]

Diana Strickland's 1/3 share descended on her husband's death in 1788 to their son Walter. By the will of his aunt Mary Tate (d. by 1778), Walter should have succeeded also to her 1/3 on the death of Mary's immediate heir, her sister Sarah Moyser. He died, however, in 1793, before Sarah in 1796, and under his will his widow Dorothy, later the wife of Charles Michell, succeeded to the Strickland and Tate shares. Sarah Moyser's own 1/3 share was left for life to another son of Constance Moyser, the Revd Richard Gee. In 1803 the Moyser estate was partitioned between Mrs Michell and

1 *Cal. Inq. p.m.* ix, pp. 429–30; *Yorks. Fines, 1347–77*, p. 223; *VCH Yorks. ER.* iv. 117.

2 *Cal. Inq. p.m.* xiv, pp. 51–2; xv, pp. 92–3; *Cal. Close*, 1385–9, 496–7, 499, 682; above, Gt and Little Driffield, soc. hist., soc. leadership (medieval).

3 *Cal. Close*, 1381–5, 589; 1385–9, 153; *Test. Ebor.* i, p. 117.

4 *Cal. Pat.* 1381–5, 74.

5 *Cal. Close*, 1392–6, 321; 1435–41, 246; *Complete Peerage*, s.v. Ros.

6 TNA, STAC 2/22/162.

7 Ibid. CP 25(1)/280/157, no. 30; for Thomas, *Test. Ebor.* iv, p. 102 n.

8 *Test. Ebor.* iv, pp. 102 n, 103 n; *Select Cases in Star Chamber*, i (Selden Soc. 16), 170 n.

9 TNA, C 1/460, no. 13; C 142/51, no. 100.

10 Ibid. C 54/434, no. 72; *Yorks. Fines*, i. 107.

11 TNA, C 54/441, no. 35.

12 TNA, C1/602/9; A. R. Maddison (ed.), *Lincolnshire Pedigrees*, 2 (1908), 480–2; *DNB*, *s.v.* Sir Thomas Heneage.

13 Above, this section, Elmswell manor.

14 TNA, C 66/1385, mm. 7–8; *Cal. Pat.* 1575–8, pp. 188–9; *Yorks. Fines*, i. 224, 356; ii. 99, 189; *DNB*, *s.v.* Sir Thomas Heneage.

15 TNA, C 66/1385, mm. 7–8.

16 *Cal. S.P. Dom.* 1603–10, 149.

17 ERAO, DDCC/111/214; Best, *Farming Bks*, ed. Woodward, 130–1, 194–5.

18 TNA, C 142/550, no. 93; ibid. CP 25(2)/525/20 Chas I Hil. [no. 1].

19 Ibid. CP 25(2)/615/1658 Trin. no 14. Heron's first wife was Jane daughter of William Spink of Driffield from whom she inherited an interest in half of the manor of Kelleythorpe: Best, *Farming Bks*, ed. Woodward, 266–7.

20 TNA, CP 25(2)/893/3 Wm & Mary Mich. no. 24; CP 25(2)/894/5 Wm & Mary Easter no. 12; CP 25(2)/895/10 Wm III Easter no. 12; HUL, DDHO/74/7; J. Foster, *Pedigrees of Yorks.* iii, s.v. Hotham. For the following, ERAO, DDLO/1/26.

21 Pevsner and Neave, *Yorks. ER.* 71.

22 RDB, AN/196/12.

the Revd Richard Gee, life tenants respectively of 2/3 and 1/3 shares. The holding based around Kelleythorpe fell to the share of Gee. It then comprised a chief house or farmhouse with 1,101 a., called Driffield Greets and extending into Sunderlandwick, and another farm, of 111 a., in Elmswell and Little Driffield. Gee (d. 1815) was succeeded, under Sarah Moyser's will, by his sister Gertrude's son, Robert Whyte, who took the surname Moyser.[1]

In 1836 Robert Moyser, then of Pilton House, Devon, sold the Driffield Greets estate to W. J. Denison.[2] Like Elmswell manor, which Denison bought in 1844, Kelleythorpe descended in his heirs to W. F. H. Denison, earl of Londesborough, who sold an estate of some 3,000 a. in the parishes of Driffield and Skerne in 1909 and 1911. After the Elmswell estate, the largest lot was that comprising five houses and almost 1,000 a. in Kelleythorpe, which H. S. Hopper bought in 1911.[3] Hopper (d. 1918) was succeeded by his widow Kate, later the wife of William Thompson. From 1936 parts of the estate were bought by the Air Council, later Ministry, for an RAF station; 225 a. were acquired that year, 25 a. in 1945, 104 a. in 1949, and 9 a. in 1952.[4] The rest of the estate, comprising a house and 608 a., passed, following Mrs Thompson's death in 1956, to H. S. Hopper's son, H. J. A. Hopper.[5] In 1966 the estate was further diminished by the sale of 147 a. to H. G. Mackrill.[6] Hopper (d. 1967) was succeeded by his son James, from whom Sunderlandwick Farms bought the estate in 2010.[7]

Kelleythorpe was evidently divided between two lessees in the 16th and 17th centuries. One of the leasehold interests probably belonged to Ralph Buckton (d. 1540), the lessee of neighbouring Elmswell,[8] and his widow Margaret (d. 1545)[9] certainly had it. Buckton's son-in-law, Robert Heneage, bought the other lease of Kelleythorpe from a London grocer, William Normanville, and presumably obtained that of Margaret Buckton, before purchasing the freehold of Kelleythorpe manor in 1545.[10] The whole of Kelleythorpe was let by Thomas Heneage and his wife in 1576 to Edward Nettleton, who then also obtained Heneage's leasehold interest in Elmswell manor,[11] and about 1600 Kelleythorpe was similarly held by James Best, lord of Elmswell manor, as Lord Hay's lessee.[12] William Spink of Driffield was lessee of half the manor of Kelleythorpe on his death in 1616. The lease was then held by his widow Margaret who married Robert Salvin of Skerne. Margaret Salvin and Alice Edwards held the whole of Kelleythorpe in more or less equal shares in the 1630s. At her death in 1654 the half held by Margaret Salvin passed to her daughter Jane and son-in-law John Heron. In 1660 Kelleythorpe was divided between Heron, then owner of the whole manor, and Michael Edwards, lessee.[13]

Manor House Some of the lords of the manor may have lived at Kelleythorpe in the Middle Ages, but the chief house on the estate, mentioned from 1374,[14] was probably most often occupied as a farmhouse by one of the tenants.[15] The house in Elmswell or Kelleythorpe with five hearths held by John Heron in 1672 was presumably the chief house at Kelleythorpe.[16] After W. J. Denison bought Kelleythorpe, he rebuilt the house there in 1848.[17] Besides the white brick and slate house, restored after being severely damaged by enemy action in the Second World War, some earlier farm buildings in red brick survived in 2004.[18]

Ecclesiastical Estates

The archbishop of York had 2 oxgangs in Kelleythorpe which by 1086 had evidently been assigned to his church of St John at Beverley (Beverley minster).[19] In 1297 the provost of Beverley was disputing the holding with Ralph de Brunne and his wife, perhaps his tenants.[20] The land was recorded again, as part of the provostry, in the early 15th century.[21] The collegiate church was suppressed in 1548, and in 1567 the Crown granted land in Kelleythorpe formerly belonging to the provost of Beverley to Thomas Heneage and his wife Ann.[22] The estate may later have been subsumed in the Heneages' manor of Kelleythorpe.[23]

ECONOMIC HISTORY

Agriculture: Before Inclosure

In the later 11th century Kelleythorpe included a berewick, or dependent estate, of Driffield manor which was probably farmed with the lord's land in Driffield, as well as tenanted land held by one or more

1 J. Foster, *Pedigrees of Yorks.* iii, s.v. Gee, which errs over Gertude's parentage.
2 RDB, FB/195/208; FB/198/212.
3 Ibid. 113/335/312; 113/410/377; 131/387/334; 135/95/85.
4 Ibid. 135/41/39; 540/268/199; 699/318/273; 810/438/358; 906/545/477.
5 Ibid. 968/500/450; 1057/335/311; 1098/72/67.
6 Ibid. 1439/447/405.
7 Ibid. 1678/490/431; inf. from Mrs Hopper, Kelleythorpe, 2004; inf. from Sunderlandwick Farms, 2011.
8 Best, *Farming Bks*, ed. Woodward, 217; above, this section, Elmswell manor.
9 *YAJ* 14 (1898), 508.
10 TNA, C 54/434, no. 72; C 54/441, no. 35; *DNB*, s.v. Sir Thomas Heneage.
11 ERAO, DDCC/111/214; above, this section, Elmswell manor.
12 Best, *Rural Economy*, ed. Robinson, 167 n.
13 Best, *Farming Bks*, ed. Woodward, 194–5, 224–5, 266–7.
14 *Cal. Inq. p.m.* xiv, p. 52.
15 ERAO, DDLO/1/26.
16 TNA, E 179/205/504.
17 Sheahan and Whellan, *Hist. York & ER.* ii. 505.
18 TNA, MAF 32/1057/5.
19 *VCH Yorks.* ii. 215.
20 *Monastic Notes*, i (YAS Rec. Ser. 17), p. 6.
21 Copy of Sheffield City Libraries, Lindsay coll. no. 69 at ERAO, DPX/56.
22 *Cal. Pat.* 1566–9, p. 46; *VCH Yorks. ER.* vi. 77.
23 Above, this section, Kelleythorpe manor.

sokemen. Like the rest of the manor, the demesne and tenanted land at Kelleythorpe was returned in 1086 as of no value.[1] Agricultural production was later restored, and in the later 13th century the whole 5–6 carucates there were rented or valued at £4 4*s*. a year. The tenant or tenants seem by then to have occupied the whole settlement, including the former berewick. Suit was owed to Driffield manor court, as well as the payment, when it occurred, of a relief of £1 6*s*. 8*d*., which suggests that the tenure there may have been that of drengage.[2] The largest holding in the settlement was probably Kelleythorpe manor, which may have been based on the earlier berewick. Subtraction of the 3 carucates of sokeland in 1086 from one of the later 13th-century totals for Kelleythorpe gives a probable figure for the berewick of 2 carucates and 6 oxgangs, and in 1374 Kelleythorpe manor was said to comprise 1 carucate held by the tenant as demesne land, or a home farm, and 1 carucate and 6 oxgangs occupied by his tenants, who comprised freeholders, tenants at will, and bondmen.[3]

The manor of Kelleythorpe may have been improved after its acquisition by the Heneages in the 1540s. It was then let by the lord for some £20 a year,[4] but by 1576 the rent was almost £106.[5] The lease of the manor made in that year to Edward Nettleton, then also the tenant of neighbouring Elmswell, gives a reasonably comprehensive view of the manor and settlement of Kelleythorpe.[6] There were then two fields in Kelleythorpe, High and Low Fields, with a combined area of *c*. 220 a.; three pastures, the largest, Sheep Pasture, of some 240 a., Cow Pasture about half as big, and the 60-a. Horse Pasture, and about 30 a. of meadowland adjoining Horse Pasture and lying in the field of neighbouring Sunderlandwick, in Hutton Cranswick. Those grounds, amounting to almost 700 a., may still have been farmed in common, but there are indications that the common lands had by then been reduced by inclosure. In 1563 part of the tillage, 'a flatt in Kelleythorpe', had been occupied by a single farmer,[7] and in 1576 the manor included *c*. 260 a. of meadow closes, among them New Close, of 20 a., and the 60-a. Great West Close.

By the 1630s Kelleythorpe would seem to have been largely inclosed, though some of the closes were in multiple occupation, and the common pastures, known from their gritty soils as Kelleythorpe or Driffield Greets,[8] remained. In 1635 the manor was divided between two chief tenants. The part of Alice Edwards included 'her sheep ground and tillage', valued at £28 a year and occupied, with some closes, by a Mrs Hardy, presumably an undertenant. Another tenant paid £20 a year for Upper and Nether Closes, perhaps parts of the earlier High and Low Fields. The other head lessee was Mrs Salvin, whose closes included the Brenks let to several farmers for £12 a year and the Summer Kine Close, perhaps taken from Cow Pasture and held by two tenants for £10. Much of her land, comprising 'Lough close, the sheep ground, and the cow pasture', valued at £45 a year, was however kept in hand.[9] Mrs Salvin exploited her share of the pastures largely by letting the right to graze between May and September to other farmers, including Henry Best of Elmswell, and various 'poor folks' at the rate of 5*s*. 4*d*. for each cow. The pasture was managed by her neat-, or cattle-, herd, who received £1; the milk of a cow; a cow gate for himself; a share of the manure, and 1*d*. for each beast in his charge. The well-watered pasture at Kelleythorpe was highly regarded as summer grazing for cattle, although Best thought its value had declined because of overstocking with sheep.[10]

Rabbit Warrens

Soon after he acquired Kelleythorpe in 1658, Heron made an embankment surmounted by a fence, later a hedge, along Kelleythorpe's western boundary to separate the greets from Eastburn's outfield, then also used mostly as grazing. The new barrier, extending from the south-western corner of Elmswell to Brick Kiln Gate, the road to Kirkburn and Market Weighton, was remade later by Moyser; about 1710 the fence along a southern stretch was renewed 'on or near the old bank', and a few years later a 'ditch of sods' was laid along the remainder. These actions may have related to the existence of a rabbit warren on the land. A large part of the pasture land at Kelleythorpe or Driffield Greets was a warren by 1707, and it was mentioned again in 1719.[11] Later in the century Driffield Greets consisted of two large warrens.[12] William Boyes who was the warrener there, also took on the adjoining Eastburn Warren in 1740.[13] His son, Bethel Boyes, who later moved to Eastburn, was the occupier of Driffield Greets in the mid 1750s.[14] Boyes was followed at Driffield Greets by Francis Brown who was the farmer and warrener by *c*. 1770.[15] The warrens were the target of poachers from Driffield, Nafferton and Hutton Cranswick in the mid–late 18th century.[16] There were

1 *VCH Yorks*. ii. 197.
2 *Yorks. Inq*. i, p. 109; ii, p. 96; above, Gt and Little Driffield, agric. (manors and land tenures).
3 *Cal. Inq. p.m*. xiv, p. 52.
4 TNA, C 54/434, no. 72; C 142/51, no. 100.
5 Ibid. C 66/1385, mm. 7–8; ERAO, DDCC/111/214.
6 The estate extended into neighbouring townships, notably that of Elmswell: ERAO, DDCC/111/214.
7 Best, *Farming Bks*, ed. Woodward, 229, 232.
8 RDB, AN/196/12; A. Bryant, *Map of ER Yorks*. (1829).
9 Best, *Farming Bks*, ed. Woodward, 194–5.
10 Ibid. 125–6.
11 ERAO, QSF/3/B/18.
12 Marshall, *Rural Economy*, 263.
13 ERAO, QSF/4/C/15; HUL, DDHO/29/9.
14 ERAO, QSF/191/C/22, QSF/203/C/8.
15 Ibid. QSF/245/C/5, QSF/256/C/23; ibid., DDGR/34/99.
16 ERAO, QSF/245/C/5, QSF/256/C/23, QSF/269/D/13; QSF/290/D/16.

thousands of rabbits on the warrens and they were regularly 'harvested'. Carcasses were sent every Monday and Friday night to Hull market in the early 19th century, and the skins went to furriers in Malton and elsewhere who processed the fur and sold it to hatters in London and Manchester.[1]

Sheep were kept in the warren; there were some 800 sheep, including 300 ewes in lamb, at Driffield Greets in 1816. The sheep and improved shorthorn cattle of the tenant Francis Brown, jun., were said then to be well known for their 'perfection and superiority'.[2]

The warrens kept by William Lee in 1817 were last recorded nine years later, but they may still have been worked in 1830 when Lee's widow gave up the farm, selling off 680 Leicester sheep.[3] The tenancy was then taken by George Hopper whose family had the farm for 180 years.

Later Agriculture

The warrens had been reclaimed by 1835 when it was said that the estate comprised 1,100 a. of 'productive' arable, meadow, and pasture land of the 'best quality' including over 300 a. of 'Old Swarth', that is unploughed pasture.[4] The last would have been part, at least, of the former warrens and area bordering Elmswell Beck and known in the 1930s as Big Pasture.[5] It 1849 this area was seemingly worked as a single 400-a. field, sown with oats, and 'having the appearance of a prairie'.[6]

The land at Kelleythorpe was said to be very productive in damp seasons in the 1840s. It was worked on a four-course rotation of 'turnips, barley or oats, (principally oats), seeds eaten down chiefly by sheep, and then oats after barley, or wheat after oats'.[7] Around 1,200 sheep were kept on the farm at this time.[8] Twenty-one men were employed on the farm in 1851, 13 male and 3 female farm servants living-in at the farmhouse.[9] By 1861 the farm servants were living in the hind's or bailiff's house.[10]

Thomas Hopper (1813–66), who had succeeded his father in 1837, brought the farm into 'an excellent state of cultivation' and in 1853 was awarded a silver cup by Lord Londesborough for the best managed farm on his estates.[11] Hopper was one of the most influential local farmers, a member of the Yorkshire Agricultural Society, president of the Driffield Farmers Club and vice-president of the Driffield Agricultural Society; he was a founder and first chairman of the Driffield & East Riding Pure Linseed Cake Co. Ltd, and succeeded his brother-in-law as captain of the Driffield Rifle Volunteers.[12] His son James continued this role as a leader of the local farming community, but was hit by two outbreaks of foot and mouth disease, amongst sheep in 1883 and cattle in 1885.[13]

Details of the farm after it had been reduced to around 600 a. by the building of the airfield are provided by the 1941 Farm Survey.[14] The farm continued to have an emphasis on livestock with 661 sheep and lambs, 101 cattle and calves and 99 pigs. There were 256 a. of permanent grass, 4 a. of rough grass, and 60 a. of clover or other temporary grasses, of crops there were 113 a. of barley, 60 a. of oats, 40 a. of wheat, 60 a. of turnips and 7 a. of rape. Eight working horses were kept as well as two tractors. The workforce consisted of 9 full-time men and one part-time.[15]

MILLING

Kelleythorpe had a water mill in 1086, and it, or a successor, was recorded again in 1297,[16] perhaps in 1592,[17] and again in 1693.[18] The mill seems to have been given up by the later 18th century.[19]

1 *HA* 11 May 1808; A. Harris, 'The rabbit warrens of E Yorks. in the 18th and 19th centuries', *YAJ* 42 (1967–70), 441.

2 *HP* 5 Mar. 1816. Brown was declared bankrupt in 1815. Ibid. 26 Dec. 1815. It was almost certainly this Francis Brown who was transported for 7 years for fraud in 1824. ERAO, QSF/463/B/1. See also ERAO, QSF/399/B/6 and *YH* 12 Mar. 1808, 19 Feb. 1820.

3 ERAO, QSF/435/B/3; *YH* 6 Mar. 1830; ERAO, PE/10/T. 99, s.a. 1826.

4 *HP* 18 Dec. 1835.

5 Corder, *Excavations at Elmswell*, 5, 7.

6 *YH* 18 Aug. 1849.

7 TNA, IR 18/11557.

8 *YH* 13 July 1844.

9 TNA, HO 107/2366.

10 Ibid. RG 9/3608.

11 MI, Little Driffield churchyard; *YH* 24 Dec. 1853.

12 *HP* 18 Apr. 1851; 26 Jan. 1855; 24 Jan. 1862; 23 Nov. 1866; *YH* 6 Aug. 1859.

13 *YH* 17 Mar. 1883; *HP* 1 May 1885; *LM* 29 Apr., 18 May 1885.

14 Annual agricultural returns for Kelleythorpe are combined with those for Elmswell: above, table 18.

15 TNA, MAF 32/1057/5.

16 *VCH Yorks.* ii. 215; *Monastic Notes*, i, p. 6.

17 TNA, C 66/1385, mm. 7–8.

18 Ibid. CP(2)/894/5Wm&MaryEaster, no. 12.

19 T. Jefferys, *Map of Yorks.* (1775).

NOTE ON ABBREVIATIONS

Abbreviations and short titles used include the following:

Acreage Returns, 1905	Board of Agriculture, Acreage Returns of 1905, from a MS copy in possession of the Editor, Victoria County History of the East Riding
Alumni Cantab. to 1751; 1752–1900	*Alumni Cantabrigienses to 1751*, ed. J. Venn and J. A. Venn (Cambridge 1922–7); *Alumni Cantabrigienses 1752–1900*, ed. J. A. Venn (Cambridge 1940–54)
BG	*Beverley Guardian*
BIA	University of York, Borthwick Institute for Archives
BL	British Library
Baines, *Hist. Yorks.*	E. Baines, *History, Directory and Gazetteer of the County of York*, II, East and North Ridings (1823)
Best, *Farming Bks* ed. Woodward	*The Farming and Memorandum Books of Henry Best of Elmswell, 1642*, ed. D. Woodward (British Academy, Records of Social and Economic History N.S. 8, 1984)
Boulter 'Ch Bells'	W. C. Boulter, 'Inscriptions on the Church Bells of the East Riding', *Yorkshire Archaeological Journal* ii (1873), 215–25
Bulmer, *Dir. E. Yorks.*	T. Bulmer & Co., *History, Topography and Directory of East Yorkshire* (1892)
Cal. Chart. R.	*Calendar of the Charter Rolls preserved in the Public Record Office* (HMSO, 1903–27)
Cal. Close	*Calendar of the Close Rolls preserved in the Public Record Office* (HMSO, 1892–1963)
Cal. Fine	*Calendar of the Fine Rolls preserved in the Public Record Office* (HMSO, 1911–62)
Cal. Inq. Misc.	*Calendar of Inquisitions Miscellaneous (Chancery) preserved in the Public Record Office* (HMSO, 1916–68)
Cal. Inq. p.m.	*Calendar of Inquisitions post mortem preserved in the Public Record Office* (HMSO, 1904–95)
Cal. Inq. p.m. Hen. VII	*Calendar of Inquisitions post mortem, Henry VII* (HMSO, 1898–1955)
Cal. Lib.	*Calendar of the Liberate Rolls preserved in the Public Record Office* (HMSO, 1916–64)
Cal. Pat.	*Calendar of the Patent Rolls preserved in the Public Record Office* (HMSO, 1891–1986)
Cal. SP Dom.	*Calendar of State Papers, Domestic Series* (HMSO, 1856–1972)
Char. Com.	Charity Commission
Close R.	*Close Rolls of the Reign of Henry III preserved in the Public Record Office* (HMSO 1902–75)
Complete Peerage	G. E. C[ockayne] and others, *Complete Peerage* (2nd edn, 1910–59)
Crockford	*Crockford's Clerical Directory*
DNB	*Dictionary of National Biography*
DP	*Driffield Post*
DT	*Driffield Times*
Dir.	Directory
Drummond's Visit.	*Archbishop Drummond's Visitation Returns 1764*, ed. C. Annesley and P. Hoskin (York, 1997–2001)
ER	East Riding
ERAO	East Riding of Yorkshire Archive Office
ERCC	East Riding County Council
ERG	*East Riding Gazette*
ERM	*East Riding Mail*
EYC	*Early Yorkshire Charters*, i-iii, ed. W. Farrer (1914–16); iv–xii ed. Sir Charles Clay (Yorkshire Archaeological Society Record Series, Extra Series, 1935–65)
Educ. Enq. Abstract	*Abstract of Answers and Returns relative to the State of Education in England* (Parl. Papers 1835 (62), xliii)
Educ. of Poor Digest	*Digest of Returns to the Select Committee on the Education of the Poor* (Parl. Papers 1819 (224), ix B)
Feudal Aids	*Inquisitions and Assessments relating to Feudal Aids preserved in the Public Record Office* (HMSO, 1899–1920)
HA	*Hull Advertiser*

HDM	*Hull Dail Mail*
HP	*Hull Packet*
HRO	Hull Record Office, now part of Hull History Centre
HUL	Archives formerly in the Brynmor Jones Library, University of Hull, now in Hull History Centre
Harrison, *Driffield*	S. Harrison, *The History of Driffield: From earliest times to the year 2000* (2002)
Herring's Visit.	*Archbishop Herring's Visitation Returns, 1743*, ed. S. L. Ollard and P. C. Walker (Yorkshire Archaeological Society Record Series 71, 72, 75, 77, 79)
Hodgson, *QAB*	C. Hodgson, *Queen Anne's Bounty* (2nd edn, 1845, with supplement, 1864)
Howorth, *Driffield*	P. Howorth, *Driffield: A country town in its setting 1700–1860* (1980)
Humbs. CC	Humberside County Council
L & P Hen. VIII	*Letters and Papers, Foreign and Domestic, of the Reign of Henry VIII* (HMSO, 1864–1932)
LM	*Leeds Mercury*
Lamb. Pal. Libr.	Lambeth Palace Library
Le Neve, *Fasti*	J. Le Neve, *Fasti Ecclesiae Anglicanae*, revised edition issued by the Institute of Historical Research
Lond. Gaz.	*London Gazette*
Loughlin and Miller, *Survey*	N. Loughlin and K. R. Miller, *Survey of Archaeological Sites in Humberside* (1979)
Mem.	Memoranda
NMR	National Monuments Record
NR	North Riding
NYCRO	North Yorkshire County Record Office
ONS	Office for National Statistics
PN Yorks. ER (EPNS)	A. H. Smith, *The Place-names of the East Riding of Yorkshire and York* (Cambridge, 1937)
PRS	Pipe Roll Society
Pevsner and Neave, *Yorks ER*	N. Pevsner & D. Neave, *The Buildings of England: Yorkshire: York and the East Riding* (2nd edn, 1995)
Poor Law Abstract, 1804; 1818	*Abstract of Answers and Returns relative to the Expense and Maintenance of the Poor* (Parl. Papers 1804 (175), xiii; 1818 (82), xix)
precentorship wills	Court of precentor of York, original wills, at Borthwick Institute for Archives
RDB	The former Registry of Deeds, Beverley, now part of the East Riding of Yorkshire Archive Office
Rec. Com.	Record Commission
Reg. Corbridge	*Register of Thomas Corbridge* (Surtees Society, volumes cxxxviii, cxli)
Reg. Giffard	*Register of Walter Giffard* (Surtees Society, volume cix)
Rep. Com. Char.	*Reports of the Commissioners for Charities* (1819–40), indexed in Parl. Papers 1840 (279), xix (2)
Rep. Com. Eccl. Revenues	*Report of the Commissioners appointed to Inquire into the Ecclesiastical Revenues of England and Wales* (Parl. Papers 1835 (67), xxii)
3rd Rep. Poor Law Com.	*3rd Annual Report of the Poor Law Commissioners for England and Wales* (Parl. Papers 1837 (546), xxxi)
Returns Relating to Elem. Educ.	*Returns relating to Elementary Education* (Parl. Papers 1871 [C 201], lv
Review of Char. *Rep.*	Humberside County Review of Charities, 1978–80, *Report* of the Review Co-ordinator to Humberside County Council
Ross, *Driffield*	F. Ross, *Contributions towards a History of Driffield and the surrounding Wolds district* (1898)
Sheahan and Whellan, *Hist. York & ER*	J. J. Sheahan and T. Whellan, *History and Topography of the City of York, the Ainsty Wapentake, and the East Riding of Yorkshire*, II, East Riding (Beverley, 1856)
TERAS	Transactions of the East Riding Antiquarian Society
TNA	The National Archives, formerly the Public Record Office
Test. Ebor.	*Testamenta Eboracensia* (Surtees Society volumes iv, xxx, xlv, liii, lxxix, cvi)
VCH	*Victoria County History*
Valor Eccl.	*Valor Eccesiasticus, temp. Hen. VIII* (Record Commission, 1810–34)
WR	West Riding

YAJ	*Yorkshire Archaeological Journal*
YAS	Yorkshire Archaeological Society
YC	*York Courant*
YH	*York Herald*
YML	York Minster Library
YP	*Yorkshire Post*
Yorks. Fines	*Feet of Fines* (Yorkshire Archaeological Society, Record Series, volumes ii, v, vii, viii, xlii, lii, liii, lviii, lxii, lxvii, lxxxii, cxxi, cxxvii)
Yorks. Inq. i–iv; *Hen. IV–V*	*Yorkshire Inquisitions* (Yorkshire Archaeological Society, Record Series, volumes xii, xxiii, xxxi, xxxvii, lix)
Yorks. Worship Returns 1851	*Yorkshire Returns of the 1851 Census of Religious Worship*, i, ed. J. Wolffe (Borthwick Texts and Calendars 25, 2000)

SOURCES

The following bibliography highlights the chief primary and secondary sources used in the current volume and should be read in conjunction with the list of Abbreviations.

UNPUBLISHED SOURCES AND MAPS

Documentary sources for the medieval history of Driffield are chiefly limited to records in the National Archives and include feet of fines, pipe rolls, inquisitions post mortem, chancery cases and lay subsidies. Elmswell is better served with early 14th-century manorial accounts in the National Archives (LR 11/51/732) and extracts from later 14th–15th century court rolls in the Yorkshire Archaeological Society archives (MD161).

There is no major collection of relevant estate papers although there are deeds, accounts, surveys and other material amongst the papers of the Dawnay family at North Yorkshire County Record Office (ZDS) and the Langley family (DDCV/215) in the Hull University Archives now at Hull History Centre. Other sources at the Hull History Centre include the papers of the Sykes family of Sledmere (DDSY) and sale catalogues and plans in the collection of Hebblethwaite and Sons, land agents (DBHT).

The most important source for tracing land ownership in Driffield is the East Riding Registry of Deeds 1708–1974 (RDB). This is now part of the East Riding Archives and Local Studies Service, at the Treasure House, Beverley, where other material includes the parish records for Great and Little Driffield, records of Nonconformity and education, inclosure and tithe awards, quarter sessions files, land tax assessments, and the 1910 'Domesday Survey'. Here are the papers of Driffield Poor Law Union, (PUD), Driffield Local Board and Urban District Council (UDDR) and the East Riding County Council (CCER). Amongst the records at the Treasure House of particular note are the farming and memorandum books of Henry Best of Elmswell (DDHV/75/48, 50), the diaries of the Revd Richard Allen (DDX/904/1/1–3) the notebook of the Victorian journalist, John Browne of Driffield (DDX/17/15), and the papers of the Broadley family (DDHB).

The records of the prebendal jurisdiction for Driffield including visitations are kept at York Minster Library and the Borthwick Institute for Archives at York University: the testamentary material, notably wills and probate inventories, dates from 1557 to 1852. Some records have survived relating to Driffield causes, or cases, which came before the dean and chapter's court; those cause papers are to be found at BIA, D/C. CP.

MAPS

The earliest map of Great and Little Driffield is the inclosure plan of 1742. The original may not have survived, but at least two copies of the plan were made in the 19th century. One of them was re-copied carefully in 1956, and that version (ERAO, IA. 41) has been used throughout this volume. The other 19th-century copy is at BIA, CC. Pr. 11/1. The two copies were clearly derived from the same, original plan, the differences between them reflecting the difficulty of transcribing the earlier versions. The Borthwick Institute and the East Riding Archives have copies of tithe maps for Great and Little Driffield, 1845, and Elmswell and Kelleythorpe, 1842.

A map of Elmswell in 1815 is reproduced in *The Farming and Memorandum Books of Henry Best of Elmswell, 1642*, ed. D. Woodward (1984), 213.

PRINTED SOURCES

PRIMARY SOURCES

H. Best, *Rural Economy in Yorks.* ed. C. B. Robinson (Surtees. Soc. 33)

E Yorks. Family Hist. Soc., *Driffield Monumental Inscriptions* (Driffield, 1989/2005)

D. Petch, *Driffield Cemetery Monumental Inscriptions* (Driffield, 2002)

The Farming and Memorandum Books of Henry Best of Elmswell, 1642, ed. D. Woodward (British Academy, Records of Social and Economic History N.S. 8, 1984)

Papers used include: *York Courant* (1749–1803), *Hull Advertiser* (1794–1857), *Hull Packet* (1800–86), and *Driffield Times* (1860–2010). Trade Directories from 1784 to 1937 are cited in footnotes.

BOOKS AND ARTICLES

C. Atkinson, *Driffield Rugby Union Football Club 1926–2001: A Brief History* (Driffield, 2002)

M. W. Barley (ed.), *History of Great and Little Driffield* (Hull, 1938)

A. D. Biggin and R. Squires, *Driffield Navigation Guide* (Driffield, 1975)

J. Bradley, *The Henry Best Estate, Elmswell: Assessment of archaeological potential*, Humber Archaeology Reports 56 (Hull, 2002)

A. T. Brand, *The Sykes Lodge of Freemasons* (Driffield, 1919)

G. K. Brandwood, *Temple Moore* (Stamford, 1997)

G. P. Brown, *Parish Church of All Saints, Great Driffield* (Driffield, 1984)

F. N. Burton, *The Changing Economic Structure and Development Potential of Driffield and its Region* (Hull, *c.* 1966)

W. Burton, *The Malton and Driffield Junction Railway* (Halifax, 1997)

E. T. Carr (ed.), *Driffield Capital of the Wolds* (Driffield, 1948)

C. Clubley, *Driffield in Old Picture Postcards* (Zaltbommel, Netherlands, 1985)

A. L. Congreve, *A Roman and Saxon Site at Elmswell, E Yorks. 1935–6* (Hull, 1937)

A. L. Congreve, *A Roman and Saxon Site at Elmswell, E Yorks. 1937* (Hull, 1938)

P. Corder, *Excavations at Elmswell, E Yorks. 1938* (Hull, 1940)

A. G. Credland, 'Alexander Mackintosh (1742–1829) a forgotten sportsman and author of *The Driffield Angler*', *E Yorks. Historian* 6 (2005)

C. Cross, 'A Medieval Yorkshire Library', *Northern History* 25 (1989)

L. Daniels, *The Workhouse, Bridlington Road, Driffield: A History of the East Riding General Hospital* (Driffield, 2001)

B. F. Duckham, *Inland Waterways of E Yorks. 1700–1900* (E Yorks. Local Hist. Ser. 29, 1973)

A. Harris, 'Francis Cook Matthews of Driffield', *E Yorks. Local Hist. Soc. Bulletin*, 43 (Winter 1990–1)

S. Harrison, A *Time to Reap: A Celebration of E Yorkshire's Agricultural History* (Driffield, 2000)

S. Harrison, *The History of Driffield from the Earliest Times to the Year 2000* (Pickering, 2002)

C. T. Holderness, *Some Driffield Incidents 117 Years Ago* (Driffield, 1908)

P. Howorth, *Driffield: A Country Town in its Setting 1700–1860* (Driffield, 1980)

P. Howorth, A *Year Gone By: A Yorkshire Town* [Driffield] *1871* (Driffield, 1991)

P. Howorth, *From White House to Workhouse: Luke White 1845–1920* (Driffield, 1998)

P. Howorth, *The Impact of War: Driffield and the Wolds 1914–1919* (Driffield, 2002)

C. P. Loveluck, 'The Development of the Anglo-Saxon Landscape, Economy and Society 'On Driffield', East Yorkshire, 400–750 AD', *Anglo-Saxon Studies in Archaeol. and Hist.* 9 (1996)

R. and A. McLean, *Benjamin Fawcett, Engraver and Colour Printer* (Aldershot, 1988)

E. H. Milner, *Centenary Brochure of the History of the Driffield Agricultural Soc.* (Driffield, 1973)

M. C. F. Morris, *Benjamin Fawcett: Colour Printer and Engraver* (1925)

J. R. Mortimer, *Forty Years' Researches in British and Saxon Burial Mounds of E Yorks.* (Hull, 1905)

G. Moses, *Rural Moral Reform in 19th-Century England* (Lampeter, 2007)

D. Neave, *Driffield: A Town Trail* (Beverley, 1981)

J. Nicholson, *The Capital of the Yorkshire Wolds* (Driffield, 1903)

M. Noble, 'Growth and development in a regional urban system: the country towns of eastern Yorkshire, 1700–1850', *Urban History Yearbook* 1987

M. Noble, 'The Land Tax Returns in the Study of the Physical Development of Country Towns', in M. Turner and D. Mills (eds), *Land and Property the English Land Tax 1692–1832* (Gloucester, 1986)

S. Parrott, 'The Decline of Hiring Fairs in the ER of Yorks.: Driffield *c.* 1874–1939', *Jnl of Regional and Local Studies*, 16 (1996)

F. Ross, *Contributions towards a History of Driffield and the surrounding Wolds district* (Driffield, 1898) [Foreword dated 1889]

G. Simmons and B. Abraham, *Strong Foundations: Driffield's Aerodrome from 1917 to 2000* (Cherry Burton, 2001)

R. Wood, *Policing from Wansford Road: A Record of Policing in Driffield during the last 100 years* (Driffield, 1997)

H. Woodcock, *Piety Among the Peasantry: Being Sketches of Primitive Methodism on the Yorkshire Wolds* (1889)

M. Wynn, *Driffield Capital of the Wolds: the Growth and Development of Driffield and the surrounding landscape* (Driffield, 2004)

THESES AND UNPUBLISHED MATERIALS

P. Howorth, 'The social and economic development of Driffield 1700–1860' (Hull Univ. MPhil thesis, 1980)

D. Neave, 'The Buildings of Great Driffield', unpublished report for Borough of North Wolds, 1977.

S. Neave, 'Rural settlement contraction in the East Riding of Yorkshire *c.* 1660–1760' (Hull Univ. PhD thesis, 1990)

M. K. Noble, 'Growth and development of country towns: the case of eastern Yorks., *c.* 1700–1850' (Hull Univ. PhD thesis, 1983)

P. A. Shaw, 'Driffield: A geographical analysis' (Durham Univ. BSc dissertation 1969) copy at ERAO, DDX/980/2/4

H. D. Watts, 'The industrial geography of rural East Yorkshire' (Hull Univ. MA thesis, 1964)

INDEX

NOTE. Page numbers in bold-face type are those of the principal reference. A page number in italics denotes an illustration on that page. A page number followed by *n* is a reference only to the footnotes on that page.